Landry's Boys

An Oral History of a Team and an Era

Peter Golenbock

Library of Congress Cataloging-in-Publication Data

Golenbock, Peter, 1946–

Landry's boys : an oral history of a team and an era / Peter Golenbock.

p. cm.

Rev. ed. of: Cowboys have always been my heroes. c1997.

Includes bibliographical references and index.

ISBN-13 : 978-1-57243-746-3

ISBN-10 : 1-57243-746-4

1. Dallas Cowboys (Football team)—History. I. Golenbock, Peter, 1946– Cowboys have always been my heroes. II. Title.

GV956.D3G65 2005

796.332'64'097642812—dc22

2005045761

This book is available in quantity at special discounts for your group or organization. For further information, contact:

Triumph Books
542 South Dearborn Street
Suite 750
Chicago, Illinois 60605
(312) 939-3330
Fax (312) 663-3557

Printed in U.S.A.
ISBN-13: 978-1-57243-746-3
ISBN-10: 1-57243-746-4
Design by Patricia Frey

Contents

ACKNOWLEDGMENTS

To Tony Seidl, you old Longhorn you, for taking the ball on this fine idea for a book and running with it to pay dirt. Mmmmmmmmm.

To Rick Wolff of Warner Books, for your patience, encouragement, and friendship. And to Rob McMahon, who was always there for me on the other end of the phone.

To Rich Dalrymple, the director of public relations for the Dallas Cowboys, and his staff—Emily Cruz, Brett Daniels, and Doug Hood—for treating me in a manner exemplary for a public relations staff: openly and with unusual trust. I was allowed unlimited access to whatever material I wished to explore, and many a time I worked late into the night at the Valley Ranch complex with not another employee in the building except the security guard. I sincerely hope the finished product is all that you expected it to be, and more.

To Carlton Stowers, for generously providing me access to his precious telephone book, which got me to my Treasure Island neighbor Maury Youmans, to whom I owe a large debt of gratitude for letting me use his Cowboys-alumni phone and address list. To Steve Sabol and Kathy Davis of NFL Films, for their encouragement and for finding for me the few players who had recently moved or had dropped out of sight.

To some of the most talented newspaper reporters and columnists in America—the late Steve Perkins, Gary Cartwright, Jim Browder, Sam Blair, Andy Anderson, Frank Luksa, Blackie Sherrod, Bob St. John, Randy Galloway, Gary Myers, Tim Cowlishaw, Jim Dent, Mickey Spagnola, Rick Gooselin, Barry Horn, Mike Fisher, Whitt Canning, Gil LeBreton, Susie Woodhams, Kevin Blackistone, Rick Cantu, Jim Reeves, Ed Werder, and Skip Bayless—who provided me with reams and reams of juicy research material through their articles, columns, and books. I hope you won't mind my hit-and-run excursion onto your hallowed turf.

To Time-Life veteran Mark Goodman, for explaining college football in Texas when he was a boy. To Kate Agmann, for sharing with me her knowledge of Texas culture and religion, and to Les Leopold, my dear friend, for reminding me about *The Graduate* and the scene in which Benjamin is advised to look into "plastics."

To David Solomon, for hours of solid research in the New York Public Library. To the staffs at the St. Petersburg, Tampa, and Dallas libraries for helping me to find tons of important material. To Ken Samelson and Bob Castillo, for your discerning eyes. To Carolyn Jack, for all your hard work. And to Alex Gigante, my law school classmate, for your legal advice.

To yesterday's warriors: Margene Atkins, Gene Babb, Rodrigo Barnes, Dick Bielski, Byron Bradfute, Frank Clarke, Fred Cone, Gene Cronin, Buddy Dial, Bob Fry, Pete Gent, John Gonzaga, Cornell Green, Alvin Harper, Thomas Henderson, Calvin Hill, Chuck Howley, Lee Roy Jordan, Steve Kiner, Tom Landry, Eddie LeBaron, Bob Lilly, Ray Mathews, Don McIlhenny, Dick Nolan, Pettis Norman, Jack Patera, Drew Pearson, Don Perkins, Mel Renfro, Tex Schramm, Roger Staubach, Duane Thomas, Jerry Tubbs, and John Wilbur, for your time, patience, memories, and encouragement. The greatest joy of these projects is in meeting and getting to know the participants. Thank you all from the bottom of my heart. You men know better than anyone just how difficult it is to be a professional athlete—before, during, and after. My hat is off to you all.

To my wonderful family: Rhonda Sonnenberg, the literary light of the family; Charles Eliot, the light of our lives; and Doris, the dog of our lives, all my love.

And last, but the opposite of least, to Neil and Dawn Reshen, whose generosity and unflagging support made this bucking bronco of a book not just successful, but possible.

Part I

The Old NFL

Chapter 1

The Two Clints

During the fall of 1958, as America was approaching the end of the tranquil Eisenhower era, Texas oil baron Clint Murchison Sr. and his wife Virginia left their two thousand–acre homestead south of downtown Dallas and flew from Love Field, Texas, to Los Angeles as guests of Californian Ed Pauley, another oil tycoon. Pauley, a former wildcatter who had literally struck it rich, was one of the owners of the Los Angeles Rams football team. As their limousine drove them to the massive Coliseum, the L.A. businessman and philanthropist enthusiastically regaled Murchison with stories that conveyed the joy Pauley derived from owning a pro football franchise.

Murchison listened politely. The Dallas oilman, known for his no-nonsense, bottom line–seeking demeanor, then asked Pauley, "Did the Rams make any money last year?"

"Oh no," said Pauley. "It's just a fun thing."

When Murchison arrived back home, he couldn't wait to tell his rash and foolish son, Clint Jr., who seemed intent on pursuing a quest to blow a large wad of Murchison dough on a pro football franchise for Dallas. Ever since Clint Sr.'s younger son had sought to buy the failing Dallas Texans back in 1952, the old man was constantly irritated at the thought that Clint Jr. wanted to invest in this toy. He couldn't understand why his 29-year-old offspring, an intellectual with degrees from both Duke and MIT, a man of great wealth and impeccable taste, would want to invest in a small-potatoes business that earned very little money for anyone.

When Clint Sr. told his son what Ed Pauley had said, his son was undeterred and unfazed, which was as his father had anticipated; he knew the worst thing you could do was tell the boy either that he was destined for failure or that he shouldn't do something. Clint Sr. suspected that despite his best advice, Clint Jr. would do the opposite: plunge ahead, unmindful of cost, secure in the knowledge that his instincts had more validity than either logic or the balance sheet.

In this respect the son was no different from his old man. The father, Ethelbert Clinton Murchison, one of the world's richest men, was a true Texas folk hero. Though he had started life with the financial advantages that come with being the son of a well-to-do banker, he earned his niche in Texas history by becoming immensely wealthy the Texas way: mano a mano, down and dirty, dog eat dog, me against you. Like the expert poker player he was, Clint's main pursuit all his life was the "big score." And if he had to win by dealing from the bottom of the deck, well that was too bad for you. For Clint Murchison, it was no holds barred and every man for himself.

As a youth Clint Sr. learned about ruthlessness from the Yankee-owned railroads. The citizens of his rural hometown of Athens, Texas, located 60 miles southeast of Dallas, had always resented the Texas & Pacific Railway because the line had passed up their town in favor of going through Dallas, where the citizens had ingratiated themselves with the railroad by buying $100,000 in T&P bonds and then pressured the state legislature to twist the track toward them. Dallas grew dramatically. Athens did not.

Murchison, moreover, was aware that the railroad habitually cheated the Athens farmers by fixing freight rates, charging higher rates for farm products than other goods. Clint also saw that the railroad hired the best lawyers, steeling itself against the little guys trying to get a fair deal. In later years, when Murchison was in the oil business, he would remember that the railroads had extracted the last penny from the citizens, and he would ask himself, "If the railroad could do it, why can't I?"

When Clint Sr. was seven, he sold animal pelts to fur traders. He also learned the art of horse and cattle trading, in which the goal is to outwit (read: *cheat*) the other guy as badly as possible, preying on his ignorance or weakness. In his very first trade, Clint himself was taken when he traded a decent horse and a healthy calf for a handsome horse he didn't know was injured. As he did all his life, Murchison learned from his mistakes and didn't repeat them. Once he figured out the trading game, Clint Murchison could look a man in the eye and overstate the quality of his steers, at the same time finding imaginative flaws in the opponent's herd. Through his cunning and his charm, as a youth Clint Murchison made more money animal trading than a lot of adults who worked full-time jobs in his Athens hometown.

In 1915 Clint interrupted his practical training when he enrolled in Trinity University, a Christian school in Waxahachie, Texas, 20 miles south of Dallas. Clint found college life unbearably tame. He became restless, stifled by the regimentation, bored with the curriculum. His prime activity at Trinity, a school run by Christian brothers, was organizing a floating crap game. When, during his freshman year, one of the other boys ratted on him, school authorities told him that he wouldn't be suspended if he revealed the names of the other participants. Said Clint years later, "I thought that was a very unethical approach for men operating a Christian school."

He opted to return to Athens to work as a teller in his father's bank, an activity that also proved too mundane. Early in his employ, he quit after an examiner complained that Clint was mixing the nickels with the dimes. He disgustedly told his father he could make more money in a day trading cattle than in a month at the bank.

Soon after leaving the bank, the 20-year-old Murchison learned that the U.S. Army needed wood. He knew where there was a supply of East Texas pine available, but it needed to be cut. He cut a deal with the army, then hired local Mexican workers for booze and a meager salary. He cleaned up.

During World War I Clint enlisted in the quartermaster corps of the army. While in the service, he took advantage of his trading skills. In Michigan he had his men collect salvage lumber, which he was supposed to burn but instead sold for $15,000 for the mess fund. He was loved by his men, though he was almost court-martialed.

When Clint got out of the army in 1918, his close friend Sid Richardson begged him to become his partner in the oil business. Richardson, Clint Murchison's childhood friend, had been involved in the oil business since 1911, hauling pipes and working on an oil-well platform at night, but also trading leases for himself. In 1918, when Richardson was 24 years old, he had made $100,000 buying and selling oil leases. Richardson and Murchison had done a lot of successful horse trading together before Clint's stint in the army, and Richardson figured that Murchison would be a natural at trading oil leases. He was right; Clint caught on very quickly.

Lease trading, like horse trading, is an art unto itself. If leaseholders sense a well near the property will come in, the value of the lease goes up. If the leaseholder sells and the well comes in, the buyers are winners. If the well comes up dry, the sellers are the big winners. Accurate news is the key to success, and Clint Murchison became skilled at locating the right people to hang around (and pay off) in order to learn the secrets of where oil was about to be found. Late in 1919 he and his partner made $200,000 selling leases just before an oil strike on the Texas-Oklahoma border.

In 1927 Murchison invested in the Hendrick oil field near the Texas–New Mexico border. The wells came in, but the oil and natural gas couldn't be shipped. A pipeline was needed, and Clint built it. He then began supplying large cities like Santa Fe and Albuquerque, New Mexico, with natural gas. By 1930 he was supplying 43 towns in Texas, Oklahoma, New Mexico, Colorado, Wyoming, and Arkansas.

In the spring of 1931 oil was discovered in Woodbine, Texas, and shortly thereafter 13 miles to the north in Kilgore, Texas. The question this time was whether the two finds were connected, whether this was a huge pool of oil or a series of finds. Clint Murchison gambled everything that it was one pool. Early in 1931 Clint drew a circle around the Kilgore strike and told his employees to lease everything they could within the circle. He financed the purchases by offering little up front but a decent return should the wells come in. "Give them a dollar, two or five, whatever it takes, but give it to them out of a quarter of their oil," ordered Murchison.

Within three years that East Texas oil field was recognized as the largest in the world, a gigantic pool holding more than 1 billion barrels of oil. To take further financial advantage, Murchison built a pipeline to take the oil west to Tyler, Texas, where he would refine it.

Clint built on his fortune using OPM, other people's money. Clint reasoned, "When you start using your own money, you start thinking you can do anything. Don't do it. Cash makes a man careless." He also taught his sons, "If you are going to owe money, owe more than you can pay, then the lenders can't afford to foreclose." One time when a banker from the Bank of Manhattan wanted to invest in one of Clint's pipelines, he asked how much Clint wanted. "All the money I can get," Clint replied. The bank loaned him more than $1 million.

After netting profits estimated at between $20 million and $30 million, Clint's next move was to drill his own wells on a large scale. Well drilling is not only an expensive endeavor but it is also extremely risky. Not even Frank, his own brother, thought it prudent. But Clint believed in his instincts, and once again he was proved prescient. Drilling a Kilgore well was as sure a thing as there ever was in the oil business. Of the twenty-nine thousand wells sunk into the 40-square-mile oil field, only 555 of them turned up dry. By 1934, when most people couldn't afford $50 for one of Henry Ford's used Model Ts, Clint Murchison was estimated to be worth $50 million.

Murchison added to his wealth by engaging in practices that were forbidden by both federal and state laws. Many Southerners had lost their land and their homes after the Civil War. Their whole way of life had been changed. And it was all because of Abraham Lincoln's government in Washington, D.C., and his damn Yankee soldiers. Then when Northerners invaded their states in order to help the ex-slaves gain the vote, their contempt for outside regulation intensified dramatically. Their lives had already been turned upside down once, and Southerners, including most Texans, swore that they would defend their land and their property and their right to do anything they wanted to do without interference of any kind from any government, including the one in Austin, and especially the one in Washington, D.C.

In August 1931 the Texas oil commissions limited the amount of oil Murchison and the other oil barons could pump. Murchison and hundreds of oilmen refused to follow the rules. Murchison had such contempt for these regulations that as a form of protest he changed the name of his company from Golding-Murchison to the American Liberty Oil Company.

The excess oil was known as "hot oil," and competitors charged that Murchison's company not only sold hot oil but that it stole oil from East Texas competitors through the installation of mysterious pipelines with destinations known only to Liberty Oil Company installers. Murchison was accused of opening hidden refineries in the backwoods, miles from the wells, enabling him to produce excess oil without getting caught. There was a saying: "The American Liberty pipeline was so hot, you couldn't sit on it."

If the state enjoined a well for overproducing, Clint would switch the property into the name of another company and keep drilling. There was only one set of rules: Clint's. Murchison's renegade reputation was such that when he later showed up in Washington to argue against federal regulation, he was told that because of his rogue reputation the most helpful thing he could do would be to get back on the plane and go home.

Murchison, though, did not care what others in the industry thought of him. He could recall how the railroads had cheated the farmers of Texas with the help of federal regulation, and he was determined to keep Washington from interfering in his affairs.

To protect their oil investments, the Texas oil barons reached out to men in high political office sympathetic to their cause. Texas Representative Sam Rayburn chaired a House Committee on Interstate and Foreign Commerce to study the question of whether the federal government should step in and cut oil production in order to raise the price. The plan was to make the East Texas pool an oil reserve. Under the plan, the U.S. government was going to issue bonds for the value of the property taken. Murchison was dead set against such a plan, even though in May 1933 oil was down to 4¢ per barrel. Clint's rallying cry was, "You are taking away my liberty."

In the end, Murchison's friend Sam Rayburn recommended the bill not pass, and it did not. It wasn't until 1935 that the Connolly Hot Oil Act was passed. According to the act, if you were caught piping hot oil, the government could confiscate it. Only then did the Hot Oil War end. The U.S. Supreme Court upheld the validity of the law. Many years later Murchison was still bitter about it.

Beginning in 1939 Clint Sr. began to diversify, to add properties other than oil and gas to his portfolio. Looking into the future and seeing potential growth of a company proved the key to his unwavering success. Clint demonstrated a genius for searching out companies with untapped growth potential based on trends in America and around the world. Clint saw the future growth of the insurance industry, and that year he and a partner, Toddie Lee Wynne, borrowed $1 million and bought the Reserve Life Insurance Company of Indianapolis and moved the corporate offices to Dallas the following year.

If the times were a-changin' and a certain company seemed ripe for improved earnings, Murchison would buy it. In the forties Clint Sr. saw the potential for curbside convenience stores. His friend Earl Cabell had founded the 7-Eleven stores. When Cabell became mayor of Dallas, he sold 75 percent of the company to Murchison. Clint Sr. wanted to open a chain of these stores all across the country. Cabell didn't have Clint's foresight, and when Cabell said he wasn't interested, Clint Sr. immediately sold out his shares to a third party. As any of us who ever needed a loaf of bread at 3:00 in the morning can attest, Clint turned out to be very right.

Clint then purchased Henry Holt and Company and saw the publisher's profits double as servicemen returning from the war bought millions of its textbooks. In 1957 Clint Murchison Sr. was listed as one of the richest people in America, along with Vincent Astor; John Hay Whitney; Mrs. Edsel Ford; Doris Duke, the tobacco heir; several DuPonts; and the Rockefeller boys, Nelson, David, John D., Laurence, and Winthrop.

Clint had married young, and in 1921 his wife Anne gave birth to a son, John Dabney, and in 1923 to Clint Jr. Two years later a third son, Burk, was born, but he died in April 1936 of pneumonia. In 1926 Anne died suddenly, leaving Clint Murchison shattered. The boys, raised by servants and nannies, were sickly and frail. When Clint Jr. was eight years old, he told his grandmother, "I'm just the shyest little boy in the world." As a child Clint Jr. hated the outdoors, much to his father's dismay, preferring to sit at home and read *Popular Mechanics* magazine and the dictionary. On their two thousand–acre farm in south Dallas, where Clint Sr. developed championship racehorses during the rare times that he was home, the boys grew up with the children of servants, seeing few white children and even fewer women.

Neither John nor Clint Jr. showed any interest in the oil business, so in the forties their father preordained their future by acquiring for them a series of companies under the umbrella of Murchison Brothers—without their knowledge.

At the end of 1949 Papa Murchison popped a surprise on the sons. He presented his two boys with a portfolio of 20 major companies. He wasn't giving them the stock in the companies. He was giving them the companies. Part of the arrangement was that John and Clint Jr. were to be 50-50 partners in everything they did. "Have at it," he told his sons.

The two Murchison boys, very different in personality, were thrown together as a team. John, the more outgoing and social of the two brothers, took to the task with great relish. A Yalie, he was conservative, too deliberate his father thought, but thoughtful and intelligent. John had flown during the war, and he loved to fly and to ski, so when a friend asked him to invest in a new ski area in Vail, Colorado, he did so. In the early sixties John built a private airport for his fleet of planes and ran it at a profit.

Clint Jr. was different from both his father and his brother. Clint Jr. was a small, owlish-looking man who, as in his childhood, assiduously avoided the outdoors, preferring an easy chair and the company of *Popular Mechanics* and scientific journals. His great loves were teaching and mathematical theory. After graduating from Lawrenceville Academy with the highest grade point average in the school's history, he went on to Duke University, where he graduated magna cum laude with a degree in electrical engineering. From there he got his master's degree in mathematics at MIT. He was an A student there as well. Shy and introverted, Clint Jr. believed himself intellectually superior to others, and he could be abrupt to the point of being impolite. He shunned social events, spending most of his time in his office, making deals.

Author Jane Wolfe recalled that one time at a party a man walked by Clint Jr. and said hello. Clint stared but said nothing.

"Why didn't you speak to him?" asked a friend.

"I saw him yesterday. How often do you have to speak to someone?"

But though he appeared to be an introverted egghead, Clint Jr. had another personality that he could pursue and indulge because he had the money to do so. Behind that sport-jacketed, buttoned-down exterior, Clint Jr. was a wild child. His best friend was Bedford Wynne, the son of his dad's former partner, Toddie Lee Wynne. In 1944 Clint Jr.'s dad had discovered that Toddie Lee had bought some oil wells without telling him. Clint Sr. was devastated, and he would have nothing more to do with Toddie Lee. But Clint Jr. admired Bedford for his outgoing personality and for his ability to have a good time, and the two were best buddies for life.

Bedford was a serious partyer, and he was more than willing to help Clint Jr. with his extramarital sexual conquests. Clint Jr. may have been shy, but after Bedford made the introductions for him, Clint Jr. wasn't without his charms. For Clint Jr., "Want to fly to Mexico for the weekend on my private plane?" was a very effective way of starting an affair on just the right note.

Clint Jr. loved the less-educated drinking crowd, partied openly with women who weren't his wife, and had as much fun as he could find. His brother John, who was devoted to his family, was often disgusted by his brother's frat-house behavior. But there wasn't anything John could do about the two brothers being bound to each other in business as lifelong 50-50 partners.

His father recognized Clint Jr.'s flaws. In addition to his son's stubbornness, his father also saw that in business he was a reckless gambler, a man who moved impulsively without giving his decisions much consideration. Clint Murchison Sr. saw that his younger son would move from deal to deal, often losing interest in past investments and leaving them unattended. He also saw that Clint Jr. was the sort of guy who did little work if his heart wasn't into it.

In 1951 the old man built 52 middle-income houses for returning servicemen, and he appointed Clint Jr. to go out and sell them, hoping it would make him more gregarious. The son's partner in selling was Robert Thompson, who would become Clint Jr.'s other best friend. It wasn't long before Thompson found himself procuring women for Junior. When Clint Sr. saw that his playboy son and his fun-loving buddy weren't going to sell the houses, he hired a go-getter, female hat salesperson to do it. Within nine months she had sold all 52 houses. Afterward, with Papa Murchison's backing, she started her own construction company, and she became rich as one of the top real estate brokers in America.

Making his employees rich was one of Clint Murchison's hallmarks. One of his credos was, "If you've got a good man working for you, make sure he dies rich."

But Clint Jr. was already rich. Money wasn't an incentive. He needed to find a line of work that interested him, and he found it in construction, which gave him an opportunity to use the engineering degree he had earned. He bought the City Construction Company, a Dallas street-paving company, and he hired his buddy Robert Thompson to run it. Clint Jr. soon expanded it into a large pyramid of construction companies. In true Texas fashion, Clint named his company Tecon, for "take on," as in, "We'll take on anything."

Clint Jr., through his actions, displayed a strong love-hate relationship with his powerful father. He was always demonstrating a willingness to take risks as big as those taken by his father. One time Clint Jr. won a bid to remove shale from a high hill near the Panama Canal. The job was risky because any shale that fell into the canal would have to be dredged out at a high cost. Murchison Sr. advised Junior not to do it. He did it anyway. Tecon accomplished it with no major disaster, and the company earned worldwide recognition.

His father was impressed, but he remained deeply concerned about Clint Jr.'s "take on" philosophy. He saw an ego (or perhaps a lack thereof) that caused his son to boast that he could beat anyone, no matter how big the opponent. In one residential development deal, despite all warnings that he was paying too much for the property and would suffer large losses, Clint Jr. went ahead anyway. He borrowed and lost $500,000. His father warned him, "You can afford to go broke once, but that's all."

During the early days of the Murchison Brothers partnership, Clint Jr., for the most part, kept his riverboat gambling instincts in check, with the exception of an occasional bad deal and the insistence that he buy a football team for Dallas. His father just could not understand why he was intent on putting serious capital into an investment that was virtually guaranteed to lose money. In 1960 pro football was a *very* marginal business. It was a mom-and-pop operation dependent almost solely on ticket sales. Money from television and radio was peanuts. A new expansion team in Dallas, Papa Murchison knew, promised mediocrity, at best, for the foreseeable future. Clint Sr. feared that Clint Jr. was unbalanced—that his boy wanted to spend his valuable money and precious time operating an NFL franchise seemed proof enough.

Chapter 2

GROWING PAINS

Clint Murchison Jr.'s passion for football began at Lawrenceville Academy, where he was a halfback on the school team, and even though he was small at 5'7", 130 pounds, he played club football at MIT. When Giles Miller, a Dallas textile mogul, bought the National Football League's financially strapped New York Yanks, moved the team to Dallas in 1952, and renamed it the Dallas Texans, Clint Jr. became an instant fan. He was one of the few thousand who traveled to the Cotton Bowl to see the first home game, the Texans against the New York Giants. To help the struggling franchise, Murchison bought 20 season tickets and gave them out to his friends.

At that game Governor Allen Shivers prematurely proclaimed it a "new era in sports in Texas." The highlight of the dismal game came when Giants defensive back Tom Landry fumbled a punt on his own 22-yard line after he was hit by Texans tackle Jim Lansford. The fumble led to a Texans touchdown. Perhaps five thousand fans saw the game, a scattering in the cavernous, seventy-five thousand–seat Cotton Bowl.

When Miller bought the team he had a vision that pro football would become a national phenomenon. Unfortunately for him, his timing was bad. It was before the age of television, therefore before pro football became a national phenomenon. In 1952 the pros had to depend on local support with little outside revenue. If a team couldn't draw fans, it was dead. And the Dallas Texans could not draw fans because the area surrounding Fort Worth and Dallas was *the* hotbed of college football in the nation. The powerful Southwest Conference boasted six Texas schools of note: the University of Texas, Southern Methodist University, Baylor, Rice, Texas Christian University, and Texas A&M. Not to mention Texas Tech, which later joined the conference.

What Giles Miller didn't understand was that Dallas was not like the industrial cities of the North where college football was weak. The sometimes-powerful University of Pittsburgh played in Pittsburgh, but other colleges near enough to NFL teams to compete with the pro stars weren't much competition. There were Columbia and NYU in New York City, Temple and the University of Pennsylvania in Philadelphia, Northwestern in Chicago, and who can even remember who played in Detroit, Cleveland, and Green Bay? Nobody. Only on the West Coast did the pros have competition, which came from the great California universities: Stanford, the University of California at Berkeley, USC, and UCLA.

Giles Miller just could not get the rabid football fans of the Dallas–Fort Worth area to either switch or add their allegiance to his team. In Texas, where the nearest National Football League franchise was in Washington D.C., pro football had been barely a curiosity, and because the Dallas Texans were a losing team, local interest in them was minimal.

Journalist and author Mark Goodman was 12 years old when he went to see the Dallas Texans as Giles Miller's guest. "It was sad," said Goodman. "Mr. Miller was doing everything he could to fill the Cotton Bowl, and the place was so empty I remember going to those games and being able to sit anywhere we wanted. Boy, Giles was giving tickets away. The only ones who cared a little about pro football were the kids, 'cause we'd send away for pictures of Otto Graham, but really nobody gave a damn. He lost a lot of money that year."

The Texans' final home game was played against the Los Angeles Rams. Before the game, NFL commissioner Bert Bell warned Rams general manager Tex Schramm, "Don't you leave that office until you get your check." After the game Schramm made certain to pick up the Rams' share of the proceeds in person. Schramm could relax only after the check cleared.

Three-quarters of the way into the season the NFL took over the Dallas Texans, and they were made into a "road" team.

Despite the poor attendance at Texans home games, Clint Murchison Jr. thought he would enjoy owning an NFL franchise, and at the end of the 1952 season he asked Bert Bell for a 24-hour grace period so he could study the books before agreeing to take over the team. Bell refused his request. Instead, Bell awarded the franchise to an old friend, Carroll Rosenbloom, who, like Giles Miller, also was in the textile business. Bell gave Rosenbloom a sweetheart of a deal, and the Dallas Texans became the Baltimore Colts.

Undeterred, almost immediately Clint tried and failed to buy a minority interest in the Washington Redskins from Harry Wismer, who at the time was part owner and play-by-play announcer for the Redskins. Two years later Clint's intention was to buy the San Francisco 49ers and move them to Dallas. Clint had been contacted by Fred Saigh, the former general manager of the St. Louis Cardinals baseball team. Saigh had been barred from baseball after a conviction for income tax evasion, and when Bert Bell told Clint that the league would not accept Saigh as an owner, Murchison dropped out of the deal. "He brought it to me," Clint told Bell, "and if he can't be a part of it, then I'm not going to go ahead."

Then in 1958 Clint came close to buying the Washington Redskins from George Preston Marshall for $600,000 and moving the team to Dallas. Under the terms of the deal Marshall would run the team for five years and then step down. At the last moment Marshall decided he wanted to stay for ten years, not five. "Tell him to go to hell," said Murchison. "The deal's off."

Clint asked commissioner Bell where he should try next. "The Chicago Cardinals might be for sale," Bell told him. Murchison was told to negotiate with Walter Wolfner, a nightclub owner from St. Louis, and his wife, Violet, who was the widow of Charlie Bidwill, the founder of the Cardinals.

At the same time, Lamar Hunt, the son of a rival Texas oil baron, also wanted an NFL franchise for Dallas. Hunt, too, asked Bell how he should go about buying a franchise and bringing it to Dallas. Bell told him the same thing: negotiate with Walter and Violet Wolfner. But like Murchison, Hunt found the negotiations fruitless. Frustrated, Hunt decided on a course that would ultimately land Murchison his franchise and lead to Hunt founding the American Football League.

If there was one man even richer than Clint Jr.'s daddy, it was Lamar's daddy, Haroldson Lafayette Hunt, a man who traded oil leases with the best of them. H. L. Hunt's son, Lamar, loved football as much as Clint Jr. Lamar surely was the richest man ever to play college football (third string at SMU behind Doyle Nix and Raymond Berry). When Lamar couldn't find an existing franchise to buy for himself, he met several times with NFL commissioner Bert Bell in what appeared to be an attempt to land an expansion team for Dallas. Hunt pumped Bell for information on the financial stability of the league. After it was clear that Hunt intended to start his own league, observers believed that his meetings with Bell were a spy mission, that his goal had been to glean as much information as he could from Bell about the NFL's finances.

In June 1959 Lamar Hunt announced the formation of the American Football League. To ensure the league's success, Hunt arranged with the American Broadcasting Company a five-year contract to broadcast its games. On August 14, 1959, the American Football League was founded in the Conrad Hilton Hotel in Chicago. The new teams were announced: the New York Titans, Houston Oilers, Minneapolis Vikings, Denver Broncos, Los Angeles Chargers, and Dallas Texans. Among the original investors to whom Hunt had sold franchises were Harry Wismer in New York, Bud Adams in Houston, Max Winter in Minneapolis, Bob Howsam in Denver, and Barron Hilton in Los Angeles (who after one year moved to San Diego). Hunt would own the Dallas franchise. There were to be two other franchises, which turned out to be Boston and Buffalo. William Sullivan and Ralph Wilson became owners of those teams, respectively.

At the same time, Hunt and Bud Adams continued to meet with George Halas, the chairman of the NFL expansion committee. But Halas had two other candidates for NFL franchises in Dallas and Houston, Clint Murchison Jr. and Craig Cullinan. And Murchison had been pressing Halas for an answer because he needed the time to negotiate a lease with the Cotton Bowl. He also didn't want Lamar Hunt's Texans to get a head start in the battle for the hearts and minds of Texas.

On August 29, 1959, Halas and Pittsburgh Steelers owner Art Rooney called Clint Murchison Jr. to tell him that Dallas would be eligible for membership in the NFL. Craig Cullinan was to get an NFL franchise in Houston, but he first had to get permission to use Rice University's stadium. (He never did get the franchise, which the following year went to Minneapolis.) Murchison was told that he had a franchise subject to the membership of the league voting its approval at the league meeting in January. Whether he would start in 1960 or 1961 would also be decided at the meeting.

On October 11, 1959, commissioner Bert Bell died watching his beloved Philadelphia Eagles playing at Franklin Field. In a meeting following Bell's funeral, all the league owners except George Preston Marshall of Washington voted to expand. The Redskins were the team of the South, watched by southerners from Florida across to Texas. Marshall had no intention of allowing a new franchise to hurt his television and radio revenues. Nevertheless, the politics of the time was that the league badly needed to expand in order to cut off the legs of the new league. On October 19, 1959, in an effort to scare off investors in the AFL, Halas exaggerated the NFL's intent by announcing that it would admit two teams in 1960 and two more, one in 1961 and one in 1962.

Murchison was reluctant to have to compete with another pro football team in the same town, and late in October 1959 he offered a partnership in the NFL Dallas franchise to Lamar Hunt. Hunt, however, told Clint he was committed to his partners in the AFL and could not abandon them without the risk of a lawsuit.

There is always intrigue when wealthy, powerful men fight over territory. Observers wondered what the NFL owners, who had enjoyed their monopoly in pro football until now, would do to counter the upstart AFL. Who would be compromised? Who would be paid off?

On November 22, 1959, at a meeting of the AFL owners, Max Winter, who had told Hunt he would buy the AFL franchise in Minneapolis, shocked the newcomers when he double-crossed them by accepting an offer to own an NFL franchise in Minneapolis. If George Halas had wanted to hurt the new league, giving franchises to Dallas and Minneapolis was the most effective way of doing it. The move crippled the American Football League in the South and kept it out of the Midwest for several years. To replace the Minneapolis franchise, the AFL hastily regrouped and put a weak franchise into small-market Oakland.

When Clint Murchison Jr. was told in August 1959 that he would be the owner of the new Dallas franchise, he still had to wait five months for the league vote. Murchison saw that Hunt and his Dallas Texans were starting up in 1960, and Murchison realized that if he waited to hire his staff in January, he would not be able to put a team on the field until 1961, putting him at a further disadvantage. Murchison saw he had no choice but to hire a general manager and a coach and sign a slew of free agents immediately in his effort to show the other owners that he was serious about fielding his new team in 1960. Accordingly, Murchison asked the advice of George Halas, who recommended that Tex Schramm, the former L.A. Rams general manager, run the new team's front office. Schramm then personally hired New York Giants defensive coach Tom Landry as the team's head coach. Because Murchison's new team was starting too late to be included in the draft of college senior players, Halas gave Murchison permission to sign personal service contracts with two college standouts, quarterback Don Meredith of Southern Methodist University and running back Don Perkins from the University of New Mexico. If the team was not voted into the league, Meredith and Perkins could then sign with whoever picked them in the upcoming draft.

The drama unfolded in Miami Beach at the annual NFL meeting held in January 1960. Murchison, Schramm, and Landry headed to Florida with the existence of their franchise at stake. Clint Jr. had also flown in a dozen or so of his partying friends and put them up at the swanky Kenilworth Hotel, owned by TV personality Arthur Godfrey. Murchison had expected the meeting to last a day, two at the most. What he hadn't counted on was that the league had to vote on a new commissioner before it could decide the fate of the new team. It would be 11 days before the feuding league owners finally picked a commissioner.

One group of owners—including Wellington Mara of the Giants, Paul Brown of Cleveland, and Daniel Reeves of Los Angeles—wanted Marshall Leahy, who was the attorney for the San Francisco 49ers. The opposing faction, including Art Rooney of Pittsburgh and Carroll Rosenbloom of Baltimore, preferred Austin Gunsel, the league's attorney. One reason they opted for Gunsel was that Leahy said he would move the league headquarters to San Francisco if he were elected. The Rooney group held enough votes to keep Leahy from getting the job. At the same time no matter who else the anti-Leahy contingent recommended, the pro-Leahy contingent voted him down, holding out in the hope that Leahy would prevail. Cleveland owner and coach Paul Brown was asked to run for the job. Brown declined. Don Kellett, the general manager of the Colts, was nominated and defeated. The standoff became an ordeal. For 23 ballots over 10 days, there was a deadlock.

The next day the pro-Leahy forces finally gave up. As a compromise choice, L.A. Rams majority owner Daniel Reeves nominated his general manager, Alvin "Pete" Rozelle, who was asked to leave the room. Rozelle went across the hall and hung out in the bathroom. To keep his nomination secret, every time a reporter came in the bathroom, Rozelle washed his hands so the reporter wouldn't be suspicious that his name was under nomination.

Rozelle was young, and he had made no enemies. After the deciding vote in his favor, Rozelle was asked to come back into the room. His hands were wet. "I can honestly say I come to you with clean hands," said the man who would lead the NFL for the next generation.

Once the new commissioner was chosen, the league's next order of business was deciding whether to give Clint Murchison Jr. an expansion franchise in Dallas.

Going into the meeting Murchison knew that his primary opponent would be George Preston Marshall, who had joined the NFL in 1932 when he bought the Boston Braves. He moved the team—renamed the Redskins in 1933—to

Washington after the 1936 season. Marshall was colorful, controversial, flamboyant, and egocentric. Marshall was an old-timer who believed that the success of the sport of pro football was due to the fact that it typified the tough, aggressive nature of the American people. He liked to say, "Football is no place for soft people."

On Sunday evenings after a Redskins home game, Marshall and his wife, Corinne, a movie star once known as the "Orchid Lady," would go to the Blue Room of the Shoreham Hotel for dinner. Bandleader Barnee Breeskin and his orchestra would be playing, and when the Marshalls entered the room the orchestra would segue into "Hail to the Redskins," which Breeskin and Corinne had written. Marshall would greet the other guests as though he were royalty.

Marshall was a pioneer in broadcasting games. In 1942 he hired broadcaster Harry Wismer to do the play-by-play, and his Redskins Network spread throughout the South. Throughout the fifties the fortunes of the Redskins declined in part because Marshall was quick to fire his coaches and in part because of his stubborn refusal to sign black players. Even after stars such as Jim Brown, Lenny Moore, John Henry Johnson, and Ollie Matson came into the league in the fifties, Marshall maintained that his fans and viewing audience would boycott if the team signed blacks. Said Wismer, who also was a minority stockholder in the team, "He was wrong, he knew he was wrong, refused to admit it, and blamed all the Redskins' failures on everyone but himself."

The pigheaded Marshall, Clint Murchison Jr. knew, would be the one formidable stumbling block to getting his franchise. It may have been in the interest of the league to expand, but it was not in the interest of George Preston Marshall, who didn't want to give up his southern audience.

But Clint Murchison Jr. was not a man used to losing, and ultimately he got his way. How he did so is cloaked in mystery and intrigue. Part of the story has become folklore. The other part was hidden behind closed doors in the back rooms of Washington, D.C., politicians. The folklore part of the story has been retold over and over, but nevertheless it says a great deal about Clint Murchison Jr. It speaks of Murchison's power, his preparedness, his willingness to turn every stone in his quest for something he badly wanted.

When George and Corinne Marshall were divorced in the late fifties, in the settlement Corinne received as her property the rights to "Hail to the Redskins," the fight song she cowrote with Barnee Breeskin. In 1959 Breeskin asked Corinne if she would sell him her rights, and she did so. Perhaps Murchison put him up to it. It's possible, as Murchison knew the society bandleader. Or perhaps once Murchison learned that Breeskin owned the rights, he knew Breeskin could use the $2,500 he shelled out to pay for those rights. Regardless, Murchison loved to tell the story of how in the fall of 1959 he gave $2,500 to his close friend and Washington lobbyist Bobby Baker to go to Breeskin and make the buy.

The month before the vote on the new franchise was to be taken, Murchison called Marshall on the phone before a late-season Redskins game.

"Does the Redskins band intend to play the Redskins fight song?" asked Murchison.

"They sure will," said Marshall.

"The hell they will," said Murchison. "Nobody plays *my* fight song without *my* permission." It was at this point that Murchison told him about his purchase of Marshall's beloved song.

Said Bobby Baker, Murchison's messenger, "You couldn't make that sort of basic boo-boo when engaged in a peeing contest with the Murchisons. Their price for the Redskins being able to continue to use the song: withdrawal of Marshall's opposition to the Dallas NFL franchise."

Clint Jr. could not be certain Marshall would value his fight song highly enough to give up his dominant position broadcasting his Redskins games across the South, and so Murchison moved against him on another front. This is where the behind-the-scenes dealings come in. He used his influence to get Congress to declare Marshall's Redskins Network a monopoly.

It is ironic that Clint Murchison Jr.—whose father hated big government, hated Franklin Roosevelt for his socialistic policies and for trying to regulate the oil industry, and hated the federal government for trying to stop him from pumping hot oil during the thirties—knew *all* the powerful people in Washington. Clint Sr. had spit on Washington; Clint Jr. embraced it.

Once again, the man he used to get the job done was Bobby Baker, who later would get in trouble during the Lyndon Johnson administration for taking payoffs. In 1967 Baker was convicted on eight counts of larceny, fraud, and tax evasion, a conviction he fought until 1971, when he went to prison to serve 16 months.

Baker was a facilitator. If you wanted something done in Washington, you went to Baker and he would make an "arrangement" with a senator or representative. To make sure your hands stayed clean, you carried out the arrangement with this middleman, or aide. After he was caught, Baker's job description changed from facilitator to bagman.

It wasn't until years later that Baker revealed to author Larry L. King what Murchison had done to assure his getting the Dallas franchise. According to Baker, Murchison delivered $25,000 to the late senator Estes Kefauver, chairman of the Senate Antimonopoly Committee, from "a group of Texans who badly wanted to gain a profitable NFL franchise for Dallas.

"I was approached by [Murchison's] courier, whom I knew as a fellow reveler and high roller in Washington. 'Bobby,' he said over drinks in my office, 'my job and my ass are on the line. I've got to lock up that damn football franchise. I have been told not to leave any stone unturned.'"

The courier was probably Robert Thompson, Murchison's right-hand man and head of Tecon, the holding company for all the Murchison enterprises. At the time of the article in 1973, Thompson was still alive.

Baker said the money was delivered to a member of Kefauver's staff in a committee office in the old Senate Office Building. According to Baker, George

Preston Marshall "was adamantly against sharing the South with a Texas-based team certain to divide regional loyalties at the expense of his pocketbook." The money, according to Baker, was designed to influence the subcommittee's "finding that . . . Marshall . . . held an illegal monopoly with the so-called Redskins Television Network." The subcommittee did make that ruling against Marshall. Said Baker, "Marshall's proprietary instinct, wholly robber baron in character, may well have been rejected by an honest subcommittee. But with millions at stake, the Texans took no chances."

When the admission was published in *Playboy* in June 1973, denials flew. Clint Murchison Jr. denied the story. Pete Rozelle even denied the story, though he wasn't involved. However, Robert Thompson, who was one of Murchison's closest friends and one of his party companions and who had probably been the courier who took the money to Baker, *loved* to tell the story of the $25,000 bribe to Kefauver. "It was why Clint hated George Marshall all those years," Thompson told a friend. "The rivalry the Cowboys had with the Redskins was strictly personal on Clint's part."

At the league meeting a pressured George Preston Marshall went from opposing the entry of the new team into a stall tactic where he asked only that the league wait one year before bringing Dallas into the league. In response, Tex Schramm, who had been hired as the Dallas general manager, explained to Marshall that the Dallas Texans in the AFL would be starting the coming season. To wait a year would be to give the Texans a one-year head start. "We must have an even start," Schramm told him.

Marshall, outflanked in every direction, finally gave in. Murchison paid the league $550,000—50 grand for the franchise and half a mil for a roster of washed-up, over-the-hill, or never-were players who were selected during the meeting.

After the meeting broke up a reporter asked Clint, "Are you prepared to come up with $550,000 cash?"

Murchison considered the huge bar bill rung up by Robert Thompson, Bedford Wynne, and his other partying buddies over the course of the 11 days of the marathon NFL meeting. "I better be," he said, "or I won't be able to get out of the hotel."

Chapter 3

TEX

By 1960 pro football was becoming a national phenomenon, though it still did not generate the mania engendered by pro baseball, with fans agog over the prospect of Mickey Mantle and Roger Maris batting back-to-back in the New York Yankees lineup for the first time. But America's addiction to television was becoming stronger, and part of the sports fare being televised from Maine to California was NFL football. Some clubs were on TV more than others. At that time each pro football franchise cut its own deal. CBS televised a cluster of teams, including the Giants, the Rams, and both Chicago teams, the Bears and the Cardinals. George Preston Marshall had his own network, which was broadcast across the South with Red Grange and Harry Wismer announcing.

Television and pro football together reached their adulthood in December 1958 when the Baltimore Colts defeated the New York Giants in overtime in the NFL championship, as millions watched from their Barcaloungers enthralled as Alan Ameche pranced through the huge hole in the Giants line to end the epic battle. Ameche's dash has been etched indelibly in the memory of everyone in the baby boomer generation who saw it.

CBS, moreover, greatly added to the mystique of professional football when it aired its first important special on the sport, called *The Violent World of Sam Huff*. Huff, the middle linebacker for the Giants, wore a microphone for this program, and as the cameras focused on him throughout a ballgame the viewers could hear the crashing of the linemen, and they could see that professional football was, in fact, a very violent game. It was riveting to sit in your living room while listening to the participants barking signals or screaming at the opposition, and when Huff put a hit on one of the big backs you could almost feel the impact in your bones. The National Football League was just beginning to wake up to the promotional potential of television, and *The Violent World of Sam Huff* showed the way.

It is interesting that the man Clint Murchison Jr. chose to be the general manager of his new Dallas team was Tex Schramm, who had been working for CBS since 1957, after a 10-year reign as general manager of the strife-ridden Los Angeles Rams. Schramm was a very bright, very astute man who was as much a competitor in his own right as any coach or player under his employ.

Schramm's philosophy was that there was always an angle to explore, a better way of doing something than anyone else did it. As with Murchison, there was only one set of rules: his rules. If Schramm needed to accomplish something, he would do it, even if he had to invent a new way of doing things. For instance, when he was with the Rams, he tired of guessing at whether a college prospect had ability or not, and so he invented a ruse that prompted hundreds of unpaid, unknowing scouts to send him information. With this information he was the first to build a scouting system, later copied throughout the league. After he was hired to run the Cowboys, Schramm did everything he could to build a team, even before the league gave him permission to begin. Schramm was a rare combination, a visionary and a businessman as tough as Jimmy Hoffa or, for that matter, Clint Murchison Sr.

Schramm had envisioned great profits to be made televising sports, and at CBS he pushed for the network to televise the 1960 Winter Olympics at a time when other executives thought there would be no interest and no sponsors. Schramm won out, and he was the first to use a central anchor for a sports broadcast, Walter Cronkite, who previewed the various events. That one idea—an anchorman—changed the way sports was presented on TV. The programming from Squaw Valley was a revelation; millions of Americans watched day after day as David Jenkins and Carol Heiss each won a gold in figure skating and the U.S. Olympic hockey team defeated the favored Russians in a game still talked about to this day.

In his three years working for Bill Paley and under Bill MacPhail, the brother of future New York Yankees general manager Lee MacPhail, Schramm was a very well-paid member of the CBS brain trust, and during that period he turned down the job of general manager with the Detroit Lions and the Montreal Alouettes in football and the Detroit Pistons in the National Basketball Association. (The NBA had even talked about Schramm becoming commissioner.)

When Clint Murchison Jr. asked George Halas who he would recommend to run the new team's front office, Halas had one choice: Tex Schramm. That time, Schramm accepted. Though raised in California, he had gone to college in Texas and was comfortable living there. Moreover, this was the challenge of which Schramm had always dreamed: the opportunity to start a team from scratch. This would be Tex Schramm's team. His fingerprints would be all over it, which meant that before long the city of Dallas would have an exciting, competitive football team.

Tex Schramm: "When I started, it was with the assumption we were going to start up the next season. I didn't have much time. I needed to hire a coach. While I was with CBS, I was living in Riverside, Connecticut, which is next to Old Greenwich, and working in New York, so I was very familiar with the Giants. I went to a lot of their games, and I was aware that their defensive team had developed a special esprit de corps. It was the first time the fans related to the defense, and they had been very successful. And apparently they had a great relationship with the defensive coach Tom Landry, so that sounded good, and in the meantime, some people here in Dallas who knew Landry had suggested we look into him, so it was tailor-made, so I went and saw him and was impressed by him.

"The Houston Oilers had also approached him, but he liked the sound of Dallas. It was a gamble for him, because we didn't even have a franchise yet. Right after the Giants lost to Baltimore in the '59 playoffs we brought him down, had a press conference, and announced him.

"I honestly didn't care that he had played college ball in Texas. That's not why I picked him. I had been in football for 10 years and had five coaches with the Rams. The only thing I was interested in was getting a great football coach, not somebody who sounded good in Texas. Where he went to college didn't make any difference to me.

"I knew we were going to be too late for the upcoming NFL Draft, so I started by going after as many free agents as I could sign. The first thing I did, I talked to Daniel Reeves, and for $5,000 he agreed to sell me the scouting reports on all the players who were not drafted. Having set it up and been there, I knew how their books were with all their information. That was found money for him, and he wanted to help.

"I hired Gil Brandt, one of the first ones that I got to go out and sign players. Gil was one of the originals of all the people they have now who are amateur evaluators. I knew he was good because when I was with the Rams we had used him when we needed some kind of project done. If I needed someone to go see someone, or for someone to find out something, he was the guy we used on that kind of stuff. And I knew he always got it. He had lived in Milwaukee, and one time the College All-Star team was training in Stevens Point in Wisconsin. We weren't allowed to scout them, so we got Gil to go over and see what the hell they were doing, and see what the players looked like. So I knew him. So in '59 I called him up and asked him, 'Do you want to sign some players for me?'

"He said, 'Great, give me the names.' And I gave him seven or eight names and a pile of our made-up player contracts.

"So we started signing free agents, even though we weren't in the league. We had started as the Dallas Steers, but that's not a very good name because you don't want your whole football team being castrated. Then we went to the Dallas Rangers, which was the name of the minor league baseball team that was supposedly moving out of town, and so we were going to use that name, and so the first NFL contracts we printed said 'Dallas Rangers.'

"Anyway, that year Bert Bell, the commissioner, had died, and a guy by the name of Austin Gunsel had been the treasurer of the league, and he was acting as interim commissioner, and I called him up, and I said, 'We're getting ready for this season, and we're going to have a franchise. Can you send me some contracts?' He said, 'You're not a member of the league. I can't send you any contracts.' I said, 'Oh? Well, OK.'

"And so either I had a contract from when I was with the Rams or I got one from the Giants, but either way I had no trouble getting one, and I sent it down to Dallas, and I asked Bedford Wynne, one of the partners in the team, 'Can you go to a printer and have him duplicate this with exactly the same paper, the same type, the same everything, for the Dallas Rangers?'

"He said, 'I think so. Let me go do it.'

"So we had these NFL Dallas Rangers contracts printed, and you couldn't tell the difference. They looked like the real thing. So I had all the contracts I needed. Next I sat with Bedford Wynne, who was an attorney, and if you can imagine it, we drew up a release for the player to sign in which he acknowledged he was signing with the Rangers, but if Dallas didn't get a franchise, we would have no obligation. And it was amazing. We went out and signed players, and those players didn't give a damn about signing that release."

Signing free agents in the NFL was often a fruitless exercise. These were the players still unattached after each of 12 teams had drafted 25 rounds of players. True, it still left thousands of college seniors to choose from, but by 1960—thanks largely to the pioneering work of Tex Schramm—teams were drafting more knowledgeably than they had in the past. Schramm realized that for him to find an undrafted college player with a shot at making the team, he had to look for unusual circumstances. One of the free agents he courted was Byron Bradfute, a big lineman who had been thrown out of Abilene Christian University for drinking beer. He had finished his senior year at Southern Mississippi, his reputation sullied by the alcohol incident. But Tex Schramm was one of those general managers who didn't care as much about Bradfute's scrape with the morality police at Abilene Christian as he did about the big kid's raw talent. Schramm's overriding concern was to build a winning team. Though Bradfute had been ignored by the NFL, he had been drafted in the 17th round by the AFL's Los Angeles Chargers. Schramm wanted the 23-year-old Bradfute. He was a Beeville, Texas, farm boy, who, Schramm argued, ought to be playing pro ball in Texas.

Byron Bradfute: "I had been drafted 17th by the Chargers in the AFL, but I signed with Tex. It was Texas. I could identify with it. All my family was in Texas, and by then I was homesick. I had been over in Mississippi, and in December I got my contract in the mail, and they gave me a $500 cash bonus, and that paid for my last semester, which I took at Abilene Christian. I got my degree and graduated with my class.

"The first contract Tex sent me was with the Dallas Rangers. I signed it and sent it back. Then he called me and said I would have to re-sign it because they changed the name. I could see they were a little short on secretaries, because in the new contract they had just marked a line through Dallas Rangers, typed in Dallas Cowboys, and sent it down for me to initial. I initialed it and sent it back to them."

Tex Schramm: "In fact, we signed 26 players, including Jake Crouthamel, a running back out of Dartmouth, who is now athletic director at Syracuse, and signing those free agents played a little role in encouraging the league to let us start in '60, because we already had 26 players signed, and they thought that was pretty good.

"I can remember we had a scout up trying to sign a free agent, and Paul Brown was trying to sign the same free agent. The guy said, 'I have a contract with the Dallas Rangers.' Paul said, 'What the hell are you talking about? They're not even in the league.' The player showed him the contract. Paul called Gunsel and said, 'What in the hell is going on? I've got somebody out there I'm competing against that isn't in the league!'

"We also went out and we signed two of the top college seniors in the country, Don Meredith and Don Perkins, to personal service contracts. We signed Meredith, and it had the blessing of Halas, who was the guy Clint was using as a contact, and then we signed Perkins in New Mexico, because Murchison was a real close friend of the senator from New Mexico, and I can't remember his name. We actually had this senator who had the responsibility of getting Perkins signed. So we got those two signed.

"The draft was in late November, and when the draft came, Halas got up and said, 'Dallas has signed these two players, so don't draft them.' Halas warned them that these two players had been signed by Dallas."

Don Meredith had become famous by his senior year at SMU. A native of Mount Vernon, in East Texas, Jeff and Hazel's baby boy was an outstanding high school athlete in both football and basketball, a sport in which he once set a single-game scoring record of 52 points in the Dr. Pepper high school tournament in Dallas. At SMU he was a two-time All-American and the holder of the record for career passing accuracy at 61 percent. During his junior year he was named national collegiate back of the week four times during a 10-game season. Murchison gave him a guaranteed $150,000 contract to remain in Dallas and not sign with Lamar Hunt and the Dallas Texans. Meredith would get the money whether Dallas was accepted into the NFL or not.

When Meredith was offered a personal service contract by Clint Murchison Jr., he jumped at it. He knew that no matter what happened on the football field, he would have a good job in the Murchison organization. Don Meredith didn't know it at the time, but his fans would follow him from SMU into the pro ranks, and whatever ambivalence the fans had for him in college would grow exponentially after he entered the pros.

While Meredith was visible and renowned in Dallas, Don Perkins was unknown. A quiet, unselfish, introverted man, Perkins played in obscurity for the University of New Mexico despite his College All-Star status. But Tex Schramm and Gil Brandt knew that Don Perkins had the makings of a great NFL running back. He was a great blocker, was tough, had crazy legs that caused him to dart every which way and made him hard to tackle, and he was explosive. Teammates would race him for 10 yards, and no one could beat him.

Perkins served as an inspiration to teammates and also as a teacher, as he unselfishly trained the new kids coming up. Once when rookie running back Walt Garrison asked him why he was helping a man intent on taking his job, Perkins told him, "If you're a better player than I am, then you ought to be playing, because I'll make more money that way. If you're not better than I am, then I should be playing." Don Perkins was a pro's pro.

Perkins, who is black, was a pioneer with the Cowboys. Along with receiver Frank Clarke and defensive back Don Bishop, Perkins came to Dallas in 1960 during the last days of Jim Crow segregation in the South. A stranger in a white-run society, Perkins came to Dallas afraid for his job. He knew his place, kept a low profile, and did his job extremely well, and eight years after he came, he left Dallas about as unknown as he had been when he arrived, but still grateful to have been given the opportunity.

At the time he quit, only four other running backs in the NFL had gained more yards than his total of 6,217: Jim Brown, Jim Taylor, Joe Perry, and John Henry Johnson. Perkins had played eight years, finished in the top 10 in rushing each year, and was named to the Pro Bowl six times. Jackie Robinson had hardly done better in Brooklyn with the Dodgers.

Don Perkins: "In my senior year I was contacted by New Mexico senator Clinton Anderson, who was somehow connected with the Murchisons. This was before Murchison even had a franchise. But he had some kind of deal with the NFL that his team could sign so many players, and 'If you get a franchise, you can keep these guys. If you don't, they'll get picked by other teams.' Anyway, I signed a personal service contract with the Cowboys. It was no risk. Baltimore drafted me, too.

"Anyway, in those days it was a very low-key thing. Football was hardly even televised in the fifties. People didn't set out to be pro football players. Not many people knew anything about pro football. It was a job opportunity, and I took it. They gave me a little money up front, and I got to keep it whether I made the team or not. I said, 'Why not?'"

Tex Schramm: "After we signed Meredith and Perkins, I put my guys on Billy Cannon, who was one of the top players that year from LSU, and Billy was ready to sign with us except that he had been drafted by the Rams, and running the Rams then, as general manager, was Pete Rozelle. He wouldn't be named commissioner for another couple of months. And Pete called me and said, 'You sign Billy Cannon, and you might have Billy Cannon, but you might not have a franchise. We have to vote on that.'

"I said, 'Yeah, Pete, don't worry.' And I told our guys, 'Get the hell away from Billy Cannon.' So that is what stopped me. That's why we didn't sign 10 of them. Don't rock the boat. But we went ahead and signed all the free agents, and then we went to Miami at the end of January to get the franchise.

"We got the franchise, but the league made it very hard for us to draft any good players from the expansion lists. Some people in the league spoke up and said, 'If we're going to have an expansion team, we got to give them a chance.' Some chance. A little chance. There was some or a little, as it turned out. They did it in such a way that the other teams weren't risking anything by the number of players protected. Everybody could protect 29 of their 33 players, a big number, and we could select one from each team. But if we picked one, then they could withdraw one name. So no one gave up very much. I can remember after we picked Buzz Guy, we gave the Giants something for them to leave Don Heinrich on the list.

"We had had an idea what players we were going to get, because we had done as much research as we could do before the time came to go to that meeting. There wasn't a lot of time to do it, but we researched all of the players on the other teams who were likely to be left unprotected, and we knew them all pretty well by the time that they did it. Our problem was that the league only gave us 24 hours to make the picks, and we couldn't call the players to see if they would play for us. The other teams didn't want the players not picked to know they had been on the list, 'cause they were afraid it wouldn't be good for morale, so they made us stay in the hotel and make the picks blind. As a result, we picked players from Texas. We figured if we could get L. G. Dupre from the Colts or Don McIlhenny from the Packers, they were better than some of the other guys on the lists, and we knew we wouldn't have any trouble signing them, 'cause they would want to come back to Texas.

"We got three good players out of it: Jerry Tubbs, a linebacker; Jim Doran, an end; and another end, Frank Clarke. We got Tubbs because he had threatened to retire. He was always going to retire with us, too. That was his big bargaining chip. He played eight years, and then he winds up coaching and never getting out of football. We got Doran because he was in his midthirties and about ready to retire, and we got Clarke because Paul Brown gave up on him.

"I knew it was going to be a rocky time, because they didn't give us anything in the expansion draft. But I *knew*—there was no doubt in my mind—that it was just a matter of time before we would start winning. I never entered anything with more confidence in my life."

Chapter 4

THE BOMBARDIER

The man Tex Schramm picked to coach his new team was unknown to many football fans. Assistant coaches usually are. But to those who had played with him and for him on the New York Giants, Tom Landry was considered a certified football genius.

Born on September 11, 1924, the son of a bricklayer turned car mechanic, Landry grew up in Mission, Texas, not far from the Mexican border and deep in the Rio Grande Valley, which boasted unending acres of flowering lemon, orange, and grapefruit trees. When the wind blew, he remembered, "There wasn't a prettier smelling place on earth."

As a child he was shy, a characteristic he never overcame. He didn't say much because he had a speech impediment, but the youngster was responsible and goal oriented, and so his disability didn't stop him from selling newspapers on the street. His dream as a boy was to become a cowboy.

Landry grew up in a segregated, deeply religious society in which the melting pot consisted of Saturday night dances when the Methodists mingled with the Baptists. His high school coach feared the corrupting influence of the opposite sex and warned his boys against letting the girls wear their letter sweaters. As a senior Landry was class valedictorian and a member of the National Honor Society. He was also a talented back on the football team, and in 1941 he led tiny Mission High School to a 12–0 record, as the team outscored the opposition 322–7. In the district championship against Aransas Pass, Landry scored on runs of 4 and 38 yards, and then late in the game he ran through the entire Aransas Pass team for a 76-yard touchdown. The celebration was short-lived, because two days later the Japanese attacked Pearl Harbor.

Landry was courted by SMU, Rice, and Mississippi State, but he went to the University of Texas after a local oilman/alum convinced him that UT produced most of Texas' leaders. And just as important to Landry was that UT was close enough to home that his parents could come to the games and watch him play. He accepted a full scholarship there.

His intention was to enter the oil business, and he enrolled in engineering. Before entering college in the fall of 1942, he worked the entire summer on the floor of a drilling rig, wrestling with heavy pipes as the driller barked orders, warnings, and threats. It was backbreaking labor, but the $4 per hour wages earned him enough money to last the entire school year.

During his freshman year his older brother Robert was reported missing in action while on a flying mission; it was later disclosed that his plane had exploded in midair. In November Landry enlisted in the Army Air Corps, and in February 1943, he was called to active duty. He sailed in the fall of that year on the *Queen Mary* to England, where he learned to fly B-17 Flying Fortress bombers.

At age 19, Tom Landry was made a copilot, one of the youngest among the American bombing squadrons. The B-17s flew in groups of four in a diamond shape with gunners from each plane protecting the others from air attack. The pilots were trained to follow closely what the lead plane was doing. Survival depended on teamwork. As in football, teamwork was at a premium, but in this case individuality could get you killed.

The return rate of these bombers was low, and several times Landry had close calls. After 30 missions, he was discharged in November 1945. He returned to Austin in the spring of 1946 to play football during the final season of coaching legend D. X. Bible, who believed in hard work and preparation and would say things like, "If you pay the premiums, you will get the dividends." Landry's philosophies would later ape Bible's.

Landry had been away from football for four years, but at age 23 he felt he could still play. He and another talented Texan named Bobby Layne, who could not have been more different from Landry, competed for the starting quarterback job.

Landry was a quiet loner. At Texas he would meet his one true love, Alicia Wiggs, and remain true to her for life. Layne, who grew up in Dallas, even as a high school student was a hard-drinking hell-raiser who enjoyed a good bar fight followed by a good roll in the hay with whatever Texas belle he could get drunk and seduce.

The two men were as different as two men could be. In his autobiography, Landry noted, "I wasn't the first person Bobby thought of when he needed a drinking partner or party company," and admitted the stories he knew about Bobby all came from others. And as great as Layne was, attaining All-America and All-Pro status, Landry's penchant for coach Bible's standards of hard work and preparation caused Landry to comment that Layne "never trained. And I've often wondered how much greater he might have been if he had." Layne, who was one year ahead of Landry, in turn would freely express his deep dislike for Landry, making fun of his quarterbacking ability and his straitlaced martinet nature.

As a junior Layne took UT to the 1946 Southwest Conference championship, a season in which Landry played little because of an injury. In 1947 Blair Cherry took over as coach and switched from the single wing to the pro-style T formation. Cherry went so far as to send Layne to Chicago to study under the Bears' resident genius George Halas and his quarterback star Sid Luckman. Under

Cherry, Landry's initial assignment was to back up Layne at quarterback and to go in for him on defense.

Against Oregon Landry badly broke his thumb making a tackle and Cherry moved him to fullback, where he became a star. In one game, Landry outgained North Carolina All-American Charlie "Choo Choo" Justice. In 1947 Layne and Landry took UT to a 10–1 record and a No. 4 national ranking. The only loss was a heartbreaking one-pointer to Doak Walker and SMU. Landry has always blamed himself for the loss, citing a play in which instead of gaining a key first down he slipped in the mud before he could take a handoff from Layne. But UT then beat famed quarterback Harry Gilmer and Alabama in the Sugar Bowl.

When Landry returned in 1948 the colorful Layne was gone, off to the Chicago Bears on the first leg of what would be an outstanding 15-year pro career. In Landry's senior year UT went only 6–3–1 but was selected to play in the Orange Bowl against Georgia. Landry led UT to a 41–28 win, running for 117 yards on 17 carries.

In 1949 Landry was drafted by both the New York Yankees in the All-America Football Conference and the New York Giants in the NFL. His long-range plan was to have a career in the oil business, and to that end he enrolled at the University of Houston in order to earn an engineering degree. His need to pay tuition made the money a primary consideration in choosing where to play. The Giants were the more established team, but the Yankees offered him the better deal, a $2,000 bonus and a $7,500-a-year salary, double what some established pro players were making. Landry also signed with the Yankees because—ironically—so many of their players had come from the state of Texas, and he figured he'd feel more at home with them than with the Giants. The heart of Texas always remained deep within Tom Landry. When he went off to training camp his wife remained in Houston to give birth to their first child. His reason: if the child ever wanted to run for governor, he or she could run as a "born and bred" Texan.

In his rookie year with the Yanks, an injury to the starter forced Landry into action as a defensive back against the Cleveland Browns, the best team in the league. Browns quarterback Otto Graham wasted no time picking on the inexperienced kid, as he threw to Dante Lavelli and Mac Speedie for over 200 yards, an AAFC record.

It was during that game that Landry realized that skill, emotion, and even determination were not enough to succeed in the game of pro football. He had gone into the game raw and unknowledgeable. Otto Graham had kept him guessing all game long with his play calling. Landry, who saw defeat as an event akin to death, had not only lost, but he had been humiliated as well, and so he decided that in order to make sure what had happened against the Browns wouldn't happen again, he would have to devise a system that would better prepare him for what he would face on the field. "The primary lesson learned that day served as the very foundation of my philosophical approach to playing and coaching pro football," said Landry years later. "Any success I ever attained would require the utmost in preparation and knowledge. I couldn't wait and react to my opponent. I had to know what he was going to do before he did it."

He learned another lesson as well: rookies should practice hard all week and sit on the bench during games. When Landry later became coach, rookies would start for him only if they were truly exceptional or he found himself with no other choice.

At the end of the year the All-America Football Conference and the National Football League merged and the Yankees folded. In 1950 Landry was signed by the New York Giants as a regional draft choice. His first year with the Giants, Landry was the second-best punter in the league behind Frankie Albert, and he played behind halfback Buddy Young. Later, when defensive back Harmon Rowe was injured, Landry took his spot in the secondary as the Giants' left cornerback. Teammates noticed that though he was not fast and not as quick as some backs, Landry always seemed to know where the play was going. Also, when he hit he did so viciously. Landry hit his man like a spike going through a board. "I had an acute hatred for receivers," said Landry. "If a guy caught a ball against me, I'd try to hit him so hard he wished he hadn't."

But what most impressed teammates and foes alike about Landry was that he hated to lose. He was an angry, sore loser. Dick Nolan played in the same backfield with Landry on the Giants, and what he recalled best about Landry the football player was that duality of intellect and assassin.

Dick Nolan: "He was a tough egg. He'd knock your brains out. I remember when we played the Baltimore Colts, Jim Mutscheller, a tough tight end for the Colts, went out, and Johnny Unitas hit him with a pass, and Landry hit him and drove up through him in the air until he had Mutscheller turned upside down. His head was straight down, and his feet were straight up in the air, and Landry was still going through him. Tom was a tough guy, a tough tackler. He was strong, and he was tough. He didn't back down from anybody."

The other habit Landry possessed that impressed others was a raging mania for preparation. After he completed his analytical engineering training in 1952, he embarked on an independent-study course in which he began breaking football down into its component parts. Before it became fashionable, Landry spent hours a week watching game films of the upcoming opponent. What he was looking for was what he called "keys." Using his analytical skill Landry figured out that when the offense lined up in a certain way, there were a limited number of plays that could be run from that formation.

For instance, from watching films he saw that if the halfbacks were split behind the quarterback, the offense would run either a long trap or an end run, or they would run a counter play. If they set up with the fullback behind the quarterback and the halfback on the side opposite the tight end, he knew the formation called for the fullback to run the ball.

Once Landry knew where the play was going to go, he could ignore the feints and fakes and the window dressing, and all he had to do was lie in wait at the location he knew the ball was going to be, either on a run or through the air. He developed his analysis to the point that he could actually anticipate what the offense was going to do by the formation and initial movement of the offensive players. Landry saw that if the opposition sent a halfback on a flare pattern toward the sideline, what the offense wanted was for the linebacker on that side to go with him, thereby leaving a big space in the middle of the field for the wide receiver to run into and catch a pass. If you knew that, Landry figured out, all you had to do was lie in wait where the wide receiver was sure to go. Teammates were amazed that, more often than not, Landry would be in perfect position to flatten the receiver with a jarring tackle or intercept the pass. By 1952 Landry had perfected his system to the point that he made eight interceptions and became an All-Pro defensive back.

From his first season with the Giants, Landry had the respect of his teammates. That year the team was preparing to play the powerful Cleveland Browns, with quarterback Otto Graham and receivers Mac Speedie and Dante Lavelli and the rest of a very powerful offensive team. The week before, the Browns had creamed the former NFL champs, the Philadelphia Eagles. To stop Speedie and Lavelli, Giants coach Steve Owen devised what looked like a 6-1 defense, with six linemen, one linebacker, and four backs. The twist Owen was bringing to the Cleveland game was that the 6-1 look was only a disguise designed to confuse the normally unflappable Graham. At the snap of the ball in passing situations, the Giants ends were to drop back into the zones, where the quick and talented receivers usually stopped to catch Graham's pinpoint passes. Speedie and Lavelli would be running into double coverage. The other key to the defense was a heavy rush from the defensive linemen.

After Owen described his new defense, with its different assignments and new pass coverage, he walked out of the room. There was a buzzing, a murmuring of confusion about what everyone was supposed to do. Landry, normally taciturn and slow with words, rose from his chair and went to the blackboard. He had never spoken in front of the team before. But his teammates were aware that Landry, with that engineer's mind, could dissect plans. Moreover, he had the gifted ability to explain hard concepts and make them understandable. When he got to the chalkboard no one questioned his right to be up there before them. He began drawing the *X*s and *O*s that make up the football vocabulary, and by the end of the session the Giants players understood Owen's revolutionary "umbrella defense."

Against the Giants, Otto Graham did not complete a pass in the first half. At halftime Paul Brown, himself a coaching genius, adjusted. He ordered Graham to throw short passes or run wide. But Owen reacted as well, and his ends, Ray Poole and Jim Duncan, kept Graham running for his life, and Landry and Emlen Tunnell came up to make tackle after tackle.

The Giants won the game, 6–0, and later in the season beat the powerful Browns again, 17–13. The Giants finished the season 10–2 but lost to the

Browns in a playoff, 8–3. In three games against the Giants' umbrella defense, the Browns had scored but one touchdown.

In 1951 the season came down to a game against the Pittsburgh Steelers, led by defensive end Ernie Stautner. After Stautner put Giants quarterbacks Charlie Conerly and Fred Benners in the hospital, Landry had to come in and run the offense. Landry had last been a quarterback in high school. Pressed into duty against the Steelers, he had to draw the plays in the dirt. Before the end of the game Stautner broke through, doubled his fist, and smashed Landry in the face through the meager face bar, breaking his nose and knocking him down. As Stautner was returning to his huddle, Landry jumped up and punched him in the back. The Steelers won, 63–7.

The Giants were mediocre in 1952, and injuries cost them dearly in 1953, as their record fell to 3–9. After the season, Giants owner Tim Mara fired Steve Owen and replaced him with former Giants end Jim Lee Howell. Howell hired a young assistant from West Point by the name of Vince Lombardi to coach the offense. To coach the defense he appointed the 29-year-old Landry as player/coach.

As a player Landry would never have been presumptive enough to try to formally teach his system to the other defensive players, but when he became defensive coach, it was his job. He designed a defense he called "the inside 4-3" and "the outside 4-3." It was revolutionary because in the past everyone played man-to-man defense. In the past brute strength had been the requisite. You lined up opposite your man, and you tried to beat the crap out of him, using a forearm or your shoulder or a head slap, or grabbing him by the jersey and throwing him off to the side in an attempt to get by him to make the tackle.

Landry's defense depended on his players knowing what the other team was going to run and stopping the lanes where the play was expected to go. The defense was also designed in such a way that the defensive linemen would control the offensive players so that no one would get a decent block on the middle linebacker, whose job it was to patrol the center of the field behind the line. Under Landry's system it was the job of the middle linebacker to fill unclosed holes and tackle the ball carrier.

When the Giants would see that the play was going to run inside, they set up in their inside 4-3. The two defensive tackles would control the lanes to the left and right of the center. The middle linebacker would fill the holes outside both tackles, the place where the ball carrier was expected to be. If the offense saw it was bogged down when it tried to run inside, then the opposing coach would set up formations designed to run wide, and Landry's defense would counter with its outside 4-3. The defensive ends would come back inside, head up with the offensive tackles, forcing the ball carrier to go outside, where the middle linebacker and safety would be waiting for him.

Landry also did something else that was new and revolutionary. He made his defensive players watch game films for hours on end. Each player had a book of skeleton sheets, and in conjunction with watching the films they had to meticulously learn each offensive formation and the position they had to adopt in order to counter it. Landry's theory was that if you knew in advance what was coming, you could stop it. His credo was that with foreknowledge you could take away what the other team was trying to do, thus creating chaos in their backfield, causing rushed passes and fumbles, and thereby forcing teams to continually operate in second-and-long situations.

All the Giants players needed, he told them, was faith in his system. To Landry, the system was foolproof. But his system went against everything that the defensive players had been taught over the years—chase the ball, attack the ball carrier. Players who were used to chasing the ball wherever it went had to hold their ground and wait for the ball to come back to them. For some players, Landry's ability to predict what play the offense would run seemed more like black magic than science. Accepting that his "keys" were accurate predictors took more faith than some had in them.

"What if they don't do that?"

"But they will."

"But what if they won't?"

"There are no *what ifs*," Landry would reply.

Because most of the Giants defensive players had played alongside Landry and respected him for his savvy nature and brilliant mind, they were more than willing to follow his lead. He continually preached that using this defense, the Giants could play a perfect football game. For four years beginning in 1956, the Giants played games that proved this was possible.

That year Landry orchestrated the first famous defensive unit in the history of professional football. During the off-season, the Giants traded for two tough-as-nails linemen, Andy Robustelli of the Rams and Dick Modzelewski of the Steelers, and from the draft they added lineman Jim Katcavage and an agile, smart, disciplined, and downright mean ball of fire by the name of Sam Huff.

Huff had been a guard at West Virginia University. But when Giants middle linebacker Ray Beck had to cut short his career to attend to his sick father, Landry made Huff the middle linebacker, the centerpiece of his inside 4-3, outside 4-3, tutoring him day and night until he knew every key, every ramification, every nuance. Under Landry's system, the linemen played off their blocks in such a way that the middle linebacker remained free of interference to make the tackle. Without an effective middle linebacker, his entire system of defense would fail. Landry needed Huff to succeed in order to succeed himself.

Everyone else told Landry that Huff was too small to play the position. "Everyone else is wrong," Landry said, and he set out to prove it. He had a projector in his apartment in the Concourse Plaza Hotel, down the avenue from Yankee Stadium. Huff also had an apartment there. Landry would call Huff on the phone.

"Sam, what are you doing?"

"Watching television."

"Good, I'm glad you aren't doing anything. Why don't you come up to my room and look at some football films with me? There are some things I want to show you."

Off Huff would go to watch game films projected on the Landrys' living room wall. There were times that Landry's relentlessness—and the enormity of the task of cramming Landry's complicated system into his young head—got to Huff, and one time the rookie packed to leave for home, along with his rookie roommate, Don Chandler. It took the bull moose persuasion of Vince Lombardi, who caught them as they were about to depart and told them, "You two might not make this club but nobody runs out on me." They stayed.

If Landry had a flaw, it was his tendency to remain the unrelenting perfectionist. Under his system the player read the key, then went to a predetermined spot. If the player wasn't there, no matter what the outcome, Landry would be in his ear to remind him. One time Frank Gifford, who was then playing defensive back, intercepted a pass and ran it back for a touchdown. Gifford had made a spectacular play, but after it was over Landry told him, "Frank, you were out of position on that play."

Perfection may have been his goal, but that same perfection also squeezed some of the fun and spontaneity out of the game. It still, however, helped turn the New York Giants into a defensive machine, half of a Giants team that began the modern age of professional football. The 11 members of the defense all became well known to their adoring fans: Andy Robustelli, Jim Katcavage, Rosey Grier, and Dick Modzelewski up front, with linebackers Sam Huff, Tom Scott, and Cliff Livingston, along with defensive backs Dick Nolan, Jimmy Patton, Lindon Crow, and Dick Lynch.

On offense Vince Lombardi, an outgoing, bellowing "pretend tough guy," as defensive back Dick Nolan called him, had a different philosophy from the stoical, impersonal Landry's. Lombardi's philosophy was to run a half dozen basic plays, but to run them with such precision that no one could stop them, even if the defenders knew in advance what was coming. To get his players to reach the perfection he was looking for, Lombardi cajoled and badgered them, but at the same time hugged them hard and let them know he loved them. Like Landry, Lombardi watched hours of films, dissecting defenses to find flaws, and when he found one, in the game he'd run the same play two, three, four times in a row until eventually the other team would slip, and his offense would be right down their throats. Lombardi created a whirlwind attack behind Charlie Conerly at quarterback, Frank Gifford at halfback, and Alex Webster at fullback.

In the locker room Landry and Lombardi were close friends, but there *was* a rivalry. They were two perfectionists who hated to lose even at checkers, and each wanted his unit to conquer whomever it came up against. To that end each demanded extra practice time from head coach Jim Lee Howell. And during games they would fight for their unit's honor. On fourth-and-one, Landry and

Lombardi would stand on either side of Howell and try to influence him. Landry would advise Howell to punt so his unit could get back out there, while Lombardi would importune him to let *his* players go for it.

Beginning in the fall of 1956, the New York Giants became the glamour team in the NFL, and these Giants players became heroes and ultimately legends. They were adopted by New Yorkers who formerly had cared only about the Yankees, or the Dodgers, or the baseball Giants, or the basketball Knicks, or the hockey Rangers. The fans appreciated Lombardi's style of play, with glamour boy Frank Gifford capturing the hearts of wives and girlfriends, as well as the male rooters. And when the offense filed off the field, those fans cheered on every play for Sam Huff and his destroyers. In third-down situations Giants fans would chant, "*Deee*-fense, *deee*-fense." And more often than not, the defense would hold, as the frenzy in the stands would escalate. When they loped off the field, they would be treated to standing ovations. This recognition for a team's defense was a first, and before the TV camera's see-it-all eyes, across the country millions of fans would watch them and root for them.

In December 1956 the New York Giants played the Chicago Bears for the NFL championship on the frozen turf of Yankee Stadium. Before the game the Giants players donned sneakers, while the Bears played in metal spikes. Giants speedster Gene Filipski took the opening kickoff and ran it back 53 yards to the Bears' 5. The rout was on. The Giants led at the half, 34–7.

During the week the Giants defenders had worked on stopping the Bears' big-play man, receiver Harlon Hill, and against the Giants, Hill did little, along with the rest of the Bears. With an offense drilled by Lombardi, the Giants moved the ball with machinelike precision as they won the championship, 47–7.

The next year the interest in the NFL grew with the start of one of the greatest rivalries in the history of the sport. The rivalry was between Sam Huff of the Giants and a rookie running back drafted out of Syracuse University by the Cleveland Browns. That back, Jim Brown, is still considered the greatest runner in the history of the game. With Brown running the ball for the Browns, Sam Huff's world did indeed become violent. The Giants-Browns games pitting Sam Huff against Jim Brown in the late fifties became legendary.

In 1957 the Browns won the East, with the Giants second, and in 1958 the Browns led the Giants by one game with one game to go—against each other. The Giants would have to win that game for the right to play the Browns in a playoff game for the Eastern title. The Giants had to twice stop Jim Brown and the Browns, a difficult task considering that Brown ran for 163 yards per game and scored 14 touchdowns that year.

In the season finale Brown eluded Huff's grasp early in the game and ran for a 65-yard touchdown. After that Huff and the 4-3 defense shut him down. Toward the end of the game, the score was tied 10–10. If the game ended in a tie, Cleveland would win the division title.

The Giants had the ball fourth-and-10 with 2:09 left. Because snow was falling and blanketing the field it was hard to see what hash mark the ball was on. Pat Summerall lined up to kick what turned out to be a 49-yard field goal. It was the longest kick he would ever attempt as a Giant. The snow swirled, making it hard for him to even see the goal posts.

As Charlie Conerly kneeled to clear a spot on the powdery turf, all seemed lost, but in one of those mythical moments, the Giants kicker swung his leg and made the football explode toward the end of the field. As it spun forward among the eddies of snowflakes, the ghostly officials standing under the goal posts signaled the kick good. The Giants and Browns would go at it in Yankee Stadium in frozen New York City one more time.

For two solid weeks Vince Lombardi had studied the Browns on film. The Browns defense put so much pressure on the quarterback, it was hard to score against them. This time Lombardi opened with a stunning surprise. Quarterback Charlie Conerly handed the ball to Alex Webster, who switched it over to Frank Gifford, who turned upfield untouched and ran down to the Cleveland 8-yard line, where as he was about to be tackled, he lateralled to a trailing Conerly, who scored. Summerall later added a field goal.

For two solid weeks Landry too had studied the Browns on film, and he had spent a lot of time tutoring Huff on how to stop Jim Brown. And in this game Landry's defense came as close as was humanly possible to reaching the perfection he had been seeking. Cleveland, led by Brown, its feared runner, was held to eight yards in *total offense*. The Giants won 10–0. It was the first time a Paul Brown team had been shut out since 1950, when Steve Owen concocted his umbrella defense against the Browns.

After the game Cleveland Browns kicker Lou Groza commented, "There's only one man who could have done this to us . . . Tom Landry. Nobody else." When Andy Robustelli was given the game ball, he turned it over to Landry. "This doesn't belong to me," said Robustelli. Head coach Jim Lee Howell praised him as well, saying, "Tom Landry is the best coach in football."

The 1958 NFL championship against the Baltimore Colts, the best offensive team in the league, is one game everyone who saw it still remembers. This was the game that propelled football into America's consciousness as a spectator sport that had the capability of rivaling baseball.

The Giants led 17–14 late in the game on a touchdown pass from Charlie Conerly to Frank Gifford. The game would be theirs if they could gain one more first down. But on third-and-four, Frank Gifford took the handoff, headed wide, and cut back inside. Colts defensive end Gino Marchetti stopped him with a crushing tackle just shy of the first-down marker. And worse, Gifford was through for the day with a broken leg. A punt put the Colts back on their own 12.

The Giants knew what Johnny Unitas was going to do, but they couldn't stop him. They tried a desperate measure, double-teaming ends Lenny Moore and

Ray Berry. Unitas hit Berry with three passes in a row. In a minute and a half Unitas had taken his team to the Giants' 13. That was when Steve Myhra kicked his field goal, tying the game, and leading to a loss that has always rankled Giants fans and Tom Landry. But because of that field goal, the game was sent into overtime and into the annals of history.

In overtime the Giants won the toss and elected to receive. Three plays later, the Giants were inches shy of the first-down marker, and Don Chandler had to punt. Unitas started on his own 20, and despite defensive adjustments of all sorts, the Giants could not stop the march of the Colts. When Alan Ameche bulled over from the 2, the Colts became world champions.

In 1959 the Giants defense held 12 opponents to 170 points, remarkable in that the Giants had allowed 49 in one game against the Philadelphia Eagles. In the other 11 games, the defense allowed just 121 points—incredible numbers. Despite the loss of Vince Lombardi, who left the team to become head coach of the Green Bay Packers, the Giants again reached the NFL championship, only to lose again to the Colts. Landry's defense had a rough afternoon against Unitas & Co., and against the Colts line of Marchetti, Don Joyce, Eugene "Big Daddy" Lipscomb, and Artie Donovan, the Giants didn't do much. The final score was 31–16 Colts. Still, in four years of using Landry's defense, the Giants had played in three championship games, winning one, and one year finished second in the Eastern Division.

Landry was primed to leave the Giants after the 1959 season. Landry's intention all along after getting his degree in industrial engineering was to go into business. After the 1955 season he had moved to Dallas in the off-season in an attempt to find a career in which he might find success in the real world. But what Landry had not anticipated was that whether he was selling storage tanks for oil fields or insurance or real estate, he floundered because for six months of the year he had to be absent coaching football, and employers didn't want six-month employees.

Tom Landry was at a crossroads in his life. His football salary was only around $12,000 per year, so he either had to find a better-paying job in football or get out of the game and go into business full-time. Rumors abounded that Jim Lee Howell would quit the Giants and let Landry take over, but no offer was made. Bud Adams of the Houston Oilers contacted Landry about coaching his team, but Landry wasn't sure he wanted to coach in an unstable new league and demurred. It was at that point that Tex Schramm offered Tom Landry the job as head coach of the new NFL franchise in Dallas. This was a chance to get out from under the shadow of Jim Lee Howell and prove his own worth as a coach. And he could do it in front of his homefolk.

Tom Landry was coming back to Texas.

Chapter 5

The Expendables

There was one other incentive pushing Tom Landry to take the job as head coach at Dallas: he could build a team from scratch and once again prove the worth of his defensive system, an impossible task, but one that appealed to him. "The idea of such a big challenge intrigued me," Landry said years later.

The key to success for any pro team is young players—unformed, eager, ready to learn, playing on legs not yet pounded and broken. In pro football the college draft is what makes a good team great, as the youngsters imbue a team with their youth and their enthusiasm, pushing the veterans to play harder, and sometimes pushing them out. It is the natural order of things. But in 1960 the fledgling Dallas Rangers did not get to participate in the college draft, because it was held *before* the NFL officially admitted the team into the league.

Only through the largesse of expansion committee head George Halas were the Rangers able to sign their two young talented college seniors, SMU quarterback Don Meredith and University of New Mexico running back Don Perkins. The rest of the Dallas players would come from a hastily compiled list of fringe players grudgingly given up by the existing NFL teams.

A half dozen of the men plucked from the hasty expansion list were pushing 30 or were older. Coaches of the existing NFL teams risked the least by placing their oldest players on the list. Even if they had been stars and still could perform, it would not be long before it was time for them to retire. If a player on the list was younger than 30, it was probably because he had been broken and hadn't been the same after he had mended, or because he had never approached his potential and was being discarded.

Making Landry's job even harder was the fact that several veterans he was counting on, like fullback Ed Modzelewski of Cleveland and center Charlie Ane from Detroit, retired rather than report to the expansion Rangers, deciding that moving teams and towns—in essence starting from scratch—was too difficult and not worth the emotional price at that point in their careers. Of the ones who did report, a few looked forward to coming and were even happy to come to this new team, angry or frustrated as they were about their status on their old teams. A few, as Tex Schramm had surmised, were pleased to come to Dallas because they were Texans coming back to Texas.

Schramm knew the players taken on the expansion list would be upset at having to leave their teams to play in a new town for a ragtag ensemble. He also knew that if he could draft players who had played in college in Texas, they would be less likely to be resentful. It was one of the considerations when he plucked running back Don McIlhenny from the draft list of the Green Bay Packers. As it turned out, Schramm was right about McIlhenny. The running back was glad to be coming back to Dallas.

McIlhenny was born and raised in Cleveland. When he entered Southern Methodist University in 1952, he was a single wing tailback, following in the footsteps of Doak Walker and Kyle Rote. But the heyday of the Mustangs was over, and the team was mediocre. In one game against Kansas, McIlhenny scored four touchdowns. But SMU couldn't beat the big boys like Notre Dame. Still, McIlhenny was named the starting halfback in the College All-Star Game, and he played in the Shrine Game and Senior Bowl Game as well.

In 1956 he was drafted third by Detroit, the same year the Lions picked Howard "Hopalong" Cassady, the All-American from Ohio State, number one. Nevertheless, Lions coach Buddy Parker started McIlhenny, and he was near the top of the league in rushing until he tore up his knee against San Francisco when Leo Nomellini drove his large body through McIlhenny's extended leg. But McIlhenny did return in time for the Western Division championship game against the Bears.

Middle linebacker Jack Patera was also happy to be coming to Dallas because he was getting away from the Chicago Cardinals, a dreary, unorganized team. Patera had been a member of a rising Baltimore Colts team, and he was looking forward to playing on a championship-winning team when during training camp in 1958 coach Weeb Ewbank asked him to switch from linebacker to the offensive line. Patera stubbornly refused. And as a result Ewbank got rid of him. Patera missed being part of one of the most exciting championships in the history of the game, the historic win over the New York Giants in Yankee Stadium in December 1958. Instead, he was shipped to the gulag in Chicago. Thus, when Patera found himself leaving Chicago via the expansion draft, he was ecstatic. Even playing for an expansion team was better than having to spend another year with the Chicago Cardinals.

Jack Patera: "Weeb traded me to the Chicago Cardinals, and if there was one team I didn't want to go to, it was the Cardinals. Our strong safety, Bert Rechichar, had been traded there in the off-season, and sometime in training camp the Cardinals had released him, and so the trade was nullified, and Bert was saying, 'You can't imagine what it's like. It's the worst thing you can imagine,' and he went on and on. And when I got to Chicago, everything Bert said was true. It was just awful. The equipment had to be from the forties, stuff they were still trying to use. The cliques on the team were obnoxious. The people in management and coaching were inferior types. Everything about it was inferior.

"At the end of the season I wrote a letter asking them to put me in the expansion draft. I figured anything would be better than playing on the Cardinals. I knew nothing about the Dallas organization and I could have cared less. It was just an opportunity to start over again."

Some of the players, including tight end Dick Bielski and guard Bob Fry, didn't particularly want to leave their old teams, but they had the sort of personality not to complain once it occurred. Bielski had been a star fullback for the Philadelphia Eagles until quarterback Norm Van Brocklin came and ordered the coach to move him to tight end. In 1959 Bielski found himself on a team headed for glory. But at the end of the season he was perplexed to find that coach Buck Shaw had put him on the expansion list. While the Eagles won the NFL championship in 1960, he was toiling for expansion Dallas. To his credit, he didn't bitch and moan. It wasn't Dick Bielski's nature.

Dick Bielski: "What made going to the Cowboys hard was that everything was different. The attitude was different. The players were all players from different groups. They all had ideas of how it should be, what shouldn't be. And it was very difficult. It was difficult because you had nothing to lean on, nothing to fall back on, nothing to get your teeth into. Everything was so different."

Chapter 6

THE DISGRUNTLED

If some players were not actively unhappy to be playing in Dallas, practically everyone else on that expansion list was. Most made it abundantly clear they were coming to play for the Dallas Rangers, soon to become the Cowboys, against their will. They were not ready to retire, but this was where the NFL was telling them they had to play. As a result they had to start over very late in their careers, and they hated the idea. But one player, linebacker Jerry Tubbs, was in the opposite situation. He had intended to retire from pro football and take a managerial job with Coca-Cola. When the job didn't materialize he joined the Cowboys because he needed the money.

Tubbs, who was acquired from the San Francisco 49ers, grew up in Breckenridge, Texas, about 135 miles west of Dallas. In three years of high school ball Tubbs' teams lost only three games as he led Breckenridge High to state championships in both his junior and senior years. Tubbs wanted to play for a winner in college, and so in 1954 he went to the University of Oklahoma to play for coach Bud Wilkinson, one of the most successful coaches in college history. Tubbs played on undefeated national championship teams his junior and senior years at the University of Oklahoma, and in 1957 he was drafted number one by the Chicago Cardinals—ahead of Syracuse running back Jim Brown. Unfortunately for Tubbs, the Chicago Cardinals were the worst-run team in football. Tubbs himself will tell you the fact that the Cards owner took him over Brown was a strong indication that the organization was in disarray. Tubbs signed his rookie year for a $9,000 salary and a $2,000 bonus. Tubbs had played middle linebacker at Oklahoma, but because he weighed only 215 pounds, the coaches forced him to play on the outside. He was given a starting role, and then three-quarters of the way through the season he was cut. After missing just one game, he signed with San Francisco, again playing outside linebacker for coach Frankie Albert. The next year he was able to convince the new coach, Red Hickey, that he should play in the middle, and in 1959 the 49ers would have been in the championships if they could have beaten the Baltimore Colts.

Tubbs intended to get out of pro football after 1959. He had played to find out if he could, and he had met the challenge. At the end of the season he went back to Breckenridge, Texas, to teach and coach at his old high school. While he was there, he was contacted by Coca-Cola and offered the job of district manager in a plant in Little Rock, Arkansas. An honorable man, Tubbs told Coke he could not leave at that time because one of the other Breckenridge coaches had left to go to another school, and he didn't want to leave the school with two openings in such a short period of time. Tubbs asked Coke to hold the job for him until the end of the school year. Coke told Tubbs they could not do that, but that if another opening came up, they'd let him know.

When Dallas got its franchise and each existing club was told to make a list of players for the expansion draft, Red Hickey called Tubbs and asked about his plans. Tubbs told him, "If a job opens up with Coke, I'm going to take it."

Hickey was incredulous: "You're going to take a job and *not* play pro football?"

"Yes," said Tubbs, "if a job opens up. But if a job doesn't open up, I'd like to play again."

The night the 49ers were making the expansion list, Hickey called Tubbs from the meeting and said, "Now Tubbs, if we keep you on the 49ers, tell me you'll play for us. We can't hold you and then lose you to retirement."

"Coach, I just can't do that."

And so Red Hickey put Jerry Tubbs on the expansion list.

Jerry Tubbs: "There wasn't any ulterior motive. I wasn't trying to get to Dallas. In fact, I really didn't like the idea of playing for Dallas, because I knew they were an expansion team, that they wouldn't do very well. When Tex Schramm called, I told him about the Coke deal. When June came, and Coke still didn't have an opening, I finally signed with the Cowboys."

The players who came to that first Cowboys training camp had several characteristics in common. Most were children of the Depression, brought up by parents who had struggled to clothe and feed them. These players, almost all white, were hardworking, honest, forthright, and self-sufficient. They had had to be. Most of them had come from hard times. Tubbs, the son of a tenant farmer in rural Oklahoma, grew up with a toughness he developed from hard times. Defensive end Gene Cronin had been part of *The Grapes of Wrath* legacy, a Nebraskan who fled the dust bowl and relocated in California, where the father dug ditches and the family lived in a tent. Defensive end John Gonzaga couldn't afford even to go to college and got his tryout with the pros after working in the steel mills. Fullback Gene Babb, who grew up in and around the oil fields of Texas, lost his father when he was eight, his mother when he was thirteen. Kicker Fred Cone was a parachute jumper in the army during World War II when he started playing football. Part of the ethic of the fifties was that you were supposed to be rewarded for your long service. These men, rather, had been betrayed, and so men like Gene Cronin of the Detroit Lions, John Gonzaga of the San Francisco 49ers, and end Ray Mathews of the Pittsburgh Steelers never got over having been dumped by their old teams. They hated leaving their friends behind and brimmed with bitterness over being cut adrift. Cronin and

Mathews had played for the hard-drinking maverick Buddy Parker, and each had loved him. Gonzaga had played for Red Hickey, whom he disliked, and demanded that Hickey send him elsewhere. Hickey sent him to Dallas, which didn't suit Gonzaga either.

When Cronin, Gonzaga, and Mathews came to Dallas, they were met by a coach who ran the team like it was boot camp, ordering their lives on and off the field. The three spent a year in Dallas chafing against Tom Landry's iron rule. This bitterness would permeate the team and subvert Landry's authority the first few years of their existence, until he could supplant them with younger, more malleable, more talented players.

Of all the expansion players, the one who made the biggest show of disrespect for Tom Landry and his system was offensive end Ray Mathews, who had been plucked from the roster of the Pittsburgh Steelers, where he had caught the passes of Jim Finks and then Bobby Layne. Mathews felt he had had Tom Landry's number when the new Dallas head coach was playing defensive back for the Giants, and now that Landry was coach, Mathews was not shy about reminding him of the numerous catches he made against him. Mathews was the quintessential freelance end, a hell-raiser like Layne. But with the Cowboys, Landry made Mathews, who had been one of Bobby Layne's drinking buddies, run specific routes and heel to his precise system. All year long he bitched and moaned loudly about Landry to teammates, even to the coach's face.

Ray Mathews: "I went to Dallas with a chip on my shoulder. I had played nine years with Pittsburgh, and I was hoping the Cowboys would send me back. But they never did. I did everything I could to get them to trade me, but they kept me for the whole year."

Chapter 7

MR. NICE

When Tex Schramm was general manager of the Los Angeles Rams, he was a pioneer in bringing black players into the NFL. Schramm had lived in California, where racial tolerance was at its highest in America in the fifties, and when he sought players for his Rams team, he didn't exclude blacks as other owners did. Tank Younger was a Rams star, as was Deacon Dan Towler, and later Schramm would introduce the NFL to Gene "Big Daddy" Lipscomb.

When the Cowboys came into existence in 1960, Dallas was still rigidly segregated. Blacks could live in one of several overly crowded areas, including South Dallas, the east side of Love Field, Oak Cliff, and the State Street–Thomas Avenue area off Hall Street. The hotels and restaurants were still segregated, and blacks still had to ride in the back of buses. In 1950 federal regulations outlawed segregation on interstate carriers, primarily trains, though after the law was passed some of the Texas conductors continued to enforce the segregationist policy. Schools were still segregated. In fact, Dallas was one of the largest cities in the South with a completely segregated school system. Despite *Brown v. Board of Education*, it was only in May 1960 that the school board moved to end segregation in Dallas, voting to desegregate one grade at a time, a plan rejected by the federal courts.

It was during this time that Tex Schramm, the general manager of the Dallas Cowboys, went to the citizens council in order to solve his own problem. Among those signed by the Cowboys were Don Perkins and Frank Clarke, black players who needed to be able to eat and sleep with the team.

Tex Schramm: "When we came to Dallas, we had no hotel where any of our black players could stay, nor could any of the visiting players who were black. At that time they had a very good situation in Dallas in which there was a group of businessmen that essentially had the influence in the town and ran things with good intentions. I went to them and said, 'Look. We got a problem. We've got blacks on our team, and the teams coming in are going to have blacks.' They were very conscious and aware of the circumstances, because they had been working with the Negro leaders to prevent things that had happened in other parts of the South, having nothing to do with football, and so the Ramada Inn on the property of the airport said they would take all the players, but only if none of the other hotels would retaliate. Back in those days, if a hotel took a black in, the other hotels would get the word all around, so the whites wouldn't go there. They got an agreement from the other hotels, and so that first year we stayed at the Ramada Inn, both the white and the black players. We stayed there after we came back from training camp and the night before games.

"We then moved down to the Sheraton downtown, and that broke the hotel barrier, though Dallas still had a restaurant problem."

Frank Clarke had come to the Dallas Rangers in the expansion draft from the Cleveland Browns. Clarke, 27 years old, had been signed by the Browns as an offensive end. He had spent his three years with the Browns playing mostly on the special teams, but he was 6' and 215 pounds, so Tex Schramm and Tom Landry liked his size and speed. What they could not know was that the combination of an abusive mother and a rigid system of segregation had caused him to feel scared every moment of his life. Clarke, like the rest of a subservient, oppressed generation of blacks under orders to "know your place," discovered that the best way to get along was to show the world that he was not a threat to others. He rarely became angry, never raising his voice. He was polite, said, "Yes, sir" and "No, sir," and hoped society would find him acceptable. "Humble" is how most of his teammates remembered him to be.

Despite his popularity at the University of Colorado, Clarke chose to keep to himself and had few friends. Pleasure was not one of the emotions in his makeup. Even when Colorado won the Orange Bowl game his senior year, he could not enjoy the victory. Despite his obvious talent, his coach, a southerner, never gave him a starting role. Clarke felt it was because the coach didn't want a junior college transfer who was black to be his star player. When Clarke was drafted by the Cleveland Browns, the men who started ahead of him were not wanted; only he was. Clarke would not even smile at the irony.

When he arrived in Cleveland, he found that head coach Paul Brown was critical and rarely supportive, and he never felt comfortable as a whipping boy. The Browns' star player, Jim Brown, went out of his way to show his contempt for Clarke. To this day Clarke does not know why.

When the Browns put him on the expansion list, it was with the tag of "unfulfilled promise." Frank Clarke had no guts, it was whispered. But Clarke was thrilled to have escaped. At age 27, he was going to get a real opportunity to prove his talent. Unlike most of the players on the expansion list, Clarke was excited about coming to the Dallas Cowboys, happy to be getting a fresh start with a new team.

Frank Clarke: "Before the expansion list came out, I had a feeling the Browns were going to put my name on it. It made sense. I had been with them for three years, and I hadn't played much. I had heard from one of the coaches that Paul reluctantly put my name in it. He knew that eventually Darrell 'Pete'

Brewster and Ray Renfro would be gone, and I was going to wake up one day and realize I was a pretty good athlete.

"But I also knew if I went to Dallas, I would be playing for Tom Landry. He had been an assistant coach with the Giants, but because I was a Brown, I knew he was no ordinary assistant coach. I knew his was the epitome of defensive football in the late fifties. Landry had an energy and an air of pure respect. This was a guy who was going to go places. And so I wasn't sad to leave the Browns, any more than I was sad to leave the University of Colorado. I thought, I'll just move on and do this."

Chapter 8

LITTLE EDDIE

The Cowboys had drafted quarterback Don Meredith, the phenom out of SMU, and Don Heinrich, who with the Giants had mostly been a stalking-horse for Charlie Conerly, starting the game, deciphering the defense, and then turning the team over to the more talented quarterback. Tex Schramm and Tom Landry didn't think Heinrich was talented enough to start every day, and they figured that Meredith, just a rookie, wouldn't have a clue for at least a year or two. On June 23, 1960, two weeks before the opening of training camp, Schramm traded a first- and sixth-round choice in the 1961 draft to Washington for four-time Pro Bowl player Eddie LeBaron, the sawed-off quarterback who had announced his retirement in 1959 after seven seasons with the Redskins. In the off-seasons LeBaron, who was known for his magical ball handling, scrambling, and passing skills, had gone to George Washington University Law School and had passed the Texas and California bars, and he had retired from football to pursue a career in law related to the oil and gas business. Schramm knew that LeBaron had had it with the hapless Redskins, and when Tex called him, the quarterback decided he would return to football, saying he wanted to play for Tom Landry.

LeBaron, who would start at quarterback for the Cowboys during their first three years, was the perfect man for the job. Like Landry, he had been in the service. Unlike most of his teammates, who would resent Landry's newfangled ideas, LeBaron believed in the chain of command, believed in respecting your coach, and was rigid about following orders. If Tom Landry wanted LeBaron to do something, he was going to do it, no questions asked. Like a good soldier, it would be his job to carry out orders and to perform to the best of his ability. At age 30 LeBaron no longer was a spring chicken, but at one time Eddie had been one of the best, and a shadow of his old self would still be plenty good. The Cowboys were lucky to have him.

Eddie LeBaron: "I retired from the Redskins after the '59 season. It had been a miserable year, and I passed the California bar in '59, and I thought, I might as well practice law rather than play. You didn't make much money in those days. I was making $18,000 my last year with the Redskins. So I retired. This was before I knew there was going to be a Dallas team. George Preston Marshall tried to get me to stay. He offered me more money. But we weren't very good, and I didn't see us getting any better. It's an emotional game, and I just didn't feel like I wanted to play for them any more.

"After I retired, I settled in Midland, Texas. I wanted to be an oil and gas lawyer, and I was offered a position in a law firm. During the time I was studying for the Texas bar, I got a call from Roone Arledge at ABC to be color man for the AFL telecasts. I said, 'Give me a day to think it over,' and fortuitously, the very next day Tex called up and said that the Cowboys would be interested in trading for me. We talked back and forth. I was a great admirer of Landry and also of Tex, because of what he had done with the Rams. I said, 'That sounds interesting.' He said, 'We need someone with experience. We have a new team.'

"I came a week late to training camp. From the beginning Tom put in his offensive system of movement and shifting. He didn't put in something simple. I said to him, 'We could beat some of these teams if you made it a little simpler.' He said, 'That's probably right, but I'm putting in a system to compete with the New York Giants and the Cleveland Browns. When we get the talent, we will beat those teams, but we have to have the system in place to beat them.'

"Tom Landry knew exactly what he was doing. And I bought it. I said, 'That makes sense.' The other vets weren't happy with it, but Tom knew that with his way, one day we were going to beat the big boys."

Chapter 9

THE FIRST HERD

By the start of training camp, the Dallas Rangers minor league baseball club announced that they were staying in Dallas, and so the new NFL franchise was forced to pick a new name. With *Texans* taken by the new American Football League team in Dallas, Tex Schramm opted for *Cowboys*, even though no steer or heifer or dogie had ever trod the streets of the city. To the west and down the highway, sister city Fort Worth was the cattle town, but not Dallas, which was known for its banks and skyscrapers more than anything else. But the more appropriate *Dallas Bankers* carried little romance, and so Schramm went with the name *Cowboys*, a nickname he knew carried with it all sorts of public relations possibilities.

Throughout the spring and summer of 1960 Schramm and his sidekick, Gil Brandt, kept their ears to the rumor hotline, scouring NFL rosters in search of other disgruntled players like Eddie LeBaron, men who had feuded with their coaches and quit, or like Jerry Tubbs, who had left the game because the money wasn't there and other opportunities outside football had arisen. One such player was Gene Babb, a halfback who had been demoted at San Francisco by coach Red Hickey. Rather than accept his demotion, Babb had quit the 49ers in order to coach football and teach art at Ranger Junior College in Texas.

Babb had signed a contract with the Houston Oilers in the fledgling American Football League. But Schramm had no depth at running back. He had Don McIlhenny and L. G. Dupre and no backup. Schramm *needed* Babb, who had been in the league since 1957. Babb kept telling Schramm he had already signed a contract, but Schramm would not take no for an answer. Schramm offered him $5,000 a year more than the Oilers were giving him; plus he sent Babb and his new bride off on an all-expenses-paid honeymoon—in part to get him to sign, in part to keep him out of reach of the Oilers prior to training camp. When Babb showed up in Forest Grove, Oregon, for the Cowboys' first training camp, he had become notorious for signing not one, but two contracts. The notoriety, of course, should have gone to Tex Schramm for making Babb the (second) offer he couldn't refuse. What would have made Babb even more notorious to the other players was that he, a journeyman, was coming to camp as one of the highest-paid players on the roster.

Gene Babb: "About the Fourth of July, my girlfriend—now my wife—and I went to Waco to visit her relatives. We were going to get married, and when we were in Waco I got a call from Vance Jobe saying that Dallas had gotten my rights from the 49ers and that they wanted to sign me, right now. The Dallas training camp had about a week to open. I told him, 'I'm in Waco and I'm fixing to get married.' He said, 'I want to come to Waco and take you and your future bride out to dinner and just talk to you.' I said, 'Mr. Jobe, I signed a contract with the Houston Oilers. And I'm happy.' He said, 'You realize that the Dallas Cowboys have your rights.' I said, 'That's fine, but I signed with Houston.' He said, 'But I want to come down and see you.' I said, 'We'll have dinner with you.'

"So he came down, and we met him at the Black Angus Steak House. We're sitting there eating, and he's visiting with me, and he says, 'Dallas is very interested in you. They want to sign you.' I said, 'I'm happy with what I'm making with Houston. I signed a contract.' [It was for $10,000.] He took out his napkin, and he wrote out, '$15,000.' He said, 'Would you come to Dallas for that amount of money?' I said, 'Well . . . I'll have to think about it.' He said, 'Let me get the phone and call Tex Schramm at camp.' I said, 'You're making it hard on me.' He said, 'Come on with me.' So he got Tex Schramm on the phone, and Tex told me they wanted to sign me, said that Tom Landry had remembered me when I was with the 49ers and he was with the Giants. So I proceeded to tell Tex I had signed with Houston, was happy, that I was fixing to get married, and I was going on my honeymoon.

"He said, 'Well, would you consider coming to us for $15,000?' I said, 'The only way I would do that would be if it was a no-cut contract.' And he said, 'You plan to get married on top of that?' I said, 'Yeah.' He said, 'Put Vance back on the phone.' So I did, and the two of them talked, and Vance and I went back to the table, and he said, 'OK, here's the deal. I'm going to spend the night. We're going to get you married in the morning. We'll drive to Dallas, and my wife will have on deposit a $1,500 signing bonus, and she'll open a bank account, and we'll get all squared away, and we will fly you to the training camp in Forest Grove, Oregon.'

"We agreed. And the next day Gerry and I were married. We drove to Vance Jobe's home in Dallas, and his wife, Anne, bless her heart, she had champagne, and they had the airline tickets for us to go to Denver that night, and fly the next morning on to Portland, and then over to Forest Grove to camp. The bank account was opened, the money deposited, we signed the cards, and she had starter checks, and my wife put them in her purse. Anne also had two apartments for us to look at, which we did in the next hour, and we put a deposit down to rent one of them.

"We went to the airport to go on our honeymoon, but the clincher was that Vance Jobe was going with us! We got on the plane and flew to Denver. When we arrived there was a Shriners convention, forty thousand Shriners, but

Bedford Wynne had influence and managed to get us two rooms on the same floor, and as we got to our door Vance said graciously, 'I'll see you kids in the morning. I'll give you a wake-up call. We have a flight leaving out of here at 7:00.'

"We went out, and it took us 30 minutes to cross the street because there were Shriners everywhere. We ate dinner in a candlelit place, had a dance or two, and went to sleep, and it seemed we had just closed our eyes when Vance was banging on the door. We got up and flew to Portland, where Gil Brandt met us at the airport. When we got to Forest Grove, the rookies were still on the field.

"As soon as practice was over, we went to the dorm. Tex came in and said, 'Coach Landry wants to visit with you.' He told me where I fit in his plans, was complimentary. After that, we signed the contract, and Tex said, 'Here's $3,000. You have a reservation over at Oceanlake, Oregon, at a resort there near the ocean, and here's the keys to the Chevrolet.' It was Wednesday, and he said, 'We need you to be back in camp on Sunday.' So Gerry and I had three days before the start of camp.

"As for the Houston contract, the Cowboys took about three hours deposing me, took my statement, and as it turned out, Houston never contested it. And so I became an original Dallas Cowboy."

The Cowboys' first training camp was at the University of the Pacific in Forest Grove, Oregon. It was in the middle of nowhere, a haul from the nearest big city, Portland. Landry intended to run a boot camp, and Forest Grove was the perfect place to conduct it away from any distractions. The town had one movie theater and one bar. Nearby was a maraschino cherry factory. The sweet, syrupy aroma permeated the place as the players sweated under blue skies.

Landry opened the first day's practice with a test of stamina the players called the "Landry mile." Backs and ends had to run a mile in under six minutes. Linemen had to do it in under six and a half. The vets thought the exercise ridiculous.

John Gonzaga: "I hated the Landry mile. I told Tom Landry, 'If they ever make the field longer than 100 yards, I'm going to quit.' But he said I had to run the mile anyway. He said, 'I don't have any time for comedians.' So I ran it."

Slowly, but at least he finished, whereas Byron Bradfute, the free agent lineman, passed out before he reached the finish line. Rookie running back Don Perkins was under the assumption that he would get in shape once he came to camp. He arrived 15 pounds overweight, and when he couldn't run the Landry mile, he considered quitting right there. But a few of the players, including Frank Clarke, were both physically fit and mentally prepared.

Frank Clarke: "I had a big, strong body and pretty good endurance, but halfway through it there was one player, Tom Franckhauser, a defensive back, who was way ahead of me. I knew I could have just finished the thing, but I got a burst of speed and stamina and I really hauled ass, and I ended up passing

Franckhauser, winning the Landry mile, and Tom said to me, 'That showed me a lot of class.' I had never heard praise like that before."

Once Landry began the practice regimen, the players were dismayed to see that it was long and brutal. A lot of the other pro teams saved most of their hitting for the season. Landry had his players hitting in practice all day, every day. The players had to absorb a daily pounding that came from the natural brutality of the game. And when they weren't scrimmaging, Landry had them in one-on-one or two-on-two drills, which could be just as brutal. The regimen was grueling, harder than anything any of these grizzled veterans had ever experienced before. And after a day of pain, there would be long, tedious meetings. If any of the players were anticipating having fun in their off-hours, they were dismayed to learn there were very, very few off-hours. Landry's training camp created strong hostility in some of his players.

Big John Gonzaga, who had come from a winning program in San Francisco, was furious about having to play on an expansion team to begin with. Making his situation worse, he didn't like Landry's impersonal nature, didn't appreciate his autocratic ways ("He even told you when to pray"), and resented Landry's omnipotence. "Tom's real strength was defense, though Tom wouldn't tell you that. He'd say he knew *everything*," said Gonzaga. Moreover, he thought all the hitting to be a waste of energy.

John Gonzaga: "It was really unnecessary. We would see guys like Ray Mathews, who had already played 10 years in the league, having to do that. They didn't need that kind of crap."

The rookie lineman Byron Bradfute had had nothing to compare to Landry's regimen, and he thought it hard, but like most young rookies he took the attitude he would do whatever he was asked. Bradfute may not have minded Landry's scrimmages, but he did mind a drill designed for the linemen by coach Brad Ecklund.

Byron Bradfute: "He had a little exercise where he took one of those big tackling dummies, put a rope on it, tied it to the crossbar, and let it swing. He'd hold that thing up high and then swing it into you, and you were supposed to hit it with your nose first. That was dumb, really dumb. The older I get, the more I hold that against him."

In addition to the hard, long practices, Landry made the players go to endlessly long meetings, where he introduced his complicated systems. Landry had had little time to build a coaching staff and had hired three stopgap assistant coaches, offensive line coach Brad Ecklund, who had been coaching in Oregon high schools; backfield coach Babe Demancheck, who had coached under Buddy Parker for the Pittsburgh Steelers; and defensive line coach Tom Dahms, who came from the University of Virginia. But these men did little except make sure the players ran their drills. The teaching was done entirely by Landry, and often players had to sit a long time in their classroom watching game films without commentary or explanation all the while stewing in wait for Landry to arrive for their personal instruction.

Dick Bielski: "It was stand around and wait for Tom to do something. I recall sitting in meetings with our offensive coaches, and they would show us films, and not do a thing until Tom got there. Not a play was put in. There was not a bit of coaching until Tom got there to do it. He did everything, because he wanted to make sure the new system was put in right. He taught the offense, and he taught the defense. And when Tom wasn't there, you sat there and watched films for two or three hours with practically no comment whatsoever. And after a while that got to be a bit boring, and you became resentful, because he was not giving us the time we thought we deserved. Here we are, marking time, treading water, waiting for the guy to come in, and there were other things we would have preferred doing. After we spent two or three hours waiting for him to come, well, you feel like stepchildren."

Very quickly the Cowboys training camp became tinged with bitterness on the part of many of the veteran players, angry that their football fortunes had sunk so low.

Bob Fry: "I could see that so many of the veterans didn't want to be there. In a way, everyone had that feeling. It's like me, 30 years old and going someplace different, doing something different. It isn't like being traded. You get traded because someone wants you. Here, someone wanted to get rid of you. So we had that feeling of having to start over again. It was hard, at our age, to have to prove ourselves all over again."

The players on the defensive line openly rebelled when they were shown Landry's defensive system. They were used to pursuing the ball wherever it went. Under Landry's system, the one he had perfected with the Giants, a lineman was supposed to recognize which formation the offense was using and glean from it what plays might be run. Then, when the ball was snapped and the offensive players began to move, he was to take his "key" from whatever players he was supposed to "read," and then wait patiently for the play to come to him. Under the system it was common for a lineman on a running play to take a block and then hold his position, even when the ball was going away from him, because under Landry's system eventually the ball carrier would find him. Had the Cowboys drafted members of the Giants' defensive line, perhaps Landry might have had allies. But the Giants had protected their defensive players, and neither offensive guard Buzz Guy nor quarterback Don Heinrich were qualified to tout Landry's defensive acuity to the defensive unit. Not a single other veteran lineman believed that Landry's system could work. Linebacker Jack Patera, who loved and understood Landry's system from the first time he saw it, recalled his teammates' resistance to Landry's way of playing defense.

Jack Patera: "Tom would tell them, 'If you can just hold your own, we're better off.' But guys would say, 'Why should I just hold my own here if I can make the play?' They didn't understand that part of their job was to not get knocked down so you can make the play or to just create a mess by cutting off offensive players who are supposed to be in pursuit. Remember, a lot of these players didn't know a whole lot more than their own position. It amazed me how many of these people just didn't know. They entered the situation and criticized it without understanding the overall program."

When he was with the Chicago Cardinals, linebacker Jerry Tubbs had had a sense that Sam Huff and the Giants always knew where their plays were going and that somehow Landry had been responsible. Tubbs was eager to learn Landry's secrets, and he supported his coach from the first.

Jerry Tubbs: "Guys were used to doing things one way. If you tell a defensive tackle who is used to getting to the ball that he has to take a step inside when the ball is going outside, this is against all the things he's done since he began playing the game. And so these older guys didn't like it. You had to have faith in Tom for his system to work. I can remember Gene Cronin and John Gonzaga, defensive linemen, were particularly unhappy."

There was not the universal griping among the members of the offensive unit that there was on the defense. The great irony was that the moaners and groaners on the defense were more talented and more cohesive than the more compliant offensive players, like Fred Cone, a halfback and kicker, who for the most part accepted Landry's system but weren't good enough to make it work against the better teams.

Fred Cone: "Landry was thorough. He talked about our opponent, and then we'd take a test with a pencil and paper. Some players hated to sit in those meetings. They lasted a long time. We'd watch the films over and over. But if you did your homework, you'd know what the other team was doing before they snapped the ball."

Bob Fry: "I don't remember any griping or sniping from the offense. I think Tom is a great person, a wonderful man, and one of the best defensive coaches I've been around. I can remember, though, our great frustration over the inability of the offensive line to stop our quarterback from getting sacked. It was *very* frustrating."

Gene Babb: "I believed in what we were doing. I liked the man, respected him. Tom Landry was one of the most dedicated men I've ever been around in my life. He was very businesslike on the football field. And the man had such a mind on him. He was always two or three plays ahead of where everyone else was."

In counterpoint to all of Tom's supporters on the offense was wide receiver Ray Mathews, who was brutally outspoken about the contempt he had for Landry.

Frank Clarke: "When Tom Landry said 'Quiet,' Ray would start talking. He showed his disrespect, and everybody saw that. Ray came when he wanted and left when he wanted. Ray was set in his ways, a rebel kind of a guy. Tom in his head knew what he wanted, and Ray said, 'Tom, I've done this my own way, and

I'm going to continue doing it my own way.' We didn't take Ray seriously, but this became a challenge and a big frustration for Tom."

Landry kept Mathews despite his constant show of disrespect in large part because he had to. The team needed him. With the Steelers Mathews had been a star at split end. The other Cowboys split ends were Jim Doran, who had had a fine career with the Lions but was reaching the end, and Frank Clarke, who had not yet proven his worth. Three players was not much depth. And Mathews did not roil Landry badly enough for the new coach to get rid of him, though there were others who did, men like Buzz Guy, a former Giant, and Bob Cross, formerly of the Rams and the Cardinals. Landry had been forced to cut them for lack of effort as much as lack of respect. Guy was perhaps the hardest loss. Offensive linemen were scarce, and Guy was the biggest and fastest of the Cowboys draftees. Landry had known him on the Giants.

Byron Bradfute: "Buzz was an Adonis. He was the fastest, most talented offensive lineman. The spot was between him and me, and he would have won it, except that he didn't want to be there."

Guy could be a wild man.

Byron Bradfute: "You know the story in the novel *North Dallas Forty* where this one guy threw the televisions off the motel balcony to see how far he could throw them? That was a true story. That was Buzz Guy. He just pulled them out of the walls and tossed them as far as he could out the window of the motel."

Before the end of training camp, Buzz Guy was gone, and the Cowboys had to make do with the rookie, Bradfute.

Another disruptive player was another big lineman, Bob Cross, whom the players recall most vividly.

John Gonzaga: "He was a small Texas-town type of guy. Cross didn't like anyone who was different. He always thought my name was Gonzalez and that I came from Mexico. He didn't hesitate for a minute to tell anybody how he felt about 'wetbacks.'"

Frank Clarke: "Someone told me he was a card-carrying member of the Ku Klux Klan. Now I don't know if this was true, but it sure opened my eyes to a lot of strange things that were going on in the world."

Bigotry does not disqualify a player. But taking the coach's 12-year-old kid on a snipe hunt is not recommended either. And that's what Cross did, according to veteran linebacker Tom Braatz, who was finishing his career with the Cowboys.

Tom Braatz: "Cross gave the boy a pan and a wooden spoon and a gunnysack and told him to go out there and beat on the pan with the spoon and pretty soon he'd have a sackful of snipe. Well, you know how it works. Tom Jr. spent most of the night in the woods, holding that sack and beating on his pan with that wooden spoon.

"A couple of days later coach Landry got wind of what had happened and Bob Cross got his release."

Landry was well aware of the problems he was facing. He knew how hard it was to teach old dogs some new tricks. He knew that if you took rejects from different teams, every player would have his own system, his own way of doing things, and chances were he would not be amenable to change. He also knew how difficult it was going to be to fuse together an offensive unit and a defensive unit with these recycled old dogs. But you can say one thing about Tom Landry: he was determined to succeed, and he worked those veterans as hard as they ever worked, making them practice three, four hours a day, force-feeding them a system he knew most of them either could not understand or would not stomach.

In his defense, Landry had some disciples from the beginning, including Jack Patera at middle linebacker and Jerry Tubbs at outside linebacker, and on offense, split end Frank Clarke.

Frank Clarke: "When I arrived in Dallas, Tom came with this 'genius' title. They were calling him a genius, and to me it made sense. He *was* a genius. He was far and above. He had a way of approaching the game of football—the *whole* game—in a way that whatever aspect of the game that Tom Landry put his arm around and embraced, that's what sparkled.

"He told me early on, 'I want you to go downfield, take five steps and then cut at a 60-degree angle, take five more steps, and look for the ball. It will be there.' I had never heard anyone say that before. I would ask him, 'How do you know?' Or, 'What about the people trying to rush the passer? How is the quarterback going to know where I am?' He would say, 'Just do it.' And it was amazing how uncanny this became. I would take the steps he wanted us to take, cut the angle, take more steps, look for the ball, and it was *there*! I'd say to myself, 'Holy smokes. This guy knows everything.' And I would see him do the same thing with the defense, and with the kicking game, and the special teams. And as time went by, more and more guys would remark, 'Who is this guy? How did he get to know so much about the game?' Whenever he was able to impart his confidence, that part of the game just sparkled."

The offensive players weren't nearly as rebellious as the ones on defense, though they had their criticisms, too. When Landry had his linemen all rise up 1-2-3 in synch before the snap count, then get back into their stance before the snap, they thought it "Mickey Mouse nonsense."

Don McIlhenny: "A lot of guys wondered, 'What the hell are we doing this for?' Looking back, Tom had a reason. We didn't realize he was as smart as he was, and we thought we were a lot smarter than we were."

Though most of the offensive players were not as resistant to coach Landry's way of doing things as the defenders were, that didn't mean they found it easy making his system work. Part of the problem was that Landry, as the former Giants defensive coach, looked at everything from the point of view of the defense, and so when he put in the plays he designated "odd" for left and "even" for right, when almost every other team designated "odd" for right and "even" for left. But Tom was looking at his diagrams from the defense's left and the defense's right, and so he flip-flopped them without considering the consequences. Throughout the year the veteran offensive players would occasionally revert to their ingrained habits, reacting rather than thinking as their brains told them "odd" was right and "even" left. During games veteran linemen would pull the wrong way, or backs would head in the opposite direction from the way they were supposed to go on a screen pass, and Landry could never figure out why.

In the beginning Landry kept his offensive playbook simple. The trick plays and the motion would come later. During the exhibition season it was pure vanilla. Landry knew his backs had no speed, saw that his wide receivers had potential, but also realized that his offensive line would not be able to stop the top teams from rushing in and grinding his quarterback into the turf. He was counting on Eddie LeBaron's quickness to keep him from getting killed.

Of the quarterbacks, LeBaron was squarely on the coach's side. The former Washington ace had been well aware of Landry's impact when the Redskins had to face the Giants. LeBaron, moreover, was the kind of person to do whatever his coach asked him to do.

Eddie LeBaron: "I had been an officer in the Marine Corps, and through many years of football had watched the good teams who were well organized, well drilled like the Cleveland Browns and the New York Giants, and you saw what it took. That was my nature. I was prepared to fit into the system."

As for his teammates, they respected LeBaron, both for his great skill and also for his ability to play the game despite his lack of size, which LeBaron insisted was never a factor.

Dick Bielski: "LeBaron was a delight. He was a treat. He was a little guy; you pulled for him; you wished him success. He was capable and talented, though undersized, but it never seemed to be a problem for him. He never approached it as a problem. We kind of all accepted him as he was."

The second-string quarterback, New York Giants veteran Don Heinrich, was respected for his worldliness. Having played in New York for so many years, Heinrich was a fixture at such haunts as P. J. Clarke's and Downey's, and he would talk about places and restaurants other players had only heard about. Heinrich was also respected for being able to figure out a defense quickly. With the Giants he had opened the game, then after figuring out the defense, would turn it over to the more talented Conerly or Y. A. Tittle. Heinrich was like a coach on the field.

Heinrich, like LeBaron, generally went along with Landry's system of play. Any reluctance stemmed from the fact he had anticipated being the starting quarterback, until the late arrival of LeBaron. His disappointment at not getting much of a chance to start never abated all season long. The third quarterback, rookie Don Meredith, hated Landry's system, wanting no part of it. At SMU Meredith had spent his career dropping back seven or eight yards and throwing bombs to his receivers. His career completion rate of 61 percent spoke highly of his skill. But Landry was too disciplined a coach to allow what he considered such a haphazard attack, and Meredith was too stubborn to want to do anything different from what had brought him success in high school and college. LeBaron would lecture Meredith on the importance of fitting into the system. Said LeBaron with a chuckle, "He sometimes declined."

Meredith knew he wouldn't have much opportunity to play his first year, and he took a laissez-faire approach to his work. One time in practice Meredith, barking signals, called out the wrong color, indicating the wrong offensive formation.

"It's red," said backfield coach Babe Demancheck, "not purple."

Quipped an unrepentant Meredith, "I was close."

The first preseason game in the history of the Dallas Cowboys took place in Seattle against the San Francisco 49ers. Four of the Cowboys' top signees—Don Meredith, running back Don Perkins, lineman Paul Rochester, and running back Jim Mooty—were not available for the game. They were in Chicago playing for the College All-Stars against the world champion Baltimore Colts.

Lineman John Gonzaga was playing his old team, and for that reason Landry had made him a captain for the game. When his former teammates asked him how he enjoyed playing on the Cowboys, he replied, "I'll tell you what, guys. Don't let them stars get in your eyes. That's all I can tell you."

The 49ers won that day, 16–10. Most of the game the Dallas offense's timing was terrible, but there was one shining moment for the Cowboys when Eddie LeBaron threw a 56-yard touchdown pass to Frank Clarke.

Against the 49ers Gene Cronin suffered a knee injury and had to spend the rest of the preseason in a cast. Also in that game Jack Patera, playing under Landry's system for the first time, learned a valuable lesson.

Jack Patera: "I had fast become a tremendous disciple of his defense. Against a certain offense, my job was to key the offensive running back, and if he went to his left, I was to step between the left guard and the left tackle. In practice, nothing had ever happened that I couldn't handle, but against San Francisco, Bob St. Clair was the tackle for the 49ers, and after watching the back, I took my step, and the next thing I knew Bob St. Clair, who was 6'8", 275 pounds, hit me so hard I landed almost at the sidelines. It was then I realized there were two parts to his defense: you key the back, and then you look for the tackle coming down on you. That made me study a little bit more, too. I started asking more questions. When we watched the films of the play, Tom and I got a good laugh out of it."

Despite a decent performance by the Cowboys, there was sobering news from the All-Star Game in Chicago: both young Cowboys running backs, Don Perkins and Jim Mooty, had been seriously injured in practice. Perkins had broken the fifth metatarsal in his foot as a junior in college and missed a few games. Doctors had performed surgery on it. At a College All-Star Game practice, Perkins planted his foot, and the g-force on the bone proved too great. The bone broke again. He hadn't even been tackled. Perkins would be lost for the entire season, as would Mooty, who called Schramm to tell him he had torn a leg muscle during drills. When the All-Stars returned in time for the exhibition game in San Antonio against the hapless St. Louis Cardinals, only two of the four top prospects, Don Meredith and Paul Rochester, remained. And Rochester, who would go on to star with the New York Jets in the AFL, did not survive the final cut.

The Cards won by only a touchdown. After the game at a gathering held in honor of the team, Ray Mathews set his hosts' teeth gnashing when he said that the men at the Alamo, San Antonio's shrine to Texas freedom, had not been heroes but rather cowards. "I talked about them running out the back door of the Alamo," said Mathews, who continually sought to find the magic words that would send him back to his old coach, Buddy Parker, in Pittsburgh.

After the Cardinals game, the Cowboys had to find a new site to continue training camp, and the team traveled to Wisconsin, about 35 miles south of the Twin Cities, to the town of Delafield. After the players settled into the dorms of St. John's Military Academy, they hated it there.

Gene Babb: "Let me tell you about this place. There were four floors in this dormitory, one of these old stone and marble buildings, ivy going up the walls, and the only bathrooms—toilets and showers—were all the way down in the basement. And it had one of these big belfries on one end, and we had to be in bed with lights out at 10:00, and at 11:00 the bells went off and the live bats would fly up and down the halls. And that became the sport of the evening. Everybody would lay in their beds, lights out, and you could feel the anticipation in the air, 'cause you laid there with your pillow on top of you, and when the bells chimed at 11:00 the bats started flying up and down the halls and in the stairwells. The halls just filled with everybody and their pillows trying to knock down those bats."

The beds were kid-size, the rooms were as Spartan as in a monastery, and Delafield was as inaccessible to the world as Forest Grove was. Twice the players hung Tex Schramm's assistant, Gil Brandt, the one they accused of finding St. John's, in effigy.

The third exhibition game was played in Nashville against the Baltimore Colts. The Colts won, 14–10. Landry should have gotten a lot of credit from his players for putting together a representative team so quickly, but to the players a loss was a loss. Jack Patera, at middle linebacker, continued to learn the benefits of playing Landry's defensive system. During the game Patera sacked his childhood friend, quarterback George Shaw. The Colts ran a play, and Patera read his "key" and reacted accordingly. Alex Sandusky, the Colts offensive lineman, was supposed to trap him, but Landry's blueprint had warned Patera that he was coming, and Patera stepped up, avoided him, and made the tackle, angering Sandusky, who accused him of "playing the play." Patera laughed. Sandusky didn't know it, but that was the way the Cowboys defense was designed.

The team traveled to Louisville to play the New York Giants, the defending Eastern Conference champions, in their fourth exhibition game. The temperature on the field reached 120 degrees. "It was the hottest night I ever played," said Patera. The Cowboys gained the first win in their history, albeit in an exhibition game. The score was 14–3. Some of the players wondered whether the Giants were really trying. "I don't know if they gave it to Landry or what," said John Gonzaga. Recalled linebacker Jerry Tubbs, "It was a combination of Landry knowing the Giants, and the Giants not caring."

In that game Eddie LeBaron proved himself to a doubtful Frank Clarke, scrambling and throwing Clarke a 73-yard touchdown pass, and then Don Meredith relieved LeBaron and hit Clarke with a 74-yard touchdown beauty.

Frank Clarke: "Eddie LeBaron was short, 5'6", on his tiptoes 5'7", so imagine big guys like Jim Katcavage and Rosey Grier barreling in on little Eddie. He could get the ball over *them*? I figured, no way. I remember running this pass route, a 'quick-in' route is what it's called, and when I looked 'in' for the ball, I couldn't even see the quarterback, so I immediately looked away. As soon as I did, that very second the ball careened off my shoulder pads. I thought, No way, man. *No way* does he get rid of that ball. But Eddie could. He did some tricky things with that ball. So I learned from early on, stay with this guy. In the Giants game I caught a touchdown pass from LeBaron and one from Meredith. That gave the Cowboys their very first victory."

If the game had a memorable moment, however, it belonged to Don Meredith. Since his return from the All-Star Game, the SMU rookie had halfheartedly attempted to learn Landry's complicated system of play calling. Against the Giants, Landry gave Meredith his first opportunity to apply what he had learned. Gene Babb recalled what happened.

Gene Babb: "Don had had to go to the All-Star Game, so he hadn't had that much exposure to Landry's system. He came into the huddle, and he said, 'OK, purple right, 46 lead.' And L. G. Dupre and I were looking at each other. L.G. said, 'Don, that's not the right formation. It's red right, 46 lead.' Don said, 'OK, whatever, let's just run it.' And we'd line up the way we were supposed to when we got to the line of scrimmage.

"Don was laid-back, very easygoing. He knew the experienced quarterback was going to play, that Don was there to learn, and he was having a great time. He hadn't yet gotten serious, the way Tom wanted him to be."

During the game Meredith's problems multiplied when Sam Huff, the Giants middle linebacker, decided to show the rookie how green he really was. This one time Meredith started his count, and when Huff saw Meredith's offensive formation, he adjusted his defense accordingly, just as Landry had taught him. Meredith then called an audible, and Huff reset his defense to counter. When

Meredith realized he was about to send his back right into the heart of the Giants defense, he didn't know what to do about it. Meredith called, "Four set! . . . Uh, red right . . . uh, 22. . . . Ah, shit, son of a bitch, timeout." Huff and the other members of the Giants defense broke out laughing, along with some of the veteran linemen on the Cowboys.

The next exhibition was against the Los Angeles Rams. The game was played in the evening in Pendleton, Oregon. What Babb recalled most vividly was that they had played the game at the rodeo grounds "on grass that had a lot of fertilizer growing there." The circus had come to town before the NFL, and the elephants, tigers, and bears had left presents behind. After a 14–14 score at halftime, Rams quarterback Billy Wade ripped the Cowboys apart, 49–14, throwing a touchdown pass to Del Shofner and two to fullback Jon Arnett.

The final exhibition game was against Vince Lombardi and the Green Bay Packers in Minneapolis. It was only Lombardi's second season with the Pack, but already he had molded it into a powerhouse. The Packers won a close one, 28–23, scoring the winner in the final minutes. Rookie offensive tackle Byron Bradfute recalled that the Packers defense was a little different from what he had been used to in college.

Byron Bradfute: "They didn't run the normal 4-3, and under our blocking formula, I thought I was supposed to pass block on the number two man on the line from center. How you start counting is determined by whether the defender is over the center or right behind him or off to the side, and the way I saw it, I was playing right tackle and Willie Davis was playing on my right shoulder, and I thought that Davis was supposed to be the number two man. So that's who I blocked—all day long. And I thought I had one of the best days I ever had.

"But as it turned out, that's not who I was supposed to block. I was supposed to be blocking the *next* guy out, and he had a field day against us. And I can remember Tom Landry showing the game films, and over and over again he kept saying, 'Bradfute . . .'"

Linebacker Jack Patera had his own particular memories of the Packers exhibition.

Jack Patera: "I remember right in front of the Packers bench some guy running near me on a screen pass. He dropped the ball, and I hit him with an elbow. The Packers all got on me. I remember Lombardi yelling, 'Cheap shot son of a bitch,' or something like that. And then Bart Starr was scrambling, and I flushed him out of the pocket and chased him. He stepped out of bounds, and I dove at him, and I ended up sliding into their bench. And Jimmy Taylor, their fullback, put a knee down, and I slid into it, and he had his helmet off, and he was yelling at me, 'You stupid son of a bitch. We're going to take care of you.' So I turned around and gave him a short jab and punched him in the nose and knocked him over the bench. That brought the bench up, and I ran across to my side.

"The last play of the game the Packers gave me the 'bootsey,' where they snapped the ball, and everybody forgot about hitting anybody but me. They were all on top of me, but there isn't a whole lot they can do. It was nothing. I didn't know who it was at the time, but from the bottom of the pile I reached up and grabbed this guy's jock strap and squeezed it as hard as I could. There was a lot of yelling. They started unpiling, and I just held on, and we got up, and I was holding Fuzzy Thurston. He said, 'You are kind of a tough guy after all, aren't you?'"

There were two full weeks between the end of the exhibition season and the first regular-season game, and Landry and Schramm began working harder than ever, inviting to camp players dropped in final cuts from all the other teams.

Eddie LeBaron: "There were 200 bodies [actually 193] who tried out that first training camp, and most of them came the last two weeks. It looked like the Greyhound bus station. As teams started cutting players, we had them trooping in and out of there so fast, you couldn't believe it. One day Don Meredith asked me, 'Who's that guy over there?' I said, 'Don, the first thing you learn is never learn their names until the last cut is made, 'cause you'll feel bad when they get cut.'

"There weren't many who were any good."

Bob Fry remembered the extra work brought on by the influx of bodies.

Bob Fry: "The Cowboys had first pick of the players cut by the other teams, so the week before the first game, we would have two practices. First the 40 or 50 guys who they were trying out would practice, and we would practice later."

Landry needed to know if any of the late arrivals could play, so he used his regulars to find out.

Jack Patera: "Tom was bringing in 20 new guys a day, and he always wanted us to scrimmage them. I don't think I ever scrimmaged so much in my life. It was like playing a game every day. We only had a handful of linebackers, Tom Braatz, Jerry Tubbs, Gene Cronin, and me. Wahoo McDaniel had tried out for middle linebacker, but he wasn't good enough to play. He had a good reputation, but he never did anything. He didn't like to practice. I loved to practice. If I could take three turns, I would take three turns. And if someone else got out of his turn, I'd want his turn. My philosophy was that if a coach never sees a player, he won't know whether he's any better than you are. So I hated to be replaced any time, 'cause if some guy could do something that was outstanding, maybe he might take my job."

No one took Patera's job. And surprise of surprises, Byron Bradfute beat out Paul Rochester, Jerry DeLucca, and Buzz Guy for a starting spot at offensive tackle. Of the 80 or so free agents to pass through the Cowboys training camp, Bradfute and Gary Wisener, an offensive end and defensive back, were the only two free agents to land spots on the team.

A handful of late arrivals cut from other training camps ended up making the Cowboys final roster. Center had been a serious problem all through the exhibition season, and a rookie, Mike Connelly, was signed despite his relative lack of size after the Los Angeles Rams cut him late in training camp. Along with the late arrivals, Schramm also signed defensive back Don Bishop and linebacker Wayne Henson from the Bears, guard Mike Falls from the Packers, and defensive back Bob Bercich from the Giants.

Despite all the bickering and the lack of stability during the exhibition season, with training camp coming to a close, some of the vets approached the coming season with their usual confidence.

Jerry Tubbs: "I went into the season thinking we would win maybe half our games. I was that confident. And we could have if we had had a little luck. And if we'd have been a little better."

Quarterback Eddie LeBaron was equally upbeat.

Eddie LeBaron: "I thought we were a pretty good football team for just starting out."

Chapter 10

0–11–1

When rookie halfback Don Perkins broke his foot during training camp, the doctors suggested he wear a special shoe to see if he could run despite the break. By the end of training camp, it was clear he would need an operation, and so Perkins was awaiting surgery in Dallas with his teammates as they were getting ready for the start of the season.

One day scouting director Gil Brandt and some of his players, including Don Meredith and Jim Mooty, were heading for lunch, and they asked Perkins to come along. Arriving at the Highland Park Cafeteria, they took trays and got in line. When one of the waiters informed Perkins, "Hey, you can't get served here," they all left.

Don Perkins: "It was the nature of the society. We were very polarized in this country at that time. The black players lived in Oak Cliff on one side of town; the white players lived on another side of town in North Dallas. You saw each other in practice, and then you split. That was it. I don't think what happened was shocking to anybody. How does it feel? Well, I had been called *nigger* and lots of things in my life by the time I was 22, so this was not the first time I had been told, 'You can't do this. You can't use the bathroom. You can't do that.' Little kids would come up to you to rub their hands across you to see whether your black skin would come off. So there was no new ground broken that day. And after the operation, I was lost for the season, and I went back to Albuquerque. I went back to school, and even though I still got paid by the Cowboys, I also did odd jobs, worked construction."

The other black player, Frank Clarke, also couldn't help but be affected by the segregationist society of Dallas. A northerner from Wisconsin, for the first time he was encountering a situation where he could not stay in hotels or eat at lunch counters.

Frank Clarke: "You could walk into a 5-and-10 cent store and see drinking fountains marked 'colored' and 'white.' I had never seen this. It kind of takes your breath away. You go, 'Holy smokes. How far away are we from lynchings?' Though we didn't have any cause to be threatened, I could not divorce myself from the fact that we were in Texas.

"Nevertheless, the fact that Dallas was segregated didn't matter to me. When we broke camp we all stayed together in a hotel as a team until the season actually started. There were no problems there, no segregation there. Then once we made the team, where I could live was limited, but I was satisfied with where I lived. Hey, man, the season goes so fast, you don't start messing with other things. My concentration was on playing good football, so where I lived was fine. I wasn't slumming it. And we weren't caught up in any civil rights movement. Our emphasis was on playing football. We just wanted to make the most of it. We were in Dallas to play football. And when the season was over, I went back to my family in Cleveland."

Don Perkins: "I never even had aspirations of a pro career while I was in college. Even after I signed with the Cowboys, it never occurred to me that I might be around for a long career. I never felt I was good enough to be playing at the professional level. I spent most of my career afraid someone would find me out, suddenly discover that I didn't have any business being where I was."

By the whites on the team, both Frank Clarke and Don Perkins were respected as hard working and congenial. Both went along in order to get along, and they were awarded high marks for that. It would not be for a couple of years, after Perkins established himself with the Cowboys, and after the civil rights movement began to pick up steam, that he would fight for the right for his son to go to an all-white private school. Black militancy was then still a decade away.

For the 1960 Cowboys players, a more immediate source of controversy was the deplorable condition of their practice facility at creaking Burnett Field. In organizing the fledgling team in only a few months' time, Schramm had had a lot of scrambling to do. When you start from scratch, sometimes you have to make do, and that was certainly the case with Burnett Field. After having to endure monkish facilities at St. John's Military Academy, where they felt like they were in a jail, once they finished the exhibition season and came back to Dallas they had to face the rats and scorpions and uncomfortable conditions that marked their practice facility. For the veterans it was one more reason to dislike playing for the Cowboys. "We really didn't have a practice facility," said Ray Mathews. "Everything was chaos."

Daily team meetings were held on the second floor of the American Automobile Association building off the North Central Expressway. After the meeting, the coaches and players would get on a bus and drive to antiquated Burnett Field, which had once been the home of a minor league baseball team. The offense would meet in the clubhouse behind first base, and the defense would meet in the clubhouse behind third base.

Eddie LeBaron: "Burnett Field was in the middle of the Trinity River flood plain. When it would rain, the showers would plug up, and we'd be standing in six inches of water. And when it rained, the field would get flooded, and we'd have to get on a bus and Tom would scout out a park that we could practice in."

Don McIlhenny: "There were rats in pretty nearly every building, including our locker room. The rats would chew the leather shoulder pads at night, and we'd come back the next day and find their teeth marks. When we got to practice, we had to take our shoes and hit them on the ground to shake the scorpions out of them, 'cause they liked the salt, liked to crawl up into moist places.

"The locker rooms were cold. Some of the guys would throw used tape and paper into a barrel and light it. One time we went out onto the field to practice, and we looked back, and smoke was coming out of the stadium locker room. It was sort of fun. The coaches halted practice and began running toward it ready to fight the fire. It did accomplish one thing. It smoked the rats out for the next couple of weeks.

"I can remember one time it had rained so much that we couldn't practice at Burnett Field, and so we got on the bus. We started driving around, hunting for a place to practice. We saw a public park over on Harry Hines Boulevard, over in the industrial district. We jumped out of the bus, went over and practiced. Not a soul showed up. Nobody watched us. I said to my wife not too long ago, 'Can you imagine today if the Dallas Cowboys got on a bus and practiced in a public park? There would be ten thousand people there.'"

The opening game of the 1960 season was against Landry's old UT teammate Bobby Layne, plus Ernie Stautner and the rest of the Pittsburgh Steelers, in the Cotton Bowl. Twenty thousand spectators (paid and comped), including the 2,100 season-ticket holders, took their seats in the huge seventy thousand–seat arena for the inaugural. To give the event a little extra Texas flavor, Schramm hired Roy Rogers and Dale Evans to ride Trigger and Buttercup around the cavernous bowl before the game. What Schramm, a Californian, didn't realize was that to Texans, Hollywood cowboys made a mockery of the genuine article, and Schramm was mortified when hundreds of Texans amused themselves by pelting an angry singing cowboy and his wife with ice cubes from their soda cups. "I'll never know why," said Schramm, "but it was one of the most embarrassing things to ever happen to me."

The Cowboys opened the game with a run for no gain. Then Gene Babb ran for one yard, and on the third play, from his own 15, Eddie LeBaron threw a short turn-in to former Detroit Lions star Jim Doran, who from his position at tight end cut across the middle, captured the pass, got a perfectly timed block from halfback Don McIlhenny, and hightailed it the rest of the way for the first Cowboys touchdown.

Eddie LeBaron: "I remember the play. It was 'brown left, X turn in.' Brown calls for the halfback and fullback to be side by side in regular position. 'Brown left' means the flanker goes out on the left side, and the 'X' is the tight end, which was Doran. The play was designed for the halfback to run a little shoot pattern on the right side and for Doran to go down and turn inside the linebacker. I got it to him, and then he took off."

The second time the Cowboys had the football, LeBaron threw a 58-yard pass to Frank Clarke down to the Pittsburgh 7, followed by a touchdown pass to end Fred Dugan. Before Steelers coach Buddy Parker and his star quarterback Bobby Layne could regroup, the Cowboys were ahead 14–0. It was the biggest lead they would have all season long.

For rookie offensive tackle Byron Bradfute, the Steelers game was his inauguration. The Steeler he attempted to stop was Big Daddy Lipscomb, the gargantuan tackle with the vicious disposition.

Byron Bradfute: "Big Daddy Lipscomb played defensive tackle for the Steelers, and on running plays I blocked down on him a lot. He was big and strong, and Lord a' mercy, he was a talker, just filthy. Steady and filthy. He gave LeBaron a terrible, terrible time. Even after the game I heard Big Daddy say things to LeBaron when his wife was with him. It made LeBaron mad just to think about it. Big Daddy was a *bad* guy."

In addition to Lipscomb, the other Steelers defender the Cowboys had to worry about most was linebacker Ernie Stautner. In that game the responsibility for stopping him fell on tackle Bob Fry.

Bob Fry: "I didn't have success, though I did all right against him. Ernie was a guy who had a super motor. He was short, but he would come at you like gangbusters every time, and he'd come hard. He wasn't a finesse guy. He was a power guy. He had a lot of strength, and boy, when you set up to block him, you had better block him aggressively. You didn't sit back and wait for him to make a move. And the thing about him, he went 110 percent all the time. There was no such thing as going into the fourth quarter and Ernie getting tired. Eventually, he would wear you down. 'Cause it was continuous, continuous, continuous."

Bradfute, Fry, and the rest of the offensive line did well enough that, in all, LeBaron completed 14 of 25 passes for 348 yards. In their inaugural game, the Cowboys scored 28 points. It would not be enough.

For the defenders, the Steeler they had to stop was quarterback Bobby Layne, and on this evening the fledgling defensive unit couldn't do it. Layne threw for four touchdowns, and during the evening he broke the career passing record set by Sammy Baugh. Baugh had managed 22,085 yards passing in 15 years. This was Layne's 13th season, and by the end of the game his total was 22,351. A 58-yard touchdown pass from Layne to Tom "the Bomb" Tracy was the game winner.

Gene Cronin: "Bobby Layne wasn't about to lose to us. No way. He usually found a way to win. He'd find a way. I saw him play hurt, bleeding, blood running off him, but he still wouldn't leave the ballgame. It was his *life* to beat you."

Eddie LeBaron: "We weren't bad, but we weren't good enough. We didn't have the killer defense, and we couldn't rush the ball. We had big, strong backs, but we didn't have a big, strong line."

It was in the next game, against the Philadelphia Eagles, that the fate of the Cowboys during their inaugural season would be sealed. The Eagles, led by their exciting quarterback, Norm Van Brocklin, would lose only two games all season long and win the Eastern Conference. Against them the Cowboys scored 25 points. They should have had 27, except the Eagles blocked two extra points by kicker Fred Cone. Three Eagles interceptions also hurt their effort. These were both games the Cowboys could have won. Perhaps two early victories would have changed the early destiny of the team. But as would happen at least five times during their inaugural season, victories turned into losses as a result of a misplay or two.

Eddie LeBaron: "All the Eagles had was a simple zone. They got really deep, and they were so easy to throw against. But I threw to the wrong man a couple of times and was intercepted. That was dumb. We should have won both of those games. We were not a bad football team. But when you don't win games you should win, then people start looking for reasons, and so the players get down. We were a disparate group, guys thrown together. We didn't have that unity experienced teams have going in."

One reason the Cowboys had to win early if they were going to win at all is that as a season goes on, injuries take their toll. Against the Eagles, the middle linebacker, Jack Patera, saw that Van Brocklin was going to throw a screen pass, and as he rushed to cover the receiver coming out of the backfield, he was blindsided and clipped behind the knee by one of the Eagles guards. Patera would miss the rest of that game and the next and would return against the Cleveland Browns. That injury would effectively ruin his career.

The Cowboys lost to the Washington Redskins, 26–14, and for the third week would play well but not well enough to win. It would be a different story against the powerful Cleveland Browns, who were led on defense by linemen Bob Gain, Floyd Peters, and Jim Marshall. On offense a powerful front line blocked for Jim Brown and Bobby Mitchell, two of the best runners in the history of the NFL. This was to be a big game for Frank Clarke, who had been cast adrift by the Browns. For the others, the challenge of playing against coach Paul Brown and his juggernaut was overwhelming.

Dick Bielski: "You watch the film all week, and even though you may not make any comment to anyone else, you say to yourself, 'Boy, this is going to be a *long* Sunday.' You know your chances aren't going to be so good against a team like the Browns, or the Packers, or the Colts, against whom we were completely outclassed. You say to yourself, 'What the hell. They can't kill me, can they?'"

They weren't capable of murder, but the Browns were more than capable of a solid maiming. It was while playing against these Browns that the talented middle linebacker Jack Patera saw his career come to an end.

Jack Patera: "I played the first half, and on the last play of the half Jimmy Brown ran a sweep to our right, and I got tangled up in a big pileup, and that tore everything in my knee. My foot was jammed up against my hip almost. It was the worst pain I ever felt. It was the one time in my life I said to the trainer, 'Just leave me alone. This hurts so bad it feels good.' I didn't want him to move me for a while. And that was the end of it. I came back the next year, got hurt in the first preseason game, twisted [my knee], and I played the final game of the season, but I had no strength in it. I had to retire."

The loss of Patera would have been far more devastating except for the fact that this was the one position at which the Cowboys had an equally talented backup. At the University of Oklahoma Jerry Tubbs had been an exceptional middle linebacker, but because he weighed only 210 pounds, pro coaches had been hesitant to let him play there. When Patera got hurt, Landry didn't have much choice. When Tubbs begged him to be allowed to return to the middle, the coach reluctantly gave in. He didn't have anybody else. For the next seven years Tubbs starred for the Cowboys as middle linebacker.

Gene Babb: "Jerry was a smart player, had a great mind on him, knew the defenses, and he was a heck of a hitter. He was the ideal guy to play in the middle of Landry's 4-3 defense."

In his inaugural game at middle linebacker, Tubbs would have the job of keying on and stopping Jim Brown and Bobby Mitchell.

Jerry Tubbs: "Jim Brown was the best runner that ever was. He wasn't the kind of back who would put his shoulder down and go in and deal a terrible blow, unless he was down on the goal line and he wanted to score or it was third-and-one and a critical situation. He was fast and tough to knock off his feet, but he wasn't a punishing runner. He didn't hurt you. But you didn't tackle him either. He had tremendous balance and strength, and he would use you. You'd go in to hit him hard, and it wouldn't do any good. He'd bounce off, use that great balance of his and keep going. Plus he had tremendous speed.

"And what I remember about him, he never said a word, no matter what you did to him. If you hit him as hard as you could, when he was down on the ground, he'd never complain, didn't gripe. He'd get up slowly and just walk back to the huddle, slowly, acting like he was hurt every time. He was telling you, 'You didn't hurt me,' even if he was dying at the time.

"And Bobby Mitchell was the perfect complement to Jim Brown. He was quick and elusive and dangerous. Boy, they had a great offensive team. And the quarterback, Milt Plum, wasn't a great talent, but he did what he had to do with that great complement around him. They started, and for the better part of the sixties beat us pretty bad."

As punishing as the Browns offensive unit was, their defenders were just as devastating. Frank Clarke recalled the verbal abuse he took from his former teammates.

Frank Clarke: "I remember the Browns players, especially Bernie Parrish, gave me a hard time. They were screaming things at me, 'You chickenshit,' using energy to try to get me distracted. When I was with the Browns, I had the reputation of being a receiver who heard footsteps. They had been teammates, but they hadn't been friends. They didn't seem to care much about me. They knew if I was going to be effective, I had to keep my cool, so they were doing whatever they could to upset me. Only it wasn't part of my makeup to view that as a form of flattery. I should have said to myself, 'These guys think enough of me to try to get me off my game.' I should have told myself they were just trying to make things even, because with my speed and talent I could beat them one-on-one."

Clarke didn't catch a single pass all day.

For quarterbacks Eddie LeBaron, Don Heinrich, and later Don Meredith, it was a day spent trying to avoid getting killed by the Browns defensive linemen.

Mike Falls: "I was playing [guard] against Bob Gain, and he was literally wearing me out, beating my brains out. I've never been so frustrated. Finally, there was a play where Eddie LeBaron was rolling out to pass. Gain was chasing him across the field and finally ran him out of bounds. The whistle had already blown, and there was Gain standing there out of bounds and I still had up a full head of steam. It was the best shot I had all day so I took it. Man, I creamed him, and, of course, got a 15-yard penalty for it, which wasn't that big a deal, really, since we were already facing third-and-20 anyway."

The final score was Browns 48, Cowboys 7. What followed the next weekend was a heartbreaking 12–10 loss to the St. Louis Cardinals, a game the Cowboys would have won had L. G. Dupre not fumbled toward the end of the game. Then came a 45–7 blowout by the Baltimore Colts, and another blowout, a 38–10 loss to the L.A. Rams in the Cotton Bowl. In that game quarterback Don Meredith made his first start, and the SMU rookie spent much of his effort running from the large Rams defensive linemen.

Byron Bradfute: "I started the day blocking Gene Brito, who was an All-Pro, who was real fast. I had to set back and be on my toes and be ready to go in either direction, react to whatever kind of move he put on you, and I was having a pretty good day against him. And then the Rams substituted for Brito and sent in a backup, John Baker, who was 6'6" and weighed about 290 pounds. Baker had to go over me to get to Meredith, and I didn't even slow him down. I mean, he came over me, and I have never felt so defenseless. I weighed 250 pounds, was reasonably strong, and he went over me like I was a child. I swear, I never even slowed him down. The only way Meredith recognized me was if he laid down on his back and looked up."

If Landry had any concern for his quarterback, his offensive game plan didn't show it. Some offenses provide a backup blocker if someone gets through. The Cowboys didn't. Landry expected his linemen to keep the brutes out one-on-one. The offensive linemen complained that the defenders got through to the quarterback as much because of Landry's flawed system of blocking as through their lack of talent. It was those flaws, they said, that made it more likely the defenders would get past them and reach the quarterback.

Byron Bradfute: "The first couple of years the only time the offense blocked the defensive ends was on pass plays. And that puts a man at an extreme disadvantage. It gives the defensive end a *terrific* advantage. I'm not trying to say we were all blessed with such great talent, but this was one of the reasons we had so much trouble stopping the defensive ends.

"The defensive end would line up over the offensive tackle. If it was a pass play or draw, we would block. And the defensive end would look for that move. Once we committed ourselves, that end immediately knew what kind of play we were running. So once we started the block, the defensive end would know it was going to be a pass, and he could just go after us wide open. That gave the defensive end an extreme advantage. It was one of the main reasons our quarterbacks were harried."

From the start, the players on the offensive unit felt a keen respect for Eddie LeBaron, but for Meredith, who obviously had natural talent, they developed a fondness. Dandy Don, as he was called, had a quick wit and engaging personality, and he liked to make jokes as though he didn't have a care in the world. This was his public persona, the one that would most often appear in the newspapers, and as a result the Dallas fans would come to regard Meredith as a happy-go-lucky party boy and a maverick, and when he failed, especially in big games, they would hold that against him. It was not a coincidence that Landry held these very qualities against him as well and would continue to do so for Don's entire career.

Chapter 11

The Righteous and the Sinners

At first blush, an observer would have assumed that Tom Landry and Don Meredith would have gotten along famously. They were both small-town Texas boys. Tom had come from Mission in the south and Don from Mount Vernon in East Texas. Both had been Texas high school and college football heroes, Landry at UT, Meredith at SMU. But aside from that, they were as different in temperament and approach to the business of life and the game of football as two men could possibly be.

Landry had been a serious young man during his playing days at the University of Texas, but after he accepted Jesus late in 1958 his emphasis on seriousness, clean living, and hard work was magnified to the extent that he had become a prophet trumpeting the Christian ethic. He was one of the few coaches who injected religion into his speeches. A lot of coaches had a minister say a prayer before a game in a ritual much like the playing of "The Star-Spangled Banner," but to Landry the Bible, Jesus, and Christianity weren't just for Sunday services. They were a way of life. His religious beliefs were important, and he felt it was appropriate to inject them into his talks to the team. After a game he might recap the game and then take out his Bible. He would say, "I did a lot of things in my life, but my life was empty until a guy in Dallas invited me to go to this prayer group. And after I went to the prayer group and read my Bible, my life changed. I got this job . . ." That was how he presented the Bible: follow Jesus, and you will succeed. And why not? That's exactly what had happened to him. Not long after his conversion, Schramm had offered him a five-year contract at $34,500 a year.

Back in 1958 Landry had been responsible for the great New York Giants defenses and had been credited for his leadership and acumen. Emotionally, however, he was feeling rudderless and found himself without purpose in life. Part of it was that pro football wasn't paying him very much, a $12,000 salary that he had tried to augment during the off-season. His problem was that employers did not want six-month employees—and each year after football

Landry would have to start over again in a new endeavor. It left him frustrated and unsettled.

In the winter of 1958 Landry, born a Methodist, was invited to a Bible study class in the dining room of the Melrose Hotel in Dallas. He sat with 40 businessmen as they discussed Jesus' Sermon on the Mount. The session filled him with what he described as "joy," and he embarked on a Bible study program in which he immersed himself in the scriptures as assiduously as if he were studying an opposing team's offenses. Over a period of months Landry found that the Bible "made sense," and in 1959 his faith outweighed his doubts. That year he committed himself to Christ.

He began to look at life from a Christian fundamentalist perspective. Life became very simple for him. In the Bible, in John 3:16, it says, "I have given you my only living son . . ." Tom Landry gave himself to Christ. For Landry, the Bible became his handbook for life, like a manual for a car. If he wanted to know how to fix his life, he went to the Bible. When he became coach of the Dallas Cowboys he also expected his players to follow its teachings as well as his own.

What Landry read in the Bible was that a person is born into the world a sinner, and then when he accepts Jesus as his savior, his original sin from Adam and sins built up from birth to the time of his acceptance of Christ are washed "white as snow" by the blood of Jesus. He is absolved of all those sins. After he is saved, Jesus then lives in his heart, and if he seeks guidance for any decision or action through prayer, he will be guided by "the still, small voice" of the Holy Spirit.

Landry believed that the problem comes when a person goes against that "still, small voice," when he knows what the right way is according to the scripture and knowingly strays. Then, according to the scriptures, that person has "transgressed," and he has to repent. And if he doesn't repent, he suffers the consequences of that transgression. Because he has had access to the Holy Spirit and the scriptures, whatever happens to him after that as a result of his transgressions is his fault.

Landry knew his scriptures and lived by those rules. And when Landry devised his ingenious systems for defense, and his Multiple Offense, he instructed his players with a certainty that his systems would work. He became like a pastor to his cleated congregation, a shepherd to his muscular flock. In the Christian tenet there is a chain of command, whether in family or in business or in football. As a good Christian, if you trust that chain of command, if you have that faith, then everything will work out. Landry believed that all his players had to do was listen to him. They didn't have to think. All they had to do was trust him and do what he was telling them to do. The problems came when they would not do that, when they refused to accept his word. It became a terrible frustration for him.

The player who frustrated him the most was his young quarterback, Don Meredith. Meredith had been raised a Methodist, but upon his arrival in Dallas had turned his back on his small-town upbringing. For kids growing up in East Texas, Dallas *was* Mecca, the big city, where the lights glowed brightly and life could be lived away from the domination of one's parents and the church. At SMU Meredith enrolled as a divinity student, but once he tried out his newfound freedom, he escaped from what he saw as the twin chains: abstinence and chastity. That escape was tied to his rejection of the more encompassing institution: his religion.

Meredith questioned its tenets. He also rebelled against what he saw as its hypocritical nature. Meredith had seen firsthand that his Christian fundamentalist brethren in the South often projected racist and sexist attitudes. He could not understand how anyone who called himself a Christian could also have such strong hatred for blacks, Mexicans, and Jews. He saw how the southern Christian society used the scriptures to justify slavery, citing the argument that the Creator had made Negroes to be servants of white men.

Meredith all his life believed that the best 11 players deserved to be out there on the playing field, regardless of color. But race wasn't the only issue. Meredith intended to be the quarterback of his own life. Somebody had to be in charge of it, and he decided it would be himself. Meredith was not the sort of person to give up control of his life to anyone—not to Jesus, and not to Tom Landry. And Meredith believed that because you only go around once, a person should have as much fun as he possibly can. And so, to Tom Landry, Don Meredith was not only a sinner, but he was also a "rebellious and stiff-necked person," like the Jews, whom God was always killing off because of their "rebellious and stiff-necked ways."

Much to Landry's chagrin, Meredith—"Jeff and Hazel's baby boy," as he would later call himself—turned out to be the reincarnation of Bobby Layne, Landry's old reprobate teammate. In fact, Meredith, who like Layne drank and partied hard and spent hours in the pursuit of Texas women despite having married the SMU homecoming queen, often paid Layne the highest tribute when he would say, "When I die, I want to come back as Bobby Layne's chauffeur."

If Landry would not forgive Layne, who was a teammate, for his profligacy and wasting of his natural talent, Landry certainly would not accept this behavior from Meredith, one of his players. It was a tug-of-war between the two that was fought for nine long years.

Unlike Landry, who tried unsuccessfully to get Meredith to leave the party life behind and act serious like an adult, his teammates didn't give a damn about his private life. For most of them, Don's steady, obsessive regimen of hard liquor and women kept them from joining him socially, but they admired him greatly nevertheless. They loved his way of keeping them loose. When the team was getting clobbered, he would sing the words of some country-western song, and they would smile. Those players who disliked Landry, but who nevertheless followed his orders because of their fear of him, rooted for Meredith not to bow to the wishes of their martinet coach. Ballplayers play harder for a leader, an independent guy who thinks he knows best, who calls the shots and makes things happen. Everyone knew Don and Landry didn't get along because of the fundamental difference in their personalities. They saw this independent quality in the youngster.

And all his teammates also noticed that Meredith, more than anything else, was one tough Texan. He was not mobile in the pocket, a dangerous characteristic when your line is as airy as Swiss cheese. Making the danger even greater for him, often times he chose to stand in there rather than run, hoping he could make something happen at the last moment. Too often the thing that happened was that he would take a severe beating. Still, he kept on getting back up.

Bob Fry: "He was a tough, tough kid. That first year he had his ribs separated, his legs hurt, he had pulled muscles, broken ankles, a broken nose, dislocated fingers, and he kept on playing. Talk about a guy who had a lot of toughness. He was as tough as any quarterback I've been around. He was hurt by his party-boy image, but he needed that. It made him feel comfortable. I know that sounds crazy, but it's true. I'll tell you what, when you played with him you were playing against one tough son of a gun."

What his teammates didn't know was that Meredith and his wife, Lynn, had split up, again, and his wife had ended up with custody of his daughter. Meredith's ulcers flared. He suffered terribly from the guilty feelings that the breakup had all been his fault, that he had brought it all upon himself. Meredith saw the brutal beatings he took on the football field each week as his just punishment, something that he felt he deserved. Meredith would tell a reporter, "In a way I welcomed those beatings after losing a wife and daughter. It felt good."

Frank Clarke: "I remember when Don and I first met in training camp. I pulled up in a taxicab and got out of the cab with my bags, and Don Meredith walked out of the dormitory, and he extended his hand, and he said, 'Hi, I'm Don Meredith, SMU.' And I said, 'Hi, Don, I'm Frank Clarke, University of Colorado, Cleveland Browns.' We always felt a closeness. I felt a nice connection. Don and I connected because we were both very sensitive people. That's the part of Don a lot of people didn't see. I don't think he was intentionally trying to hide that part of him. He was unskillful in manifesting that. He didn't know how to let it come out and blossom. My problem was the opposite. I didn't know how to hide my sensitivity. It was easily identified, and people used it against me.

"And I can remember in the early years the offensive line wasn't strong, and as a unit we weren't together. We didn't have confidence. We were just a bunch of guys. Sometimes when I would move into a slot position or play tight end, I had occasion to block linebackers in certain defenses, and sometimes I would go to sleep or totally miss a guy, and the guy would just cream Dandy, really smash him, and I would go back to the huddle, and Don would just look at me like, 'Frank, you sure let me down on that one.' I'd say, 'God, Dandy, I'm sure sorry about that.' But Don wouldn't say anything."

After the pounding by the Rams, the Cowboys' record was 0–7. The next opponent was the Green Bay Packers, led by coach Vince Lombardi and an all-star cast. This was only Lombardi's second season in Green Bay, and already the coach with the big grin and the loud bark was becoming a legend.

Gene Cronin: "We had a rough afternoon against the Packers. They had Lombardi, which is a plus for anybody, and they had the people. Before Lombardi came, they had Paul Hornung, Jim Taylor, Bart Starr, Hank Gremminger, but they weren't used the right way. Lombardi came, and he put it all together. His trademark was the Green Bay sweep. It's a play that was in everybody's playbook. Everybody ran it. But Vince Lombardi believed in the running game, and that was his bread-and-butter play, and they worked and worked and worked and worked on that. They lined up in the split formation to the wide side of the field, and you knew it was coming, and they ran it and still made yards because they had some darn good people running it. They had Paul Hornung carrying the ball, and Jim Taylor blocking on the end, and they had two guards, Fuzzy Thurston or Jerry Kramer, out front blocking. On that play Jim Taylor would come after me. He was a tough football player, an excellent blocker."

Against the Cowboys, Jim Taylor ran for 121 yards and three touchdowns. The Pack dominated, 41–7, for Cowboys loss number eight. The next game, against the San Francisco 49ers, brought a 26–14 loss on a cold and rainy afternoon in an almost empty Cotton Bowl. The game after that was a 17–7 loss to the Chicago Bears, one of the better teams in the league. Don McIlhenny caught a 64-yard touchdown pass from Don Heinrich, and the defense played its best game. After the game McIlhenny went up to Landry and told him that it was the first time he had felt the Cowboys were an NFL team. And yet, despite a fine effort, on the books it amounted to just another loss, the 10th in a row.

Dick Bielski: "The losing became hard. It became a struggle. It becomes all the things that are unpleasant, because you are losing. What it's telling you is you're not good enough.

"It was hard for guys who had come from great situations and were used to winning. I can remember one time L. G. Dupre stood up and looked at all his teammates and said, 'What the f*** is going on?'"

For others, however, the losses were hard to take, but their morale continued to be good.

Fred Cone: "I wasn't demoralized. Jim Doran wasn't. Every game you went out and did the best you could, did everything we could to win."

Gene Babb: "We didn't like losing. We played hard. We were blown away by good teams, against people who had played together a long time, had good personnel who weren't learning a new system.

"With the Cowboys under Tom Landry's system, every week we got a new game plan, a new way to run the same play. Each week the blocking schemes would change, the formations would change. Some became exasperated. The core of the team came closer together."

The next game was to be played in Yankee Stadium against the New York Giants, a powerhouse. The Giants defense starred Andy Robustelli and Sam Huff, and on offense were a number of all-time Giants performers: Frank Gifford, Kyle Rote, and Alex Webster in the backfield. The quarterback, George Shaw, was subbing for an aging, banged-up Charlie Conerly, and that was a break for the Cowboys. But the Giants were still 13-point favorites.

On the flight from Dallas to New York, the team plane flew above the Statue of Liberty. Dick Bielski and Gene Babb called Byron Bradfute, who had only been as far east as Mississippi, to see it.

"What do you think of that?" the rookie Texan was asked.

"It looks just like the Bee County Courthouse," Bradfute replied.

Babb recalled the intensity with which Landry approached the Giants game on the bus ride from Newark Airport into New York.

Gene Babb: "We were on the bus the day before the Giants game, and Alicia, Tom's wife, went along on the trip. To give you an idea about Tom's ability to concentrate, we'd landed in Newark, and we were on the bus going to the Manhattan hotel, and it was a city bus, and you had the long seats up at the front by the door. And Mike Dowdle and I were sitting across from Alicia and Tom, and as we were heading in, Alicia was just talking up a storm. Mike and I were sitting there, and you couldn't help but overhear. She said, 'Maybe this evening we can see so-and-so, and give so-and-so a call, and perhaps have dinner with so-and-so,' mentioning all these people they knew. Mike and I both looked at Tom, and of course Tom had his hat on, and he was looking straight ahead. And I don't know that he heard a word of what Alicia was saying, 'cause we both knew that he was already at the ballgame on Sunday. And that's just the way he was."

When the team arrived in New York, Bradfute noticed a heightened excitement that emanated from the normally sphinxlike Landry. This was his coach's former team, and Landry wanted his new charges to put on a good show.

Byron Bradfute: "Psychologically everybody wanted to beat them because Tom wanted to beat them. I've read where he said it didn't make that much difference, but I don't remember it that way. My perception was that he wanted to beat them real bad."

When Tom Landry's name was announced over the public address system before the game, the huge Yankee Stadium crowd gave him a welcoming ovation. And when the Cowboys—led by three touchdowns by Dupre, two on receptions and one on a five-yard run—played the Giants even, a significant portion of the Giants rooters found themselves cheering for the Cowboys.

With the Giants ahead by a touchdown, their running back Joe Morrison fumbled and the Cowboys' Bill Herchman recovered. Eddie LeBaron then took the Cowboys down the field, scoring the tying points on a touchdown to split end Billy Howton, who had starred for years in Green Bay and had been acquired from Cleveland. The touchdown gave the Cowboys a 31–31 tie, the team's first non-loss. Some of the players celebrated as though it had been a victory.

Eddie LeBaron: "We started out the season pretty good, but we didn't win, and then we went to New York. Number one, we had practiced against New York's defense every day, because that was our defense. We knew it pretty well. We knew what they could do. And secondly, Tom had scouted the Giants beautifully. Also, we matched up pretty well against them. They had a great defense, but we just knew how to attack it, because that's what we did every day in practice. They used Tom's patented defense, a man-to-man defense with a free safety. Tom would tell us, 'If this guy steps this way, then it will be . . .' He knew the defense really well, so we could read it.

"I always got inspired playing in Yankee Stadium. I had some of my better games there. It wasn't a loss, so we were happy. Just to look halfway decent was more important than the wins or the losses at the time."

Frank Clarke: "It was like a victory, man. I loved it. And what I remember, it was so typical of New York fans, they were cheering for us. I suppose part of it had to do with Tom Landry coming from the Giants, and also it was an empathy thing: 'Wow, this might be the only game this team might not lose.' And the fans in New York were loving it. They were seeing a good football game, nothing sloppy. Both teams played really well."

The final game of the 1960 season took place in Detroit against the Lions. The game was played in the snow, and the Cowboys lost 23–14 to finish with a season record of 0–11–1. The game was marked by an uncharacteristic outburst by Landry, who berated officials for allowing LeBaron to be roughed up by the Lions defenders. It was also a game in which rookie quarterback Meredith learned an important lesson.

Don Meredith: "Eddie had been playing well, and I was dead certain he would go all the way, so the night before ol' Don decides to spend the entire evening introducing himself to the Motor City. That was the first time in my football career I had ever made a complete night of it. But, shoot, I wasn't worried. In fact, by the time the sun came up I wasn't even feeling the cold anymore.

"When I arrived in the clubhouse, Tom Landry told me I was starting against the Lions. I was sitting there with my pads on, my jersey, my socks and shoes, trying to figure out how I was going to make it through the day, when Nate Borden looked down at me and said, 'Boy, you are gonna need a lot of help today.' I told him, 'Hey, man, I'm ready.' Well, he started to laugh his head off and then said, 'Maybe it would be a good idea, then, to put your pants on before we go out. Which I understand we're going to do in just a very few minutes. It's a little cold today.'

"Then at the last minute Landry decided to start LeBaron. Don Heinrich and I sat on the bench smoking cigarettes. LeBaron started the second half, but then got his hand stepped on. They thought something might be broken, but he stayed in the game, as I kept throwing to keep my arm warm. I sat down again. In the fourth quarter Landry told me to warm up again. This time I told him I would not do it.

"I didn't play any football that day, but I learned a couple of things. First, I found out that all-night partying is OK if you don't have to play a football game the next day.

"And it was on that afternoon that I first began to realize that Tom and I were going to really have a lot of fun together."

Gene Cronin: "It was no damn fun. But I thought all along that Tom Landry would be successful. He was a dedicated man, smart about a lot of things, not only football. You knew he was going to persevere and succeed."

Jerry Tubbs: "We had a team party after the season, a lot of drinking, and Ray Mathews was loud and vocal blasting Tom."

Gene Babb: "Those who were disgruntled didn't last long. Tom Landry had a plan, and he intended to go a long way with it."

Chapter 12

Big Bob and Hogmeat

It was hard to imagine that the 0–11–1 Cowboys could improve themselves in the 1961 draft considering that they had traded their number one pick to the Washington Redskins to acquire quarterback Eddie LeBaron. But the Cowboys had a general manager of great cunning, a shrewd competitor who could not only ferret out a jewel in a competitor's slag heap, but could also find a way to get around the system and then take advantage of it. As a result, despite the team's inferior position in the draft, Tex Schramm was able to acquire for the Cowboys two of the finest defensive players in the history of the franchise, 25-year-old linebacker Chuck Howley and 22-year-old rookie defensive lineman Bob Lilly. In his second year with the Cowboys, middle linebacker Jerry Tubbs would have some help, and the defense would improve as it began to grow younger.

Howley, a five-sport letterman at West Virginia University, had been the number one draft choice of George Halas and the Chicago Bears in 1958; then in 1959 he tore up his knee and retired to run a service station back home in West Virginia. Don Healy, a defensive tackle who had come to the Cowboys from the Bears in the expansion draft, touted Howley to Schramm. Howley had wanted to come back to football, but he wasn't the sort of guy to pick up the phone and ask Halas for a job. As a result, Schramm acquired Howley from the Bears, and Howley played outside linebacker for Dallas from 1961 through 1973.

At 6'4", 235 pounds, Howley, whom his teammates called "Hogmeat," had the agility of a big cat. He could outmuscle, outjump, and outrun just about anyone who came his way. He also had an uncanny instinct for playing defense. Many times Howley would ignore his assignment, roaming not where he was supposed to go but where he was sure the ball or ball carrier would be. To the amazement of his teammates, most often he would be right, and as a result, during his 13-year career, the six-time All-Pro often made the big play, blitzing to throw a runner for a loss, backpedaling and roaming to make an interception, or sniffing out the ball and recovering a fumble.

Tex Schramm: "He was working in a gas station, and the Bears weren't that high on him, and we traded a song for him, and he turned out to be one of our greatest players."

Chuck Howley: "My first contract from Mr. Schramm was $9,000, which was an improvement. I went to St. Olaf College, where they had their training camp, and that was the year they drafted Bob Lilly. My position was linebacker, and when I got there I felt I was a starter and so it was my position to lose. I was a first-year Cowboy, and Bob was a rookie, but we looked at each other like we were veterans. And a clique began to develop with us and Jerry Tubbs, Larry Stephens, and Nate Borden. We all kind of fell into our responsibilities.

"There is no doubt that we had a collection of everything. You had older players, who had a tendency to be stuck in their ways. I was still young, and I felt like a rookie, even though I had been in the league three years. With the Bears you tried to let instinct take care of you. With the Cowboys, Tom had a system we didn't know a whole lot about. Tom was trying to preach to us, 'Forget your instincts. Do what I tell you.' And we didn't want to believe that if the ball was going away from us, we shouldn't pursue it. Tom kept telling us to do what the defense told us to do, but it was very difficult building that confidence in his system. Most all defenses up to that time were pursuit defenses.

"When I came to camp, they handed us a playbook, a big fat thing two inches thick. Tom did his best to make us as responsible as coaches. He wanted us to know the responsibility of every man around us, and as the years progressed we learned that. I didn't dig in and study it out of the book as was his intention. When I got done with it, my playbook ended up being about 10 sheets of paper. What related to me, that's what I concentrated on, and I think most of us did that, because it took so long for it to sink in. If we had been all straight-A students—not that we were a bunch of dumb jocks—we'd have picked it up in a month and believed in it.

"Remember, we played football because we have hard heads."

The other new defensive standout, rookie Bob Lilly, had more to do with the later success of the Cowboys than anyone. He was the most physically talented defensive lineman ever to play football, so talented that Landry would design an entire defensive system around him. Lilly's responsibility was to use his speed and quickness to beat his blocker and foil the play. Almost as often as not, he did that. Bob Lilly could foil an opposition's offensive plan all by himself. His teammate Walt Garrison once said of Lilly, "He was like some damn animal, like a wild lion out on the savanna in Africa. Just born that way. They put him on a football field, and he'd just eat people alive."

Lilly should never have been available when the Cowboys made their first choice in the second round of the 1961 draft. Lilly, who weighed in at 250 pounds on a 6'6" frame, was one of the quickest large men ever to play the game of football. At Texas Christian University, Lilly gained fame as a defensive lineman who could set up on the line and, at the snap of the ball, jump like a flash into the backfield and get to the quarterback in almost the time it took the ball to get there. Schramm was able to get him because Lilly, who came from the small Texas town of Throckmorton, told everyone and anyone who asked him that he would play pro ball only in Texas. In any other era a club could ignore such a demand, but in 1961 the NFL was competing for players with the American Football League, and Lilly had been drafted by the Dallas Texans. The other NFL teams were afraid that if they drafted Lilly, he would make good on his threat to play only with a Texas team and sign with the AFL. The one hope the NFL had to keep Lilly in the league was if he signed with the one Texas team in the NFL: the Dallas Cowboys. And so when it was Dallas' turn to make its first pick in the second round, the hulking Bob Lilly was still unplucked. Schramm, who very well knew how lucky he was, quickly took this man-child.

Like a lot of players from his generation, Bob Lilly fought his way up from hard times. After a drought baked West Texas for a half decade, in 1956 Lilly's dad was forced to quit the farm and Texas as well, moving the family to find a job near relatives in Pendleton, Oregon. Lilly played his senior year for a Portland high school, then returned to Texas to go to Texas Christian University, where he became an All-American. Because of his insistence on playing pro ball in Texas, he anchored the Cowboys defensive line for 14 glorious seasons. Before he was through, Lilly would be rated the finest defensive tackle ever to play the game.

Because Lilly was left-handed, Landry initially placed Lilly at left defensive end, a position ill-suited to his talents. Ends have to run long distances to chase down ball carriers, and Lilly did not have long-range speed. On many plays his job was merely to watch and make sure the play did not come back in his direction. Lilly was adequate at end, but uninspired. The first two years of Lilly's career were a nightmare for him. He was so talented that despite playing out of position and despite a hurt knee, two sprained ankles, a broken thumb, a broken wrist, and five broken ribs, his first year he was named to the All-Rookie team. Nevertheless, during practice he would become so frustrated he would start smacking the offensive linemen around. He felt so overmatched that he considered quitting.

Bob Lilly. "I knew the Cowboys hadn't won a game in '60, but it didn't bother me a lot because I knew they were a new team. I hadn't been in the pros, so I didn't realize how hard it was to build a team from scratch. Landry was pretty lucky the first year 'cause he got Don Meredith and Don Perkins, and my first year we got Chuck Howley. I don't know how we got him, but I do remember he had torn his knee up, ran a service station, and the Cowboys got him from the Bears, and I can recall Chuck had a big scar on his knee.

"So there he was when I arrived for training camp, and Jerry Tubbs was there, and so we had a little bitty nucleus of good football players. Between Tubbs and Howley, they made about 80 percent of the tackles for a couple of years there.

"I went to St. Olaf College in Northfield, Minnesota, for training camp. That was a beautiful campus, except you had to walk down 386 steps—I counted them—to get from the dorm to the playing field, plus I was on the third floor of the dorm.

"When I returned from practice for the College All-Star Game, I noticed that some of the older veterans were bitching all the time. They made fun of Landry. They were almost as old as he was, and they made fun of his new system because they had come from other systems, and this hampered his building a team in those early years. We could have done it faster if he had just gotten all new guys. And looking back, I suppose he was getting rid of guys as fast as he could. But the bickering caused us to have doubts about the system, too, just because the veterans had been in other places, and I didn't know. I admired coach Landry, but I wasn't going to sit down with him on a first-name basis and talk to him. I was in awe of him really. And yet, here were these older players talking about 'rinky-dink' this, and how 'stupid' that was, and that destroys your confidence a little bit.

"We played a 4-3 defense, and I was playing defensive end the first two years. The playbook called for me to 'read' my man, and I had never done that. I had always just reacted. And my first couple years half the time I would run toward the quarterback, and he would bootleg and go the other way, and I'd be standing there as he was throwing a touchdown. Or I'd be rushing in as fast as I could, and they would pull a reverse on me. I finally learned that if somebody was letting me get in real easy, something was wrong, that it was going to be a screen or something tricky.

"Coach Landry wanted me to 'key' the tackle and guard, but I also had to look at the fullback if he was lined up in a certain position. And I couldn't do all that. I just wasn't used to it. It would take a few years before I learned to do those things. In some systems, you can be productive in your first or second year. But under coach Landry's system, you had to be thinking all the time, and I was never sure what I was doing, and I wasn't real productive. Basically, I was just lost those first two years.

"I felt sorry for Jerry Tubbs those first couple of years, when we didn't have much. He had two, three guys, especially me, who weren't doing their jobs, and he'd have to cover for all of us, plus his own responsibilities. Jerry helped us as much as he could, and he was hurt himself, playing with a bad back, bad knees, and yet he would make 20 to 30 tackles a game. He was the only one who could catch them. When I'd forget to close off my man, Jerry would give me some fatherly advice. He'd bark at me, 'Lilly, close the trap. You're going to get me killed.' I'd say, 'Jerry, I'm sorry.' And I was. I felt bad.

"My first year I hurt my knee, sprained both ankles, broke my thumb, broke a wrist, and cracked some ribs. They weren't totally broken. The worst thing was my knee. I had never been hurt, and I wouldn't have been hurt then except my own man shoved me. Against Minnesota we were playing on the field where the baseball team also played. And we were going down on a punt return, and I was just fixing to get ready to make the hit when a teammate behind me got hit and ricocheted, and out of a reflex shoved me. And when he did, I went up in the air, and I came down on the pitcher's mound, where it was hard, right on the point of my knee, and it tore the cruciates a little bit. The knee swelled up.

"We only had four defensive linemen left, and me. I wasn't supposed to play the next week, but the coach told me I had to play, so they taped my leg stiff and I went out and played. And it was a good lesson. I limped through it, got killed out there, but I played the whole game. And in a couple weeks it quit hurting.

"At the same time my thumb had broken and gone through the skin just a little, and they put it in a cast, and every week I broke it again. My arm was made relatively useless. That was my best arm, the one I used to grab somebody. And then my ribs hurt, but they put pads there and it didn't bother me too much. And they use novocaine, too. They shoot you to kill the pain. And you went out there, and it would wear off, and that was a problem, but you at least got out there and played.

"Coach Landry knew an injury was going to affect the way you played, but he wasn't sympathetic about being hurt. I think part of the reason for that was that we only had 35 players in those early two or three years. There just weren't any replacements, so that's why he wasn't very sympathetic. He always said, 'The mark of a pro is if you can play hurt.' He said, 'Everybody gets hurt. If you can't play hurt, you can't play in the NFL.' So that's really the way it was. You just accepted the pain.

"As I said, the problem my first year was that even though we had some pretty good football players, we weren't all on the same page. A lot of them were playing their old way, and a lot of them like me didn't know what page they were on. All I remember was that the guys were always talking, 'We shouldn't be doing this. We should be doing that.' And then in the game there would be a lot of bitching in the huddle. Tubbs had to shut everybody up, because they were all griping at each other, blaming each other. Half the time they were bitching about me, and I didn't blame them. That was a humbling experience, playing defensive end in pro football without ever having played it before. I just didn't fit. Those two years I hated football. I could not stand being out there at the end. I wanted to be in the middle of things. When you're the end, you're never free to really go out there. You can't pursue, because you're waiting for a fake or a lateral, a rollout, a keeper, a reverse, or a screen play. And so you're always sitting out there, watching. And half the time you don't even get hit. They're just screening you off. I *hated* it, and if I had continued at end, I probably wouldn't have played much longer. In fact, [Landry] probably would have gotten rid of me."

Commensurate with the influx of new blood was the excising of some of the old. Kicker Fred Cone, at age 34, quit to take a job recruiting for his alma mater, Clemson University. Quarterback Don Heinrich, at age 28, unused and frustrated, packed it in. He was replaced in the 1962 draft by 6'7" TCU quarterback

Sonny Gibbs. LeBaron, quietly sensitive about the many references to his 5'6" height and the constant wonderment that his lack of height should have disqualified him from being able to play in the NFL, was master of ceremonies at a banquet at which the gangly Gibbs was also a guest. While introducing the young quarterback, LeBaron publicly asked him, "Sonny, did it ever occur to you that you're *too tall* to play quarterback in the NFL?" Gibbs, unsure what LeBaron was referring to, said, "Huh?" It got a good laugh. Gibbs never made it with the Cowboys.

Disgruntled lineman Gene Cronin found himself traded to the Washington Redskins. Another lineman, John Gonzaga, reported to training camp at St. Olaf angry at having to play another season with an expansion team. Then the hot weather, the rain at night, and the mugginess, combined with Landry's killer workouts, finally made him snap.

John Gonzaga: "I thought about it one night, and the next morning at breakfast I went to see Tom Landry and told him he had 10 days to get me out of there, because 'I consider myself a Cowboy no longer.'

"After about four days, I asked him if he had anything going for me. He said, 'I was kind of hoping you'd change your mind.' I said, 'I have. I'm not going to wait the 10 days. I'm leaving now.' I was going back home to go to work. As far as I was concerned at that point, football was over.

"The Cowboys took me to the airport, and at the airport I was paged. I got to the phone, and it was E. J. Anderson from the Detroit Lions. He told me that he owned me. I enjoyed five years more than I even dreamed I could."

Don Perkins' return to health caused Landry to make a couple of personnel shifts. Landry informed the incumbent, Don McIlhenny, that to stay on the team he had to gain some weight and play fullback. Two games into the preseason Landry informed him he was too slow to play fullback. "But you're the one who told me to gain the weight," said McIlhenny. No matter. The veteran back was dispatched to the San Francisco 49ers. Another back, Gene Babb, was switched from offense to defense, where he was installed as a linebacker. Another player might have balked. Babb didn't care. He just wanted to play football.

Gene Babb: "Now I'm over there trying to learn the Landry defense, and that's no easy chore. I'd played both ways in college. Back then things were different than they are today. Back then it was 'Yes, sir,' and 'No, sir.' This day in time it's 'Why?' and 'What for?' It's a different outlook. I just wanted to play. I loved to play. The money wasn't the thing. The tail wasn't trying to wag the dog. Since I had played linebacker before, it wasn't a big change for me to move over. They had an opportunity for me, and I took it. I really never ever gave it a second thought."

With such additions as Lilly, Howley, and Perkins, the other players felt encouraged because of the injection of talented new blood and because after a full season, they were more organized as a team. But many of the players, especially the veteran defenders, continued to buck the way Landry wanted things done, and there was some consternation when Lilly began fighting with Tom as well.

Jerry Tubbs: "In those early years Lilly really got frustrated. Lilly was a griper. For a lot of years he complained. A lot of players do. Nothing wrong with that if they perform. And boy, was Bob talented. But Bob griped about anything and everybody. Part of it had to do with Tom's system and his relationship with Tom. Lilly knew he had great natural ability, and sometimes he would want to do something different from what Tom wanted him to do. He always liked it in a passing situation when he didn't have to worry about the run. But he'd get frustrated against the run. He'd say to himself, 'I can trap the quarterback.' Lilly *knew* what he could do. But Tom wanted him to hold his ground And so he felt held back by the system. And this was also true when he was later moved to tackle.

"Bob Lilly was our superstar for so long. They would have two or three guys blocking him. It was unbelievable how he could beat one man every time. He was the best player we've ever had, and we've had some great ones."

If many of the players continued to resist doing what Landry asked of them, there were also a few converts to his way of thinking. Wide receiver Frank Clarke was one.

Frank Clarke: "We were starting to believe more in Tom as a leader. 'Maybe this guy knows what he's talking about.' Tom was saying, 'If we're going to play football, why not play to win?' We were waking up to that. There was a newness, an intensity that was starting to be ignited in us."

The 1961 season began against the Pittsburgh Steelers. Don Meredith started, and he was playing well until he threw a pass that Johnny Sample intercepted and ran back 39 yards for a touchdown to give the Steelers a 24–17 lead. When Landry substituted LeBaron, Meredith joked with a couple of players on the bench, went to sit by himself, and cried.

With 56 seconds left in the game LeBaron capped a 75-yard drive by throwing a 17-yard touchdown pass to tight end Dick Bielski. Linebacker Jerry Tubbs then intercepted a Bobby Layne pass on the Cowboys' 38. There were five seconds left in the game.

LeBaron threw a long pass down the left sideline to Billy Howton, who ran out of bounds on the Pittsburgh 22.

Eddie LeBaron: "Billy was a *great* end. He wanted the ball *all* the time. The only trouble I had with him was that he'd say, 'I can get behind him,' when he was reaching the age where he wasn't getting behind them nearly as well as he could cut in front of them. But he was still a really good receiver.

"On that play I had to run out of the pocket to the left, and then he broke it off and got behind the corner and underneath the safety, and I threw about a 40-yard pass. He didn't score, but it gave Allen Green the chance to kick a field goal to win it."

One second remained. Green, a graduate of Ole Miss, had missed two field goals and had had a punt blocked that led to a Steelers touchdown. When he came into the game for the final time, the Cotton Bowl crowd roundly booed him.

Allen Green: "I had definitely not had a good day. Big Daddy Lipscomb had been putting tremendous pressure on me all afternoon, blocking one and forcing me to rush all afternoon. I was getting pretty roundly booed every time I came off the field."

He managed to kick himself into the record books with a straight and true 27-yarder. Tom Landry and his Cowboys had gotten the monkey off their backs.

Allen Green: "It was a great feeling to come off the field that day knowing I had made a contribution to the first regular-season win in the team's history."

It was to be Green's one and only season with the Cowboys. The second time they played the Steelers, a defender hit him during a punting attempt and chipped his anklebone. LeBaron had to replace him as punter. In the off-season Green was traded to the Packers.

The second game of the season was against the second expansion team, the Minnesota Vikings, coached by Norm Van Brocklin and led by a young University of Georgia quarterback, Fran Tarkenton. The Cowboys won again, this time by the score of 21–7. The defense was effective, and on offense the star of the game was Don Perkins, who ran for 108 yards on 17 carries. He also caught five passes for 61 yards. From the start, Perkins' impression was a lasting one.

Bob Fry: "Don Perkins was a great football player. Perk was as smart as any back I've been around. He knew his assignments, knew what he had to do, knew how to do it. Ermal Allen, the coach who ran the offense, would ask something, and even though he was only a rookie, Perk would be the one to ask, 'Is this how you want me to pick it up?' Or, 'Do you want me to do it this way?' He was right into it. He picked up Landry's system. So he was a leader among the backs even as a rookie."

Don Perkins: "When I came to Dallas I can't say that I was overwhelmed by Tom's system. At every level of competition it gets a little more challenging, and as a running back, you have to instinctively find things, and you better find them quick. I don't have a feel for how different or complex his system was. This was my first year playing at that level. You go in, take your shot, and see what happens.

"I thought Tom was very thorough, very patient, a professional. He was not emotional. He didn't feel it was his job to be a cheerleader. He prepared you, and you played. His attitude was, 'I've got my job, you've got yours. Let's go do them.' I thought it was cool. I didn't need anybody to wind me up. I knew what my job was. And my first year, there may have been a whole country believing we couldn't win, and for the most part, we didn't, but I don't think we ever went into a game thinking we could not win. How could I possibly critique what was going on in the offensive or defensive line, or anyplace else? I had enough of a job as a young person trying to hold down a running back slot."

In the third game of 1961 Cleveland dominated, 25–7, but the next weekend the Cowboys shut out the expansion Vikings in their second meeting, 28–0, as the defensive line sparkled. In this game Landry inaugurated a system of shuttling quarterbacks in and out, a system that has raised the hackles of his field generals over the years. In this case, his veteran, Eddie LeBaron, the good soldier, accepted the arrangement. The young kid, Don Meredith, hated it.

Eddie LeBaron: "I thought it was a pretty good deal. I thought the system was very good. And it was interesting. If you were the first- and third-down quarterback, you got to throw a lot. If you were the second-down quarterback, you didn't.

"I know Don didn't like it. He was young, and he felt he wanted to be in there all the time. I don't blame him, but . . . all I know was that in one game against the Steelers in which we were alternating, I threw five touchdown passes. It wasn't something you could not have a good day in."

Don Meredith: "What I didn't realize then was that all along Tom knew what he wanted. It must have been tough for him, because he received so much criticism the way he did things, but he never altered.

"In '61 I really wasn't impressed with anything. I became rebellious and antagonistic about the whole situation. I really thought Tom was wrong, and it became sort of a personal thing, which is the worst thing that could have happened to me. I wasn't hurting him, just myself."

In the blowout against the Vikings, Perkins scored on a short run, and Clarke showed Landry something, with touchdown catches of 16 yards from LeBaron and 52 yards from Meredith. Clarke, finally, was beginning to live up to his potential.

Eddie LeBaron: "When Frank came, he hadn't played a lot at Cleveland. And he had a bum rap on him: they said he couldn't catch the ball across the middle.

"I used to work with him all the time, because he was really a talented guy, and he loved to stay out after and work, catch the ball, and we spent a lot of time together. We practiced a lot, worked out our own routes together. On a pattern I might tell him to run a 'zig-in,' or a 'zig-out,' which might be different from a regular pattern. When he first started, he had good soft hands, but he didn't always watch the ball. I think part of any rap he might have had, he just didn't watch the ball closely. As time went on, he really became a great receiver. He was a very durable player. He never got hurt, and he had that great speed, and he was a great guy to work with."

After three early wins in 1961 the Cowboys' bubble burst with a 31–10 drubbing by the New York Giants before forty-two thousand fans in the Cotton Bowl. The home crowd was substantial, because Dallas fans believed the team had turned the corner. But the early start had been illusory, and the lopsided loss disappointed a lot of them.

Tex Schramm: "We had won a couple of games, and people got a little interested, and we had forty-two thousand people, and we got the hell kicked out of us, and the next home game we had sixteen thousand. We hadn't become established."

The Cowboys had toyed with their fans' emotions, not for the last time, as once again Sam Huff toyed with Don Meredith.

Frank Clarke: "Sam Huff was playing middle linebacker. What would happen, Meredith would call an audible, and the Giants wouldn't move. And at one point Meredith even looked at Sam Huff, and moved his head, like he was telling Sam, 'You're supposed to move over this way.' He nodded his head toward his right shoulder as if to say, 'Tom Landry told us, Sam, that when you saw this formation, you were going to move over there, so damn it, get over there!'"

After a 43–7 demolition by Sonny Jurgensen and the Philadelphia Eagles, the Cowboys flew to New York where, before sixty thousand Giants fans in Yankee Stadium, they defeated an excellent Giants team, 17–16. Once again an Allen Green field goal won it. And after that the game wasn't in hand until Don Healy stopped a final Giants drive by intercepting a Y. A. Tittle pass.

It was a joyous triumph for Landry, who was uncharacteristically whooping and hollering in the locker room after the game. At four wins and three losses, some players were under the illusion that there was a possibility of making a run at the championship. But in the final seven games, all the Cowboys could accomplish was a tie against a terrible Washington Redskins team. Their triumph over the Giants would be the last win in what would turn out to be a 4–9–1 season. The Cowboys just did not have enough talent.

Bob Fry: "Don Perkins was a good running back, and we had a couple of wide receivers, but you have to have 11 guys to win consistently. It only takes one weak link. When you throw a pass, if just one lineman doesn't block, if you're playing against Deacon Jones or Merlin Olsen . . . it's tough, unless you have people to match them."

Against the Washington Redskins, former Cowboys defensive lineman Gene Cronin proved exactly what Fry was talking about. Tackle Byron Bradfute had torn cartilage during the exhibition season and returned in time to face Washington, who had won just one game in their last 34 exhibition and regular-season games. This game would end in a 28–28 tie. Bradfute, a second-year player, recalled the beating he took from defensive end Gene Cronin.

Byron Bradfute: "In the middle of the season the Cowboys cut Charley Granger and activated me, and so I felt, 'This is a great chance to bring my old high school coach up here,' and so I brought him to Dallas to watch us play the

Redskins. That was my first game to be activated, and there was no way I was supposed to play. So I partied a little bit too much the night before with my old high school coach and then went out there to play the Redskins. In the first quarter Bob McCreary got kicked out of the game, and I had to play the rest of the game. An ex-Cowboy named Gene Cronin was playing defensive end for the Redskins, and he had an absolute field day against me. He'd have made All-Pro if he had played against me all season. In fact, that's what he told me. We'd line up, and he'd say, 'Bradfute, I'm going to make All-Pro against you.' And boy, he did, too. In fact, they moved me over to the other side and put Bob Fry on him, and really, I didn't stop him and nobody else did either."

Despite the 4–9–1 record in 1961, quarterback Eddie LeBaron had a strong feeling that his team was progressing.

Eddie LeBaron: "We were getting better. Oh yes, you could see it. The defense was getting better. We had Bob Lilly and Chuck Howley. On offense we had Frank Clarke and Don Perkins. We were just getting better people.

"In the next draft we got speed. Cornell Green was going to play tight end when he came up from Michigan State, and they made him a defensive back. Lee Roy Jordan, George Andrie, Dave Edwards, and Mike Gaechter also joined the team on defense. And we added tight end Pettis Norman, who had so much talent. Tex Schramm was starting to put together the nucleus of a very good football team."

Chapter 13

Pettis and Cornell

When Tex Schramm was running the Los Angeles Rams, he had one overriding drafting philosophy: if you mine where everyone else does, you'll be mediocre like everyone else. As a result, Schramm looked for talent, regardless of color, the size and reputation of the school, or whether an athlete had even played football.

Even though in 1947 Jackie Robinson had proved the ability of black ballplayers to compete alongside whites, in the early fifties owners and general managers of many sports teams still were reluctant to sign blacks for fear they would drive away their white fans. George Preston Marshall, the owner of the Washington Redskins, flatly refused to sign black players, fearing the appearance of a black player would alienate his southern audience. It wasn't until 1962, with the trade for halfback Bobby Mitchell, that the Redskins finally fielded a black player.

Schramm was acutely aware that his Cowboys were playing in the Bible Belt, but he refused to allow the collective feelings of his Deep South constituents against blacks to affect his chances of winning football games. In the early years with the Cowboys, Schramm thoroughly investigated the black players he signed in an attempt to eliminate malcontents and to determine that the players he hired were smart enough to learn Landry's systems. As the years went on, Schramm saw that to win, a team needed a lot of black players, and he even did away with those tests. For the most part, if Schramm saw a player he thought could help the Cowboys, he would sign him regardless of race. It would not be long before the Cowboys would field more black players than just about any other sports team. According to Schramm, this lack of prejudice had been passed on to him by team owner Dan Reeves, his friend and boss on the Los Angeles Rams.

Tex Schramm: "Dan Reeves never got the credit for integrating football the way Branch Rickey did in baseball. Of course, there had been a few black players in the NFL, players like Fritz Pollard, but the last one had played in 1934, and there wasn't another one until Kenny [Washington] and Woody [Strode] played for the Rams in '46.

"When I joined the Rams, we signed Tank Younger, the first player signed out of Grambling, and we drafted Dan Towler from William & Mary.

"When I began drafting players with Dallas, I just kept doing what I had been doing, drafting the best players I could find, regardless of color."

Finding great black football players in the fifties and early sixties wasn't as easy as it is today. The institution of segregation kept black players out of the great southern football schools like the University of Alabama, the University of Georgia, the University of Oklahoma, and all the big Texas schools. The best of the black players either played for those northern schools that were integrated, or they played for the many unpublicized all-black colleges around the country.

During the fifties teams didn't scout in an organized manner. There were no staffs for scouting prospects. Word of mouth, newspaper clippings, and statistics produced draft choices, and aside from the All-Americans and the record setters, teams often had a miserable time picking competent players.

Schramm realized that if he could get the athletic directors and coaches of hundreds of the small colleges—white and black—from across the nation to do his legwork for him, he would have a significant advantage over the opposition. That's where his brilliantly conceived Tom Harmon All-America Team came into play. Each year these so-called awards honored the best football players from the little-known small schools by publicizing the names of the winners. No one knew who was behind them, but since the legendary University of Michigan and pro quarterback Tom Harmon was the name sponsor, no one thought to question it. Had someone, anyone, investigated, he would have discovered that these "awards" were but a vehicle for Tex Schramm and his Rams football team to learn the identities of the best players at these small schools. It was a drafting ploy that benefited Tex financially, while at the same time heaping lots of glory on Tom Harmon and the honored football players. To this day the coaches and athletic directors who filled out the questionnaire for the Tom Harmon awards never knew their ulterior purpose. More than anything else, this ingenuity in finding players marked the genius of Schramm as he struggled to make the Dallas Cowboys into a competitive football team.

In addition to Schramm's contacts, the Cowboys also had the benefit of having Gil Brandt running the scouting department. Brandt was a real-life Walter Mitty, who as a collegiate at the University of Wisconsin was one of the very first "draftniks." He would write to college sports departments to borrow game films in order to advance his hobby of making a list of the top pro prospects.

After Brandt worked part-time for Schramm in L.A., Tex hired him in 1960, and it wasn't long before Brandt, who the players said had the heart and mind of a bunko artist, developed a huge network of informants among college coaches, trainers, secretaries, and athletic directors in colleges large and small. If a coach needed a favor, he would go to Brandt. In return, Brandt wanted information. It was his scouting reports that for many years gave Schramm and Landry the advantage in drafting unknown players in the lower rounds and free agents.

In 1962 a total of 13 of Schramm's draft picks and free agents made the Dallas Cowboys. The guys who made it in 1962 were typical of the Cowboys. The top choice, TCU quarterback Sonny Gibbs, didn't make it. A few picks came from major colleges—defensive tackle Don Talbert from the University of Texas, offensive tackle John Myers from the University of Washington, and Mike Gaechter from the University of Oregon—but of the 13 rookies, a remarkably high number were unheralded low draft choices and free agents from colleges few had ever heard of. Among the Cowboys' choices were a defensive end named George Andrie, who hadn't even played his senior year because his college, Marquette, had dropped its football program. There was linebacker Harold Hays from Southern Mississippi; a defensive back, Don Davis, from Southern University; a fullback, Amos Bullocks, from Southern Illinois; and a free agent offensive end named Pettis Norman from a small, black North Carolina college, Johnson C. Smith University.

Pettis Norman, unlike black teammates Frank Clarke and Don Perkins, had grown up in the Deep South, subject to all the rules and regulations—and crushing indignities and limitations—imposed on him by segregation. Growing up, Norman faced all obstacles with honesty, industriousness, determination, and intelligence. He demonstrated the ability to get knocked down and get back up, traits that would serve him well both on and off the football field. His motto was to never let anyone, or anything, defeat him. In addition, he maintained a moral strength that helped carry him to success, both on the field and off. It was that sense of righteousness that he would use to help change the segregationist climate, first on the Cowboys and later in the city of Dallas itself.

Norman spent his first 11 years in rural Georgia, working with his nine brothers and sisters to help his father sharecrop the land. After his father died his family moved to Charlotte, North Carolina, but the size of his new school petrified him so that Norman stayed in Georgia for two more years to continue his education in the two-room schoolhouse that he had been accustomed to. When he returned to Charlotte as a seventh-grader, the 14-year-old boy played tackle football for the first time in the sandlots. Despite the culture shock of going from sandlot ball to big-time high school football, he made the team his junior year but didn't start until he was a senior. His intention was to join the air force, but he was recruited by the coach of Johnson C. Smith University, which was located near his home in Charlotte, and he developed so fast he was named the team's MVP as a freshman.

Norman was a sprint star on the track team and was named All-America as an offensive end on the football team, but he was not drafted by an NFL team after the Dallas Texans in the AFL falsely told everyone he had signed with them. When the Texans tried to strong-arm Norman into signing, he became angry and broke off negotiations. He signed with the Cowboys as a free agent, starring as a tight end for Dallas from 1962 through 1970, when he was traded to the San Diego Chargers for split end Lance Alworth.

Pettis Norman: "Before the NFL Draft, the word got out—on purpose by the Texans—that I had signed a contract. And so when the Cowboys called, Gil Brandt said, 'We wanted to draft you, but you've signed a contract.' I told Gil I hadn't. He said, 'We don't want to waste a draft choice, but if you're not drafted, we want to sign you to a free-agent contract.'

"Part of it was they were afraid I had signed a contract, but part of it was, and I didn't know it then, but I do know it now, it was a cheap way of getting me.

"Well, sure enough, right after the NFL Draft, Gil Brandt called and said he wanted to come up. I called the Texans and told them the Cowboys had called, and they told me over the phone, 'You can't sign a contract with them, because you've already signed a contract with us,' which wasn't true. We got into a dispute. I felt they had lied to me and tried to cheat me, and I told them I didn't want to deal with them any more.

"Gil and I went out and had a hamburger. He had five hundred $1 bills, and he was flipping through them on the table like they were a pack of cards. He offered me an $8,500 contract, and we agreed, and as a bonus I got those five hundred $1 bills.

"When I signed I was happy, and for a number of reasons. It was more money than I had ever made at any one time. Eight thousand five hundred dollars was more money than my college professors were making at the time. And at that time my mother had had a second stroke. She was an invalid, and we were poor, and she needed medical attention, and so I could use that money to help defray the medical costs. And so I signed with the Cowboys and reported to training camp."

Another free agent signed by Schramm and his sidekick, Brandt, had played no football in college at all. Rather, Cornell Green had played basketball, and with great ability, at Utah State University. It was Schramm's theory that if an athlete had size and enough ability, he could learn to play the game of football. Over the years Schramm would occasionally gamble low draft choices on college hoops stars, including Green; Pete Gent, who starred in basketball at Michigan State University; Minnesota's Lou Hudson; Kentucky's Pat Riley; and Ohio State's John Havlicek. He would also sign track stars Mike Gaechter from Oregon and Olympic hero Bob Hayes of Florida A&M and lose Olympian Carl Lewis to a professional track career.

Tex Schramm: "If you start an expansion club, and if you're going to be able to compete, you have to do more, spend more money on scouting. We did. We had more people and did more things. One of the things I did was go after great athletes. I especially wanted a star basketball player who fell in the gray area of not being tall enough to make it as a forward in the NBA, and not being quick enough to be a guard. 'Cause you're never going to get the *top* college basketball players. If they played basketball all four years in college, they are not going to come in as a tryout in football. Among the players we drafted over the years were Lou Hudson, Pat Riley, and John Havlicek. They would have made great football players. Unfortunately, they all made it in the NBA.

"Gil Brandt, our scouting director, knew as many basketball coaches as he knew football coaches, and he would ask them, 'Who do you see who won't make it in the NBA but who's a hell of an athlete?' That's how we found Cornell Green at Utah State. It's how we found Pete Gent. The ones who made it were the exceptions.

"In other words, we fooled around with a lot of guys, and some of them worked, and some of them didn't. One time I drafted Carl Lewis, who came out of the University of Houston. But Carl was the first one who wanted to make track a livelihood, and he was good enough to do it. But you have to do something different. If you do the same thing, you're going to be in the same spot they are."

Cornell Green was an All-American hoops star at Utah State who was swayed from playing in the NBA because the Cowboys made him an offer he couldn't refuse. Green, who hadn't played football since high school, originally was going to play tight end, but he was turned into a defensive back by coach Landry and his defensive coordinator, Dick Nolan, and Pettis Norman was given the tight end job. Tall at 6'4", athletic, fast, and most of all smart, Cornell Green found himself starting for the Cowboys when the 1962 season started, despite coach Landry's intense dislike of having rookies on the field. Green was an All-Pro selection four times (1966, 1967, 1968, and 1969) and was named to the Pro Bowl five times. He retired after the 1975 season.

Green, a black player from Southern California, had played on mostly white teams in high school and in college was one of a handful of black students on the campus of Utah State in Logan, Utah. Green came to Dallas, lived where he was told, but otherwise found he could do pretty much whatever he pleased.

Cornell Green: "I really didn't encounter any racial problems, nothing, when I came to Dallas, because I was told where to go and where to stay. A lot of things I saw for the first time down here in Texas amazed me. I was from California, and I had never seen a system where people had to live in only a certain section. That was where you had to be in. It had nice houses, very nice homes, but just the idea that you had to stay in a certain section amazed me. I had never seen an all-black college. In my whole high school, grammar school, growing up, I only had one black teacher in California. Here, all the teachers were black in the school.

"In our own way we came down here fighting the system. The system was being fought at *every* turn. We didn't do anything to get our names publicized. We would go and do things against the system knowing there wasn't a whole lot they could do about it because I was a Cowboy, a member of the NFL.

"A lot of white guys from up North didn't understand the system either. Take a guy like Mike Gaechter, who was also a rookie that year. Gaechter and I would go wherever we wanted. We never said, 'We can't go in here.' Or 'I'm not supposed to be in here.' And I don't remember anyone challenging me. Just by my being there I was integrating the city."

When Pettis Norman and Cornell Green reported for training camp, the Cowboys roomed them together. Since 1960 the Cowboys had always roomed black players with black players and white players with white players, consistent with the racial policies of the Deep South. It would be a few years before Pettis Norman would act to change the system of room assignments.

Pettis Norman: "Everything back then was by race. We were separated by race within the dorm. You roomed by race. Cornell Green was my first roommate. I hung out mostly with the black players because of that, though there was very little socializing in Marquette, Michigan. Most times, you stayed in your room studying, keeping to yourself.

"The first practice we had lifted my spirits. After the scrimmage, coach Landry put the film on, got it all set, and before he turned the camera on, he said, 'If you all want to know how to play football, watch Pettis Norman in this film.' For coach Landry, that was really a high compliment. I'll never forget that.

"That first year I didn't have a great appreciation for Tom Landry as a coach. I appreciated that he didn't seem to get rattled, and that he didn't berate players if they made mistakes. He didn't try to embarrass the player. Rather he took every situation and tried to make it a teaching situation. He made some bold statements like, 'By 1965 we're going to be a winner,' and it was hard for me to see that based on what I saw.

"Still, there were things that happened during the course of the season that had you begin to build confidence in him. You began to know if you followed his instructions to a T, if you took exactly 10 steps, and everyone did his job, chances were you were going to catch the pass and be successful. So you began to develop that kind of respect.

"I started camp as a split end, blocked well in a game, knocked people down on the run, and then one day Tom Landry came up beside me as we were walking to practice and he said, 'I really want to move you to tight end.' I thought to myself, I thought you said I was doing well. Why do you want to move me to tight end? I asked him why he wanted to do that, and he said, 'I want to take advantage of your blocking.' And so he moved me to tight end.

"Eddie LeBaron and Don Meredith were the quarterbacks, and early on they helped me tremendously, especially LeBaron. He was the veteran. He really took me under his wing, and he would stay out with me after practice every day, and would stay out there as long as I wanted to stay out, and he'd throw balls to me. He'd teach me little techniques, how to catch the ball better, how to relax.

"Don Meredith was a happy-go-lucky person, but a nice person as well, and he also worked with me. He was such a young guy, much younger than Eddie. Don was certainly very nice about staying out and working after practice as well, but Eddie just made me feel so comfortable. He would come over and say, 'Do you want to work some extra time today? Anytime you want to work, just let me know.' He was really, really nice, and for a rookie it makes all the difference in the world. See, I grew up on Eddie LeBaron, watching the Washington Redskins in Charlotte, North Carolina. I knew exactly who he was. He had been an idol of mine when I was in high school and college. He was *the* quarterback for the Washington Redskins, a magician. So it was a real pleasure to be on the same team with him.

"At Dallas, too, he *was* a magician. Had Eddie been three or four inches taller, there is just no telling how great he could have been. He was very good as it was, but there is no telling how great he could have been, 'cause he really had the ability to fake the ball and hide it, and threw just a wonderful pass, and although he was only 5'6", he had a way of getting that ball to you.

"We were not a good team in '62. We finished 5–8–1. The main weakness was that the team was still made up of a lot of guys who were castoffs, and they thought of themselves as castoffs. They never thought of themselves as people who were going out to win. They thought of themselves as people who were going to go out and lose games. They were going to stick around as long as they could to make that money. That was over half the team.

"The other half of the team was made up of rookies, because in '62 we had 13 guys in my rookie class to make the team. Some of us really believed we could win and had a winning attitude, and some of us played a lot during that rookie year, and others played in a support role. So we had a lot of inexperienced players, in addition to the castoffs who thought of themselves that way.

"We could look very good one week, and very bad the next, and you never knew which one was going to show up."

Chapter 14

INCONSISTENT D

Even with this influx of talent, there were glaring holes. The biggest was on the offensive line, which was hurt badly when tackle Byron Bradfute suddenly quit before the season began in 1962. Tom Landry had hired as an offensive coach a man by the name of Jim Myers, who had worked under Bear Bryant at Texas A&M. Myers was the sort of coach who constantly yelled criticisms at his players, and during the last week of a rigorous training camp, Bradfute decided he had had it with Myers and the business of football. Football was paying him $8,000 per year. Outside of football, Bradfute knew he could do better and have more fun doing it.

Byron Bradfute: "During the off-season I had worked for one of Clint Murchison's companies. Because of football I had plenty of money, but I was trying to build a career, so I started at a sand and gravel pit with a shovel in my hand making $1.25 an hour. By the time the off-season was over, I was making time-and-motion studies and involved in control standards in production and doing marketing as an assistant to the president. And it was not because I was in football. It was because I was doing the job. And so I perceived that I had a real good career in front of me with Clint Murchison's companies. And as it turned out, I wasn't with them much longer after that, changed companies several times, but the point is that during the off-season my mind was challenged a lot. I was really doing something I had gone to school for, and it was exciting. When I went back to training camp, I had to listen to Myers telling me, 'You dumb son of a bitch,' that kind of stuff, and I kept wondering why I was doing this.

"One night a lot of us couldn't sleep. About five of us, Dickie Moegle, Bob Lilly, Mike Connelly, L. G. Dupre, and I were going to quit. We sat up talking until about 3:00 in the morning. It was training camp. It was a low point.

"The next morning I went to Tex Schramm and demanded that he trade me. When Tex said he couldn't guarantee who I'd get traded to, I said, 'Well then, I'll go on home.'

"I've talked to Lilly about it since then. He said, 'The next day it looks different.' And he stuck it out one more day. That's what the others did, stuck it out one more day, and then one day turns into another day, and before long, the season starts and you get paid. So quitting at that point is the dumbest thing you can do, because we were only getting $50 a week during training camp, and only when the season started did we get paid. I was dumb. They were smart; a lot smarter than me.

"I went and told Tom I was leaving. Tom said I hadn't given it enough of a chance. I was at the point of crying, not sure of what I had done when I told one of my better friends on the team, Bill Herchman, about it. His was the first commiseration. He looked up at me and said, 'Since you're quitting, can I have your shoes?'

"So I gave him my shoes and left camp. That kind of put it all in perspective."

To fill Bradfute's offensive tackle spot, Schramm was able to acquire 25-year-old Monte Clark from the San Francisco 49ers. When Clark arrived in camp that Monday, Schramm told him he would start just as soon as he was able to learn the offense. Clark studied every waking moment, hoping he could win a spot in the starting lineup in three or four weeks. Six days after arriving in Dallas, he started.

The other vulnerable spot was defensive back. After the 1961 season Dick Nolan had been released by New York Giants coach Allie Sherman, who was dumping a lot of Jim Lee Howell's vets, and Landry immediately asked the 30-year-old Nolan to join him in Dallas as his defensive coordinator. Coach Landry had been coaching both the offense and defense, and he desperately needed help. Landry knew that Nolan had been a disciple when they were together on the Giants. Landry figured that leaving Nolan to teach the defense would allow him to spend more time teaching the offense.

The day before the opening game of the season against the Washington Redskins, Landry approached Nolan.

"How about playing again?" he asked.

"When do you want me to start?"

"Tomorrow."

"Tom, if you want me to, I'll give it a try. You know I haven't done any conditioning to speak of."

Said Landry, "Dick, I know you. You'll do just fine. By the way, I activated you yesterday."

And so in addition to taking the job of head honcho of defense, he would also have to play corner as part of that defense. Nolan discovered he had a *big* job ahead of him.

Dick Nolan: "When I went to Dallas in '62 as a coach, we had a bunch of ragnuts, never-wases, and never-will-bes. In '62 there was no defense at all. They had a bunch of dogs. The offense won the games. On defense we were struggling for our lives. . . . The simple fact that I had to come back and play was a pretty good indication of how much we were struggling.

"Part of the problem was that Tom was different, and sometimes because somebody is different than you are, you take a dislike. Tom was a very stoic guy.

He kept to himself, distant. I know Tom and Don Meredith had their differences. Don was a very emotional guy, and he wished somewhere along the line that Tom would be a pal or a friend. Don would have liked to have had Tom say, 'Hey, Don, you did a great job,' and pat him on the back. But that was not Tom. He was not that way.

"Perhaps if Tom had had a little more of Vince's personality he might have been better able to motivate his players. I know there were times Tom could be intimidating. I can remember Tom and I used to set up quizzes the night before study sessions. We'd tell the players, 'Fold up your books and put everything away.' I'd fire questions at guys. I'd say, 'OK, Bob Lilly, what happens if we're on our goal line, five yards out, and they have first down, and you're in an inside 4-3, and so-and-so calls a Rita. What are you going to do?' And he'd say, 'I go into a Rita position.' I'd say, 'That's right. What are you going to do?' 'Key to the inside.' Then I'd say, 'What's the force on that side?' He'd say, 'Belt force.'

"Well, when I was running the meeting I would ask Chuck Howley 10 questions, and he'd have the answers so fast you wouldn't know what would hit him. But every time I'd bring Landry in there, Tom would ask Howley one question, and he would get so tongue-tied, he couldn't get it out. I'd say to Howley after it was over, 'What the hell is the matter with you? You knew it, but you made me look like a jerk. Why don't you answer? You can give it to me. Why can't you give it to him?' He'd say, 'Geez, I don't know.' I finally told Howley, 'I'll tell Tom to leave you alone.'"

Chuck Howley: "Dick was a lot of fun. He was one who communicated well with the players. He was a player, but yet he was a coach. He respected Landry, because he had played so many years with Tom. We liked him as a player, and from a player/coach relationship, Dick shared a good relationship with all the players."

Dick Nolan: "Even though it took a lot of the players a long time to accept Tom's system, once they did, under Tom's system the players virtually became coaches on the field, linebackers like Chuck Howley and Jerry Tubbs, and later on Dave Edwards and Lee Roy Jordan. They had his system down pat. They knew where everything was, and they'd tell people where everything was. They'd stop the others from making mistakes. They'd be talking to them all the time about what they were going to do, if they were worried the guy was going to do it.

"They knew so much football. Tubbs would call a defense in the huddle, and he'd say, 'It's third-and-eight, and you know what they like to do here.' And he'd remind them, 'Be ready.' He'd remind everybody, and boom, they'd be out of the huddle, ready.

"When it came to teaching, Tom knew how to teach. The players knew he knew his football. No question about that. They never could say he didn't know football. Ask any of them."

Bob Lilly: "In 1962 we beat the Washington Redskins badly. They didn't score until late in the game. It was one of those freak games where we did a lot of things right, where we were more coordinated, and we were stopping things they had done. There were several turnovers in that game, and George Andrie and Chuck Howley had real good days. Let me say this, too, when you're a very poor team, no one takes you very seriously. That's why we were able to beat the Giants the year before, because they looked at the films, and they just couldn't get very excited about us, so they didn't approach it on the higher intensity level that they would if they had been playing the Green Bay Packers or somebody like that. That's one thing that happened to a lot of those teams that we beat. They would watch our films and see us get beat 40–10, and they just couldn't get up for it. And we were up, because we wanted to beat somebody. That's one reason you see a team one week win big against a good team and then the next week play a mediocre team, and get beat, 'cause they just didn't take it very seriously. It's hard to stay on that high plane. Just a few times can you do that. But that's what happened when we won. We surprised them that we had more ability than they thought, and we were up for the game and they weren't.

"We had talent. We were getting a lot of good talent in those early years. The talent is not that much different from team to team. It's just a matter of whether all of you are going in the same direction. What surprised a lot of teams was that every once in a while we would jell a little bit. We would have a good game. Everyone would be coordinated, and they would be doing the things that we did the best against.

"But I do remember that Washington game, because that was the first time we beat anybody really bad, not that anybody noticed. You went to a Cowboys game, and if it was raining and everybody was underneath the eaves, you couldn't tell that anybody was there. So in Dallas they were just out there writing 'So what?' Because we were very inconsistent."

On December 2, 1962, the Cowboys played one of the finest games ever, shocking the powerful Cleveland Browns, 45–21. Don Meredith had his finest day as a pro, and on defense the Cowboys virtually stopped cold legendary fullback Jim Brown.

Chuck Howley: "In our third-to-last game, against Cleveland, in 1962 we held Jim Brown to just 13 yards. Jim Brown was a great athlete. He had power. You knew that when you tackled Jim Brown, you needed a lot of help. So we were keying on Jim all game. We just didn't want him to get started. He was a great breakaway runner, one of those superb runners. If he had a weak point, it was pass protection. We all have our weaknesses, and we felt Jim Brown was a person who didn't like to block on the pass rush, so as linebackers we didn't pay a whole lot of attention to him. He'd set up, and we'd just run by him. Because Jim just didn't want to block. I'm not saying he never did, but it was his weak point. Most of the time they used him in pass patterns rather than in pass protection.

"We'd watch the game films, and Tom would say, 'This guy doesn't like to block, so even if he sets up to block, don't pay too much attention to him.' That didn't mean you weren't going to get popped. But when we studied him in game preparation and saw him set up to block, we could see defenders buzzing right on by him. You could see in the films that if you gave just a little bit, he was not going to come after you."

The next week, in the next-to-last game of the season, the Cowboys were crushed by the St. Louis Cardinals, 52–20. St. Louis quarterback Charlie Johnson threw five touchdown passes against the defense, throwing three long bombs in the final minutes.

Defensive consistency was still several seasons away.

Chapter 15

CLARKE STAR

On offense the Cowboys could put the points up on the board. The 1962 team, led by backs Don Perkins and Amos Marsh, rushed for 2,040 yards, second only to the Green Bay Packers, and its passing yardage was comparable to the top teams'. Wide receiver Frank Clarke, after years of living under the cloud of his self-doubts, proved in 1962 that he was as good as anyone, that year catching 47 passes for 1,043 yards, and a league-high 14 touchdowns.

Frank Clarke: "We beat some teams in '62. We beat the Rams, the Eagles, and against the Pittsburgh Steelers in Pittsburgh, when Eddie LeBaron threw me three touchdown passes. I was *good.* I had some of the best moves that any NFL end had. I could run corner routes; I could run turns. I could run some of the best routes a receiver could ever run, and when you ran them with my speed and size and my ability to catch the ball, it was really fantastic, really something.

"The toughest loss that year was by two points to the Pittsburgh Steelers in the Cotton Bowl. We had the ball on our own 2-inch line, just barely not touching our goal line. The play came in from the bench for Eddie to throw me a fly pattern. I spread wide to the left, facing Brady Keys, and I just did a number on him, 'cause I was very fast and very deceptive, a tight end playing wide receiver, and they'd relax, 'cause they'd say to themselves, 'He's not going to beat me.' But before they knew it, I was gone, and they didn't catch me. So I was flying, scalding the dog down the sideline, and Eddie laid this ball right in my lap. I caught it and ran like the dickens into the end zone. The play went 99 yards.

"There were not many people in the stands, certainly not more than twenty thousand people in the big, cavernous Cotton Bowl, but they were making all kinds of noise. I ran the 100 yards, made the turn, and looked back down the field, and I could see all the players still down there. The defense didn't leave to go to the sideline, and the offense didn't leave either. I thought, 'Hey, wait a minute. What's going on?'

"I walked back down to the other end of the field, and somewhere near the 30- or 40-yard line, Tom Landry was talking to the official. He was livid. Tom was saying, 'You *better* make it good.' And the people started booing. They made more noise than anybody I ever heard. Literally, I had to take off my helmet, because the boos were so loud it was making a funny sound in my head. I thought, 'Look at all these people going crazy.'

"I didn't know the officials had called the play back and gave the Steelers a safety because Andy Cvercko was holding in the end zone. Hell, hardly anybody did. We did not understand that the rule was that if you're caught holding in your own end zone, it's a safety. Because we were thinking that the whole thing was going to be played under protest.

"To this day people talk about it. Somebody sent me a book of all the crazy things that happened in the NFL. It talked about this play, calling it 'The NFL's only eight-point play.' If someone asks you, 'Can you name an eight-point play in the NFL?' that would be it.

"For me it was one of those never-take-me-out-of-the-record-books chances. And what I remember most was how livid Tom Landry was. Tom Landry showed something that he had never showed any Cowboys fan ever. He met the official on the hash mark, and I can still remember Tom screaming at the referee as he was telling Tom he was going to explain it to him. 'You better explain it, and it better be good,' Tom was screaming. Tom, with all his knowledge, didn't know the rule, but it was in the book. That official came out smelling like a rose.

"In '62 I was on the verge of breaking a 17-game-in-a-row touchdown record. I had 14 games in a row with 3 games to go, and against Washington I got hurt. I got banged up real bad. I was coming down to block the linebacker, and some guy—I do not remember who it was—viciously took his knee and with all of his force, hit me in the thigh, and gave me real bad internal bleeding.

"I was still on the sideline when the Giants beat us bad, and I had to miss the next game when we lost to the Bears by a point. I watched from the sideline as Dandy had a great game, threw four touchdown passes. Do you know what else I remember from that game? I remember seeing the Bears' Mike Ditka catch passes and look for people to run over. He was amazing. I never saw any receiver catch the ball and *look* for people and then run over them. He was amazing. Of course, you pay the price when you want that kind of contact. At the end of his career, he could hardly walk. I didn't play again that year until the third-to-last game of the season, against the Cleveland Browns."

Meredith in that game threw Clarke a two-yard pass for the big end's 14th touchdown of the season, tops in the NFL.

The Cowboys appeared to be up and coming.

Chapter 16

A Season Dies with a President

Unfair as it might be and even though he had a five-year contract, Tom Landry in his own mind believed that if he didn't produce a winner in three years he would be fired. Nineteen sixty-three was the start of his fourth season. He had faced an impossible task building a team from scratch, but he was a keen analyst of situations as well as football strategy, and history had proved over and over that team owners as a group seemed to have less patience than the average fan or hometown beat writer. When the 1963 season began, Landry figured that every day he lasted on the job would be "gravy."

Despite the ominous noose hanging over him, Landry had reasons for guarded optimism. For one, Clint Murchison, the owner of the team, didn't seem to care whether the team won, nor did he seem to mind that it wasn't drawing very well. Clint loved being part of this team, and he treated his players like they were part of his family. When he asked a player, "How is the wife and family?" he was sincere. At Christmas he gave gifts to all the players. One year it was TV sets, another year jewelry. But more than the gifts themselves, the players appreciated that Murchison was thinking of them. What was important to Murchison was to be able to walk to the back of the plane after a game and chat quietly with his players.

In fact, the year before on a flight home from a game the Cowboys plane experienced engine trouble. The pilot made an emergency landing in Memphis and pulled the plane to the gate farthest from the terminal, where a three-man emergency repair crew was waiting in a Jeep. As the players stood up, preparing to deplane, Murchison rose from his seat and hollered, "Look sharp, men! This may be our biggest reception yet."

Tex Schramm, too, showed no impatience with the progress made by the team. Schramm steadfastly maintained that in time the team would be a winner and a top drawer. The team would get a boost beginning that year because it would no longer have to compete head-to-head against the AFL's Dallas Texans. Lamar Hunt was offered a guarantee of twenty-five thousand season tickets by the municipality of Kansas City, Missouri, and as a going away present Murchison agreed to pay his pal a nice chunk of change for moving out of state. From then on, the Cowboys would be the only Sunday game in town.

As for his own team, Landry was pleased that he was slowly replacing his disgruntled retreads with talented young kids, and in 1963 the Cowboys added another jewel, number one draft choice Lee Roy Jordan, an alligator-quick, tenacious, cussed, Bear Bryant–trained junkyard-dog linebacker to bolster the defense. Bryant once bragged to a reporter, "If the runner is in bounds, Jordan will tackle him."

A two-time All-American at Alabama, Jordan was thought by some to be a risk because at 6'1" and only 200 pounds, he gave away 20 to 30 pounds to some of the beefier linebackers. But despite his apparent lack of size, Jordan had something football fans would talk about during his illustrious 14-year career: he tackled you with the force of a sledgehammer crushing a tin can. And in addition to his bone-jarring ferocity, he provided needed leadership. It would be a couple of years before he started for the Cowboys, but once he took over for Jerry Tubbs he became the soul of the defense. "Who's gonna make this tackle?" he would growl in the huddle. During scrimmages, Jordan pushed his teammates, and as a result the Alabama farm boy would be criticized by several offensive players on the Cowboys for being a redneck, but the men on the defensive unit, white and black, found him to be an inspiration. They raved about his intensity and sense of mission. Few in the college or pro game played with the dedication, determination, and love for the game that Lee Roy Jordan did.

Lee Roy Jordan: "When I was drafted number one by the Cowboys in '63, everyone questioned my size. As a linebacker I was 6'1", 200 pounds. What the heck, you didn't have time to gain weight at Alabama, because coach Bryant believed in endurance, not size. We worked out all the time, ran cross-country, ran everywhere on the field. You never walked. You never jogged. Hell, you ran from one drill to the next. And in all drills you ran full-speed. He believed the guys who were in the best condition would always win in the fourth quarter because you'd outlast the other team. And he believed that if you had more energy, you would think better because you were not tired, wouldn't make mistakes.

"As a matter of fact, when I weighed in the first time at the Dallas training camp, I weighed 203 pounds, and the trainer said, 'Oh, my God. Man, I thought you were bigger than this.' I said, 'Well, maybe I *will* get bigger.'"

With the addition of Jordan some experts were noticing that the Cowboys, at least on paper, were looking very strong. In a *Sports Illustrated* cover story Tex Maule, Schramm's former assistant with the Rams and then the football pundit of America's leading sporting weekly, predicted that the Cowboys would win the Eastern Division of the NFL. It was a prediction that surprised and annoyed just about everyone on the Cowboys.

Bob Fry: "When Tex Maule predicted we'd win the East, I thought maybe he was a little crazy. I don't know where he got that from. I was amazed. It put the pressure on the whole organization."

Frank Clarke: "In 1963 Tex Maule predicted that the Cowboys would win the East. Thanks, Tex. We didn't like reading that. It was like, 'Hey, come on, we don't need to hear that.' We were afraid the opposing players would start looking at us in a different way. 'Hey, wait a minute? You mean we have to play these guys harder?' Oh, that was weird to see that.

"We started out in '63 losing six of our first seven games. That's what I mean. Tex Maule didn't do us any favors at all. That was a mean thing to do.

"Despite the fact that we only won four games that year in '63 the offense was really coming nicely. Don Meredith took over at quarterback for Eddie. By that time my confidence in Tom was so strong that I knew he was doing the thing that would make the team continue to move forward. It had nothing to do with Eddie, nothing to do with Don. It was Tom Landry saying, 'Stay with me you guys. We're going to heaven.'

"My feeling was, if Tom Landry said it, I was happy to do it. Aw, man, yes. Landry was saying, 'I have been testing him, and I like what I see.' And against the 49ers in Kezar Stadium, Don threw for 460 yards, and close to 200 of that was mine. Man, it was fantastic. God, it was wonderful. The 49ers had pretty close to the same yardage. I mean, their offense was pretty potent, too. John Brodie was the quarterback, and it was one of those games where the air was filled with passes, and it was wonderful to play so well in that foreign territory, to be so far from Dallas, and to play so well, 'cause we had a rhythm going. There was something happening with the club, and to produce like that offensively was really a high thing for us.

"And after that game we upset the Philadelphia Eagles, and Don again was brilliant, and we were practicing, getting ready to play the Browns in Cleveland, when we learned that President Kennedy had been killed."

The Kennedy assassination was the worst in a series of ugly events that prompted outsiders to brand Dallas the City of Hate. Four days before the 1960 elections, vice presidential candidate Lyndon Johnson and his wife, Lady Bird, came to Dallas for a Democratic Party luncheon. Lyndon, a senator from Texas, angered conservative Texans by agreeing to run with Kennedy, who was hated for being Catholic and for being a "nigger lover." The Johnsons were confronted by an angry, screaming crowd of demonstrators who shook insulting signs at them—"Smiling Judas Johnson," "LBJ Sold Out to Yankee Socialists"—and taunted them as soon as they got out of their car. Lady Bird was genuinely frightened. Some demonstrators spit on them.

The demonstrators were livid that Johnson would join a ticket with a Catholic. W. A. Criswell, pastor of the First Baptist Church of Dallas, in July 1960 declared, "The election of a Catholic as president would mean the end of religious liberty in America." He had also preached against the evils of school integration as contrary to the Bible's teachings. In a sermon Criswell endorsed Richard Nixon.

The Dallas Morning News, meanwhile, blasted Kennedy for being a "Socialist" and for his liberal views on civil rights. When *News* publisher E. M. "Ted" Dealey went to a White House luncheon, he infuriated President Kennedy when he told him, "The people in Texas and the Southwest need and want a strong president who would get off Caroline's tricycle and lead the nation from horseback."

On October 26, 1963, United Nations ambassador Adlai Stevenson was invited to town to speak. The John Birch Society, a far right-wing organization opposed to the United Nations as an institution, staged a demonstration during which fourteen hundred protestors, led by former army general Edwin Walker, blasted Stevenson, the UN, and Supreme Court Justice Earl Warren, who had ordered desegregation years earlier. Walker told the crowd that the Communists and "the Alger Hiss crowd" were behind the founding of the United Nations.

Lee Harvey Oswald was at that rally stalking Walker. Six months earlier he had tried to assassinate Walker, shooting at him with a rifle from an alley while he sat in his office working late. Oswald was not as accurate as he would be accused of being later.

The next day Stevenson was scheduled to speak. That morning the Walker group distributed handbills with pictures of John Kennedy with the words: "Wanted for Treason. This man is wanted for treasonous activities against the United States." Among the charges were that he permitted "known Communists" to abound in federal offices. When Stevenson got up to speak, he was shouted down with a bullhorn. After the speech, as he was getting into his car, one woman hit him on the head with a homemade sign. A college student spat on him. It was all recorded for television's all-seeing eye.

The city leaders were aghast by this incident. Mayor Cabell and dozens of city leaders sent telegrams of apology to Stevenson. In a letter the former presidential candidate recalled the days when the Ku Klux Klan had reigned in the city and made it the "hate capital" of the Southwest. He urged Dallas residents to reject the radical right just as it had ultimately rejected the Klan.

For four days the event rated front-page newspaper coverage. Said *The Dallas Times Herald*: "We must quit preaching hate. We must stop spreading the believing of the ridiculous stories of suspicion and distrust of our fellow citizens from the seeds of uncontrolled frenzy."

In a few weeks President Kennedy, the primary target of that fury, was coming to Dallas. Because he felt he needed the Dixie vote, Kennedy had sat on the sidelines during the sit-ins and the first freedom rides in 1961 as blacks began to demand the vote, but in 1962 as black students were integrating the state university system in Mississippi, Kennedy sent federal troops. Then after a black demonstration in Birmingham, Alabama, in April 1963, in which white mobs set upon the protestors with clubs and dogs, Kennedy called Birmingham officials to negotiate a settlement. Public facilities were integrated. When Martin Luther King's motel was bombed, Kennedy sent three thousand federal troops into position near the city. He also ordered the National Guard to protect two students enrolling at the University of Alabama.

On June 11, 1963, Kennedy made a speech on national television. He asked, "Who among us would be content to have the color of his skin changed and stand in his place?" A few hours later NAACP field director Medgar Evers was shot in the back and killed in the driveway of his home in Jackson, Mississippi. In September 1963, soon after a church in Birmingham was blown up, killing four little girls, Kennedy asked Congress for the most sweeping civil rights bill in American history, a law preventing discrimination at all facilities that served the public. He also came out against school segregation and for voting rights.

By then the South's outrage at Kennedy had increased so much that Adlai Stevenson wondered whether the president should even go to Dallas, and so did some of the city's leaders. Stanley Marcus, the owner of Neiman Marcus, the famed department store, told Lyndon Johnson to urge Kennedy not to come. Johnson knew Kennedy well. He told Marcus that Kennedy would be coming, so "go out and raise money."

The Dallas players remember November 22, 1963, because they were all out on the practice field. Even though President and Mrs. Kennedy were to ride down the streets of downtown Dallas, an experience attended by a huge throng that day, Landry refused to allow his players to skip practice—not for the president or for any other reason.

Though a couple of the southern players would say they were glad that Kennedy had died, his death was a cruel blow to most of the players, especially the blacks. To them, Kennedy's death raised an alarm. With Kennedy gone, who in the federal government would care about them, take up their cause? The death of John Kennedy would haunt the Cowboys for the rest of the season and into the next. Like the city of Dallas itself, the team would be associated by the rest of the country with the murder of President John F. Kennedy.

Chuck Howley: "When we heard what had happened, we really didn't believe it. We were as stunned as the rest of the world was. We were very concerned how it would affect us as a team. In fact, we were playing in Cleveland that weekend. They were going to cancel, and then the National Football League decided that they had to go ahead and play those games, and I remember trying to ship a suitcase because Cleveland was close to my hometown in West Virginia. I had taken a suitcase full of Christmas presents home with me on that charter, and I was trying to ship them by Greyhound the rest of the way. And the Greyhound employee saw that I had a Dallas return address on it, and he said, 'I'm not going to do this. You're from Dallas.'

"So the general tendency among people was to blame the people of Dallas for this, and it was a great tragedy, as we all know. In Cleveland we all stayed close to the hotel, stayed close to each other through that particular weekend, and we played that game, and we got out of town as fast as we could."

Bob Lilly: "It was devastating, and then we found out we had to play that week, which we did not want to do. No player wanted to. We had to go to Cleveland, and when we arrived there we had to unload the plane, haul our own luggage, because nobody would do it for us.

"And then when we went to the stadium, we didn't know if we were going to get shot or what. They called us everything, murderers, everything, from the stands. Like we had something to do with it. It wasn't much of a game. We were beaten that week. The death of President Kennedy was pretty disheartening. I really think that destroyed our '63 year. I know it did for me, and I think most of us felt the same way. We didn't get over it for weeks. We didn't get over not only our own personal feelings, but the stigma. It affected us, no question about it.

"It was extremely distracting, because we never got over it. We never got over the stigma when we played other teams. But the other thing was, it was too distracting, an ongoing saga of what happened. For weeks, months, in the paper, the media, everywhere you went, people asking you where you were that day, what you were doing, this and that. And we felt kind of disgraced that it had happened in our town. We'd go on the road, and people booed us because of that. It was *very* distracting."

Frank Clarke: "We went to Cleveland a couple of days later to play the Browns, and we were still numb. I remember being there in Cleveland, and I remember playing the game, but I don't remember *being there.* It was just numbing. Everything was just thrown off, so surreal.

"I wish you could have experienced Cleveland Stadium. I used to play there a lot. It was like, 'Why are we even doing this?' Because some people were saying, 'How could they not cancel the NFL games that week?' It didn't make sense. It *didn't.* It was really weird to play that game. Because we weren't ready to play at all.

"His death affected us. It affected us a lot. There were a lot of people commenting on the fact that we were from Dallas, where our president was killed, almost as if *we* had something to do with it. My goodness, what a numbing thing for our country to go through."

Cornell Green: "John Kennedy affected everybody's life. He meant that as a black man, I would have a chance. We weren't so worried about segregated housing at the time. I didn't care if you lived next door to me or not. It didn't hurt me. I didn't want to live next door to you either. It's just that: don't discriminate against me in the job field. Don't hold my being black against me when it comes to getting a job. And they were. That was the main thing. That was it. And with Kennedy as president, the feeling among the blacks was that it was ending.

"I was numb for three or four days. It doesn't sink in what magnitude this is going to be. And then after a while, as it goes on, you start thinking about it, what is really happening, what's going to happen, and you think about who did it, and a lot of things. When they made Lyndon Johnson president, I had no idea even who he was, and probably nobody else in the country did either.

"At one time they thought everybody from Texas was responsible for it, really. If you were from Texas, then you heard, 'You son of a bitch, you killed Kennedy.' Even some towns we went into to play football, the Texans were looked at as people who killed Kennedy. But that was just people's own ignorance. It never really affected me one way or the other, 'cause I knew where I was that day and what I was doing. I just was sorry that the man was dead. A great man had died."

Pettis Norman: "Incredibly, it was almost like I had had a premonition about it. Frank Clarke and I were on the field practicing, running pass routes, and we were engaged in conversation. The practice field was right by the trainer's room, and the trainer had a radio out on the back porch of the trainer's room up loud, and we could hear it. They were describing the presidential motorcade while we were running passes.

"A lot of us would have loved to have been there, because President Kennedy represented a whole new concept of a president, a very, very engaging, gregarious young man, everything the presidents before him had not been. He just captivated the country. And I remember saying to Frank Clarke, 'Wouldn't it be something if some nut tried to shoot the president?' And the reason that thought came to my mind was I saw how mean-spirited the people in Dallas had seemed to be toward Kennedy and the Kennedy people. I got a sense when I first came to Dallas that white people, unlike in urban Charlotte and other urban cities I had been to, really wanted to relegate blacks to a lower status. As little as white people in other cities appreciated blacks, it was even less in Dallas. It was a mean-spirited thing I had picked up, and so coupled with these thoughts and my feeling that everybody talked alike and thought alike, 'Wouldn't it be something if one of these nuts with this Texas mentality were to shoot the president?' And within a matter of seconds of saying this to Frank, the trainer ran out and said, 'They just shot the president.'

"Frank and I looked at each other and thought, 'This guy is lying. He heard us talking.' And we said, 'You've got to be kidding me.' 'No, no, listen,' and he turned the radio up loud, and then louder, and we heard it, and we still could not believe it. We stood there and looked at each other, and our mouths just dropped open, and I felt a sense of innocence, of loss at that moment that I could not explain. It was a sense of devastation. I thought, 'What are we going to do now? They have shot the president.'

"The other thing I remember was that when we were sure that President Kennedy had died, some of the players—I won't say their names—they were almost happy that it had occurred. The perception was that Kennedy was doing things for minorities, and I knew that was behind a lot of that strong sentiment against him by whites in Texas at that time. It just reinforced some things that we knew, that we really had people on the team who had such a hatred for our people.

"I felt such outrage. I couldn't help but feel that these people were basically moral cowards, that they could only be brave behind sheets or in large gatherings of folks of their kind. They could never go out on a limb, like the civil rights workers who had to fight against long odds for a chance to be equal.

"Kennedy's death affected the team the rest of the year. It was *always* in the back of the team's mind, and you could never 100 percent focus on what you were doing. It was like that for most people in Dallas; it was something we could not get out of our minds. It was enough in your subconscious, and so we just went through the season. We were 4–10, nowhere near what we had envisioned."

Frank Clarke: "In the final game against St. Louis, a team we had never beaten, we were down by 10 points late in the game, but Don led us back to win it on a pass he threw to me. I had never done that before, and I never did it since, been on the receiving end of a game-winning touchdown. That was neat.

"Over the years as he gained more experience, Don got to where he took a lot of the lift out of the ball, but in '62 and '63, he was getting a rise out of the ball—what I mean, he used to throw a lot of passes that took off on the receiver. The ball would look like it was coming to shoulder height, but because of the way he threw it, that baby kept going up, so by the time it got to you, you had to either jump or stretch real high to catch it, and that's OK, but you take away from the receiver's potential by doing that. There aren't many quarterbacks who come into the league who already know how to do that. They have to work at it. By the time he learned and gained the confidence, Don could throw a sweet pass."

The 28–24 win over the Cardinals gave the Cowboys a 4–10 record. Landry's overall record after the four years was 13–38–3. Four of the losses in 1963 were by 10 or more points, and the Dallas sportswriters, led by the rapier pens of Gary Cartwright and Steve Perkins, called for Landry's firing, if not his lynching. Many of the Cowboys faithful agreed. There were unconfirmed (and untrue) rumors that Oklahoma coach Bud Wilkinson was in the wings to replace Landry.

Tom Landry: "I began wondering if it was time again to start thinking about life after football. Maybe God wanted me to be doing something else."

Tom Landry prayed for guidance.

Eddie LeBaron: "I can remember when everyone was on Tom. The papers were on him badly. I was upset that the reporters didn't realize how good Tom was, and it made me mad that even after they found out, a lot of writers still didn't like him because he didn't have the personality that some of them might like. Tom's reputation was that the Cowboys were a clinical, cold-blooded team that relied on science and skill and not the razzle-dazzle and shoot-'em-up type of guys, and yet the truth was, our offense was very exciting. And no one ever gave him credit for that."

Frank Clarke: "Toward the end of the '63 season, there was some talk in the papers that Landry would be fired. But I'm almost certain there were not many players who came close to even thinking that. As a matter of fact, it would have been more in line to give this guy a long-term contract. Oh yeah. That's the way we felt.

"I know for a fact—I was there—there was *nothing* buzzing around our locker room that had anything at all to do with Tom being seriously considered for not being there. Not with what he had done. Not with what we were *feeling*. The press didn't know this. They did not feel what we were feeling. It wasn't that they didn't bother to ask. With all due respect, it was more that they didn't know *how* to ask."

Bob Lilly: "Some of the older players wanted their own coaches to come. Some of them wanted Bear Bryant, and I did hear Bud Wilkinson's name. Everybody had a different opinion on what it took to win, and there was hope among some of the players that Tom would go and we would get another coach."

Fortunately for coach Landry, only Clint Murchison, not the reporters or the fans, could make the decision on whether to retain him or not. Clint was a guy who was taught by his father to pick the best person to run his outfit and then let him do his job. He also believed in loyalty, and Tom Landry had given him that. And so Murchison, the Dr. Jekyll–and–Mr. Hyde oil baron with the taste for expensive hobbies, cheap scotch, and dyed blondes, confounded everyone by going out of his way to give Landry a rousing vote of confidence. Murchison was one of those Texans who refused to let himself be pushed around, not by any two-bit newspaper reporter nor by ignorant fans. Clint never once lost faith in Tom Landry, and neither did Tex Schramm.

Murchison, rather than firing Landry as the throng demanded, instead gave him the richest contract in the history of football up to that time, presenting him with a 10-year contract extension to begin after his present one expired at the end of the 1965 season. The players who believed in Landry's genius understood and agreed.

Pettis Norman: "Out of the clear blue nowhere, Tom got a 10-year contract. This told you something about Clint Murchison. That was done as much out of a deep sense of loyalty and commitment as his foresight into what was going to happen."

Bob Lilly: "Clint Murchison did a very wise thing signing Tom to a 10-year contract, because once Tom signed that contract, then all the players knew where they stood. And at that point was where Coach really started building the team. He got rid of all the bitchers, people who were not for him, and that's what he had to do."

Chapter 17

MEL AND MAURY

In selecting future Cowboys in the 1964 draft, the brain trust of Tex Schramm, Gil Brandt, and Tom Landry again showed both guts and ingenuity. Their second-round draft choice was a running back from the University of Oregon by the name of Mel Renfro, a lightning-fast sprinter who had run anchor in college on the world-record-setting 4 x 100 meter relay team along with Cowboys defensive back Mike Gaechter. Renfro, called "Suds" by his teammates, would have been a surefire first-round pick, but on the day John F. Kennedy was killed, he was so distraught over life's fluctuating nature that he punched out a glass mirror and severed tendons in his right hand. Renfro's hand was still a mess at the time of the draft, and so when it was the Cowboys' turn for their second pick, Mel Renfro, who would be an All-Pro performer 10 times, was still available.

Mel Renfro: "The day of the NFL Draft, I was sitting in a hotel room in downtown Eugene with four or five scouts from around the country. They all had me pegged number one, the first pick. The Cowboys drafted first, and they started calling around to check with my doctor about my hand to see if it was OK. Well, they had a tough time getting ahold of him, and Tex held up the draft. While I was sitting around in the hotel room, people were wondering what was going on with the Cowboys. And when they finally picked, they didn't pick me. They drafted Scott Appleton, a defensive lineman out of Texas, and traded him immediately, and then they spread the rumor that I had cut my hand off, that I wouldn't be able to play pro ball. No question the Cowboys did that. They admitted it. Because they came right back in the second round and picked me up just like that, and so they got two first-round draft choices. They pulled a coup, and everybody else had egg on their faces."

Tex Schramm: "We were interested in Mel Renfro, but he had cut his hand and severed the nerves or tendons. At that time he didn't have any feeling in three or four of his fingers. The word got around the draft room in Chicago that he'd be who we'd take on the first round.

"Before we made our first pick, we held up the draft several hours. Buddy Parker was offering us a trade for Buddy Dial, and we were spending all that time trying to work out that deal. Everyone else thought we were checking on

Renfro. The season wasn't over, so we couldn't say anything about the trade because Dial was still playing for Pittsburgh.

"When we drafted [defensive tackle] Scott Appleton on the first round, the word spread that obviously we'd found something wrong with Renfro, so nobody else drafted him on the first round. Then when we came back and took Renfro on the second round, everybody screamed they'd been taken."

In football, as in life, there can be funny bounces. Renfro became a defensive gem for the Cowboys. In the deal to acquire Buddy Dial, the best wide receiver in the league at the time, Schramm sent Appleton to the Steelers, who turned up empty-handed when the big tackle signed with the Houston Oilers of the AFL.

On the face of it, the pundits saw the Cowboys as the big winners. But Schramm knew something no one else knew, and it would haunt him, but only because he was the sort of person who always wanted his cake and to eat it too: had the Cowboys not traded for Dial, they were prepared to draft and sign a player they had tucked away in a hotel room in Columbus, Ohio. Had Buddy Parker not popped the Dial idea, said Schramm, "We probably would have drafted him number one because of the doubt with Mel's hand." That player was star receiver Paul Warfield of Ohio State. Warfield would help defeat the Cowboys in important playoff games as a member of the Cleveland Browns.

When Buddy Dial hurt himself early and did little with the Cowboys, Schramm would mull the what-ifs of ending up with a Warfield-Renfro duo. Any misgivings, however, certainly were lessened because in that same draft in 1964 Schramm picked in the seventh round a track star and football player from Florida A&M University by the name of Bob Hayes, a future Olympic medalist and the man who would be branded as the "World's Fastest Human." Because of his commitment to the U.S. Olympic team, Hayes would not be available to the Cowboys until 1965, but when he finally arrived he would change the game of pro football with his explosive speed. (In the 10th round in 1964 Schramm would gamble and pick a player who wouldn't show up for another *five* years, Navy quarterback, Heisman Trophy winner, and *Time* magazine cover boy Roger Staubach.) But, Tex being Tex, he would always wonder: how many Super Bowls would the Cowboys have won if they had come away with Renfro, Warfield, *and* Hayes in 1964?

For coach Landry, the key addition in 1964 was Renfro, who had been an outstanding runner at Oregon. Landry had figured that with his athletic ability, even with a bad hand, the fleet Renfro would make a great defensive back. As it was, Landry felt Renfro was too frail to be a runner in the pros, and after giving him a shot during training camp, Landry decided the risk of Renfro getting hurt running the ball was too great and made him his free safety instead.

As usual, Landry was right, and as a rookie Mel Renfro became the Cowboys' weapon for stopping the other teams' fastest receivers. Renfro would be a mainstay of the defense for 11 years. In Cornell Green and Mike Gaechter, the Cowboys had had some solid speed in the corners. With Renfro, they had a rocket man with magical ability who seemed to have a sixth sense to divine where his man was going to go. Hooked into Tom Landry's system, Renfro, a quiet man, was virtually unshakable. He had a methodical deftness to his movements so that he always seemed to be in position against his man. And if the pass was completed in front of him, he was a sure tackler, too.

In practice, wide receiver Frank Clarke had to scrimmage against Renfro often. He well knew just how great Mel Renfro was.

Frank Clarke: "Mel was *so* good. Man, yes, I can tell you about Mel Renfro. He was *incredible*. It was like he knew where you were going. I can only say that he had that sense great defensive backs are born with. You just could not shake this guy.

"We'd scrimmage, and on most defenders I could plant that right foot and go, but I couldn't do that with Mel. He had this hip movement that allowed him to be right there with you no matter what cuts you made, no matter where you moved, no matter what you did. And he had the quickness of a jaguar or one of those cats that has speed *and* quickness, too. This was Mel Renfro, speed and quickness, and no matter what you did, he was there. And it got to be really frustrating, like, 'Mel, God, get off of me!' And you'd realize, this guy is going to be *real* good. It seemed he was *always* in position, and I say to myself that that kind of skill is innate, inborn. This was not something that some coach at Oregon taught him. He was amazing."

On defense, the Cowboys were improving steadily. The front line was anchored by Bob Lilly, who had been moved from defensive left end to defensive right tackle in mid-1963 to take better advantage of his strength and quick bursts. But defensive end George Andrie had been hurt much of 1963, and the Cowboys had had to trade for veteran Larry Stephens of the L.A. Rams. The line was still in flux and was a question mark, though the linebacking corps of Jerry Tubbs, Chuck Howley, Dave Edwards, and Lee Roy Jordan was improving every year. In the backfield Green, Gaechter, and Renfro were joined by Jim Ridlon, who had been the other back at Syracuse University along with Jim Brown and who had played for six years with the San Francisco 49ers before being acquired by the Cowboys in 1963. Landry's system was built for Ridlon, who was both athletic and very smart.

Jimmy Ridlon: "By the end of my first season with the Cowboys, I was comfortable with his style of coaching. It was a great experience to learn from him. To be honest, I don't think there were a lot of people in our group who fully understood what he meant by playing the game with the mind. What it boiled down to for me was first the fact that we were going into the game with far more information than players on other teams. We were prepared, knew what we were expected to do. When you've got that kind of information, you've naturally got to be more confident. You play the game without the element of fear getting in the way. He didn't want a team going on the field all excited. In his style of play, emotions get in the way. What he wanted you to do was use logic, conception, and reaction."

To shore up the defensive line, Landry and Schramm acquired from the Chicago Bears a 260-pound tackle by the name of Maury Youmans, who grew up in the Syracuse area. After a year at prep school, he went to Syracuse University on a scholarship under coach Ben Schwartzwalder, a former paratrooper who had made the D-day jump. Under Schwartzwalder, Youmans learned that his coach valued toughness more than anything. A player could miss a play only if he had a broken leg.

In 1963 Youmans, playing for the Chicago Bears, tore up his knee. In an exhibition game in Washington against the Redskins, he took an outside rush, but the lineman covered his outside. Youmans grabbed the lineman's shoulders and planted his own left foot to pull the lineman to the inside, but his left knee could not take the pressure. The cartilage gave out, and all the ligaments were torn. Unfortunately for Youmans, the doctor who did the operation allowed him to leave the hospital while he still had a fever and a bad infection. He should have been back in six weeks. He could have returned to play the World Championship game against the Giants, but his leg had atrophied, so Halas kept him out of the game, won by the Bears, 14–10. And Youman's replacement got the game ball in the season finale.

At that point Youmans got a call from the Packers' Jim Ringo, one of his teammates at Syracuse. Ringo said to him, "Maury, the old man [Vince Lombardi] likes the way you play. How would you like to play for the Packers?" Ringo told him that Lombardi was fed up with defensive end Bill Quinlan, who was giving the other tackle, Willie Davis, problems because Davis was getting more publicity than Quinlan could stomach.

Figuring he was going to Green Bay, Youmans asked Halas to trade him.

Maury Youmans: "The next thing I know, I got a call. I was traded to the Dallas Cowboys, which at that time was a disaster. I thought, 'Holy geez.' I was traded for an end named Gary Barnes. He lasted a year in Chicago."

When Youmans arrived at Thousand Oaks in California for training camp in 1964, what struck him more than anything was the difference between the rough-and-tough Bears and the more gentlemanly Cowboys.

Maury Youmans: "When I arrived at Thousand Oaks I couldn't believe how it was like going to Sunday school in comparison to the Bears. The Bears were an old-line team, rough-and-tumble guys. With the Cowboys the players were such *nice* guys. When they would party on Sunday after a home ball game, they would party together at a little brewery, in a little room, very quiet, very mild compared to the Bears.

"The Cowboys practices were a little more difficult than those of the Bears, because the Cowboys would run through ballplayers at that time. In practice you would hit. I remember double sessions, and we would hit with shoulder pads and helmets on. That would be our morning drills. And then in the afternoon we'd scrimmage. Full pads at Thousand Oaks and hitting. So you did a lot of hitting.

"With the Bears you got in shape yourself. You didn't hit much with the Bears. You hit a lot with the Cowboys. My shoulders were so bad there my last year in Dallas that I took Demerol after every ballgame to get to sleep. Both shoulders were gone, just beat up, and that was all from hitting through training camp. I could not roll over either way. Then after Wednesday I'd be fine.

"The Cowboys system was harder to learn because everything on the defense was coordinated. The playbook didn't startle me as much as did the learning process, because all of a sudden you had to know every offensive formation. No longer was it read and react. It became key and react. You read your key and reacted at the same time. Once you learned it, it was a much easier defense to play. Also, you knew where the breakdowns were.

"When I arrived in '64 a lot of the vets *still* didn't understand Tom's system. Tom is a very quiet, almost impersonal individual. He has an engineering personality. That's what he is. But he had a way of convincing you that if you really learned his system and you really all played it, you could play the *perfect* defensive football game. He made me believe that we could play the perfect defense. He would walk away after a ballgame convincing you that, 'Next week, if you work and continue to learn the system, you can do it.' That's how I felt. By '64 we really believed in Tom's defense. And the more you played it, the more you felt comfortable in it, the more you learned it.

"There was some dissension, but the dissension went less against Tom than it was offense against defense. The defense was better, as you probably know, than the offense, so the consequence was that we would blame the offense for the loss, or the offense would say, 'Aw, it's your fault.' That went on more than blaming the coach.

"The defensive players were frustrated and angry at the offense. Keep in mind the way the Cowboys set it up, the offense did everything on its own, and we did everything on our own, so it was almost like we were two teams. So you didn't develop the community that you would normally develop. It would have been smarter, in hindsight, to do that, because you want unity as a team. You naturally pulled for each other, but there was still a certain amount of rationalization—if you were going to blame somebody, if you wanted to rationalize, you were going to blame the other guys, and unfortunately during that period of time, the offense was not as good as the defense."

Chapter 18

BUDDY AND DON

The reason the Cowboys appeared to be choirboys compared to the barbarians on other NFL teams was that Tom Landry preferred them that way. Landry was heart-attack serious, and he believed that his players should be as serious about life, football, and family as he was. To Landry the perfect player gave 100 percent during practice or in a game, returned home to his wife and 3.2 towheaded kids, studied the game films or read the scriptures in his spare time, and went to church every Sunday. That's what Tom did. That's what he wanted his players to do.

What Tom was constitutionally unable to tolerate were players whose mission in life was to go out and have fun, and if they could make their living playing football, so much the better. Tom had contempt for such players, because no matter how great they might have been, all he could see was unfulfilled promise, and to Landry that was a sin he could not forgive. Players who laughed on the practice field or who tittered during film sessions or who got rip-roaring drunk at night were just trying to break the grinding tension of pro ball. To Landry they were creating sacrilege, making a mockery of his chosen profession. Tom handled such players in two ways. If he could replace them with an equal or better player, he did so as quickly as possible. If he could not, he would continually lecture that player on the importance of taking the game—and life—seriously.

The first in a growing bush of thorns in Landry's side was a talented kicker by the name of Sam Baker. Baker, a running back at Oregon State, is the top punter in the history of the Cowboys, with a 45.1 average. His longest was 75 yards, a total of 90 yards from where he kicked the ball. He never had one blocked. He was also a field-goal and extra-point specialist, and in the two years he was with the Cowboys, he led the team in scoring, with 92 points in 1962 and 75 points in 1963. Despite all that, he was released at the end of 1963. Right or wrong, Landry didn't want the carefree, back-talking Baker around any more.

Part of the reason Baker was tossed aside was that neither Landry nor Tex Schramm ever had any respect for kickers, believing them to be easily replaceable. The other part was that Baker continually balked at having to be serious, responsible, focused, and sober, the way Landry wanted his players to be.

Baker's resentment of Landry's solemnity and authority caused him to taunt and make fun of the coach, even in front of others.

When Baker reported to the Cowboys in 1962, Landry had written out the requirements for his Landry mile. He gave the time expected for the backs and the time for the linemen. His instructions did not include the kickers, and Baker tried to argue that he was exempt as a result. When Landry ordered him to run, Baker did so while reading a book. He cut corners, acting like the entire exercise was foolish, and ran the slowest time in Cowboys history.

Another time after a game, Baker missed the team plane back to Dallas. When he finally arrived, it was early in the morning. Gil Brandt met him and took him to see Landry. Baker knocked on Landry's door at 4:00 A.M. When Landry opened the door, Baker snapped to attention, saluted, and said, "Baker reporting, Sir." Landry told him he was fined $1,000 for missing the flight. Another time Baker showed up for a game in Pittsburgh carrying a potted orange plant and looking quite drunk.

Baker never seemed to say the right thing in front of Landry. One time he made it seem that he was laughing at Landry's religious beliefs.

Sam Baker: "We were in a team meeting one time, and Tom was talking about his philosophy of team dedication. He said, 'If I thought it would help this team in some way, I'd climb on top of this building and sing "Glory to God."' Bill Howton was sitting in front of me and said, 'Hallelujah,' and I started laughing. Landry turned just in time to see me crack up and, obviously, thought I was laughing at him."

At another team meeting Landry was lecturing the players that the team would have to exhibit more harmony if the Cowboys were to accomplish anything. To show his willingness to harmonize, Baker responded with a loud, humorous, "Hmmmmmmmmmmmmm." Some of the players tittered while Landry frowned and burned inside.

By 1964 Baker was gone, replaced by a rookie kicker, Dick Van Raaphorst. At the end of the year Baker and Van Raaphorst had almost identical records, and Landry slept better at night. The levity, however, did not disappear from the Cowboys team. Landry still had to endure the shenanigans of his starting quarterback, Don Meredith, who continued to exhibit his Wild West, drink 'em up, shoot 'em up outlook. To the dismay of the abstemious and monogamous Tom Landry, Don pursued his late-night emulation of Bobby Layne, at times showing up for games hungover and sorry looking, and there were times when he would sass Landry. Once Meredith said about his coach, "Landry's the kind of guy if he was married to Raquel Welch, he'd want to know if she could cook." Sometimes to show his contempt, Dandy Don even sent the messengers carrying Landry's plays back to the sidelines. The whole time Landry would lecture him and wonder when Don would finally tilt toward adulthood.

Pettis Norman: "Meredith was a happy-go-lucky guy who didn't take himself too seriously, who approached the game of football with a lightheartedness that I had not been used to in college. Don would be on the field, and in the middle of the huddle he'd crack a joke and not remember the play Landry had called and just say, 'OK, run the last play all over again.' We had that happen a number of times.

"Landry lectured him about being more serious, but he would not do it in front of the team, unless it was, 'Get your head in the game.' And Don could be quite flip with Landry at times, and part of that flippant attitude was when Landry would send a play in and he'd tell a joke and forget the play, and he'd say, 'We'll run the last play, on two.' That was Don's way of being flippant toward Landry. So it was really very interesting, if you consider Landry on one hand, and Don Meredith on the other."

In 1964 Meredith found a "pardner" in receiver Buddy Dial, himself a born-and-bred Texan who had been a huge star at Rice University. Dial was one of them fallen fellas, a Layne disciple, not a Landry disciple. He was one of them renegades, and how could the fun-loving Dial have been otherwise in that he had been Layne's primary receiver and running mate in Pittsburgh? Layne and Dial were freelancers, and they had become so close they could almost read each other's minds. They played instinctive football, and there wasn't a better passing combination in all of football. Over the previous four seasons Dial had averaged over 1,000 yards per season catching Layne's passes. In five years, he hadn't missed a single play because of injuries. He was also a guy with a guitar, looking for a bar in which to croon a tune and honky-tonk women with whom to sing along. When Landry traded for Buddy Dial the receiver, he also got Dial the country-western singer. It would not be long before Landry wished he had signed Paul Warfield instead.

When Dial arrived at camp in 1964, he made the fatal mistake of being out of shape. Under Buddy Parker and the Steelers, the players had worked their way into playing shape during training camp. In Dallas, the players were supposed to come to camp ready to go full-out from the first day.

Dial wasn't in shape to run the Landry mile, and he wasn't ready to run the 40-yard dash. Before the end of the first week of training camp during an afternoon scrimmage, practice was coming to an end and Don Meredith wanted another score. He called a long pass to Dial down the left side. Dial made the long run and then had to jump high and extend himself to catch the ball. As he launched himself upward, he heard and felt the sickening snap of a muscle in his thigh.

Dial practiced another two weeks before the doctors realized that a muscle had pulled off his knee, and he was sent back to Dallas for an operation. The doctors sewed the muscle back together, but when they reattached it to the knee, they made it too tight, and when he began working out again, the muscle pulled off the hip. In 1964 Dial played against the Steelers the third game of the season, but he didn't get to play again until the last game, also against Pittsburgh. In between, Dial provided his teammates with a lot of songs and a lot of fun.

Buddy Dial: "Don and I were roommates, and I was a terrible influence on him. I played the guitar, and he loved to sing and drink, and we just stayed in trouble all the time. We almost stayed in jail for three years because of Landry, 'cause he never knew what we were going to do. So Tom finally demanded that Meredith mature a little bit, and they got rid of me due to injury, so Don, he kind of grew up and got serious a little bit, but not all that much.

"I'll tell you, Meredith was, and is, a *very* classy guy. I mean, he is a high-caliber person, a clean guy, and the people got down on him, because he didn't have an offensive line at the time and he was a free spirit. He'd come to the huddle, and he'd be singing. We'd been in Vegas, seen Dean Martin's show, and Meredith would come back to the huddle singing one of Martin's songs, and he'd call a play, and Danny Reeves—he knew more about the offense than anybody except Landry—and ole Danny Reeves would say, 'Dandy, that ain't the way we call that play.' And ole Don would say, 'Hell, you call it, Danny.' So Don was slapstick, but boy, he played hard. And he practiced hard. But he was a very classy guy, and he still is.

"I'll tell you one thing, nobody got the better of him. No one ever came on top of Meredith, 'cause he was so witty and articulate. He's just a winner.

"And, you know, Landry was tough on Don. Don was just a free spirit, and Tom was as serious as the Holocaust every time you saw him. If Tom laughed, his face would break. Don just didn't buy the life-or-death struggle that Tom said we were involved in, and so Tom caused Don to be criticized a lot, because he would cut Meredith up, 'cause Don would mess up. And you know, Roger Staubach was so serious. He was the opposite of Meredith. He paid the price, and he was so successful, and so Don really never got credit. Don brought a lot of class to that ballclub and to that city, and people never gave him credit. I think he got even with them, because he was such a smash on *Monday Night Football*. The people in Hollywood worshiped him. We'd train out in Thousand Oaks, and we'd go to town, to Hollywood, and the people would just fall out wanting to meet Meredith, and the women, I mean they loved him like a god. Who was the other guy? Blackie Sherrod. He was good to Don, because Blackie was a class act. But those other guys, [sportswriters Gary] Cartwright and Steve Perkins, aw, they crucified Don, and you know, Cartwright and Perkins, they just seemed to see who could get the dirtiest stuff about Meredith. And if it hadn't been for Blackie carrying on a little class act personally, Meredith would have been crucified all the time.

"And as a result, it carried over to the other cities. We'd go up to play in New York or Cleveland or Pittsburgh, and the opposing players respected Don, but the press would treat him like they did in Dallas, because of the influence the Dallas press carried."

On the field the team did not miss Dial, because in 1964 Frank Clarke became an All-Pro receiver. Clarke was a bright spot in a 5–8–1 season during which

Meredith was injured over and over, crashed to the ground by ferocious linemen with little to stop them. During the preseason Meredith tore up his knee, but he didn't sit on the bench. Rather, he played the entire year with torn cartilage, missing just one game in what Tom Landry would call "perhaps the most courageous and gutsy season any professional quarterback ever played." Said Landry, "What made it worse was that our line couldn't have protected a healthy quarterback, let alone a hobbling one."

Early in the season, one Dallas writer suggested a new statistic, "Yardage lost attempting to live." Every week Meredith took a pounding, suffering one injury after another. Despite the pain, he refused to quit.

Frank Clarke: "In 1964 the Cowboys traded for two outstanding receivers from other teams in the league, Tommy McDonald and Buddy Dial. Of course, when that happened, it was real clear: people were saying that 'Frank Clarke is expendable. Frank Clarke is gone.' I was taking a look at that, and I was talking to myself in ways I had never done before. I was saying to myself, 'By golly, if I'm going to do the things I'd like to be able to do in this game, I have to do it this year. This is the time to do it.'

"And everything I did from training camp all the way through that '64 season was otherworldly. Things were happening. I became consistent in my blocking. It was almost as though the team itself got a sense of my sincerity in what I was doing. And Dandy was calling on me in third-down situations, and I felt *so* fantastic, so good, because I was answering the challenge. But most of all, I felt as though I was fitting into what I strongly aspired to do, and that was to follow Tom Landry's tutoring. I really wanted to do it for this guy, 'cause I just had a good feeling about *everything* about him. To me he was the same sort of general that a lot of guys thought of George Patton, that they would do anything for him.

"In the third game against the Steelers, the team lost when it couldn't score from inside the 10 right at the end of the game. In the final minutes, Don Meredith's knee buckled, and he had to come out of the game. Going into the game, his knee was weak, and I was just amazed he could perform as well as he did with all the injuries he had.

"Dandy had such bad legs. He would look at my legs and then he'd look at his, and his were pretty spindly, *really* spindly, and he'd point to his, grab his calf, and say, 'Thoroughbreds.' He'd look at mine and grab mine and go, 'Clydesdales.'

"He was hurt a lot, and unfortunately, he came to the Cowboys at a time when our offensive line had a lot of holes in it, and I know, because I helped make it porous. It was not intentional. But we had a lot of mental lapses. And the quarterback paid the price. I'm sure they paid him pretty well, but they didn't pay him nearly enough.

"Don was hurt in the Redskins game, and so he didn't play against Green Bay, a game we lost, and when he came back against Philadelphia he was sacked time and time again and got hurt again. Against the Steelers, he went back out, and he was sacked seven or so times, and again he got hurt. It's hard to win when that happens. And except for that Green Bay game, he played in every game."

After the final 1964 game, a win, Landry went over to congratulate Meredith, who had to shake with his left hand because he'd injured the right one in the first quarter. Landry said to him, "You did a fine job in a tough situation this year. We're gonna get you more protection next year."

Said Meredith, "Promise?"

Don Meredith: "It wasn't really a matter of courage as much as of determination. Nobody is going to beat me. I knew if I didn't get up, they would have beaten me. I couldn't stand the thought of that."

Frank Clarke: "In spite of the losses, our momentum was building. We were not a doldrums team. We kept our focus in spite of all of that. I don't know what kind of schedule Tom Landry had us on, but I felt like we were either at it or ahead of it during those times, in spite of those things.

"Not everyone felt the way I did, but when it came to Tom Landry, there were a lot of players who were willing to go along with him, more on the offense than the defense. We knew we had something on offense, and we were just waiting for the defense to catch up. So was Tom. That's why every year they were drafting defensive players. And ironically, most of the bitching by this time came from the defensive guys, and it's funny, because the offense was better than the defense, and yet the defense was always complaining about the offense."

Chapter 19

PETE

When Tex Schramm sent out a questionnaire to Big Ten basketball coaches and athletic directors asking them to name some college hoopsters who might make it in the NFL, Michigan State's freshman coach Danny Petersen included on his list the University of Indiana's Van Arsdale twin brothers, Tom and Dick, and as an afterthought wrote in the name of Michigan State's top scorer, forward Pete Gent. Petersen figured that the 6'5" Gent had the quickness, agility, and size necessary to play pro football.

When Gil Brandt came to East Lansing, Michigan, to sign Gent, Brandt swore to him that the Cowboys were only bringing in three defensive backs. (When Gent got to camp, there were 100 rookies, and 17 of them were defensive backs.)

When Gent arrived at camp, Tom Landry had little use for him. However, the Cowboys offensive coordinator, Red Hickey, saw in Gent the making of a fine receiver. Hickey liked his soft hands and his aggressiveness, and he kept Landry from cutting the effervescent, free-spirited free agent. Thanks to Red Hickey, Gent became a Cowboy in 1964, and he remained on the team through the 1968 season, long enough to see the highs and lows of the great years of the Don Meredith Cowboys. After Gent retired from football, he wrote a controversial, hard-edged novel, *North Dallas Forty*, a book about how a football team takes advantage of its players and treats them like faceless cattle. In the book Gent used all he saw and heard, adding embellishments for dramatic effect. Cowboys owner Clint Murchison, himself a rebel, loved *North Dallas Forty*. Tex Schramm and Tom Landry, who were protective of their image and were portrayed as manipulative, uncaring men, passionately hated it.

Gent may not have been the greatest player to ever perform for the Cowboys, but certainly he was one of the more observant and entertaining.

Pete Gent: "I was beginning to get the feeling they were getting ready to send me home, and one day in practice they were running single routes, man-on-man coverage, and they didn't have a whole lot of receivers. They had drafted a bunch of them, but none of them turned out well. We still had 10 defensive backs and only had four or five receivers. So Red Hickey, who had obviously heard in one of the coaches' meetings that I was being cut pretty soon anyway, called me over to run routes, just to even things out. And I caught 10 balls in a row, including some circus catches. The thing was, it's real easy to catch a football. A football is made to catch. You just catch it and fall down. Try catching a basketball at full speed and having to make up your mind what you have to do in a step and a half. And so the concentration part of it came real easy. All I had to do was get past hearing footsteps. That wasn't difficult either. I had learned that in basketball because you were playing so close to the crowd.

"Immediately Red called me aside, and he said, 'Look, I've had a couple guys who were basketball players.' He mentioned R. C. Owens, for whom he had developed the alley-oop pass. Red said, 'You have the ability to be a receiver, but you're going to have to work. And I'll stay out with you every day and teach you,' which he did. And of course, the other thing you know, when the coaches are in a meeting, when they are trying to decide who to cut, you've got a guy who is in your corner, who is arguing for you.

"When I came that year, the receivers were Pettis Norman, who would eventually become an All-Pro tight end, Lee Folkins, who was a good tight end from Washington, and they traded for Tommy McDonald and Buddy Dial at wide receiver, and Frank Clarke. And they were only planning to keep five. Because of Red, they made room for me as the sixth, but Tom Landry didn't plan to play me much, which he didn't.

"To keep me, they had to cut Sonny Gibbs. Sonny was their number two quarterback, but Sonny was too erratic as a passer. He was a big [6'7"] guy from TCU, a nice guy. He ended up making golf clubs."

From the start Pete Gent and Tom Landry did not see eye to eye. Landry was a member of a postwar generation that venerated conformity, consensus, rules, and regulations. A nice girl was a virgin who didn't smoke cigarettes. Guys wore saddle shoes and sang "Love Letters in the Sand." Dwight and Mamie Eisenhower (and Pat Boone) represented that era of the fifties, and on TV the favorites were Robert Young and Jane Wyatt in *Father Knows Best* and Ozzie and Harriet Nelson.

Gent, like many who were kids when Elvis Presley came along to excite a generation, saw himself as a rebel against his parents' drab lives. Gent and his generation listened to and were thrilled by Jerry Lee Lewis, Chuck Berry, and The Big Bopper, the bad boys of rock and roll, and they began to rebel against their parents' lifestyle. Once in college they questioned the prudery that called for curfews and wanted to know why they couldn't entertain girls in their rooms. In October 1964 the students at Cal Berkeley erupted in protest over the college policing their moral lives. In January 1965 the free speech movement began on campuses all over America.

In college, Pete Gent began to question things. A Methodist like Landry, he wondered how a person could love Jesus and still hate his fellow man just because his religion or skin color was different. Cynicism began to creep into Pete Gent's view of those who were dogmatic about their religion, and he developed doubts about whether there really was a God. That cynicism also caused him to attempt to use religion to his benefit in training camp as a way of influencing Landry to keep him on the 40-man roster.

Pete Gent: "In those days they posted the starting times for the area churches on the bulletin boards. A lot of the guys in those days were Catholic, and they rode together to Mass. Landry was a Methodist, and I was a lapsed Methodist—that's an agnostic. Anyway, when I realized he was a Methodist, I signed up. My theory was, 'I'm going to get this first Sunday punch,' even though church had been distasteful since I was a kid. To me it was stupid. But I figured if I went to church with him, it had to have some effect on him, and maybe that would be enough to make the team.

"It turned out the only Cowboy beside me going to the Methodist church was Landry. So that first Sunday, who do you think was riding in the front seat next to him? Me.

"I never went again. I wasn't going to go twice—'cause there could be a God. But this was just football."

Once Gent became an offensive player, the teammate he gravitated toward and who gravitated toward him was his quarterback, Don Meredith. It's not hard to see why Don liked Gent, though Gent was a Yankee who had never even played college football. What Gent was was very bright, very witty, and the sort of person willing to go anywhere or do anything Meredith wanted to do. Over the years the two became close, as anyone who read *North Dallas Forty* could see. The two main characters, Shake Tiller and Seth Maxwell, were close, brothers almost. So were Gent and Meredith. Gent would become Meredith's primary confidant and amateur psychologist as the Cowboy quarterback's life became more and more topsy-turvy as the years went on. And in the battle of wills between Don Meredith and Tom Landry, Gent would always side with his buddy.

Pete Gent: "Meredith's approach to the game was the realization he had to lead the team. Don was the Old NFL, which I still think is right. The quarterback should call the plays from the field. That's where you get your best information. And the other thing was, here was a losing team that would get so depressed and so down on themselves, they needed someone to lead them and keep them feeling up. Don had seen the Cowboys year after year just corkscrew right into the ground as their season went on. So in '64, what I saw was this happy-go-lucky guy on the outside and this very serious guy on the inside. His first marriage had broken up. Don had been a divinity student, for Christ's sake, who had turned into a drinker and a womanizer.

"Don's life off the field was just one incredible tragedy after another. Horrible bad luck and mistakes and just circumstance. And he *always* blamed himself. He was not a guy who did not take the blame. Don was a guy who beat himself unmercifully. He constantly tortured himself with guilt. He was absolutely guilt-ridden. It wasn't religious guilt. It was personal guilt, deeply felt. And because it wasn't religious guilt, there was no way for him to cleanse himself of it.

"How did he survive? The guy's character was incredible, and I don't think I was the only guy who noticed that. I always noticed that wherever we were, Don Meredith was *the* focus. In football the defense hates the offense, because they think no matter what they do, the offense loses the game. But Meredith was the one guy who nobody on the team ever, ever said a bad word about.

"And Meredith felt—we *all* felt, and I still believe this to be true, it's why the NFL is not as interesting as it used to be—that the quarterback should call the game on the field. If the quarterback can't remember the plays, then why are you paying him all that money?

"Tom Landry's whole theory, on the other hand, was industrial. Football was a machine with replaceable parts. This came as a result of his experiences as a bomber pilot, I presume. He didn't want to know the gunners. He didn't want to know them, because they were probably going to get killed. It was the biggest struggle between Landry and Meredith.

"I sided with Don on that issue. I've been around sports long enough to know that everything is great in theory, but you also have that human factor that elevates you even higher. And if you get that working for you, then you've got everything. And that's what Landry wanted to eliminate. And that was the huge philosophical gap, which you could never cross. And within that huge gap, all sorts of turmoil developed. Landry didn't like Meredith's lifestyle. Meredith would walk out onto the field, and he wouldn't be serious enough for Landry. But that whole style that Meredith had adapted was designed to take pressure off the players and keep them believing that if Don was happy and feeling good, then we must be OK.

"Nineteen sixty-four was a disaster because Meredith stayed hurt, his substitute, Billy Lothridge, was hurt, and John Roach, who came from the Packers, never did figure out the offense. In '64 we did not have a real good line coach, and we did not have a very good line. Jim Myers was the coach. He got better as we got more talent. Until Dave Manders took over, in '64 our starting center was Mike Connelly, who was only 215 pounds. We had a tackle who was only 220. The guards couldn't pull. Don barely got back into the backfield to throw, and the defense was waiting to pounce on him. Of course, he was scrambling to try and throw, while Landry was trying to get him to stay in the pocket, which was insane. There was no pocket. And what happened was, with Sonny Gibbs gone, Meredith got hurt in the exhibition season. He tore up his knee.

"Our punter, Billy Lothridge, had been a quarterback at Georgia Tech, and he took over when Don got hurt. Billy got injured almost immediately. We were down on the goal line, and he was trying to run a play, and he fumbled. And when he bent down to pick up the ball, the defense ran by him and he ran in for the touchdown, but he tore a muscle, so now Billy was hurt.

"At the time Meredith was hurt, there was still time to set the roster, so they brought in John Roach from the Packers, 'cause they wanted a quarterback with some experience. Roach went out there, and although he had all this experience, it was running the Packers offense, which is the absolute opposite of ours literally in every way. In fact, that was Landry's whole theory: his defense was specifically designed to stop Vince Lombardi's offense.

"Landry always was obsessed with Vince Lombardi. They both had been coaches with the Giants. Lombardi got the first head job. Lombardi's theory was this: 'We got six running plays. We got six passing plays. I don't care what you do. You know we're going to run it. We'll tell you. Just try and stop us, 'cause we're not going to make a mistake.'

"Landry's theory was the opposite: 'We're going to run a lot of different defenses, and multiple offenses with shifting backs. I'll bet you can't guess what we're going to run.' His theory was, you make everything much more complicated, but you get smarter players. He used to give us intelligence tests because they didn't want guys who were dumb, but they were always concerned about guys who were too smart. And I think that came because of me. I heard from Gary Cartwright, who was then the beat reporter for *The Dallas Morning News*, that I was the only guy who ever scored higher on the IQ test than Landry. And you took these personality tests, the Minnesota Multiphasic Personality Tests, to find out if you were aggressive and hostile enough. Well, that test was easy to figure out. You always wanted to do the most violent thing, and your answers always tried to show you had to have organization in your life and a willingness to cooperate.

"After the team was set in training camp, Landry would explain his system to the rookies in a long speech he would give. First the trainer would talk to you about how to behave, what you should do. And the equipment man would tell you how to pick up your equipment. The publicity man, Larry Carl, would tell us, 'Boys, remember, this is show business. Your first job if you have an interview is to show up. If you have a photo session, show up.' You got fined if you didn't do it.

"And then Landry would come and speak, and the first thing he would explain was the history of the development of his offense and of modern football, and he would cite the Packers as the perfect example of the opposite of what we did. He'd talk about the simplicity and execution and talent of the Packers. He'd say, 'The Packers are this, and we are the opposite end, but we are willing to give up a few more mistakes, because we're going to beat them on the big play. Ultimately we will break down and give up things and we'll have a few turnovers, but we will get better and better as we execute better and better, as you know the offense more and more, it can't be stopped.'

"As much as Landry and I fought—and we fought like cats—Landry was a fascinating guy. He was a guy who at 19 years old was flying B-17s over Germany, and then he had to deal with us. We were fighting the Vietnam War, and we'd come drunk and stoned to practice. As a man, as a presence, still to this day, he was the most impressive coach I've ever been around. He just knew everything."

Chapter 20

Bob Lilly and the Flex

Soon after Maury Youmans was traded from the Chicago Bears to the Cowboys in 1964, the two teams played in an exhibition. George Allen, who had been one of Youmans' coaches on the Bears, came over to make small talk. "Maury, how's it going?" The big tackle couldn't wait to tell him about Tom Landry's eye-opening defensive system known as the Flex.

"George, this is great," replied Youmans. "You won't believe it. The defense here is so interesting. You know every place you gotta be, where you line up, what you gotta do. It's all coordinated." Youmans told him, "George, I learned more football just in this training camp than I did in the four years with the Bears."

"No kidding," was all Allen said.

After the 1964 season was over, Youmans was living in Treasure Island, Florida, where his wife's parents owned the Buccaneer Motel. That winter he received a call from Allen, who was vacationing down the beach in nearby St. Petersburg. He said, "Maury, I'm going to be down your way. Do you mind if we get together?"

Youmans, glad to hear from the personable coach, said, "Sure."

They met at the Biltmore Motel; Allen was sitting at the bar when Youmans arrived. Allen said, "Maury, I brought a projector along. I'd like to get together with you and go over your defenses."

Youmans was taken aback. Finally, he said, "George, I can't do that. I'm playing for the Cowboys now."

Maury Youmans: "He wanted to pick my mind. And George ended up the head coach of the Washington Redskins, our archenemy. You can imagine if I had given him all that information.

"That was George. Tom Landry once accused him of having spies, and it was true. George would do anything to win. Well, he learned it from the master, George Halas. There were rumors, and I'll never know if it was true or not, that Halas had microphones in the visiting locker room at Wrigley Field to hear what was going on."

Landry's famed Flex defense made its debut in 1964, when the Cowboys used it on occasion to test whether it would work. In 1965 it became a regular part of the defensive system. That year, for the first time, the Dallas defense became effective. In all but three of the fourteen games, the defense held the opposition under 24 points.

Dick Nolan: "Over the years Tom had watched and studied all the films, noting the formations, and plotting all the plays that were run from those formations. All of a sudden, he saw a master key to it. Those keys told us in advance what the other team was going to run. At the same time, he devised a defense to disguise what *we* were going to do to attack an offense. What Tom came up with was the Flex, a combination of the 4-3 inside and the 4-3 outside defenses. On one side of the line you're playing an inside, and on the other side, you're playing an outside.

"We had been strictly an inside-outside 4-3 team, like the old Giants, and then in '64, we used the Flex as a change-up defense in different spots, just to work our way into it, see what it was all about, to see how it worked. In 1965 we went to it big time. Bob Lilly was the key to the defense. He had moved from left end to right tackle, and boy he was quick as a cat. He was so quick off that ball, the center couldn't block back and get him. If the center did try to block back on the line of scrimmage, he'd knock his own guard off trying to pull. That's how quick Bob was. The only way that center could get him was straight down the line of scrimmage—not on an angle. And the guard would be knocked off, 'cause Bob was so quick.

"See, Lilly wasn't a sprinter of any kind. He wasn't a great 40-yard guy. But he was so quick for five or ten yards, and brother, once he got his hands on you, he was so strong, too, you couldn't get away. And he'd throw you any way he wanted to.

"Let me try to explain the Flex to you. Let's say the Packers set up in a split backfield. The two backs are split, Paul Hornung behind one tackle, Jimmy Taylor behind the other. What we did, we took our left defensive tackle and put him head-up on the line of scrimmage with their right guard. Now, you take your left defensive end, and you bring him back off the ball by two feet, head-up on their right offensive tackle.

"We then took our right tackle opposite their left guard, and put him *off* the ball. His job was to read the head of the guard. Whichever way the head of the guard went, he was to go with him. And the defensive end on that right side, he plays on the outside shoulder of the left offensive tackle.

"As soon as the Packers set up in a split backfield, under Tom's system of reading the keys you have to anticipate that one or both of those guards will be pulling. In this formation, it was the job of our right tackle, in this case, Bob Lilly, to explode on that guard.

"Let's say the other team tries the old Lombardi sweep. When that guard pulls and that center tries to choke back to get Lilly, he can't get to him quick enough because Lilly can just go around him, and the center will fall on his nose trying to block him. Lilly will be running right behind their guard, and Paul Hornung will be running the ball, and Paul Hornung can't come back, because if he does, he'll be running right back into Lilly, who is running down the line of scrimmage with him.

"So now, when he does that, the right defensive end, who is head-up on the tackle off the ball, he's keying the guard, too. If that guard pulls away, he'll follow him, take it down inside with him, go along the line of scrimmage, so if they try to cut back behind Lilly, who is chasing the guard, Lilly will pick up the guy cutting back that far, and the defensive end will pick up the rest of it.

"And then what you do also, you can give them that Flex look, and all you would play was the normal inside 4-3 and *not* the Flex. The next time you could play the normal outside 4-3 from that look and *not* the Flex. So they didn't know *when* to pull or *who* to pull.

"When the defensive end is head-up on that tackle, he can key the tackle if he wants to, just read his head. If the tackle tries to cut inside of him, cut him off in the pursuit of the play, he'll get by his head. See, if he fires straight out at him, he'll say, 'Fine, I'll straighten you up and control your inside.' If he tries to reach to his outside, he'll say, 'OK, I'll step into you and control you on the inside by knowing that the play is trying to come there.'

"The only thing that would hurt me as a defensive end off the ball and looking at the tackle is if the tackle sets for a pass, and then they try to run something underneath me. Then I'm in trouble. Because I'm taking the influence of a pass, and I see it as a pass and nothing else. Well, as a defensive end, if that guy did that to me, the first thing I would do would be to go right back to the guard key. Now I don't care what you as the tackle do. You can set back to pass; I won't even look at you because the guard is telling me what's going on. So that's the truer key. But the end was an easier key. He used to be on all fours just like a tackle. He'd be off the ball looking down at the guard.

"And *nobody*, not me, and probably not even you knew what we were doing. [It had to be experienced on the playing field, which is why it took three years for the average player to learn the system.] They didn't know, because we gave them the same look, and they'd say, 'Here's the Flex,' and it wasn't the Flex at all. It was nothing but the inside-outside 4-3. And the next time we'd play the Flex, and they wouldn't be ready for it. That's how we got to control most people.

"And sometimes what we'd do, too, off that same look, we'd play a regular blitzing defense, the 4-3 storm, where both inside linebackers would be coming hard full-tilt, and you have every gap shut off. So you'd blitz your linebackers. You weren't playing a Flex, but it looked like a Flex."

Maury Youmans: "Larry Stephens had played for Texas when we played them in the Cotton Bowl. Larry was probably one of the brightest ballplayers on that team. He picked up the system better and quicker than anyone else on the Cowboys at that time. Larry had some talent as a football player, but when you ran Landry's system, you didn't have to have all the talent in the world to be a good football player. With the Bears a linebacker might cover an end, but he made the play just on physical ability. With the Cowboys, you covered the end because Tom's system told you to do it before the play ever began. You knew exactly where the play was going to go. As a consequence, Larry became a *really* good football player with the Cowboys.

"None of us were as studious as we should have been, except for maybe Larry, and for Larry it was almost like osmosis. It wasn't that he just sat down and studied; it was that he had a quick mind and picked it up. He's a schoolteacher now. And a really good guy.

"George Andrie was our left end. George Andrie was a terrific player, but he didn't get much credit because it's a little hard when you have a Bob Lilly on the team. George was as good as any of the defensive ends at that time. He was a hard worker. I don't think he had as much ability as he had heart, and that led him a long way. And he learned Tom's system very well. George made the Pro Bowl a few years, so he did get *some* recognition.

"Bob Lilly, our right tackle, was *the* most agile football player I ever saw. Bob could do 'kip-ups' with pads on. A kip-up is where you lay on your back and kick up onto your feet. He would lay on his back and kick himself up. He was that agile. And he was strong. He had a very good upper body. And he had the right mental attitude for a football player. He was just hard-nosed, not mean, but intense. There was never one tackle who could block him on a pass defense.

"In fact, I guess you know, they designed the Flex defense *for* him. I was playing the right end next to him the year the Flex came in, and what they did was, they put Bob head-up closer on the guard. Instead of having my left shoulder to the left shoulder of the tackle, I had to go head-up on all fours. And the whole object of that was for me to watch the helmet of the tackle. If he closed down, I had to close that hole. Lilly was so quick that when they pulled the guard, he could follow and make the tackle on the halfback. The offense had the sucker play where they would pull the guard and run the halfback up through that hole, so they needed to cover it with the defensive end, and so it was the job of the defensive end to step into that hole. That was my job or Larry's job. We didn't like it because if it turned out to be a pass play, it took our rush away. There is *no way* you're going to get a rush coming around. You don't even have a start on it. First, you're waiting to see what the helmet does, but it was because of Bob's quickness that we could do it."

Bob Lilly: "We were starting to get into Tom's theories more and more, and I call them 'theories' because that's what they were when he came to Dallas. He implemented them slowly. By my third year, that's when we got into the Flex defense.

"The Flex defense was a gap defense. I don't care what defense it was, everyone had a responsibility for a certain gap. A lot of teams back in those days played a gap defense where the men were actually *in* the gaps. They had a defender between center and guard and another one between guard and tackle. The defensive end was out wide, and the linebackers were in the gaps that weren't covered. And therefore the guy in front of you knew exactly what you were going to do. But with the Flex, what we tried to do was disguise it, to keep our strategy from the offensive linemen.

"When I first began with the Cowboys, we played what we called the inside-outside 4-3. The linebacker would call it, depending on what formation we had, and that meant we had to step with our right foot if it was an outside 4-3, and we'd be responsible from the head of the guard to the head of the tackle. That was my position. Lee Roy Jordan, our middle linebacker, had responsibilities from the head of the center over to the head of the guard. And so forth and so on. And then if it was an inside 4-3, then I'd step with my left foot. I had inside responsibility, and so did the other tackle, and Lee Roy had to fill either gap between the guard and the tackle. The defensive ends had the gaps on the inside. Our goal was to push the play up the middle to Jerry Tubbs or Lee Roy."

Lee Roy Jordan: "I've seen a lot of good players, and I'm not sure that Bob Lilly still isn't the best one I've ever seen. If Bob Lilly had had the weight program like they have now, I'm not sure Bob would have been controllable. And if he had had a mean streak like some defensive linemen, you would have had to outlaw him. Bob would tackle quarterbacks and lay them down on the ground, where other guys would tackle them and throw them onto the AstroTurf with their 300-pound bodies and maybe break a rib or shoulder or something. But Bob wasn't that way. Bob really didn't try to injure anyone, but his escape from offensive people trying to block him was unbelievable. He was like magic. He was just an unbelievable athlete. His foot coordination, his hand and arm strength, were unbelievable, especially for a guy who didn't lift weights.

"We would go back and watch films after games, and he was 'Mr. Amazing.' We'd say, 'Let's run that back. I can't believe Bob Lilly did that.' He would have three guys on him, and he would go through them like there were little doors in between each one of them that they were opening for Bob Lilly. And he did it week after week, year after year.

"A whole generation of great linemen never got written about because they were playing alongside Bob. And I don't really think it bothered the other linemen, because we all got to watch him in person and on film, and we were so amazed. Hell, I know my career lasted as long as it did because I got to play behind him. I might not have lasted five years behind some other defensive line. I was not the main problem. Hell, they had to worry about Bob Lilly first.

"If you were coming across the middle, I did create some problems, but like us, the other team had to set its priorities, and the other team's number one priority was to block Bob Lilly. And then they could say, 'OK, once we contain Lilly, we have to block the linebackers. You have to keep Jordan from working the Flex if you're going to run on them.' I had a couple holes to fill on the Flex, and if they couldn't get me blocked, there was not going to be a hole for them to run in."

Bob Lilly: "In 1964 we went from the inside-outside 4-3 into the Flex, and I don't know if that was part of Tom's long-term plan, or whether he did it for me,

I have no idea, but the Flex defense was identical to what we had been doing, only we brought the defensive end on the short side on the outside shoulder of the offensive tackle. If I was on the weak side, I'd be head-up with the guard, right on the line of scrimmage, whereas the tackle on the other side would be three feet back. George Andrie would be right over the tackle, and instead of being on his outside shoulder, he'd be head-up, three feet back. He would be keying my guard. I also keyed my guard.

"We got to where we could play the inside-outside from the Flex look. I don't know whether Tom designed the Flex defense as something else to do off the inside-outside 4-3, or whether the Flex was the major defense, but we would play our old inside-outside 4-3 to give them a different look.

"Anyway, that's what football is all about, disguising the defense and never letting them know what you're doing."

When Bob Lilly was told that coach Landry had designed the Flex defense specifically to take advantage of Lilly's superior play, the big tackle seemed surprised. "I was never told he designed that for me," he said. "But I loved it, I'll tell you that." Lilly explained why he and the Flex were made for each other.

Bob Lilly: "Back in those days the other teams ran 65 percent of their plays to the right. So I was in wonderful pursuit. I could catch the offensive guard *before* he could get out of his stance. I'd usually grab him by the back of the jersey and let him pull me right into the play.

"Also, I had a good inside move for a pass rush, which is the fastest way to get there. I don't know how many traps I had. I know one year I had 18 or 19, but mainly I was able to force that quarterback out of the pocket, and then our other tackle and our two defensive ends could get after him. But it was a natural position for me. I *loved* it. I finally felt at home.

"By '65 we were playing pretty consistently good defense, not every game, but if you look at the whole season, we accomplished most of our goals. Dave Edwards didn't start until '64. That's when Jerry Tubbs came up with the idea of switching Dave and Chuck Howley. Dave wasn't quite fast enough to play weakside linebacker [where the assignment was to guard the flanker] so Jerry came up with the idea of switching our linebackers, putting Dave on the strong side [where the assignment was to guard the tight end] and Chuck on the weak side so that no matter how they lined up, Dave played opposite the other team's tight end. And what Dave added was a lot of strength. He could hold a tight end and stand him up when they tried to block him, so they couldn't run around that side. They never could get a clear block, no matter who it was, even Mike Ditka, didn't matter. Dave was strong enough to hold up any of them. He could stand 'em right up on the line of scrimmage: Jackie Smith, Ditka, even John Mackey at Baltimore. They couldn't push him around. So that's what he added. Plus, he was a smart football player, never made a mistake. Tom liked that about him.

"Mel Renfro came in '64, and he was an All-Pro. He was the finest cornerback I saw, with maybe the exception of Mel Blount, during my years of watching football. They wouldn't throw at [Renfro]. They just wouldn't throw because he always intercepted it or knocked it down. And Mel was also a great return man. He had been a running back in college. Mel forced the other team to go all to the other side, and that way we could set up our defenses. Tom was able to create the situation where they had to throw over there, and we had some good cornerbacks, but unfortunately not another one like Mel. Cornell Green was a good cornerback, but he wasn't as fast as Mel either. Charlie Waters was a good one, but he wasn't as fast as Mel.

"Then in '65 we added defensive lineman Jethro Pugh, and before long he became an excellent football player, adding an awful lot to our team. We started playing good defense, because we were consistent. We got beat sometimes when we didn't play well, but 10 out of 14 we played pretty good defensive games. Our statistics were good as far as yards per carry, yards per catch, total offense, total points. We had goals for all those, and we kept pretty much within those goals, which, according to coach Landry, should have won the game, but we weren't winning some of those games because we weren't scoring consistently enough. We might have averaged 25 points, but we'd score 45 points in one game, and we'd score 10 in another.

"The problem was our offense was erratic. They would score 50 points one week, and we'd play a good team and get beat. In '64 and '65 on the defense we were judging our offense a little bit, and we shouldn't have, but we did, and it took us until '66 to stop—after we started winning. The few years we bitched about our offense, we created a division in our team. In '63, '64, and '65 we were bitchin', and when we had a bad game, I suspect they were bitching, too.

"I don't know that Tom was aware of it. Then again, part of that was that we didn't have enough coaches. We went three years without having even a defensive line coach. We just had an overall defensive coach, Dick Nolan. So we were kind of on our own, and we could get together and bitch all we wanted to. We could bitch and raise hell and all that.

"Through '65 the offensive line was leaky, and Don Meredith was playing on bad legs, and we continued to chirp about the offense. We liked Don. It wasn't personal as much as it was frustrating. It wasn't that we didn't respect him. It's just that we could never seem to get together in a big game. Either we'd let them down, or they'd let us down. It got to where they let us down in the big games more than we let them down. That's what we bitched about. And that's what you can't have. And a lot of that was due to our having a little bit of a porous offensive line, and because of that, Meredith was beat up, hurt a lot. Don played with everything, even broken fingers. He played one time with a broken nose. His nose was *so* big I took a picture of it—his eyes were covered up. We had a lot of respect for his toughness."

Chapter 21

VARMINT

Pete Gent grew up in northern Michigan in the same sort of farming community as many of the other players did. His father, a former marine, had been hired out at age 12 to another farmer as a laborer. As an adult he worked on the railroad mail, but in his spare time he was an environmentalist before the term was even coined, walking alone over several hundred acres planting pine seedlings and then hand cultivating them. When he sprayed insecticide, Gent's dad saw the dead birds and realized that in his attempt to make the fields grow, he was killing wildlife. And during the age of Joe McCarthy and the Red Scare in the fifties, Gent's father, a staunch Republican, would ask, "Why are we afraid of the Communists? If we think Communism is so dangerous, let them try to feed the world for a while and see how good their system is."

It was from his dad that Peter Gent inherited his individuality and a certain disdain for those in seats of authority. When he came to Dallas, he saw discrimination that offended him, and when the war in Vietnam began to heat up, he was one of those who questioned its wisdom.

Of the many influences in his life, though, it was the game of football that changed him most. When he joined the Cowboys, Gent was a mild-mannered, well-behaved kid who didn't drink, didn't smoke, and whose idea of a perfect marriage was Ozzie and Harriet's. He had spent a frustrating first season with the Cowboys, and after passing the law boards, began attending SMU Law School at night with an eye toward a law career. Gent had worked in Chicago for a few months in the advertising firm of Foot, Cone, and Belding. A life of middle-class respectability seemed to await. And then, during training camp in 1965, Gent roomed with one of the wildest Texans ever to play for the Cowboys, Don Talbert, called Varmint, one of four brothers known as the Varmint Brothers. Gent's life would never be the same again.

Pete Gent: "Most of the '64 season I lived by myself near the Cowboys practice field. I mostly hung around with Dave Manders, his wife, and his two kids and with Frank Clarke and his wife. I didn't know anybody else. I made no other friends. It was stultifying only because I couldn't figure out how to live. I was real lonely, and every time I tried to do something with Billy Lothridge or Don

Meredith or any of the partyers, it wasn't any fun, because I didn't drink. So after my rookie year I realized if I went back into football, I was going to have to do what all those other guys on the team who I liked and liked being around were doing.

"In '65 I ran into Craig Morton, a rookie, and Craig drank vodka gimlets, and I could get those down. You didn't have to drink a lot of those to feel it, and by the third one you didn't care what it tasted like. And I immediately became a drunk, going from not drinking at all to drinking every day.

"I had hurt my knee playing basketball in the off-season. I was getting what they called joint mice, little pieces of cartilage the size of a quarter floating around the joint, and then they'd lock in the joint. That happened in midspring, I had it operated on, and then I worked to get ready for camp. And I was in camp the second day, and some more broke off. So I came back to Dallas, and they went in and made a small hole, just did a small incision and got the small piece of cartilage out.

"I stayed in Dallas till the first exhibition game and started working out, and when I got back to camp, I was walking in at around 10:00 at night, had my suitcase, and standing naked in the hall was Don Talbert, who had been in Vietnam, who I had never met. He was about 6'5", 250 pounds. He'd gone in to do his six months in the reserves, got frozen in the service, and got sent to Vietnam. You think he wasn't pissed? He missed a complete year. He spent it in Saigon as an MP in 1964. He was so mad they had sent him over there.

"I had seen Don the first couple of days, but I had yet to meet him, and there he was standing there, and as I walked by him he said, 'Hey, motherf***er, I need a roommate—and you're it!' I went down to my room thinking, 'Oh, f***, I can't say no to this guy.' So I roomed with Don Talbert, and it changed my whole life.

"We lived in this apartment called the Four Seasons, and the only people who lived there were single football players, Dave Edwards, Mike Gaechter, Colin Ridgway, Obert Logan, Talbert, and me, and we lived next to four stewardesses from American Airlines. This apartment house had luxury apartments. Dave Edwards had one that had a champagne fountain next to his bed. I don't know how he put in the champagne.

"In Dallas in those days you could not buy liquor over the bar, except in private clubs, and that apartment complex had a private club called the Fifth Season. Talbert was a drinker, and so Don and I went to that club every night after practice. Every night after practice we'd get drunk.

"Talbert and Edwards and all those guys from the South barbecued all the time. Outside the back door of the club Edwards had his barbecue on the deck, and we'd eat and get drunk. It was insane. Oh God, Talbert and I did shit like get drunk and play golf in the apartment. We put divots in the carpeting with 9 irons. We tried to hit the ball out the door, put it through the window, off the walls, Jesus. It was nuts, but oh God, it was really fun.

"Talbert was one of those guys, when he would step into a club, everybody would look at the door and they'd be saying to themselves, 'Oh boy, I hope he doesn't sit down with us!'

"Don had a brother, Diron, who was still at the University of Texas. Diron was also 6'5", about 250 pounds. He later played with the L.A. Rams and the Washington Redskins. Charlie, his older brother, was in law school at the University of Texas, and then the youngest was at the University of Colorado.

"Don would do absolutely anything. He had no fear. There was nothing you could do to scare Don. How were you going to threaten him, kill him? What were you going to threaten him with, to send him back to Vietnam?

"I met Don Meredith through Talbert. Talbert and Meredith had played together in Dallas before Talbert went to Vietnam. When I started running with Meredith, that's when my life *really* changed."

Chapter 22

Turmoil and Dandy Don

Pettis Norman: "In '65 we had broken training camp and were staying at the Holiday Inn, and it was a Wednesday night off, and we had a get-together. I walked in, one of the last to walk in, and everybody was standing around pretending to have fun but watching for me to come in the door. As I walked in I saw this group of people in the center of the room. Don Talbert was over there pretending to be dumping some bread into this cage and tapping on the cage.

"Dave Edwards and Pete Gent came up and started talking to me. As we were talking, I was looking out of the corner of my eyes at Talbert. I asked, 'What is Don doing?' Dave said, 'You're not going to believe what that crazy Don Talbert is doing. He has a wild mongoose.' I said, 'A mongoose?' They said, 'Yeah, a wild mongoose. Come on over and look at it.'

"Dave Edwards and Pete led me over there, and I said, 'What are you doing?' Don said, 'I'm trying to feed this mongoose. The crazy thing won't come out and eat.' I said, 'A mongoose? What is a mongoose?'

"He said, 'First of all, they are vicious. A little hairy animal, but very vicious. You don't want to put your hand in the cage or your finger through the wire, because man, it will rip your hand apart.' I said, 'Don, what would you want with a mongoose?' He said, 'I was out hunting, and I saw him, and I caught him.' And knowing Don, he would be a guy who would do that with his bare hands.

"I looked into the wooden cage with a little round hole in it and a hairy tail sticking out of the hole. Don said, 'He won't come out. They are as stubborn as I don't know what.' Don was knocking on the side of the cage, saying, 'Come on out, you mongoose, you lazy so and so.' And as he was beating on the side of the cage I started leaning down closer to see.

"He started rattling the cage, and I was leaning down closer and closer, and I said, 'This thing must be sleeping.' Don said, 'He's just lazy. And he's ornery. He just won't come out.' So I leaned farther, and Don hit a switch for the trap door, and this tail jumped out of the cage at me, and I had a can of beer in my hand—even though I don't drink beer. Someone had given me the beer. But boy, as I saw that tail coming at me, it looked like a lion! I can swear to you that tail had teeth and fangs, and as I saw them coming through the air getting ready to devour me I leaped backward. I mean, I hold the world record for leaping backward from a standstill. I must have leaped 20 feet in the air backward, and as I was leaping, I threw this container of beer at that tail and hit it. I thought I was going to die of a heart attack. It was incredible, and everybody in that place just laughed until they couldn't stand up. I mean, they got me *real* good.

"It really was fun. You had Don Talbert, Don Meredith, Pete Gent, and several others who didn't take themselves too seriously, who approached the game of football with a lightheartedness that I had not been used to in college.

"There were times we could pick up a flippant attitude or statement by Don Meredith, and on the other hand, you had Tom Landry, who was a very serious person coaching this bunch, and tolerating them, and yet they respected Landry to a degree, so it was a divergency that existed among this group of players. And it was really interesting. As I look back, how would it have been if we didn't have them on the team? We might have been too serious. Because out of that we developed a winning mixture. So it was really a very interesting mix, if you consider Tom Landry on one hand, and Don Talbert, Don Meredith, and Pete Gent on the other."

Traditionally, when the coach spoke, a player obeyed without questioning him. But with the cynicism brought by the controversy over the murder of John F. Kennedy and a growing revolution against race discrimination and the burgeoning Vietnam War, some of the formerly malleable players began to challenge authority. They wanted to know *why* the coach was doing what he was doing. And if it didn't seem right, the player no longer kept silent.

Pete Gent was one of the first to speak up if things didn't make sense, at times angering Landry. This generation war started as a battle between Landry and Gent. By the end of the decade there would be an army of other players just as vocal, but more cynical and vicious. This generation gap between coach and players widened until the end of the decade, when it became the size of the Grand Canyon.

Pete Gent: "The first thing you had to do when you got to training camp was run the Landry mile. You did it before they gave you your physical, before you did your electrocardiogram, before anything. You had to go out there in 85-degree heat and run a mile in under six minutes if you were a back or end, and under six and a half if you were a lineman. In '65 Bob Lilly held out and came late to camp. Lilly, of course, hadn't worked out in months. We had all been in camp, so the only player to run the mile that day was Lilly. We were all waiting for him to run the mile, and he came out loaded up on Dexadrine. On the third lap he went blind. He had Larry Stephens on one side and George Andrie on the other, running with him around the track. Landry made him finish, and he was blind! He finished the mile, staggered off, and fell into the dummy shed, a small sheet-metal building that was like an oven. While we went on with practice, Lilly was just lying there. After lunch he was still there. And he was our best player.

"The next year Pettis Norman almost went into cardiac arrest. And that was the last time they ran the Landry mile. It was just nuts. That was still post–World War II era coaches. The game was about meanness and toughness. If you went blind, you ran blind. It didn't make any sense at all."

Another of the players with whom Landry didn't see eye to eye, Don Meredith, began the 1965 season on the wrong foot with his coach. For four years Landry had been preaching seriousness and commitment to his quarterback, and in return he was treated to country-western songs in the huddle and raucous behavior that seemed to him to belie a lack of maturity. In one preseason scrimmage a Meredith pass was intercepted by Cornell Green. Meredith took off his helmet, held it high as though he was going to whack him with it, and began chasing Green, who was laughing. Landry didn't find it funny.

Not long after Meredith informed coach Landry that he "fell in a puddle of water" in his dorm and badly hurt his shoulder and elbow. Landry was not happy or sympathetic.

Buddy Dial: "During training camp in '65, Don and I went to town, and we bought a bunch of water guns. They were like machine guns, and we were having a war in the hall, and he slipped on the wet floor and hurt his arm. Of course, I got blamed for it."

It was the first in a string of injuries that would keep Meredith from being effective for much of the 1965 season and that would bring turmoil to the entire team. It's bad enough for a quarterback to have a bad arm, but to Landry this injury was inexcusable because of the way it had happened. There was no question, though, that Meredith had to play at a serious disadvantage.

Frank Clarke: "Dandy started the season with a sore arm. We knew Dandy's arm was really painful, and it became a challenge for us: do we stay with our style of running these routes and know he's going to get the ball to us, or do we make the mistake of getting out there and starting to think about making some kind of compensation so that we can catch the ball or make it easier for him to throw it to us? And the answer was don't think, just run your routes, because if he's supposed to be there, he'll be there. If he can't do the job, then he *shouldn't* be there. And that was it: no compensation, no compromises. Run your route and keep your concentration. It was something intuitive, something I did on my own.

"The coaches weren't making any big deal out of it, because mentally if you bring these things up, the players start to think about it. It was not anything we talked about, but the intuitive part of us said, 'Pretend Dandy's arm has never been stronger.' But it certainly did pain him."

Backed by only two rookies, Craig Morton of Cal Berkeley and Jerry Rhome of Tulsa, Meredith was *the man*, and Landry was counting on his arm, for this year the team was adding one of the most exciting offensive weapons in the history of the game of football. His name was Bob Hayes, and he was billed as the World's Fastest Human. He could run the 100-yard dash faster than any man alive, which meant that there wasn't a defensive back in any league fast enough to catch him. Before he came to camp the only questions were whether he had the skills to get open and, if he could get open, whether he could catch the ball.

Pete Gent: "Hayes had been in camp several days before me, and when I got there everyone was saying how bad he was. The problem was that he was catching Craig Morton, who only threw at one speed, which was like shooting the ball out of a cannon. In fact, I was the only guy in camp who could catch Craig.

"In fact, I said to several guys, 'I'm going to start here because nobody can catch this kid but me.' Craig literally threw a pass so hard to Bobby Hayes that it split his hand in half between his two middle fingers, and it took 17 stitches in the webbing to close the split.

"And then Red Hickey started working with Bob, and I would stay out with him, too. Red taught Bob how to cradle the ball, how to handle the ball, and by the end of camp there was no doubt in my mind that he was going to be something special. You don't think there is much difference between a 9.3 sprinter and a 9.1, but when Hayes turned it on, the 9.3 sprinters looked like they had stopped to walk and Hayes had just been shot out of a cannon. And it changed the game. It literally changed the whole game. When Hayes was in there, I *always* had single coverage. They had to put everybody over on Hayes' side.

"And halfback Dan Reeves, who was another rookie in '65, became a key receiver, because we could run him out of the backfield on Hayes' side, and there would be nobody there. Everybody was chasing Hayes."

Frank Clarke: "I had made All-Pro in '64. Tommy McDonald and Buddy Dial were real quiet. The talk of the Cowboys and in the league was the rise of Frank Clarke, because I had a sparkling season, played well, blocked well, and I was smart, and everything just happened for me. And so there I was, an All-Pro. It stunned me.

"But the Cowboys knew they had Bob Hayes coming, and Tom Landry knew this guy was going to be great. He *knew* it. And so to make space for Bobby Hayes and to utilize my physical talents and pass-catching ability, he moved me to a slot position, because he was going to give the wide receiver spot where I just made All-Pro to Bobby Hayes—as a rookie.

"That's quite a statement, isn't it? To take an All-Pro and move him to another position and move a rookie in, a guy you've never seen play? Bob hadn't played a down. And this was fine with me.

"If Tom Landry wanted me to put on a 70s number and play tackle, I would have done it without a word—I had surrendered to his tutelage. I knew this guy was incredible. He had a mental approach to the game that astounded me, and I knew how important it was not only to have physical ability but mental ability, and this guy had it, so if he wanted me to go to another position, I didn't question it whatsoever. I knew it was in the best interest of what we all wanted.

"I didn't even question it until I started hearing from some close friends who were fans of the Cowboys and until it came out in a couple of sports articles, where sportswriters said things like, 'Well, this smacks of some kind of racism.

They take this black player who just made All-Pro and move him,' and I resented that somebody would come to me with this kind of baloney. I thought it sucked, and I still do, thought it was really in poor taste. And I told everyone that. I stood up for Tom."

Pettis Norman: "In the opening game of '65, coach Landry started Frank Clarke, Bob Hayes, and Buddy Dial instead of me, and I was troubled by that move. I knew from past history that we were a running team, and I knew I could block with the best of the tight ends in the league. I knew also that when given the opportunity, I could catch with a good portion of them, because I had done this all through my college career. So I was troubled by that. As much as anything I thought it was done to accommodate the trade for Buddy Dial. Tom was trying to experiment with a passing offense and hoping the run would somehow be adequate. It didn't work out that way. But I was troubled by that move. There was also speculation he did it because Dallas wasn't ready for three black receivers all on the field at the same time. Interestingly, I didn't say it, but I had a lot of teammates who did, a *lot* of African-American teammates who were very vocal about it. They were saying, 'Landry just doesn't want to start three black receivers in this town. This town is not ready for that.' That's what *they* were saying.

"I didn't think about it like that because I guess I just didn't look at it like that. I could never really understand why I was benched, because I had consistently proven myself in every training camp and every other time that I could handle that position. The switch couldn't have been made for speed, because I was the third-fastest guy on the team behind Hayes and Mike Gaechter. Mike was a 9.6 sprinter in college, and I was a 9.7 sprinter, and so we'd just be nip and tuck in the 40-yard dash. When Bob Hayes came, he was even faster. I was always a team player. I would give whatever I had whenever I was out there. So that was a troubled season for me, trying to reconcile that."

The Cowboys won the first two games of the 1965 season by the scores of 31–2 over the New York Giants and 27–7 over the Washington Redskins. The buzz was that the Cowboys were the most exciting young team in the NFL.

Frank Clarke: "In the fall of '65 we beat the Redskins on three long touchdowns to Bobby. He was starting to get a lot of coverage in the papers, but more important he was also getting a lot of coverage defensively. People were starting to double up on him as best they could.

"We were all quite stunned watching him run. It was really a tribute to Don Meredith how quickly Don got to where he could get Bob Hayes the ball. He didn't underthrow Bob very much, and we were very impressed with how quickly Dandy was able to do that. One of the things that helped, Bob Hayes and Meredith practiced a lot after our regular practice. They spent a lot of time together.

"Bobby was such a joy to watch running routes. He not only had this great way of practicing his moves and working on his moves, practicing as though he didn't have this great speed. He practiced the moves and got the timing down and used his peripheral vision, his way of looking at the whole secondary so he could see if they were rolling into a zone or if the linebackers were going to blitz, because he would have adjustments to make. And it was as if he was doing all of this mentally as if he just had normal speed. When he got into a game, it was amazing how quickly he made all these adjustments, and he turned these great moves into getting behind defensive backs. Once he got behind a defensive back, it was *over*.

"Bobby was committed to succeeding. Because of his work ethic and because of his connection with Meredith, he became a dominating player."

If Meredith could stay healthy, Landry and the Cowboys would finally reach their long-term goals. But the 1965 Cowboys had an Achilles heel, their offensive line. In the season opener the Giants sacked Meredith five times, and against the Redskins he wrenched his back when he was violently thrown to the ground. Added to the elbow injury incurred during training camp, Meredith entered the third game against the St. Louis Cardinals banged up and severely damaged.

Buddy Dial: "In '65 we did not have a great line. We were weak at guard and didn't have a real good center—it was a patchwork offensive line, but Don, he had a devil-may-care attitude. He released the ball late, and he loved to go deep. And if he wanted to throw deep, he was going to throw deep. Coach Landry would beg him to get rid of the ball and not take such a beating, but Don, he just was fearless. He knew if he had a little second, he could go deep against anybody. I can remember in our second game against Washington, the Redskins had some veteran ballplayers, really a good defense, and Myron Pottios hit him and hurt him.

"In the next game against St. Louis, Don was throwing late and real high. That was a night game, a Monday night, a weird night, and Don was off. I remember he threw me a turn-in, and Meredith threw it real high, and I went up to catch it, and Larry Wilson, the free safety, a tough hitter, hit me in the ribs, and I broke four ribs and my spine, and they didn't tell me. They doped me up, and I kept playing, but that messed me up pretty good right there."

One of the reasons Landry kept playing Dial was that he didn't have any faith in Pete Gent. Assistant coach Red Hickey kept pleading with Landry to put Gent in, but Landry was adamant. Gent was a rookie—a free-agent rookie at that. The dispute added to the unrest.

Pete Gent: "That same year I became a real sore point between Tom and Red Hickey, who felt I should be playing a lot, if not starting. I wasn't playing much at all. I was almost 6'6", and I weighed about 220, but my problem was that Red was a great technician at telling you how to catch the ball, but nobody knew how to show you how to run routes. And the only guy who ran really beautiful routes who would show me was Frank Clarke, but Frank had such a unique running style, it was like he was on roller skates. I kept trying to run like that and couldn't do it. He'd make these fluid cuts. Tommy McDonald and Buddy Dial were no help. Dial was a one-on-one receiver who Bobby Layne had made famous with the Steelers. He never really did well with Dallas, and Tommy McDonald was just such a mean little bastard, he just, God . . . So as a rookie I had nobody to teach me how to run routes, and I was not making the right kind of moves, because I was using basketball fakes."

After starting the season with two big wins and then losing to the St. Louis Cardinals in a game in which the offense in the first half could gain only 47 yards and make but two first downs, Landry shocked the team by benching Meredith, citing his inability to hit the open receivers. His teammates, who knew how banged up Meredith was, could scarcely believe it.

Frank Clarke: "Dandy played injured against the Cards and threw some interceptions, didn't play well, and Landry benched him, but Landry never said, 'I'm benching Don Meredith because he's hurt.' It was always, 'I'm benching Don Meredith because he's not performing.'

"It did seem as though this would have been quite a blow to any player's ego, to have been injured and then to be benched not because you're injured but because you're not doing the job. And that was real hard. I'm certain if Dandy spoke frankly about that, he would say that might have been one of the seeds for his retirement at the end of the '68 season. In fact, that probably was *the* seed, because Dandy never overcame that."

Buddy Dial: "Against the Eagles, coach Landry alternated Craig Morton and Jerry Rhome. But see, Don was playing under a handicap. He was playing with strange receivers, guys who they had traded for, and they hadn't worked together enough, and the timing was off, and Don got dumped on for the whole damage, and it was *not* his fault. He had me and Tommy McDonald alternating, he had Frank Clarke out of position, he had Pettis Norman at tight end, and Pettis was a good blocker, but not a good receiver as yet. No one gave Don credit. And Landry never backed him. Never. But I'll tell you what, Dandy, he didn't forget. He kept a record, because he was that smart. He didn't want to hurt anybody or get even; all he wanted to do was win, and that's a class act. I mean, he could have been vindictive, because he was unjustly crucified for losing, but he just kept it to himself, and he said, 'I want to win.'"

With Don Meredith fuming on the bench and the two rookies trying to get something going, the Cowboys lost to the Philadelphia Eagles and the Cleveland Browns. Meredith returned in the Cleveland game, but a large Browns lead made it impossible for the Cowboys to catch up.

Frank Clarke: "We lost to Cleveland, then lost to Green Bay, our fourth straight loss. Tom kept changing quarterbacks, and it was definitely chaotic. Our constant march to improve was being strongly challenged, in terms of our confidence in ourselves and in our leader, Tom Landry. These things were playing on our minds, and we couldn't dismiss it right away, and it made a difference.

We were beginning to question ourselves, to get our confidence challenged at that time."

The turmoil on the team was becoming so destructive that even the defensive players were beginning to take notice.

Bob Lilly: "When Tom did it with LeBaron and Don we didn't mind, because we had such a lousy team it wouldn't have mattered anyway. With Meredith and Morton, it did. We wanted *one* of them in there. We didn't care who. Just somebody. And Meredith was the natural choice, because he *knew*, sensed a lot of things out there that Craig was going to have to develop to know."

Landry decided to start Meredith against the Pittsburgh Steelers, a bad team he figured he would beat. But Meredith was only able to complete 12 of his 34 passes for 187 yards, and the Cowboys lost 22–13, the team's fifth straight loss.

After the game, when Landry walked into the locker room, no one looked up. The usually stoic Landry walked to the middle of the room. He began to address the team. His voice seemed to quaver. He said, "In the six years I have been with the Cowboys, this is the first time I have felt truly ashamed of the team's performance." No one looked up.

After a minute—a silence that seemed eternal—he continued, "Maybe the fault is in the system, with the approach we are . . ." His voice broke, and then he coughed, and then came a slow rivulet of tears down his cheeks. Tom Landry began to cry.

Don Meredith, who admitted later that he had tried very hard but had done poorly because of the pressure he was feeling, stood up and most gallantly apologized to his teammates for not playing better. "I tried my hardest," he said, "but I'm going to work even harder, and we will start winning again."

The players knew that the fault did not lie on the valiant shoulders of their beat-up quarterback. They were four-square behind Dandy Don. Any resentment they were feeling was being directed at their coach. When he cried in front of them, some were moved more than others. Despite the tears, the players who loved Dandy Don could never fully forgive Landry for not being more supportive of their leader.

Bob Lilly: "After we lost to Pittsburgh, coach Landry told everyone to get out of the locker room except the players and coaches. He told us he came to the Cowboys and had studied football for 50 years in New York, going back to the archives, had devised the Multiple Offense and the Flex defense, and that he thought those were the types of philosophies that were going to carry us for the next 20 years. He wanted to thank all of us for giving him 100 percent, and this and that, and then he broke down and started crying. That touched every one of us. And it seemed like it went on for about an hour, though it was more like two or three minutes. But he was just crying, and he couldn't control it.

"He said, 'I very likely won't be here next year.' And then he just broke down, and boy, that touched us. We were touched—very deeply. I think it humbled all of us. From that point on we were much more attentive and much more diligent.

We saw a real man up there. We had always taken coach Landry for granted, and this time we saw a real person, and we wanted to fight for him. And we did. And I don't think we planned it that way. I know he didn't. It just happened. And I never saw him cry again."

Frank Clarke: "When I saw him crying, I felt a swallow, one of those swallow things you do because you feel like, 'This guy's tears might be contagious.' And I don't know how many other guys might have felt that, too, but there was a quietness at that moment. It's very possible that every one of us might have felt that same way at that time. And we got a sense of what kind of commitment this man was willing to make."

Pettis Norman: "He [Landry] was apologizing for allowing too many things to happen. He was not settled in his own mind about who to play, when to play them. He did not exhibit the kind of confidence in a lot of players that he should have, Meredith included. And so consequently, you can't be prepared as a team when you don't know who's going to start at quarterback, and you don't know who's going to be pulled in what quarter. You don't know who's going to start at tight end or wide receiver or running back. And a team can't prepare like that. And so he was saying, 'It wasn't your fault. It was *my* fault.' He was saying in effect, I have allowed doubt to set in myself, and I passed it on to you all, so you couldn't play any better than how you've been playing. It was remarkable, because Tom was not the type of person to admit his faults. And I don't remember him doing it again."

During the 1965 season Landry was using his all-important statistics for guidance, and he didn't like what he was seeing. Later Landry would say that the press and fans were justified in their sharp criticism of Meredith and that he had been justified in benching him by citing his completion percentage.

Tom Landry: "He had only completed an embarrassing 38 percent of his passes all season. We couldn't possibly win with that kind of performance. I had to go with one or both of the rookies."

It was an assessment with which a number of the players found fault. Pete Gent, for one, found Landry's use of statistics arbitrary and self-serving.

Pete Gent: "Tom Landry finally showed that what he was doing was unmaintainable. You couldn't demand these things and expect them to work. The other thing you couldn't do was lie to yourself. You couldn't say, 'I'm judging everyone on their statistics,' and then play the guys you liked and wanted. Because if you believe that, you better live with that. Because then you could live with your wins and your losses if you really, truly believed what you were doing. But see, he broke down and cried because he believed he had been betrayed, but he couldn't figure out who. Well, he was betraying himself."

The way the players saw it, Landry should have chosen his quarterback and then let him play. In their opinion, his decision to replace Meredith with two rookies was foolish from its inception, and in doing so he had doomed the entire ballclub.

For three days Landry mulled over what to do. He truly did not like Meredith, not as a player and not as a person, and even perhaps for reasons he himself did not understand. Had he had an acceptable replacement, surely Landry would have junked Dandy Don. But after experimenting with Morton and Jerry Rhome and seeing the team display a bitterness bordering on open resentment, Landry decided that he had to sink or swim with Meredith.

According to his autobiography, Landry tossed and turned for two nights. He prayed for wisdom to make the right decision.

Tom Landry: "Finally I called Meredith into my office. He sat down, his face somber, ready for the blow he knew had to be coming. When I looked at him and said, 'Don, I believe in you. You're my starting quarterback the rest of the year,' Don began to cry. Then we both cried."

On November 3, 1965, Landry called a press conference. He told the reporters, "Our offensive team is very young. We have three rookies starting, and Leon Donahue [at guard] is a veteran who has been with us only two months. The only veterans with experience on our offensive team are Jim Boeke, Don Perkins, and Frank Clarke. We need a quarterback to lead us to our potential, and that's why I have made my decision. . . . Don Meredith will start the next seven games this season."

Landry continued, "After five straight losses a decision of this nature is difficult, but I had to go with the man I felt everyone on the team had the most confidence in, the man I felt could make the team rise up and play well enough to make up the seven to ten points we've been losing by all season." Concluded Landry, "I have no doubt Don can win."

It was what his teammates had been saying all along.

Pettis Norman: "In small groups the players were criticizing him for experimenting too much, saying, 'Landry has to get set on who's going to quarterback the team, and who's going to play the other positions, and let people play. And he has to stop jerking people out every time they make a mistake.'

"And after he finally announced that Don would be our quarterback, the doubts went away, and we were as good as any team in the league the rest of the way."

Buddy Dial: "After the Steelers game, Landry gave the ball to Meredith and let him call the plays. We had been so frustrated. We finally decided it was garbage time, and we had a little freedom to play, and we did pretty well. We won five of our last seven."

Frank Clarke: "We were all very much involved in this quarterback controversy. It wasn't just Meredith; it was the whole offense. And when that decision was made, things were just looser. There was an air of lightness we hadn't known in several weeks. Prior to that string of defeats and faux pas, dropped passes and switching quarterbacks, we had been building up to a nice sense of confidence, and then three or four weeks of crazy things put us at the brink of having our confidence destroyed. But as soon as Tom said, 'Don Meredith is my quarterback,' that was over with. We all became Don, and we all got lighter. It was almost as if we could predict that we were going to have a fine close of the season, that we would do well."

In the next game, Meredith led the Cowboys to a 39–31 win over the San Francisco 49ers, winning the game with 4:18 remaining on a 34-yard pass to Bullet Bob Hayes, one of two Hayes touchdowns. Hayes also ran back a kickoff 66 yards.

Frank Clarke: "When Don came back against the San Francisco 49ers, he had aches and pains. His knee was very weak, and he probably still had trouble with his back, too, but he was relatively healthy. For Meredith, he was relatively strong, and we beat the 49ers, and we beat the Steelers, 24–17, and then we played the Browns."

Pettis Norman: "After losing to Cleveland [24–17], in the paper the next day Gary Cartwright of *The Dallas Morning News* really put the knock on Don. [Meredith had thrown two interceptions, including one from the 1-yard line for which Cartwright seemingly could not forgive him. Cartwright paraphrased Grantland Rice by writing, 'Outlined against a gray November sky, the Four Horsemen rode again Sunday. You know them: pestilence, death, famine, Meredith.']

"It was devastating to Meredith. It angered a lot of players. It probably was the sour grape that really made the Gary Cartwright era in Dallas as far as players were concerned, made him a real outsider, because a lot of players felt Gary was someone who would criticize everybody on everything and who was there just to tear people down. I remember people started talking, saying they didn't want to be around Gary Cartwright any more, and a lot of them avoided him from that point on. Lee Roy Jordan wanted to beat him up. I can remember people cursing Gary Cartwright like he was really a piece of dirt, so it was a good thing he wasn't there at that moment."

Lee Roy Jordan: "After Cartwright wrote that article about the Four Horsemen, some of the players wanted to beat him to a pulp. I was one of them. Gary deserved it several times and never got it the way he should have."

Buddy Dial: "We didn't lose the Cleveland game because of Don Meredith. We lost it because of the coach. You know what happened there? The play came in from the sideline. Meredith had the play he wanted to run, and Landry's play was the opposite of Don's, and the team wanted Don's play. Whose fault was that? It wasn't Meredith's. But Meredith had to do what Landry wanted 'cause Rhome and Morton were on the sideline, and Landry was over there, and he'd have had his head in his helmet.

"On the play from the 1-yard line, Don threw to Frank Clarke, it was tipped, and intercepted, and the next day Don was just crucified in the papers by Gary Cartwright. Oh boy, and that hurt so bad, because typical of the situation it wasn't Don's call, it wasn't his play, it wasn't his fault."

Pete Gent: "Meredith was such a decent man. We had a team meeting after the Four Horsemen article, and everyone wanted Gary dead. They wanted to kill him. And I tried to tell Cartwright that, but he'd say, 'No, they like me. They have their job, and I have mine.' I said, 'Gary, you think your job is to cost us our jobs. These guys are pissed.' And Meredith would calm them all down.

"The other half of it was that because it was Landry who was the one always criticizing Don, none of the other players, except myself, defended Meredith in any of the papers. The reason for that was that the worst thing in the world that you could do was be in the paper saying that Landry was wrong, or worse, lying. Danny Reeves wanted to be a coach. Danny was young, a kid, and he was very smart, and look where he is. Walt Garrison's remark was, 'I like rodeo better than football, because it has a better class of people.' Walt just didn't get into the politics of it. He did his job, and he felt that was enough. And he was a good friend of Don's. Privately Walt would defend Meredith to anybody. But you were taking a *big* risk going public against Landry. But see, for me, I realized that Landry was *never* going to warm up to me. I knew I would never be able to do enough to satisfy him."

The next game was against Sonny Jurgensen and the Washington Redskins. Meredith played an excellent game, throwing for 249 yards and two touchdowns, including a 53-yarder to Frank Clarke late in the game that appeared to be the game winner.

But Jurgensen, who would go on to have a Hall of Fame career, took the Redskins 64 yards for a score in just four plays. Even then Meredith almost pulled it out, losing only when Danny Villanueva missed a 45-yard field goal. When the game was over, some of the players couldn't believe they had lost.

Frank Clarke: "It all happened so fast, even though it may have taken three minutes. First of all, as a pro athlete, you don't sense that something bad is going to happen. You think, 'We're going to stop Jurgensen. Our defense is so good, our guys are going to stop him.' And you keep that feeling, until you realize you're taking off your jersey and shoulder pads in the locker room, and you go, 'Hey, they beat us.' You don't even get a chance to think about it during the game. Later on, you say to yourself, 'I can't believe that happened.'

"That was the way we felt, too, especially about our defense. We were feeling really good about the way our defense was playing, 'cause they were really catching up in terms of the offense and catching up statistically with the best defenses in the league. So when Jurgensen and those guys were moving the ball, we had a sense, 'We're going to stop them. We're going to win.' And then we looked up at the scoreboard, and it was, 'Hey, they got more points than we did.'"

After the game Meredith met his ex-wife at Dulles Airport for the purpose of accompanying his daughter, Mary Donna, back to Texas. Their rocky relationship had been a constant strain on Meredith, in addition to all that Landry had put him through over the years.

Peter Gent: "Don's ex-wife Lynn was working in Washington as an aide to a congressman, and she came to the airport and brought their daughter so that Don could have her for a week in Dallas. Mary Donna was either going to fly back or her mother was going to come to Texas to visit her family.

"Losing the game was tough, but what was most difficult for Don was the realization that he was spending a lot of his time away from his daughter. During much of the flight she was sitting in his lap.

"I was standing up leaning on the chair in the row in front of Don, and Don kept looking at me and then looking with his eyes at this beautiful little girl, who was curled up in his lap with her head against his shoulder. He was looking at this great tragedy. Here was this little girl he had not been able to provide for in terms of being around as her father, and I think Don felt a great sense of failure at that point, not as much as a football player as his desperate attempt to be a good husband and father.

"And he was looking at her and then looking at me, that's when he began crying. He was crying and saying out loud, 'I am not a loser,' and I always took that to refer to his personal life, about his personal relationship with his daughter and wife more than the fact we had lost the football game, 'cause Don was just heartbroken about not being able to be with her. My heart just ached for him. In fact, I was engaged at the time, and I remember when I got off the plane, one of the first things that went through my mind was, 'I am never going to get married and get in that situation,' because you could literally see him being torn in about five different directions. Because Don really liked Lynn, his first wife, but it was just impossible to make that marriage work. They had been the king and queen of the SMU campus, and then he ended up in that madhouse called professional football."

Of the other players who saw Meredith's pain and heard his words, "I'm not a loser," they thought Meredith was talking in a football context. Their hearts went out to him just the same.

Pettis Norman: "Other players were trying to comfort him and assure him that he was not a loser. He felt really bad about that, because he had not gotten over the wounds of being benched earlier on and of Gary Cartwright's vicious article, and I think what happened, he expected he would be crucified and vilified in the papers the next day, and even maybe benched. He had developed a defeatist attitude, started believing the self-fulfilling prophecy, and he was talking to himself, trying to convince the players, 'I'm not all those things my benching might have suggested, or Gary Cartwright might have suggested.'

"Don was a good friend of mine. I've always considered him a good friend of mine. I was one of those guys who always tried to lift everybody else's spirits. I told Don he was a good quarterback and to hang in there. We all told him we supported him."

It was the lowest moment of Don Meredith's professional life, until the day he finally retired. But it was at this point that Don Meredith proved to himself, and to his critics, that he was not a loser, as he quarterbacked the Cowboys to victory in the final three games of the season despite the continual mauling he endured. Meredith led the Cowboys to a win against the Eagles, despite playing in the fourth quarter with a dislocated finger, and against the St. Louis Cards, he was 16–30 for three touchdowns in the first half alone, finishing the game with 326 yards passing despite getting sacked so hard he did not know his teammates.

Buddy Dial: "Against the Cards, he was hit so hard he couldn't remember his teammates' names, and Landry left him in the game. Landry would send out the plays, but Danny Reeves had to interpret them for Meredith. I'm telling you, it's hard enough to play when your head is on straight, but when you get the crap knocked out of you, it's a little hard to remember who to give the ball to, never mind which team you're playing for."

The Cowboys had a final game against the still-tough New York Giants. A win would give Dallas second place and a spot in the Playoff Bowl in Miami.

Meredith threw two touchdown passes to Bob Hayes and broke the game open in the fourth quarter with a 29-yard touchdown pass to Buddy Dial, as the Cowboys won 38–20.

In the last seven games, Meredith had thrown 16 touchdown passes as the Cowboys offense proved itself the equal to any in the league.

Pettis Norman: "We won the final three games of the season, beating New York in the last game of the season. The win enabled us to go to the Playoff Bowl. I was so happy, I didn't know what to do. After the Giants game, I threw my helmet into the air, singing 'Moon over Miami.'

"It was one of the happiest moments I can think about in pro football. People ask me, 'What was one of the happiest moments you can remember?' and most of them think it was playing in the Super Bowl, but really, truly, beating the Giants that day was one of the happiest moments I can remember, because we became winners. The team had reached a milestone. We were *winners*. We had won as many games as we lost. We were going to go to an extra game. We were going to Miami to play in the 'Losers Bowl.'

"You reach milestones in your lifetime. You have to appreciate the moment when the next step you take represents a *real* milestone in your journey. Beating the Giants was a major milestone in our journey. Whoever couldn't be happy about that just didn't understand its significance. Going to Miami was what was important. It was the fact we had gotten ourselves in a position to go by winning that game by beating another team on their home field to become winners for the first time, to be able to say that we had won as many games as we had lost. We had never been able to say that before."

Some of the veterans felt that going to the Playoff Bowl in Miami against the Baltimore Colts was a waste of a weekend. They called it the "Losers Bowl," and they liked it even less when Landry treated it like the Super Bowl, making the players work hard during the week while the Baltimore Colts players were enjoying themselves in sunny Miami Beach. In the game, Colts halfback Tom

Matte, filling in for injured quarterbacks Johnny Unitas and Gary Cuozzo, taped the plays to his arm and led Baltimore to a 35–3 win.

Don Meredith: "We knew Johnny Unitas wasn't going to play, so we thought it would be a breeze. We forgot Unitas didn't play defense. Their defense killed us."

Bob Lilly: "When we went down I don't think we took the game very seriously. We were just happy to be there. I remember [offensive guard] Ralph Neely and Don Talbert and George Andrie and I drove around in a Cadillac convertible, and we went to the jai alai games, the dog races, went out and ate at a nice restaurant. We didn't have our wives down there, because Tex Schramm wouldn't let us, and I think that we had a resentment toward Tex Schramm starting then. Because we really fought those last seven games to get where we were, and here we were in a playoff game, and the Colts were staying just down the street from us, and Carroll Rosenbloom, the owner of the Colts, took their wives down, paid their way, put them all up, had an open bar where they could go in and have a drink after practice and even sign his name. And the Colts players were telling us how well they were being treated, and here we were, eating as a team, not allowed to bring our wives. It was probably childish for us to feel that way, but that's the way it was. It was a joke among the team that a whole front office of 27 people went down there, and we couldn't even bring our wives.

"One night Don Meredith ended up signing Tex Schramm's name to the checks, and we all got a letter about that in the off-season. We just went down there and had a good time. I honestly don't know why we did that.

"It was the first time we had been in any kind of playoff, but it wasn't something we were proud of, particularly, because we didn't have that good a year. But we knew we were going to be a lot better team. We *knew* that."

Chapter 23

ICONOCLASTS

When an entire nation turned on the city of Dallas after the Kennedy assassination, its residents looked for something that would give them pride, that would make them forget. The outlet for their depressed emotions was one they had turned to in the past on both the high school and college level: football. But the Cowboys were a team that represented the entire city, and not only were the players young, flashy, and talented, but they were also winning some games. One hundred and twenty thousand fans had flocked to the Cotton Bowl for the first two 1965 home games, only seventy-five hundred fewer than the *entire* 1964 attendance.

And then on November 21, 1965, a crowd of 76,251 flocked to see the Cowboys host the Cleveland Browns, and even though the Cowboys lost that day, from that day on a horde of fans would make their weekly influx into the city to watch what was arguably the most interesting football team in the NFL. A stoic Tom Landry fascinated everyone, as he stood on the sideline wearing a suit, topcoat, and a serious hat made of houndstooth, looking to all the world like a humorless stockbroker. But for many of the Dallas fans, Landry represented exactly what they had been raised to believe in: God, hard work, and faith. In his case, the faith had been in himself. For six years the Cowboys had stumbled, and only once, out of public view, had Landry let on that he was questioning himself. With the resurrection of Don Meredith, however, the crisis passed, and as the 1966 season began with five straight preseason victories, including a win over the Green Bay Packers, that two-year-old prediction by Tex Maule that the Cowboys would win the division title seemed to be coming to pass.

The 1966 Cowboys, at least, were a team to be reckoned with. They could score on big plays from anywhere on the field. Don Meredith was the quarterback, Don Perkins had a good year running the ball, and catching Dandy Don's passes was a corps of exciting talent led by Bullet Bob Hayes, the World's Fastest Human; Frank Clarke; Buddy Dial; Pettis Norman; and the unknown former basketball player, free agent Pete Gent.

Pete Gent: "In training camp of '66, I hit my stride. We beat the San Francisco 49ers in an exhibition game after I caught two touchdowns, one a circus catch about 45 yards over Jimmy Johnson, even though he had me step for step. They are reading your eyes so I just pretended like I was running, and then just caught the ball falling into the end zone backward. I ended up with five catches for two touchdowns. And I got coldcocked by Matt Hazeltine. Then when I got back in, Meredith threw an across-the-field pass to me in the open a little high, and it bounced off my hands, and I was finger-tipping it, trying to pull it in, but it slowed me up just enough for him to hit me, and I didn't hold on to it, or that would have been a third touchdown, and that would have gone for about 80 yards, so I'd have had close to 200 yards. But the next game I beat Clancy Williams in Los Angeles for a 35-yard touchdown, and then against Detroit in Tulsa I didn't do a whole lot, but we beat them pretty easily. My job when you got against those teams was to catch the early passes until we could open up Hayes. By the end of the '66 season Bob Hayes and I were the leading receivers on the team."

On defense the team was greatly bolstered by the addition of defensive line coach Ernie Stautner. Bob Lilly, George Andrie, Lee Roy Jordan, Chuck Howley, Mel Renfro, and Cornell Green were then recognized names, and they were beginning to play excellently on defense. It took the addition of Stautner to instill the one missing ingredient: ferocity.

Dick Nolan: "In '65 Tom said to me, 'Let's get a line coach the next year,' and Ernie Stautner had been fired by the Redskins. When Bill McPeak was released as coach, Ernie was out, too, and I got a hold of Ernie, because I knew Ernie was a guy who would work like a horse. He was good, and he was smart, and I brought him down to Dallas, and I taught him the Flex defense. So now I had a line coach to do some of it, along with Jerry Tubbs to coach the linebackers, so we were pretty solid.

"Landry let me run the defense, and he ran the offense, and he never bothered me at all. I used to go to his home on Wednesday nights, and we'd sit down there for hours just to go over what I was going to do on defense, and I'd tell him, 'This is why I'm doing it,' and of course, I was schooled by him so much, he knew I was going to be doing just what I did. I put some things in there that worked pretty good. We used them. But the thing was, we almost always ended up rated one or two on defense."

Bob Lilly: "Ernie Stautner came to the team in 1966. I can remember that when Ernie played for the Steelers, Bob Fry, our right tackle on offense, in practice used to tell George Andrie, 'George, all I want you to do is beat me up every day, beat the crap out of me, hit me in the head with your hand, your fist, your forearm, 'cause that's what Ernie Stautner is going to do.' And that's what Ernie did. He just beat him up. Boy, every game Bob was just bloody all over. And Ernie hit Meredith like that a few times, too.

"So we had a lot of respect for Ernie. He had been at Washington for one year to coach, then he came to Dallas. Ernie started computerizing the defenses, computerizing the plays, and so he brought that with him. We had done that a little bit, but he was the one who was responsible for having a good computer program where they had high school coaches who would come over and grade film, take off all the plays of the opposition, write 'em down, and program them in, and they'd have a printout of all the plays they ran, against what defenses, what down and distance, what end of the field, so we knew all that.

"During the game he'd get in our face, right in it. He would try to be nice, and then he'd get carried away, kind of like Mike Ditka. When he became a coach, Ernie was always a gentleman. He never hit anybody, never cursed anybody. He was a good teacher, very patient.

"Ernie helped us a lot. He *really* helped our defensive line because we had been on our own. We worked hard, but you're never going to accomplish as much unless you have somebody pushing you a little harder than you want to go, and we didn't have that. Once we had Ernie in there, he made us study harder, he made us work harder in practice, and he made us much more aware of our job during the game. We weren't doing a bad job during that time, but he put us up another level."

Year by year Landry had built this team, taking the best athlete available. For some reason that "best athlete" was usually a defensive player. In 1966 for the first time Landry directed his attention to molding a line that would keep Meredith from his weekly mauling. Landry drafted in the first round a behemoth guard from Iowa, John Niland, and teamed him with a second-year man, the 6'5", 257-pound Ralph Neely, a guard from Oklahoma who had signed with the Cowboys despite also signing with the Houston Oilers.

Neely was huge and agile, with the hand and foot quickness necessary for pass protection. He also had great strength to block on running plays. A quirky character, Neely could expound on any topic. At the same time, he loved to complain. The beer was never cold enough. The sun was always too hot. Nothing was ever good enough for Neely. His teammates had a nickname for him: "Rotten." But he could block. He may have been the finest offensive lineman the Cowboys ever had.

But to keep him, Tex Schramm would have to really pull a rabbit out of his hat, especially after the U.S. Supreme Court ruled that at the end of the season Neely would become property of the Oilers.

These hulks, Neely and Niland—who had quirks of his own—were the final pieces of a puzzle that would lead the Cowboys to the steps of greatness.

Buddy Dial: "In '66 we were strengthened by the addition of a couple of offensive linemen, Ralph Neely and John Niland. What horses they were, especially Neely. Neely was the finest offensive lineman I had ever seen, until he hurt his knee bad later on. You talk about a phenomenal athlete.

"Niland was from Iowa, a typical dumb guard, but No. 76 could play a little football. John talked a lot, and he thought he was smart, but he was dumber than dirt, you know. He drove people crazy. One night in Dallas he ran through a neighborhood buck naked, just crazier'n a loon. Here was an All-Pro guard running buck naked through a neighborhood, and Don Meredith saw him to be an inspiration. I mean, would you like to have your life on the line protected by a lineman running naked through your neighborhood?

"And at tight end Pettis Norman began to play a little more regularly, and he was a good blocker, and he caught some good balls, too. Pettis was a really competitive guy. On the field he was mean, a wild animal. But off the field he was a real kind, gentle person.

"Old Pete Gent was tough. I'm telling you, he got killed. If the ball was anywhere close to Pete, he knew he would catch it. We often wondered who was going to get off the plane and get in the ambulance first, Meredith or Gent. Many times they'd bring the ambulance to the airport and take Meredith or Gent to the hospital. We'd all get off the plane and get in our cars and drive home, and they would take one of them to the hospital."

In addition to Neely and Niland, the Cowboys signed as a free agent another talented offensive lineman, John Wilbur from Stanford University. Wilbur was different from most of the Cowboys players who came before him. His father had not been a struggling farmer, a postman, or a baker. Rather, Wilbur's dad was a well-to-do attorney who raised his son in a Jewish, white-collar suburb of Los Angeles. The boy attended L.A. Rams games with his dad, who had owned season tickets since 1948.

Because his father had attended Stanford Law School, the son always loved Stanford football. As a boy, he could sing all the Stanford songs, including "Join the Band," "The X Cheer," and "The Golden Bear." In high school Wilbur played baseball, football, and volleyball and participated in water sports including swimming and water polo. A California beach boy, in his spare time he loved to body surf.

After his senior year, the University of California at Berkeley expressed a willingness to give Wilbur a scholarship, but since he didn't need the money, his intention was to play football for Stanford, with or without a scholarship. After seeing Wilbur play in an All-Star game that pitted the top L.A. high school stars against San Diego's counterparts, USC and UCLA also began talking scholarships. Wilbur told them he was going to Stanford.

Stanford ultimately took him, but not on an athletic scholarship. Wilbur didn't care. His future was law, not football.

Wilbur's sophomore year John Ralston became head coach, bringing with him some legendary assistants, including Bill Walsh and Dick Vermeil—a who's who of future NFL greats. Wilbur played on good Stanford teams. He never did beat USC or the University of Washington, but he did well enough to be drafted after his junior year as a future prospect by the Kansas City Chiefs in the American Football League. When it came time for the NFL Draft, Wilbur was nowhere to be found. Rumors were that he had signed with the AFL, and so he wasn't drafted. When Gil Brandt learned he had *not* signed with the Chiefs, he made Wilbur an offer he could not refuse.

John Wilbur: "At the time of the NFL Draft, Bobby Beathard was babysitting me and Gary Pettigrew for Kansas City. We didn't realize it, but he hid us away in a hotel so the other side couldn't get ahold of us. We thought we were just getting a free room and booze and food. We weren't reachable, and Beathard started a rumor I was signing with him, and so I didn't get drafted in the NFL.

"After the draft, the Cowboys contacted me, because they were really big on free agents, along with several other NFL teams. My dad handled the negotiations. Kansas City offered a bonus of $1,000, and the Cowboys offered four grand, with a salary of $12,000. That was a lot of money then, about what I owed Stanford, so I took it. Gil Brandt was really good at the PR, sending stuff about the Cowboys to college seniors. They hadn't won yet. They were 7–7. They had a good record of free agents making their team, so I did the deal.

"Dallas was not my favorite place. In those days it was the 'Changing South,' but it was a town I didn't want to be in during the off-season. Dallas was in the middle of nowhere, had no ocean, was cold, and everybody spoke southern and said racial things, was prejudiced, and in addition, the night clubs closed early.

"Prejudice was everywhere. Danny Villanueva, our kicker, used to get hate calls, obscene calls, harassing calls all the time in Dallas from fans who hated Mexicans. He was scared to death. He had threats against his family. His being on the team unleashed the racial tensions existing in Dallas at the time.

"The black players had to live in Oak Cliff. That's why Pete Gent called his book *North Dallas Forty*. The blacks lived in South Dallas. I wasn't a civil rights activist, but civil rights activism had been all around me. I had come from Stanford, and we had participated in the Mississippi Project. I was sympathetic to their cause and gave money and time.

"I wasn't into the good old boys of the team. The good old boys were the staff, Landry, Jim Myers, and Ermal Allen, and George Andrie, Bob Lilly, Dave Edwards, Ralph Neely, Chuck Howley, Harold Hays, and Lee Roy, the guys who still live in Dallas, the 'let's go hunting' guys.

"My rookie year I had a fan club in Dallas, the 'John Wilbur Fan Club.' I was an anachronistic hero, kind of an antihero. The guys made banners, 'Go John Wilbur,' made buttons. They had cards, because they liked my style on special teams, a wedge-buster. That's where I made my reputation when I started out. These guys called and asked me if they could start a fan club. They were always there after a game. It was kind of cool for a rookie to have a fan club. So they had the Most Popular Cowboy Contest. On the expressway they had a billboard: Oak Farms Milk, with players' pictures and a running tally. And the way you voted, you got a milk carton and cut out a ballot and sent it in to them—a big promotion. Whoever's name was on it got a vote. So my guys got behind this. They got this smart idea to go down to the city dumps, and they scrounged everywhere in all the dumps in Dallas for milk cartons, 'cause each one had a ballot on it, and they cut them all out and put my name on them.

"I got a call late in the year, 'You're invited to come down to the Quarterback Club. You're going to win something.' I said, 'OK,' and I went down there. And they went through the announcements, and they were announcing that day the winner of the Oak Farms Most Popular Cowboy Contest. Curt Mosher, the PR guy, came up to me, and said, 'Look, we never have a second place for this award, but you're the second-place winner. We have a $1,000 check for you.' First place was a round-trip ticket to Hawaii to stay at the Kahala Hilton first class for two people.

"They announced: 'The winner of the Most Popular Cowboy is Bob Lilly, and the second-place award goes to John Wilbur.' I got the $1,000 check. I figured what had happened was that I had won, but they couldn't give it to me because I had no name, nobody knew who I was, and there was no PR value to the milk company. So they gave me the second-place award.

"That's the way the Cowboys worked. Unfortunately, the fix was on. And the fix was *always* on. That was a Tex Schramm, Gil Brandt signature. Because of Vietnam a lot of guys were in the reserve. In fact, the way the Cowboys could get rid of guys they wanted to redshirt was to get them in the reserve. Dave McDaniels, a draft choice one year, couldn't play. They didn't know what to do with him. They thought he had potential and wanted to season him, but they didn't want someone else to pick him up, so they put him in the army reserve. They had all kinds of ways to get guys out of the military. There were two or three guys that way. The fix was on, like the Most Popular Cowboy Contest."

When Schramm signed him, he was unaware that John Wilbur would be nothing but trouble for the Cowboys, participating in everything from civil rights activities to antiwar protesting to what Schramm considered the worst sin of all: representing the Dallas Cowboys players for the hated players union.

John Wilbur would play with the Cowboys from 1966 through the 1968 season, when the Cowboys would ship him off to the lowly St. Louis Cardinals. When he refused to go, he was able to get himself sent home, to the L.A. Rams and George Allen. Wilbur insists that he was traded by Schramm only because of his politics. That he became an All-Pro guard for the Washington Redskins makes his suspicions plausible.

As the team (and the country) was being populated more and more with what from Tom Landry's perspective seemed to be "radicals," the job of head coach of the Cowboys would become more and more trying. Now he had John Wilbur *and* Pete Gent.

John Wilbur: "Tom Landry did have a sense of humor. He had a *great* sense of humor. When you got him to smile, it would light up a room, because he was usually so taciturn. Pete Gent would try to get him to laugh. He would wise-crack. If Pete had a shot, he'd take it. Landry didn't mind it much the first two years I played. Then he moved Gent from flanker to split end to tight end to traded. Pete worked his way down the line."

When a person is constitutionally unable to give himself over to authority, he becomes tagged a rebel, like James Dean in *Rebel Without a Cause*, or like Marlon Brando in *The Wild One*. Pete Gent, along with John Wilbur and Don Meredith, became part of the Wild Rebel Bunch on the Cowboys. As a football player, Gent would play an integral role in the team's success in 1966, fighting for every yard, and he would sacrifice his body to the game he loved to play, but it would be his quick wit and sacrilege that people would remember. Like the time in training camp that Gent walked up to a rookie who was reading his playbook. "Don't bother reading it, kid," Gent told him. "Everybody gets killed in the end."

Gent saw himself as the hero in a popular TV series at the time, *The Fugitive*, someone on the run who had to keep one step ahead of management, and that included Tom Landry. At the end of the 1965 season the Cowboys sent questionnaires to their players, asking them to make suggestions to the coaching staff. According to the instructions, the responses would be anonymous. Gent didn't believe a word of it.

Pete Gent: "The only way I kept up with Landry, I read a lot of psychology—abnormal psych.

"They knew they were having problems with the coaches, so after the '65 season, they sent out a questionnaire that was supposed to be anonymous. You were supposed to say anything you wanted about any of the coaches.

"I had just gotten through reading how you could send out supposedly anonymous questionnaires, but they could find out who was actually answering by coding the return addresses in pinholes, and not two weeks later here comes this questionnaire from the Cowboys. I held that son of a bitch up to the light, and there are the f***ing pinholes.

"I wrote that everybody was wonderful."

It did not take Landry long to determine that Gent was a "troublemaker." Early in 1966 Gent found himself in Dutch with Landry for seemingly contradicting him in the newspapers.

Pete Gent: "In training camp Bob St. John interviewed me for a column in the *Morning News*. He asked me, 'How do you think you're going to do?' I said, 'We're going to win the East. I've been here two years now. I know we're going to win it.' At that time you just played the Eastern teams home and away, and you played just one Western Division team. By my third year, I knew who we had and I knew what the other teams had. And I knew what we had in Don Meredith. That ability to lead is so important, to get other guys to do what has to be done and think like you're thinking. Because instead of having 11 guys going in all different directions, you've got them following the game plan and going in the direction that the quarterback is thinking. And so Meredith would call a play, but he would also remind guys in the huddle what they were doing, and tell them, 'Make certain to make this adjustment,' even though it wasn't in the game plan. And lots of times he would call a play designed to do one thing, and he would do something else off of it. The other thing Don knew, when you are like Landry, you are predictable. Pretty soon, even with all the shifting, you could break his game down by percentages, and so Don was just incredible at coming in at the last minute and changing everything and making those drives we had to have. So when St. John interviewed me, I said, 'We are going to go 10–4, and we will win the East.'

"And then he interviewed Landry, who said he hoped to go 8–6 or 9–5, who said he didn't think we had the talent yet to win it.

"Well, Bob St. John ran the interviews like Landry and I were having a conversation with him at the same time, and when it came out, Landry was just f***ing furious. I don't think Landry ever forgave me for that. No. Oh, no. And of course, we went 10–3 [actually 10–3–1] and won the East."

The real trouble between Landry and Gent occurred when Landry didn't start him, even though he was producing and playing well. In the past, when Landry started one player over another, no one said a word. Pete Gent wasn't like that. Gent not only felt that Landry was treating him unfairly, he said that to Landry's face and also told it to the world.

Pete Gent: "In '66, I had a great exhibition season, and Meredith and I had a really good rapport. We were running together. He'd been married and divorced, and married again, and I'm married, and now we're two married guys. He married a woman named Cheryl King. Her father was a big trucking executive in Forth Worth. He married her in the off-season after '65. Yes he did, because I got married in June of '66, just before camp, and after I had been in camp for a while—he had met my wife before we got married, although she was at Michigan State and only came down and visited—he sidled up to me, trying to hem and haw around, wanting to know whether I ran around on my wife. I said, 'Well, not really,' but I liked him so much, I loved running around with him, so we went out every night.

"Dick Nolan was in charge of curfew, so we were in L.A. every night. Of course, we'd get drunk, and Meredith would come back and complain that his arm hurt and miss morning practice, and I'd be out there having to run around, dying. But to me it was a classic example of Meredith knowing what worked, particularly dealing with Landry. You had to stay loose, or you just went crazy. So I had a really good exhibition season, then opened the season against New York, and just blew them away.

"I didn't catch the ball, but otherwise I did my job. I blocked. I was an excellent blocker for a flanker, and in those days you could crack back, so I blocked the linebackers a lot. That's why Dan Reeves had such good running stats, because they always ran to the strong side, and I cracked back on whoever showed up first, a linebacker or whoever, and you'd get such a huge pileup, lots of times it would knock down two or three guys. Anyway, in the Minnesota game, we started out slow. Everybody was having trouble, and Minnesota got up on us by a touchdown. He pulled me at the half, put Buddy Dial in, and Dial caught a five-yard down-and-in for a touchdown. I lost my job.

"And this was how you found out you weren't starting from Landry: when you're starting, he tells everybody his assignment. 'Bobby, you're doing this. Pettis, you're going to do this. Danny, you'll be coming out of the backfield.' And then he said, 'And the flanker will be doing this.' Well, as soon as I heard that, I knew that I wasn't the flanker. And sure enough, come the first full workout with the game plan, Dial was the starting flanker.

"I took it to his face. I went to him. I said, 'This is bullshit.' I told him, 'You say the numbers count. Look at my numbers. Look at Buddy Dial's numbers. He drops more than he catches. You got him out there, and he won't block anybody. You got an offense that has a flanker that has to block. Your outside game isn't there if he doesn't block. He hasn't touched a guy in two years. You have me sitting on the bench.'

"So immediately the papers wanted to know why I wasn't starting. And I went public.

"Landry told the paper, 'I never considered that Gent had the job.' He also said, 'I consider that I have two starters.' But I didn't get off the bench."

Gent would not become a factor in the Cowboys' success in 1966 until the team hit a midseason slump and end coach Red Hickey had to bully Landry into giving Gent another chance to play.

Chapter 24

SUCCESS—AT LAST

In 1966 Tom Landry told his players he was putting more of an emphasis on winning the exhibition games because he wanted to "establish a pattern of winning." He told them, "I want you to get used to feeling the emotions of winning." His players nodded, went out on the field, and won all five preseason games, including their first win ever against Vince Lombardi's Green Bay Packers.

Pete Gent: "The biggest difference in the Cowboys in '66 and the Cowboys I had known in the first couple of years I was playing for them was that now the players were convinced Tom's system was right. When I first joined the team there were a lot of guys on the team who questioned what he was trying to do. There were a lot of personality conflicts between players and coaches, and coaches and players. But Tom Landry stuck to his beliefs and finally won everyone over. You could see the confidence in him growing toward the end of the '65 season. By 1966 he was in charge of the situation.

"I can remember having a long talk with Meredith about it, and at the time I was a little surprised to hear Don defending Landry so strongly. He said, 'Hey, the guy has shown me a lot.'"

Frank Clarke: "We were focused on surrendering and following this amazing leader of ours, and sometimes wondering what he might do next. We could look back to see how and why we got where we were, and we just became more and more and more confident in our offensive ability. By this point, Landry's system was ingrained in us. And during the exhibition season of '66, for the first time, we were even able to beat the Green Bay Packers.

"What we were looking at, we were hearing it from Tom Landry, we were seeing it in the newspapers, we were seeing it in the results of each practice, each week, each game, each experience of competition with other teams, good teams, and the bottom line was: 'We've got every phase of our game covered.' Our running game was going well. We were blocking well. I mean *everybody*—wide receivers like Bob Hayes, who weighed 180 pounds tops, blocking well from out there, enabling guys to get extra yards. We were sharp. The thing I remember most, we were no longer making the mental errors that we used to that had really hurt us a lot, hurt our confidence and also hurt our ability to be a solid offensive team.

"It made sense that we were winning games, that we were beating the teams that used to beat us . . . but when you think about where we were in 1960—how people used to push us around, that we were a laughingstock—in the '66 season that gave us a strong impetus to be even stronger, 'cause we knew that those days were over. We saw how we got where we were and that we could be totally responsible for it, totally responsible, and feel good about it. That was a great feeling to be able to take a look at the complete picture of the Cowboys, from its inception to that '66 season and realize how strong we were, and it was a wonderful, wonderful experience to be a part of that."

When Pete Gent came to the team in 1964, many Dallas sports fans didn't even know who or what the Cowboys were. But by 1966, the Cowboys had indeed become America's darlings.

Pete Gent: "When I was a rookie in '64, I found an apartment directly across from the practice field, where they eventually built the Cowboy Towers. At the time the Cowboys offices were in a temporary building down the street a ways, and across the street on Mockingbird, by the Central Expressway, was a shopping mall. In it was a TV store run by an acquaintance whose father was the sports information director for SMU.

"I wanted to buy a television so I went down there, and since I never had any money, it seemed to me the way you bought everything was on time, and so I filled out a credit report, and he looked at this, and he said, 'The Dallas Cowboys? What are you, in a rodeo?' Now this guy's father was not only in the sports business, he was only a block away from the practice field and the offices, and he didn't even know who the Cowboys were. People in Dallas didn't know who the Cowboys were. The crowds were thirty thousand people, and half of those were black because they were playing in the Cotton Bowl, which is on the black side of town. They were the greatest fans in the world. The end zones were always full.

"In 1964 if you bought an adult ticket, you got five kids in for nothing *and* a free football. Tickets in the end zone were $1. An adult ticket was only $5 or $6 anywhere. The only time we filled the stadium was when Green Bay came.

"By '66 we were sold out every game. In just two years we went from our not being able to get a seat in a restaurant in Dallas to literally being America's guest. I can remember I was driving back and forth across the country then, and if I wanted to drive 100 miles per hour from Texas to Michigan, I just pulled on my Dallas Cowboys practice shirt. I had a souped-up Ford. A state policeman stopped me in Iowa one time. When I got out, the cop saw I was with the Cowboys, and he said, 'Jesus Christ, we needed a plane to catch you. Slow down.' They knew who I was and let me go.

"But you also saw a change in the players. Ralph Neely, when he came in as a rookie in '65, was a sweet kid. By '66 Neely was cruising around in a Mercedes with a car phone going to his oil wells. And Don Meredith and I just used to laugh about it. You saw all these guys believing that suddenly *they* were different. It didn't dawn on them that what had changed was everybody else. *We* were the same people. And interestingly enough there were only a few guys who really grasped that, guys like Don Perkins, Frank Clarke, and Meredith, the guys you'd expect, and also the really bright thinkers in the offensive and defensive lines, guys like Blaine Nye and Larry Cole, John Wilbur, Leon Donahue, Dave Manders, Jim Colvin, and of course, Bob Lilly, who had an innate brilliance about him."

Bob Lilly: "We scored 52 points against the Giants in the opener. We always played well in the opener. Don threw five touchdown passes, two to Bob Hayes, and we were saying to the offense, 'Save some of those for next week. We understand you only have so many of those in you. You don't want to waste them all in one game.'

"In the second game we beat Fran Tarkenton and the Vikings, 28–17. Fran was the greatest scrambler I ever saw in my life. He made an awful lot of yardage and touchdowns out of scrambling. He was a little bit short for quarterback. I think that's why he had to scramble a lot, because we held our hands up, and he couldn't see over us. But boy, he made you really have to watch your pass rush, because you couldn't really cut loose on him.

"The best way to control his passing was to maintain your lanes, as we called it, and keep him in a pocket. When he started rolling out, that was when he killed you. He was a great quarterback. For his size he was one of the best quarterbacks who ever played.

"I can remember that day: it was 90 degrees, and we were exhausted. We called timeout, and Tom sent in one guy as a replacement. All four of us left the field for him to replace us."

Then came a romp over the expansion Atlanta Falcons, 47–14, and a 56–7 stomping over the Philadelphia Eagles. After these offensive showings set a team scoring record, Buddy Dial said about Meredith, "Don was so accurate that he could spit in a swinging jug."

The undefeated Cowboys tied the undefeated St. Louis Cards, as linebacker Larry Stallings led the defense against Meredith, who didn't have much time to operate. But this was a new day for the Cowboys, and even the skeptical Don Meredith was beginning to see that Tom Landry was indeed a master, not some quack with weirdo theories, as had been suspected before.

After the Cards game, Meredith told reporters, "When the Cowboys start winning, we're going to win more consistently than any team who ever won in this league. More than Cleveland, more than the Giants, more than Green Bay. And the reason is Tom.

"Tom is right. You get tired of a guy being so right so often. You almost wish he could be wrong some time. The hardest thing about this system is believing Tom every time.

"I used to fight believing Tom. I really rebelled against it. It was immature and I was stupid, but we were losing and I wasn't used to losing. When every man on this team learns and accepts this about Tom, Dallas will be the world champion."

Against the Cardinals, just before the half, the Cowboys were losing. Buddy Dial had not caught a pass, and from the press box Hickey began screaming down to Landry to send in Gent. The Cowboys had the ball with less than a minute to go in the half.

Pete Gent: "I caught about a 45-yard post in between Larry Stallings and Abe Woodson and fell on the 3. Dan Reeves got in on the next play for a touchdown. We were back in the game. 'Cause you could never blow St. Louis out, they were always tight games. And I caught one other pass in the second half that set up Danny Villanueva to kick the go-ahead field goal, but with hardly any time left in the game, Bob Hayes fumbled a punt, and they moved it down and Jim Bakken tied the game at 10–10. So now, although I played a great game, we didn't win. So now I didn't know what Landry was going to do."

Landry, a thoughtful man, must have agreed that he had been wrong to bench Gent without telling him first, because before the game between Dallas and Cleveland, Landry announced to the players that in the future he would tell a player to his face when he was being benched. In the newspaper that day Landry also announced that Gent would start at wide receiver for the rest of that season. It was a replay of the Meredith drama the year before, only this time no one much cared one way or the other except Pete Gent.

Adding to the intensity of the next game against the Jim Brown–less Cleveland Browns was the publication of a newspaper article written by Joan Ryan, the wife of Cleveland quarterback Frank Ryan, saying that the Cowboys in general and Don Meredith in particular were "losers." She made this observation in a column in *The* (Cleveland) *Plain Dealer* after watching Dallas and St. Louis tie at 10–10.

Pete Gent: "I started against Cleveland, and in that game Don and I went back to our old routine, opening up with quick passes to me, and then the rest of the game I blocked for Don Perkins up the middle. I would come across and generally catch middle linebacker Vince Costello unaware. What Landry did with me was have me cut down my split, and I would just come across the middle and take the middle linebacker on myself. Ask Sam Huff. Sam Huff hates me to this day 'cause it was such an insult for him to be blocked by a wide receiver. And in that Cleveland game we needed a touchdown, and I came across the middle, and I was off-balance so I didn't get down to block Costello, but I got in his way, and Perkins cut off my hip and went in for the touchdown."

Despite Gent's heroics, the Browns won, 30–21. Meredith had one of his worst days. He was intercepted four times. Andy Anderson in the *Dallas Press* wrote that the Cowboys had "choked."

Some of the players agreed with Anderson.

Frank Clarke: "When we went to Cleveland and lost, they wrote that we choked, and it *was* a choke. When we played Cleveland, for some reason or another, we played them like we didn't know who we were. They had a way of just showing up, and we'd forget who we were, and it *was* a choke. When you write about it, that's *exactly* what it was. It's the only thing you could call it. We panicked when we played Cleveland. I don't know what it was. And it wasn't just me, though I felt it. Cleveland was more than just the team I used to play for and wanted to do well against and all this other crap.

"But yeah, that was very well put. We could relate to that. It felt like a choke, but you know what else it felt like? I remember this, too, it also felt like it was a wake-up call that we needed to get, that we aren't there yet, and we know what we need to do 'cause we aren't where we want to be."

Athletes are very sensitive to what is being written about them, and some of the Cowboys players were furious with the negativism of the Dallas sportswriters. The contempt for the writers by some of the players was intense.

Pete Gent: "It was only our first loss of the year. Even though our record was 4–1–1, the headline in the paper said, The Cowboys Choked. For any of us, reading the paper was never a pleasant experience. I would pick up the paper and see an article and glance through it looking for my name to see if I was in trouble. But I wouldn't sit there and read it. Early on I learned from these guys that they weren't talking about what was happening. It was one of the reasons I got the idea that I ought to write a book. That media view of the game, I know, isn't right. That's also why I have no faith in newspapers. Thirty percent of the people buy the paper for the sports pages, and the sportswriters are not correct about *anything*. All they wrote about was numbers, like in Vietnam the way the correspondents wrote about body counts. And this was going on at the same time. 'Cause I would go speak somewhere, and you'd talk to these people who were getting their information from television and the newspapers, and they had such a totally different idea of what was happening in professional football than what was *really* happening."

After a 52–21 shellacking of the Pittsburgh Steelers, the Cowboys lost their second game, this time to the Philadelphia Eagles, when with 90 seconds left in the game second-year back Dan Reeves, who was running for a touchdown, thought he heard a whistle. Relaxing, he was tackled so hard he fumbled, and it was bye-bye ballgame when the referee ruled he had been hit *before* the whistle. In that game Timmy Brown ran back two kicks—of 90 and 93 yards—for touchdowns. On the latter play John Wilbur threw his knee out trying to tackle Brown. Said Wilbur, "He made me cut so radically, my cartilage tore." Wilbur had to have a knee operation and was out the rest of the season.

The next game was against the Washington Redskins. It was the game that made believers out of *everybody*. The Cowboys trailed 30–28 with 1:10 left on the clock. They were on their own 3-yard line, 97 yards away from victory. And they had no timeouts left in the game.

The first play was a 26-yard rollout pass from Don Meredith to Pete Gent. On the next play the Cowboys QB rolled right for 12 yards and then ran out of bounds. After an incomplete pass, Meredith threw a swing pass to rookie Walt Garrison, good for but a yard. It was third-and-nine with 48 seconds left.

Meredith went back to Gent, who gained 25 yards and ran out of bounds. The lanky QB rolled right for 6 yards, and when Redskins linebacker John Reger hit him late, another 15 yards was added to the play.

The Cowboys, miraculously, were on the Redskins' 12 with 15 seconds left.

After the roughing penalty, the ball was moved to the middle of the field, where Danny Villanueva calmly kicked a 20-yard field goal for the 31–30 victory. Said Villanueva after the game, "What if I'd missed it? I'd have gone home. What would I have said to those guys?"

Said Gent about Meredith, "You can't imagine how much this team loves that guy."

Bob Hayes: "We did love Meredith. We really did. We loved him, because he had taken so much abuse. He would go out there and play for you when he should have been in the hospital, and you've got to like somebody like that. I don't know anybody who didn't think a lot of Don. Don would have been at the very highest level if he hadn't gotten killed and got bad-mouthed so much that he just wanted out."

Frank Clarke: "Against Washington we won in the final minutes. Don took us just about the whole length of the field in the Cotton Bowl with no timeouts to win it. The crowd was going berserko. That was so fantastic.

"I know this for a fact: during that drive there were at least six plays that were picture-perfect from what Tom Landry had conceived, put on paper, and we had talked about in our meetings. I can see him now telling Bob Hayes to go down, curl in at 15 yards, and him telling the tight end to run a post or a corner route, which would take this linebacker and this safetyman with him, and it would enable Pete Gent to come underneath and catch the ball, and then flare out to the sideline. This happened for at least five or six plays of that drive.

"Each of us on the field knew that we were doing exactly what we were supposed to do. Those plays were designed to connect so that we could move with that kind of precision for 97 yards without a timeout. Nobody was making a mistake, and everything was happening absolutely perfectly. Walt Garrison or Gent or Reeves was getting the ball, because the play was *exactly* designed for that person to have the ball. And Landry probably was even getting the extra yardage that he wanted out of each play. 'We need 12 yards on this one? Let's get 13.'

"Danny Villanueva kicked a field goal to win the game, and it was absolutely amazing, because we all knew that this was the first time the Cowboys had ever moved the ball with that kind of confidence.

"It probably was the most important moment of our Cowboys offensive history. As you know, the teams that win consistently are the teams that move the ball like that. And here we were—in our infancy! 'Cause we were still a young team, in the league just seven years. To have that experience, you say to yourself, 'Oh my goodness, this is fantastic.'"

Chapter 25

Two Feet Away

The 1966 season ended with four wins in five games, including a spectacular 26–14 Thanksgiving Day victory over Frank Ryan, Leroy Kelly, Paul Warfield, and the rest of the Cleveland Browns in front of 80,259 howling, berserk fans in the Cotton Bowl. The players had not forgotten Mrs. Ryan's article. Before the game in the silent locker room Tom Landry told his players, "I have all the confidence in the world you'll win this game." Afterward, Landry would call the win "the biggest game in our history."

Frank Clarke: "The Cleveland game on Thanksgiving in '66 was the best football game I personally have ever played. I caught the ball well, blocked well, and I was part of this wonderful offensive movement. We were *so* good that day, and I think for the first time, I got a sense of having *fun*. It was beyond a methodical following directions, following our instincts, following our mentor Landry. It was like, 'Wow, man, maybe we can do this consistently.' And God, that was a fun game.

"We had deserved that 'choke' label against the Browns the first time. But we were able to set that aside in terms of, 'Don't lose concentration about who we are and what we're doing here. We're not where we want to be, so yes, when we make a mistake, we're going to learn from it, and we're going to keep moving forward.'

"By the time we came to that week, we had an intensity of purpose. It was a night game, so we practiced late under the lights of the stadium, and I remember during that week that there was an air of confidence around everything that we did, and every movement of our practice. In retrospect, when you saw how we played, it just made total sense. We were ready. All the games we had played in the seven years of being in the league prepared us against Cleveland.

"And it was fun for me, because I had come from Cleveland. These guys *had* given me a hard time, and it was fun to see all of that laid to rest. I knew it was final. It was finally just laid to rest because our offense, aw man, we played so well. The defense did, too, but it's easy for me to remember how easily we moved the football. It was the sweetest victory I can ever remember."

A 34–31 loss in the final four seconds to Washington on a field goal by Charlie Gogolak followed by a 17–7 victory over the New York Giants gave the

Cowboys a regular-season record of 10–3–1, as they won the Eastern Conference championship for the first time. Under the two-division organization of the time, the Cowboys would play the Green Bay Packers for the NFL championship. The winner of that game would play in the first ever Super Bowl, a game arranged as part of the June 8, 1966, merger agreement between Tex Schramm and Lamar Hunt of the AFL. (As part of the new era of good feeling, Tex Schramm and Bud Adams, the owner of the Houston Oilers, agreed that Dallas would get to keep Ralph Neely. In exchange, the Oilers would get a number one draft choice, and most important to Adams, the Oilers would get to play a string of preseason exhibition games against a team that was now being called "America's Team.")

Getting the opportunity to play the Packers for the title meant tremendous satisfaction for the players, but it was especially so for a player like Frank Clarke, who had been there at the beginning.

Frank Clarke: "The NFL title game was against the Green Bay Packers. For Tom and Don and me it meant that hard work, determination, and self-sacrifice had paid off. The Packers had the reputation as being the NFL's best. Their style of play was envious, and it was also well known. They told people: 'We know that you know what we're going to do, and we're not trying to disguise it'—which is the opposite of what the Cowboys did.

"By the time we were playing the Packers in the NFL championship game of '66, their reputation was, 'We're going to do it because we're better than you are.' So that in '66 when the Packers came onto the field to play us in the Cotton Bowl, they *knew* that they would win, and we knew that they knew that. The difference was that we *thought* that we could win, but we didn't *know* that we could win. And that was basically the difference in the game."

Buddy Dial: "The thing about Green Bay was they were not going to beat themselves, and if you made a mistake, you'd lose.

"I remember during our preparation for the game, coach Landry had our whole team together. He was up at the blackboard, and Bobby Hayes and Meredith and I were sitting at the back of the room. Hayes was sitting at his desk, and he was leaning back against the wall. And ole Tom turned around to the blackboard, and he said, 'All this year, Bobby, you have been going deep and Dial and Gent have been coming across the middle.' And he said, 'This week for Green Bay, Dial, you and Gent are going to go deep, and Bobby, you're going to come across the middle,' and from the back of the room we heard Bobby Hayes say, 'Shiiiiiiiiit.' Hell, Landry nearly dropped the chalk. We all fell out of our chairs when Bobby said, 'Shiiiiiiiiit.'

"And in that game he did not run across the middle."

Although it was only nine years since the Giants-Colts championship of 1958, the Packers game was billed as the Game of the Decade. The Cowboys started poorly. On the opening drive the Pack drove 76 yards, as Bart Starr hit halfback Elijah Pitts for a score, and on the ensuing kickoff Mel Renfro fumbled and Jim

Grabowski picked up the ball and ran for a touchdown, making the score 14–0 before the offense had even touched the ball.

Lee Roy Jordan: "We were trying to do too much defensively in the secondary. Under the game plan we were trying to set up our defenses depending on how wide the split end was set. If Boyd Dowler was eight yards out, we were going to play one defense, and if he was fifteen yards out, we were going to play another defense.

"And the first time the Packers got the ball, Dowler moved from a wide position to a closer position, and I didn't see it, didn't hear the call, and so I played the defense for his original position, and in the spot where I was supposed to be, Elijah Pitts caught a pass for a 17-yard touchdown. If I'd have been playing the right defense, I'd have come his way, but because of my mistake it left a big hole in the area where the halfback was running, and Bart Starr picked it up and hit the right guy, and boom, it was a touchdown. They then came back and returned a [fumbled] kickoff for a touchdown, and we were down 14–0, and our offense had never been on the field.

"We were a very inexperienced team wanting to show we could compete against a Green Bay team that knew they were good and had all the confidence of a veteran team that had been in the playoffs and championships. At the end of the game we were throwing at the end zone from five yards away, and that's a great position to be in for the young football team that we were. Had we not made mistakes early, we would have beaten them. But at the time we were just not mature enough to handle them as a defensive football team."

Dallas managed to tie the game at 14–14 before Green Bay scored twice late in the game. In the third quarter Landry began substituting wholesale, prompting some of the players to wonder whether he had given up.

Frank Clarke: "My father was there, my mother was there from Dallas, my brothers and sisters, and I remember catching a 68-yard touchdown pass in that game from Meredith that was really fantastic. The play was red right motion X post. The offensive formation was red right, where I'm at the tight end spot, Pete Gent is the flanker, and Bobby Hayes is the wide receiver. Danny Reeves goes in motion to the left. X is the tight end spot, and what happened was, when Danny Reeves went in motion to the right, Packers linebacker Dave Robinson, who was on my nose, went with the motion man, so it left me uncovered. Now I take off, and I have this wonderful shot at defensive back Tom Brown; I'm looking right at Tom Brown's number, nobody to block me, nobody to mess with me, and I run down, and I make this great inside move, and he goes for it. And then I make another move toward the corner, and he recovers, but as he's recovering, the greatest thing that could happen to an offensive receiver happened: the defensive back fell down. He tripped over his own legs trying to keep up with the offensive move, and that was wonderful, man. You know you have done your job when that happens. So Tom Brown tripped over his own legs trying to keep up with me, and now I break toward the post, and nobody is near me, and

Meredith lofted that ball up there fantastically, but the key to the whole play was not this, 'cause I *knew* I could beat Tom Brown, or any defensive back, one-on-one, no question about it; the key to it was what Bob Hayes was doing over on the other side and what Dandy did. Bob Hayes was split wide to the left on Bob Jeter, and he went down, and he did a great sideline route, and then looked like he was going up, and by his going up toward the end zone, like he was running a fly route, this momentarily made Willie Wood, the weak safety, hesitate. By Bob Hayes momentarily running that route, it froze Willie Wood for just a fraction of a second, and that's all it took, because by the time Meredith put that ball in the air, Willie Wood, with his great speed and ability, was not able to come over in time to catch me running this post route. He dove, and he did clip me, and I can still feel his hand on the back of my left heel, but it wasn't enough. I sped into the end zone with the ball.

"And for a second it seemed as though everything was still. I couldn't hear myself breathe. I could hear nothing. And it seemed as though the Cotton Bowl crowd erupted in this thunderous explosion. I ran into the end zone, ran up to the Cotton Bowl wall, and I handed the ball to a man in the stands there. I later found out that this guy was a Green Bay Packers fan, and he knew I was from Beloit, and he sent me a note thanking me for the ball.

"I went back to the bench, and our defense went in the game, and there were four minutes left in the game, and then, fantastically, the Cowboys got the ball back. We held, four downs. Don Chandler punted, and it went off the side of his foot, a lousy kick. And we're saying, 'We're *supposed* to win this game.' So we went into the game, and we had another third-down call, and we did the same thing, but here's what we did: Dandy said, 'Red right motion, X corner.' So instead of going for the goal post this time, I went to the corner. And everything worked out just fine. Dan Reeves went in motion, and Dave Robinson left me uncovered. I ran down, and this time I made a real strong inside move, and Brown went for it, because he figured we were going to hit a quick post this time. And then when I planted and went back toward the corner, he said, 'Oh my God,' and he was close enough to me to grab my arm, break my stride, but the official saw it and threw the flag, but the ball was still very close because of my power to keep going. I still almost got to the ball, which meant if I had caught it, we would have tied the game.

"And that's when we got the ball on the 1-yard line. And then on the first play, Dan Reeves ran right into the middle of the Packers line, and he was knocked senseless by Lionel Aldridge, and the next play tackle Jim Boeke jumped before the snap, and that put the ball back on the 6. Don threw a swing pass to Dan. We didn't know it, but Dan was seeing double, and he dropped the ball. On third down Don then threw to Pettis, who got down to the 2."

Buddy Dial: "After the Boeke penalty, we were pushed back to the 6. Meredith had a play he wanted to call, and I remember what it was. He wanted to throw to me coming across from the weak side, 'cause I was open all night doing that. But Landry called another play, and Don hated it. Landry wanted to call a turn-in to Pettis Norman. Well, Meredith tried to throw the turn-in to the tight end, and it was crushed up on that side, and it only got us to the 2.

"Don knew what the defense was going to be, but Landry didn't have any confidence in me at that time. Pete was more productive than I was, but Gent was so beat up. It was a weak position at that time, but I remember coming across so open, and oh, mercy, the throw was made to the tight end."

Frank Clarke: "The next play is one that I still wonder about to this day. On short-yardage plays anywhere on the field or in goal-line situations on the field, I was always the tight end. Bob Hayes would come out of the game. I always played the tight end, and Bob Hayes always came out of the game. In this particular situation we had fourth-and-two with 45 seconds left. The Packers had a seven-point lead. A touchdown and extra point would have tied the game. On this particular play, the tight end was supposed to block linebacker Dave Robinson. For some reason or another—and it stunned me, I couldn't figure it out—Tom Landry sent Bob Hayes *into* the game for me. And it was supposed to be the other way around. I was already on the field, so I was getting ready to line up for that short-yardage play. And I couldn't figure out what was going on. I thought, 'This is unlike Tom to try something different. Not in a situation like this.' Perhaps I should have said, 'Excuse me, Coach, for calling timeout, but . . . what's going on? Is this what you want to do?' But I didn't even consider it. Not even close.

"And on that particular play, Bobby Hayes, who had never done this before, had never even practiced doing it, basically he didn't know what to do. Dave Robinson, the big linebacker, just brushed by Bobby like he wasn't even there, and he charged in on Meredith, who was rolling out to the right to throw the pass, and Dave Robinson foiled that. Meredith in desperation threw the ball up in the air, and Tom Brown intercepted it, and that was the game. And I've often wondered, 'Did Tom Landry in his astute way of seeing himself as a coach, did he in that moment want to see that happen, because he knew that if the Cowboys had won that game it would have turned our whole destiny in another way, that it made sense that the Packers would win that game?' 'Cause I was trying to figure out, 'Did he choke? Was it a situation where Tom Landry, the head coach, lost his concentration for the moment?' That might have happened, but I've often toyed with that other idea, that he certainly wasn't trying to lose, that would be impossible to imagine, but did he in some way feel that the destiny of the Packers was that they should win that game, because Tom had a timetable where he was going, and the road map showed the Packers winning that game?

"My primary sense tells me that we were so close to beating the heralded Packers. Even though we were seven points down, there was every reason to believe if we had scored that touchdown, we were going to win in overtime. It might have been so overwhelming to him. He had never been in a situation like that before. His former peer, Vince Lombardi, was heralded. The so-respected

Packers—he had a chance to beat them, so that he probably could not quite get it together. But why would he have sent Bob Hayes into the game? It just stuns me that he would have done something *so* out of character. How do you explain that?"

Pete Gent: "Everyone blamed Boeke's jumping offside for the loss, 'cause NFL Films got such good shots of that. Why did they think that cost us the game? He jumped offside, and we got a five-yard penalty, but we got the down over, and we got the yardage back. It is hard in any game to isolate a single thing and say it is the reason you lost, but a couple of things come to mind more quickly than Boeke's jumping offside.

"Really what cost us the game was that Danny got poked in the eye. He was in the huddle, and we couldn't get him to leave. Danny was one of those competitors. He bought that old philosophy that you played whether you were blind or not. Reeves was seeing double. Hayes had gone right to the end zone and taken everybody with him, and Danny was wide open. That ball came at him, and he needed six pairs of hands to catch the ball. And *that's* what cost us the game.

"It's so strange because you see the play from so many different perspectives. You never really remember where you were. Right now I picture that play as though I were Meredith throwing the ball, 'cause the ball hit Danny right in the chest. But see, Tom Landry loved Danny. So Danny wasn't going to go in for any blame. Danny was man enough to accept blame. He didn't try to dodge it. I have heard Danny talk about how he should have taken himself out of the game. He was a kid. He didn't know what to do.

"I honestly think that the main reason so much attention was dealt to Boeke's mistake was the fact that NFL Films got some really good shots of it. They played that thing over and over, using several different angles. And there was always that deep bass voice of John Facenda dramatically saying how the 'Cowboys' hopes died with that play.'

"They didn't. Shoot, we moved the ball back down to the 2. But again, that points out what was right about what Meredith and I believed, that you have to make the decisions on the field. If you've got half your players paralyzed to move because they are afraid of what the coach is going to say, then Frank Clarke is going to stand there on the sideline when he should be in the game, and Danny Reeves is going to stay in the game when he should take himself out.

"And those are your breakdowns. Those are the breakdowns that kill you. Mental breakdowns kill you 10 times worse than physical breakdowns. If you make mental mistakes, you're going to lose. Everybody makes physical mistakes. The game is played in your head."

Buddy Dial: "After the game, I came off the field, and I walked up to Landry, and they showed that picture before every broadcast of me talking to Landry after the game. Aw, I can't say what I called him. Aw, I was so bad. I called him an ill-advised name. I had a little single-bar face mask, and I was right in his face. It was very embarrassing for me when they replayed that. But we wanted to win so bad. You never saw so many guys cry after a ballgame as we did after that one.

"I blamed Landry for making the wrong call. But he had no reason to have confidence in me. In my heart I wanted the chance to catch it. But everybody did at that point. I didn't justify the ball being thrown to me. I had not been that significant that year. And I really wonder, because that was the type of play I had made all my life. And it was thrown to the other side. And essentially, that was the end of my playing career.

"I know, when watching the film, how wide open I was, because I split out way wide to the left, and came across, and they went strongside, and golly. . . . But it was very frustrating for Meredith and the guys who really deserved to win. I hadn't done anything for the team, but Don really deserved to win that night. But we were real close, running a strong side play, and aw, we should have won that game. Don would have had the satisfaction of winning a championship and going to the first Super Bowl.

"We should have won it. The defense played brilliantly. And the offense had a good day, too. That should have been the beginning of the Cowboys' victory seasons, right there, but we broke down and got beat. If we had won that game, Don would have been the winner he wanted to be, and it would have allowed him to stay at his own choice. But because we lost, there was so much pressure on him. The next year Roger Staubach was behind him, and he did not want to go through another LeBaron/Morton/Rhome episode, and before long he quit."

Frank Clarke: "It was at the end of this game that I was beginning to take stock about 'What in the world is all this about?' Like 'Whoa.' And I remember going into the locker room after we played that game, and it was like a wake, like somebody had died. And I could *not* relate to that. I didn't say it to anybody, but here I was thinking, 'Wow, this is *not right*.' This is really weird. We had had a fine season. We had reached many of our goals. We had even surpassed some of them. And here we had just played one of the best teams in the history of the sport. There had been no NFL playoff game quite like that since 1958, and we had every reason to be proud and pleased with how we had done. It was the last game of the season, we weren't getting ready for another game, and we should have been thrilled.

"I wondered, 'Why are we feeling like this? This does not make sense.' And that's when I started saying to myself, 'Maybe I'm just not cut out for this. Maybe I don't have what it takes.' And I really began to question, 'What the heck is really going on here?' And it was at that point where I felt that, 'Am I looking at a flaw in a coaching philosophy? Is this going to help us, or is this going to tear us down?' 'Cause I felt as if the coaching leadership at that point should have praised us. It would have been a great spot for one of the coaches to say something about the wonderful season we had just had, and that winning or losing that game at that point didn't have anything paramount to do with what we had accomplished. And it wasn't there, and it really took something out of me, and one of the reasons I was feeling that way was because I had just played maybe the finest offensive game I had ever played in terms of producing. I caught four or five passes in that game, and they were either third-down plays or touchdown plays. And I blocked well, and all in all, our offense was coming through, and it was just a great game.

"I didn't express this to anyone, because it didn't seem as though the other guys felt that way. I wondered, 'Why was our Cotton Bowl locker room so damn dismal after that game?' It just did not make any sense at all. So I doubt very many guys were feeling the way I was. If more guys felt that way, it probably would have had a way of manifesting itself, a way of lifting the doldrums of that place.

"And in the papers, Landry *wasn't* praising us. He was saying, 'We blew it.' That's when I began to question something that I had never questioned before. It was, 'Maybe I don't know what this guy sees. Maybe I don't see what he sees.' How could this be the feeling, especially at the end of this fine season? My God.

"I don't know, Tom might have seen his faux pas for leaving Hayes in for me on that key play. He might have been feeling so responsible that he couldn't bring himself to say what he might have otherwise said to his team after such a great season, 'cause it did not make sense, did not click that we should feel the way we were feeling after such an outstanding season.

"It was so weird. 'Tom, what's missing here?' Something is missing. And we looked to him. I know I did. I thought about it. But after that experience I knew I was playing one game at a time. I knew that I wasn't going to be there, and even if I was there, I wasn't going to be there, because I didn't know what it was going to take. I got a sense of it, what it took to be on an NFL team, on a Landry team, as close to the brink of champion as we were. And I saw I didn't fit in there."

Chapter 26

Lance on the Flank

Pete Gent: "In '65 we had been sitting in a meeting at our old practice field, the first one of the regular season. It was raining, a miserable day, and Al Ward, the assistant general manager, a really nice guy, came in and announced, 'We have word that Lyndon Johnson has plans to accelerate the war in Vietnam, and the draft lists are going to go way up. So any of you guys aren't in a reserve unit, get in one.' Ward said that football was no longer going to be a safe haven and that they were holding guard unit spots for everybody. And this was before anybody had seen a word in public print.

"John Hannah, the president of Michigan State, was a friend of mine, and so my first year with the Cowboys the college carried me as a student, so I still had a 2-S deferment, even though I was living in Texas. The draft board I was under was twelve hundred miles away in Paw Paw, Michigan, and their high school was in the same conference as my high school, and they hated me and my brothers. We always kicked their ass. So it wasn't long before they found out I was in Texas playing football, and the next year, '66, I didn't get away with a 2-S deferment, so on Al Ward's instructions, I decided I better get into a guard unit.

"My board in Michigan waited six months and then called me up for a physical, which I failed, and they did that every six months from 1965 to the spring of 1967. So I had taken four physicals down there, flunked them all, and by May of '67 the trip to the mailbox had become a literal nightmare. Finally one day, I walked to the box, and I saw another letter from Selective Service, and I thought, 'Aw f***,' another physical, another trip through that nightmare. But instead, it was a letter telling me I had been inducted, that I had to report to Fort Wayne on July 13, which was two days before training camp was to start.

"In February, I was desperate. I couldn't get any help. No one would help me. I didn't know what to do. So I went to the Cowboys, and I said, 'You have to help me.' Tex Schramm said, 'Don't worry, we'll help you.' And immediately Tex traded for Lance Rentzel.

"I imagine the Rentzel trade was already in the works, but it sure was strange. 'Yeah, we'll help ya.'"

Gent had reason to be worried. The weekly casualty rate for American servicemen in Vietnam was reaching an alarming level. In April 1967 heavyweight champion Muhammad Ali, formerly Cassius Clay, refused to go based on religious grounds, and he was stripped of his title. Officially, we were winning the war. Said General Westmoreland, "We are winning slowly but steadily." No one who faced induction cared much whether we were winning or not.

Gent got his deferment only after fate intervened. He became drinking buddies with a lawyer who represented the Buick dealership that sponsored his five-minute weekly radio show. The lawyer, who had fought in World Wars I and II, was a retired inspector general, and he wrote letters appealing Gent's draft status to every Democratic representative from Texas. In July 1966, two days before Gent was to begin down the path leading to Vietnam, Texas senator Lloyd Bentsen stopped his induction and got Lewis Hershey, the head of the Selective Service, to order a medical deferment for Gent and to write him an apology. (About that time Gent's brother was also inducted, but he never served because on the way to the induction the Detroit riots forced police to turn back their bus. Their papers got lost in the bureaucracy, and none of the people on the bus were ever called.)

Gent's body may have been saved from shrapnel wounds, but his days with the Cowboys appeared numbered with the arrival of Lance Rentzel in 1967. In Rentzel the Cowboys were getting a talented kick- and punt-return specialist who had the speed to become an excellent receiver. Rentzel had suffered in Minnesota from not getting along with Vikings coach Norm Van Brocklin. Like Gent, Rentzel was an odd mix of intelligence and jock. His mom had wanted him to go to Princeton, but Rentzel instead went to Bud Wilkinson's football factory at the University of Oklahoma, where he played with one of the most famous football crazies in American sports, the uncontrollable Joe Don Looney. Also on that Sooners team was Cowboys tackle Ralph Neely, who himself gained notoriety for signing contracts with two pro teams while in school.

Rentzel's attraction toward the opposite sex brought him his share of negative publicity. Before the Senior Bowl in Mobile, Rentzel was attacked in the bed of a beautiful German fräulein by her pissed-off boyfriend. The police had to be called.

Rentzel played two years as a Viking, mostly on special teams, running back punts and kickoffs. On May 2, 1967, the Vikings traded Rentzel to the Cowboys. Rentzel was an exhibitionist, and his compulsive disorder had become somewhat public after an incident in Minnesota. No mention was made of his prior problems in any of the articles in the Dallas papers.

Pete Gent: "When Lance came to camp in '67, he was there to take my job. I knew that. And by this time I had enough experience, had seen all the tricks you could play on a guy. I had seen that if you can't beat a guy on the field, you f*** with his head. Already the rumors were around about him. So I figured I would take his head away from him. We'd get out on the field, and we'd start running pass routes, and I just wouldn't let him ever run when he wanted to.

"You'd line up and take turns, and I would always make him run with the second- or third- or fourth- and fifth-string quarterbacks so he couldn't get any timing with Meredith. I just pushed him out of the way and stepped in front of him. I was just dominating him. And he was a real sweet kid.

"He was already having problems, because guys like Lee Roy Jordan knew all about Minnesota, so they were already calling him a 'fag,' which he wasn't. That wasn't his problem. And so even when he was playing for Minnesota, everybody *knew* he was an exhibitionist. Van Brocklin, the Vikings coach, would call him a 'flasher' in team meetings. So that was an open secret when he came to the Cowboys, although nobody talked about it. He and Ralph Neely had played together in college at Oklahoma, and Ralph knew, but everybody went into denial except guys like Lee Roy, who were so cruel to him. Lee Roy thought being an exhibitionist was the same thing as being a fag and a child molester, and treated him accordingly, so there was all that pressure on Lance, plus the pressure to perform, which comes with playing the game. And here I was, just f***ing with him, just playing with his head. He was a big, tough, muscular kid. He didn't take any shit. And maybe he couldn't have kicked my ass, but he would have hurt me.

"One day when I tried to do it he turned to me with the saddest eyes, and they just welled up with tears, and he said, 'Why are you so mean to me? I didn't do anything to you.' And I stepped back, and I thought, 'My God, I'm doing the very thing that I resent guys like Lee Roy Jordan doing. Look what I have become.' And after that, we became friends."

When Rentzel came to the Cowboys, he became the regular flanker and Gent became a backup, which only made the outspoken Gent more biting and sarcastic in his jibes at Landry and what he perceived to be the coach's humorless approach to what he felt should have been a fun game.

One time after Bob Hayes was injured during a game in Pittsburgh, on the return flight Landry decided he'd move Gent from flanker to the other side, split end, where he'd start against Philadelphia in Hayes' spot. Landry walked to the back of the plane and told Gent, "Pete, you'll be moving to the other side this week. So get ready."

"You mean, Coach, that I'm going to play for Philadelphia?"

Landry inhaled deeply and walked back up the aisle.

In the second preseason game Meredith cracked two ribs, and against San Francisco, Craig Morton came in and won the game. Morton played outstandingly the rest of the preseason. Instantly there rang a chorus that Morton should be the number one quarterback.

Frank Clarke: "Don got hurt, cracked two ribs in the second preseason game, so then Craig Morton came in and won, and immediately the fans started calling for Morton to be the quarterback. I don't know why. What did those people want from Don? When you hear about some of the things that go on in our great Southwest . . . The fans were saying they wanted him traded, and don't you know, Don was deeply hurt."

In addition to fans calling for Meredith's benching, trade rumors persisted. Gent blamed Landry for allowing them to spread.

Pete Gent: "In '67, in the preseason, there were all these trade rumors, which I never believed, because Clint Murchison never would trade Don, he was too close to him, but there was a strong call from the fans to trade him. And again, this all came from Tom Landry. A lot of it was a result of Landry's inability to control Meredith.

"Landry wanted to control Meredith, and when he couldn't, whenever anything went wrong, Tom allowed the blame to fall on Meredith, rather than ever shouldering it himself. Most of it seemed to fall on Don Meredith, and I liked Meredith, and what fell on me—a lot I drew on myself, but I also felt it was my job to protect my quarterback, even if I had to protect him from the coach."

It was to be a year in which Meredith would need a lot of protection—from his coach, from the Dallas fans, and from defensive behemoths intent on breaking his bones. His agony began in the very first exhibition game against Green Bay at home when he was booed during the introductions. In the next game Ernie Ladd of the Houston Oilers grabbed him with 41 seconds to go in the game and KO'd him with a body slam and broke his nose. Against San Francisco his ribs hurt, and they were reinjured against Baltimore in the second quarter of the final exhibition game. Meredith escaped further damage in the season opener in a big win against the Cleveland Browns, and he was relatively unscathed against the New York Giants, though Gent was seriously injured when middle linebacker Vince Costello kneed him hard in the back, cracking several ribs. After a loss to the Rams, Meredith led the Cowboys to a stirring win over the Washington Redskins when he completed a 36-yard touchdown pass to Dan Reeves with only 10 seconds left in the game. A few plays earlier Redskins linebacker Chris Hanburger had broken Meredith in half when he crashed through and mashed the Cowboys quarterback into the ground.

After the game a reporter asked Landry why he hadn't noticed that Meredith was woozy and why he hadn't taken him out of the game. Standing near his quarterback, Landry said sarcastically, "Well, I can't tell the difference."

On Sunday and Monday night Meredith had trouble sleeping. On Tuesday he went to Presbyterian Hospital in Dallas, where doctors found fluid in his lungs. As a result of Hanburger's hit, Meredith had suffered a partially collapsed lung. He lost 20 pounds and would miss the next three games.

Pete Gent: "If you look at the clips of that Washington game, Meredith was getting hit by two and three guys all the time. He was getting sandwiched between two defensive linemen continually—somebody had to help him to his feet after each play—and when in that last drive he punctured a lung, he still got up.

"On fourth down, Meredith hit Dan Reeves down the sideline, and Dan ran in for the winning touchdown with 10 seconds left in the game. Two days later Don was in the hospital, having his lung pumped up. I snuck into the hospital, had to sneak by the desk, and got to see him. They were pumping his lung back up, and he was just in agony, crying. After they finished, we talked for about five or ten minutes, and then I went to the practice field.

"When you got to the practice field, the first thing you did was get dressed and taped, and then you went to the team meeting. You have a general meeting, and then you break up into groups. Before looking at the films, Landry would make general statements, comments, and at this meeting he never said anything about Meredith being in the hospital with a punctured lung. And then during the films he tore Don apart.

"For me that was the last f***ing straw with that guy. I wanted out of there. I knew I was only going to play if they needed me, and the minute they didn't need me, I was gone. And I knew that it didn't matter how well I did. I could call Tom an asshole to his face, and he wasn't going to trade me until he had somebody to play my spot, and the moment he had somebody to play my spot, I was gone. And so from then on, that was my attitude toward Tom Landry and the rest of the organization going all the way up to Tex Schramm."

Chapter 27

AGONY

With Don Meredith out with a collapsed lung, quarterback Craig Morton filled in and showed skill, winning games against the New Orleans Saints and the Pittsburgh Steelers before losing to the Philadelphia Eagles. Meredith announced he would return against the Atlanta Falcons, promising the offense would score 35 points against the second-year team; the final score was 37–7. Meredith hit running back Dan Reeves six times for 114 yards and two touchdowns. In that game Reeves, playing in his third year, scored four times, a club record. With Tom Landry's new strategy at work, only one pass went to a wide receiver all game long; Bob Hayes caught it for 34 yards. At the end of the game Meredith told reporters, "Don't let this get around, but we are going to win the whole thing."

In the next game Meredith led the Cowboys to a 27–10 win over the New Orleans Saints before 83,437 unruly drunks and drunkettes in the Sugar Bowl. The highlight of the game was a 56-yard touchdown run on a reverse by Frank Clarke, who most of the season was playing part-time, coming in at tight end in short-yardage situations to take advantage of his superior blocking. This scintillating run indirectly led to Clarke's decision to retire at the end of the season.

Frank Clarke: "I had a good game against the Saints. On an end around Dandy gave this great reverse to me, and I went untouched, unscathed, at scalded-dog speed, 56 yards for a touchdown, and that was enough for our victory. That came at a good time, too, because we were losing to an upstart team that we should have beaten easily.

"After the game we went back to Dallas, and on Monday the television reporter, Verne Lundquist, called me and said, 'Meet me downtown. I want to do an interview with you.' I said, 'Sure.' So we were talking about the game and my career, then in its 11th year, and he asked me, 'Frank, do you think you might play two or three more years?' And that sounded very reasonable. I wasn't slowing down. I said, 'No, Verne, it's possible that this could be my last season.' And then we went on to talk about other things.

"The next morning in *The Dallas Morning News*, the headline said, Frank Clarke Announces His Retirement from Pro Football. I said to myself, 'Aw, you guys did it again. Aw, man.' So that was the way it came out.

"Neither Tom Landry nor Tex Schramm said anything to me, and I didn't say anything either, didn't go to Tex Schramm and say, 'Let's set the record straight.' I didn't tell them exactly what happened. I don't know why I didn't. One of the reasons I didn't, I guess, was fate, that I really *was* supposed to retire. That's the only answer I could have to why I didn't go to them at that time."

Meanwhile, throughout the season the battle raged between Tom Landry and Pete Gent, who never stopped trying to get his job back after Landry gave it to Lance Rentzel. The anarchistic Gent went so far as to put himself into ballgames behind the coach's back.

Pete Gent: "I figured he wouldn't notice. If I put myself in the game ten times, he would catch me four, and then he'd send the guy back in and glare at me when I came off. And that would be it.

"We had quite a thing going. I'm the only guy he would ever call into his office to tell me I was going onto the bench. He'd call me in the first of the week, have a long talk with me. We literally had meetings every week or so."

Gent was tough, and he was persistent. It took a broken back suffered the third game of the season against the Giants to keep him out of the lineup, and even then it was not for long.

Pete Gent: "Against the Giants I caught a ball in the dirt over the middle. I didn't want to get up. I knew the moment I did, somebody was going to kill me. I had gotten the first-down yardage, so I just laid there. Well, Vince Costello, the Giants middle linebacker, rather than touch me, decided he would jump about six yards through the air and bury both knees into my lower back, and from the waist down I was paralyzed. I had no feeling. My left leg drew up, for some reason, was pulled up. My knee was up in the air and my foot was on the ground, and it was just dead. There was no feeling. I could not feel my leg. I couldn't lift it or get it to straighten out. And my right leg was just burning like fire, and then on the left side I had absolutely no feeling. And the trainers and team doctor came out, and I said, 'I've broken my back.' And they said, 'No, no, you haven't.' I said, 'I *have* broken my back. I can't feel anything in my left leg. I can't move it.' They said, 'Move your left leg.' I said, 'I can't move my leg. It doesn't move. I've tried.' 'Move your leg.' 'I can't do it.' So they just lifted me up by the shoulders and dragged me off the field at the 18-yard line and laid me facedown on the sideline and left me there. They went back to the bench.

"And this was in the first quarter. It took me until halftime to get to the bench, about 20 yards. I crawled back to the bench, and I said, 'I have to go in. I'm hurting.' I was on my feet, but I hurt so bad I couldn't stand. I kept falling. So I got up and I was almost to the tunnel when halftime broke, so when the team ran over, a couple guys helped me into the locker room, where they laid me down on the training table and then called an ambulance, took me to the hospital, x-rayed my back, and I had fractured vertebrae in the lumbar region of the spine.

"The doctors didn't give a shit. They literally did not care. It was a bad injury. What the Cowboys wanted to do was waive me through, but the Falcons and the

Giants kept trying to pick me up, so they had to put me on injured reserve, kept me out 30 days, but I was back out trying to run the next week. And it hurt so bad. And what I didn't realize was that I had truly paralyzed some muscles. I had lost muscles from the mid-lumbar down to my hip, and to this day I have no feeling there, and so to run, I had to learn to throw my left leg. I couldn't run in the normal fashion. I had to throw the leg, and that's how I learned to run, and so I was really ready to play by playoff time. I was running at a pretty good rate again, and I was taking a lot of painkillers.

"They tried to play me the next week, shot my back full of novocaine, and I got halfway through the warm-ups against the Rams, and so then they put me on injured reserve. And then against the Cleveland Browns in the conference championship playoff game I got in for one play, and I broke my leg.

"Tom put me in for Hayes for one play. One play! I was to crack back, and we were going to run to the weak side, so I was in for Hayes, who had just run a fly route and wanted out. So he signaled me, and since I was in, we decided to run a quick pitch to Walt Garrison to the weak side, and I was to crack back on whoever showed up first. It was the cornerback. While I was blocking him, the safety went at Garrison, and my recollection is that Garrison spun him off and swung him around, and he hit me right above the ankle with the heel of the shoe. Well, I thought I had just been kicked, so I pushed off that leg to keep blocking, and my foot turned around backward. And I went down, and I looked at it, and at first I thought I just knocked my shoe off. And then I looked at my foot, and uh uh, I'll never forget it, the official came by, and I grabbed him by the pant leg and I pointed down to my foot, and I said, 'I've broken my leg,' and he said, 'Well, do you want to call a timeout?' And I looked at him for a minute, and I said, 'I can't. I'm not the captain.' He said, 'Oh, OK,' and walked away. And I laid there for what seemed like an hour. It hadn't hurt yet, but I knew it was coming. And finally, Craig Morton, who was standing over me, called timeout.

"I was in a hip-length cast for 13 weeks after that. I can remember looking down, remembering my shoe had been knocked off, because it was backward at such an odd position, and then I saw my foot was in it! My ankle was so messed up I had to be in a hip-length cast. They had to operate that night, put two screws in it. All the ligaments were torn out."

Gent was through for 1967; his friend Don Meredith, meanwhile, had continued to suffer from one injury after another. In a win against Philadelphia in the second-to-last game of the season, Don broke his nose. And just before halftime in the finale, a loss to the San Francisco 49ers, linebacker Stan Hindman threw him to the ground with an armhold with such brute force that he lay on the ground holding his left knee, writhing in pain. Meredith did not return the rest of the contest, and there was concern that he would not be able to perform in the playoffs.

Finishing at 9–5, the Cowboys had won their division the second year in a row, but this year they would have to defeat *two* teams to reach the NFL finals.

Because of the merger with the AFL and expansion there were now four divisions, and the first opponent was the champion of the new Century Division, the Cleveland Browns, led by Frank Ryan, Paul Warfield, and Co. Only four days before the game the Cowboys grieved for Bob Lilly after his seven-week-old daughter, Carmen, died suddenly in her crib.

Bob Lilly: "That was so sad. I'm the one who found my daughter. She was already . . . Earlier in the morning I had heard her. It was pretty early when I went up, around 7:00. I assumed everything was fine. We had all our kids upstairs. There were three others. Anyway, she had already turned blue and was starting to get kind of hard. I screamed, and that's when my wife went up, and she screamed. It was sad; it was tough. Then we had to do the funeral and get ready to play, and it was very difficult.

"My teammates were very supportive. We had a big funeral. Everybody was there from the Cowboys. Then they did an autopsy, and it was really terrible. It was crib death. Her lungs had filled up. It was one of those deals.

"Practicing was my only way of getting relief, and I wouldn't have missed that game for anything. But it was very sad. It was one of those times. It ended up helping to destroy my marriage. I married again a couple of years later. It just happened, one of the things in life that happens. It's like the Kennedy weekend. It's hard to remember. I just went out there against Cleveland and played as hard as I could."

The Cleveland playoff game was a crowning achievement for both Bob Lilly—who had one of his greatest days, sacking Frank Ryan three times and batting down two passes—and for Don Meredith, who discarded his specially made face protector, wrapped his aching knees, and played an almost flawless ballgame, going 10 for 12 for 212 yards and two touchdowns, including an 86-yarder to Bob Hayes. The Cowboys won this big game, 52–14, in front of 70,786 screaming Texans in the Cotton Bowl. Before he left the field, Meredith shook hands with each of his offensive linemen.

On defense the line of Willie Townes, Jethro Pugh, Bob Lilly, and George Andrie stopped Leroy Kelly and the Browns' running game. Defensive back Cornell Green stymied Browns star receiver Gary Collins and ran an interception back 60 yards for a touchdown.

Cornell Green: "In '67 we played the Browns in the first round of the playoffs, and Don Meredith had one hell of a game. We weren't on the field a lot. The defense was very seldom on the field. I remember every time Meredith got the ball, he would walk them right down the field and score. And then you'd get a punt, and here he comes again, walking them right down the field.

"The offense makes it easier for the defense. If you have your offense putting points on people, that determines what they can do to you. If we *know* they have to pass to catch us, it makes it easier playing defense. In other words, a strong offense makes our job easier because as long as our offense is holding the ball, the other team can't get on the field to score against us. And that's exactly what happened that day."

The Cowboys for a second year in a row were one game away from playing in a Super Bowl. To get there they would once again have to defeat Vince Lombardi's Green Bay Packers.

John Wilbur: "Vince Lombardi was a monkey on Tom Landry's back. He had been an old teammate on the New York Giants. I expect if you look deeply into his history, you'll find that Lombardi was always the monkey on Landry's back. Lombardi wanted the players to do what he wanted them to do, to depend on him, and at the right time come together, and history shows they did. And in the end Landry didn't. Landry never did conquer Lombardi's world. Lombardi always outsmarted him."

Chapter 28

The Ice Bowl

This game, played in frozen Wisconsin on the coldest December 31 in Green Bay history, would forever be known to those who played in it as the Ice Bowl.

Frank Clarke: "We arrived in Green Bay on Saturday. We landed in Appleton, Wisconsin. It was a wonderful day. Practice was great, the sun was shining, it was beautiful, 35 degrees, the field was fine. God, we were *high*. We just *knew* we were going to play well. When we met the Packers the year before, we *thought* we could win. This time we *knew* we were going to win that game. No doubt whatsoever. We didn't have an ounce of doubt that we were going to play well and win.

"But in that part of Wisconsin in December, anything can happen. It could snow. It could be 0 degrees for days. Sunday morning, the day of the game, the operator called us. We got that wake-up call, just so we'd be in rhythm. I still remember answering the phone. The operator said, 'Good morning, boys. It's 7:30 in the morning. It's 13 degrees below zero.'

"I said, 'I beg your pardon. Thirteen degrees *below zero*?' Ow, God. We weren't prepared for that, so it was demoralizing. I just was not ready for that. It was almost like, 'Are the heavens against us again? What is this? How could this be—to go from such a fantastic day?'

"In just a few hours the field was totally frozen, and not only that, the winds were due to pick up. So we not only had very cold weather, but added cold with the wind blowing. It was so bad people risked really getting hurt playing in that kind of weather. But there was no way the game was going to be postponed, absolutely none, so consequently the game went on."

Bob Lilly: "Everyone says there are some things in your life you never forget, and one was when our president was shot, and another was the Ice Bowl. I may have forgotten a lot of other things, but I will never forget the Ice Bowl.

"Lombardi had installed a system of pipes underneath the ground that were warmed by water going through them, and the day before the game we went to the stadium to work out. The field *was* in good shape, though just a little bit damp. You could wear real cleats. The turf was pretty good, and the temperature was nice, the wind wasn't blowing, just a pretty day, and when we warmed up we didn't even feel the cold at all, so we were all happy. We all knew a cold front was coming, but it wasn't supposed to get there until after the game, sometime the next night. So we weren't concerned about that.

"We had our meetings. We were in great spirits. We were finally relatively healthy. The Packers were beat up pretty bad. We hadn't had a great year, but we had become better and better as the year went on.

"The next morning George Andrie, my roommate, got up and went to Mass at about 6:30 or 7:00, and he came back about 7:30. I was up, watching TV. He came in and didn't say a word. We were in a Holiday Inn. He got a glass of water and threw the water on the plateglass window. Half the water froze before it got down to the windowsill. He said, 'Bob, it's cold. It's already 10 below, and there's about a 35-mile-per-hour wind out. It's supposed to be 20 below by game time.'

"We were pretty somber at breakfast. We went on out to the field, got dressed, and as we were going to go out and warm up, he said, 'You and I are going to have to be leaders out there today. I grew up in this weather,' and he talked me into not wearing any longhandles or any warm-up jacket, because we were going to show these guys that it wasn't that bad.

"And so I walked out that door, and when I did, I said to myself, 'You fool, you fool.' I looked at George, and I said, 'Don't ever ask me to do anything like this again.' I froze to death. I had icicles hanging out my nose about four inches. And I was absolutely freezing. I just barely got through warm-ups.

"We went back into the locker room, and I put on everything I had. I got my longhandles out, put Saran Wrap on my feet, put an extra pair of socks on. Ernie Stautner wouldn't let us wear gloves. Ernie said, 'Men don't wear gloves in this league.' We went back out, and every guy on Green Bay had gloves on, and as a result we all got frostbite. I didn't get much, but we all got frostbite. And we about froze to death.

"I remember the first play vividly. The referee blew his whistle, and it froze on his lip. He pulled part of his lip off, and the blood froze down his chin. After that, they wore Vaseline.

"That was the beginning of the game, and as it went on the conditions got worse. The field wasn't totally frozen when we started, but by the first quarter I had already taken my cleats off and put on my soccer shoes. We were starting to slide around. I was really having a field day then because Gale Gillingham had on his cleats, and he was trying to figure out what was going on, because I was getting around him so fast. So he put on his soccer shoes, and by the time the end of the game came, we were on a solid sheet of ice, all the way from the 20-yard line in."

Lee Roy Jordan: "In my mind we were a better football team than Green Bay that day. We were a pretty darn good football team at that time, but the conditions eliminated a lot of our offense. We were a speed team. We depended on Bob Hayes and Lance Rentzel, and to win, those guys had to make big plays, and I don't know if Bob caught a pass all day. He had his hands down his shorts trying to keep them warm, and hell, it *was* cold. I went out there at the start of the game to show them how to be tough. In warm-ups and the first series I didn't wear any gloves, because Ernie Stautner wouldn't let the linemen wear gloves, and I was one of the leaders on defense, and I wasn't supposed to do anything to show the guys I was a pansy. But about the second series I went to the equipment manager, and I said, 'Where are the gloves? I don't care what it shows. I want a pair. I'll be a pansy if you want me to. I got to have some gloves. My hands are killing me.'"

Frank Clarke: "Midway through the second quarter, a few minutes before the end of the half, I was lined up in my tight end spot, and I ran down this frozen field. You can't imagine what it's like to play on concrete in cleats—so many of the things you did well and easily were totally negated. Hell, you were just trying to stand up, just trying to stay on your feet, let alone throw a block or make a catch.

"I ran a play where I threw a block at a safetyman, Tom Brown or Willie Wood, and I was walking back to the huddle, and I got about two feet away from Ray Nitschke, and he turned, and he started screaming at me, 'Get away from me, you son of a bitch. I'll break your f***ing neck.' And I looked and he had white froth in the corners of his mouth, and I could see this glare through his face mask. It was like Nitschke was going to literally rip me apart merely because I was so close to him.

"Willie Davis came over, and he put both his hands on my shoulders, and he turned me away from Ray, and he said, 'Don't worry about it, man. Just go on back to the huddle.' This was Willie Davis, his own teammate.

"I thought, 'What in the world is with this guy? He is really strange.' I had never heard about Nitschke doing this. I had played against him before. But there was something about him that day. Man, he was weird."

The Packers led at the half 14–10 on two Bart Starr touchdowns to their little-noticed big-play man, Boyd Dowler. The Cowboys scored on a fumble recovery and seven-yard run by George Andrie and a Danny Villanueva field goal, as the conditions stifled the Dallas passing offense.

Pete Gent: "Had I not been injured, the Ice Bowl is one game I would have played, because I knew Bob Hayes couldn't play in that cold. The nature of his hands were that he had no moisture in them. His hands were extremely dry, and that cold just split his hands open. A lot of the guys got frostbite real bad, and it still bothers them to this day."

Of the receivers only Lance Rentzel was effective, and when in the fourth quarter he caught a 50-yard bomb from halfback Dan Reeves over a slipping and sliding Packers defense, the Cowboys took a 17–14 lead.

Frank Clarke: "We played admirably, under those conditions and meeting the challenge as we did, leading in the game up until the end like that. I remember catching a couple of passes in the game, but basically what I liked was the way our offense did keep moving. We didn't just fall flat under those conditions. Most people thought that because of the weather the Packers had the advantage, but we knew that was bullshit, because *nobody* had any advantage. The Packers didn't practice in that kind of weather. It wasn't as though they were used to it. In fact, they probably had as many guys as we did from the South, and there is no way they could be used to that. They never played in it before.

"I can't begin to tell you how cold it was. There was *nothing* warm about me. Nothing. Our hands couldn't get warm. They had these hot air blowers that seemed to blow hot air on you, but you had to be standing right in front to get any sense of beginning to warm up, and the second you stepped away from it you were cold again."

With the Cowboys ahead 17–14, the Packers took over on their own 31-yard line with 4:50 left. The last 10 times the Packers had the ball, the most they could advance was 14 yards. It appeared that there was no way Starr could move the ball under such adverse conditions and that the Cowboys would fulfill their destiny and get into Super Bowl II.

John Wilbur: "I was counting on my trip to the Super Bowl."

The final drive was Packers quarterback Bart Starr at his best. He threw short passes under the coverage to backs Donny Anderson and Chuck Mercein, and he had a little help from the officials.

Cornell Green: "They had some lucky plays, and then the ref made them a big call, pass interference on Dave Edwards. That was a big play, and I say that was the worst call I've seen in history. It was *really* a bad call. I was standing right by him. Bart Starr passed to Donny Anderson, and Donny Anderson had Dave beat, and Dave was running trying to catch him, and the ball hit Dave in the back of the helmet, hit him in the head, and the ref called pass interference, saying Dave face guarded him, and Dave was just trying to catch him. Anderson was three yards ahead of Dave, and Bart Starr just threw a bad pass. And the referee called a penalty and gave them a first down. That would have been a *fourth* down. That was the game.

"I started yelling, complaining, and the ref told me, 'It was face guarding.' You can call it anyway you want, but the only way you can face guard, you have to put your hands up in the air and wave them. If the ball hits you in the back of the helmet, you're just running. That ain't no face guarding. That was just a bad pass."

Frank Clarke: "I was watching a guy named Chuck Mercein be heroic. It was the only time I can remember being in a game when I felt pissed off. I thought, 'This is not right.' Our great linebackers, Chuck Howley, Dave Edwards, and Lee Roy Jordan—there were none better—went for Chuck Mercein to stop him at the line of scrimmage, just routine tackles, and Chuck Mercein, for heaven's sake, a guy who had been around, been with four or five different teams, all of a sudden he's making it look like he's the star of the NFL championship?

"Edwards and Howley would slip on the frozen field, and Mercein would make enough yardage to make a first down. This was the way they moved the ball down there. Remember how they got the ball down there? It was not great football. It was *lucky* football, which was what I hated, and what I was feeling pissed off about. I was thinking, 'The best team is not going to win this game, the luckiest team is.' For the first time in a game, I was feeling, 'God, this is not right. Who's against us?'"

Chuck Howley: "They were running but two plays on us, an option deal, and I remember vividly my frustration that if we defensed one, they hit the other. The offense had the advantage because as a linebacker I had to help my defensive halfback on a down-and-in pattern, which he couldn't cover when he had to cut. I'd get back to take away the down-and-in, and they'd throw a little circle pass, which was my responsibility. I wasn't able to get back as quick. And I was faced with having to make an open-field tackle, which I did about half the time, because on a frozen field, you have one shot, and it better be the right one. So it was a frustrating game for us, and for myself individually. We lost that game on a quarterback sneak, and that's what makes the game of football so great."

The Packers had the ball fourth down and six inches to go at the goal line. There were 13 seconds left in the game. Green Bay had no timeouts. In their prior two plays, back Donny Anderson made plunges from the 1, but each time was stopped by the dogged Dallas defense.

Starr was at a loss what to do. If another running play failed, the game would be over. Nevertheless, Starr decided he would call his own number and run a quarterback sneak. He figured the defense would be keying on the backs. The play called for center Ken Bowman and guard Jerry Kramer to double-team defensive tackle Jethro Pugh, and Starr would follow right behind. At the snap, the Cowboys' Willie Townes submarined tackle Forrest Gregg, and with Bowman and Kramer driving forward on the slick ice, Starr squeezed between them. The six inches would be the difference between victory and defeat.

Bob Lilly: "Right before that last play, I was trying to dig a hole for traction, but I didn't have any success. That's when I wished I had had my cleats on.

"I knew Starr was going to run up the middle. They had just tried a play around the outside and fell. I am pretty sure I told Jethro and Lee Roy that they were going to come up the middle. In fact I told Jethro, 'We ought to call timeout and get a screwdriver out there and dig a couple of holes.' Because we were on a sheet of ice. I don't know why I didn't do that. I should have. It's one thing I'll always wish I had done. But I did think about it. I had the presence of mind to think about it. 'Cause I didn't think there was any way we could stop them if they put two men on you. You're just on ice, and you can't get under them, because they just scoot along. And that's what happened to Jethro. I don't know where I ended up. I've seen the picture of that play. I must have been underneath. Because I never have seen myself."

Jethro Pugh: "It was like standing in a pot of ice. My feet were so numb, a bucket of ice. I said to Bob Lilly, 'We've got to call a timeout to get an ice pick.' We had to dig holes for our feet. But we didn't know if we could. I tried scraping the ice, but I couldn't feel my feet. My hands were in my pants. I didn't have gloves on because the coaches didn't want us to hurt ourselves in the pass rush. I was sliding back because I was standing on ice.

"We played the percentages. Bart Starr didn't like quarterback sneaks. He was going to call the play to Donny Anderson. But Kenny Bowman and Jerry Kramer double-teamed me for the quarterback sneak. Kramer moved before the snap. He was offside. And Bowman threw an even better block from the other side. It was like a gunfight. Somebody pulls the trigger first, and it's too late to do anything."

Chuck Howley: "When we lined up, we knew we had to stop the run. We felt it was going to be some kind of a power play, and we had to gap them. We were keying the fullback, Jim Taylor. It didn't happen, and they got the surge off the line of scrimmage, and that's all you need on a quarterback sneak, 'cause the ball was on the 1-inch line. All he had to do was get the momentum. We would have had to collapse the offensive line, which would have been hard to do because they had the snap count. But we knew it was going to be the last play.

"I was laying on Bart Starr's back as he went across. He kind of went off to the side, and I was able to knife the gap, but my momentum was going down the line, and as he penetrated behind Thurston and Kramer, to make the tackle I had to lay on the runner.

"I thought it was a gutsy play. It was a great game."

Lee Roy Jordan: "On the final play I was lined up over the fullback. I was watching the fullback, Jim Taylor, closer than I should have been. I should have been watching Starr closer. When the ball was snapped, I took a jab step the wrong way. I don't know where I could have made the tackle if I'd have known he was going to run a quarterback sneak and gone straight for him, because there were a lot of people between me and Bart Starr.

"About seven years later we were riding on the bus to a game, and coach Landry turned to me and said, 'Why did you take a step to the left when Bart Starr scored up there in Green Bay?' I said, 'Coach, are you still worried about that play?' Seven years later he still thought I could have won the game."

Cornell Green: "I was on the line of scrimmage right by where Starr snuck over for the winning score. They made it out to be such a big play, a big deal, and said what a great block Jerry Kramer made, but he didn't do a damn thing. Hell, Jethro and Bob Lilly were standing on ice. All you had to do was push them, and they'd slip down. And they knew the snap count, so they were going to get off first. Our guys got to catch your blows when you push them, and they did, and Bart Starr just walked in. They talked about 'great blocks' and all that. Wasn't nothing great about nothing. None of the blocks. But Jerry Kramer wrote a book on it, and made a fortune, and I guarantee, hell, I could have blocked

Jethro, or anybody else on that line that day, 'cause we hadn't played in the end zone, and it was just ice. You ever stand on ice and have somebody push you? That's what it came down to.

"When Starr scored, there was no time left, and that was it. At the end of the game, nobody said anything. Everyone just got dressed and left. There weren't any speeches or talks or anything."

Bob Lilly: "I remember after the game we took a shower, and the water temperature was around 60, but it felt hot. The water wouldn't get hot, but it felt hot, and the happiest feeling in my entire life was when we climbed up that stairway in the tail of that 727 and got on that warm airplane, and when we left the ground, I thanked the Lord that we were out of there.

"After the game my lungs were in bad shape. I used to smoke cigars a lot. I inhaled them, and I smoked a few cigarettes. After that game I quit all smoking. And my lungs have never been the same since that game, ever, because of the cold. I don't know what did it. I can't be in a room with smoke. I can't stand the diesel fuel from trucks. Exhaust or anything of that nature gives me asthma or some sort of an allergy immediately."

Don Meredith took the loss so hard that on the airplane he talked with Tom Landry about retiring. Landry told him he was being too hard on himself, that the conditions had been "dreadful." Chuck Howley overheard Don. Reporter Steve Perkins overheard Howley.

Chuck Howley: "As we were flying back on the plane, I was in the front of the plane with Phil Clark, and we were sitting there talking, and we were all kind of despondent from losing the ballgame, and I said to Phil, 'Hell, Don's going to retire, and I'm thinking about retiring,' and Steve Perkins of the *Herald* heard me and wrote a story about Don retiring. It came out in the headlines, Meredith Retires.

"Don called me up on the phone, and he said, 'Chuck, what the hell is going on, baby? What do you mean I'm going to retire? I got all these damn endorsements. I have my phone ringing off the hook.' Don was pretty well pissed. I can't blame him. Here's a sportswriter who takes something out of context and makes a story out of it. I mean, after a game you're despondent, the players are talking off the cuff laying back in their seats, you're making all kinds of statements, and to me it's a little bit irresponsible when a sportswriter such as Steve Perkins takes something like that out of context and makes a story out of it.

"I apologized to Don. That's the only thing I could do. I said, 'Hell, Don, I made a comment. Yeah, I said you're going to retire. You made the same kind of statement. We all made crazy statements after that game. We were all kind of down, and we were making statements.' I said to Don, 'For someone to come out and write an article like that based on hearsay, that's not the right thing to do.'

"Within a week, Don put the story to rest.

"Controversy sells newspapers, and someone who's a sportswriter presenting his views is different than a player giving his views. To me, the player is more qualified to give his views than a sportswriter. What experience does a sportswriter have other than following the sport itself? Yes, he has an opinion. The media has that unique position. And yes, after we lost, we got a lot of criticism and so did Don."

Because of the conditions that day Meredith did not recover from the pneumonia he had contracted until February. Five Cowboys—George Andrie, Jethro Pugh, Mel Renfro, Willie Townes, and Dick Daniels—were treated for frostbite.

The Cowboys had fought valiantly against a legendary football team, with field conditions adverse to their style of play. They had come within six inches of winning.

None of this mattered either to Tom Landry or to the press or fans. All that mattered to them was that the Cowboys had lost. In the streets, at restaurants, at parties the talk was how the Cowboys had "choked." For some of the players, the response to the loss was far worse emotionally than the loss itself.

Pete Gent: "After that game the press turned on us with a vengeance. They said we couldn't win the big game. Well, what else are you going to say? Landry was not going to say, 'Boy, what a stupid thing I did to run a prevent defense, when they are running in the face of a 40-mile-an-hour gale and the windchill is around 50 below zero.' So now it was: the Cowboys can't win the big one."

Lance Rentzel: "All of this created problems—serious problems. We heard it so often, a part of us wondered if it were true, and once that set in, once that cancer started to work, the whole organization began to contend with its image. This resulted in the so-called self-fulfilling prophecy."

Frank Clarke: "When we got back to the clubhouse after the game, the mood in the clubhouse was worse than it had been the year before. Double times worse. It was *more* gloomy, *more* down, *more* negative. Again, I felt, 'Whoa, no way this is . . . this is not . . . I just . . .' It just felt so weird that this would be going on with grown men.

"Two years in a row, man, we had done something that hundreds and hundreds and hundreds and hundreds of athletes would have given their pinkies for, just to be a part of that. And here we were, after back-to-back stellar seasons, very reputable, very enviable years in which we had challenged the world's great Vince Lombardi–led Packers, and we feel like this? This did not make any sense at all. And there was a part of me that said, 'Maybe I *should* get out of this. Maybe I'm not meant to be a part of this.'

"At the end of the season I got involved in doing radio and television. And I was doing a pretty good job, and when it came close for the preseason to start, I started to say, 'Maybe one more year.'

"I called Tom Landry and said I wanted to talk to him about the '68 season, and he encouraged me *not* to come back. He didn't say, 'Don't come back.' But he had always let me know where I stood with his plans. It was almost as if he sensed and he knew that I didn't have the kind of energy that he needed to get to the Super Bowl. And he was right. I did not have it, and there was no way I wanted to manufacture it.

"After our meeting I immediately felt down, depressed, because I had wanted him to say, 'You deserve to come back for one more chance. We think we're going there, and there is no reason why we can't see ourselves as Super Bowl contenders, and you're the kind of player who's helped us get here, and we want you around for one more year.'

"But he just listened to what I had to say. But the other thing, too, that was a downer for me, not one of my friends or anybody else on the team said anything like, 'We want you to come back.' It was as if everybody had accepted that fact that once they saw that newspaper article about me retiring, that was it. They knew just by my personality if Frank says that's what he wants to do, he's gonna do it, and that's it. But it did hurt. There was a part of that that really hurt me, that I would go out that way."

For some of the other players, the criticism was justified. They had not won it all. They had not gone to the Super Bowl, and so the following year there would be only one thing to do: work even harder.

Chuck Howley: "After the Ice Bowl loss, Tom announced that the next year he wanted everyone to work harder. If you don't achieve what you're trying to achieve, there is only one way to achieve it, and that is to work harder. Even today, I say to myself, 'If I had worked harder, I could have been a better player.' I can look back and think, 'Yes, we had goals for ourselves.' Tom taught us how to do that. He was a great goal setter. He saw these were the things we could pull out within ourselves that we didn't know were there. These were the words that were frowned upon: 'We need to work harder.' But he was right. We hadn't won. We may have been 12–2, but Tom wanted a world championship.

"Because we had come so close, after that it was expected. And when you make it to the top, they are not content unless they repeat. The fans are the same way.

"In the early years all the Dallas fans wanted was a winner. Maybe that's human nature. Fans want to support a winner, not a loser. In the early years, they all wanted to be associated with a winner. It took us 11 years to do it.

"A fan does not look at it in the reality or the context. If you ask anyone who buys an NFL team if he'd be satisfied to go to the Super Bowl in 10 years, he'd take you up on the deal. But the fan says, 'I'm only concerned with *now* and what you're doing *this* season. I'm only interested in the Cowboys so long as they're winners.'"

Chapter 29

UNCIVIL WAR

Nine thousand American boys were killed in Vietnam in 1967, and that summer there were bad riots in cities across America. In the fall, antiwar activists looked for someone to oppose Lyndon Johnson. In January 1968, the Vietcong mounted the Tet offensive, overrunning Saigon and more than 100 other cities and leaving Americans to wonder whether Vietnam was worth the price. The myth of American invincibility was shattered, and Johnson's popularity sank.

And then on March 16, 1968, Robert Kennedy, the younger brother of the slain president, antiwar and pro civil rights, announced his candidacy for president. Two weeks later, President Johnson announced he would not run for renomination. Though vice president Hubert Humphrey announced he would run in Johnson's place, it seemed that most of the nation was embracing Kennedy, and it certainly appeared he would soon inhabit the White House.

For Cowboys guard John Wilbur, it was an exciting period because Robert Kennedy seemed like someone who would champion the cause of those who, like Wilbur, staunchly opposed the Vietnam War.

John Wilbur: "I met Robert Kennedy during his campaign in '68. I had met John Kennedy, and we all idolized him. I'd followed Bobby's path and what he had been doing, and I liked the Kennedys' philosophy. They were willing to stand up against any wrong. Later when I was traded to Washington I worked with Ethel Kennedy to raise money for her charities, and I became socially involved with the whole family. Ethel is a very dynamic woman who has done a wonderful job raising her kids. I am very close to them, and I will always be a Democrat and always be a Kennedy person.

"And so in '68 when Bobby's campaign asked for help getting out the votes in the black community in Los Angeles, I got involved with a group of athletes including Cornell Green, Bob Hayes, Rosey Grier, and Rafer Johnson.

"I would have been with him when he was killed in Los Angeles, but I had to go to training camp. And when Bobby was killed, I backed off from politics until '72, when I went to work for George McGovern."

On April 4, 1968, Martin Luther King Jr. was assassinated. Riots swept through more than 100 American cities. On June 5 Robert Kennedy narrowly defeated

Minnesota senator Eugene McCarthy in California, leaving him as the only antiwar candidate capable of defeating the mainstream Hubert Humphrey. That night he was murdered. This time there were no riots, only a pall of sadness. With the deaths of Dr. King and Robert Kennedy, the optimism of the sixties had come to an end.

John Wilbur: "On the team in 1968 you had your conservative southern elements, and there's no question many times we heard the word *nigger* among our white teammates—I won't say who, but there was a racist element on the team, and a racist element in the management and on the coaching staff.

"And on the other side was that radical element, the antiwar guys, all the guys who stood up for Mel Renfro when he was denied housing in North Dallas, Pete Gent, myself, Pettis Norman, and Bob Hayes. Bob really didn't come out publicly, but in private. Don Perkins, Cornell Green, Rayfield Wright, Jethro Pugh, and Mel Renfro were also people who were not going to put up with the racism that existed in Dallas at that time and constantly would talk about it, bring it to our attention. We were young men searching for perfection both in our football team and our lives and in our society. Some mirrored the elements of the society they came from, and others were looking for a better world."

Pettis Norman: "King was the person I had looked up to for a long, long time. I had been involved in the same kind of issues he was involved in. I knew him through all the things I saw and read and believed in, which were the things he preached and lived and practiced. He was really a major hero, as far as I was concerned. When Robert Kennedy died a couple months later, I was in a state of disbelief, but it was far worse when Martin Luther King was killed. It was the feeling of, 'Who can pick up the mantle and lead this movement?' It had come a long way, but it was very much incomplete, and I knew that. I just did not see anyone on the horizon who could galvanize people and pull them together to march toward some form of equality. And so there was a tremendous void, a sense of almost hopelessness for just a little while.

"I somehow realized that we could not live in a state of hopelessness, and each one of us had to do what we could wherever we were to change things. In essence, we could be as effective, if not more effective, if enough of us picked up the mantle and did our own little piece. And so that's what I attempted to do as an individual and tried to encourage others to do as well. And a lot of other folks had the same notion. That was my feeling with Martin.

"And even now when I think about him and see his speeches, especially that last one the night before he was killed, I have flashbacks to that time, and I still feel that tremendous void that I felt in me at that time. No one has really stepped forward to fill that void. A lot of people have contributed on a major level, but not to the extent that Martin did.

"And when Bobby Kennedy was killed, I was watching TV. I just sat there in total disbelief, and once again, it was another symbol of hope gone. It seemed like the light had flickered out for a brief moment. And I was thinking that this would be the fate of anyone who steps out and really becomes an advocate for change. And so it was a moment of disbelief and a moment of sadness, a moment of hopelessness, and then you realize you must move beyond that point.

"In 1965 I went to Tex and told him it was time to stop the living arrangements of the players by race. I said, 'We need to do something about the way we assign roommates. We need to stop assigning roommates by color, but by last names. We play together, we eat together, and it's time to take the next step.' He said, 'Let me think about it,' and he called me and Dave Manders, and he said, 'We want you two to room together.' And we did in training camp, got along fine. Dave was a great roommate. We had fun together. We liked each other, and what we showed, regardless of color, you had the same concerns: you wanted to make the team, you wanted to make money, you had a family back home you loved, you wrote letters, you called at night on the phone. We shared the phone. We had respect for each other. We showered together, and no black or white rubbed off in the shower. We were two human beings who just happened to have slightly different hues of skin.

"And after that training camp, that was the last time players were assigned by race. Because we broke training camp, and during the season we were assigned roommates by last names. And it worked out fine. I don't know of any incidents. There were probably incidents where players had different personalities and requested some other roommate, but for the most part, I don't know of any major blowup.

"But I can tell you that when Dave and I roomed together, that opened the team's eyes. And when it happened with the whole team, it began to open eyes of other guys on the team who had ideas about what would happen if the races came together. It was interesting to watch individuals grow even beyond football, and how people gained a much greater appreciation for people, no matter what color they are.

"Dave Manders and I call each other 'roomie' right now. We still see each other. After my first wife died, I got remarried, and he came to the wedding.

"The Cowboys really had some influence on a lot of things in Dallas. Though the black players lived in South Dallas and the white players in the north, a lot of guys would get together and socialize in the midsixties, have aftergame parties, and a few guys would visit each other's homes. Some white guys didn't like it when that happened. But that's what happened. People began to know about the team staying together, eating together as a team, and it became much more acceptable. It gave the white community a chance to relate to the African-American community better, on a whole different level, from kind of a hero-worshiping type level. Little kids would wait after the game to get my autograph, just like they would anybody else's. And so all of this began to subliminally have an effect on the city."

When Mel Renfro moved to Dallas in 1966 from Portland, Oregon, he immediately encountered the kind of segregation experienced by all blacks at that time.

Mel Renfro: "I wasn't in Dallas three days when I got a dose of Jim Crow. It was borderline Oak Cliff, South Dallas, where there were a lot of white businesses. There was a white restaurant and a black restaurant right next door. It looked like the white restaurant was a little nicer, so I walked in there to have breakfast. I was refused service. I was told, 'We don't serve coloreds here. You go eat next door.' I said, 'I didn't order a color. I ordered breakfast.' That didn't stand too well with them. And I went next door and had a great breakfast.

"I learned my lesson. I remembered what my dad said, 'If they don't want you, get away from it. Don't rock the boat, because you'll get hurt.' So I started looking for places where I knew I'd be accepted, mostly black restaurants. Very few times would I go to North Dallas or a white area unless it was a team thing, or somewhere where we knew we could go."

For two years Renfro sought to live in North Dallas, closer to where the Cowboys practiced, and time after time was rebuffed. In 1968 Lyndon Johnson signed the Civil Rights Act, which made discrimination on the basis of race illegal, and that year Mel decided he no longer would be silent about the indignities of being denied housing. Against the wishes of Tex Schramm and the Cowboys, Mel Renfro sued to be allowed to live where he wanted.

Mel Renfro: "It's funny, because when I moved to Dallas as a rookie in '64, the first place I drove to was the Cowboys office, and they directed me to an apartment complex in South Dallas where four or five other black ballplayers were living. It was just automatic. It was OK. It wasn't a slum. It was the Cedar Crest Apartments, one of the nicer apartments for blacks in that area. But just to automatically say, 'This is where you go . . .'

"I remember going into the Cowboys, and they wrote me a map: 'Go down Central South 75, and go through town and hit Corinth Street, and go up Corinth, turn left here, and here you are. That's going to be your home, buddy.'

"I can remember when the team would go to an area where there was segregation, Tom Landry used to say, 'Fellas, we know what's going on here. We don't particularly agree with it, but that's the way it is, so we have to do what we can so we don't create unnecessary problems.'

"And sometimes we would joke about it. I'll never forget Willie Townes. He called coach Landry 'Presbyterian Tom.' We'd say, 'There goes Presbyterian Tom again.' Here's a guy who was supposed to be a Christian, and yet he's condoning segregation. He's saying, 'This stuff is happening, and though we may not agree with it, we'll ignore it and stay in our lane.' I'm still a very sensitive person to things like that. But the way I was brought up, my dad told me, 'Just get away from it. Don't challenge it.' But still, you have to be a man. Be a man. And after being denied housing three or four times, the fifth time I said, 'I'm not going to stand for this.'

"I would find an apartment or duplex that had a For Rent or For Lease sign on it, and I'd go up, and immediately it was not available. Several times when we'd call on the phone and we'd get there, it was always leased or it wasn't available. I understood what it was, and I didn't want the problem of fighting it. I'd just go on to the next thing. But then, in 1968 my wife and I went and looked at a duplex, and there were ads in the paper and For Lease signs, and we actually went in and talked to the people, and they actually said there were three or four units available, and did we want to sign up?

"We said no, because the rent was kind of high. At that time $375 a month was a little more than we wanted to pay. I had a game that weekend, so I flew to Philadelphia, and she went home. And while I was in Philadelphia I told my wife, 'Aw, what the heck. You only live once. We want to live in a nice place out near the practice field. Go back in and make the deal.' So she went in, and from the time we had been there, all the signs had been pulled out of the ground and there were no more units for lease, just for sale, and I was so livid I could hardly play the game. I discussed this with my teammates, just told them what happened, and it was really no surprise to anybody that that had happened, because they were experiencing the same thing.

"But Oscar Mauzy, a state senator in Dallas, had heard about what happened, and he contacted me and said, 'Mel, you want to fight this?' I said, 'You bet I do.' He said, 'I'll represent you for free.' So we sat down and talked about it, and we took it to federal court, and when the Cowboys found out I was taking it to court, Tex Schramm called me in, front and center. For 35, 40 minutes he said, 'Mel, you can't do this. You just can't do this.' I said, 'Tex, this is not the first time. This is the fifth time this has happened. And I can't handle it anymore.'

"He said, 'Mel, you can't do this. This is going to hurt you.'

"I said, 'I've been hurt by being denied housing.'

"I found out later, Tex was afraid of the white hierarchy in Dallas, the real estate industry. I guess the real estate industry had been putting pressure on him to have me not do this. Because it drastically changed the laws.

"When he realized I was going to do it, he jumped up behind his desk, got between me and the door, and he just said, 'If you're going to do it, I'm with you all the way.' I had gotten my own lawyer, but the Cowboys later claimed they had hired the attorney to represent me, which they did not.

"I went in to court, and these real estate people actually thought they were going to win. They fought this thing and spent a lot of money. We were in court a long time testifying.

"I said, 'It's the simple truth. I went in to lease the place and they denied me. Why did they deny me? Because I was black.' And this guy, a big builder, he knew if he lost then that would open the doors for other blacks to move into places that they didn't want them.

"Actually, I got a lot of good letters, a lot of good phone calls from people saying, 'We're glad you're doing this, because they're not messing with us any more. Now we can get a place to live and not be denied.' Then on the other side of the coin the hate mail came. It was ugly. I told my wife one time, 'Don't ever open a letter that looks strange that has no return address on it.' It scared her to death. And what I did, I took a couple of them and put them on the bulletin board at the practice field, and they weren't up five minutes before someone took them down. Never found out who. But they came off in a hurry.

"I thought I was going to lose, because of the way they were presenting their case. I was saying to myself, 'What's going on here?' They were asking these stupid questions for me to answer. It was to the point, 'If you did and if that hadn't happened and this . . .' And I'd say, 'No, it was none of that. It was cut-and-dry.' You know how lawyers are, they work the questions so if you answer it, you're going to incriminate yourself or sound bad. Many times I refused to answer the question, and the judge would say, 'No, he doesn't have to answer that question.'

"The judge was Sara Hughes. She was very sympathetic. She knew what was going on, but she had to act like a judge. It was a very difficult thing for me to experience.

"And after I won, the owner of the complex said, 'Take your pick. You can move into any one you want to.' But I didn't because of all the negative publicity and the hate mail that came in, because the public knew where it was. I said, 'There is no way I'm going to subject my family to people knowing where I live. There are some racist idiots out there that were saying and writing some nasty things.' I said, 'If they take the time to write a nasty letter like this, they could do anything.' And my daughter was a little baby. My boys were three and four. I said, 'No way.' And so I didn't move in there. I moved into an apartment complex in the north side about a half a mile from that complex.

"After all the publicity behind it, the doors really opened up in the housing industry. I know that was so because of the many letters I got from people, including from mixed couples who were also having problems.

"The black ballplayers were elated, because it opened the doors. And it put a spotlight on the problem. It was right at that time that Dr. King and Bobby Kennedy were assassinated. And that was some ugly stuff. That tore me apart. That *really* tore me apart. I stayed drunk for a week after the King thing, and I got real militant, and had an attitude, and of course, the Cowboys didn't like that. I was the premier player, myself and Bob Lilly and maybe one other, and they couldn't do anything to me, although they sure wanted to. They fixed me by not paying me any money. That was the way they got to me."

Chapter 30

JORDAN VERSUS GENT

A most brutal internal war was waged between Lee Roy Jordan and Pete Gent. The two did not get along on any level. Jordan, like Landry, believed a player should practice as hard as he played, giving 100 percent at all times. Gent believed in having fun in practice, and even in games.

Jordan, a product of the Deep South, preferred country-western music to rock and roll and, like America's conservative bedrock, firmly believed drug users should be thrown in jail and unpatriotic antiwar protestors should be thrown out of America. On the issue of integration, Jordan had one test: if a man dedicated himself to the game, he wanted him for a teammate though not necessarily as a friend. His black teammates understood Lee Roy's rural Alabama background, and even if he did say the n-word every once in a while, the great majority of the Cowboys—black and white—understood it was because of his upbringing and forgave him, at the same time admiring him for his dedication and what he meant to the success of the team.

Because Jordan believed it important to play as viciously in practice as he did in games, a whole generation of Cowboys offensive players held Jordan's ferocious nature against him, and a few took his hard hits personally. Several, including Pete Gent, John Wilbur, and Bob Hayes—all offensive players—castigated him as a "redneck racist." In his own defense, Jordan says he never, ever acted prejudicially toward his black teammates.

Lee Roy Jordan: "Hell, I don't know what *redneck* is. If that's being from the South, I'm a redneck. But if that means I didn't respect Bob Hayes as a person just because of his color, I have to question that, because I judge every guy as an individual, no matter what color he is. Show me a guy who won't compete hard to win, and I won't like him. I don't care what color he is. You show me a guy who competes hard to win every play, I'll love him because that's what I'm all about."

Several black teammates concurred.

Pettis Norman: "I've always had a lot of respect for Lee Roy Jordan. He has changed a lot. I've always had a lot of respect for him, especially for his playing ability and his approach to the game. And he always treated me very, very nicely. Never, never was there one incident when he wasn't very nice. In Dallas, a lot of people changed over the years, and Lee Roy was one among many."

Mel Renfro: "Pete Gent and John Wilbur probably saw the side of him we didn't see. Because they were white. He probably sat around with a group of his buddies, and they passed some words around that weren't so nice about black people, and I'm sure Pete heard that and John heard that. But like I said, none of that 'Down with the niggers' talk came across when I was with him, not like it did with some of the other players that were not so friendly. I know who Lee Roy was, where he came from, how he grew up, but as far as his treatment toward me, that was gold."

Cornell Green: "I didn't think Lee Roy was a racist, and I was as close to him as anybody. I thought Lee Roy was a gung ho, ready-to-play, want-to-play, want-to-win type of guy, and though I didn't know that much about his personal life, on the field I thought he was ready, he wanted it, he would be there, a hard hitter, ready to play. Yeah."

Lee Roy Jordan: "They've been in the huddle with me, and they know how important it is to win, and they know that because we stuck together and believed we could do things that we got a lot of things done."

Gent, who was often the target and victim of Jordan's viciousness during scrimmages, does not remember it that way.

Pete Gent: "I hated the guy. Oh, I hated him. He was a racist, sorry bastard. I have absolutely no respect for him as a man. In those days I didn't live in that great a neighborhood, but where some of the blacks lived was far worse. When we went on the road Dickie Daniels and Mike Johnson were afraid to leave their personal belongings in their apartments where they lived, 'cause it was in the paper they were out of town, so they would load up their stereos, TVs, and radios in their cars and drive over to my house and park them in my driveway, because we had firemen next door so there was always somebody watching the house. At the time the blacks still had problems finding hotels. I remember the first time we went to New Orleans in '66, we stayed at the airport hotel, 'cause no hotel downtown would take us. It was horrible. Those guys had such a tough time. They had to try and act like it wasn't happening.

"It was well known that Lee Roy and I didn't like each other. Alabama governor George Wallace was often our favorite subject. I would tell him to his face what a racist asshole Wallace was. In practice drills, Lee Roy would clothesline me half the time. But Lee Roy was a great player. He was tougher than shit, but I hated him for his racism. Most of the receivers were black—Frank Clarke was one of my best friends—and Lee Roy hated that.

"Interestingly enough, the outside linebacker who played behind Chuck Howley, Harold Hays, who was white, came from Hattiesburg, Mississippi. Lee Roy and I had gotten into a fight at some point on the field during a scrimmage, and I remember I was in the shower alone with Harold after a particularly ugly incident with Lee Roy. I don't remember which ugly incident it was, we had so many, and physically I always came out on the short end. Harold and I were in business together, and Harold was sitting there with me, and I said, 'That guy is not a f***ing human being. That's bullshit. I don't care if he's your friend or not, Harold. F*** that.'

"And Harold said, 'You know, Pete, what you've got to try and understand is, when I go home to Mississippi I still have to tell my grandfather we have separate showers for the whites and the blacks. We're in Dallas. We're still in the South here. You come from the North. You've got to understand where Lee Roy is coming from. Lee Roy isn't going to change.'

"As he aged, though, Lee Roy did change, as Dallas changed. If Lee Roy was going to make it in business he was going to have to deal with black people."

Between the southern conservatives and the northern liberals, there was no common ground. The team was even split in its choice of recreational drugs. For the good old boys, whiskey was the standby. The Protestant ethic was to "just say no" to drugs, but never to Jack Daniel's. The creed of the sixties antiwar, antiestablishment was that so long as no one got hurt, it didn't matter what you put into your body. As long as it felt good, "Just say yes." It was the pleasure principle, and drugs—first marijuana, the drug of the flower children, then the hallucinogen LSD, and then the addictive, destructive cocaine—played a large role in it.

The counterculture smoked grass because it felt good and it was fun. Dopers made fun of the nine-to-five corporate execs and their housewives who stayed home and took Valium. Eldridge Cleaver, the head of the Black Panthers, claimed that blacks needed marijuana as a bolster against onslaughts on their manhood by whites. It was the straights versus the heads, us versus them.

In 1968 the national youth mania was smoking marijuana. In the age of Aquarius and free love, it was everywhere, including among those Cowboys who did not feel cowed by Texas' 50-year sentence for getting caught smoking it or by cultural and religious inhibitions. And just because the good old boys shunned pot because it was illegal, that didn't mean there weren't substitutes. The potheads on the team found it amusing and hypocritical that their straitlaced brethren sought their kicks in pot substitutes such as amyl nitrate and speed.

John Wilbur: "Just about everyone was smoking pot at that time, though I would not say the southern redneck contingency of the Cowboys were experimenters. But one thing they did experiment with was amyl nitrate. You used to be able to buy it in the drugstores. So we'd go to the beer bars, the cowboy bars, and these amyl nitrates would get you high for 30 seconds. You'd giggle. It was the redneck way of getting high. We'd snort amyl nitrate to get high and laugh and get light-headed and drink beer. It sounds like a country-western song. 'Mama don't let your children grow up to be Cowboys snorting amyl nitrate in cowboy bars.'

"The euphemism was: we were all experimenting with the fruit of the times, whatever the fruit of the times would be—amyl nitrate, mescaline, speed, pot.

"This period was precocaine. There was *a lot* of speed. In fact, the team used to dispense it. I was a rookie, and I was in the locker room before the game, and there were these little white boxes in everybody's locker, and I was wondering, 'What's going on? What the heck is that?' I asked one of the older guys, 'What's that?' 'Dexamil.' 'What does it do?' 'It makes you feel good. It's a performance enhancer.' So I said, 'I want some of that, too.' So I got on the list. They were pretty good about not letting the new guys do it. It was just for the old guys. I was kind of into the beer and the speed. The precocaine era. The speed generation. Beer and speed. Beer and speed. And amyl nitrate."

To those steeped in the Texas culture who had not strayed from biblical ways, marijuana was seen as the devil's weed. Pot smokers were viewed as fiends as exemplified in the movie *Reefer Madness*. When Lee Roy Jordan somehow learned that Pete Gent was smoking marijuana with Don Meredith and other teammates, Jordan was horrified. He was convinced that Gent was an evil influence on Meredith and the team, and he did what he could to get Gent off the team, including an attempt to maim him during practice.

Lee Roy Jordan: "Pete was a basketball player in college, and he didn't like contact, and I can understand that from some people. But I didn't think Pete was real committed to football and committed to winning. And I thought Pete wasn't a good character to be a part of the team because Pete experimented with anything that came along, and I think he was a guy who was helpful in exposing some other people to those kind of things, helping them to experiment with them, because he had them available.

"I didn't respect that, and I didn't like that because I thought it was detrimental to our football team. And basically that's it. I like everybody who has a real interest and commitment to helping us win. I respect *anyone* with that commitment. I don't care who you are.

"The [drug] thing *really* angered me, and in practice I probably attacked him more than I should have—no, let me take that back, I don't think I could have. If I could have made him quit the team, I felt like we would have been better off. Because I felt like Pete was a bad influence as far as work ethic. I don't think he had a work ethic as far as really wanting to win and having it a major thought in his mind every day in practice and after practice and the next day when he came back.

"I would get on Pete for playing his music loud in the clubhouse. If I thought it was interrupting my concentration, or someone else's, I would, because I didn't think he was going to help us that much anyway. It's kind of like what Don Meredith said after the movie [*North Dallas Forty*]. He said, 'If I had known Pete had been that damn good, I'd have thrown him a lot more passes.' That's the way I felt about Pete. If he had been as good as he felt he was, shit, he'd a caught a lot more balls."

Pete Gent: "Lee Roy turned me in to league security as a guy who was passing out drugs on the team. I wasn't doing that. He knew that Meredith would come to my house, and that Don and I were smoking dope together. When we smoked it on the team plane one time, everybody thought the plane was on fire. They didn't know what the smell was. That was the closest they came to catching us smoking it. We were in back of the team plane, and Don went into the bathroom and smoked half a joint, and I went into the bathroom and smoked the rest, and the stewardess came back and said, 'Jesus, what's that smell?' They thought the plane was on fire. We were sitting there praying, 'I hope it is on fire.'

"So Lee Roy turned me in to league security. In the off-season after the '67 season and all during '68 they followed me. They had guys on me for one whole season. I can remember one time a neighbor told me, 'Pete, now don't look, but there is somebody sitting in our parking lot with binoculars.' I went out the back door, got in my car, and came around and pulled next to this car, and there was a woman with a baby in the front seat, and she had a pair of binoculars, looked like a German tank commander. She was watching my house. I said, 'What are you doing?' And she looked over at me, and her jaw dropped. I said, 'Why are you watching my house?' I had already gotten her license number. She said, 'I'm not,' and she dropped the binoculars and roared off. I gave my lawyer—the guy who got me out of the draft—the license number, and he called me back the next day and he said, 'I don't get this. This license number traces to a judge in Oak Cliff.'

"One time I was driving along, and I looked back and here are these two guys following me, and I said to my wife, 'We are being followed, looks like by two cops.' She said, 'No, you are paranoid.' I said, 'Watch,' and I made a U-turn, and these guys made a U-turn right behind me in front of a patrol car and hit a parked car. The patrol car's lights went on, he walked to that car, and in less than a minute he turned them loose, and they came right after me. And they just kept following me. We were on our way to Casa Dominguez to eat, and when we came out, there they were, parked across the street.

"And then I was getting calls from guys who went home in the off-season like Leon Donahue, who called from San Jose. Leon used to come to my house a lot. Leon said, 'I just had two guys from league security here, and they wanted to know what you are doing.' He said, 'One, they know there are a lot of black guys over at your house, and two, somebody has told them you are doing drugs.' And about that point, Meredith got real paranoid. I went to see him, and he sort of got all over me about my behavior, saying it was me leading him on. I said, 'Look, Don, I never ran your life. I ain't running it now.' Don said, 'I just think you better be careful.' Then I knew the word had come down.

"I found out it was Lee Roy from Bob Thompson, who ran Tecon for Clint Murchison. Lee Roy did it out of a conviction that I was destroying the team because I was introducing recreational drugs, as opposed to the amphetamines and steroids everybody was taking. Everybody thought it was much better to drink a fifth of whiskey before a game than to smoke two joints and go to sleep. Remember, I was in Dallas, a very conservative place. I was seen by Landry and particularly by guys like Lee Roy as the bad influence on Meredith. Whereas the way I looked at it, when I came to that club, they were losing, and when I left, they were winning.

"What I found so fascinating was that the southerners on one side and the northerners and blacks on the other didn't agree on anything, had nothing in common, didn't get along at all. There was no unity—until we stepped on the field. I always marveled at it, too. In *North Dallas Forty*, all through the book and movie, all week long Elliott and Joe Bob would fight, but right before, during, and after the game, they would have a moment of communion where Joe Bob would actually tell him he did well, and then it would be over. And the next week the fighting would start, and it would be the same battle all week long, until the next game.

"It was a constant. It's still amazing to look back at, to see what we would go through each week, and then how the day of the game we were all so focused on what we had to do, and how we counted on each other, black, white, redneck, limousine liberal, whatever you were, you were focused to win that game, because that's who you were. You were football players. If you didn't do that, everything you did during the week was useless. You were meaningless. To me, that explains everybody's behavior, from Don Perkins' to mine to Lee Roy's. We all understood at one level that we were football players. That's all we were. Practices were tough enough, because your job would be on the line every day in practice. But on Sunday, your *life* was on the line. You f***ed up on Sunday, your life could be over. If you were no longer a football player, you were no longer anything, 'cause you'd been doing it for so long. It was the only thing you had in your identity."

Chapter 31

TRIALS AND TRIBULATIONS

Cornell Green: "In '68 we started 7–1, and then after we lost to the Giants 27–21, you'd have thought we were the worst team in football. But that was Tom Landry's deal: Even when we won, Tom Landry would go to the media, and you'd think we'd lost, after every game. I have no idea why. Tom had trouble saying we played a good game. He had a *problem* with that. For his whole career, you could beat someone 52–0, and he'd find something wrong with it. And he could do it for two and a half hours. When he did that, though, I kind of cut him off. I didn't even listen half the time. You'd get in the habit of not even listening. Let him ramble on."

Pete Gent: "I must tell you a certain part of what Tom Landry was doing there was some sheer genius. But there was another part of it that was just blind foolishness, and dishonesty, and that's what you kept seeing in the press. That's where the dishonesty showed up, because we were 7–2. Yet the press was saying, 'We're terrible.' How could we not be a good team? Who was telling them that? I wasn't telling them that. Who was telling them, 'We're terrible'? It had to be Landry. He was already preparing the ground for his landing."

After the loss to the Giants, the Cowboys did not fulfill Landry's dire prophecy and sink further, but rather rebounded with a 44–24 shellacking of the Washington Redskins, a game in which Don Meredith passed for 295 yards. In that game Meredith suffered a torn ligament in his leg, and he had to sit out the 34–3 mauling of the Chicago Bears as Craig Morton led the team on offense while Bob Lilly, Chuck Howley, and the rest of the defense held the Bears to a lone field goal.

The next game was a rematch against Washington in the Cotton Bowl, a 29–20 victory that was televised nationally; the Dallas fans spent much of the game booing Don Meredith—despite the 9–2 record and his success in the game. Fueled by Landry's criticisms and the many negative stories written in the Dallas papers over the years, the relentless booing of the fans let Meredith know that they did not approve of him. Meredith was so upset after the game that he refused to talk to reporters. A few days after the game Don and his wife went into a Dallas restaurant, and some men at the bar recognized him and began booing. They continued to do so until Don and his wife, embarrassed, left. The team won the rest of its regular-season games, but Don Meredith would never forget the insults.

Pete Gent: "We had pulled back together, and we didn't lose again. We won 12 games. And yet, in a game in the Cotton Bowl against the Redskins, Meredith was getting booed by the fans. We quit introducing the starting lineups on offense, 'cause they would boo Meredith.

"Don and I talked a lot about why he wasn't getting the respect he deserved. I was always harping on what I thought it was. We couldn't agree. We were now slowly moving into separate camps. Mine was, 'You f***ed up. You handed back control. You never should have given that up.' And he would say, 'It's not that.'

"Because of the injuries I suffered, I had lost my starting job to Lance Rentzel, and so because I was no longer a starter, and no longer potentially ever going to be a starter, Don now looked at me more like a guy who was a complainer and a malingerer, which really irritated me, because I played hurt all the time.

"About that point is when Lance married Joey Heatherton. I'm convinced he married Joey Heatherton because it was the Cowboys' way of solving his problem, by getting him publicly married to a sex symbol and who continually, when he would go to practice, would take off for L.A. And Lance would try to get my wife or Meredith's wife to stay with her, so she wouldn't run off.

"I remember we went out to dinner one time with Lance and Joey and a choreographer in Fort Worth, a guy who was wearing more makeup than Joey, and Joey looked ratty, dirt under her nails. She was loud and obnoxious.

"We went out one night to a diner, and she was so bad that we just laid the money on the table and left. I said, 'Come on, Lance. We gotta get the f*** out of here.' My wife went outside. I said to Lance, 'Grab her and let's go.' We got out into the parking lot, and Lance was so upset he walked over and threw up. Joey was driving him crazy."

Meredith led the team to a 28–7 win over the Pittsburgh Steelers, a home game in which Craig Morton was booed in the fourth quarter. In the final, meaningless game against the Giants in New York, Meredith needed to play only an average game to win the NFL passing title.

The night before the game Meredith and some teammates attended a party thrown by author and former Detroit Lions quarterback-for-a-day, George Plimpton, the paper Lion. Meredith drank heavily, and during the game he played listlessly, without fire. It was windy that day, but that was only part of the reason for Meredith's 1-for-9 day, a performance that cost him the passing title. Halfway through the second quarter Meredith told Landry he "didn't have a feel for the game." Landry replaced him with Craig Morton, who saved the day for a 28–10 win over the Giants.

During the Giants game it had snowed, and when the players filed onto the Braniff 727 at the airport, the wings were covered with white. It was a flight that the players remembered for their fright as much as for Don Meredith's cool.

Pete Gent: "We were taking off, and Don Meredith was sitting in front of me. They gave us two beers, and we would smuggle whiskey in. Don said, 'I'm going to drink my first beer before we take off. I'll save the second one for later.' I was playing my record player, smoking a cigar, finishing my beer.

"We started down the runway, and we heard this tremendous *bang*. Everyone just sat up straight in their seats. The plane shut down, and we skidded to the end of the runway. I could hear guys whimpering in the back of the plane. Dan Reeves' face was down.

"The pilot came on and said, 'Aaaaaaa, we think we just had a little snow that blew through the engine. We're going to try it again.' And I can remember George Andrie and other guys broke into tears.

"Meredith turned to me and said, 'I think I'll have my second beer now. I don't want to waste it.' So I put the Beatles' *White Album* back on, and somebody in the back yelled, 'Gent, you motherf***er, shut off that record player.' I said, 'F*** you. If I'm going to die, I'm going to do it listening to the Beatles.' And we took off.

"The only guys who had any humor about it were Meredith and Walt Garrison, who looked back at me and gave me this wry grin that he always had. Garrison always looked at playing football as punishment. He always said, 'I'd rather be in the rodeo because I meet a nicer brand of people.' I loved Walt. He was a wonderful guy with a great sense of humor."

Walt Garrison: "It was snowing like shit and this sonuvabitch takes off and the whole plane shudders. It sounded like a bomb went off. *Boom!* They tried climbing again and *boom!*

"We'd been sitting on the ground for about two hours while they deiced the plane three or four times, and, in the meantime, Lilly musta drank a case of beer. So Lilly was ripped. Lilly stands up in the aisle and says, 'We've all had it, baby. It's alllll over.' And he's still chugging his beer.

"The plane is flying at about a 45-degree angle because they can't get its ass in the air, and all Lilly's beer cans start rolling down the aisle. One of the stewardesses comes skidding down the aisle on her hands and knees. The beer cans are flying by her, and she's screaming, 'We're in trouble. We're in trouble.'

"'Oh no.'

"Everyone is scared to piss. Pete Gent yells, 'Joe Don, Joe Don, we're gonna crash.' But Meredith is still sitting there, and, finally, he takes a long drag on his cigarette and a big swig of beer, and he says, 'Well, it's been a good un, ain't it?'

"Now that's cool. I'm thinkin', 'It's been a good one? What the hell are you talking about? We're gonna die.' But Meredith never even blinked. He just kept sipping his beer. He could have cared less if that plane went down. He didn't actually care. And everybody knew he wasn't bullshitting either."

The plane, of course, didn't crash, and the Cowboys began their march to the title with a game against the Cleveland Browns, a team they had clobbered 52–14 in 1967 and had beaten 28–7 in late September. After beating the Browns in what was supposed to be a formality, the Cowboys were to play the winner of the Colts-Vikings game for the right to go to Super Bowl III. The Cowboys were heavily favored. No one thought the Browns would win.

Against the Browns in Cleveland, in mud up to the players' ankles, the Cowboys played tentatively. The score was 10–10 at the half. The first play of the second half was a pass from Meredith in the left flat to Hayes, but Browns linebacker Dale Lindsey, who was not supposed to be there according to Meredith's keys, batted it up, intercepted it, and ran 27 yards for a touchdown.

On the next possession Meredith threw a pass that hit Rentzel. The ball should have been caught, but Rentzel let the ball bounce off his hands, and a surprised defensive back named Ben Davis intercepted. On the next play Leroy Kelly ran 35 yards for a touchdown.

The game was but two minutes into the third quarter when Landry panicked. He replaced Meredith with Morton, and Meredith did not go back into the game again. He sat on the bench, his head buried between his knees, hurt and depressed, as the Cowboys lost, 31–20. Meredith had played for the Cowboys for nine seasons, but through that whole time Landry had never placed his faith in his country-western-song-singing quarterback. In 1968 Meredith may have given himself to Landry, but against the Browns, Landry made it clear that the surrender was not mutual. When Landry pulled his star prematurely, he ended all chances the Cowboys had of going to the Super Bowl. During the final minutes of the game, Schramm walked over to Meredith on the sideline and threw his arms around him. The two men cried.

Pete Gent: "The idea of replacing your quarterback to have an effect on the team is just nuts. Who pulls your starting quarterback in the third period of a playoff game when you're only one or two touchdowns behind? Particularly when you're a team that's as explosive as we were? He had quit. He was planning for next season. Game over.

"The only guy who *ever* had an effect on the Cowboys by being put into the game was Roger Staubach. Otherwise, every time Tom ever replaced a starting quarterback with a backup quarterback, he lost. And Craig was probably the worst guy to ever put in, because Craig suffered from the same problem that coaches cited for why they never liked to let black guys play quarterback—'cause they always felt that black guys at quarterback would always throw long. That was their theory, like in basketball where they say the black guys never give up the ball. Well, that was the way Craig was. He'd get in and call three long passes rather than try to work his way down the field. And so we lost that game when we might have won if Tom hadn't panicked."

John Wilbur: "This was a very dicey game. It was in Cleveland, colder than shit. Obviously, we weren't prepared. We didn't play good offense, and not too good on defense either.

"After that game, Blaine Nye said, 'It's not whether you win or lose, but who gets the blame.' He didn't invent that comment. Obviously, Landry and the coaching staff blamed Meredith.

"After the game we were all wondering where the hell Don was when he got off the team plane and took that trip to New York. I was a little surprised. I wondered, 'Where is he?'"

Pete Gent: "After losing the Cleveland playoff game, Meredith and I jumped the team plane and went to New York. Our team plane was a 727, and we walked in through the tail. We were sitting there. Meredith and I were on opposite sides of the aisle in the back, and he lit up a joint, handed it to me, and I didn't know what to do, because now guys knew what it was, so I put it out. He looked at me and said, 'Let's get the f*** out of here.' And he grabbed his bag and jumped up, and I got up and we walked out the tail of the plane.

"When we walked into the Cleveland Airport, we were walking by all the gates, and Don said, 'Let's find the first flight out of here. I don't care whether it goes to L.A. or New York. Let's just find one.' We were walking along, and there was a flight to New York, and it was going to leave in 25 minutes, and when we walked over, there was Frank Gifford, who had broadcast the game for CBS. We sat down and started talking with him. And we went to New York with Frank.

"We sat in the last row of the first-class section of the plane to New York. Meredith was on the window, I was on the aisle, and by accident we ended up sitting next to Gifford. Giants owner Wellington Mara's wife was on the other window seat.

"We sat down, and Don lit up another joint, handed it to me. I puffed and handed it back to Meredith, and then he handed it over to Gifford, who looked at it and immediately put it out in his drink. I looked at Frank and just shrugged my shoulders as if to say, 'The guy's on a death trip.'

"We ended up at Gifford's house for a couple of days. Frank took us out to see where his puppy was buried. It was a schnauzer pup that Don had given him, and it had died. Roy Clark had this record out, *Yesterday, When I Was Young*, and it was on the record player, and Frank laid his head against the speaker of the record player and began to cry. When I went by, he looked up and said, 'This is my song.' I looked at him and said to myself, 'Life after football is going to be really tough.' He lived in this beautiful house in Westchester. I thought, 'He's got everything, and he's crying about not being out on the football field getting the shit kicked out of him.' Frank said, 'I'd give anything in the world to trade places with you.' I said, 'Frank, you are so f***ing dumb. I'd give anything in the world to trade places with you.'

"When Frank was first with CBS, he would ditch the crew and come stay with me when they were in Dallas, but I've noticed lately he's just been leaping into these personal attacks against me. When the video of the 75-year anniversary of football came out, he was asked what he thought of it, and he said, 'They didn't have me in very long. They had Pete Gent and Al Davis, two rebels and guys who caused all that trouble.'

"The first nine pages of Frank's book launched off in an attack on me, saying I wasn't a loyal friend of Don Meredith like he was. It was so far out of context. He's going back to *North Dallas Forty* and assuming that character Seth Maxwell is Meredith 100 percent. What I find interesting, Meredith was offered that part for the movie, and Don was at Elaine's one night talking with Bud Shrake, Gifford, and several others, and Don said, 'I just don't want others to think that's me.' And Gifford said, 'Well, it *is* you.' That was 15 years ago. And now Frank's attitude is that I somehow ruined Don's reputation.

"After our stay with Frank, the thing I remember, after we flew back to Dallas, Meredith immediately went back to Landry and apologized. I didn't. I just went back to my house. F*** him. The season was over.

"Landry hadn't known we were gone until they were almost in Dallas, and some of the writers came back and said, 'Meredith and Gent left.' Of course, it became all my fault."

The loss to the Browns did not end the 1968 season. The Cowboys had to travel to Miami to play the Vikings, losers to the Colts in the other divisional playoff. After the game in Florida, Meredith's life would take a darker, sadder turn.

John Wilbur: "Don played very well in the 'Losers Bowl' game in Miami against Minnesota. We won 17–13. Don was voted the MVP of the game. That was a great game. We had a good time down there. It was a lot of fun. We went to the Jockey Club, had a good time. No curfew. We stayed right on the beach. Good fun. Don probably knew it was his last game. It was the last hurrah for everybody, 'cause at the end of that year everybody got traded or quit."

Two players who quit were Don Perkins and Don Meredith. Perkins had played nine seasons and no longer wished to absorb the physical punishment. Meredith, who came with Perkins that first season of 1960, also quit to end the punishment, but the pain that did in Dandy Don was mostly mental. For eight years Meredith had tried to develop a friendship with his coach, but failed. From the time Meredith took over as starting quarterback Landry had allowed him to shoulder all the negative criticism from both the press and fans. Finally, after the vitriol from sportswriters after the Cleveland debacle, Meredith decided he had had enough.

Lee Roy Jordan: "You can accept criticism; all of us got a lot of it through the years, but it was one of those deals where no one—not Tex Schramm, not Tom Landry—ever really took the blame for anything that happened. The players always had to take the blame for the losses. If Tom had a bad game plan or if he called a bad play, it was always the players' fault. It was the defense or the secondary, the linebackers or linemen, or it was the quarterback and the receivers. It was, 'They lost the game. Don threw an interception. We had this guy open. Don missed him.' That was just Tom. And a lot of guys never accepted that, and I think it still bothers Don.

"Don and Tom were so different. Tom felt that he couldn't manage people and make decisions on who got cut and who stayed with the team if he got to be personally involved or close to people. Also, Tom had a hard time visiting with people when he wasn't talking about steps in a defense, movement on the Flex defense, halfbacks running a route. He was shy. And really sometimes he seemed cold, because he would be thinking about something else, and you'd see him in the hall, and Tom might not even speak to you. He might not do that for a week. And all of a sudden you're thinking, 'Gosh, the coach is mad at me or doesn't like me,' and it wasn't that. Tom was thinking about something in football. He wasn't thinking, 'Here's one of my players. I really should speak to him to let him know I know he's alive.' Early in my career it really bothered me, but once I got to know him, it was, 'Hey, this is coach Landry. He really doesn't talk to anyone.' And probably the guys it hurt the most were the quarterbacks who really felt like as much time as they spent with him, there should have been some kind of personal relationship there.

"We all would say, 'We should have a little relationship with him,' but we also accepted and understood, 'Hey, that's Tom.' At the same time you always said, 'God, I wish I had gotten to know coach Landry better.' I know it hurt Don Meredith, and that was one reason Don retired as early as he did."

At the time there were also comments made by coach Landry that Don was retiring because of personal reasons. For Meredith, bombarded with constant criticism, playing football had lost its appeal. At age 30, Don Meredith, one of the most valiant, exciting, memorable athletes to ever play the game of professional football, quit prematurely. If the constant criticism wasn't bad enough, family burdens made continuing impossible.

Pete Gent: "When we were in Florida, Meredith's wife was pregnant, and in late June their daughter Heather was born with birth defects. And they didn't know what had caused it. Don felt tremendous guilt. He blamed his wild life and all the sleeping around that he did. He was sure that played a part in what happened to the baby.

"The baby was badly retarded. She was institutionalized within a year. When I was living in Wimberly, Texas, in the early eighties, she had been at the Brown School for retarded kids in San Marcos at least 10 years. Cheryl brought her over to visit us. She was blind and almost deaf. It was a horrible, horrible story. Talk about trouble on top of trouble. Don just had tragedy after tragedy. Two weeks after the baby was born, Don told Landry he was retiring. He was only 30.

"Don came by my house right after he did it, and he said, 'I've decided to do this, but I thought Tom would try to talk me out of it.' But Tom never did. So it seems possible that Landry intended to replace Meredith after that year anyway, and so Meredith retiring just made his decision easier.

"Landry said that the reason he didn't stop him was that Don was having personal problems and that the personal problems were so great, the best thing for Don was to quit. But Don had had personal problems from day one. Don *always* had personal problems. Meredith's personal problems were monumental from the first day I ever met him. And after he retired Don just went on a binge of self-destruction. He literally was trying to kill himself."

Chapter 32

SELF-DESTRUCTION

In April 1969 Tex Schramm sent Pete Gent a form letter: "Dear Player, We are not required to renew your contract, but we're making you an offer of 10 percent off your salary . . ."

Insulted, Gent sent back a form letter of his own: "Dear General Manager, Here's what I want, and if you don't give it to me, don't bother me."

The next month Tom Landry ended his feud with Gent when he called the receiver into his office for the purpose of informing him he was being placed on waivers. Normally a waived player learns his fate in the transactions columns of his local newspaper, but Landry apparently wanted to tell Gent in person, just to see the look on his face. "I think you've made a mistake," said Gent.

With Frank Gifford's help, Gent was given a shot with the New York Giants. His tenure was short. He saw coach Allie Sherman as incompetent, hated Fran Tarkenton, whom he called "one of the worst people in the world I ever met," and after he called Giants owner Wellington Mara "crazy," his football career came to a sudden end, and he returned to Dallas to live as a civilian.

After Don Meredith retired, he turned his back on football and gave his full attention to the stock brokerage business. It took Meredith about a year to lose just about everything he had. Down to his last grubstake, Meredith headed for Baja California with Pete Gent. It was a wonder either came back alive.

Pete Gent: "Oh God, Don was just so self-destructive. Don really had a death wish. He always wanted someone to accompany him, and I always was stupid enough to go along. Of course, he was tougher than I was. His whole theory was, 'When I die, then I'll stop.' But if I died, that was God's signal for him to slow down!

"In '69 he and his wife and me and my wife were invited to go to the Baja Peninsula in Mexico as the guests of Jantzen, the swimwear company that had a sports advisory board with Don and Jerry West and Larry Mahan, the rodeo cowboy. They put their pictures in *Sport* magazine. It was the exact opposite of the *Sports Illustrated* swimsuit edition.

"Don had gone broke in the stock brokerage business. He had $1,000 left. Before we left for Mexico, Don's father found the $1,000 in cash, and he thought Don had gotten it from me because I was dealing dope. Aw, his parents hated me.

"When we got to Mexico, Don left the $1,000 cash in the room, and when he got back, someone had stolen it. That's how his luck was going.

"We were staying in Cabo San Lucas on the coast. Literally there was nothing there, one hotel and a dirt airstrip. The next hotel was 40 miles away. We went out fishing one day on a boat with a guy from a fishing magazine who wanted to get pictures of Meredith. I was riding along, and what they told you was, 'Don't swim in the bay.' Because they cut bait in the bay, and the bay was full of sharks. We were out on the boat, and it was just gorgeous on the Baja Peninsula, and so we came into the shore, about 200 yards out, and Meredith, who was not a strong swimmer to start with, said, 'Let's swim to shore.' I said, 'Don, Don, sharks, sharks. They said there were sharks here. We shouldn't swim.' He said, 'Boy, sometimes I just wonder about your manhood.' And then he dove in. Ten seconds after he dove in, a big shark swam under the boat, and I was thinking, 'Oh, God, he's going down any minute.' But Don swam right to shore. Nothing got him.

"David Halliburton, who owned a big oil company, showed up in his 60-foot yacht. We went out on Halliburton's boat, and he was just a complete ass, what you'd expect an Oklahoma oilman to be. He had two motorbikes on his boat. Meredith said, 'Come on. We want to borrow them.' Halliburton said, 'Now Don, don't be damaging them.' So we took them out, and we drove to the other motel, 40 miles across the desert. There was nobody there, a couple of maids, nothing open, we couldn't get any drinks, and so we drove back until we saw this tin-sided, tin-roofed shanty, a cantina that had seven or eight Mexican workers all wearing machetes. We went in there, and Meredith had four or five beers, got drunk, and he started talking pidgin Spanish, insulting these Mexican guys. The first thing these guys did was move all the way down to the other end of the room so they didn't have to kill us. The bartender came over and said, 'Please, please, I don't want no trouble in here.' And I was trying to shut him up, too. Don was just saying all sorts of shit. '*Chinga de madre*.' And these guys were about ready to kill us. The bartender hustled us outside, and now Meredith was pissed at me.

"He said, 'Gutless bastard, we could have whipped all their asses.' And he jumped on that motorbike, and it was getting dark, and he took off down the road, opened it flat out. I got on my bike, putt-putt-putting along, until I came up over this hill, and there was Don's bike just scattered across the desert. I didn't see him anywhere.

"I looked off into this ravine, and there he was, down about 20 yards. He had landed on the only sand on the Baja Peninsula. The rest of it was just rock. He had dislocated his shoulder and had a spiral fracture in his right arm.

"We were out there in the desert 20 miles from the hotel, and it was getting dark, and I didn't know what to do. I said, 'Don, I'm going to have to go back to the hotel to get help.' Just about then a truckload of Mexicans came out of nowhere, and they picked him up and put him in the back and took him to the hotel.

"I got Meredith back to the room, and I went down and found two doctors, who were dead drunk. It was fortunate they were there, because the guy who ran the hotel said that two weeks before, a girl had sunburned her eyeballs, and the only medication they had to give her was sleeping pills. And the nearest x-ray machine was 60 miles away in a dentist's office.

"The two doctors saw his shoulder was dislocated, and they popped it back in in the normal fashion, pulled and jerked, without any idea that he had a spiral fracture of the arm, and then they shot him full of morphine, and went back to the party.

"About two hours later they came back, and they were *really* drunk, and they said, 'Look, we don't want him waking us up in the middle of the night for another shot of morphine when we got hangovers. So we're going to give it to him now.' Well, they overdosed him. He went crazy, screaming and yelling, reliving his past. So my wife and I just sat up with him all night, making sure he never fell into a deep sleep, because he'd never have woken up.

"The next day the models came in, and one of the models was Jo Ann Pflug. Don and Jo Ann had this thing before she found Jesus, and so when she got there, he was taped up with electrician's duct tape. His arm was taped to his chest, and as soon as he saw her, he took the duct tape off to screw her somewhere, and his shoulder fell out of joint, and at that point I said, 'I've had it. I'm leaving. Somebody is going to die here, and I'm going to get blamed.'

"Before Don fell off the bike and wrecked his shoulder, Don and the Cowboys were talking serious about his coming back in 1970. They were not happy with the team they had, and Don had gone broke in the brokerage business. So he was thinking about making a comeback, until he took the header off the bike, until he went and dislocated his shoulder and ended up with a spiral fracture of his throwing arm."

Don Meredith did not stay out of the limelight for long. He became a TV star, an entertainer loved by millions of football fans when he fashioned a second career as one of the stars of ABC's *Monday Night Football* with Howard Cosell and Frank Gifford. Don was a natural, singing songs the way he had in the Cowboys huddle and just being his own natural self.

Pete Gent, who had been discarded by the game because he angered management with his logic and humor, has never gotten over it, which is true of so many former professional athletes. After football, Gent channeled his energy into writing books, including three highly acclaimed novels, *North Dallas Forty*, *The Franchise*, and *North Dallas After Forty*. All three are remarkably fine works that reveal the inner workings of the game and the thoughts and emotions of the players in plots devised from the mind of one cynical, angry, beaten, and semi-tough human being.

Because of *North Dallas Forty*, Don Meredith and Pete Gent will be forever connected through their characters Seth Maxwell and Phil Elliott, played by film stars Mac Davis and Nick Nolte. They were the wild ones, painting the entire team with that image. Most teammates will point out that after reading *North Dallas Forty*, they did not recognize much of what went on, and that is because many of the players stayed home with their wives, while Meredith and Gent ran roughshod over Texas and the NFL.

Their retirement after the 1968 season marked the end of the Old NFL. Those who followed would be just as talented, or more so, but none would be as colorful, as salaries would soar and briefcases would replace lunch pails, and investments in stocks and bonds and fancy restaurants would replace the dog track and the ponies.

Meredith and Gent stayed friends after football, though their friendship faded after the release of the movie version of *North Dallas Forty*. Part of the reason was that Meredith had made peace with his past, and Gent still had not. Nevertheless, Gent has never lost his affection for his old running mate.

Pete Gent: "By the time I met Don, he had so many demons in his life, and he tried so hard to deal with them, and I always felt Don did pretty well. I don't know if I'd have done everything exactly the way he did it, but look at the end result, look at where he is today, compared to where he could be. He is not somewhere gagging on his own blood. He's sitting up in the mountains in Santa Fe.

"Jerry Jones and his PR guys have tracked down all the old Cowboys, got their phone numbers, and mailed them out to the rest of us. All Meredith gave was a post office box and a fax number. I intended to buy a box of crayons and fax him an obscene picture, and write on it, 'Remember her, Don?'

"I was talking to Frank Clarke, and the first thing he asked me was, 'Have you talked to Don?' I said, 'Not in 10 years.' Don just drifted away. Don is just drifting, slip-sliding away. Apparently Frank has tried to get a hold of him, a lot of guys, but he won't respond. A fax number? Give me a break.

"Why is this guy this way? Does this mean he never meant any of that stuff? Is he afraid we're going to find out? We saw his nightmares. We *all* had our nightmares. But we never thought any less of him."

Don Meredith is in hiding. It's as though he's in the NFL witness protection program. He doesn't list an address, only a post office box. He refuses to give a phone number, only a number to fax him. When his former teammates fax, they say he doesn't respond. He avoids most football functions. He has become football's equivalent of Joe DiMaggio, the Yankee Clipper, who made ceremonial appearances but fiercely protected his privacy. Why Meredith is so reclusive seems a mystery. As Gent asked, "Why is this guy this way?"

Innocently, I began my correspondence with Meredith by sending him a letter—by fax—asking for an interview. Nothing. I sent a second request, and that time he called me. I told him how much his input would mean to the book, because he was such an important part of it, but he made it clear he would not talk to me about his Cowboys days. I asked if he would talk about his childhood. His voice hardened, and he let me know in no uncertain terms that he would not answer any questions—period.

For a time after football Meredith was a Hollywood star. He had the lead in the TV drama series *Police Story*, and while working in L.A. he met his present wife, Susan, who had been married to a prominent actor. Today, she is not only his wife but his business manager as well.

Some actors protect their privacy and are rarely written about because their agents and managers work hard to control what is written about them. This is apparently what happened with Meredith. My friends at NFL Films told me that when Don agreed to an interview, Susan insisted on seeing every question before he could go on camera. That's control.

After I wrote the final draft, I sent Don several of the early chapters and requested comments. Athletes for the most part love to talk about their lives. This was especially true of the Dallas football players, who loved the game and each other with a ferocity I hadn't seen before. Meredith's refusal to take part in this project with his teammates was puzzling to me, much as his refusal to participate in Cowboys events had been to his teammates. But of one thing I was certain: I was getting the Hollywood freeze-out. One of Don's handlers and spin doctors, in this case his wife, was putting me on notice to watch my back. At this point, I was frustrated and a little bit angry myself, because my experience is that those who refuse to be interviewed are always the first to holler that your account of them is awry when the book comes out. I again asked his wife if Don would be willing to talk about any of this. Again she said he would not. She was not friendly.

I decided to fly out to Santa Fe to learn more about Don Meredith's life. Santa Fe is one of this country's most spectacular locales. It is a jewel of a city built in a valley below the towering Sangre de Cristo Mountains in north-central New Mexico. For two days I visited shops and asked townspeople if they knew him. Most said, "I've seen him around. He used to play football." None were friends of his. Most were of the opinion he was retired, like many residents of the posh adobe city with its trendy art galleries and nouvelle New Mexican cuisine. None knew his address. A reporter on the sports staff of *The Santa Fe New Mexican* knew only that he lived somewhere off the Old Santa Fe Trail. The reporter reiterated Meredith's desire for privacy, relaying to me an account of how he had once tried to interview him as part of a benign piece he had done. He said he had called Meredith's attorney several times to try to arrange a meeting. "I never got anywhere," he said.

I drove past the main square of the city and started up the Old Santa Fe Trail toward the shrub-covered mountains. To the right, the high desert spread out for miles, with adobe houses randomly dotting the landscape. Dozens of dirt paths cut off to either side of the trail, many made unnavigable by heavy steel gates, others disappearing from view into the brush. I marveled that the former Cowboy from small-town Texas was living in this land steeped in the culture of the Pueblo, Hopi, and Navajo. It also seemed a long way from L.A.

After riding aimlessly through the dusty, hot desert on this narrow road with its romantic name, I turned around and drove back toward the city. I saw a sign that read "Museums" and drove to the Museum of International Folk Art, one of the many historic treasures of Santa Fe. After being overwhelmed by the number and quality of the toys and dolls on display, I sat in a museum alcove on a bench staring out at the desert. "If you want to hide, this is as good a place as any," I thought to myself. A security guard came by. I asked him—as I had asked dozens of others—if he knew where Don Meredith lived. Surprisingly, he said he did.

I drove to the spot down a dusty unpaved road off the Old Santa Fe Trail. If the guard's directions were correct, the Merediths live in a large, beautiful adobe home dotted with indigenous trees and cacti with a spectacular view of the pink and purple mountains. They are living in paradise, though one desperately in need of reliable central air-conditioning.

I went to knock on the door. There was no answer. The blowing of the desert wind was the only sound. Was this in fact his house? There were other houses in the neighborhood, but I was loath to start canvassing the area. If it was Don Meredith's house, he remained a ghost, invisible, just as he wants it. Still, I was sorry Don didn't answer. It would have been my opportunity to tell him how much I admired him as a quarterback and as a commentator on *Monday Night Football*. And he wasn't bad in *Police Story* either.

I flew home, thinking of how this boy from Mount Vernon had become a national icon, both in the NFL and as a fixture for football fans on TV. And yet so much about Don Meredith seems shrouded in mystery. He remains, for his fans as well as for his teammates, a towering, if reluctant, hero.

Part II

The New NFL

Chapter 33

THE NEW ORDER

With the unexpected retirement of Don Meredith and the forced dismissal of his sidekick Pete Gent, the law-and-order leadership of Tom Landry regained control of the hearts and minds of the Cowboys, a shift that was reflected nationally with the election of Richard Nixon and his vice president, Spiro Agnew, in the fall of 1968. It would be a strange few years, filled with wonder and horror. A black man, Charles Evers, would be elected mayor in a southern town, Fayette, Mississippi. Neil Armstrong would step on the moon. But Mary Jo Kopechne would drown in Senator Edward Kennedy's automobile after a drunken night of partying, and a week later on the other coast Charles Manson's followers would brutally murder Sharon Tate and four others. A week after that, Woodstock would draw a throng of hippie music lovers, which was followed by news of the My Lai Massacre of 567 old men, women, and children by American soldiers in a faraway Vietnamese village.

It was a time for seriousness, reexamination of purpose. With Gent gone, Lee Roy Jordan could go back to beating up on the opposition and Cowboys management could call a halt to the narc patrols, though drugs would surface as an issue in another year and continue to be a serious problem throughout the coked-up seventies.

With Meredith gone, Landry would no longer have to fight with his quarterback over play calling. The clash of lifestyles between the puritanical coach and his sinning quarterback, however, would continue as Dandy Don's heir apparent, Craig Morton, a left-wing California intellectual who loved to read, was a rock and rolling night owl in his own right. Walt Garrison, the stocky fullback from the Texas country-western, bull-roping rodeo mold, was impressed with Morton's stamina.

Walt Garrison: "Morton was like Meredith. Football was not his whole life. He was more dedicated than Meredith, but that wasn't saying a lot.

"Craig was famous for his partying. That boy could rock and roll, let me tell you. He spent money like it was fertilizer, and he had a couple thousand head of cattle. And boy, he had some good-looking girlfriends. I don't know any of their names, but he'd come to a party and he always had somebody shiny with him. But hell, he didn't have a wife or family and he was the quarterback for the

Dallas Cowboys, which was glamorous as hell, and he had a big contract, so why not enjoy it?

"Morton proved he was a great athlete. You'd have to be great to stay out as many nights as he did and do all the crazy stuff he did and still make practice. The guy was phenomenal."

If Morton provided the nightlife, a gimpy-legged tight end with the disposition of a snorting bull by the name of Mike Ditka added rowdiness. Getting Ditka, a future Hall of Famer with a reputation for bloodlust, was Landry's idea. A few days after the 1969 season, Landry called Ditka, who had feuded with coach Joe Kuharich in Philadelphia while spending much of his season with the Eagles drinking heavily. Ditka was thinking about retiring, even though he still had a year left on his contract.

Landry told him, "We don't even know if you can play anymore, but we're going to bring you down and take a look at you and see if you can play a few more years." Ditka had always hated the Cowboys because of their arrogance and their goody-two-shoes image, but he had despised Kuharich more, and he agreed to come if Landry could swing a trade for him. Just prior to the 1969 season the Cowboys shipped Dave McDaniels, a second-round draft choice who turned out to be one of Gil Brandt's mistakes, to Philadelphia in exchange for the eight-year veteran.

Ditka created headlines a week before the 1969 season began when he was involved in an early-morning accident after a night on the town. He weighed 235, and because of his fat jowls halfback Walt Garrison started calling him "Monk," short for "Chipmunk." Garrison, who enjoyed watching a good train wreck, was fascinated by the unpredictable Ditka.

Walt Garrison: "When Ditka joined the Cowboys, defensive backs Charlie Waters and Cliff Harris used to taunt Ditka: 'Yeah, Mike, you got some great moves.' And they'd swivel their heads back and forth indicating the extent of Ditka's moves.

"In practice Charlie and Cliff would cover Monk like paint. They'd be all over him because he couldn't beat them deep and they knew it. So they didn't have to be honest. Ditka would try his damndest when he was running his routes to get those two little bastards up close enough so he could give them a forearm to the chops. Right before he made his cut, he'd try to cream our cornerbacks. That was Ditka."

With the retirement of Don Perkins, their indestructible back, the Cowboys were looking to Garrison to be one of the starters in the backfield. Garrison, who grew up in Lewisville, Texas, was the perfect Tom Landry ballplayer, an over-achiever who worked as hard as he could to do as well as he could. As a high school boy Garrison had worked in the local peanut mill from midnight to 8:00 every Friday and Saturday night to help make ends meet. The man who owned the nut factory was the brother of the governor of New Mexico, and as a favor to Garrison's dad he helped the kid get a scholarship at Oklahoma State.

Garrison starred at fullback on a bad team that made history his senior year, when OSU beat the mighty Oklahoma Sooners of Bud Wilkinson in a stunning upset, 17–16.

Garrison signed as a free agent with the Cowboys in 1966, sat on the bench for three years, and with Perkins' departure, was finally getting his chance. In Texas, Garrison became a crowd favorite because not only was he a Cowboy but he was also a cowboy who knew how to rope a bull and ride a bucking bronco, and he actually performed and did well in rodeos. He *was* Texas. He dipped snuff, and his commercials for Skoal and Copenhagen made him nationally famous. The other thing he did was whittle, though one time it nearly cost him a finger. This was one tough son of a gun Texan.

Walt Garrison: "One time before a game Bob Lilly brought in a hunting knife for me to sharpen. So I put a hell of an edge on that puppy. Then I decided I'd whittle a little bit. I had a block of wood I carried with me and a couple of pocket knives. I wanted to cut a chunk off that block, so I thought, 'Man, Lilly's knife looks ideal.' Only thing was, it was so sharp it went right through that wood and cut my index finger down to the bone. The whole finger was just hanging there. Blood was gushing out all over the place. It was making such a mess, I had to pull a wastebasket over and let it bleed in there. And I like to fill the damn basket up.

"Charlie Waters was rooming with me then, and he threw up, freaked out, and fainted all at the same time. Then he started screaming, 'Walt, you cut your finger off! You cut your finger off!'

"Charlie called down for the team doctor, but, of course, he was out eatin'. So I told Charlie to go down to the trainers room and get me some tape while I held my finger together. A few minutes later Charlie came back with the tape, and I taped the finger back on. Then I got a big bucket of ice and stuck my finger in it and went to sleep.

"Only Charlie couldn't sleep a wink all night. 'You pissed me off so bad that night,' he said. 'You were sound asleep with your hand in that bucket of ice, and I stayed up all night. I thought you were gonna bleed to death, so I kept checking to see if the ice bucket was filling up with blood.'

"The next morning I went out to the stadium, and the doctor sewed me up. He put 19 stitches in my finger right before the game. And I told him, 'Don't tell Tom.' 'OK, but just don't fumble.'

"I ended up having a great day. I caught seven passes, one of them in the end zone for a TD, and gained 120 yards on the ground. And Charlie played the worst game of his career. And all because I needed something to relax."

The other penciled-in backfield starter in 1969 was another veteran, Dan Reeves, but because the versatile back needed surgery and was on the downside of his career, in 1969 the Cowboys' number one draft choice was a surprise pick, a bruising running back by the name of Calvin Hill. The surprise was that Hill had attended Yale University, an Ivy League school not known for turning out pro football players. (Cowboys fans bristle when reminded that Chuck Mercein, who helped the Packers win the Ice Bowl in 1967, went to Yale.) When the pick was announced, Cowboys fans were incensed. What were Tex Schramm and Gil Brandt doing drafting a player from the lowly Ivy League? But in Hill the Cowboys were getting an intelligent, thoughtful man, just the type of player Landry enjoyed working with. But they were also getting an idealist, a divinity student concerned with right and wrong, good and evil, justice and mercy. And this was one player not afraid to speak out on issues such as Vietnam, racial equality, and players' salaries, much to the Cowboys' chagrin.

Calvin Hill: "In 1969 I went from Connecticut during the civil rights era and the anti-Vietnam era to Dallas, which was much more conservative. That was going into a different culture. What I saw was a place that was more conservative. On a personal level, I had assumed, for example, that most people, white and black, saw Martin Luther King as a responsible, nonviolent figure, and I realized that some people in Dallas didn't see him that way. They saw him as a rabble-rouser. And it was an interesting perspective for me, because while on the one hand I was coming from Yale, I was also a Dallas Cowboy and I was in Perkins Divinity School at SMU, where I was a little more to the left than the prevailing theology in a lot of churches in Dallas. Perkins was very progressive, and I was able to find like-minded people, but I was accustomed to *everyone* being where I was, and in some respects I was a little different."

Though Landry was skeptical that a player from Yale could start at halfback, he was counting on the 6'4", 225-pound Bulldog to play somewhere, perhaps linebacker or tight end, and during training camp Landry had the quiet rookie practice at those positions as well.

Calvin Hill: "Nineteen sixty-nine was an interesting year for the Dallas Cowboys, because after the '68 season three things happened that they really had not planned on. For one, Don Meredith retired, so they knew they had to get a new quarterback, but they still had two-thirds of the backfield intact with Don Perkins and Dan Reeves, and so they drafted me, and after that Don Perkins retired and then Reeves wasn't able to come back, and so the question was, 'Would Dan be able to come back from his latest knee surgery?' And if he did, probably I would have played another position.

"At first they weren't quite sure where they were going to play me, and I went off to the College All-Star Game. And when I got back, Craig Baynham, who had taken Danny's place the year before and was the second running back, got hurt, and so in the second exhibition game against the 49ers I got to start at running back, primarily because no one else was able to play. And I did a lot better than anybody expected.

"I had just been back for a week or so. Typically in the training camp before the vets come in, they spend the first week with the rookies spoon-feeding them, and then when the vets come in, they put things in very quickly. The vets pretty much know what's going on anyhow. So you have to try to understand what they are putting in, but they are doing it at such a quick pace that you can very easily get lost, and what happened, I had a wonderful coach, a man named Ermal Allen. He was just an unbelievable coach and understood the game. Ermal had a great ability to analyze the game and to break it down, and he ultimately got involved in research and development. There was nobody better. But Ermal was also kind of cynical, and he was honest, and sometimes he hit the wrong nerve, but my sense with Ermal was that beyond the cynicism was a lot of truth. I got along very well with him, because I listened to him and I tried to learn from him, and I learned a lot from him.

"In spite of the force-feeding, I didn't know half the time whether I was getting a pitch or whether I was getting a handoff, so that first exhibition game I was uncomfortable. Despite that, in football there's a certain level where you are instinctive. When you're a running back, and you have the ball, you know people are trying to hit you, so you try to avoid them as much as possible. I wasn't completely out to lunch."

John Wilbur: "In 1969 Calvin Hill was a rookie. That was a pretty good choice by the Cowboys. Calvin was an inspiration. I'll never forget his first exhibition game. Calvin had just come back from the All-Star Game, and they completely changed practice around so that he could get work in for the San Francisco game. He came in, and for one week we had what they called 'Calvin Hill drills,' drills just for him. He was the only running back. He'd run the plays, and the coaches would explain them to him. And we'd run another play. And we did this every day for four, five days. He would get daily coaching, and it would be a ballet for Calvin Hill in practice.

"The game came, and we were playing the 49ers at Kezar Stadium, and Calvin went out and ran for 106 yards. After the game he was sitting next to me on the team bus, and Calvin said to me, 'God, John, I don't think I did very well. I did terrible. I played one of the worst games I ever had in my life. I blew this play, and I blew that assignment.' Little did he know it was the start of a brilliant career, and he had played a wonderful game."

During the six years he was a Cowboy, Calvin was outspoken on the issues that were important to him, and he made Cowboys management nervous.

Cornell Green: "Calvin made a big impression, because he was the closest thing to Jim Brown I've seen. People don't realize that Calvin was 6'4", weighed 235 pounds. Calvin could fall forward for five yards. He could get yards without even passing the line of scrimmage. I just thought he was a great back.

"There were people at the top of the Cowboys organization who didn't like him, people were just thinking he was going to change the status quo too much, or he was going to ask for too much money."

Those people would be right on both counts. With the coming of Calvin Hill and a bumper crop of young, politically savvy black men, Schramm and Landry would have to justify their actions and learn to get along with these players for the next decade. Over time, and after making several mistakes in the way he handled rebellious stars, Landry would learn that he would have to adapt to them, not the other way around. As the sixties came to a close, so did the era of the silent, grateful, hat-in-hand football player. In the future these players would demand fairness, rationality in decisions, and above all, respect—or else.

Chapter 34

ROGER

It must have been fate, because there is no other way to explain how Roger Staubach ended up becoming the symbol of the Dallas Cowboys in the seventies. Staubach began his pro career in 1969, and before his retirement a decade later, he would be known as Captain America, the leader of America's Team. He would quarterback the Cowboys to four Super Bowls and be hailed as one of the great players of his generation.

He had been drafted in the 10th round his junior year at Navy all the way back in 1964 by Tex Schramm and Gil Brandt, and after five long years—in sports a lifetime—he was finally free from the navy to begin his pro football career. Tom Landry had been willing to wait. Landry, after all, himself missed four years while flying bombers in World War II and then returned to the University of Texas. And Landry knew Staubach had been someone special, a Heisman Trophy winner his senior year at Navy, a naval officer, a man dedicated to whatever he attempted. In 1968 Staubach had spent his two-week leave attending Landry's quarterback school, and Landry had been impressed with the fine shape he was in and with his work-hard attitude. Whether he was a skilled-enough passer, that was another issue.

But for Staubach to become the Cowboys' quarterback, a series of events had to transpire, and eerily, those events all took place. The first came in June 1969 when third-string quarterback Jerry Rhome demanded to be traded and was granted his request. The next came a month later when Don Meredith unexpectedly retired. Without that one event, it is doubtful Staubach would ever have remained a Cowboy, for he would have been backing up *two* veteran quarterbacks, Meredith and Craig Morton. The 27-year-old either would have rotted on the bench, or, more likely, he would have demanded to be traded. But with Meredith in retirement, Staubach came to camp accepting his backup role—for the first year, anyway.

When Staubach reported in the summer of 1969, to most outsiders he began as a curiosity. It didn't seem conceivable that he would ever play in the NFL, never mind take Craig Morton's job. But those people didn't know what made Roger Staubach tick. All his life Staubach had started low on depth charts and had worked his way up to fame and glory. Frank Merriwell was a dime-novel character who usually won the game in the final moments by doing something implausibly heroic. But he had nothing on Roger Staubach.

Roger Staubach: "I grew up in Cincinnati. I was an only child, and my parents lived their Catholic faith, and so I grew up in a Catholic grade school, like back in the good old days, with nuns that beat a lot of sense into my head. I feel the nuns had a great influence on me. I had a very positive experience as far as my faith and my education, and it carried on through high school. I went to Purcell High School, an all-boys Catholic school, and I would have gone to a Catholic college, like Notre Dame, but it wasn't meant to be.

"I played football, basketball, and baseball at Purcell. I also played baseball in summer leagues. I played against Pete Rose. He was on a team called S&H Green Stamps, and he went to Western Hills High School. I was highly rated, along with some others like Eddie Brinkman, who went to the same high school as Pete. Pete wasn't at a high level at that time, but he developed. Pete was kind of a scrawny kid in high school, but he had these intangibles, and he continued to develop. He got better, stronger.

"In football I played tight end and defensive back as a freshman, and my sophomore year our coach, Jim McCarthy, switched me to quarterback. In my junior year I broke my hand, so I played only at defensive halfback. So my senior year was the first year I really played quarterback.

"We were a running team. We had a T formation offense, so we didn't throw very much. I threw the ball maybe five or six times a game. I didn't think that was going to be that exciting, but that switch changed my life. I had this instinct for running. I improvised, and I ran. No one really knew about my arm. I had a real strong arm from baseball, but no one knew if I was going to be a passing quarterback.

"I signed a tender that if I went to any Big Ten school, I'd go to Purdue. Ohio State had recruited me, and also Northwestern and Michigan, and the quarterback coach at Purdue, Bob DeMoss, felt I had the arm, saw that I was tall, saw my running abilities, and saw my baseball arm, so he wanted to groom me as a college quarterback, so I really liked him. I was very close to going to Purdue, but it was one of those things in life where you're not sure, and I was torn between going there and going to the Naval Academy, which was also talking to me.

"I would have gone to Notre Dame, but they never recruited me. When you're in Cincinnati and you're a Catholic kid, Notre Dame is a big deal. I could have gone there. But they didn't contact me until June after I played in a North-South high school All-Star game. The head coach's nephew was the quarterback, and he kept moving me around, so in that All-Star game I played weak safety, wide receiver, and in the fourth quarter I played quarterback. The college scouts were watching, and after that game Notre Dame offered me a scholarship, but it was too late. I was committed to go to the Naval Academy.

"I actually went off to junior college first, to New Mexico Military Institute. I had high grades, but to get to Navy you had to get a 500 on the SATs in both

English and math, and in English I had a 480. I had 600-something in math. I only took them once, and I didn't want to take them again. I just said, 'Forget about Navy.' I wasn't sure what I wanted to do.

"They then sent this coach from the New Mexico Military Institute to see me. All the service academies had an arrangement with New Mexico Military. I didn't want to go to prep school because I didn't want to waste a year. I didn't think I had to prep for anything, but the coach talked about the school, said the Navy foundation would fund my scholarship, and it turned out to be one of the real blessings in life. Academically it was just a fantastic school, and it was like a redshirt year for me athletically. If I would have gone straight to the Naval Academy with only a year of high school football under my belt, I think it would have been difficult. I don't know what would have happened. And going to New Mexico really helped me develop militarily. I struggled to adapt, not that I was undisciplined, but I got a few demerits. Shining your shoes and doing a lot of stuff like that just didn't seem important, though it really was. It was part of the system, and you had to live with the system, and I had to adapt to that. And that helped me also. And in football we played a very tough junior college schedule.

"When I entered Navy, I really didn't know what my plans were. I knew I wanted to get a good education. The navy would have to sell me on a career, and that's what they do. A lot of kids go there with the dream of being a career marine or naval officer, and they don't do it. And a lot of them with no plans all of a sudden say, 'This is my life.' I didn't really know. I went to Navy because I knew I'd get a good education and also because Navy said I could play both baseball and football. At Navy, you're regimented. You don't have a lot of time to goof off, and I thought it was important if I was going to play sports in college that I just didn't want to skate through. That was fortuitous for me to be thinking that way. I might have spent too much time at sports and not on academics, but at Navy they really made you study.

"As a plebe I had a very good football season. My sophomore year we had two senior quarterbacks, a sophomore quarterback, and a junior quarterback, so on the depth chart I was fifth team going into varsity practice. Our coach, Wayne Hardin, knew about me, and he was counting on me for maybe my junior or senior year, but one of the seniors got hurt and then the sophomore lost a kidney in practice, so now I was third team, though it didn't seem that what I did was going to be very important.

"The senior quarterback, Ron Clemek, was very good. He had had a good junior year, and Bruce Able, the junior quarterback, was good, had a great arm. I was very worried. I was working my tail off.

"We got off to a tough start, lost to Penn State and Minnesota, and I played a little bit at the end of those games. The team was struggling. Our next game was against Cornell, which hopefully was going to be an easier game, but Ron got off to a shaky start, and coach Hardin put Bruce in, and he had a bad series, so

Wayne was ticked off, and so he threw me in there, and we went in and scored, and we won something like 41–7, and so the next week I started against Boston College, and after the first series he took me out. Ron came in, and he didn't do much, and [coach Hardin] put me back in, and I never came out again. We ended up beating Boston College.

"I was a scrambling quarterback, and our team needed that. Ron was a great passer, but we didn't have the protection, so I ended up doing a lot of scrambling and making things happen, and that was it. I stayed in the rest of the time.

"In college I ran a lot, and people thought, 'Well, he's a runner.' But if I was just a runner, I never would have made it. In college I had a high percentage of completions. I was a passer, too. But that scrambling confused people. The scouts were wondering, 'Is Roger a scrambling quarterback or is he a passer?' At Navy we had a pro offense. It wasn't a running offense. Wayne would rather have his quarterback drop back and throw the football. He was worried about injuries the same way Landry was later, though in college it's not as bad. And I was not like that. I was different. If I was in trouble I ran. So Wayne adapted to me, because he was like Landry. They knew I wanted to win, and they put up with it.

"I was drafted by the Cowboys as a junior in 1964. I was eligible because I had spent a year in junior college. No one thought I would ever play pro ball. I had another year at the Naval Academy and then four years of military service. But Tex Schramm and Gil Brandt saw I was eligible, and so the Cowboys drafted me in the 10th round, and Kansas City did the same thing in a later round.

"I almost signed with the Chiefs. Lamar Hunt came to see me in Annapolis. He designed a contract that would pay me a bonus of $10,000, pay me $500 a month while I was in the navy, and if I left the navy, I'd get a contract for a certain amount.

"I called Paul Borden, a navy legal officer, and I said, 'Paul, can I do this? This is more money than I'm making in the navy.' Paul checked it out, and he said, 'There's no obligation to leave the service. The navy has no problem with it.' I thought, 'Gee, this is a windfall for me.' So I mentioned it to Dan Petersen, an assistant basketball coach at Navy. Danny, who was close to Gil Brandt, had led the Cowboys to Pete Gent, and Dan said, 'You ought to talk to the Cowboys about it.' So I mentioned it to Captain Borden, and he called and talked to Gil Brandt, and Gil said, 'Yeah, we want to talk to him.' The next weekend the Cowboys were playing Philadelphia, so Captain Borden flew up there and met with Gil and Tex while Clint Murchison was in the room, and he called me and said that the Cowboys would do the same deal. I said, 'Fine.' 'Cause at the time they were in the NFL, not the AFL, and they had drafted me higher than Kansas City, so I called Lamar Hunt back and said, 'I appreciate everything, but . . .' He said, 'We'd like to negotiate a better deal.' I said, 'That isn't the issue.' I didn't want to get into a bidding war. I just wanted to get it behind me, and I felt Dallas was the right thing, so I signed with Dallas. If you think about it, the $500 a month is almost ludicrous today.

"When it came time for my selection, my choices were to be a line officer in the staff corps, to fly or be an officer on a ship, to become a marine, or to go into the supply corps. When I entered Annapolis, it was discovered that though my vision was perfect, at a distance, certain dark colors look alike to me. Dark green and black look the same to me, and as a result it prevented me from being a line officer. They didn't want to train someone to go into a staff corps and be disqualified from flying. The marines wanted me, and I thought very strongly about that because, though being in the supply corps was a great responsibility, at the Academy if you're gung ho, you want the navy line or the marine corps or flying. The civil engineering corps or the supply corps is less prestigious. So at the last minute I was thinking of the marines. The marines are special. They are great, dedicated, but the marines wanted to be marines from the time they entered as plebes, and that wasn't me. I didn't feel like I was one of them. So when I went in for my selection, I still wasn't sure what I was going to do, and I decided to stay in the navy, and so I went into the supply corps. I had a lot of responsibility in Vietnam. Later I learned a lot at Pensacola. I had a big job at the Pensacola Air Station. It helped me as a businessman.

"I volunteered to go to Vietnam. The choices I had were to go out to sea for a couple years or if I went to Vietnam, I'd go for one year and then be on shore duty. At the time my wife, Marianne, was pregnant. We had just had a little girl. Vietnam meant I'd get home sooner. And Vietnam had this aura about it that you felt you wanted to participate. Even though I wasn't going to be out there fighting, I was still in a big, big support role. In fact, in an article in *Stars and Stripes* I said I felt guilty I wasn't doing enough in Vietnam, and everybody in the supply corps got ticked off at me. But I didn't mean it in a negative way. When you're a competitor, and you're not out in the middle of things . . . and because my classmates were out there fighting, and I was behind the scenes supporting . . . that was my job.

"In 1968 I was running the supply arm of the Pensacola Naval Base, and I took a two-week leave and went to my first Cowboys training camp. I had two weeks with the rookies and a very short time with the veterans.

"I was playing for the Pensacola Goshawks after hours. Two months before I was scheduled to arrive, I developed tendinitis in my throwing shoulder. It was serious, because I had never had any trouble with it before. I would go out and throw, and the next day it would be sore as could be. And I was really worried about it. I could not have gone to training camp the way my shoulder was. But I got one shot of cortisone in that shoulder, and I had two very good weeks of training camp.

"I impressed them that I was in good shape, and Landry gave me a playbook, and I was allowed to keep it, which was a real vote of confidence. When I went back to Pensacola, I made up my mind for sure I was going to get out of the navy and play football, and in the spring of '69 I went back to training camp. I was there with Don Meredith and Craig Morton. Jerry Rhome did not go. They were in the middle of trading him.

"And Don Meredith was great to me. He was a fun guy. He was a player's player. They liked him a lot. Craig Morton was a very nice person. Craig is one of the finest. He'd give you the shirt off his back. He was a heck of a football player. I got along with him. But I knew my age was a factor, and I wanted to play, whether it was in Dallas or someplace else.

"I remember when the Cowboys PR guy called me and told me Meredith had retired, I was excited. Because even though I had had a real good camp the year before, I didn't know if I was going to make the team. They probably would have kept the three of us. But I wanted to play. I was thinking, 'Gee, I'm 27, I've got *two* veteran quarterbacks in front of me.' Don was only 30 years old. Now at least I knew that I would definitely be the number two quarterback. I figured I'd spend the first year learning the NFL. But I was thinking that long-term I didn't know where I'd be."

Chapter 35

THE DEPTHS

When Roger Staubach joined the Cowboys, he didn't fit into either of the two camps. He was at odds with the liberals on the team in that he had been in Vietnam, understood why America was fighting there, and defended the policy. And he did not fit into the conservative group of southern hellions in that he was married and square, went to the movies instead of the bars, wasn't hesitant about socializing with the black players, and was such a nose-to-the-grindstone religious straight arrow that he made the Jim Beam crowd uneasy.

Walt Garrison: "Roger Staubach was the epitome of what Landry thought a quarterback should be. He was the most dedicated guy you'll ever be around. If somebody did 100 sit-ups, Roger was going to do 101. If somebody ran a mile in 6 minutes, Roger would do it in 5:59. If somebody threw the ball 60 yards, he was going to throw it 61.

"Landry felt that when you've got a guy as dedicated as Roger was, it was very easy to get the other players to go that extra mile to win, because your leader was out there doing it. Besides that, Roger was a good Christian, went in and served his country, and had a great wife and kids. Landry thought he'd died and gone to heaven.

"Now you've got to admire that kind of dedication. The principles Roger stood for, he wouldn't waver from. If a guy won't compromise his beliefs, no matter what they are, you gotta respect him.

"Roger is not a hypocrite. He doesn't say, 'Hey, you oughta do this.' And then he does something else. Roger just says, 'This is what I do.' He doesn't try to tell you what you oughta do. He ain't a bit phony. One thing about Roger Staubach, I've always respected him. I always will. I don't want to spend a lot of time with him, but I sure do respect his ass.

"See, Roger just wasn't given to having a good time. He's against having fun. It's in his genes or something. Anything that's fun, you're not supposed to do it. That is the way he feels. One time somebody said, 'Boy, wouldn't you love to have your kid grow up to be more like Roger Staubach?' And Meredith said, 'No way. I'd want my kid to have more fun.' That's the way I feel about Roger. I could never figure out why he couldn't loosen up and have more fun."

Garrison and the other good old boys made fun of Staubach's prudishness. Staubach didn't smoke, drink, or run around at night, and the others would prey on his naïveté.

During training camp in 1969, Roger noticed that a very sexy young woman was watching practice. She had on tight shorts and a thin blouse. She was dating one of the players on the team, and after practice, the player called Staubach over and said, "Roger, you're a Catholic, so I'd like you to meet Sister Teresa."

Roger was very polite and respectful.

"I knew I'd never seen a nun who looked like that," Staubach said later, "but I kept thinking, maybe she really was. I fell for it. The girl told me she was on leave from a convent. I went around the entire camp thinking she was a nun. Every time I'd see her, I'd say, 'Hello, Sister Teresa.' Can you imagine how those guys were laughing at me?"

One time Walt Garrison had Roger try snuff, only he didn't tell him he had to spit it out. During a team meeting Staubach threw up twice, and he was sick for two days, missing practice. He didn't forgive himself, or Garrison.

Yet another time during practice, not long after Walt and his wife had their first son, Roger said to Garrison, "I don't know, gosh darn, my wife and I have had four kids and they've all been girls. And the first one you have is a boy. How did you do it, Walt?"

And Garrison said, "Well, I really can't explain it, Roger. But I'll tell you what, if you bring Mary Ann by the house I'll try and getcha one."

According to Garrison, Roger "was pissed off at me for five years about that crack."

Said Garrison, "Seemed innocent enough to me. Just trying to help out a friend any way I could."

When Staubach joined the team in 1969, right away there was a quarterback controversy. Morton had played behind Meredith and had five years of schooling in the Landry system. Staubach was just an untested rookie. Each could be effective in his own way. Roger had an uncanny ability to scramble that left defenses with their tongues hanging out. But Morton was a disciplined veteran who knew the advantages of staying in the pocket and sharing the load. The offensive players wanted Morton.

Walt Garrison: "The team was split. The defense liked Roger because he made things happen. But the offensive guys loved Craig. We thought he was a better quarterback. He knew the offense better than Roger. He could read defenses better. He had a better feel for the game and a better arm. And Roger hadn't played professional football for very long, whereas Morton had been playing for six or seven years."

If Staubach had one advantage over Morton, it was that he worked harder. In fact, Staubach worked harder than Sisyphus, the mythical figure who every day had to push that big rock up the steep hill, only to see it roll back down at the end of the day. Perhaps part of Morton's laissez-faire attitude was that he had sat behind Don Meredith so long, he was not able to immediately readjust his thinking to his new, more important role.

Pettis Norman: "He would have had a better shot at greatness had he taken over in an orderly transition. *Nobody* expected Meredith to retire. Meredith was very young, 30 years old. Other quarterbacks were going until they were 35, 38 years old. Nobody expected Don to retire, and it was a shock. I know it was a shock to Craig. So instead of Craig going to training camp and being the number two guy, all of a sudden he is the number one guy. 'Here's the ball. Get out there. This team is expected to win.'

"We had been to the championship game for two years, and we were expected to win, and that was a tremendous assignment for a young guy who did not have a decent apprenticeship."

In the end Morton's departure from Dallas had nothing to do with his attitude. It had everything to do with his lack of mobility and his bad luck to be playing alongside Staubach, a competitor who pursued his job with pit bullish ferocity. To keep Landry from replacing him, Morton would have had to avoid injury and win the Super Bowl. In the third game of the 1969 season, against the Philadelphia Eagles, Morton was outstanding. He was 15 for 20 and threw for 239 yards, including touchdown passes to Lance Rentzel, Dan Reeves, and Mike Ditka. That's how good Morton would have been had he remained healthy. But Morton was a gutsy pocket passer who stood his ground to pass, even when defensive commandoes were about to lower the boom. And Landry's offenses did not feature protecting the quarterback as a priority. Morton was injured first during the exhibition season and then against Atlanta in the fourth game of the season, giving rookie Roger Staubach his first opportunity to play.

Roger Staubach: "In '69, Craig's first injury, which wasn't serious, was his finger in the Jets game. He messed it up, so I got to finish the game. I came in and pulled a comeback. It was one of those stories, though it was just an exhibition game. But I was all excited. Here I was, given a chance.

"The next week we played the Baltimore Colts, who had a really good team, and I ran like a wild man that day. I ran for over 100 yards. I did not have a good passing game. I threw four interceptions, though some of those interceptions were kind of iffy . . . one was tipped. But all of a sudden the Baltimore Colts players, like Bubba Smith, were saying, 'I hope we don't have to play this guy again,' 'cause it was a hot night, and I was running all over the place. The fans liked it. But Landry was sitting there saying, 'Geez, what have I got here?'

"In the season opener we played the St. Louis Cardinals, and Morton couldn't play, and Landry's comments in the paper were, 'We're starting this rookie quarterback.' It *was* an unusual deal, a rookie quarterback starting. For him it was really amazing. But I was a little bit older than the usual rookie. Landry said, 'I don't know what's going to happen with Roger.' In other words, I can't predict what he's going to do. And after practice he would stay out with me. We'd work on, 'Hey, this is what you need to see. Larry Wilson is the weak safety. We're going to run this post pattern to Lance Rentzel, and you pump Wilson, and I promise you if you keep looking at Wilson and pump to the other side, if you don't look at Rentzel . . .'

"He gave me a lot of coaching points, and sure enough, the first time we ran that play, Rentzel ran a turn-in, and Bob Hayes did a hook, and I pumped to the hook, and Wilson took two steps forward, Rentzel ran a post and beat the cornerback, and we hit a 60-yard touchdown. It was my first touchdown. It was the most exciting feeling I ever had as a player.

"The rest of the game went very well. I ran well, didn't throw any interceptions. I hit Denny Homan on a long pass that he should have scored on, but a guy caught him from behind. And after that we played the Saints the next week, and Craig came back and had a really good game, and then in Atlanta, he got hurt badly. Morton scrambled out of the pocket, and Claude Humphrey tackled him, and Craig suffered a partial separation of his shoulder. We were playing the Eagles the next week, and he wasn't supposed to play—I practiced the whole week—but in the pregame warm-ups he said, 'I can go.' So he started and had a great game. Craig threw four touchdown passes, but as the year went on his arm started to become a problem."

Calvin Hill: "Until Craig got hurt, he was the leading passer in the league. Craig was playing at a very high confidence level, and though he had had one knee operation prior to my coming there, physically he was in great shape.

"I remember when he first came into training camp, to me he looked like a million dollars. He was a vet, he had a cannon for an arm, and he knew all the keys. And I got along fine with him. I was a rookie, so he spent little time with me, but he was helpful to try to make sure I knew what I was doing.

"Craig and Roger were in the same class, but Roger had been away for four years in the navy, so again, so much of the Cowboys system was understanding, and Craig had understood it, and Roger was trying to play catch-up, and it was difficult."

Morton's quandary was that after his shoulder injury against Atlanta, he should have undergone an operation. But Morton had waited four long years to become the Cowboys' starting quarterback, and when the doctors told him he could play despite the injury, he opted to go on, pain or no.

On his return, Morton threw very well. He kept playing, too, even while the shoulder kept getting worse. Toward the end of the season he lost the feel for throwing the ball. His passes had little on them.

Morton used the running ability of Rookie of the Year Calvin Hill, who broke the Cowboys single-game rushing record with 138 yards in his second game, and that of Walt Garrison. And behind an outstanding offensive line of Ralph Neely, Tony Liscio, Rayfield Wright, John Niland, John Wilbur, and centers Dave Manders and Malcolm Walker, he threw 12 touchdowns to Lance Rentzel. The wounded but still effective Craig Morton, in his first year as the new Cowboys quarterback, skillfully led his team to an 11–2–1 record. In 1969 the

Cowboys lost badly only to Cleveland and by a single point to the Los Angeles Rams in a game marked by the absence due to injury of Hill, Neely, and Jethro Pugh. Hill, who finished the season with 942 yards—second in the league only to Gale Sayers—had fractured his foot in mid-November against Washington and was slowed the final three games. The injured foot would keep him from the vaunted 1,000-yard mark and plague him for the rest of his career.

Craig Morton should have been lionized in Dallas. He was talented and gutsy. His offense was tops in the NFL, quite a feat for a first-year quarterback. Instead he was vilified after the Cowboys were blown out in the conference championship playoff game by the Cleveland Browns, 38–14, in the Cotton Bowl. The game began on an ominous note, when a Browns punt accidentally touched Cowboys lineman Rayfield Wright. The Browns recovered, and the rout was on. In the first half Morton completed just three passes, and Hill and Garrison ran for just 22 yards on seven carries as Cleveland took a 17–0 lead behind the passing of Bill Nelsen to Paul Warfield. After Morton threw a pass that was intercepted by Walt Sumner and run back 88 yards for a touchdown, Landry put Staubach into the game in the fourth quarter to mop up.

In the Cowboys locker room following the game and in the papers afterward, the players' criticism was not directed toward their quarterback as much as it was toward Landry, who as part of the defensive game plan had switched Mel Renfro and Otto Brown between safety and cornerback, depending on the situation, in an attempt to keep Cleveland from isolating Warfield on Brown.

Cornell Green: "Tom Landry had Otto Brown and Mel Renfro switching back and forth between safety and cornerback 'cause Tom thought he could hide a weakness that way. Otto was the weakness, and with Paul Warfield, you knew Cleveland was going after Otto. I was playing the other corner, and Gary Collins was the other end, and they thought me and him would be a wash, so he left that alone, and went the other way, directly at Otto. And so in certain formations, he put Mel out there and put Otto at safety, and on certain formations he switched back, and I have no idea what that was for, because I thought it was stupid. And Cleveland proved it was stupid."

The other criticism felt by the players was that because of Landry's changes in the game plan only days before the game, the confidence of some of his players on both defense and offense had been shaken.

Lee Roy Jordan: "Changing game plans close to game day caused us to doubt ourselves, and in his pep talks before the game and during halftime coach Landry had some doubts about us being able to beat that Cleveland team. And it came through to the team that he doubted we could win. In the locker room just prior to the second half, coach Landry let slip that he had doubts the Cowboys would win the game.

"We were a good football team. We were as good as or better than the Browns were any time we stepped on the field, but after halftime coach Landry was making his 'get ready' speech for the game, and all of a sudden it slipped out that he didn't know whether we could win the game, but 'Let's go play them a good game.' I looked at the face of every guy around me there, and I could see the shock on every guy who was sitting there, because all of a sudden they felt, 'Coach doesn't believe we can win. He doesn't believe in us as a unit.'

"So it was really a shocking thing, and I know it slipped out, but you have to say, 'It was in his mind or it wouldn't have been on his lips.' It was a shocking deal, and we went back out, and in the fourth quarter they intercepted a pass against Craig and ran it in for a touchdown, which is the worst thing in the world that can happen to you as a football team."

Pettis Norman: "In the locker room after a game in which we had expected so much of ourselves, it was just total devastation. I took losses as hard as anybody. I would be the last person to leave the locker room, just because I would sit there trying to replay the game in my mind to figure out how it could have gone the way it did, realizing that you don't have another chance to redeem yourself. This time it was not a home-and-home situation. This was it. We lost, and we were going home. A lot of things would run through my mind on a day like that. It was a low point."

Roger Staubach: "To me, Landry's low point was after that playoff loss to Cleveland my rookie year in 1969. We were getting ready to board a flight to Miami for the Playoff Bowl. People were crying for his scalp, and he looked like a beaten man that day. We had a meeting at Love Field before taking off, and he was the lowest I've ever seen him. He was ashen. He'd had it, and he was down."

After the Browns beat the Cowboys in the 1969 championship, Meredith called Landry at home and told him he wanted to drop by to talk to him. "The first and last time I was at his house," said Meredith. Meredith was deeply concerned about his coach's emotional well-being and advised Landry to retire.

Don Meredith: "I listened to some of the game on the radio, and it had to be the worst game I ever heard. It was kind of sad for such a dedicated, disciplined man to wind up in such a situation. We used to be at odds on a lot of things, but we learned to respect one another for different reasons. We're not exactly identical personalities.

"Here was a man who devoted 10 years to this year. His philosophy was challenged and all but destroyed. He had taken a torpedo in the hull and was drifting.

"Tom asked me, 'What can I do?' And I told him to hang it up, forget it, get out. Obviously he didn't follow my advice. He is such a fine man . . . it was kind of sad for such a dedicated, disciplined man to wind up in such a situation."

At the Playoff Bowl in Miami the defensive players staged a rebellion of sorts. They had lost confidence in the Flex defense, and they petitioned Landry to allow them to play defense the way they wanted to play, by just using their natural instincts rather than reading keys and moving as those keys dictated. Landry allowed the defense to line up in a 4-3 and play any way they wanted.

They lost to the Rams, 31–0. End of rebellion.

Chapter 36

CRACKING DOWN

At a Fellowship of Christian Athletes banquet in Atlanta in late June 1968, Tom Landry gave a speech just a short time after both the Martin Luther King and Robert Kennedy assassinations. In that speech he didn't address the root cause of the civil disobedience bubbling up in America. Rather, in speaking about the changes in society, he concentrated on what he saw as a loss of the puritan ethic, with too many people not working hard for what they got. Too many people, he noted, were coming to expect something for nothing. His solution: finding Christ. "The hearts of men must change," he said. "Only Christ can change men so drastically."

In his speech he described how athletes had changed through the years. He said, "I am starting my 20th year in professional football, and I have seen a change in the athlete coming into pro ball. In 1949 all the athletes were a product of the Depression years and World War II. Coaches could treat them any way they wanted and the athletes would respond because to them success was important. The alternatives they had seen had not been attractive.

"In the midfifties, the athletes entering pro football were the products of the postwar era—plenty of everything—and we observed more independence, and motivation became an important factor. Job opportunities were plentiful in other lines of work.

"In the sixties, I have seen the decay so prevalent in other areas of American life start to take its toll on the athlete. Competitiveness is being eroded; the will to win and determination to be the best are not so important anymore. There are easier ways to get by. Now is the time we must reestablish a competitive spirit in America that has made it the greatest nation on earth with the highest standard of living."

Later in his speech he said, "If you love your neighbor as much as you love yourself, you will not want to hurt or cheat him, or kill him or steal from him. If we would all do that, it would take care of everything else. But until that happens, we need a value that may be the most pressing at the moment. That is discipline."

He told those in the audience to either play by the rules or suffer the consequences. He cited Police Chief William Parker of Los Angeles, who had said, "I don't care what color they are or what cause they represent. They're breaking the law and there's only one place for them, in jail." Concluded Landry, "It is high time we define clearly the rules for playing the game in the USA. And it is high time we had the intestinal fortitude to make them stick."

The lines were drawn. It was "My way or the highway." Whether Landry could stick to his guns and continue to win would be a continuing drama throughout the seventies, as a cast of talented but troublesome players Landry considered "rebels and misfits" would come and go through the Cowboys locker-room door.

One of the first of these rebels to come to the Cowboys was a talented linebacker by the name of Steve Kiner. The Cowboys drafted Kiner in the third round in 1970 after a solid career at the University of Tennessee. The Cowboys were impressed that Kiner was a hitter. What they didn't know about him was that he was an enigma by Texas standards: the son of a career army officer, he was fervently antiwar; a root-for-the-underdog guy, he had befriended black teammates in both high school and college; and he loved to smoke dope. Football and marijuana were his two loves. He loved to play hard, and off the field he loved to get high. When Kiner reported to the Cowboys for rookie training camp, he told the media, "Chuck Howley is getting old, and I'm here to take his job." The vets noticed, and on the night the rookies were made to get up and sing, Kiner was made to sing "Happy Birthday" to Howley.

During training camp Kiner's roommates were the Cowboys' number one draft choice, Duane Thomas, a talented running back from West Texas State, and Margene Adkins, a superfast, talented pass receiver who had left college early to play in the Canadian League. Adkins was a second-round draft choice. What made the arrangement somewhat unusual for the Cowboys was that Kiner was white, and Thomas and Adkins black.

Steve Kiner: "During the Cowboys training camp I moved in with Duane Thomas and Margene Adkins, who are black. I can honestly say there were no other white players on the team that were comfortable in that situation. And so I moved right in, and that drew the lines right there.

"Duane was the number one pick, and Duane and I became best of friends. I'm not trying to sound cosmic or anything, but Duane and I were sort of drawn together. It's hard to explain, but I felt real comfortable and he felt real comfortable, and we liked each other. Duane was a very gentle, pleasant guy, and he had a charisma, an aura about him, whether it was because he was the first-round pick or because he was Duane Thomas, I don't know, but beside the fact he was an incredible athlete, he was a likable person. He wasn't at all like—and this is going to be stereotypical—he wasn't at all like what you would imagine a black athlete—that's not fair to say either—'cause I was thinking of some of the negative stereotypes. Well, he wasn't the typical ghetto kid. He was smart and thoughtful and sensitive, and I just liked him. Another reason we became friends, I liked to smoke reefer—pot. And he used to like to smoke pot, so we'd smoke pot together. We did that all during camp.

"The only thing I knew about Duane was pretty much that something had happened to his parents, they had died when he was young, and that he had been raised by a family member in L.A. and then he had gone to West Texas State to play football. And where the hell West Texas State was, I had no earthly idea. It was in Canyon, Texas. I remember asking him, 'How the hell did you survive in Canyon, Texas, for four years?' Evidently he would go back to L.A. when there were breaks, just did what he had to do. Football was his only avenue up.

"Tom Landry's camp was a reflection of Tom. Tom was an engineer, and he expected accountability. That was a transition for me, like, 'I'm supposed to be a man now. I'm no longer a kid. I'm out of college. This is a job, and I'm a man.' It was 'I'm going to hold you accountable because you are a man, and this is what I expect you to do.' And he was very meticulous.

"The only time I ever heard him make a quip or even attempt any humor was this one day, a fog choker. It was pouring down rain in Dallas. This was after we had broken camp, and I pulled into the parking lot, and there were no parking places left except the head coach's spot. And I pulled in and parked and went inside. And later on Tom came in and he was soaking wet, *soaking* wet, and Ralph Neely and Mike Ditka turned around to me and said, 'Oh man, your ass is grass. He's going to eat you for lunch. You're dead.' And I was numbed out again, and he got up there and he was wringing wet, and he said, 'I would like to know who parked his car in my parking place.' And I raised my hand, and I said, 'Coach, I did. It's raining really hard out there. It was the only place left.' And he said, 'I really like a man who lives dangerously.' And everyone went, 'Ho ho ho,' and that was it. That was as humorous as he ever got. That was the only funny thing I ever heard him say."

Mel Renfro: "Steve Kiner was *very* different. He was a different kind of animal. As we saw it, Steve was a rebel without a cause. He was a guy coming out of Woodstock, the type of guy who let it all hang out, no inhibitions, just do what you want to do, feel free, antiestablishment, be your own man, all those things. A terrific athlete, had great football ability, and a good person, a good soul. But of a different mind-set, like a flower child.

"Steve was not arrogant at all. He was just a free spirit. He was a drug guy, but he was a good guy, a good person, and I got along well with Steve even though I didn't know drugs, never knew drugs. Oh, I had tried marijuana once or twice. I sat in on a session or two with that stuff, and it about killed me. So that was the end of that. I couldn't handle that. But he was into it, boy. I didn't know what it was all about. And the little taste I got of it scared me so bad, I ran and never looked back.

"As far as Steve's relationship with Tom Landry, it was like oil and water. The organization and Tom did not like that type of personality. He was too independent. It went against the grain. He was an early Thomas Henderson, and by the time Thomas got there, they were going to have to accept the fact that they were going to get players like that, that were totally of their own independence."

Margene Adkins, the third roommate of the Kiner-Thomas-Adkins triumvirate, was independent in his own way. Margene was a freelancer. He believed his athletic ability would take him as far as he wanted to go, and never mind the way a play was supposed to be run. "Just get me the ball." Margene had been a true pro all his life. After a stellar high school career, Adkins would have gone straight to the pros if he could have, but under the agreement the NFL had with the NCAA at the time, he was forced to wait to play NFL football until after his college class graduated. So after first attending Henderson Junior College, and after accepting a solid cash-and-gifts offer from Wichita State University, he instead went legit in the Canadian League, where he starred for the Ottawa Roughriders, leading the team to two Grey Cup Championships. He was playing in Canada when the plane carrying the Wichita State football team crashed and burned, killing everyone on board.

Margene Adkins: "I never got an opportunity to start for the Cowboys. Who started was supposed to be based on the exhibition season. What was so cold about it, I had a better exhibition season than any wide receiver. But I never got the opportunity to start. Exactly why, I'm going to let that alone. I'd prefer to let that go. Let me just say this: during the year of 1970, two weeks before I was drafted, I was called to preach by Jesus. For 13 years I would not preach, and a lot of things that happened during that time were because I did not accept my ministry, and that's one reason why a lot of things went on that weren't to my advantage. I'm going to let a lot of it go."

Adkins played two years with the Cowboys. Because he lacked the discipline required by Landry, he failed to break into the starting lineup.

Mel Renfro: "Margene had great athletic ability, could run, jump, catch, but couldn't follow directions. Could *not* follow directions. If Tom said take two steps to the left and one to the right, he couldn't do it. He just could *not* do it, and I don't know if that is dyslexic. I remember we had a receiver named Sim Stokes who was the same way. I remember watching coach Landry try to get Sim to run a route a particular way, and he did it five times, and Sim never came close, but a tremendous athlete. And Margene was that way, just couldn't follow directions."

Following directions became very important to Landry following the defeat at the hands of Cleveland in playoff games in both 1968 and 1969. After the first Cleveland debacle, Landry announced to the players that he wanted even more dedication, more seriousness, more hard work.

Lance Rentzel: "The impact of our playoff defeats hung over everything and everyone. Tom Landry had an idea that maybe there was too much kidding around at practices, that the team was not serious or dedicated enough, causing us to fail in crucial situations. He made it clear he wanted everything to be strictly business, that if everyone was completely dedicated to football for the entire season, we'd win it all."

After the 1969 Cleveland loss, Landry felt that to help the team get to the Super Bowl, he needed to involve his players. Landry's way wasn't individual meetings but rather a player survey. Every player was mailed a meticulously written long questionnaire about each and every aspect of life as a Cowboy. Landry wanted the players to help him change procedures to get the team into the Super Bowl.

Roger Staubach: "At the end of the '69 season Landry sent out a lengthy questionnaire to all the players. He's a control-type person, and he was that way to the end, but he wanted more input into what to do. He was trying to send a message to say, 'I can't do it all myself.' And it was taken in the right vein. He wanted to know a lot of things, everything about the system, our opinion of the coaches. Ermal Allen, who I thought was a very good coach, was moved from backfield coach. Jim Myers, the line coach, became the offensive coordinator. The one thing we didn't have for a long time, which I would have liked, was a quarterback coach. Ray Renfro used to help me as a coach, but he was a receiver. Landry would spend time with the quarterbacks, but during the game he was worried about the defense, and I'd come off the field and be talking to the other players, but it wasn't the same as talking to a quarterback coach. Later Dan Reeves became that. I would have loved to have Dan involved earlier in my career.

"Landry made some discipline changes on the field at Thousand Oaks. He increased discipline by doing a lot of little things. You couldn't lay your helmet down on the ground, for instance. You had to hold it. We made some changes how practice was run, changing the routine. We changed from Tuesday to Monday to watch films and had Tuesdays off."

Cornell Green: "In the questionnaire I told him he should play the younger guys in preseason more. For my whole career I played every preseason game the whole damn game, and I just thought the time to see who to keep on your team, to play the backups, the young guys, was during the preseason. And then you'll know how good they are. That was the only thing I wrote on it. Tom said that was one of the things most of the older guys said, to play the young guys in the preseason."

The survey led to substantive changes for the 1970 season. Landry decreed that there would be less reliance on the big plays, the bombs to Bob Hayes and Lance Rentzel, and instead there'd be a greater reliance on the running game, with running back Calvin Hill as the focus. He moved Ermal Allen from backfield coach to scout, gave assistant coaching responsibilities to Dan Reeves—who continued playing as an all-purpose back until 1972—decreed that there be a year-round training program, and most important, that seriousness of purpose be put at a premium. The key to the 1970 season, he said, would be discipline.

Work harder. Play by the rules. Be disciplined. These were Tom Landry's solutions for his Cowboys, and for the nation. But as Landry turned up the pressure on his players, not all of them had the emotional makeup to withstand his relentless whip. Beginning in 1970, the Dallas Cowboys would reach the Super Bowl five times during the decade, but the price exacted would be that over the years a number of the Cowboys players would crack under the terrible strain.

Coach Landry has the attention of Eddie LeBaron (No. 14), Pettis Norman (No. 84), and Amos Bullocks (No. 22) during a 1964 game in the top photo, and Craig Morton (No. 14) and Don Meredith, shown below in 1967. Photos courtesy of the Dallas Public Library.

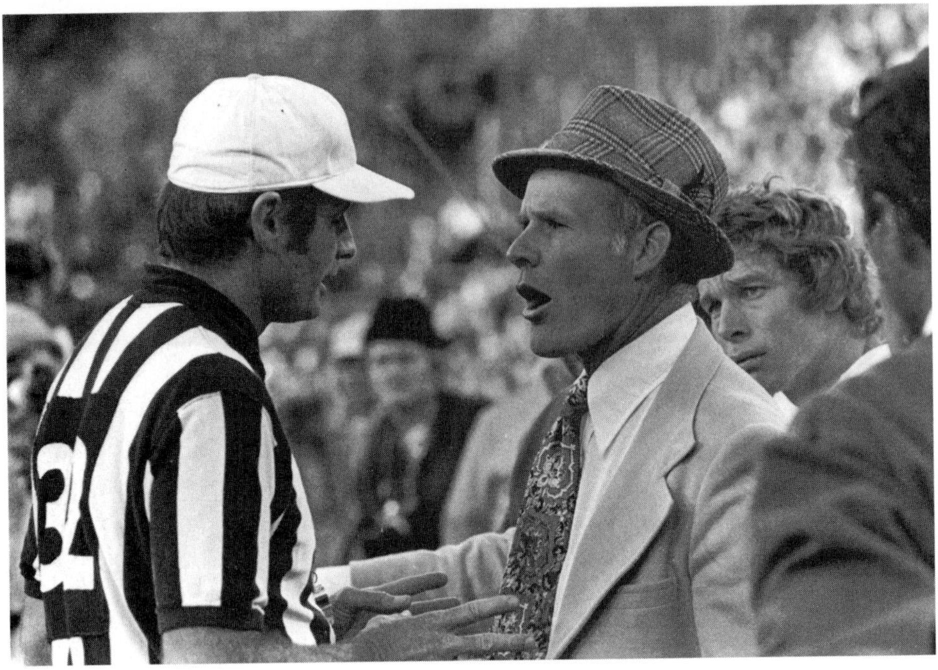

The coach makes a point during a discussion with an official in the top photo, while O-linemen (below, from left) Tony Liscio, Malcolm Walker, and Ralph Neely catch a breather. Photos courtesy of the Dallas Public Library.

Linebacker Lee Roy Jordan and coach Landry take in the action from the sideline (above), as do Dandy Don Meredith and Bullet Bob Hayes (below).
Photos courtesy of the Dallas Public Library.

Lance Alworth and Don Meredith (above), before Meredith took a hit that required a doctor's attention. Photos courtesy of the Dallas Public Library.

Don Meredith takes the snap from the center (above), and Roger Staubach ushers in Landry's finest era (below). Photos courtesy of the Dallas Public Library.

The love affair between Cowboys fans and coach Landry was always a two-way street. Photos courtesy of the Dallas Public Library.

Nicknamed "Rotten" by his teammates for his grumpy nature, Ralph Neely also earned more than a few compliments. "The finest offensive lineman I had ever seen," said Buddy Dial. Photo courtesy of the Dallas Cowboys.

Dan Reeves (No. 30) and Bob Hayes fight the heat in the top photo, while Bob Lilly (below) looks ready to fight anyone who gets in his way. Photos courtesy of the Dallas Public Library.

Chapter 38

Monday Night Humiliation

At the start of training camp in 1970, Tom Landry informed all the players that no job was safe, that he was establishing minimum performance levels, and that if a player, no matter who he was, didn't meet those levels, he would lose his starting job. Bob Hayes, who for five years had set Cowboys pass-catching records and was the leading touchdown catcher in the NFL, was one of the first to lose his job under the new regimen. Hayes, the fastest athlete in the NFL, was the sort of player who used the training camp to get in shape. Landry had mandated an off-season training program, and Hayes had rarely shown up for it. Landry wanted his players in shape beginning the first day of training. Landry also reiterated that his intention was to mount a running game very much like the old Vince Lombardi Green Bay offense and keep away from the bombs. Hayes, feeling persecuted, was furious at the way he was being treated and sulked, making his situation even tougher.

Pettis Norman: "We had been close a couple years and had fallen back after we had been in championship games against Green Bay. I suspect that Landry examined the team and felt that if we were going to be champions, we had to step it up a notch. You can't have players not carrying out their assignments to the fullest, even when they are not involved in the play. Coach Landry was a stickler about everybody carrying out their assignments. Tom's thing was, 'You never know when the play is going to break, and you can throw the key block, and if you're loafing, your man might be the one to make the tackle on a run.' And so that was it as much as anything, and it probably was to set an example to any other players who would look at Bob Hayes and say, 'If Bob can do it, I can do it too.'"

When Landry benched him, Hayes was contemptuous. The outspoken Hayes was certain he was being punished not because of any deficiency in his play but because he had entered the season playing out his option and had publicly complained about Tex Schramm's low salaries.

There were a lot of headlines, and also charges of racism, because Dennis Homan, a slower white guy from Alabama, was the one who took Bullet Bob's job. Said Hayes, "That was the big thing. He never had anything to say to the blacks on the team so it made for a kind of uptight situation."

It was then, according to Hayes, that he began to get the phone calls. At first they were sympathetic, and then they turned angry, with threats of violence to Hayes' tormentors: "We're Cowboys fans, and we're going to get even with Tom Landry for you. We're going to bomb his house. And if that doesn't work, we'll put a bomb in his car. Maybe we'll even bomb Tex Schramm's house while we're at it."

Hayes says he tried to reason with the callers to get them not to do it. "It's only a contract dispute," he told them.

"You're either with us or against us," the caller said, "and if you're not with us, we're going to kidnap your wife or maybe your daughter."

Hayes said he asked the caller if he would take money to leave him alone. He said he would. Hayes said he had $200 in cash. The caller told him where to leave it at a spot on the playground near the William Brownmiller Elementary School. "I was convinced they were violent people," said Hayes, who didn't tell the story until a year later. "I was afraid of what they might do if I went to the police or the FBI."

In addition to keeping Hayes on the bench in the opener, Landry also benched Craig Morton and offensive lineman Ralph Neely for not reaching performance levels. Landry was miffed that Morton had not returned from his shoulder operation in better shape. Staubach started the first two games because of the soreness in Morton's shoulder.

Roger Staubach: "Craig had his shoulder operated on, but during the off-season Craig didn't discipline himself, and when he came to training camp he was still having trouble with his shoulder. He hadn't gotten his shoulder back, so when he started throwing, his elbow started bothering him, and as a result I started the opener in a win against the Eagles and then the next game against the Giants.

"At halftime against the Giants we were losing, and I knew when we were walking up the tunnel he was going to take me out, so I said, 'Hey, Coach, I don't want to come out losing. Just give me a chance in the second half.' I wanted to make up for the first half. And I think I changed his mind right there. And so I played the second half, and we ended up beating the Giants. But I knew Landry was ready and waiting to get Morton in there.

"The next week we played the St. Louis Cardinals, and though Craig was getting healthy again, I started the game and actually hit Lance Rentzel in the end zone for a touchdown, but he dropped the ball. I was in a groove, and then I threw an interception to Larry Wilson, and as soon as I threw that interception, I *knew* he was going to take me out. I wanted to keep playing until I *really* screwed up, but Craig came in. Craig was the veteran. And so all I got to play was the first quarter. And I was *very* disappointed. It was a tough deal. I didn't say anything."

The Cowboys lost the Cards game, 20–7, and after an impressive display by the defense in a 13–0 win over the Atlanta Falcons, Morton was battered in a 54–13 shellacking by the Minnesota Vikings. During the trip to New York City several weeks earlier, Morton had picked a fight with a guy in a bar, and when he stepped outside, Mafia thugs had beaten him badly. After the Vikings mugging, Morton's body would be in bad shape the rest of the year. That Morton took the Cowboys as far as he did was certainly a credit to his experience, his guts, and his talent.

Roger Staubach: "The next game was against the Vikings, and I had a bursitis problem. The Friday before the game it swelled up, and they drained it and advised me not to play on Sunday. We were getting murdered, and I went in, and I did play part of the game and went into the hospital after that because they were afraid of my getting a staph infection. When the team plane landed, they took me to Baylor Hospital. So I didn't even dress for the Kansas City game, and Craig had a good game, beat the Chiefs, and Duane Thomas had a big game, ran for more than 100 yards.

"We beat the Eagles on three long touchdowns by Craig, and then lost to the Giants at the very end of the game, when Fran Tarkenton scrambled and threw a touchdown pass.

"And then on Monday night on national TV we got beat 38–0 by St. Louis. I came in at the very end of that game. Craig was having trouble with his arm. It was the beginning of some problems for him. People in the stands were yelling for Don Meredith, who was up in the TV booth, so I was feeling horrible."

Steve Kiner: "I played the whole damn game. I remember St. Louis had a fullback named Sid Smith. He was about 6'2", weighed about 270. And they had a tailback who lined up behind him named MacArthur Lane, and they would run out of the I. And they would block down, and here came Sid, and Jesus, it looked like a runaway train. They ran all over me. Ran up the field and down the field.

"And after the game, Landry cried. When I say he was crying, there were tears running down his cheeks. He didn't sound like he was crying. He didn't whimper. As tears ran down his cheeks he said that he was real disappointed in the team, because at the beginning of the year he had felt that we had a chance to go to the Super Bowl, and here it was with five games left, and we were 5–4. I remember him saying he was sorry he hadn't done a better coaching job, that he had let us down, and basically he said it didn't look like we were going to make it to the playoffs this year, that we had pissed away our opportunity.

"As a younger player, I just had a tremendous amount of respect for him. I had never seen a head coach take the blame for anything. And here was this guy standing up and apologizing in front of all these other guys with tears running in his eyes. I was impressed that 'This guy really is human, that he really does want to win as badly as I want to win.'"

Roger Staubach: "Coach Landry came in the locker room and pretty much said he didn't think we could win."

After the game, after the reporters had left, Bob Lilly told his teammates, "Aw, we got 'em right where we want 'em now. We'll trick-f*** 'em." That line became the battle cry for the season. Lilly told the entire team to forget about Landry. "He doesn't win games; we do," he said.

"Hell with him," said another player. Then Lee Roy Jordan spoke.

Lee Roy Jordan: "After the game the big thing is we had a team meeting. Just the players. We got together, and I said, 'Hey guys, there is no one pulling for us but us, the guys right here in this room. Hell, the coaches aren't pulling for us. They've already given up. Most of the wives have given up. We know damn well the press has been against us forever, so they're not pulling for us. And most of the fans are not excited about us anymore.' I said, 'Guys, it's going to happen right here in this room or it's not going to happen.' Several of us talked. We said, 'We are going to do it *for us*, not for somebody else, not for the coaches or the fans or Tex or anyone else.' We were going to do it for *us*."

Pettis Norman: "A lot of things affected us in 1970. There was the strike, a change in running backs, in the quarterback, in an emphasis on the running game. We were not cohesive as a team in the first nine games. After we lost to the Cardinals 38–0, our record was still 5–4. I remember saying to several teammates in the locker room that night, 'If we win the rest of the games, we'll have 10 victories.' And I remember saying, 'I would take that record any day and let the Cardinals shoot at me.' My point is, that's a tough record to beat. 'We can win the last five games. Give me that record today, and I'll let the Cardinals shoot at us, and I'll bet the money on it that we'll be OK. We can't do anything about the past, but we can do something about the future, so let's go out and play.'"

Roger Staubach: "There are a couple schools of thought about that. One was that after that the players took over, and that really got us going again. I don't look at it that the coaches gave up on us.

"The thing that disturbed me was that Craig was definitely having problems, and here I was, ready to go. I thought I was going to get a chance to start after that St. Louis game, and then Landry said, 'Craig Morton is going to be my quarterback.' That's what disturbed me."

Chuck Howley: "In the next game against Washington, we were losing 7–3, and I recovered a fumble and ran it close to the goal line, and Duane Thomas scored, and we ended up beating them big.

"And we made football fun again. We started winning ballgames—because we had the talent. We had the ability. But something had caused us to lose the edge. And we found that edge again."

Lee Roy Jordan: "After that meeting the intensity changed. We got after each other. The next day in practice we were competing against the offense, and they were competing against us, hard.

"See, what happens to every team after they start losing is loss of intensity. They lose intensity on the practice field. When you don't practice intense against yourself, you don't play intense against somebody else. Shit, it just won't happen. You just don't have that level. You can't turn it on Sunday at 2:50 when the game starts at 3:00. You've got to have it build up to that level every day during the week, every week, or you don't have it.

"And by golly, we beat Washington. It wasn't a real great game, but we played hard, won the game, and then we went to Green Bay and held them to three points, and now all of a sudden everyone is getting excited about us again. The coaches got to coaching real heavy again. And my attitude was, 'Hey, guys, we're going to use what we think works for us, and if we don't think it works, I'm not going to call it.' And that's what we did. We talked about game plans with the coaches, and we were much more involved in expressing our feelings about what we were doing in the game plans. Guys got to where they believed certain things would work, and when something else came out and we didn't believe in it, we told coach Landry, 'The guys don't think this is a good idea. The guys feel like we're trying to do too much, and we should be doing more letting the athletes take care of it.' And in a lot of cases Tom was receptive. He understood and made alterations in the game plan. I have to give him credit for that.

"That was Herb Adderley's first year. We got Herb from Green Bay, and we had Herb and Mel at the corners, and Cornell at one safety and either Charlie Waters or Cliff Harris, who were rookies. That was a heck of a defensive football team."

Chapter 39

Rentzel's Compulsion

When Tom Landry inaugurated his Spartan nose-to-the-grindstone training camp in 1970 and switched the offensive emphasis from long passes to four yards and a cloud of dust, the confidence of some of the players, especially Bob Hayes' and Lance Rentzel's, sagged dramatically. With the humiliating 38–0 loss to St. Louis, the shaky Cowboys suddenly appeared washed up. Before they had been chokers; now they were bums. When several of the players went to a restaurant following the debacle, patrons got up and left.

Bob Lilly: "There were many fans who were cordial and nice, but still, the impact of the media when it's negative toward someone, it affects them not just in the newspaper, but it affects your fans and their mentality, their idea of you. So when the media is on you and you go places in Dallas, you're not really welcome. It was really bad, and that happened a lot.

"It happened after we lost to St. Louis 38–0 in 1970. I was playing defensive end again because Larry Cole was hurt. We had a lousy game. We played hard. It wasn't like we weren't trying, but they just beat the crap out of us.

"Well, the next day or two, several of us went out to eat, George Andrie and Lee Roy and Ralph Neely and me at a restaurant on the north side of Dallas. And we sat down, and I noticed these people were into eating, and when we sat down they all got up and left. They wouldn't even look at us. I was thinking, 'I didn't realize how bad it is.' They didn't even want to be in the same area in the restaurant with us."

One player feeling the pressure of defeat was Lance Rentzel, the Cowboys' glamour-boy wide receiver. In addition, Rentzel's marriage to Joey Heatherton was on the rocks, and the supper club he had started was failing. On November 19, 1970, Rentzel got into his car, drove to a local Catholic girls school, and waited for the little girls to play on the playground. When he found a 10-year-old who appealed to him, he walked over to her, opened his raincoat, and revealed to her that he wasn't wearing any clothes underneath, showing her something she had probably never seen before. The little girl not only gave a description of the blond flasher to one of the teachers, but she was also able to give the make and model of the car, which quickly led police to the identity of its owner.

This was a ritual Rentzel had been playing out for years. He was a classic flasher; psychiatrists call the disorder exhibitionism. Pressures build, and the only way an exhibitionist can reduce them is to expose himself to a young girl. Rentzel had done it in Minnesota, and he continued his flashing with the Cowboys. Several of the players knew about his disorder.

Since coming to the Cowboys in 1967, Rentzel had exposed himself enough times that Tex Schramm and Tom Landry certainly knew about his problem. But instead of getting Rentzel psychological help, they continued to keep their little secret under wraps, hoping Rentzel would play out his career without his problem becoming public.

Pete Gent: "I watched what was happening to him. My lawyer knew that he had been busted in Dallas before it actually became public. And when I was with the team, I kept going to the guys on the team who claimed to be his friends, guys like Ralph Neely and Don Meredith, and I would say, 'Lance is going to get busted. Somebody has got to talk to him.' And they kept saying, 'Come on. I don't want to hear that. You're just pissed because he's got your job.'

"When Lance did it to a girl who was the daughter of a Highland Park lawyer who they couldn't buy off, Lance was f***ed. They treated it in the papers like a presidential assassination."

Pettis Norman: "Lance getting in trouble was a tremendous distraction. The man was very popular. We all liked him and really regretted what had happened with him as well as with the young girl. It was a tragedy as far as I was concerned, and a lot of people were hurt as a result of that.

"I remember talking to Lance, expressing my sorrow, because I recognized that that was some type of illness in him and just regretted that he was ill like that. And I wished him luck. And at the same time I remember feeling very sorry for the little girl."

Rentzel's teammates voted for him to remain on the team and play, but Schramm and Landry overruled them. In meeting with the players Rentzel told his teammates, "No matter how bad things get, I won't ever quit. Ever. It may take me a while, but I'll be back. So long."

Rentzel thought he was going to be suspended for a couple of weeks. But Schramm traded him to Los Angeles, ending the possibility of his return. As soon as he was gone, the Cowboys returned to the task at hand.

Steve Kiner: "When Lance was arrested, I was surprised by the reaction of the older players. I was like, 'Whoa, this guy really has a problem.' And then it was, 'Ah well, we'll put it behind us.' That was just sort of a bump along the road."

Chapter 40

The Mountaintop

When the Cowboys were manhandled 54–13 by the Vikings in Minnesota in the fifth game of the 1970 season, there wasn't much to cheer about. Craig Morton had been viciously tackled and had the ligaments of his right knee dangerously stretched. Roger Staubach had replaced him, despite an infected right elbow. Calvin Hill was suffering from a serious back injury, and Walt Garrison, the bulldog running back, had also been injured, so the Cowboys offense was looking impotent and helpless. But when Duane Thomas entered the game, the rookie running back immediately impressed everyone with his moves and his ability to bounce off tacklers and keep on going, the way Jim Brown had once done. The rookie ran for 79 yards, and he showed an ability Brown never had, catching five passes for 45 yards. And against the Super Bowl champion Kansas City Chiefs he carried 20 times for 134 yards, including a 47-yard touchdown. On the play Thomas bounced off defenders, got into the clear, and outraced the defensive backs for an exhilarating touchdown run. Tom Landry was impressed.

Hill returned and played two games under the handicap of his injuries, and after the 38–0 beating at the hands of the Cardinals, Landry announced that Thomas would start in Hill's place. In the following game against Washington, Thomas ran for 104 yards on 18 carries and scored three touchdowns. On his final touchdown run, Thomas seemed to be stopped, but he spun completely around, broke free, and ran ahead of his pursuers down the sideline. Cards defensive back Pat Fischer sought to derail him at the last second, but Thomas brushed him off like an elephant flicking a flea, and he went in to score.

To prove it was no fluke, two weeks later in a rematch in the Cotton Bowl, Thomas was again outstanding. Though he didn't score, he gained 102 yards in the first half in helping the Cowboys to defeat the Redskins 34–0.

Mel Renfro: "Duane was such a talent, tremendous, the next Jim Brown, really. Duane was smooth. He seemed to know where the hole was. He wasn't a power runner, although he was strong, and he could break tackles and elude, but he was just like a big antelope, just those giant powerful steps, and the way he'd weave in and out, and just a magnificent specimen. I just loved to see him run. He was such a complement to everybody else. We had a power running game.

He was a guy who could run inside, outside, catch the ball, break tackles, go the distance. You got something when you got a guy like that. He had deceptive speed. He could run away from linebackers and defensive backs."

But with his ascension to star status, his teammates noticed that Duane Thomas was becoming more and more withdrawn from the rest of the team. Duane was complaining about his contract, and they were wondering whether his dissatisfaction with his contract had something to do with the way he was behaving or whether it was something else.

Duane Thomas: "My problems started with my agent, who was embezzling money from me. I had gotten him through Mercury Morris, my teammate in college at West Texas State. Merc was going through changes, so he didn't tell me about this boy, who stole 10 grand from me. The agent would tell me he was paying bills, and he'd send me statements that the bill had been paid, and the bill hadn't been paid. He said he was paying estimated quarterly taxes, and then the IRS called me up and said, 'You owe us $10,000.' I said, 'What?' They said, 'Your taxes.' I called him up, and he started ducking and dodging, and the IRS was on me very strongly, so I had to call a friend of mine who worked for Levi Strauss, and I said, 'George, I need 10 grand.' He said, 'How quickly do you need it?' I said, 'Yesterday.' He said, 'I'll wire it to you.' And he did. Imagine someone giving you 10 grand in 1970. I paid him back every penny. I never did get my money back from that agent. He got away with it. But it shattered my trust. I didn't know who to trust now. I hired another agent, but he never got anything done either.

"I went to Tex Schramm. I had large debts. I was supporting relatives, an ex-wife, and I was hurting financially because my agent had not only made a terrible deal but had stolen much of it from me. I asked Tex to help. You know what he said in his actions? This was his response: 'OK, Duane, drop your pants, and we're going to stick it to you now.'

"You know, money was an issue, but it was more about principle and honesty. They were taking advantage of the idea that I played more for the love of the game than anything. On an amateur level you are doing it for the love. The word *amateur* comes from the Latin *amatore* or *lover*. It's one who loves what he is doing. But Dallas—and when I say Dallas, I mean Tex Schramm and his boys, the decision makers, the administrators—took advantage of my love of the game. Because skyline caps were making more money than I was. One time I went to tip a skyline cap at the airport, and he told me to keep the money. He said, 'Duane, I make more money than you.'

"How could it not upset me?"

Mel Renfro: "Duane was a strange bird. He wasn't only strange to the management and to the white players, he also was strange to most of the black players.

"His head was a little messed up to start with, but when Tex did to him what he did to him, the kid just totally flipped, and I think a lot of the reason for that was the drugs. I didn't realize the amount and the use, because when we came up, there was a pep pill here and a benny there and an aspirin here was about all we got. These guys went into acid. I remember one morning Duane was out early in the morning counting blades of grass—at 6:30 in the morning. I said, 'Whoa.' I said, 'Poor Duane. Poor Duane.' He just spaced out. It had to be the drugs.

"But he was still an athlete. He could still perform. He could still do the job."

Duane Thomas carried the offense on his back through a rough part of the schedule, keeping the Cowboys winning until Landry's Flex defense, which was ridiculed and abandoned by his own team at the end of the 1969 season, turned impregnable.

Beginning with the Cowboys' 16–3 win over the Green Bay Packers, the defense—led by Bob Lilly, George Andrie, Pat Toomay, and Jethro Pugh on the line; Lee Roy Jordan, Dave Edwards, and Chuck Howley at linebacker; and an All-Star defensive backfield of Mel Renfro, Cornell Green, Herb Adderley, and two rookies, Charlie Waters and Cliff Harris—went on a record-setting touchdownless streak. In the final four games of the regular season, the defense did not give up a touchdown against Green Bay (16–3), Washington (34–0), Cleveland (6–2), or Houston (52–10 [the touchdown was scored by the Oilers defense after a fumble recovery]).

Acquiring All-Pro veteran cornerback Herb Adderley from the Green Bay Packers had been a master stroke on Tex Schramm's part.

Cornell Green: "Tom Landry came to me when they were going to trade for Herb Adderley, and he said, 'You or Herb is going to have to move to safety.' He said he thought with our defense it would be easier for me to move than Herb. I said, 'Fine with me.' And so Herb and Mel and I gave us three guys who could play man-to-man in any combination, and we had Charlie Waters and Cliff Harris, two rookies, who we could put in at free safety, where they didn't have to lock up in man. We were a tough defensive team. All of a sudden, we were a *real* good defensive team. You had three guys who could lock up on any receiver in the league. And the kids, they would hit you. They might be in the wrong spot, but they would be going full speed. They'd be *all* the way wrong, never half wrong."

When Adderley came to the team, he saw that many of the players were cowed by Landry's second-guessing during film sessions. Scornful, he convinced the defensive players that if they could ignore the criticism and play their game, they could win it all.

Mel Renfro: "Everyone felt miserable because they were concerned about the Monday film sessions. Herb got my attention when he said, 'It doesn't have to be this way.' He came in like he had been there forever and said, 'Get off your butts and stop crying in your soup. Let's get out and kick some butt.'

"His leadership hit pretty quick. When he started talking, guys started standing at attention. Their antennae went up, almost immediately. His presence, just the way he carried himself, the way he talked, he always talked with confidence. Herb was so fiery, and he had such confidence. He had come up under those Lombardi days where winning wasn't everything, it was the *only* thing. And that's what he instilled in us: 'Guys, you can win, and you're gonna win. *We're* gonna win.' And that was all there was to it.

"He was always a team guy. It wasn't that he bridged a gap between black and white. It was a *team* thing. There was *no* color there. He said, 'Guys, the only way we're going to do it is to come together. White, green, red, all blacks, all whites, all reds, we have to come together as a team and do it.'

"What Herb did, he instilled within us the belief that we could win and win big. I remember one time we lost a game, and Herb got upset. He said, 'You guys are a bunch of miserable losers.' He put it right in our face. We had lost a game, and everyone was sitting around with their heads between their legs, and he said, 'You guys are a bunch of miserable losers, and you don't have to be losers.' Herb was always upbeat, always positive. 'Brother Fro, we're gonna get them, Brother Fro. We're gonna do it.'"

The Cleveland game was especially meaningful for the Cowboys. The Browns had kept them from the Super Bowl the previous two years. The Cleveland defense was as tough as anyone's. The question was: could the Cowboys defense keep the Browns from scoring?

Mel Renfro: "We beat the Browns 6–2 in the freezing wind in Cleveland. That was a milestone, and I remember it like it was yesterday. Jethro Pugh, Dave Edwards, Lee Roy, everybody was just muddy and dirty, and we just rose to the occasion. Here was Lee Roy cursing and screaming in the huddle, 'They're not going to score. They are not going to score. We're gonna stop them,' and we did. That day, Lee Roy was incredible.

"It was just like an angel was there and was protecting us and moving us and making us do the things that we did, 'cause it was like something that was divine. I can remember a third- or fourth-down play on our 2- or 3-yard line. If they had scored, they would have beaten us. Leroy Kelly was carrying the ball, and I happened to be in on the play as one of the tacklers. It was on the weak side, so Jethro was there. We just came up, rose to the occasion, and stopped them on fourth down. That was the game.

"We had lost in that Cleveland Stadium so many times when we were the better team. To be able to win and win like that, when we were down, down near the Dog Pound in that old, ugly end zone near the cheap seats, with the fans on our back, the wind was blowing, it was cold. All the things John Madden talks about that make football football, that's what happened down there at that end of the field that afternoon.

"You've heard of doomsday. That's what they called us, the Doomsday Defense. Three downs and out. The defense was much more known than the offense, and so it was the Doomsday. We literally put a hurt on people."

In the final outing, against Houston, Craig Morton had his finest game, hitting 13 of 17 passes for 349 yards and *five* touchdowns. Bob Hayes, finally returning to Landry's good graces after sitting out the first five games, caught four touchdown passes—from 38, 38, 15, and 59 yards out. Had Landry not benched him, Hayes would surely have been the Pro Bowl wide receiver. Duane Thomas carried 17 times for 115 yards. The silent rookie finished the season with a very credible 803 yards rushing.

Roger Staubach: "The way we started to win in '70 was a ferocious defense. Other than the one game against the Houston Oilers, where Craig and Bob Hayes had a fantastic game, we went into the playoffs really with a defensive team. Because of Craig's injury, his confidence was shot. *Sports Illustrated* ran a story that ours was a team without a quarterback. I was thinking, 'I'm the backup quarterback. This is really absurd.' I was *very* confident I could play and perform. Though we had other players who were upset, I wasn't complaining, but once we hit the field our guys played hard, and that last stretch our defense really got some momentum. But from my perspective with our great running game we should *never* have lost that Super Bowl against Baltimore."

The Cowboys finished the 1970 regular season with a record of 10–4, including five straight wins following the 38–0 clobbering at the hands of St. Louis and the deportation of Lance Rentzel. The first playoff game was against the Detroit Lions. Duane Thomas ran the ball 30 times for 135 yards. A disabled Morton could complete only 4 of 18. The Cowboys scored on a safety and a field goal. The Lions were shut out, 5–0, as the Cowboys defense extended its no-touchdown streak to 21 quarters. Any time during the game the Lions could have won with a touchdown, but they never got one. The Cowboys players weren't worried.

Pettis Norman: "The score was very low, but I always felt we would win the game. We just seemed to be able to move the ball any time we wanted to. We just couldn't score. That part was frustrating. Normally when you get into a game like that, you start thinking, 'We are really blowing some opportunities.' I can remember I never had that feeling that we weren't going to win the game."

Lee Roy Jordan: "The Lions had an excellent football team, but I'll tell you what: we had a tremendous belief and confidence in ourselves because we felt we had come back from some extreme doldrums, that we had really been deep in the hole after that St. Louis game. Everyone had quit on us, and all of a sudden we were a team that had reached down and got some extra intestinal fortitude and desire to be the best we could be as a team."

Late in the game on fourth down Bill Munson threw a long pass to Earl McCullough. Charlie Waters went for the interception instead of trying to knock down the ball. He missed the ball, and the Lions had a first down on the Cowboys' 29. There were 54 seconds left.

Mel Renfro: "The crowd was in a frenzy. They completed another sideline, about 12 yards. But that was OK. I said to myself, 'If they keep doing that, I'm going to get one.'

"They were between the 15- and 20-yard lines. Munson threw it down and in, and he actually made a bad throw. He had been throwing so many outside routes, he wasn't real sharp on his inside route, so he led Earl a little too much, and he overthrew it. It may have hit Earl in the hands, but it went up in the air. I never remember seeing the ball. I remember feeling it hit my hand. And I just pulled it in around the 11. I was tackled, and then came the elation that the game was over, even though there were a few seconds left.

"I remember going to the sideline and hearing the accolades, 'Way to go, Mel. Way to go, Mel.' I was sitting there by myself, because everyone else was up near the field, just having a good time, celebrating. I just went over and sat down. I thanked the Lord Almighty for letting it happen. And I remember Lee Roy coming over, and D. D. Lewis coming over.

"People talk about my most exciting game in my career. Well, I would say it was that Detroit game, and then the San Francisco game, and then Super Bowl V."

The NFC Championship game was against the San Francisco 49ers, a team that could rarely beat the Cowboys, despite a solid team and a successful coach in Dick Nolan, who had taken Landry's Flex to the Bay Area and duplicated his friend's success with it.

Against the 49ers, Landry made an offensive game plan designed to establish his powerful running game. If Morton was to pass, it was to be short, to the backs. Since the Cowboys' 6–2 win over Cleveland, there was not a doubt in anyone's mind that the Cowboys would win the game.

Pettis Norman: "Dick Nolan ran the same defense as we did, and I think that made it easier for us, because we had to run against our own defense for a long time in scrimmages. And I felt very confident against the 49ers. The whole team did. I felt we would beat the 49ers. I thought we were better than the 49ers."

With the score tied 3–3 in the third quarter, Cowboys linebacker Lee Roy Jordan made a spectacular diving interception of a John Brodie pass. When he was tackled, the Cowboys had the ball on the 49ers' 13. From there Duane Thomas ran it in, the key run in a game in which he ran for 143 tough yards.

Walt Garrison gained 71 yards rushing and caught some key passes. He had come into the game suffering from muscle spasms in his back and a sprained ligament in his knee. By game's end, he had sustained a sprained right ankle and a fractured right clavicle. He had to be carried to the locker room when it was over. His teammates were amazed the gritty back was still alive.

In the third quarter Mel Renfro made another key interception, and Lee Roy Jordan grabbed his second of the game in the final period. Though San Francisco finally scored against the Cowboys defense, stopping the streak at 23 quarters, no one on the defense complained, because for the first time in Cowboys history, Dallas was going to the Super Bowl.

Mel Renfro: "John Brodie and Gene Washington were the offensive weapons. They stood between us and the Super Bowl. It was a defensive struggle, blood and guts right up the middle. There was a lot of hard hitting. Lee Roy played an absolutely perfect game. He intercepted two passes and made great plays. We shut them down. They couldn't throw the ball.

"Late in the third quarter Brodie was trying to go deep to Gene Washington, and I intercepted it and brought it back for a few yards, which broke their backs. We put the stamp on it, and talk about the locker room after that game. That was it. There wasn't any better feeling after being next year's champion four, five, six years, and finally getting there. Like Tom Landry said in the locker room, 'You don't know what we've gone through. You don't know how good this feels.' Because we had finally gotten to the mountaintop."

Chapter 41

ALMOST SUPER

Duane Thomas stole the headlines before Super Bowl V against the Colts in Miami. When asked, "Is this the ultimate game?" Thomas answered, "Well, they're playing it next year, aren't they?" The line was repeated from coast to coast. The national media didn't know what to make of the Dallas rookie.

The same could be said of his teammates. The morning of the game Craig Morton was walking along the beach by the hotel where the team was staying when he noticed Duane.

Craig Morton: "I saw Duane sitting there on the curb with his head down. He looked zonked. I don't know what he was on, but it scared the hell out of me. I mean, here was a guy who was supposed to be my main man this afternoon. Well, he got back to the hotel, and before the kickoff he gave me this big wink, so I knew he was all right, I guess."

The players discovered that getting to the Super Bowl for the first time was the *real* prize, that the emotion of playing the game would not match that of the game that got them there.

Pettis Norman: "The 49ers championship game was better from an emotional standpoint than the Super Bowl. First of all, there was a two-week lag time. To me, you lose some edge when you wait like that and then you try to get it back. We went to the Orange Bowl in Miami, and the atmosphere was not quite real. It was really kind of boring. You get tired of going through thousands of interviews, posing for pictures, this and that. You were all of a sudden thrown into this unnatural setting on which everything was superimposed.

"It was like picture day when you break training camp. That's a dreadful day 'cause you get dressed, stand around, have pictures taken, stand around some more, take more pictures. It was a day you wanted to get out of the way. And the Super Bowl was like a week of that. So it was kind of a drag. You had to be here at this time and there at that time, be here for this interview, there for that photo, and then it was game time.

"And I kept waiting to get as high for that game as I did the 49ers game, and I never did feel the oomph of the Super Bowl. The emotion never came. And I think it was because of moving into so many unnatural settings. We did not get involved in going to the parties, so we never got caught up in the atmosphere, and you just kind of got to the point where you said, 'I'll be glad when this is over with.' That's how it was with me, and normally it doesn't take much to get me up for a game.

"The game itself, as it turned out, was not real. So many things happened to us, tipped passes that weren't tipped, and fumbles that we recovered and other folks got, and interceptions at the last minute, and you look back and say, 'This game was as unreal as the week leading up to it.' It was like a picture show."

Lee Roy Jordan: "To this day I can't understand how it was that we lost to the Baltimore Colts. We certainly gave it away. We made lots of mistakes.

"Their first touchdown was on a tipped ball. But that doesn't matter because we should have won the ballgame several times later."

The Cowboys had gone ahead 6–0 on two Mike Clark field goals. Then in the second quarter Colts quarterback Johnny Unitas—who would later be knocked out of the game following a hard hit by George Andrie and relieved by Earl Morrall—called a pass play designed to go to receiver Eddie Hinton. Unitas' pass hit Hinton's hand, whizzed past Mel Renfro, who was guarding him, and landed in the arms of Colts tight end John Mackey, who ran for a 75-yard touchdown while Cowboys back Charlie Waters, who should have been covering him, was complaining to the officials.

Renfro ran up to one of the officials to tell him that Hinton had tipped the ball, that the touchdown to Mackey should not be allowed, because at that time two receivers could not legally touch the ball one after the other. The referee told Renfro to shut up.

Mel Renfro: "The refs said the ball touched me, which it could have, I suppose. But I had no sensation of touching the ball. That was my right hand, the hand that was messed up when I punched the mirror back at Oregon. That was the hand I have no feeling in those three fingers. If it hit me, it had to have gone off the finger next to the thumb. I have no feeling in that finger, and if it hit my finger, that's the finger that it hit. But still, when I look at where the game was at that time, it had no consequence. And actually, it wasn't my fault. I was going up to intercept the ball. And it went over my head. My guy was covered.

"The Colt who caught the ball was the tight end, John Mackey, who was the responsibility ultimately of the free safety, Charlie Waters. And he was jumping up and down worrying about the double tip when he should have been tackling John Mackey.

"Even after I returned two punts for TDs in the Pro Bowl and was named the Most Valuable Player, the thing that was uppermost in everybody's mind was the tipped pass. It ate at me for a long time, because of the question, 'Did you touch that ball?' Well, so what? Right after the game I answered the question. I said, 'I may have touched it, but I had no sensation of touching it.' That's exactly what I said. For the rest of my life, I get the question, 'Did you touch that ball?' I say, 'If you had been listening after the game when I told them, I had no sensation of touching it. I may have. I never said I didn't touch it. Never once did I say I didn't touch it.'

"And I will say this: I know Mr. Murchison is not with us anymore, but one time Mr. Murchison stopped me in the hallway, one of the rare times I had ever seen him other than on the field or in the locker room, and he said, 'Why did you lose that Super Bowl for us?' He was talking about the tipped pass in Super Bowl V. It totally blew my mind. I'm thinking, 'For the owner of the team to say that to me with some sincerity, what are they talking about at those meetings? What is the brass talking about to lead this man to think I lost the Super Bowl?' That play had *nothing* to do with the outcome of the game. At the time we were still tied in the ballgame. This was the second quarter. And Craig Morton threw two fourth-quarter interceptions, one off the hands of Dan Reeves, to lose the game, and Clint Murchison asks me, 'Why did you lose that game?'"

After Mackey's catch was ruled a touchdown, the Cowboys blocked the extra-point try, then, following Landry's game plan calling for short passes to the backs, went ahead 13–6 on a seven-yard pass from Craig Morton to Duane Thomas.

The Cowboys kicked off to open the second half, and Colt Jim Duncan fumbled and lost the ball on the Colts' 31. In five plays, the Cowboys drove to the 2, from where Morton handed off to Thomas for what appeared to be the clinching touchdown.

It was the crucial play of the game—and perhaps the most questionable call by an official in the history of the Super Bowl. As Thomas was crossing the goal line, the Cowboys' John Niland heard one official say, "He's over, he's over," just as Colts linebacker Mike Curtis hooked the ball loose. The ball bounced back across the thick white stripe, and Cowboys center Dave Manders fell on it inches from the goal line. "It rolled right under me, and I fell on it," Manders said.

With Manders clutching the ball, Colts lineman Billy Ray Smith began yelling, "Our ball, our ball," pointing in the other direction. Referee Jack Fette was so moved by Smith's acting skill that he signaled that the Colts had recovered. Nearby, Manders was cradling the ball.

Manders got up and handed the ball to the ref with a big smile on his face. When the referees gave the ball to Baltimore, Landry couldn't believe it. It was enough to send the normally placid coach running down the sideline under his trademark hat, screaming at the officials.

There isn't a single Cowboy to this day who can understand how the Colts ended up with the ball. You can still hear the bewilderment in their voices.

John Niland: "I know [Manders] recovered it. I was right there on the ground next to him. There was no way it should have been Baltimore's ball. Some official just came running in from out in left field and made the call. That was the turning point of the game. If we had made the touchdown we would have been up 20–6 and it would have been almost impossible for Baltimore to come back. I couldn't believe it when I heard the call. I still can't."

In 1980 Niland was eating in a Dallas restaurant when he looked across the room and saw Billy Ray Smith.

John Niland: "I looked across the room and there was Billy Ray Smith having dinner. I yelled over to him, 'Hey, Billy Ray, you still wearing my ring?' He knew exactly what I was talking about. He raised his hand and showed me his Super Bowl ring."

With the Colts playing the run as the game went on, Morton tested his injured wing and came up short. Two second-half interceptions, both on balls that bounced off the hands of receivers, "proved" to the pundits that the Cowboys truly were a "team without a quarterback," as *Sports Illustrated* had so cruelly commented. Defensive players were saying that Landry should have played Staubach in his place, and their opinion was strengthened when they learned that Morton had sought help from a hypnotist prior to the big game.

Lee Roy Jordan: "Late in the game with the score tied, 13–13, Morton threw to Danny [Reeves] and the ball hit off his fingers and into the arms of Mike Curtis, who ran the ball down to our 28 with about a minute left in the game. And then No. 80, I can't remember his name [Jim O'Brien], he kicked that field goal, and that may be the only one he ever kicked to win a game. A year or two later he was out of the league.

"And after the ball went through the uprights and we lost, Bob Lilly threw his helmet about 300 feet in the air, and when it hit the ground it splattered into pieces. Pieces just flew everywhere. I can't believe he threw it that high in the air.

"But we were all so disappointed and devastated because we knew we should have won the football game a number of times. Earl Morrall came in and made some big plays, but not nearly enough to win had we not made some mistakes ourselves."

Mel Renfro: "You know when I got really angry at Craig? On the bus ride back to the hotel. My wife and I were sitting there crying our eyes out, and I looked back, and he was back there goosing his girlfriend and laughing. I mean, he was sitting two seats back, and they are laughing, goosing each other. And my wife and I were sitting there crying our eyes out. That's when I got angry at Craig."

Super Bowl V was the beginning of the end for Craig Morton, who had been sufficiently skilled to take the Cowboys to the threshold of the mountaintop. Three tipped passes had beaten him, however, and they would ultimately grease the skids for his replacement by Roger Staubach, who would lead the Cowboys through the rest of the decade. After too many years quarterbacking a mediocre New York Giants team, Morton would lead the Denver Broncos against the Cowboys in Super Bowl XII. But Morton would get little credit for that feat either. In pro football, it seems, going to the dance just isn't good enough.

Roger Staubach: "Against Baltimore, all we had to do was have a halfway good passing game. And after that game, that was the lowest I ever felt. Because before that Landry had said to me, 'It takes four years to become a starting quarterback.' Plus, I wasn't young anymore. I didn't know where I was going. If I couldn't play in a game and really help the team with Craig injured, what was I going to do when the guy was healthy? After the game I felt that was possibly going to be it for me in Dallas.

"We were flying back to Dallas, and Tom Landry came back and sat with me for a few minutes. I was sitting with my wife, and he said, 'You *will* get your opportunity to be a starting quarterback this coming season.' And when he said that, I was rejuvenated, and I had a great off-season, worked hard, and in '71 Craig came back in great shape, and we competed for the job."

At the end of Super Bowl V, Lee Roy Jordan was saying, "I'm not taking any shit about this game. We'll be back. We've got good personnel, we're playing the defense . . . all we need is a little better passing game. We will be back."

Lee Roy was right, but not before another rocky season of Sturm und Drang as the combination of drugs and an intransigent Tex Schramm would cause their enfant terrible, Duane Thomas, to become so alienated and act so strangely that neither Tom Landry nor any of Thomas' concerned teammates knew what to do about it.

Chapter 42

DUANE VERSUS THE PLASTIC MAN

By 1971 everyone was familiar with the stern figure of Tom Landry standing on the sideline, staring impassively at the action, his felt hat and cloth coat defining for a nation a successful, serious corporate leader. In the clubhouse, behind closed doors, Landry was that way with his players, whom he kept on edge with his brutal postgame reviews in an attempt to squeeze every ounce of effort from them. By 1971, even though the Dallas Cowboys were a formidable football team that had gone to the Super Bowl, no one on his team was very happy playing football. It was that year that Duane Thomas put into words what many on the team were thinking when he called Landry a "plastic man."

Mel Renfro: "Tom Landry was a brilliant coach, a brilliant general on the field and in the classroom. We all know his stoic presence on the field and in the media, and he was also that way with the players. There was no warmth or real friendship that was developed between the players and coach Tom, and we preferred it that way—because of his personality. He just wasn't a fun person to be around. You did your job for him, you listened to him, you paid attention because you knew what he told you was the right thing to do. He was a brilliant coach."

Margene Adkins: "Let me say this: Duane at this time, he took a stand by himself. But one man could not break the system. He didn't have enough blacks standing with him at that particular time, because when he called Tom Landry a 'plastic man,' at that time he was right. See, we'd be having a meeting, and say we'd have lunch break. We'd be in there laying on the floor or eating or playing cards, and we'd see Tom come through, and when he walked through, you could see he wanted to stop and hold a conversation with you, but he was the type of man, he could not do it. He never could hold a conversation with us, wasn't talking to any of us. And another thing about Tom Landry which we all knew: Tom was one intelligent coach, one of the greatest ever, and see where Tom made his mistake, he wanted to coach *everything*. Like on film day, he went over special teams, went over offense, went over defense. He did it all. And he didn't give his other coaches a chance to do anything. That was his problem, and I heard he broke over the years, that later on through the years he began to talk to his men, black and white."

In 1971 Clint Murchison moved the Cowboys home games from the venerable, dilapidated Cotton Bowl to his magnificent new arena, Texas Stadium, located in the Dallas suburb of Irving. Murchison had wanted city money to build a new stadium downtown, but then Mayor Erik Jonsson, one of the founders of Texas Instruments, told Murchison that city money would be made available only to refurbish the Cotton Bowl.

In late 1966 Murchison shocked the city fathers when he announced he had paid $1 for 90 acres across in Irving, seven miles from downtown, and was building a new stadium there.

A horrified Jonsson asked Murchison, "If you take the Cowboys out of [the Cotton Bowl], what are you suggesting we put there instead?"

Said Murchison archly, "What about an electronics plant?"

The new stadium cost $25 million. It was built without any public funds. Fans paid $18 million in bonds. Murchison picked up the rest. Suites, many of which were sold to corporations, cost $50,000, in addition to the seat prices (12 tickets at $1,296 each). Fans sitting between the 30-yard lines had to buy a block of four seats plus four $250 bonds in addition to the price of the tickets. The first-year cost: $4,272. If they didn't want to lose the bond money fans had to buy their seats for 32 years. The blue-collar, black, and Spanish-speaking fans who had come to see the Cowboys in the Cotton Bowl long before they became fashionable complained that they could no longer afford to go to Cowboys games. Replied an unrepentant Murchison, "If we discriminated against them, we discriminated against them, but no more than all America discriminates against people who don't have money to buy everything they want."

Murchison built a cathedral, with a large oval hole in the roof so the fans would stay dry when it rained on the field. At a dinner party a woman asked Clint, "Why did you leave that great big hole in the roof of your stadium?"

He told her, "So that God can see His team play."

Most of the players disliked the move, because the Cotton Bowl had a grass field and Texas Stadium had a much harder, more injury-prone artificial surface. Others were unhappy because from now on only the well-to-do could get in to see the Cowboys play.

Cornell Green: "I was sorry to leave the Cotton Bowl. I liked the crowd better there. They were rowdy. I liked all the beer drinkers, the loud people. And when we moved to Texas Stadium, a lot of those fans couldn't even go anymore. At Texas Stadium, it was more like a country club. And at Texas Stadium they put in AstroTurf [actually Texas Turf], and that was the next bad thing. Football was becoming more corporate. People started wearing minks to the game. Yup. They'd get fully dressed. No more jeans and T-shirts."

Mel Renfro: "I loved the Cotton Bowl—*loved* it. My only feeling about Texas Stadium was that we *had* to go. I didn't want to go, but we had to go. It was very disappointing to me because it eliminated a lot of black Americans from attending the games. It eliminated the crowd that we used to have with the excitement and the noise. It was just different, like you were playing in your living room. It was a bunch of rich people who you couldn't get excited about anything. It was just a totally different atmosphere. I didn't like the move at all."

Tex Schramm insisted that the Dallas Cowboys be run according to the same strict guidelines as any other well-run corporation. Tex wanted his players hard working and obedient. He wanted "team players," which he defined as players who worked like dogs and didn't complain about the hosing they were taking in the salary department. Schramm didn't like "troublemakers," and if they could be replaced, he got rid of them. On Mother's Day in May 1971 tight end Pettis Norman, a Cowboys pillar since 1962, led a march and boycott with about 100 blacks along Main Street in downtown Dallas. The group was protesting that the Citizens Charter Association, the town leaders who controlled such appointments, had double-crossed the black community by not appointing a local black businessman the mayor pro tempore, after promising to do so. Norman, the first black ever to be made an officer of a bank in Dallas, in a speech accused the group of affronting all African Americans in the city.

At the news conference after the march, the first question a reporter asked Norman was, "How is it going to feel to be traded to Kansas City?" Replied Norman, "If that's what it takes to be a man, then Kansas City here I come."

Norman was traded less than a month later—not to Kansas City but to San Diego—for wide receiver Lance Alworth. Though coach Landry swore to Norman that he was traded not because of his political views but because San Diego wouldn't give up Alworth unless he was in the deal, the black community suspected otherwise and was furious at Schramm and the Cowboys. They saw the Norman trade as retaliation for his making waves in a city where the Cowboys sought support from the government and the city's white power brokers.

The morning after the announcement of the Norman trade, black citizens congregated at the bank where Norman was working, threatening to march to the Cowboys office building and burn it down. Norman went on television to ask for calm.

As smart and powerful as any business executive, Tex Schramm kept an iron hand over the Cowboys, especially their purse strings, keeping to his budget as though he and not the Murchisons were the owner of the team. During the sixties, when the NFL was beginning to grow, the Dallas players knew they were getting peanuts to play but didn't resent it because no one else seemed to be making all that much either. But as the TV contracts swelled and television was beginning to generate substantial ad dollars, players on other teams (especially the Washington Redskins, where George Allen felt it important to pay his players generously) began making six figures while even the Cowboys stars were making half that. With the start of the players association, the Cowboys players began comparing notes with players from other teams, and they discovered that the Cowboys were among the worst-paying teams in football.

Schramm would not pay his players a fair wage, but there was nothing they could do about it, not yet anyway, and with might making right, Tex would chisel them down financially while at the same time fueling a PR machine that was making them nationally famous. Many players settled for the fame, figuring that their renown would lead to a secure financial future after football. Sadly, most would be very wrong about that.

If you were uncomfortable with the changes in society brought by the coming of the big business age or if you found yourself the victim of corporate ruthlessness, it could literally drive you crazy. If you believed in flower power, believed that if you loved your neighbor everything would work out fine, or if you believed in equality as promised in the Bill of Rights, or if you believed in the goodness of your fellow man, the reality of corporate America was a rude awakening. Making money had little to do with morality or equality or love. Move it or lose it. It was lead, follow, or get out of the way. The result was a new generation of disillusioned young people shrouded in a blanket of either hopelessness or anger heretofore unseen in American life.

Among the younger blacks, as segregation evaporated but opportunities remained scarce, anger rose dramatically. A small group of militants called the Black Panthers scared the pants off J. Edgar Hoover and the white power structure. They wanted real equality, and they wanted it immediately. Their slogan "Black Power" made everyone jumpy. At Cornell University a group of black students was photographed carrying large guns on campus. Malcolm X, Bobby Seale, Stokely Carmichael, and other young, angry blacks talked about "war against whitey." Malcolm X's group of Muslims, antiwhite-talking men with names foreign to American ears, made it sound like there was going to be a race war in the near future if the "honkies" didn't watch out.

These were the two social forces—the rise in corporate America and the visibility of the Black Power movement—that came into play when in the summer of 1971 Duane Thomas complained that the Cowboys had saddled him with a bad contract and then in bad faith refused to renegotiate it. He called Tom Landry a "plastic man, no man at all" and said that Gil Brandt was a liar. He called Tex Schramm "sick, demented, and dishonest," to which Schramm replied, "two out of three ain't bad." When Schramm made it clear he would not give in to his demands, an angry Thomas told Landry he wanted to be traded.

In addition to releasing antiblack sentiment within the white community of Dallas, Thomas also let loose a torrent of anti–Dallas Cowboys sentiment from all across the rest of the country, mostly from the counterculture, the huge swell of younger anti-Vietnam, anti–Richard Nixon, anti–Jim Crow football fans.

Young fans from all the other NFL cities for years had resented the button-down Tom Landry and his glamour team. In 1971 Thomas had spelled out *why* they had hated Landry and his team. It was because Landry was plastic and his team corporate. For the rest of his life, to his detractors Tom Landry would be known as the Plastic Man.

And for the rest of his life, Duane Thomas would be remembered as being "that crazy nigger who refused to talk to the press," though sometimes his more racist critics would replace *crazy* with *dumb*.

But the funny thing about stereotypes is that they don't always match the person attached to them. In this case up until the time that the pressures of playing pro football got to him, Duane Thomas was a person any mother would have been proud to call her son. Besides his immense talent, Thomas was very intelligent. He spoke eloquently. He was observant.

In the journal he kept his first season he wrote how impressed he was with the camaraderie of the Cowboys defensive stars and with the men who blocked for him on the offensive line:

> When I saw Bob Lilly and Jethro Pugh, my two favorite defensive linemen, working in such unison with Lee Roy Jordan, I said, "Look at what they have going together." I said, "Look at what we have . . . a championship team," even though some people didn't realize it. Cornell Green, the brilliance of his play was thrilling. . . . Blaine Nye, Dave Manders, Rayfield Wright, John Niland, impeccable at the point of attack.
>
> I was so thankful to be surrounded by such men on the field. The team was like an orchestra. It was so beautiful to watch the flow of execution on that team, consistently unstoppable, the scoreboard going like a pinball machine.

This was not the musing of an uneducated street urchin. Here was a young man who appreciated his teammates and wasn't afraid to say so. Here was a *team* player. He was *thrilled* to be a Cowboy. He worked hard. He was soft-spoken. He was polite. And he was trusting.

He believed in family values. Though his mom died when he was a junior in college and his dad died a year later, he never forgot his duty to his younger brothers. When brother Bertrand got in a car accident and lost three fingers, Duane paid his bills. When brother Franklin had kidney trouble and needed expensive medical care, Duane was there for him, too.

Duane had married his high school sweetheart and had two children, but once he entered West Texas State on scholarship, he discovered that under NCAA rules he could get only room, board, and $15 per month for laundry. Several times he tried to leave school to go to work to earn money, but the coaches always sat him down and persuaded him to keep at it. All his young life he had trusted his coaches, because he had had no one else to rely on. At West Texas State, his coach, Joe Kerbel, had been a mentor and a father figure.

When he was named the Cowboys' number one draft choice, the 21-year-old Thomas figured his money worries would be over. When he was first drafted, Tom Landry, superscout Gil Brandt, and president Tex Schramm all hustled him, assuring him that he could place his well-being in their hands.

Calvin Hill: "In terms of Duane, or a Bob Hayes, who wound up in prison, the sad thing is that I don't think Tom ever understood how much they depended on him."

The string of events leading to Thomas' famed Plastic Man appellation began a couple of months after Super Bowl V in the winter of 1971, when Thomas charged that the year before his agent and Schramm had sold him down the river by agreeing to a lousy contract. Thomas felt betrayed. He had trusted his agent, giving him power of attorney. He had trusted Brandt, who had put his arm around Thomas' shoulder and said, "Don't worry. We'll take care of you." He had trusted Schramm. He was also upset that Schramm wouldn't pay off on the clause in the contract that called for him to receive a bonus for gaining 1,000 yards. Thomas, who finished with 862 yards, argued that the only reason he came up short was that Landry hadn't played him very much early in the season.

Thomas told Schramm that his $20,000 salary wasn't enough to live on, that he owed the IRS $10,000, that he had an ex-wife with two kids who was demanding alimony, and that he couldn't live on the money he was making. Schramm looked him in the eyes and told him no.

"But you renegotiated Rayfield Wright's contract," Thomas told him.

"Sorry, son."

Thomas was haunted by what he saw as the unfairness of the situation: "I saw no appreciation from them—for my hard work, my dedication, and my sincerity. All of this was being exploited." Thomas was not wrong, and he knew he wasn't wrong. When Schramm told him he was stuck with his bad deal, all Thomas could think about was the unfairness of his situation. He became fixated on Schramm's rejection of his plea to pay him what he felt he deserved after helping to take the team to the Super Bowl. "I figured they didn't dig me," said Thomas. "I wasn't the stereotype passing type of nigger who comes in and says, 'Please, Mr. White Man, do this for me.'"

In March, Thomas told CBS television he was retiring. He said that the Cowboys would not have gone to the Super Bowl without him and said it was he who the fans came to see, not Schramm, and he said publicly what he had told Schramm: he wanted his fair share.

When the articles in the paper the next few days and weeks came out foursquare against him, Thomas sank into a deep depression. Not only did the reporters take Schramm's side, but they called Thomas "cocky" and "greedy."

Thomas did not report to training camp, and Schramm waited him out, fully expecting him to give in. He finally arrived in July with a man wearing a dashiki,

Ali Ha Ka Kabir (nee Mansfield Collins) and demanded that Kabir be given a tryout. Schramm refused his request. Thomas called a press conference and again requested a trade. It was at this press conference that he blasted Landry, Brandt, and Schramm.

Calvin Hill: "There was a rumor going around camp that Duane and the Muslims were going to kidnap Tex. Next morning Tex had four or five guards around him. It was wild."

On July 31, 1971, Schramm and Landry thought they had rid themselves of their Duane Thomas headache when they traded their star back to the New England Patriots, along with lineman Halvor Hagen and wide receiver Honor Jackson, for Carl Garrett and a number one draft choice.

Garrett immediately put his foot in his mouth by saying how glad he was to come to Dallas and to get away from the Patriots' leaky offensive line.

Schramm and Landry figured the tandem of Calvin Hill and Garrett had the ability to return them to the Super Bowl. A bitter Thomas angered a lot of his teammates when he told the press that the Cowboys would never make it back there without him. Others felt it was best for Thomas to be playing in a new environment.

Cornell Green: "I thought when they traded Duane to New England it might be the best thing for him. It hurt me to see what he was going through, but the only problem, when you tried to talk to him, he wouldn't listen. He *didn't* listen. I don't have time. I had two kids of my own to raise."

When Thomas reported to the Patriots, he clashed with coach John Mazur. A month before the Thomas trade, the Cowboys had sent Steve Kiner to the New England graveyard. Kiner had been infuriated when Landry coaxed Chuck Howley out of retirement and gave him the linebacking job Kiner thought he deserved. When Kiner was sent to the Patriots, he was in a position to observe what happened between Duane Thomas and the Pats.

Steve Kiner: "I had been in New England for about a week or two, when their coach, John Mazur, called me in and said, 'Steve, I'm thinking about trading Carl for Duane. Can you tell me about Duane?' I said, 'The guy is phenomenal. He's the best damn running back in the league.' They made the trade, and after Duane was in New England about three days, Mazur was just beside himself, 'I thought you told me this guy was all right.' I said, 'He's not all right; he's a great running back. You just gotta handle him differently.' And John couldn't. Duane just blew him away.

"John wanted Duane to get in a three-point stance, and he wouldn't. All he could do was line up with his hands on his knees. He could not run out of a three-point stance. If John had said, 'Hey, Duane, here's $1,500, I need you to get in a three-point stance,' that would have worked. And see, that's where Duane had lost perspective of everything. Here's what it was about: he thought he had positioned himself where he could make all these demands, and what he found out was that he couldn't.

"Duane got a lot of misinformation from the older, militant, black players in the league, militant in the sense that they were disgruntled, and he would listen to them, and he felt he was going to make a difference. I could see Duane was looking at the world differently than I was. I was looking at, 'He's cutting his nose off to spite his face.' And I begged him not to do that. I told him, 'This is just not good for you.' But he couldn't hear any of that. It was a real hard position to be in.

"All Duane wanted was for the Cowboys to renegotiate his contract. If they had torn that up and given him $30,000, $40,000, and $50,000, he'd have been happier than a pig in shit. For a crummy 10 grand, Tex Schramm cost the Cowboys a couple of Super Bowls and threw this guy's career away. And not just his career—as far as I'm concerned, threw his whole life out the window. And that's the tragedy of the sport. When you turn around, they are going to say, 'Well, he's a man. He's an adult. It was his responsibility.' But we were just kids."

After Thomas spent five tumultuous days in New England, the Pats called Schramm and demanded that the trade be canceled. "They [the Patriots] told me to leave—face-to-face—just like that. So I came home," said Thomas.

Tex didn't want Thomas back, but NFL commissioner Pete Rozelle voided the trade and forced his return to Dallas, where he would lead the Cowboys to another Super Bowl. A sheepish Garrett had to return to the Pats and their porous offensive line.

Thomas was put on the inactive list and missed the first three games of the 1971 season. He returned to action on a Monday night against the New York Giants, and he played on the special teams as though possessed. In the first half, on one play, he tackled his former college teammate, Rocky Thompson, forcing a fumble. On two other kickoffs he also made tackles on the fleet Thompson.

On the fourth play of the second half, Calvin Hill was injured, and Thomas went into the game. Despite having missed the entire training camp, Thomas looked as though he hadn't missed a beat, running 60 yards on nine carries.

Mel Renfro: "When Duane starred against the Giants after missing all of training camp, I wasn't surprised, 'cause he was a talent, just like Jim Brown. Jim Brown could have walked on any field at any time and kicked everybody's butt, and Duane, who was a tremendous athletic specimen, was potentially that way."

After the game Thomas, still angry that the Dallas media had taken Tex's side against him, announced his refusal to talk to the press. Said Thomas, "There is nothing to say when you're working." For the rest of the season, their articles about his refusal to talk to them made him sound petty, childish, and flaky, which further fueled Thomas' resentment of the newspaper reporters in particular and white society in general.

In addition to becoming a celebrity, Thomas had also become a marked man. It bothered him terribly when strangers would stare at him, like he was a curiosity or a freak in a circus sideshow. "Everyone used to look at me strangelike," said Thomas. "I'd be doing something, and they'd act like they were hypnotized. I know I hadn't told them anything and neither did anyone know anything about me. I thought I was in the twilight zone."

But those teammates who respected hard work and dedication to the game of football overlooked the sideshow and saw a football player who stayed in shape, studied the game plan, and gave his all on the field.

Lee Roy Jordan: "Duane Thomas and I got along perfect. I loved Duane Thomas. I respected him when he went into the deal about not talking. I told him, 'Duane, you have chosen the right thing. You have chosen to concentrate on football. And if you can't handle all these other things, I admire you the priority you have taken in committing to football.'"

What hurt Thomas worse than anything was the double standard that he saw on the Cowboys in the way he was being treated. He saw that when Mike Ditka got drunk and crashed his car at 4:00 in the morning, when John Niland got drunk and brawled with cops, and when Lance Rentzel got busted, the media ran one story and dropped it like it had never happened. But here was Duane Thomas whose crime was not talking to the newspaper writers, and he couldn't believe it when the media made a bigger stink about that than any of those other, to him more serious, incidents. The reason, said Thomas, was because the white press excused the behavior of the white players, but not his, because he was black. "It was accepted as just a bunch of good ol' boys having fun. No big deal."

Thomas bristled at the stereotype of the lazy, unexcited black athlete being placed on him. "People accuse me of not being excited for games. Well, compared to them [his good old boy teammates] I wasn't excited, because I wasn't using all them damn bennies they were taking. How many times did I see guys hungover for the games . . . in the fourth quarter they were breathing heavy in the huddle, and I was just getting started."

Said Thomas to journalist Howie Evans, "The thing that bothers me is the unjust attitudes many football people have toward black athletes. It's something I find not only in pro football but in life in general. It's the way they talk to us, the way they look at us, and what they really think of us. There are a lot of black players who are afraid to speak out on the grievances they have, and the injustices they know are being inflicted upon them."

The bottom line was that Duane Thomas couldn't stand not being respected and appreciated in a town where he had just helped its team win the prize sought since 1960: the Super Bowl. Said Duane's brother Bertrand sometime later, "The people of Dallas don't want to recognize my brother's ability, and he can do so much for the Cowboys."

Thomas' black teammates saw how the press used Duane's anger against him, how the reporters kept the flow of stories about him coming. They wanted to stop it, but they were powerless to do so. And then when he refused to talk in his own attempt to end the controversy, the stories took on a life of their own: silent Duane, the crazy Cowboy. His teammates could only shake their heads.

Pettis Norman: "Other players could have been angry and not gotten what Duane got. And to the extent I saw incidents in which the press treated African-American players five times worse than what it did had it been someone else. The press continually went after Duane, when they should have recognized that this was a 21-year-old kid who really didn't know his way around this ballpark, and instead of us doing it the way we're doing it, let's try to get to another level and make some sense of it. Let's try to understand things from Duane's standpoint, instead of making fun of a lot of the things he said. These writers were adults. They were grown men who had been out there for a long time. Duane was just a kid. But it never happened. They just continually wrote about the negative Duane, and the public got to the point where they thought Duane was a demon, and Duane was not a demon at all. But they never wrote the good things about Duane. To them, he was just an angry football player who signed a contract and didn't want to live with his contract. But they never got beyond that to say that this was an interesting young man who made a lot of sense when you sat down and talked to him."

Thomas defended his decision not to talk to the press: "I didn't feel like talking so I didn't talk. If I read the Constitution right, it gives me the freedom to do as I please. There's no stipulation that says if you play football you have to talk. I don't get paid for talking. I get paid to play football." When Landry told a reporter Duane had to change his attitude, Thomas called Landry "unfair and dishonest."

"There is nothing wrong with my attitude," he said. "My attitude is a winning attitude. I have felt that my attitude coincided with the goal of the team." He added, "I never go around and complain about him [Landry] not talking."

Frustrated and bitter that he had to play under a system that he hated in a town where he felt unwanted and unappreciated after a daily pounding in the press, Thomas even cut off most of his own teammates.

Mel Renfro: "When Duane came back from New England, he just clammed up. He wouldn't talk to anybody. He wouldn't say a word. And I lockered right next to the guy. I remember one time, the guy hadn't said anything all year, and all of a sudden he said, 'Fro, how you doing? How are the kids?' Totally freaked me out! I said, 'Duane, the kids are fine.' He said, 'Good.' And he didn't say another word for two weeks."

Mike Ditka: "Once we were playing the Giants in Yankee Stadium. I always made a habit of going up and wishing everybody good luck before a game. I went up to him and just patted him on the back and said, 'Good luck.' He didn't acknowledge it. I went on my way. We played the game. The following Tuesday, I was sitting beside my locker reading the paper in Dallas before practice, and he came up to me and said, 'Hey man, don't ever hit me on the back before a game. It breaks my concentration.' I said, 'Hey, Duane. Go f*** yourself.'

"That was our conversation."

Walt Garrison: "People always asked me, 'How did you and Duane get along?' Well, I liked Duane. I always liked him. I liked him when he was weird.

I didn't give a damn if he ever talked, because he played. And I don't say that even about a lot of guys who did talk.

"One time Duane scored a touchdown against San Francisco in a playoff game in Texas Stadium. They called an audible at the goal line, and Duane went to the wrong side of the formation. I told him, 'Duane, other side.' He moved over. They pitched out to him, and he scored a TD.

"A writer asked me after the game, 'Did you line up in the wrong spot?' And I said, 'Yes.'

"They found out later that I lied to them and they came back. 'Why didn't you tell us Thomas was lined up in the wrong spot?'

"'Because y'all been on his ass all year.'

"Hey, I liked the guy."

Ironically, the Duane Thomas situation put Landry in a lose-if-I-do, lose-if-I-don't situation. Thomas was disruptive, but he was a great performer. During practice Thomas at times refused to run in simulation of the opposing team, making the vets mad at both him and Landry, who didn't call him on it. The good old boys on the team—and the majority of Dallas rooters—saw Landry as the good guy in the drama for going out of his way to turn the other cheek when Duane was being disruptive.

Walt Garrison: "I think Landry looked at Duane as his one big failure. He wanted to get Duane back on the right track. Tom wanted to save him, wanted to give him a chance to get back to being a human being again. But it didn't work.

"That's when Landry really lost the respect of the veteran players, because all of a sudden we now had a double standard.

"Ironically, Landry's failure with Duane showed the strength of his character. It showed how much he really did care about his players. If Landry was truly like his image—cold, calculating, humorless, and unemotional—he would have cut Thomas without a second thought.

"Duane ran us right into the Super Bowl that year, and it just about destroyed the team. A Super Bowl is supposed to bring everybody together, and here we were holding up the Super Bowl trophy and everybody is pissed off."

All because Tex Schramm stupidly, stubbornly refused to pay Duane Thomas what he deserved.

Chapter 43

ROGER TAKES THE HELM

Roger Staubach: "In '71 Craig came back in great shape, so that season we competed for the starting quarterback job. We were 6–0 in the preseason, and that was when Landry announced at the start of the season, 'We'll have *two* starting quarterbacks.'

"I was going to start against Buffalo in the first game, but I broke a vessel in my leg against Kansas City in the last exhibition game, so he started Craig. [Calvin Hill scored four touchdowns, and Morton was 10–14 for 220 yards and two touchdowns in a 49–37 win.] Landry said we were going to alternate, so I started the next weekend in Philadelphia.

"On the third play of the game, I threw a pass that was intercepted by Bill Bradley. On the play this guy Mel Tom knocked me out from behind, a dirty shot. [The 260-pound Tom was fined $1,500 after delivering a forearm blow to the side of Staubach's head.] All of a sudden I was over at the sideline, and I was so woozy I didn't know what was going on.

"Craig came in, and we won 42–7, so coach Landry said, 'I'm going to keep the momentum going,' so he started Craig against Washington, and we lost the Redskins game [20–16], so he started me against the Giants in the Cotton Bowl.

"We were winning 13–6 at halftime. I didn't have a great first half, but we were winning. And Landry took me out, which for me was the end of it. I went crazy. I said to him that I needed to be traded, to get out of here. Of course, Landry was a phenomenal coach and we had a great career together, but I don't think he totally understood me as far as someone who could handle pressure and problems. Maybe I wasn't having a good first half, but we were still winning. That was the worst thing he could have done to me. It was what I had said to him the year before, that when I started a game, I wanted to finish what I started. Taking a quarterback out in the middle of the game is the ultimate insult. [A 48-yard Craig Morton–to–Bob Hayes touchdown pass beat the Giants 20–13. Duane Thomas and Calvin Hill played side by side for three plays when Hill was injured. After missing all of training camp, all the preseason games, and the first three regular-season games, Thomas carried nine times for 60 yards.]

"We played the next week against the Saints. Craig started, and we were losing 14–0, and he put me in in the second half, and we had a chance to pull it out. We scored twice, came back to 17–14, but we fumbled a punt, and we didn't get the ball back. [The Cowboys lost 24–14.]

"Our record at that point was 3–2, and then we played the New England Patriots in Texas Stadium, the first game we ever played there, and I started that game and had a real good game. [In a 44–21 win, Staubach threw two touchdowns to Bob Hayes and ran for a third. Duane Thomas scored on a 56-yard run the fourth play of the game.]

"So now the next day Landry announces in the team meeting, 'We're going to have two quarterbacks alternate plays.' I was sitting there, and I looked over at Morton, and he was looking at me, and I couldn't believe it. This was the most ridiculous thing I ever heard of in my life. But Tom believed in his system. He believed if he had two robots, it would work. What he was really saying was that he felt it didn't matter what player he was inserting into his system, if you did what he wanted you to do, you'd win.

"He didn't understand the emotion and the other human aspects, I don't think, of the notion that a person can make a difference, especially over a long season, and it may be in critical games. You just can't send a guy in there and say, 'Hey, mechanically, if he can throw a football, if you do what I tell you to do you'll win' 'cause a quarterback is a leader, somebody who can bring emotion among other players. So the team was now thinking, 'Well, we have *two* quarterbacks.' It was a divided team, and that is never good.

"We alternated in the Chicago Bears game. Landry called the plays and sent them in with us, and as the game went on, we had phenomenal yardage, something like 480 yards, but we didn't score much. We had this really erratic game. We lost 23–19, so now we were 4–3, kind of like the year before, and he played Craig at the end of the Chicago game, left him in for the two-minute drill, and I was thinking, 'It's the same deal, the same decision.' I'm figuring, 'Craig's going to be the quarterback again this year.' To me that was going to be the end."

After the loss to the Bears, the Cowboys, at 4–3, were two full games behind the Washington Redskins at 6–1, and the media once again was declaring the Cowboys dead. Moreover, Landry was taking a beating in the papers and from his players for his insistence that under his Multiple Offense system it didn't matter who was playing quarterback, that even if he alternated quarterbacks, the team should win.

The next day during a national telecast of *Monday Night Football*, former quarterback Don Meredith, who had never publicly criticized Landry before, told his audience, "It's Landry's responsibility as the head coach to pick a quarterback. Now after all this time he still has no idea which one is the best. Then get another coach. I'm somewhat disappointed, but I'm sure not nearly as disappointed as Morton and Staubach, not to mention the other 38 players who are involved in this wishy-washy decision."

Meredith, of course, knew of what he spoke.

Lee Roy Jordan: "The big thing with the players, it really didn't matter to us *who* started, but let's pick one and stay with him. 'He's our guy. He's the one who's going to do it for us from here on.' Because alternating players makes it seem like you don't have confidence in anyone. It's like, 'We'll try this and maybe one of them will get lucky.' That's the way the team looked at it. So we just wanted to have a permanent guy in there, to use his talents whatever they are and we'll win with him and it'll work for us eventually."

Mel Renfro: "Our preference was Roger. We knew that Craig was more experienced and Roger was an upstart, but we saw what Roger could do at certain times with his scrambling ability. We knew he had a lot to learn. We said to ourselves, 'Just make a decision and go with it.'

"We did not say these things publicly. We were not allowed to. There was one thing we found out about coach Landry: don't open your mouth, even if he asks you. You don't want it to come back and slap you in the face. Yeah, that happened a few times. He'd say, 'Air your grievances and there won't be anything said about it. We just want to know how you feel.' And so we did, and it wasn't long when those grievances started slapping us in the face. So we said, 'We'll know better next time. When they ask us to air our grievances, we'll say everything he wants to hear, not what we want to say.'"

Making matters worse, the next day Ralph "Rotten" Neely, the All-Pro offensive tackle, broke his leg. And on that day it was thought that George Andrie, the fine defensive end, had suffered a heart attack.

Neely's teammates told Landry that he had been out riding horses, that his horse had been spooked by a rattlesnake, reared, and dumped Neely to the ground, breaking his leg. That was the cover story.

What really happened was that the good old boys were out raising Cain, riding their motorcycles over rough terrain, and Neely took a mean tumble that put him out of action the rest of the season.

Walt Garrison: "A group of the Cowboys started riding motorcycles. On Mondays after the game, we'd usually go out to Grapevine Lake and ride out in the dirt all day. Mike Ditka was with the Cowboys then, and he bought a 125cc. Dave Edwards had a 125. Me and Lilly and Cliff Harris and Dan Reeves had one. And, of course, that meant Ralph had to have one, too.

"Rotten couldn't ride worth a damn. He kept falling off all day. But that didn't make any difference. His bike had to be bigger and better than everybody else's. So Ralph went out and bought a Husqvarna 400, an absolute man-eating monster. Comes with a chain and a whip.

"Anyway, we'd been out riding all day and we're packing up to go home, and off in the distance I could see Cliff coming in and his eyes are as big as silver dollars. And I thought, 'Oh, shit, what happened?'

"Cliff and Rotten had been riding together, and Ralph says, 'Cliff, let's jump some hills.' And Cliff was thinking, 'Christ, Ralph, you can barely ride. And now you want to jump hills?' Plus, he knew Ralph had a herd of ponies under him like to scare the shit outta Cochise. But he figured, 'Ah, what the hell.'

"There was a grass field out where they were riding, and at the end of it was a hill that went up at a nice pitch. Nothing too scary. So Cliff gunned his 125 and went right up the hill and waited for Ralph there.

"Ralph guns his monster and gets about halfway up and falls over. So he gets up cussing. 'Damn motorcycle ain't worth a shit. They don't make nothing worth a damn anymore.'

"Good ole Rotten.

"So Ralph goes back down and tries again, only this time he really cranks that puppy up full throttle. Here comes Ralph *eeeeee,* thumb, *eeeeeee,* thumb, *eeeeeeeee,* about 60 or 70 mph and he climbs right up to the top . . . and keeps right on going. He shoots into the air about 20 feet.

"Ralph's legs are real long and instead of putting them on the footrest, he used to ride with them dangling along the ground. Well, he lands on his back and starts rolling down the hill with those big ol' legs going every whichaway. When he finally stops he looks back up at Cliff and says real calmly, 'Ah, Cliff, I think I hurt my foot. Look at it, would you?'

"And sure enough his leg was pointing up the hill and his foot was pointing down. He'd broken it in three places, dislocated his ankle, and tore a bunch of ligaments. Out for the season.

"They throw Rotten in the back of Ditka's truck with the muddy old bikes, and every time they'd go over a bump Neely would scream. But nobody gave a damn about Neely's pain. All they kept saying to him all the way home was, 'Don't tell Landry we were riding motorcycles. Let's tell him we were riding horses. Ya, we were riding along and a snake bit Ralph's horse.'

"So they take him over to the hospital and that night there was a team party. When I got there, somebody comes running up to me and says, 'Did you hear what happened?'

"'Hell, I was with him when it happened.'

"'You were there when George Andrie had his heart attack?'

"'What? Andrie had a heart attack?'

"'Ya.'

"'Didn't you hear about Neely?' I asked.

"'No.'

"'He broke his leg.'

"'How'd he do it?'

"'He stepped off a curb and it snapped.'

"'No shit.'

"Turned out Andrie never did have a heart attack. It was just indigestion. But it sure helped take Landry's mind off Neely's foot and how he did it. The funny thing was there were seven of us Cowboys all happy as hell that George was dying of heart failure. Just as long as Landry didn't find out we'd been riding motorcycles.

"Who says you don't get close with your teammates?"

That evening Roger Staubach was feeling discouraged and lost. He was moping around when assistant coach Ray Renfro took him aside. "Please don't tell anyone I'm telling you this," Renfro told him in a whisper, "because it could cost me my job. You're not supposed to know this, but you will be starting this week."

Chapter 44

SUPER

When Tom Landry informed Roger Staubach that he would be the team's starting quarterback for the rest of the 1971 season, Staubach told him, "I won't let you down, Coach." And he didn't. Though Staubach had started only 11 games prior to Landry giving him the job, the Cowboys didn't lose another game the rest of the season as the Navy Heisman winner completed 60 percent of his passes (126 of 211, 15 TDs) and ran 41 times for 343 yards, an average of 8 yards per carry. Staubach directed a punishing ground attack and augmented it by hitting the fleet Bob Hayes for eight touchdowns, as Bullet Bob led the league with an average of 24 yards per catch.

All the while, Landry was in a constant battle with Staubach, who insisted that he be allowed to call his own plays. Despite the perception that Landry and Staubach were close friends in that they both were deeply religious, nothing could have been further from the truth. Staubach and Landry argued incessantly, and over the years Landry would be forced to accept the reality that Roger at times would countermand his play calling and go off on his own.

Margene Adkins: "At meetings, Staubach and Tom had a few problems. Staubach wanted to do this, and Tom wanted to do that. In games, Tom Landry would want to call a play and Staubach wouldn't like it. Staubach wanted to call his own plays. So Tom'd send a play in, and Staubach might not have liked the play, and what Staubach would do, he would audible that play, but it always worked, and so by it working Tom couldn't say anything. It wasn't to the point where they got angry, where Staubach wanted to run the team and Tom Landry wanted to. It was just a little problem there."

The combination of Tom Landry and Roger Staubach proved to be one of the most successful in league history. Landry would design the game plan, and he would call the plays, but Tom also came to see that if the team was in trouble late in the game, Staubach would figure out a way to pull them out of it. As quarterback of the team through the seventies, Staubach pulled their toes out of the fire 23 times. Landry never stopped begging Staubach not to run with the ball, and Staubach never heeded his advice. But over the years the two developed a deep respect and understanding of each other, as Staubach would take the

Cowboys to three Super Bowls and come within a hairsbreadth of getting there several other times.

Roger Staubach: "The beginning of our momentum in '71 came in my first game against the St. Louis Cardinals. We beat them 16–13. It was a great game. And St. Louis was a good team at that time.

"We beat the Eagles while Washington was losing to the Bears, putting us only a half game behind them, and then in Washington we shut out the Redskins, 13–0, in a tough game, to take the lead. I called a pass play to Alworth, but when I saw the left side was open, I ran myself the 29 yards to score. The press asked Tom if he had designed that play for me. I guess they didn't know Landry.

"We beat the Rams Thanksgiving Day, 28–21. That was a tough one, too. Duane ran for the winning touchdown. In that game I threw a 51-yarder to Bob Hayes and a shorter one to Lance Alworth.

"After we beat the Jets, 52–10, in a game in which Duane scored a touchdown and Calvin three, we went to Yankee Stadium to play the Giants. Duane and Calvin were great again, and Bob Hayes had his best day. He caught two long touchdowns. One of my big thrills was throwing an 85-yard touchdown pass to Bob over Spider Lockhart. I was a big baseball fan, so throwing a long touchdown pass in Yankee Stadium was *great*. But Bob could do that.

"We won the final game of the season against the St. Louis Cards to win the division title. Duane Thomas scored four touchdowns. Duane was so great.

"Going up to Minnesota for the first playoff game, we had this momentum going. We just played a good game. It was a key game, because the Vikings were pretty unbeatable in Minnesota, and I was fortunate that cold weather just didn't bother me a whole lot. The good thing about it, the weather really wasn't a factor in the game. Fortunately, it wasn't windy.

"We won the game, 20–12. After Duane scored a touchdown, I hit Bob with a pass for a nine-yard touchdown. On defense, we played a great game. We intercepted four passes and recovered a fumble.

"The NFC Championship against the San Francisco 49ers was a tough game. They had John Brodie at quarterback, and they were a very good team. Our offense moved the ball a lot, but we didn't do much. We had one big series. On a long scramble where I really could have been trapped in our own end zone, I threw the ball out to Dan Reeves, who limped down the right sideline and set up Duane's touchdown to put the game away, 14–3.

"It was just a very solid game. Our defense was outstanding. The big play in that game was George Andrie intercepting a screen pass near the goal line."

Lee Roy Jordan: "John Brodie was the quarterback, and the running backs were Ken Willard and Vic Washington, damn good running backs, outstanding runners. They had an outstanding receiving corps, Gene Washington and tight end Ted Kwalick, an outstanding football player, a great receiver and great blocker. Dave [Edwards] had to handle him, and all the linebackers worked on him, along with Cornell Green, our strong safety.

"Our preparation for the game was so good. Once we became confident that we could control certain things, we just knew it wasn't going to be any problem. Like we decided, 'We're going to stop the running game,' and in that game we stopped them. And after stopping the running game, we then had to concentrate on the receivers, and stopping Gene Washington, their number one receiver. And we were able to do that. We were able to dominate them. Bob Lilly spent the whole game on top of Brodie.

"I intercepted one of Brodie's passes early in the game, near the sideline. A few years ago I ran into John in a senior golf tournament here, and he said, 'Man, what in the hell were you doing way over there on the sideline? There is no way you're going to go over there and catch a ball.'

"I said, 'I don't know why I was there. There must have been some reason in the backfield that made me feel I knew where the ball was going.' But there's where I ended up, and I made the interception, and it set us up with good field position.

"That was special. So was George Andrie's tipping a ball on a screen pass to Ken Willard, catching it and lumbering down to the 1. Calvin Hill scored to give us our first points."

Mel Renfro: "As we celebrated after the game, you had to give credit to the defense. Give credit where credit was due. We held them to three points. George Andrie intercepted a pass to give us a touchdown. We could have beaten anyone with that defense. The Doomsday Defense. And it wasn't just that year or the year before; it was the same guys playing together, Bob Lilly, George Andrie, Cornell, Lee Roy, Dave Edwards, myself. We were all there, Doomsday, playing together."

In the clubhouse after the game, Duane Thomas angered the San Francisco reporters when he told them, "Man, don't ever try to interview me after a game."

They trooped over to ask Landry what his running back's problem was. "I don't know if I can enlighten you," Landry said, adding, "Thomas acts like he is not part of the team, but he *is* part of the team. We've never asked him why he doesn't talk to reporters or sign autographs. The team wants to understand him."

At the time he was traded to New England, he had boasted that the Cowboys would never win the Super Bowl without him. Said AP sportswriter Denne Freeman, "In a mysterious way, maybe he was right."

The team traveled to New Orleans to play the Miami Dolphins in Super Bowl VI. Miami featured quarterback Bob Griese and their outstanding running backs Larry Csonka and Jim Kiick, along with the sensational pass catcher Paul Warfield. Don Shula was the coach.

Ten days before the big game, Duane Thomas set tongues wagging when he was absent from a Thursday practice amid rumors he would skip the Super Bowl if his salary demands were not met. Tex Schramm insisted that his contract would be renegotiated *after* the game.

Thomas refused to tell Landry or anyone else why he had skipped practice except to say, "Personal reasons." Landry told reporters, "He just would not talk about it at all. Football really isn't important to his life. He told me, 'My job is football, and I will do my job.' He just doesn't think anything else enters into it." Concluded Landry, "He didn't specifically say, 'I will play in the Super Bowl,' but you have to assume he will, because he's here."

In the Cowboys locker room before the game, the players didn't feel any of the doubts that they had had against Baltimore in Super Bowl V the year before.

Chuck Howley: "It was a totally different feeling going back the second time. The trauma all year long was that we should have won the year before. We didn't win, and we felt we *had* to go back. The way we looked at it, we had X amount of games to go through in order to repeat and do what we didn't do the year before. That's the way the Cowboys looked at it. We did what we had to do and went back to the Super Bowl.

"The week we spent down there, you just felt it within you. Nobody questioned the fact that we were going to win. It wasn't cockiness; it was a feel. I just knew there was no doubt we were going to win that ballgame.

"We had control all the way. It wasn't lopsided, but we had total control. We knew it from the first kickoff, right through to the end. And we finally achieved what everybody in the NFL tries to achieve, and that's to have that Super Bowl ring. It's what we all strive for."

Mel Renfro: "Against the Dolphins, Tom used the KISS theory: Keep It Simple, Stupid. He let us play football. We knew we had to eliminate Warfield. We had good talent at linebacker, so we could control their tight end, which allowed us to double their wide receivers. And Bob Lilly and the rest of them were all over Bob Griese all day. That was the key to defense.

"There were no outstanding plays to speak of, not really. When you play defense like we played defense, everybody contributes, and everybody plays well. You have to with the coordination of the defense. Everybody has to do his job. So we were a team that day. We totally dominated, a lot of three downs and out. We won 24–3, and it should have been 31–3, but Calvin fumbled on the 3-yard line at the end of the game.

"The offense played so well. Between Walt Garrison and Calvin Hill and Duane Thomas, it just doesn't get any better than that. You've got Lance Alworth and Mike Ditka catching key passes. It was a total team effort. And Roger was the quarterback. He was the man. Roger scrambling and picking up the key plays. Roger was such a tremendous individual. He has never changed. My kids grew up with his kids, and to this day that's the first thing he'll ask, 'How are the kids?' And they are all grown. Roger is a great person."

Lee Roy Jordan: "Tom worked hard studying the film, analyzing the routes Miami took, and they came up with a defense they thought we could play on both sides of the field. It was designed to shut out Paul Warfield on one side and their tight end, Marv Fleming, who used to play with Green Bay, on the other. When they set up, we would take away their favored routes from both sides and have an opportunity to intercept the ball.

"We worked on it, worked on it, and by game time we absolutely went in with the confidence that, 'Hey, this is *the* thing,' and this time coach Landry made no changes. He was confident from the beginning, all the way through the preparation, and in the game we executed the defenses.

"We also got Larry Csonka to fumble a couple times, something he had not done in the previous year or two. And Bob Lilly, George Andrie, Pat Toomay, and the guys put a lot of pressure on Bob Griese. I remember on one play they trapped him 30 yards downfield. He ran one way, and we had three guys, Bob, Larry Cole, and another guy, chasing him, and he turned one way and couldn't get away, and so he turned back the other way, and he ended up 30 yards downfield.

"When we won that Super Bowl it was certainly a great thrill, but for us, it was more a lifting of a heavy burden that we had been bearing since 1966, when we lost that first Green Bay game. So many of us after the game were so happy to have that lifted off of us, the victory itself wasn't that big. It was almost anticlimactic—it was more important to get the bridesmaid-but-never-a-bride tag removed from us.

"I talked to a lot of guys after the game. Instead of being on an emotional high, everyone was just, 'Hey, man, I'm so relieved, so happy, so delighted. We're Super Bowl champions, and nobody is going to be able to take that away.' Because until that final whistle, we were still in a position to have those negative articles written about us—by this time the job had been passed on by Gary Cartwright to other guys who liked to write plenty of negative stuff about us."

Cornell Green: "When it was over, I just said, 'Fine, we won one.' And I ran off the field. A lot of people started carrying Landry around. I didn't have time for that. I was getting out of there and getting to the locker room. So I didn't hang around to celebrate. It was, 'We finally did it.' That's it."

Chapter 45

DUANE THOMAS' LEGACY

The star in the victory over the Miami Dolphins in Super Bowl VI clearly was Duane Thomas, who after pissing off everybody on the planet, including his coach, his teammates, the press, and the fans, defied every convention when he thumbed his nose at the sports world's displeasure by playing spectacularly. The silent Thomas, whom contemptuous sportswriters had dubbed the Sphinx, carried the ball 19 times in Super Bowl VI for 95 yards against a tough Dolphins defensive unit led by linebacker Nick Buoniconti.

But Thomas was not given the MVP award (or the Corvette that went with it), because the editors of *Sport* magazine needed to find somebody who they knew would smile and say, "Thank you," in the locker room on national TV after the game. In looking for a more suitable recipient, *Sport* editor Larry Klein saw that Roger Staubach had played his usual fine game, completing 12 of 19 passes for 119 yards and two touchdowns, and he made the presentation to a sheepish Staubach, who knew that Duane should have been the one to get the prize.

Roger Staubach: "Duane would have gotten the MVP if he would have talked to the press. Down in New Orleans, Duane hadn't talked to anybody. That's the only reason he didn't get the award. They were looking for someone else to give it to, and they gave it to me."

Thomas had led the Dallas Cowboys to not one but *two* Super Bowl appearances, and despite his achievements, the snubs and negative comments hadn't stopped. On the field, Thomas was King; off the field, he was an object of scorn and derision. And what made the situation especially unbearable to the running back was the fact that it was far too late to do anything about it. After the victory over the Dolphins, Thomas skipped the team celebration. He went back to his hotel room, lay on the bed, and stared at the ceiling. Said Thomas years later, "I was upset that the season was over. I didn't ever want to stop playing. I didn't want to come off the field and deal with the outside world."

Two weeks after the Super Bowl, Thomas and his younger brother Bertrand were driving from Dallas to the West Coast, where, Tex Schramm believed, Thomas had been involved with drug use the winter before. Schramm had asked Thomas not to return to Los Angeles, but Thomas had refused. Though Schramm has denied any involvement in the incident, what followed makes sense only in the context of an attempt by Schramm to keep Thomas from reaching L.A.

Duane and his brother had not gotten very far before they were arrested in Greenville, Texas, for possessing one marijuana joint. The two arresting policemen said they'd stopped the brothers because a white Pontiac like the one they were driving had been reported stolen. The police report said one of the policemen smelled the odor of marijuana and found two matchboxes of marijuana.

According to Thomas, the police searched the car without a warrant, then planted the drugs he was accused of possessing. According to Thomas, the judge told him if he didn't hire a particular defense attorney, he would "sentence him to life."

"The whole thing was scripted," said Thomas. "It had to have been set up."

Pete Gent, who lived in Dallas after his retirement and remained friends with both executives and players on the Cowboys, felt that the Cowboys had "been behind the whole episode."

Pete Gent: "Ask yourself, 'What was Duane doing in Greenville, Texas, with dope on him?' Duane wasn't stupid. Greenville literally had a sign over the Main Street that said, 'The Blackest Land, the Whitest People.' So what was he doing up there with marijuana on him? I'm not saying he didn't do drugs. I'm saying, 'What would he be doing *there* doing drugs?'

"It had to be a setup, because he didn't do any time for it. You have to remember at that time in Texas, the average time served—not sentenced, but served—for first-time possession was nine years in Huntsville. At approximately that same time, they sentenced a guy in Houston to 30 years for the possession of one joint. Duane got probation. So obviously, this wasn't an accidental deal when they got him. Someone wanted to give him a warning shot across his bow."

Duane Thomas: "Dan Reeves said, 'Everything turned bad when Duane went to California. He met some wrong people out there.' I told Dan, 'I met some wrong people in Dallas, and would you believe, you're one of them.'"

The bust cost Thomas—and the Cowboys—dearly. Thomas pleaded guilty to drug possession and was given five years probation, and it took him sixteen years to clear his name. All that time Thomas was denied work in many fields because of his conviction. He received a pardon from Governor Mark White, who waited almost four years to sign it, for fear his opponent would crucify him in the next election. After White lost that election, he finally signed it in 1988.

If Thomas was feeling unloved and persecuted by the Cowboys and the state of Texas *before* his arrest, after the incident in Greenville he became even more removed and hostile. When training camp began in the summer of 1972, his teammates saw that his alienation was worsening. His behavior would continue to be more erratic than in the past.

Roger Staubach: "Duane looked the same. You would not believe this guy could have been using drugs the way he looked physically, but *something* was affecting his mind, whether it was drugs or the bitterness he had about his contract. Whatever it was, he could not deal with anything, period.

"In practice one time I threw him a pass, threw it a little behind him, and he barked, 'Throw the ball to me.' He'd make comments like that, but he'd be doing everything he was supposed to be doing, working hard. I was thinking, 'God, I have to make sure to throw the ball just perfect to Duane.' And another time Dan Reeves, who was coaching the backs, asked Duane to switch from halfback to fullback. He knew both positions. Duane was unbelievable at fullback, but he didn't like to play it, and this day Duane said, 'No, I'm going to stay at tailback.'

"I said, 'Hey, Duane, why don't you do what Dan says?'

"He said, 'You shut up. You don't interfere.' I got along with Duane, but that did tick me off when he said that. So it was definitely going downhill. You could feel it. You wanted to stop it, but it was snowballing, and it probably was drugs, because he was someone you could not reason with anymore.

"Because we were the Super Bowl champs, we played in the College All-Star Game. Duane didn't run out onto the field with the team. He was leaning up against the goal posts, just leaning. And then when we came back from the game and resumed practicing at Thousand Oaks, he actually refused to go out to practice. The next thing I knew, the Cowboys shipped him off to San Diego."

The Cowboys traded Thomas to San Diego for two young talents, wide receiver Billy Parks and running back Mike Montgomery.

Roger Staubach: "When we played in San Diego, during the national anthem Duane wouldn't stand. He sat on the Chargers bench, which is a stupid thing to do with all the navy people out there. Then in the pregame warm-up, he just stood there with his hands on his knees. I said to [Chargers quarterback] John Hadl, 'Johnny, are you having a little trouble with Duane?' He said, 'Oh, my God. I don't know what to do.' I said, 'You're just like all of us. We were on eggshells with the guy.' So they just let him do what he wanted to. There he was, in the middle of their warm-ups down by the end zone, standing with his hands on his knees."

Thomas never got into a game with San Diego. In 1973 and 1974 he played for Washington's George Allen, the coach of lost causes, backing up Larry Brown. In 1975 he went to the World Football League, playing in Hawaii. In 1976 he called Landry and asked for another chance. Landry agreed, but by then Thomas had lost his speed and missed much of training camp with a pulled hamstring. In 1976 Thomas' anger was gone, and he worked hard and was as affable as anyone. His teammates rooted hard for him to make it, but the great talent had been spent. At the end of preseason he was cut.

Pete Gent: "I once interviewed Duane when he was with the Redskins, and he was a psychopath. He couldn't even talk. We sat in the hotel room and didn't even turn the lights on, and he said, 'I'm just trying to get through today.'

"Four or five years later, Duane called me several times, wanting to talk *business.* He said he thought he had been wrong and Landry and Schramm had been right, that he had been a bad boy. And it was heartbreaking to see that. When he called me, I didn't know what to say to him. My feeling was, 'I've been running on thin ice since 1969. The two of us don't need to get side by side and both go under.'"

Duane Thomas' legacy is a reflection of how people felt about him when he played with the Cowboys. The executives, Landry, Schramm, and many of his white teammates saw him as trouble. There was no acknowledgment that he had brought the Cowboys two Super Bowl appearances, that he was a key player who had made them a potful of money. Their bottom line, rather, was that Duane had been disruptive, had brought chaos to their order, and so they were glad he was gone.

Most of his black teammates saw Thomas as a hero, a man who had refused to accept shabby treatment and who had fought back and lost. To them, Duane Thomas was a martyr to their cause, much like the Reverend Martin Luther King Jr. In 1981 Cowboys defensive back Everson Walls told Thomas, "You have paved the way for a lot of us."

Like Don Meredith, Duane Thomas was not an easy man to locate. I had heard he was living in Dallas, or California, or Hawaii, and even his brother Franklin, the contact for NFL Films, said he didn't have Duane's phone number. But in the summer of 1996 Duane called Pete Gent, who happened to mention the call, and Gent was gracious enough to give me the number of Thomas' Del Mar, California, home. In a lengthy conversation, Thomas proved the thoughtful, idealistic soul the men close to him had said he was. Still stung by all that had happened to him many years earlier, Thomas said he continues to work toward forgiveness and understanding.

Duane Thomas: "I often wonder whether I would have risen to the heights I reached had Dallas not been the way they were. What I do know about me is that I am self-motivated. And I also know I could have done more. It's not wishful thinking or regret in any sense of the word; it's just an attitude that I have as to who I am.

"After that situation in Dallas, everything was ruined for me. I couldn't get a black taxi in South Dallas. I went out and started meeting people who I knew in Dallas. I knew initially when I'd meet people, they'd be in awe, and once I sat down and started talking to them one-on-one, they'd be saying, 'Duane doesn't match the image of him that was portrayed in the media.'

"After a while I became involved with the Northwest Mutual Life Insurance Company. The company had great self-development programs, which I pursued, and I also pursued courses and subject matter that interested me when I was in college but couldn't [get into] because of sports.

"I'm done with insurance, and today I work in the field of import/export, which enables me to travel all over Europe and to Africa. I met my wife in Los Angeles in '87, and she has been one of the best things to ever happen to me.

"When I left I told them they couldn't win the Super Bowl without me, and that infuriated them. Who does he think he is? But I was right, and they didn't like that either. They didn't like a lot of what I had to say."

Chapter 46

CRAIG FILLS IN

Before the 1972 season, Craig Morton asked Tom Landry for the opportunity to win back his starting quarterback job. But Landry had made up his mind that Roger Staubach would be his man, and rumors that Morton would either ask for a trade or retire floated around. He did neither, waiting patiently for his chance. During the winter Morton had disavowed his fast-track life and joined the oxymoronic Lovers Lane Episcopal Church in Dallas. Observers wondered how long Morton, even having been born again, would be willing to sit on the bench.

The question became moot when in the third exhibition game against the Los Angeles Rams, Staubach suffered the worst injury of his career, a badly separated shoulder delivered by middle linebacker Marlin McKeever.

Roger Staubach: "I separated my shoulder in an exhibition game against the Rams, and that whole season was screwed up. The injury was my fault. I was running down near the goal line, and typical, I tried to get a few yards more. I turned to cut back inside just as McKeever was coming at me, and I hit him full force with my right shoulder. Back then I had these little quarterback shoulder pads, and my shoulder was separated severely. I knew I was in bad shape.

"As I lay on the ground I was thinking, 'I wish I could get up for one more play and drop back in the pocket and get hurt in the pocket.' Because I knew everybody was going to criticize me for getting hurt running, which happened. And that was really the only injury I ever had running. After that, I ran just as much. So I wasn't really injury prone, except for the concussions, which later became a problem. But that separated shoulder was the only serious injury I had with the Cowboys.

"McKeever didn't do anything wrong. In fact, he sent me flowers in the hospital. He was getting sentimental in his old age."

The 1972 season had yet to begin, and the Cowboys were facing a long campaign without their two top stars, Duane Thomas for good and Roger Staubach for eight to twelve weeks. It was during this season that the incredible Cowboys depth made itself felt, as the team, haunted by the ghost of Duane Thomas, got to within one game of their third straight Super Bowl.

Craig Morton, who had been a good soldier in 1971 as he sat on the bench behind Staubach, got the job back. Said Landry, "Craig Morton is a great quarterback. That's what I tried to tell everybody last year even after he lost his job to Roger. Now that he has the chance to prove what I've been saying, I don't think there's any question how he'll do."

Calvin Hill, who had spent two years of frustration nursing injuries and playing behind Thomas, returned as a starter and became the first Cowboy to gain more than 1,000 yards.

Roger Staubach: "Craig took over and played very well. Craig was a heck of a quarterback. And Calvin was a heck of a player, too. Calvin had some injuries, but boy, he was a good runner, even though Calvin really took a backseat to Duane for a couple of years. Calvin played very well when he played."

Other new players provided excellent talent and also a diversity in personalities. With President Richard Nixon still in office and the youth culture still squarely against him, the arguments between the liberal players and the conservatives became heated. In June 1972 E. Howard Hunt, Gordon Liddy, and three others were arrested for breaking into the Watergate Hotel, and as the scandal widened, players like talented receiver Billy Parks and Calvin Hill, who were fiercely antiwar, spoke out often and loudly against the Nixon regime. Jean Fugett, a 20-year-old receiver drafted out of little Amherst College, also spoke out against the war, racism, and Richard Nixon. All were sorely disappointed when Nixon defeated Democratic candidate Senator George McGovern in a landslide. Roger Staubach had been to Vietnam, and he continued to stoutly defend America's right to be there, but what surprised some teammates was his siding with the blacks on the racial issue. His black teammates saw that Staubach wasn't on the sideline when it came to civil rights. Through the years he actually spoke up and supported them, earning him the eternal gratitude of many of his teammates.

Roger Staubach: "I would be in a room with Cornell Green and Mel Renfro, and we'd be talking, and they were fantastic to be able to keep the bitterness down. They were competitors, and they were treated poorly. Even today, we have a form of racism that is just as serious as in the past, because people's expectations are greater than they've been before, and deservingly so. Back in those days it was more prevalent and more obvious.

"It was over Vietnam that I had most of the arguments. We had a few fellas who were against Vietnam. Billy Parks was really antiwar. Parks loved to get into political arguments, loved to bait me. He and I would be in the locker room, and we'd have knock-down-drag-outs, but they were healthy. We got along very well.

"I remember in '72 Mel Laird, the secretary of defense, came to a game. The Cowboys were honoring him, and Billy almost decided not to play. We were in the tunnel going out to the field, and he just went ballistic. He said, 'I can't believe this. I'm not going to . . .' He said he would not play. And he was serious. He was really rabid. Billy beat to his own drummer. But he did play."

One of the players defending Nixon, the war, and the old South was Lee Roy Jordan. He recalled the ideological battles.

Lee Roy Jordan: "We had some players on the team who didn't agree with me, and I can name Calvin Hill, Pat Toomay, Billy Parks, and Jean Fugett who I would think would be very ultra, ultra liberal types of people.

"Pat was a very free-thinking, writer type of guy who—I don't know what to say about him. He was a good pass rusher on third down. Let me say that about him. That's what I say about Pat. He was definitely a character. He was long-haired, hippie-looking, and Pat didn't have a real work ethic. He thought this deal ought to be done without any work being put into it. Pat didn't like that hittin' too much. He was great on the outside pass rush because you didn't get hit much out there. So he didn't play the run a lot for us, but Pat . . . shoot, I admire Pat and think a lot of him, but we sure had some differences of opinion on work and football and politics and a lot of other things.

"Jean Fugett was a bright, smart guy, as he went on to be the president of the Beatrice Foods Company, had a great career there. After his friend died, he became president of it. Beatrice Foods is one of the largest companies in the country. It's some story about Jean and what he's done and where he is right now.

"Jean was outspoken about racial equality, and in certain areas, being from the South, I was appalled at some of the problems we had early on, with the inability to stay in certain hotels and eat in certain restaurants in some of the cities where we went early in our career, that was . . . I think that was a terrible thing. But that's the way the country was at that time."

Though ideologically split in 1972, on the field the Cowboys showed a strong united front immediately, defeating Philadelphia with a touchdown run by Calvin Hill and a passing offense featuring passes from Craig Morton to Bob Hayes, Lance Alworth, and Ron Sellers, who had come from New England for a draft choice. Alworth, who had starred for San Diego for a decade, came to the Cowboys with a career record of 83 touchdown catches, second only to the legendary Don Hutson, who topped the list with 99. Against the Eagles, Alworth caught a touchdown and won the next game against the New York Giants with a 13-yard touchdown reception. Green Bay won the next game on a field goal, but the Cowboys came back to Texas Stadium to defeat a tough Pittsburgh Steelers team, 17–13. The defense didn't give up a single touchdown, though Mel Blount scored on a fumble return, one of five Cowboys turnovers. Dallas won on a 55-yard halfback pass from Hill to Sellers.

The Cowboys fans gave Morton a terrible booing during each home game. By the end of the season, the booing was becoming a crescendo. Said Morton sadly, "I don't understand it, and really I don't know what to say about it. I'm not going to let it get me down. I'm not going to let it have a detrimental effect. Hell, I think I'm a bigger man than that. But certainly I hear it . . . a deaf man could hear those people."

Craig had his best games on the road. In the fourth game, in Baltimore, he was superb, completing 21 of 30 passes for 279 yards and two touchdowns in a 21–0 win. The Cowboys defense put on a clinic, as Jethro Pugh time and again harassed Colts quarterback Johnny Unitas, sacking him four times.

Lee Roy Jordan: "We were not great early in the year, but after the fifth or sixth game, the defense came on and really was consistent. We got a tremendous streak going in the latter part of the year. At that time we played the run extremely well. I don't think anyone played the run as well as we did. We forced people into passing situations. I can remember in one game we shut out the Colts, sacking John Unitas four times. John was a great passer and even at this point in his career was still very competitive. John Mackey and Willie Richardson and other targets of John's were outstanding receivers, and we respected them but we also felt like we could pass rush their football team, that we could beat their offensive line with Jethro and Lilly and George Andrie and Larry Cole at left end. We felt like we could pass rush them most of the time and put a lot of pressure on John."

The rest of the season went without a hitch, as Morton did his job beautifully, executing Landry's game plans, directing Hill and Garrison in a punishing rushing attack, and passing to his receivers, Hayes, Alworth, and Sellers, for 15 touchdowns. He finished seventh in the league in passing but would have been third had it not been for 21 interceptions.

Under his leadership, the Cowboys finished the regular season 10–4, second in the division behind their archrivals, the 11–3 Washington Redskins. Calvin Hill finished the season with 1,036 yards, a Cowboys record. In just four years, Hill had rushed for 3,023 yards, third-best in Cowboys history. But 1972 was a tough year for Bob Hayes, who did not catch a touchdown pass all season long.

Morton came down with pneumonia the week before the final game with the New York Giants, a game in which the Cowboys looked so listless in a 23–3 loss that Landry played a rehabilitated Roger Staubach in the final quarter. For the opening playoff game against the San Francisco 49ers, who'd given the Cowboys their worst regular-season beating, 31–10, once again the controversy blazed: who should start, Morton, who had led the team all year, or Staubach?

Landry, as expected, went with Morton. He had been the general all season long. It certainly wasn't Morton's fault that Vic Washington ran back the opening kickoff 97 yards, but then on the next series Morton fumbled, lost the ball on the 15, and the 49ers scored again. With just 17 seconds gone, the Cowboys trailed 14–0. Their season appeared to be over. A Morton interception led to a third score, and then Hill fumbled a handoff on the 1 to give San Francisco another easy score.

The Cowboys were trailing 28–3 when Morton threw a touchdown to Lance Alworth. Another Cowboys field goal left the Cowboys trailing 28–13 at the end of the third quarter. Morton launched a 50-yarder into the end zone to Bob Hayes, but Hayes could not hold onto the ball and it fell away.

A desperate Tom Landry decided to try Roger Staubach and see what he could do.

Roger Staubach: "We had had a good season, but there was something not right. We weren't in synch all the time. And so we went out and played San Francisco, and they ran a kickoff back for a touchdown, and it just looked like it was their day. It was one of those weird deals in the fourth quarter—I don't think anyone really believed we had a chance at all. By the middle of the fourth quarter many of the 49ers fans were gone. Half the stadium was empty, and their players, Dave Wilcox, all those guys, were saying to us, 'Now you guys know what it's like to lose in the playoffs.'

"And then we had a long drive. Calvin Hill had some really good runs, and we had some passes, and we kicked a field goal to make it 28–16 with eight minutes left. We could win the game with two scores. But it was still a long-shot deal.

"And then we got the ball back, and they got a little conservative. Billy Parks made some great catches, and then he caught a post for a touchdown with a minute and a half left. When Billy scored, everyone was thinking, 'There's hope.'

"The score was 28–23, 49ers. So now we had to get the onside kick. The onside kick is still one of those long shots. But Toni Fritsch kicked it with his other foot, and their guy was surprised, and the ball hit him in the chest, and Mel Renfro recovered it. Had we not gotten it, we would not have won.

"We started close to midfield. Parks was on a roll, so I was going to try to get the ball to Billy. The first play, I dropped back and ran for 20 yards. And then the next one I was figuring we could beat them on a corner, so we ran a corner, and sure enough Billy caught it going out of bounds around the 10 or 12.

"Landry then sent in an 83 pass, a sideline, and as I was breaking the huddle, Ron Sellers said to me, 'I can get open.' I said, 'Hey, Ron, if you get open, I'm going to look for you.' Ron was not the main receiver on the play. I was going to try to throw a sideline to Parks.

"I broke the huddle, and as soon as I took the snap, I saw man-to-man coverage, so I went to Sellers, and he caught the ball in the end zone. Boom, a shock! We won the game 30–28 with only 58 seconds on the clock. I still see the film of Larry Cole rolling on the ground. And Wilcox threw his helmet 50 feet in the air.

"It was one of those comebacks where you almost don't deserve it. It was one you figure was not going to happen. It just didn't seem like it should have happened. But it all went right. As for me, I was feeling healthy again. When I got into the game, I was thinking, 'This is my only chance to look good,' because I wanted to come back the next year and be the starting quarterback. I didn't know we'd score 17 points to win the game. So it all just turned out well. And it killed the 49ers. I don't think they recovered from it. Dick Nolan told me, 'That just killed us.' That was the third year in a row we beat the 49ers in the playoffs."

Most of the players wanted Morton to start against Washington in the game for the NFC Championship. In the two regular-season games against the Redskins, Morton had posted 54 points. Craig, moreover, had always had success against the Redskins. And finally, the offense was used to playing with Craig. They had been together all season long.

But Landry had been moved by Staubach's performance against the 49ers. He was hoping Staubach would once again show the form that had allowed the Cowboys to catch lightning in a bottle.

Roger Staubach: "The Redskins just killed us. We lost 26–3. And after the game Diron Talbert made a statement that he was glad that I started the game, which really . . . I *know* he didn't wish I started the game. But Talbert was baiting me, and that became something that really goaded me the rest of my playing career. You know, we never lost another [key] game to the Redskins for the next seven years.

"So Talbert really got to me. First of all, I was feeling bad enough that we lost. I know when I have a bad game, and I *didn't* have a bad game that day. We just didn't do anything. We got behind so quick, and they completed these big passes. Billy Kilmer threw two long touchdowns to Charley Taylor.

"We kept trying to run the ball. And then we couldn't run. And as a quarterback I didn't throw. I don't think we threw enough. And we had this new formation of receivers, and we had a lot of confusion there. Landry put in a new system for that game, four wide receivers, and I don't think Billy Parks paid a whole lot of attention to what he was supposed to do that game. For some reason he didn't have the same enthusiasm for that game that he did in San Francisco the week before.

"When Billy was out there, he played hard, but football wasn't his deal. He could take it or leave it, and I think it really hurt us in that playoff game against the Redskins in '72. He was a player, but because of his not making football a priority, they traded him.

"It was just the Redskins' day. It was their time. But it was close at halftime. Toni Fritsch missed a real easy field goal right before the half. So it was a tough loss."

Chapter 47

A Study in Black and White

At the start of the 1973 season, there was a great deal of uncertainty. Some of it had to do with changes in the coaching staff. Four assistants—Sid Gillman, Ray Renfro, Bobby Franklin, and a bitter Dan Reeves—left for other jobs. Reeves was angry with the way Landry had "coddled" Duane Thomas in 1971, then became even angrier when Landry let Sid Gillman run the offense and not him. Reeves left football entirely for a year and went into real estate. In early July offensive coach Ermal Allen suffered a heart attack and had to be replaced.

Adding to the turnover, Chuck Howley again retired, this time for good; George Andrie retired because of back spasms; the Cowboys forced Herb Adderley to retire; and Lance Alworth, unhappy with an uninspired passing game and stuck with having to block for the Cowboys backs for two years, also quit. Tex Schramm shrugged, saying rookie Billy Joe Dupree would take his place. Moreover, Schramm traded Ron Sellers to the Miami Dolphins for the fleet Otto Stowe, who had become dissatisfied sitting on the bench behind Paul Warfield. The last of the sixties pass-catching corps, Bob Hayes, would soon find the Cowboys trying to force him out, too, as Landry attempted to replace him with Golden Richards, the speedy rookie with the great name from the University of Hawaii.

For the players who remained there was a lot of turmoil over money. Players were so frustrated with Schramm's stubborn stinginess that they went to the press with their unhappiness. Craig Morton, Mel Renfro, Bob Lilly, and Lee Roy Jordan led the chorus. Morton was just as bitter, moreover, about not starting the NFC Championship game against the Redskins. "It wasn't explained, and I don't think it ever can be," he said. His contract had a slew of incentive clauses in it, and Morton knew if he had to sit behind Staubach, he would be penalized both ways, and he wanted his contract reworked. Schramm said no. Morton walked out of camp in mid-July. "If I'm going to be used like a yo-yo," he said, "I should be financially rewarded for it."

When Morton was absent a week, Staubach was assured he would be the starter in 1973. When Morton finally returned, little was written or said about him.

Center Dave Manders wanted a no-trade clause in his contract, and when Schramm said no, Manders said he wanted $5,000 instead. Again Schramm refused.

"I'll take $2,500."

Schramm said no.

"I'll give it to charity."

"No."

So Manders retired in disgust. Schramm was convinced Manders would come back by the end of training camp, but this time Tex was wrong. Manders sat out as the Cowboys time and again during the exhibition season watched his replacements bungle too many long snaps for punts and extra-point and field-goal attempts. First, rookie Jim Arneson rolled a snap past backup quarterback Jack Concannon on an extra point in a one-point loss to the Oakland Raiders. Then, against the Miami Dolphins, Arneson cost the Cowboys three points, as one bad snap ruined an extra point and another rolled through the end zone for a safety.

Schramm decided he needed Dave Manders, and he gave the veteran center a token raise to come back. His return was made public at a surprise birthday party for Clint Murchison. A friend of Murchison's asked Manders to dress up in a tux and hide inside a big birthday cake. Out popped Manders. After Manders returned, the long-snap problem ended.

The one and only player ever to win big against Tex Schramm was Lee Roy Jordan. As was his practice, in 1973 Tex stalled Jordan about his contract until it was time for training camp, then held to his $50,000 offer. Jordan wanted $100,000, which was the going price, what other teams were paying for middle linebackers not even as good as Jordan. Dick Butkus was making close to $150,000 with the Bears.

Jordan waited until Schramm and Landry had cut the last backup linebacker, then he held a press conference and said he would hold out until he got his money. Jordan's tactic left the Cowboys with only Dave Edwards, D. D. Lewis, and a rookie linebacker from Rice University, Rodrigo Barnes. Landry, who hated to start rookies, was horrified. Schramm, who hated to be outsmarted, had no choice but to give Jordan much of what he was asking. And because Jordan had outwitted him, Schramm kept Jordan from being named to the Cowboys' hallowed Ring of Honor. Only after Schramm was dismissed in 1988 did Jordan get his deserved honor a year later.

Lee Roy Jordan: "I kind of surveyed the linebackers around the league, and the top ones were making $150,000, and I was making $40,000. And I told him what I was expecting to make, and it wasn't what Butkus or Ray Nitschke were making—it was well below them—but it kind of fit in with some of the players I could fit in with.

"And he was absolutely horrified that I thought I was worth that. He started by saying, 'You're getting up in age. I don't know how much longer you're going to be able to play.' And that's the way he negotiated. It was disappointing. We didn't have agents back then, and we should have, no matter how much we were making.

"And so we negotiated a couple more times, and all of a sudden it was June, and I said, 'Damn, Tex. Let's get this thing done.' He said, 'Well, Lee Roy, we're a long ways apart.' I hadn't come down much, and he hadn't come up *any*. So finally in my last meeting with him, I said, 'Well, Tex, I don't think we're going to be able to do anything. I'll just have to play out my option.' He kind of gave me the backhand. He said, 'Go ahead and play out your option, son. It doesn't matter to me.'

"And so I went to training camp, had the best training camp I ever had. I was smoking everyone. And not another word was said about the contract. We got down to it, and they made the last cut of the year before the regular season started, cut the last backup middle linebacker. So the next day I just don't show up for practice. Jerry Tubbs called and wanted to know what was wrong. I said, 'Jerry, I'm not going to be there until I get a contract. I don't have a contract. I'm not playing out my option. And I'm not going to play somewhere else next year. I'm going to finish out my career in Dallas.'

"Then coach Landry and Tex called me. Finally, we got together in the next day or so, because the starting right linebacker was D. D. Lewis, and he was going to have to replace me at middle linebacker, and his backup was going to have to replace him at right linebacker.

"And so it worked out that I got some increase. I got right at $100,000, but a lot of it had to be in bonus clauses, 'cause Tex couldn't let me make any more than $75,000 salary. He said, 'Roger isn't making much more than that, and coach Landry isn't making that much, so . . .' I said, 'If you want to give me some of coach Landry's stock . . .' And that stopped that talk in a hurry.

"And Tex didn't like me ever again after that. I don't know whether he even respected me. It really doesn't matter. I've got my opinion of him, and he has his opinion of me. I just didn't think he was fair to people, and you can do what's fair. I didn't think we were treated that way."

Two players—Tody Smith and Billy Parks—who were unhappy with the way they were being treated by the Cowboys, also asked to be traded. Both players were members of the "new breed." They resented Landry's strict regimen and wanted to be respected as people, not treated like cattle by the coaching staff. But in 1971 Landry didn't yet understand or hadn't come to grips with the changing society, and his response to both players was the same: if you're not happy, we'll be happy to get rid of you. It didn't matter that both had great talent. It didn't matter that they both needed pats on the back, needed Landry to be a father figure. If they couldn't fit into Landry's system, they would be jettisoned.

You couldn't be sensitive and play for Landry. Tody Smith, the team's number one draft choice in 1971, had suffered all his life from being the brother of All-Pro defensive end Bubba Smith. He had gone to Michigan State to follow in his big brother's footsteps, but after an injury and an unsympathetic coaching staff, he transferred to the University of Southern California. He injured his knee in a basketball game just prior to the Cowboys training camp in 1972, underwent surgery, and once in camp was ordered to start practicing before he felt his knee was ready. Lacking confidence and feeling depressed, Smith walked out of camp. When he returned a couple of days later, he revealed that what was bothering him more than his knee was his feeling of being unwanted by the Cowboys. He told reporters, "I feel like a stranger here. I don't feel I'm needed."

Smith was too sensitive for pro football. He refused to take part in rookie hazing rituals, alienating him further from the veterans who cared about that sort of thing.

He told reporters, "There's no way I'm leaving again." Then he added a caveat: "But if my mental health becomes a factor, that's different."

Smith replaced an injured Larry Cole at the start of the 1972 season. In one interview Landry complimented Smith, saying he was as quick as Bob Lilly. Then Smith contracted mononucleosis late in the season. Before a game with Philadelphia he couldn't get out of bed he was so debilitated, but he played. At the same time the Cowboys doctors were telling Smith it was all in his head. Said Smith, "Before the Thanksgiving game my parents begged me not to play, but I did. I finally went to an outside doctor, and he said my spleen was enlarged, that there was a possibility of killing myself if I played again like that. Yet they [the coaches] said I had a bad attitude."

After the season Smith spent five weeks in three hospitals, including the Mayo Clinic. In the spring of 1973 an angry Smith demanded to be traded, saying he didn't want to play for a team as callous as the Cowboys.

Even before he came to Dallas, wide receiver Billy Parks had a history of wrestling with his conscience over whether even to play football. As a rookie with San Diego in 1970, he quit the Chargers early in the campaign and spent the rest of the season working in a bookstore. He returned in 1971 and led the AFC in receiving before suffering a broken arm. He walked out again in 1972, and then after Chargers head coach Sid Gillman joined Landry in Dallas as offensive coordinator, Gillman convinced the Cowboys to trade for him. Gillman loved Parks' talent. "He has as fine a pair of hands as I've seen since I've been in football," said Gillman.

But Parks was a sensitive West Coast intellectual who didn't even like to *talk* about football. He once said, "How droll to talk about post patterns. There are kids out on the playground running them just as well. How do you deal with that?" Parks felt that the nation's emphasis on football was untoward. He saw postgame interviews as ridiculous. "It was like somehow the world had changed," he said, "that some significant event had happened. It was absurd there was so much attention."

With the Cowboys in 1972 Parks played erratically. That year he caught only 12 passes in 14 games. But more than anything else, Parks was too *different* to be acceptable. After the miraculous playoff win over San Francisco, Parks said he could not answer questions because, "I've been advised by the trainers not to speak." After Parks played without spirit in the subsequent playoff loss to Washington, some of the coaches expressed anger at his attitude. Parks told reporters, "We should be able to accept victory and defeat on the same level. They're interchangeable." He added, "To me, losing isn't like dying. If everyone does his best, how can you be sad?"

If the white players coming out of college in the midseventies were looking for meaning in their lives, the black players were looking for justice. *Soul on Ice,* by Stokely Carmichael, and the writings of Malcolm X preached to young blacks that they were entitled to being treated like men, that nothing short of that should be acceptable. While Martin Luther King Jr. had counseled patience, the new generation of black leaders was announcing that they wanted their rights, and they wanted them *now*. And as a result, an entire generation of intelligent, outspoken black men arose to claim their rights under the Constitution and the Bill of Rights. And they wanted them *now*. But the society was not about to give them those rights *now*, and as a result, many of those young black men suffered because of their impatience and the frustration of discovering that getting society to change was a lot harder than they thought.

In 1973 the Cowboys drafted in the seventh round one such young black man, a linebacker from Rice University by the name of Rodrigo Barnes. At Rice, Barnes had starred in football. He had also been one of the organizers of the Black Student Union. When the school dragged its feet on the issue of hiring black teachers and a black coach, Barnes threatened that unless Rice acted on their request, he and the other black players would boycott the rest of the football games. Barnes succeeded, but he was reviled for it. Word spread among pro scouts that he was "trouble." Barnes saw his effort on behalf of black students as a benefit to the college. He saw the diversity as something positive. But the college officials saw Rodrigo Barnes the way white America saw Malcolm X: he was big and black and wasn't afraid of them. They, however, were certainly afraid of him. Had Barnes not been such a militant, he would have been drafted much higher than seventh.

When Barnes came to the Cowboys, he was different from most of the rookies. He wasn't afraid of the vets, wasn't afraid of the coach, wasn't afraid of losing his job. The truth was, he wasn't afraid of anything. When he came to camp Landry wanted him to play outside linebacker, but Barnes did not want to replace Chuck Howley, whom he revered. No, Barnes felt he was a better player than middle linebacker Lee Roy Jordan, who at age 32 was on the downside of his career. Barnes told the press that the job he intended to take was Jordan's.

When Landry wouldn't hand him the job, even after he'd proved his excellence during exhibition games while Jordan was sitting out during his contract battle with Schramm, Barnes fumed. Warning lights began flashing in Barnes' brain, the same way Duane Thomas had seen warning lights when he led the Cowboys to a Super Bowl and then was forced to play the next year at $22,000. So Rodrigo Barnes believed that he was a better player than Jordan but found himself sitting on the Cowboys bench because of what he perceived to be Landry's racism. Barnes knew his Cowboys history. He knew that Landry had had only white players at linebacker since 1960. He knew that the Cowboys had had only two middle linebackers since 1960, Jerry Tubbs and Lee Roy Jordan. He knew that the middle linebacker was one of the captains of the defense. And Barnes became convinced that Landry wouldn't let him play middle linebacker for only one reason: he was black.

Lee Roy Jordan was still a fine performer, and Barnes could not possibly learn the Flex overnight, but that did not keep Barnes from becoming resentful, angry, and then bitter toward Landry and the Cowboys.

Rodrigo Barnes: "I didn't want to go to Dallas. I didn't think they were going to let me play. I didn't think they respected my game. I didn't think they wanted what I had to bring to the table, because of my color, not because of my game. And I was correct.

"Tom Landry wanted somebody who could play *like* me. He probably prayed for a guy who could play with the ability I had. Because I could run a 4.5 40. I would win the 220. I was quick, agile. I could do it all. I could play all the linebackers' positions. I could play strong safety. But Landry wanted a white boy who could do that, not a black boy—and not a black *man* who was assertive. And so they had a big choice to make, because if you were a linebacker on the Dallas Cowboys, you were a leader, and did they want to give that leadership role to me? And the answer was no.

"The linebackers at the time were white boys: Lee Roy Jordan was in the middle, and Dave Edwards and Chuck Howley—who was the best linebacker I had seen at the Cowboys—were outside. I played middle linebacker, and I was going to be *the* star. And they could see it. When I played against the Miami Dolphins I stopped Larry Csonka on the goal line three times in a row. No linebacker did that back then. I played against Kansas City and graded out a 10-plus. No linebacker ever graded out 10-plus on the Cowboys before then. And so I did some things there to let them know I had the game, but Tom Landry did not want me to be the star. And it was because he knew he didn't have control over me. They weren't going to have control, because I got paid to play football. I didn't get paid to be a boy. And I wouldn't be nobody's boy, because they can keep that other money. I was just there to play football. And I'm not selling myself for no game. That's stupid. The game is just not that big to me. It was something I can do, but it's not *me*.

"Landry *did not* want me to make the team. During the exhibition season the Cowboys would have me practice at outside linebacker, and in the game they played me in the middle. If they practiced me in the middle, in the game they'd put me on the strong side. So that was setting me up to make a mistake. You got cut based on how you played in those games. But I survived because I was a ballhawk and I understood football.

"Lee Roy and I didn't have any problems. I respected Lee Roy. I wanted his job, and I didn't have a lot of patience to wait on it, but I respected him.

"I remember we were getting ready to play Kansas City. I was in the shower after we got through practicing. It was our last defensive practice that week, and the fullback, Walt Garrison, he was in the shower with me and Lee Roy, and Walt said, 'Hey, Lee Roy, man, I sure hate you not playing this week. We're going to get our butts kicked on Sunday. They're going to run right up the middle. So and so, so and so, so and so . . .' I was standing right there taking a shower. Walt knew I was starting, so he was just dissing me right in front of Lee Roy. He didn't care. He wasn't saying to me, 'Have a good game. You can do it.' It was like in your face.

"It may have been them trying to psych me up. I didn't know. And it *did* psych me up. I had no fear. I knew I could handle the situation. And after I had such a great game, it shocked them. Shocked them. They never were the same, because they knew I was ready. You see? Lee Roy couldn't do anything I couldn't do. I had more speed, quickness. I hit harder. Everything. His day was just up. But Landry wanted to keep him there.

"I should have had the job—really and truly. Landry tried me and saw I could handle it. When we played against Kansas City, he saw I could do the job. That wasn't the problem. The problem basically was that he did not want the package. The package was the problem."

Two days after the final exhibition game in 1973, one of the Cowboys stars found himself in the headlines after what appeared to be an acid trip that went bad, though this was never confirmed. John Niland had been troubled his whole life. He was orphaned and adopted at a young age by a 50-year-old woman and grew up in Amityville, Long Island, in relative poverty. In 1994 in an article in the *Fort Worth Star-Telegram*, he told journalist Christopher Evans that he had been emotionally and sexually abused as a child.

An only child, he lived in an industrial area near the railroad tracks. He had his first job at age 10 or 11, pumping gas for 50¢ a night and a free pizza pie.

Niland grew up to be a large man, weighing 255 pounds, and he was a talented enough football player to earn a scholarship at the University of Iowa, where he became an All-American.

Niland was drafted in 1966 in the first round by the Cowboys, and during a 10-year career, he was picked for six Pro Bowls. He was artistic, and he was popular. Only Roger Staubach attended more high school awards dinners. He was also quick with a quip. One time he attended a press party at a local spaghetti joint and observed that the "only thing Arkansas produces are hookers and football players."

"Wait a minute," said an indignant man in the audience. "My wife is from Arkansas."

"What position does she play?" Niland asked.

During his career and later in his life he abused alcohol and amphetamines and for a time used LSD, which caused him at times to become involved in violent antisocial behavior.

Mel Renfro: "I liked John—a nice guy. Whenever he was at the practice field or around us, he was as nice as he could be. But then he'd go out and get crazy with drugs. And he'll admit it to this day."

Niland's life has been plagued with incidents, from fights in bars to a 1988 prison term after he was convicted of trying to obtain a loan by fraudulent means. Niland had signed a document for a friend, a too-common occurrence for naive ex-athletes who allow friends to get them into trouble.

Niland's problems stemmed in part from a failing marriage. In 1967 he married Iree Van Cleve, a Braniff flight attendant. She was preparing to fly Military Aircraft Command planes carrying Vietnam troops to Singapore and the Philippines when they up and eloped.

Unfortunately for Iree, she discovered that Niland had an insatiable appetite for female flesh, alcohol, and drugs. She soon was on to him, and part of their relationship involved her surveillance of him in an attempt to keep him out of the arms of other women. Niland freely admits the infidelity of his former life: "I was coming out of a bar on Lemmon Avenue with this girl, and I saw my wife sitting over there in a car," said Niland. "So what did I do? I brought this girl out, we get in my car, we go 100 miles an hour down Lemmon Avenue, I lose Iree, then finally come home later and deny the whole thing."

For six years, their relationship continued in this vein until Iree finally had enough. They separated in 1973, and she moved to Aspen, Colorado.

She was back in Dallas on the night of September 10, 1973, when she and Niland were invited to the home of a mutual friend to watch the television show *In Concert*. Niland took acid, and he was sitting around with Iree and his friends when, Niland said, he was overcome by an "intense feeling." "I felt as if I couldn't breathe, as if I was being gassed or something. I had to get out of that house," Niland explained to Frank Taggart of *The Dallas Times Herald*.

Without saying a word, Niland got out of his chair and walked out the door and away from the house. "But when I got out of the house, I still had that feeling, and I started to run." Niland said he started running down the middle of the street as fast as he could. He was running so fast, he said, he lost his shoes along the way. "I actually felt like I was going to die."

Meanwhile, back at the house, his wife and friends at first didn't think anything of Niland going outside. They thought he had forgotten something in his car and had gone to get it. It was only when he didn't come back that they became concerned.

After running about a mile from the house, Niland, exhausted and out of breath, slowed down and then stopped. "I said, 'God, if you want me, if I'm going to die, take me.'"

Niland began to hallucinate. All of a sudden, Niland said, he began to see visions. "I saw Landry, Jim Myers, my offensive line coach, Paul Anderson [a former world champion weightlifter turned evangelist], and Pat Boone, among others. I still don't understand why I had visions of these people. In fact, I don't even like Pat Boone as a singer," he said. "Looking back on it, most of the men I saw in the visions were Christians. And I understand that Pat Boone went through a similar experience as I did a long time ago. So maybe that's why I saw him," said Niland.

Continuing the story, Niland said he again had the urge to run, only this time he felt totally different: "It was as if I had died and had suddenly been reborn. I felt elated. As I picked up momentum, I started to speak in tongues. I couldn't control my lips. They kept saying things as if I had no control over them. It was as if God was speaking through my mouth for me."

He said one of the first things he began to mumble were the words *player/coach*. He was asking himself whether he should stay in football, and those were the words that came in reply.

Niland said in the article that he still didn't know what it all meant.

Then, he said, he started to say, "'Find Iree. Find Iree.' Again, I don't know why I was saying it. But it was as if God was telling me to find my wife and reunite with her.

"All this time I was running and saying, 'Find Iree.' But suddenly I stopped in front of a house. And I asked myself, 'Is Iree here?' not really thinking she was back at my friends' house. My mouth kept saying, 'Find Iree. Find Iree.'"

He knocked on the door of the home of a rabbi, who asked Niland if he could help him. Niland asked if he knew where his wife was. Niland said the rabbi directed him to a house across the street. He went there while the rabbi called for an ambulance to pick up an incoherent behemoth flipped out on a bad drug trip and take him to a hospital.

At about 2:20 A.M. officers were called to a home near Hillcrest and Royal Lane by a retired business executive. He said Niland was yelling and banging on his door, thinking this was where he would find his wife. The man didn't know Niland and wouldn't let him in. He called the police.

The police came to take Niland home. When the officers arrived, he was not coherent. They said he was not drunk. (They didn't say he was on acid.) Niland said he would go by himself, but the police were concerned for his safety and the safety of everyone else, and they told him they wanted to take him to see a doctor. Niland then went totally bonkers, and it took seven men to subdue him and force him into the patrol car. He was taken to Parkland Hospital, where he was admitted. The Cowboys doctor was summoned to attend to him.

After the effects of the drugs wore off, he was back to normal, and the very next day Niland returned to the team. John Niland may have been crazy, but not crazy enough to keep him from playing in the season opener.

Several days later Niland explained that he had had a religious experience: "The best way to sum it up is to say that I gave my life to Christ. I became a Christian. Now I have to live the life I foresee coming. I have to fulfill a promise made to God."

Niland told the press that the first thing he asked his wife when he saw her was, "Are you ready to accept Jesus Christ?" She said she was. Niland said they were back together and had found a new meaning to their relationship.

Said Niland, "Coach Landry and I sat down and talked about my experience the Thursday after it happened. He seemed real happy about it. But more important, for the first time I understand what coach Landry has been talking about all these years. I found out what it means to be a Christian."

Niland even got backing for his born-again saga from the local rabbi at the home he first visited the night of the incident. Frank Taggart of the *Times Herald* interviewed the rabbi, Max Zucker, who said he believed Niland's religious experience to be "genuine." "There are just too many coincidences that cannot be explained in any other way," said the rabbi. "For instance, of all the homes that Niland could have visited on that night, he went to a rabbi's home. Why did he choose to go to a rabbi's home? I don't know."

Zucker said he had never met Niland and that there was no way Niland could have known he was a rabbi. However, said Zucker, he was not surprised when Niland showed up at his door that night. "I've had a number of people, not necessarily Jewish, come knocking on my door at all times of the day and night. I have helped quite a few nonreligious people find God in their own way." Zucker said he called for an ambulance because he wasn't sure what kind of help Niland needed. "It was the neighbors across the street who became frightened and called the police."

What was not amusing about the incident to the Cowboys was that Niland was injured during the fracas. He had a badly cut elbow and some possible nerve damage in his right hand. Being handcuffed for a long period didn't help things.

In a subsequent game against Chicago, the elbow was hit and became infected. Niland had to play the season one-armed and one-handed.

Rodrigo Barnes: "You have to understand: John didn't go crazy. John used good sense. He saved himself from going to the penitentiary. He kept himself in the league, kept the paychecks coming, and later, when he got worse, he went to a psychiatrist.

"If a black guy had done what Niland did, there's no doubt he'd have gone to jail for 10 years, but black people have been taught to live in this country differently than white people. You're told, 'You can't act like that. That's for the white man.' The only problem white folks have is when a black guy gets treated as good as a white person.

"The veteran black players told me all the time, 'Boss, I'm scared for you.' I said, 'Scared for me? If you'd taken care of this, I wouldn't have to be dealing with it.' That's why the Cowboys players didn't like me. That's why I didn't get invited to a lot of the parties. I told them, 'Somebody has to do it, because I can't live like you. I can't go to sleep and wake up in fear like that.' That's why a lot of them didn't like me. They thought I was a troublemaker. But my thing was, 'Hey, I'm not going to be scared. I'm not going to be like that.'"

Chapter 48

THE FREE AGENT

While Rodrigo Barnes was fighting for justice, another Cowboys rookie, a little-known free-agent receiver by the name of Drew Pearson, scratched for a spot on the Cowboys roster. Pearson, like Barnes, had been a black rights crusader in college, albeit reluctantly. Pearson had grown up in New Jersey and had experienced no racism until going to college in Oklahoma. At the University of Tulsa he helped lead an insurgency against the school athletic director, who was forcing the coach to play his son at quarterback. The black players felt that Pearson was the better quarterback, but they realized they could not unseat the AD's son unless they took a stand. After the black players threatened to boycott games, Pearson became the starting quarterback and the team went on to win the Missouri Valley Conference.

Pearson was as practical as he was talented. He realized the only way he was going to make it in the pros was to switch to wide receiver, so his junior year he became an end. When no pro teams drafted him, Pearson was free to sign with whomever he wished. Influenced by the Cowboys' avalanche of propaganda touting their prior success with free agents, he signed with Dallas for a bonus of $150. When he came to camp he was listed as the number eight receiver on the depth chart. That Drew Pearson would go on to become an All-Pro and a certain future Hall of Famer seemed inconceivable at the time.

Drew Pearson: "At the end of February the Cowboys invited all the rookies for a minicamp. We came in, had our camp, and then the rookies who were impressive in that minicamp, whether they were drafted or free agents, you got invited to the minicamp with the veterans, which was at the end of the next month. Off-season conditioning wasn't what it is now. Matter of fact, the Cowboys with those minicamps initiated off-season conditioning, now a big part of the process of becoming a professional football player.

"After that rookie minicamp, they invited me back down to the veteran minicamp, and I was shocked, but happy. All of a sudden here I am in the locker room with Roger Staubach, Bob Lilly, and Lee Roy Jordan, Walt Garrison, Bob Hayes, thinking, 'Oh my God, this is great.'

"That was an inspiration to me to really get after it to make this team. I had a pretty good minicamp with the veterans. It was mostly learning and watching and seeing how they did some things I needed to work on, like my strength. When we had the rookie minicamp, the rookie quarterbacks were there, and I was catching everything they threw with no problem.

"And then I went to this veteran minicamp, and you had Roger Staubach, Craig Morton, Jack Concannon. They were throwing the ball, and I was dropping more balls than I ever did in my life. I remember I ran a post pattern, and Roger zipped it in there, and it zipped right through my hands. I just couldn't believe it, because I was always noted for catching. I couldn't believe it, so I knew that I had to go back to Tulsa and get on the weights and strengthen my hands and my upper body so I could hold on to those passes.

"They kept inviting me back with the veterans at the end of these minicamps, and then finally the school year was over at Tulsa. I didn't graduate on time, but at the end of May I decided to pack up everything I owned, took my wife, and we loaded up everything into a Volkswagen Bug and went down to Dallas and moved into an apartment; the Cowboys set it all up. It was right next to the practice field. It was called the Premises. To me it was beautiful, the Taj Mahal. From where I had just moved out of in Tulsa, this was *great*, man. The Cowboys arranged a job for me. I worked at Merchants Van Lines, loading the big 18-wheeler trucks with merchandise. I was making six, seven bucks an hour, which I thought was great. So I was doing that, and I was also working out. The main thing was to be over there at the practice field working out.

"I would work out in the morning, get up early, do distance running, then go to the field, and whoever was there ran routes in the morning, and at 1:00 I was supposed to be at work. I'd work from 1:00 to 7:00 and then leave there and go home and run at night, distance running. This was the month of June, and not many Cowboys were there, because that was their time to take vacations with their families, so when I'd go to the practice field, most of the time there'd be no one there. Then Roger Staubach came, and he would always be there, and we just got to running routes. From the minicamps he knew I was a receiver, and he saw a little promise in me, and I mean, we would run routes all morning long, back and forth. He'd say, 'Drew, are you tired?' My tongue would be hanging out down to my cleats, and I'd say, 'No, sir.' He'd say, 'Do you have any more in you?' Even though I was so tired, I'd say, 'Yes, sir.'"

Until Pearson arrived in Dallas in May to begin working out in preparation for training camp in 1973, no one had worked as hard as Staubach. Day after day it would be the two workaholics, the famous quarterback and the unknown rookie free agent, running pass pattern after pass pattern. Of course, it wasn't enough that Pearson was dedicated. Staubach soon saw that in addition to his great desire, the skinny kid from New Jersey had good speed and great hands as well.

Roger Staubach: "Some of the veteran receivers hadn't come in yet, and I would throw to whoever was out there, and Drew was out there all the time. Also, he was really good. There were other free agents who were OK, but I could really see that Drew was good. And we kind of clicked. I had a lot of confidence in Drew.

"Drew made it because he worked so hard. He came out and worked, and he was good. If he hadn't been good, it wouldn't have mattered how hard he worked, 'cause when he came I didn't know him. All I knew was this guy was out there, and he had a lot of talent. He wasn't the fastest guy in the world, but if you look at film, when he got behind a defender, the guy didn't catch him. Drew was a heck of a football player. He had good instincts, basketball instincts. He knew how to get in position. He'd catch balls. If you threw it to him, you wouldn't get it intercepted. You just felt good about throwing it to him. You knew he was going to be where he was supposed to be and he was going to battle for the ball. Drew had those instincts and intangibles that they didn't recognize in the draft."

Drew Pearson: "When you're a free agent like I was, you go week by week. Actually, first you go day by day, and then you get into the exhibition games, and you try to get in that game to do something on the field to get you another week in camp and get to the next exhibition game in hope you get another game. And I was fortunate in that every time I got a chance to get in a game, I made plays, a pass catch or a block or whatever, a punt return or kickoff return. I was continuing to make plays, and I ended up making the roster."

Chapter 49

ROGER TO DREW

Drew Pearson: "Before I joined the Cowboys in '73, I hated the Cowboys so I didn't follow their history. I was a New York Giants fan, a New York Jets fan. I could tell you all about those teams. But I didn't follow much of the Cowboys history, so I didn't know there had been a feud from the Super Bowl between Roger and Craig, and I didn't know of Landry's indecisiveness as far as making the call who should be the starter and who shouldn't, and I didn't even realize all that was part of what Roger was dealing with and what he was going through.

"When I joined the team in '73 Craig was there as well, and it appeared to me they were both vying for the starting job, but there was no question in my mind who was the better quarterback from what I was seeing. Nothing against Craig Morton, who was a good quarterback, but in my opinion when I got a chance to be close to him in '73, Roger was clearly the better quarterback."

Roger Staubach: "Craig took over and played very well in '72. I got a chance to play again at the end of the year. Craig was a heck of a quarterback, and so we had another quarterback controversy going into training camp in '73. I told myself that if I wasn't the starter in '73, I was going to ask to be traded.

"I had been hoping to play, but with Tom you never knew. I still think he had this . . . that I was not his kind of quarterback. As far as desire and wanting to win I was, but I was a freelance, gambling, change-the-play-and-run guy. Yet we won, so he believed in me, but I think he still felt, deep down, that the reason we won with me in there was that I was executing the system. I felt my leadership aspect was positive, but after that '72 season, I had no idea what he was going to do."

Landry really was in a bind. After the exhibition season, Staubach had the better statistics, but Morton looked in top form. Staubach finally forced the issue. He told Landry, "You need to make a decision and stick by it. If you aren't going to start me, I want to be traded. If I have any choice in the matter, I'd prefer you trade me to Atlanta."

Landry told Staubach, "You're going to be the starter."

Roger Staubach: "About that time I found out my mother was dying of cancer. My wife, Marianne, was a nurse, so we took care of her here. The good thing was that my mother was very independent. She had been working for General Motors. She would never have come down here if she knew how bad it was, so we didn't tell her the truth until we got her down here. She was tough as could be and never complained. It helped that I was with her every day, but it was a bad deal.

"I was really in a dilemma then, because I had just moved her down to Dallas so I could take care of her. I told my wife, 'I still can't stay here in Dallas if I'm not starting.' If Tom would have said, 'Roger, you're going to be my number two quarterback,' then I would have been sitting there with my mother's situation. But I made up my mind that I would just move with her.

"Tom asked to meet over at the practice field, and I knew it was a meeting to talk about who was going to be the starting quarterback. I really didn't know what he had in mind, because he didn't say, 'Roger, I'm glad you're back healthy again. You're my starting quarterback.' He asked me, 'How do you feel?'

"I said, 'Coach, there are no hard feelings, but obviously if I'm not the starting quarterback for Dallas, I'm not going to be back. It's your decision. I'm not trying to be difficult . . .'

"I don't know if that's when he made his decision or not. I really don't. But it was unusual for him to ask how I felt versus coming out and telling me, and at the end of the conversation he said, 'We're very comfortable that you're our starting quarterback.'

"And that year Craig was very good as our backup quarterback. I was surprised Craig didn't force Tom to trade him. I would have. For the team's sake, it would not have been good for me to have been there. I just could not have handled it. And I'm not saying whether that's right or wrong. I would not have reported. I would have sat out. I would have said, 'That's it,' and they would have been forced to trade me."

In 1973 Roger Staubach led the NFL in passing. That same year Calvin Hill ran for 1,142 yards, but he also led the club in receptions with 32 catches for 290 yards. Those statistics were one indication of the turmoil surrounding the receiving corps.

During the early part of the season the team struggled, in part because of injuries and the inconsistency of the new crop of receivers, including their number one draft choice, tight end Billy Joe Dupree; Otto Stowe; Billy Truax; and rookie Jean Fugett. Another part of the problem was that the Cowboys were trying to force-feed rookie Golden Richards into the system while at the same time attempting to force Bob Hayes out. Richards had speed, and he had great PR value. He was a white guy with the name *Golden*. How great an attraction would he be if he could become a star? Bob Hayes had not only lost favor with Landry, but his confidence was down so low he was demanding that the Cowboys trade him. Rookies Drew Pearson and Rodrigo Barnes watched the way Landry was treating Hayes and wondered.

Drew Pearson: "I could see very clearly what the Cowboys were trying to do to Bob Hayes, because it was that obvious. Golden Richards came in, a second-round draft choice, and they brought him in as the heir apparent to Bob. And granted, Bob might have been on the downhill side, but I mean, there is nothing Golden Richards could have done to replace Bob Hayes, unless they *wanted* to replace him. And they really *wanted* to replace Bob. They really pushed Golden. They pushed Golden in practice by giving him more opportunities to catch the ball, sending him deep all the time. They really thought this guy was going to be the heir apparent to Bob Hayes. So I could see that.

"And Bob could see that. Bob and I were good friends. He's one of the guys who took me under his wing. Bob had revolutionized the game, made zone defenses a part of the game.

"It was the Cowboys way. What I mean by that, as long as you're out there producing and being effective, you're great—'We'll do anything for you.' But when your skills start to diminish and you start on your downhill side, then, 'We're getting rid of you. You're going out the door.' And I've seen a lot of players go through that, and the thing about that, it wasn't a black-white thing. It happened to *everybody*. It was a football player thing. Even though Bob may not have been as effective as he used to be, he was still faster than anybody out there. If he had had a little more discipline, a little more direction, if a little more appreciation had been shown to him, respect shown to him for being who he was, I think Bob would have adjusted and dealt with the pressure, instead of succumbing to it, and saying, 'If you guys don't want me, trade me. Get rid of me.' He succumbed to the pressure instead of dealing with it.

"When I saw the kind of pressure they were putting on him, the things they were doing to him, the lack of respect they were showing him, yeah, you could see why he came out and said, 'I want to be traded. I want out of Dallas.' But Golden Richards was their boy. That's the guy they wanted to push, so that's why they were pushing Bob out one door and bringing Golden in another.

"Jean Fugett was there a year ahead of me. Jean was a guy who was ahead of his time. He projected an image that he was a little too smart for his britches. He was a smart guy, came from Amherst, very bright, very sharp, very articulate.

"Jean didn't try to disrupt the system. All he did was question the system. He wanted to know 'why.' And once he got the why, he'd say, 'Why don't we do it like this instead of this?' And he made sense. And coach Landry didn't react to that very favorably. It was, 'How can you question me? This is the way we've been doing it.' You don't come in and question that. But Jean was a little too smart and a little ahead of his time.

"And Rodrigo Barnes. There is no question, he would have been a super, super football player for the Cowboys if they had given him the opportunity. He just was a radical at a time when radicals weren't popular. Today, Rodrigo would fit in nicely with anybody. The things he did, if he did those things nowadays, they wouldn't even be questioned. There wouldn't be any big deal about it. But he came in questioning the system, and you could see the sort of racial undertones that the system was projecting. What conclusions can you draw when you see they are pushing Bob Hayes out, but they were not pushing Lee Roy Jordan out? And Rodrigo couldn't understand that. And I'm telling you this stuff because it's true. I was there.

"Whether the Cowboys think it was that way, I'm sure they will give you another story. Do I have negative feelings against the Cowboys because of this? No. But I'm just telling you what I saw and observed and what was actually happening there while we were being labeled America's Team and everybody thinking everything was rosy down here in Dallas, Texas. And it wasn't, 'cause if you're a black player observing this, you're wondering when your time is going to come. How are they going to get rid of you? How are they going to push you out of the door? How is the hammer going to come down on you, because eventually it comes down on everybody? And you're wondering how it's going to come down on you, but again, it wasn't so much or all toward blacks, it was the way they did *all* players back then.

"It's like with me, after I made the team I had to compete with Golden about who was going to suit up that week and who was going to be on the taxi squad. And it should have been a no-brainer. I could play both wide receiver positions, I was running back kickoffs, I was running back punts, I was covering kickoffs—my real value was as a special teams guy. Golden wasn't doing any of that. But every Friday I had to go through the anxiety, who was going to go? Thank God, of the 14 weeks of the regular season I went each and every one of those 14 weeks, and there were many times when Golden was left at home or didn't suit up for home games. But for what I did in training camp that year, the plays I made, there shouldn't have been any question who was going to go.

"But Golden was the number two draft choice, and I was a free agent, and man, he was the golden boy. They wanted him to make it bad. He was going to replace Lance Rentzel, Lance Alworth, Billy Parks. He was *the* guy."

Rodrigo Barnes: "Bob Hayes was a tremendous athlete, speed out of this world. Landry got Golden Richards to get rid of Bob Hayes. He got him just to do that. They changed Bob into the flanker and let the other guy run the bombs. And it was stupid, because Bob was the clear-out man. But Landry didn't want Bob."

When the Cowboys opened 4–3 in 1973, part of the reason was that Richards, a rookie, was making rookie mistakes. Also, injuries took their toll. Otto Stowe had broken an ankle and had to miss a month of the season, Billy Truax had ulcers from the aspirin he took for pain, Billy Joe Dupree had a sprained right foot, and Jean Fugett had a strained hamstring.

Rookie Mike Montgomery replaced Stowe, but against the New York Giants he suffered a severely pulled groin muscle and had to miss three games. There was only one eligible receiver on the roster: the skinny free agent from the

University of Tulsa, Drew Pearson. Landry disliked starting rookies, but here he was starting a *free-agent* rookie. It was unheard of.

In this case the Cowboys would gain glory from their seeming misfortune. It's possible that had the receivers on the depth chart above him not gotten hurt, Pearson might have rotted on the bench before being given a chance to play. It's also possible he might have sat on the bench for three or four years before breaking into the starting lineup. But because of the spate of injuries during training camp and then the midseason injuries to Stowe and Montgomery, Pearson got to play his first season, and he went on to become one of the greatest receivers in Cowboys history.

Pearson gained notice in his very first game, against the Giants, and then in the 14–7 loss to the Dolphins, he caught seven passes for 71 yards and made another big play when he picked up a Walt Garrison fumble and ran it 28 yards. Very quickly, everyone began to notice that this free-agent rookie could really play the game.

Drew Pearson: "I was ready to go. I tried to have a great, great week of practice, and I did. I was catching everything. I ran so many routes that week, I wanted to build not only Roger's confidence but coach Landry's confidence and the rest of my teammates' confidence in this rookie starting in this critical part of the season. So I ran a lot of routes in practice and tried to get their confidence. Coach Landry, he's a pretty smart guy. He knew he had all these other weapons. He knew he didn't have to rely on me to win in this game. So he gradually worked me into the game and into the game plan. He threw me that little bone, that little sideline route, just to get me acclimated. And then we played four days later on Thanksgiving Day against the Miami Dolphins, and then he wore me out. He ran me *all* these routes. I ended up catching seven or eight in that game, and they were all inside routes, turning, tough-catch routes.

"And for some reason a quarterback really loves a receiver who will go inside and make those tough catches for him. Even though they might have the greatest receiver to go deep on, he's going to draw an attraction to that receiver. And from that game, Roger started having more and more confidence in me, and you could see it building."

In that loss against the Dolphins, Staubach found himself a big-play, go-to receiver. After that same game, Staubach lost the autonomy that Landry had given him at the start of the season.

With the world becoming more and more radical, Landry was fighting for control of the things over which he had influence. At the beginning of the year he had ceded the play calling to his quarterbacks, but after Staubach called an audible and failed to make a first down against the Dolphins, Landry revoked his quarterbacks' freedom. How Staubach would respond to the challenge posed by Landry's desire to be in control would determine the fate of the Cowboys.

Roger Staubach: "We won our first three games, and then in the fourth game, against Washington, I got a bruised knee, but I finished up the half. We were winning at halftime. But I got banged up, and that was the excuse Tom used to take me out. And I had told him I wasn't hurt. It was a real strange deal. We lost when they stopped Walt Garrison on the goal line.

"There was no quarterback controversy, because Tom said after the game that I hadn't played because I was banged up. So that was a weird deal.

"I wasn't playing particularly well, but we were winning. We were 6–3 going into the Thanksgiving Day game against the Dolphins. Our offense was scoring. We had just put my mother back in the hospital. She was dehydrated, and she had only a matter of a month to live. Against the Dolphins we trailed and we had a third-and-one; I audibled to a running play, a sweep. I felt it was the right audible, but we didn't score.

"We lost, 14–7, and after the game Tom said to me, 'Your mother's situation, I know how bad it is. You've got too much on your mind. I want you just to worry about formations and reading defenses and not worry about memorizing the game plan. I'm going to call the plays.' That was his reasoning, that I had 'too much on my mind.'

"I told him I'd rather call the plays and said I felt I was able to do it. In training camp during the preseason Craig and I had made a deal with him to allow us to call the plays, and we had had a really good preseason. But his reasoning was that I had too much on my mind, and I should let him worry about the plays. And of course, really, he was reverting back, because he had done it before. That was his deal. Of course, the trend was going that way with coaches trying to see what was going on on the field, recognizing and sending plays in after viewing everything from the press box. We were using a lot of multiple looks, two tight ends, and if you're calling the play, you have to make sure you have the right players in the game, so his thinking was, 'We have too much going on. We can send the play in and the right players for that play.'

"It was about control. For him to be personally calling the plays made it even more a control thing. It should have been the job of the offensive coordinator, but Tom coached both defense *and* offense. When the offense left the field, he was there with Ernie Stautner seeing to the defense. Even during the week he'd spend time with the defense, and then he'd come into offensive meetings. Tom is a brilliant guy. Tom Landry is *brilliant*. But you can get to the point where you are doing too much trying to run the whole show. Who called the plays was somewhat of an issue, but when you're winning, you sure can't complain about it."

With Landry calling the plays, the Cowboys finished the season beating Denver; their hated rivals, the Washington Redskins; and the St. Louis Cardinals to finish 10–4. Staubach's mother had died the week before the Cardinals game, and he returned in time to complete 14 of 19 for 256 yards and three touchdowns. Pearson caught five passes for 140 yards and two of those touchdowns. It was a remarkable performance.

Drew Pearson: "Roger's mother had died before the Cardinals game. And Roger played a great game. To this day, Roger is a special kind of a guy. Talk about thick skin, there is no question he had that. His parents raised him with a lot of discipline, and so in doing that, he's been taught a lot of the values you really need. And Roger is the type of teammate, even though this tragedy happened in his life, he knew that his mother wanted him to continue to go out there and play. He didn't want his anguish, his grief, his problems to become our problems, and that's just the kind of guy he was. He played that game being mentally injured, because his mother had passed, and you know what you have to go through dealing with that, but he played many games where he was physically injured, and he was always out there, always giving his all, and even though he was injured he never pulled back to try to avoid further injury. I mean, he was just that type of guy, and because he was that type of guy, it made me that type of guy. It made me want to be the same way. And I wasn't the only guy on the team who wanted to be like that. It made me tougher, not only physically, but mentally as well. And it made me look at life differently, made me respect morals and values. When I made that Cowboys team, I said to myself, 'That's the guy's pocket I need to get in. If I do things like Roger Staubach, I'm going to be OK.' I don't have to be his great buddy, go to his house for dinner every night so his wife has to tell me, 'Drew, it's time to leave.' We never were that kind of friends. But the respect was there, and I *knew* he was the guy you needed to model yourself after.

"Roger set a lot of the foundation for me as an adult. He set a lot of the foundation for me as a parent. He set a lot of the foundation for me as a businessman. I owe a lot to him. If I ever make the Hall of Fame, it's going to be hard to pick and choose a presenter because Tom Landry and Roger Staubach meant so much to my career. They meant *so much* to my career, how could I leave either one of them out?"

It was in that St. Louis Cardinals game that Staubach figured out how to "play" Landry. Late in the game, Landry called a play, but in the huddle Pearson told Staubach he could get open by breaking off his route in the seam of the Cardinals zone. As a result Staubach ran his own play, not Landry's.

The throw, into double coverage, was almost over Pearson's head, but the lithe rookie leaped up and grabbed it. The momentum of the throw bent him backward, and defenders hit him from all sides, but he hung on for the touchdown.

When Staubach came back to the sideline, Landry did not ask why he had changed the play. Rather, he congratulated him. Staubach made note of that fact.

Landry had insisted on calling the plays for Don Meredith, and Meredith had been so browbeaten and cowed by his domineering coach that he didn't have the nerve to change plays, and as a result Dandy Don had not been able to figure out a way to deal with his deep resentment of Landry. But Staubach would be different. He was not afraid of Landry the way Meredith had been. Staubach became convinced that if he changed a play in a tight situation and was successful, Landry would look the other way. And time after time, especially in crucial, last-minute situations, Staubach would go against Landry. And time after time, his improvised plays, like the one to Drew Pearson in the Cardinals game, would succeed. Handling Landry would turn out to be the true genius of Roger Staubach. And so Staubach would succeed where Meredith had failed. Even so, the issue of who would call the plays would remain a sore subject between Staubach and Landry for the next seven years.

The next Sunday, in the first round of the playoffs against the Rams, Pearson and Staubach concocted another improvised play. Ahead 17–16, Landry ordered a deep sideline pass to Bob Hayes. In the huddle Staubach told Pearson to change his turn-in route to a post pattern.

Drew Pearson: "The Rams had all the momentum, and remember, Roger was taking a chance on a rookie. He had just been sacked, and he told the line to give him maximum protection. I took off on the post and was double covered by Eddie McMillan and Steve Preece. No way should Roger have thrown it, but here it came. The defensive backs ran into each other, and I was gone for an 83-yard touchdown. Tom was *shocked*. That was the backbreaker."

Roger Staubach: "We had gone ahead of the Rams 14–0, and the Rams came back. The momentum had changed dramatically. The score was 17–16 with under 10 minutes left. We lost yardage when Calvin Hill got hit in the backfield on a sweep and fell on his elbow, suffering a crippling injury. It looked bleak. We were third-and-long, and if we didn't do something, we would have had to punt from way back.

"And in that same series we hit a play to Drew Pearson that broke the game wide open. It was an in-route for 83 yards, and we were all excited, and we ended up winning. It was a 16 route, a route Drew and I had started to feel real comfortable with. It was a timing play over the middle. He had to get by the linebacker. Most receivers worry about a safety trying to take your head off, but Drew was the type of guy who didn't worry about that. When I threw it, I knew we'd score. Sure enough, Drew was coming out of his break, and the safety was coming over to try to coldcock him, and he caught it between the safety and the cornerback, and he took off and went 83 yards.

"My mother had died two weeks earlier, right before the St. Louis game—we had a great game to win the division—and so after the Rams game and that touchdown to Drew, I told everyone, 'My mother threw that one.'"

The Cowboys played the Minnesota Vikings for the NFC Championship and the right to go to the Super Bowl. It was no contest. Led by Fran Tarkenton and running back Chuck Foreman, the Vikings kept the Cowboys defense guessing all day long. Rookie Rodrigo Barnes, his anger growing with each game, placed the blame on the shoulders of Lee Roy Jordan, the Cowboys vet he felt all season long he should have replaced.

Rodrigo Barnes: "I should have started, should have played the game. Jordan had a poor game, a real poor game. They ran right up the middle. It's in

Staubach's book. He wrote the book about '73, said that Jordan just had a bad game that day. I don't know what happened to him. And I don't guess he was the only one, but they ran right up the middle, right where he was. They ran right by him. I don't know if Lee Roy was hurt, it was something, and then at half-time I got hurt, so I couldn't even replace him if I wanted to, but Landry should have made the move earlier. He should have played me because you can't get better unless you play. You need a hitter, and the Cowboys didn't have a hitter. You got to have a hitter, and when you have a hitter, you have to make room for a hitter. A hitter is as important as an interception on defense, and when you've got a good hitter, man, you let him play. Well, those guys didn't understand that hitters cause fumbles, that they are going to cause a whole lot of things. They didn't understand that. But that game, our defense was intimidated, and Minnesota beat us. We should have won that game. We should have won the Super Bowl that year.

"We paid the price by not playing the people we needed to play to win. You can't win by playing who you want to have play. You win by playing the guys who can hit and make the plays."

Staubach had a different analysis. He blamed the loss on the injury to Calvin Hill, to bad luck, and to the worst pass he made in his entire career with the Cowboys.

Roger Staubach: "Calvin getting hurt at the time really killed us the next week against the Vikings, because they didn't worry about our running game and went after me the whole game. We had two tipped passes for interceptions. It was a miserable game. It was the worst game I had ever been in.

"We had some shots. Golden Richards ran a punt back for a touchdown to make the score 10–7 Vikings. We recovered a fumble, and we had a big play to Billy Joe Dupree. I hit him as he was coming across the middle, but the ball hit off his body instead of him catching it, and it bounced into the hands of Jeff Siemon, one of their linebackers, and that killed us, because we possibly could have gone in and scored.

"And then I threw a pass that was just terrible. It was a motion pass. Bob Hayes was in motion going across the field, and he broke a sideline route, and I tried to throw it across the field, and Bobby Bryant intercepted it and ran it back 63 yards for a touchdown. If I'm not mistaken, it was the only pass in my career that was run back for a touchdown. But Bryant ran it, man. He caught that thing and ran right down the sideline. I had *no* chance to get him. He cut right in front of Hayes. It was probably the worst pass I ever threw. The momentum of that game was going in our direction, but my job was to turn it around, and I didn't turn it around. So I think that was the worst game I ever had. We lost that day, 27–10, and then the Vikings lost to Miami in the Super Bowl."

Drew Pearson: "I was really sick after losing that game to the Vikings, because the Super Bowl that year was going to be played in Houston, and I couldn't think of any better climax to my rookie season than playing in the Super Bowl as a rookie, and as a starter at that. We thought we could beat the Vikings. The Vikings are one of those teams, man, they frustrate you so, because they don't do anything fancy. They just come at you and play football. They come out there on the field, and there's no rah rah. They just do their jobs, and they kick your butt, and they leave town. They don't talk no shit, or nothing. They kind of piss you off because they are so businesslike, so professional-like. It all permeated from Bud Grant, wearing the black shoes, those ugly uniforms, and they were out there kicking our butts."

Chapter 50

Come the (Short) Revolution

Since 1967 the Dallas Cowboys had been the most successful franchise in the NFL, despite Tex Schramm's policy of paying his players about half the going rate. Even when athletes on other teams began mocking the Cowboys players for accepting such low wages, the players would inevitably end up signing and swallowing hard. Schramm knew he could afford to do so in part because there wasn't much his beef on the hoof could do about it, and also because the team was successful. Amazingly, during all the years of Schramm's penury, the success on the field never was affected by it. If a player didn't like what he was being offered, Tex would tell him he could play somewhere else. But with the excellent chances of going to the Super Bowl almost every year, few wanted to miss being part of that.

Then in 1974 the World Football League was organized, and suddenly there *was* a somewhere else, and for the first time, if Tex wanted to keep his players in Dallas, he would have to pay them the going rate. The Cowboys' first-round draft choice, Ed Jones of Tennessee State College, signed for a reported $400,000 salary for three years, as much as double what he would have gotten had the Detroit Wheels not also been vying for his services.

The same day Jones signed with the Cowboys, the Houston Texans of the WFL proclaimed the league's long-range strategy when it was announced that Craig Morton had signed to play with the Texans starting the following year, in 1975. Morton was said to be getting $300,000 for three years. Calvin Hill revealed he had signed a future contract with the Hawaii team of the WFL, then Mike Montgomery said he had signed a contract with Birmingham to join that team in 1975. Said Montgomery, "They'll certainly have to take a look at the organization to see why folks are leaving them. Maybe this will help them to get a more human-type relationship into the organization."

The next day Schramm retaliated. He got a restraining order from a district court judge to stop the WFL from negotiating with players whose contracts had not expired. Morton, Hill, and Montgomery, moreover, were enjoined from trying to sign other Cowboys players for the new league. The ruling seemed illogical and wrongly decided, but such was Schramm's power in Dallas. On appeal Judge Harold Bateman of the Texas Court of Appeals reversed the decision. As a result, third-round draft choice Danny White, the talented quarterback from Arizona State, signed with the Toronto Northmen. White said his offer was double what Schramm wanted to pay him. White was the first draft pick lost by the Cowboys since E. J. Holub signed with the AFL in 1961.

Schramm, hearing threats from Lee Roy Jordan that he would listen to offers from the WFL, signed Jordan and gave his quarterback, Roger Staubach, a multiyear contract extension. Staubach was never a hard bargainer, which made his teammates upset with him, because Schramm would always say to them, "How can I give you that when Roger only makes this?"

Lee Roy Jordan: "Roger was making pretty big money in the off-season, so they'd get Roger signed quick and get him to sign low. After football, after we retired, I told him, 'You're the reason no one else could ever get a raise, 'cause they based all the salaries off yours. We had to be X number of percentage points close to you.' I told Roger, 'You're making $200,000 in the off-season, and I'm making $200. There's a lot of difference in that.' He was embarrassed.

"But it is true. It's *very* true. I think that was just like the deal with Tom and his salary. They kept that down so they could put up to the players, 'Tom is only making $50,000. How could you make more?' I don't know what kind of bonus he'd make, and I know he owned some stock, and that was appreciating very nicely. That was the leverage they had on us, and most of us weren't making enough to split with an agent or an attorney, so we didn't have anybody else involved. And if you brought an attorney, then you *really* got on Tex's bad side."

Roger Staubach: "The one problem I had with some of the players was that I did my own contracts, and they felt I was setting the team's salary level because I was the quarterback. I didn't think of it that way, and looking back on it, I wish I would have done it differently. I didn't think I was affecting somebody else, that there was this food chain.

"But I've never particularly wanted someone trying to represent me, trying to fight for money. I'm the same way today. I have a fee, and that's the fee. I don't negotiate. I had a price, and that was my price.

"I have never been greedy per se, but financially I was in the real estate business, and at the time I was making more money in real estate than I was in football. And I was making moneymaking endorsements. So I was satisfied with my salary. I looked at it all as a total package. I wasn't thinking, 'How was that affecting other players?' which was a shame, because I was satisfied. And I thought I was getting a big salary. Looking back, I wish I had done it differently. I would have tried to raise the level for my teammates."

In addition to having to battle the WFL to keep his players, Schramm also had to contend with those players when the NFL Players Association (NFLPA) went on strike on July 1 over the issue of free agency. When training camp opened, the veterans refused to report. They wore shirts that proclaimed "No Freedom, No Football." The College All-Star Game had to be canceled.

Four players—Bob Lilly, Lee Roy Jordan, Pat Toomay, and John Fitzgerald—refused to cast a strike vote, and Ralph Neely announced he would not support the strike. These were men who didn't like Big Government, didn't like unions, didn't like being told what to do or think. Jordan, for one, didn't believe in striking. He didn't think the players who went on strike would ever benefit themselves sufficiently to make up for the money they lost going on strike.

Lee Roy Jordan: "I thought the free agency deal was not a good plan for us at the time. Maybe it turned out to be great for everybody now, but at the time I felt what we needed more were benefits. Our pension is horrible. The retirement plan they have for NFL players is absolutely horrible. I'm getting mine now, and it was $600 a month, but one of the lawsuits was finalized and they put more money in it, and I'm up to $800 a month, so you can see I'm really knocking them down. And I played 14 years. Just think of a guy who played five years. He's not going to get a lot. Normally four-point-something years is an average career in the NFL.

"And at the time my difference of opinion with the leadership made some of them pretty angry. Len Hauss was one of the early guys who was for the union up in Washington. He hated my guts because I didn't go along with the deal. I said, 'Hey, Len, that's just the way I am. I don't believe in what you're doing. If you could convince me otherwise, I'd vote for it.'"

In response to the five defectors, some of the black players began to see the strike in racial terms, which only stirred up further animosity. Bob Hayes made a veiled threat, saying they would be marked men "looking out of the corner of their eye." Said Hayes, "If they are not going to back us, to hell with them. They can feed them to the fish as far as I'm concerned. I feel this way. If a guy doesn't want to back us, why is he part of it? I just can't see why a guy wouldn't want to be part of something that stands to benefit his family."

Mel Renfro: "The players who spoke out against them for the most part were the young, strong bucks that were into the power thing—I don't want to say black power—but stand-up-for-your-rights power, and these are rights that will help minority players, and here were some white guys not going along. They were the guys who would speak out. They were the ones who would forge new territory, who would go where others wouldn't go. That was their personality."

Twenty-year-old Jean Fugett was one of the leaders of the strike, and for him it was a crushing experience. Fugett was idealistic and thought the players could win out against the might of the Cowboys organization if only they could stick together and not give in. What he hadn't anticipated was that Schramm was as tough an opponent as any corporate CEO fighting to keep out a union and that enough of the players were content with the status quo that the strike didn't stand a chance.

By the end of July, there were two types of articles in the local papers: rumors of certain players signing with the WFL and reports of other players reporting to training camp. In the first wave of camp attendees were the Texans and the guys who needed to have that paycheck coming. Dave Manders and Walt Garrison reported. Said Garrison, "I ran out of rodeos and I figured I might as well report to camp." Golden Richards reported, saying, "Frankly, the Cowboys have given me everything I have, my car, the clothes on my back, everything. And economically, I'm just not prepared to sit this thing out."

Rodrigo Barnes: "The union sold out everybody. Whenever you're going to strike at the beginning of a work week, at the beginning of the season, that's stupid. If you're going to strike, you strike at the end of the season when people have gotten paid. So to my mind, the whole striking was to defeat the players. It wasn't to win. Ed Garvey [head of the NFLPA] didn't have any intentions of helping the players. His own thing was to work with the owners. He sold out. That whole thing Ed Garvey did in '74 and '75 was a sellout. That striking at the beginning of the season was a sellout. It was stupid. If you're going to strike, strike at the end of the season, right before the playoffs. So to me, it's real obvious. All of it is obvious to me."

It wasn't long before Schramm began making veiled threats aimed to pierce the vets' feeling of security, as he and Landry pumped up rookies in the papers to make the strikers feel doubtful about their futures, insinuating that if they didn't come back to work soon, they would be replaced. One by one, the players began crossing the picket lines. Roger Staubach reported along with Lee Roy Jordan. Said Jordan, "If they're going to negotiate, they will. My staying out of camp won't affect it." The next day Bob Lilly reported.

Calvin Hill, seeing that the strike was going badly, had harsh words for Schramm. He said, "Duane was run out of town because he was an individual. Supposedly his individuality was bad for the team. Now management is *encouraging* players to be individuals and report to camp. It's hardly consistent. We should all be for the team or should all be individuals."

Hill denied the players were losing the strike. He said, "I think we're right, and if you're supporting something, something you feel is right, you're not losing."

Hill said that before Staubach left the strikers and reported, the practices lacked organization. "You can't do a lot when the quarterbacks are gone," said Hill.

After Staubach reported to camp, Garvey said snidely, "I'd hate to have been at Pearl Harbor with him." The remark finished him with Staubach and some of his teammates.

Staubach bristled, charging that Garvey had mixed reasonable player demands with foolish ones. He accused Garvey of arrogance: "He immediately made the owners mad, which doesn't seem like a good way to me to begin negotiations." Concluded Staubach, "It makes more sense to me if a person stands up for what he believes is right rather than go along with a man who had no more common sense than to make an analogy like that one about Pearl Harbor. I just think this man has done a lot of harm." Bob Lilly called Garvey the Jimmy Hoffa of the players association.

John Niland reported, citing Bible passages, including Ephesians 6:5–9; Colossians 3:22–25; and Timothy 6:1–2. "I am trying to follow God's word by the law and be a servant to my master, but through my love of Christ and wanting to serve God I've decided to report," said Niland. Niland said that because he was a Christian, he was reporting. He said that if he hadn't been a Christian, he would have stayed out, because "my own personal will is one of siding with the players on some of the issues."

Charlie Waters reported August 7, and then the first of the black players, Rodney Wallace and Benny Barnes, came to camp. Then the flood: Drew Pearson reported.

Drew Pearson: "I supported the strike, but I didn't want to. I supported it because it was the union, and I thought it was the right thing to do. But I certainly couldn't afford to go on strike. After making $14,500 my first year, and my wife was pregnant, getting ready to have a baby in July. And here I am. . . . I needed to go to training camp. I needed that check. My money had run out, even though I worked in the off-season and made some extra money. But I stuck with the team, the majority of the players, and supported their cause. But I didn't know what the hell was going on."

Then Mel Renfro reported, shocking his teammates.

Mel Renfro: "I was very low-key and benevolent, and I was under the feeling that we would agree to disagree. But these guys didn't want to do it. These other guys did want to do it. These guys don't like that these guys don't want to do it, so what? Let's go find a place to drink beer and go have a good time.

"Once the season began, I didn't think there was any bad blood. Once we hit the field, we put the strike behind us. That's the way I felt."

By August 12, the NFLPA had lost, but to save face it announced a cooling-off period and said the strikers could report to camp. In the end there were 10 veterans manning the picket lines: Jean Fugett, Calvin Hill, Bob Hayes, Billy Gregory, Otto Stowe, Jethro Pugh, Rayfield Wright, Rodrigo Barnes, Blaine Nye, and D. D. Lewis.

When eight of the last ten reported, Landry commented, "They'll be treated like everybody else until they prove to me they don't deserve to be treated like everybody else."

With the strike over, Landry extended the training camp two weeks and worked his players like Trojans. Every morning at practice, the players had to run a nearly two-mile course over rough terrain that the players called the Ho Chi Minh Trail.

In late August the Cowboys put Otto Stowe on waivers, hoping to trade him. End coach Mike Ditka accused Stowe of "not applying himself." Said Rayfield Wright, "I hated to see that man go. He could have helped us win the Super

Bowl." Cliff Harris and Mel Renfro called Stowe the "best receiver on the team." Said Renfro, "It doesn't surprise me the way things are going. Otto's the best, but Tom has his opinion about what was happening, and he's the boss."

In response, Stowe went to bat for Calvin Hill, accusing the Cowboys of maligning Hill for political reasons and ignoring his accomplishments. "Calvin gained 1,000 yards back to back, and no other Cowboy has done that," he told *The Dallas Times Herald*. "He signed with the WFL, and [the Cowboys] said his success was because of the line. He was a good back, but it was the line. Any back could have done the same thing, they said.

"The fact is they've had Duane Thomas, Danny Reeves, and Walt Garrison, good backs who've never gained 1,000 yards. Other players see how they treated Calvin and myself and Mike Montgomery and say, 'Wow, if that could happen to them, then any day it could happen to me.' It's a bad place to be, a bad situation to be in."

Drew Pearson: "In preseason of '74 the Cowboys pushed Otto Stowe out the door. Otto said his ankle was sore. Landry said he wasn't trying hard enough to get in shape. And Landry and them were listening to doctors as opposed to listening to the player himself. Coach Landry didn't look at Otto Stowe for Otto Stowe. Otto was not the kind of player to slough off. When Otto Stowe says his ankle isn't right, you should take heed to that and say, 'If he's saying his stuff isn't right, it must not be right.'"

On October 6, the Cowboys traded Stowe to the Denver Broncos for a draft pick. Ten days later, it was reported that Rodrigo Barnes, the outspoken backup middle linebacker, had quit the team. In addition to wanting more money, Barnes complained that he couldn't stand that everyone wasn't treated alike, and that Landry wanted him off the team because he couldn't stand to have a player who spoke up for what he believed in.

After almost a full month went by, on November 11 Barnes was traded to the New England Patriots. He was too radical for whomever he played for, refused to wait his turn to play, and ultimately ruined a promising career long before it should have been over.

The 1974 Cowboys season was marked by tension and division. Quite a few of the players had signed with the WFL, and their teammates accused some of them of not putting out for fear of sustaining an injury that would hamper them in their new league. Some players continued being upset over low salary, and others were too angered by the failure of the strike to do much. Injuries were the other factor hampering the Cowboys. Staubach was recovering from a foot operation and was slowed down.

Craig Morton finally got fed up and demanded to be traded. The 10-year Cowboys veteran was dealt to the New York Giants for a first-round draft choice in 1975 with barely a *thank you*. Morton's replacement, Clint Longley from Abilene Christian, had a great arm but lacked discipline. Clint had little interest in learning the keys. All he wanted to do was throw long. He drove Landry crazy.

The disorganization hurt the Cowboys in the early part of the season. After an impressive 24–0 shutout of the Atlanta Falcons, the Cowboys lost four extremely close games in a row to the Eagles, Giants, Vikings, and Cards. Each loss was more incredible than the last. For the Cowboys, it was as though they were in the twilight zone. Once past the 1–4 start that doomed their playoff chances, the 1974 Cowboys finished out the season 7–2 and at the end played as well as any team—all for naught.

Roger Staubach: "Every off-season I'd work out like gangbusters, but after the '73 season I had problems with my ankle. I had an inflammation of the tendon on my Achilles heel, and it just killed me. I couldn't set up, couldn't run, so I really couldn't work out. It was very frustrating. I tried acupuncture, tried everything, but when I'd go to work out it would bother me. So I finally had my ankle operated on in June. They scraped my Achilles tendon.

"By the time I got to training camp, I had this open sore that was oozing blood, but my ankle felt good. It was a weird deal. It finally closed, and it was the first time in seven months that I really could run.

"We went into the exhibition season, and I pulled a hamstring, 'cause I really wasn't in shape yet, so I didn't play the exhibition season.

"We opened up against Atlanta, and we had a good game, and then we went into the tank for four straight—the worst streak we ever had. We lost four in a row, and then we were out of it.

"But that streak was unbelievable. We had the Philadelphia Eagles beat. We were up there in Philadelphia. I handed the ball to Doug Dennison across the goal line for the game winner, and he fumbled. Joe Lavender ran it back 96 yards for a touchdown. If Doug had scored, the game would have been over. In fact, the Eagles were warming up another quarterback to replace Roman Gabriel. So Roman came back into the game and pulled them back. So we ended up losing to the Eagles. I threw an interception at the end of the game.

"Against the Giants we lost 14–6. We couldn't score until right at the end, when I threw a touchdown to Bob Hayes, and then we missed the extra point. I was intercepted three times. I was trapped six times.

"We were playing the Vikings in Texas Stadium, and literally I was miserable against the Vikings, until the fourth quarter, and we came back and had a sensational fourth quarter and went ahead. We were winning. They got the ball at the end of the game, drove down and fumbled, and we should have recovered. The ball bounced near five of our guys, and it bounced back to Chuck Foreman, who had fumbled. It was just a screwed-up deal. So with 10 seconds left they kicked a field goal, and their kicker, Fred Cox, booted it and then put his head down, because he thought it was wide, but all the fans in the stands were up cheering and screaming, and the refs called it good. Really, everybody thought it had missed. The kicker thought he missed it.

"Then we played St. Louis, and we were tied with them. We kicked off, and they ran the kickoff back to about the 30, and with a minute left Jim Bakken kicked a field goal to beat us. So we lost four games, the freakiest four-game stretch, and then after that we played pretty good.

"We had a game on Thanksgiving Day when Clint Longley came in and beat the Redskins in a game we should have lost. By that time we were out of it, but it hurt the Redskins for the home-field advantage. We ended up 8–6.

"We lost to the Raiders the last game of the season when we should have beaten them. We fumbled on the 1. The Raiders won on a touchdown pass by George Blanda. Hell, we played a good game, but we lost. We still could have gotten a wild-card spot if the Rams had defeated the Redskins in their final game. But it didn't happen."

The Cowboys failed to make the playoffs for the first time since 1966. Experts were predicting that the Cowboys were getting old and would slip into mediocrity.

The experts would be very wrong. Coming were the Glory Days. Soon the Dallas Cowboys would officially become America's Team.

Chapter 51

So Long, Bob Hayes

In the spring of 1975, the NFL Players Association sued the team owners in federal court in an attempt to gain free agency. To succeed, they had to overturn what was known as the Rozelle Rule, an edict from the commissioner that provided that if another team signed a free-agent player, Pete Rozelle would decide what the proper compensation should be.

In court, one of the players who risked his career by testifying was Bob Hayes. The Cowboys star agreed to demonstrate just how duplicitous the NFL was in telling players they were free to leave and play for another team while at the same time relying on a rule that effectively killed any chance a player had of doing just that.

Under oath Hayes testified that in 1969 he was making a salary of $23,000, and in 1970 he asked for $75,000 but was turned down by Tex Schramm. He said he played out his option, taking a 10 percent pay cut, with an eye toward signing with another team at the end of the season.

Hayes said Landry told him before the 1970 season, "You are important to our game plan." But, he said, once Landry learned he was playing out his option, the coach sought to make him seem much less attractive to other teams by keeping him on the bench much of the season. According to Landry, Hayes was benched because he wasn't blocking like he should.

Even so, the Washington Redskins approached Hayes' agent to sign him for the 1971 season. But because of the Rozelle Rule, George Allen was afraid that Rozelle would punish him for not abiding by the hands-off-free-agents understanding by forcing the Redskins to give up younger star receiver Charley Taylor as compensation, and Allen decided against it. Similarly, the Miami Dolphins also wanted Hayes but were afraid Rozelle would rule that compensation would be Paul Warfield.

In 1971 Hayes was offered a five-year contract for $55,000 per year, plus a yearly $10,000 bonus, and a deferred payment of $60,677. Schramm was giving him his $75,000 per year. In the hearing in 1975 Hayes' attorney, Ed Glennon, said that Hayes was still making that same $55,000 salary and $10,000 bonus.

On July 18, 1975, Hayes was traded to the San Francisco 49ers. Two days later Bob Lilly would retire to mounds of press adulation and torrents of words of praise from Landry. But even though Hayes had revolutionized the game with his blazing speed, catching 365 passes for 7,295 yards and 76 touchdowns during his 10-year Cowboys career, he departed virtually unnoticed. He had fought Schramm and Landry for too long, and with his skills on the wane, they were glad to be rid of him. The reporters followed their lead.

With Rodrigo Barnes traded, Calvin Hill moving to Hawaii in the World Football League, and Hayes gone, the criticism of Schramm and Landry by the black players quieted considerably. Jean Fugett, the last of the outspoken blacks, would be gone in another year. With the Vietnam War over and the Black Panther movement dead along with many of the Black Panthers, peace returned to America and to the Cowboys. In early August 1974, President Richard Nixon resigned as president, and his successor, Gerald Ford, gave Nixon a full pardon. He said his act would "spare Nixon and the nation additional grief in this American tragedy."

Another American tragedy concerned what happened to Bob Hayes. To this day some of his teammates have not forgiven the Cowboys for the way they treated Hayes. After so many years of outstanding service to the Cowboys, Hayes was summarily cast aside, unappreciated for all that he did for the Cowboys, they say, because he dared speak up, for himself and for the other black players. And the other thing they cannot forgive: that the Cowboys did not do more when Hayes found himself the target of a very fishy drug bust.

In April 1978, Hayes was making his way from sports to the business world as vice president of a telemarketing firm called Dycon International. One of the secretaries at Dycon was dating a Braniff Airlines pilot named Dennis Kelly. Through the secretary, Hayes met Kelly.

Kelly, who worked as a part-time undercover officer for the Addison, Texas, police, says the secretary told him that Hayes was selling prescription drugs at Dycon. He said he became friends with Hayes for the purpose of busting him. It took Kelly three months to succeed.

First, Kelly had to get close to Hayes. It was easy. Bob Hayes was the sort of person who loved to make friends and admirers. Always generous, teammates said he would do anything for them. It was this compelling need to be liked by everybody that sealed Hayes' fate.

Hayes and Kelly were friendly enough that they regularly ate lunch together and talked on the phone. To earn his trust, Kelly initiated talks about a deal in which his friend would make Hayes a partner in a restaurant in exchange for the use of his name.

Once the friendship deepened, says Hayes, Kelly asked if he could buy a couple of quaaludes. Two other times he asked to buy a gram of cocaine. Hayes was faced with the quandary that every person faces who is asked by a friend to get him illegal drugs. If you say no, you're not being a real friend. If you say yes and your friend turns out to be a narc, you face going to jail. It becomes a question of faith and trust. Hayes, who bristled at bigotry, was not himself a bigot.

Maybe Hayes would have been better off if he had himself been prejudiced and not trusted Kelly simply because of the long history of hatred of blacks in America by the Irish. But that wasn't Bob Hayes. Hayes could not imagine that his friend was an agent of the government asking him to do favors for the express purpose of putting him behind bars.

Hayes got Kelly both the quaaludes and the coke from a neighbor by the name of Ben Kimmell, who was given a sentence of probation. Sure, Hayes knew the drugs were illegal, but his friend was asking him a favor, and a lot of people in the nightclub circuit were doing drugs at the time, and Hayes was the sort of guy who would go out on a limb for a friend. Hayes took Kelly's money and paid Kimmell for the drugs. (Hayes has an affidavit from Kimmell swearing that Hayes was not a participant in the transactions in question and that Kelly told Kimmell, "We don't care about you. We want Bob Hayes.")

Kelly then asked Hayes if he could get him a pound of coke and a pound of heroin. This is the point at which Hayes should have said to Kelly, "I wouldn't do that for my mother." Hayes had a serious problem. He wanted to do this for his friend, but, says a friend who was around when it happened, Hayes didn't have the connections to get that much dope. When he started asking around, the whispering began. Dealers who could have come up with it were told that Hayes was not reliable enough to make a deal with, that he was too much of a rube. They were told, "Stay away from Hayes. He doesn't know what he's doing."

Hayes, persistent, told Kelly he had a friend who he thought might be able to fill Kelly's order. Hayes—who was *never* a dealer and used cocaine in only small amounts—told Kelly to call the friend. Kelly did. Nothing came of it. A second meeting was scheduled, but this time Hayes backed out.

At 3:00 the next morning Hayes was arrested on charges of selling cocaine and quaaludes. Dennis Kelly was knocking on the door of his Stone Canyon home in North Dallas, leading the arrest team. According to Hayes, he was naked when his "good friend" Kelly walked in and screamed at him, "You f***ing nigger, where's that coke?" Kelly, indeed, had been a narc all along.

After Hayes was arrested, his lawyer figured a black client involved with drugs had zero chance of getting off in the all-white Dallas suburb, and so rather than mount a defense, he advised Hayes to plead guilty and then throw himself on the mercy of the court. Unfortunately for Hayes, it was to be a court with very little mercy.

Hayes' lawyer brought in a string of famous character witnesses including Tom Landry, Drew Pearson, Roger Staubach, and Pettis Norman from the Cowboys and a couple of Olympic teammates. All pleaded for the judge to sentence Hayes to probation. Hayes was sentenced to two five-year sentences for two cocaine sales, and to seven years' probation for selling the quaaludes.

Months following his release from prison in February 1980, the Texas Court of Criminal Appeals reversed his two cocaine convictions, citing improper wording in the indictments. To this day Hayes contends that he has never sold drugs in his entire life and that the only reason he went to jail was that Dennis Kelly did to him what he could have done just as easily to any other human being in his position.

Dennis Kelly disputes much of what Hayes has to say, but he cannot dispute one naked fact: Hayes would not have found himself behind bars if Kelly hadn't befriended him for the purpose of destroying him.

Robbed of his dignity, Bob Hayes would never be the same man again. The drug convictions ruined all chances Hayes had of surviving in business. He couldn't get loans. Clint Murchison offered him a job in the real estate business, but he could not get a realtor's license because of his record. Roger Staubach hired him to manage some of his properties, but that arrangement ended. Hayes turned to alcoholism, and finally, in the spring of 1985, he entered an alcohol rehabilitation clinic.

After the rehabilitation, he started drinking and doing drugs again. Staubach caught him. Hayes entered another program. Staubach paid for it.

Hayes then returned to his hometown, Jacksonville, Florida, where he lived with his relatives.

Bob Hayes' outstanding football career with the Dallas Cowboys earned him his rightful entry into the Cowboys' Ring of Honor. He swas elected posthumously, in 2001.

What saddened Hayes was that he could not go to each and every Dallas Cowboys fan and tell them, "You have to believe me, I am not a drug dealer." Though he was not wholly innocent, he was not a drug dealer. He was a guy trying too hard to please who became a patsy.

Pete Gent: "Ten years ago I was flying on a Braniff flight, before they went bankrupt. Braniff had been our charter plane when I was playing. I was up in first class, and the guy sitting next to me was a Braniff pilot deadheading back, and he looked familiar. We both finally realized he was the guy who used to fly our charters years back. We got to talking, and the subject came around to Bob Hayes, and I said, 'God, wasn't that tragic.'

"He said, 'Listen, I was involved in that. My copilot, Dennis Kelly, was an auxiliary cop in Addison, Texas. His girlfriend worked for the company where Bobby Hayes was working, and Bob thought they were friends. They'd go out drinking all the time, go out for dinner.'

"'Kelly kept asking Hayes to get him some cocaine, and Bob said, "Cocaine? I don't do cocaine. Forget it."'

"I know Bob didn't do much dope, because we had those conversations. Bob was a boozer. And Bob was the kind of guy who would slough anything off, even stuff he didn't mind doing. But finally the guy nailed him down, and Bob said, 'All right.' And at that time there were a lot of black clubs in South Dallas near the Cotton Bowl. I went to a couple of them with Willie Townes, and there was cocaine around. What Bob did was drive down there, park in the parking lot, go in, and come out with a tinfoil-wrapped gram of cocaine.

"Now the guy got Bob to go back to his apartment and sit in front of a one-way mirror, while the guy wrote Bob a check for the cocaine. And God knows what that really was in the tinfoil wrapper. And Bob took the check, and the guy says, 'Now, can you get me $50,000 worth?' And Bob laughed. Bob said, 'I can't get you anything,' and the next morning the guy put him under arrest.

"Bob was no longer playing football. Nobody would help him, except for Roger Staubach. He quickly ran out and got Racehorse Haynes' partner, Phil Burleson. Hayes felt that since he was out of football and no longer had money, Burleson just treated his case like it was another cocaine deal and plea-bargained him out.

"So instead of a defense of entrapment, what Bob ended up with was Landry going down, Staubach going down, several of the players going down and speaking as character references. That was his defense. He was no longer playing for them. He'd gone to San Francisco to play for Dick Nolan for a while. And that was it. That was separate from the Cowboys altogether. That was one of those where once you're out of the game, life kills you."

Chapter 52

Two Number Ones

After a disappointing 8–6 season in 1974, followed by the defection of star running back Calvin Hill to the World Football League, the Cowboys' future looked even bleaker when in mid-June veteran back Walt Garrison suffered a career-ending leg injury in a rodeo competition in Bozeman, Montana. The 30-year-old Garrison was competing in the National Intercollegiate Rodeo Association steer wrestling championship when he dropped from his galloping horse onto the steer.

He landed too far forward and as a result put too much weight on the animal's head, and both rolled onto the arena floor. Garrison did not get up. He underwent an operation to repair a ligament in his left knee. He had been bulldogging since he was 12, and it was the first time he'd ever gotten hurt doing it.

When contacted, Garrison told reporter Bob St. John, "I'm not going to kill myself. You know, it's a long time till the end of the world."

If there was any good news for the Cowboys, it was that the WFL seemed to be folding, as Tex Schramm had predicted all along. Schramm had said that the league didn't have enough millionaire owners, and he bitched that their salary structure was too high. As a result of the WFL's weakness, the NFL could breathe a sigh of relief when in May 1975, 65 NFL players, including Joe Namath, became free agents. Those players knew that because of the Rozelle Rule, no other team would sign them. But with the rumblings that the WFL was on shaky financial footing, few left the NFL. Several Cowboys, including D. D. Lewis and Pat Toomay, had been considering the WFL but were at a crossroad when the new league threatened bankruptcy.

Lewis had signed to play with the Memphis Grizzlies in 1975 and Toomay with Birmingham, but when Birmingham announced it was broke, Toomay refused to report. The day before Lewis was to report to the Memphis Grizzlies, he was paid $5,000 by the Grizzlies to get out of the contract. Had he reported the next day, the Memphis team would have been obligated to pay him another $40,000, the second half of their signing bonus. Said Lewis, "They didn't want to pay my salary. They also wanted to trade me to Philadelphia, but I had a no-trade clause. I didn't want to go."

The Cowboys were delighted.

The joy over retaining D. D. Lewis was short-lived, though, because three outstanding veterans—center Dave Manders, defensive back Cornell Green, and Hall of Fame lineman Bob Lilly—announced they were retiring. The praise for Lilly came in volumes. Said Tom Landry, "Bob was the best lineman I ever saw. He combined great strength with quickness. It was kind of uncanny the things he did. Two or three men blocking him every play, and he still goes in and traps the passer." Said Roger Staubach, "He's the only player I ever remember who, when we'd watch our defensive films, other guys would ooh and aah and talk about what he did."

If the Cowboys were going to improve, they would have to depend on their draft choices. Schramm had once again displayed his brilliance in his trade of quarterback Craig Morton to the New York Giants. The Giants had been slogging along under Norm Snead and wanted better, particularly Morton, and so Schramm was able to extract from Giants owner Wellington Mara their first pick in the 1975 draft. Morton's problem with the Giants was that the New York line was a sieve, and so the immobile Morton spent much of his time on his back as the Giants finished at the bottom of the NFL, along with the Baltimore Colts, a team crashing under the yoke of one of the new breed of pro sports owner/tyrants, Bob Irsay.

Baltimore and New York flipped a coin to see who would get the first pick, and Baltimore won. Baltimore then traded its pick to the Atlanta Falcons so that the Falcons could draft quarterback Steve Bartkowski from California. Because of the Morton deal, the Cowboys had the next pick, and they selected the best defensive player in the draft, Randy White of the University of Maryland. White was large and mobile and was one of the strongest men in the world. He could bench-press 475 pounds. He was so strong, his nickname was "Manster"—half man, half monster. In games he was known for his great intensity, charging hard from the first play to the last, close game or not. The only question was whether White would be better at linebacker, which was Landry's inclination, or at down lineman, which was what line coach Ernie Stautner wanted. Either way, White looked like a solid addition to the Cowboys defense.

Lee Roy Jordan: "I liked Randy right off. I thought he was going to be a great middle linebacker because you knew he was going to be a great something. He had all the tools and attitude, the work ethic, and toughness—he had all of it. But he had been playing down lineman, and he just couldn't quite get used to the steps from a standing position, and that frustrated him, because he wasn't able to compete and play. He played on all the kicking teams, and he probably didn't think he was going to take my job the first year. He thought it would take a year or two, but he was frustrated that he couldn't play more than just the kicking teams and on some special defenses we had put together that had him as a standup linebacker."

In addition to Randy White, the Cowboys still had their own first-round draft choice, and they used it to pick a small-college defensive standout, a tall, powerful, extremely quick linebacker by the name of Thomas Henderson from Langston University, 35 miles north of Oklahoma City.

Before he was drafted, few had even heard of Thomas Henderson, but when he reported in July, he grandly announced he was after D. D. Lewis' job. Trumpeted the rookie, "I'll tell you, I'm going to make him that much better a player . . . that is, if he sticks. All I can say is I'm after that job and may the best man win."

Henderson made it clear he would not be like the usual rookie. He was his own man, and he would bow down to no man, not even Tom Landry. Henderson had had to grow up quickly. At 12 he saw his mother gun down and seriously wound his stepfather with a .22 rifle. He saw his best friend die after an accidental shooting. A survivor, he decided to get out of Austin before he, too, was dead. Over his mother's objections, he moved to Oklahoma City to live with his mother's estranged stepmom, found a job, became a high school football star, and even after none of the big universities recruited him, he persevered, walking on at the local all-black college, Langston University, where he became an All-American. He was named NAIA All-America his junior year along with Ed "Too Tall" Jones and Walter Payton. He had made it—on his own.

Thomas Henderson: "I can remember the day after they drafted me, there was a picture in the paper of Landry shaking hands with Randy White, the other number one. I saw it, and I understood it, and it pissed me off. I understood he was the first player picked, and it was customary for the owner or the head coach to take a photograph with the number one draft choice. But in this year they had *two* number one draft choices, so I felt Landry slighted me. Here again, I didn't feel racism. I felt pissed off. I was pissed off that they had traded Craig Morton to the Giants and gotten that second number one pick. Otherwise, I would have been the guy in the picture. Because I was their 18th pick that year. If not for the trade, I'd have been *the* guy. So there were several things happening there, but again, it's important that I didn't think racism. I just thought it was unfortunate. And when Landry picked a bunch of guys—white guys—to go to the College All-Star Game, but didn't pick me, I understood that, too. Landry was saying, 'Thomas Henderson comes from a small school. He needs to get all the work he can get here.' As a matter of fact, I thought he was smart to do it, because I was not ready or prepared to become a student of football. I just wanted to play.

"I disliked Landry's football system, because it is for disciplined players, and I was not a disciplined player. Whenever there was a concept that I saw that had restraint and that limited my ability to play the position, I balked at it, wouldn't do it.

"By my last season with the Cowboys, I contend that I was the hardest-working man in the franchise. I was playing defense, third-down defense, kickoffs, kickoff returns, punts, punt returns, field-goal rush, field-goal block. I was playing *everywhere* except offense. I remember Gil Brandt said to me one time after I asked him for a $250,000 salary, 'We don't even pay Roger Staubach $250,000.' I said, 'He doesn't work as much as I do.'

"There was one thing I liked about Landry. He taught me something. He said, 'When you keep your shoulders parallel to the line of scrimmage, you're the most powerful thing on the field.' So my little skinny 215-pound ass had to have every possible trick, and that was one of the great ones. And I used to knock 300-pound tackles and guards on their ass by squaring up to the line of scrimmage and just knocking the shit out of them.

"That was the thing he taught me that helped me. As a matter of fact, Landry would come out sometimes and try to give me instructions on how to play linebacker, and I'd say, 'But you never played linebacker, did you? I know how to do this. Why don't you go and talk to those defensive backs.' And the team would just die laughing.

"It never occurred to me to be afraid of Landry. It never occurred to me to take him as seriously as he thought he was."

Chapter 53

THE DIRTY DOZEN

In addition to first-round picks Randy White and Thomas Henderson in the 1975 draft, the Cowboys made other excellent choices, including linebacker Bob Breunig, defensive back Randy Hughes, center Kyle Davis, offensive linemen Herb Scott and Pat Donovan, fullback Scott Laidlaw, and punter Mitch Hoopes, all players who would help the team immediately. Of course, for them timing was everything. Any other year they would have had vets like Bob Lilly, Cornell Green, Pat Toomay, Calvin Hill, Bob Hayes, Walt Garrison, and Dave Manders in front of them. This year, Landry had to put aside his reluctance to play his dozen rookies. The Cowboys were depleted, and he needed these rookies badly.

In the exhibition season the Cowboys finished 2–4, giving little reason for optimism. But once the season began, the Cowboys defense gave glimpses of greatness, with Ed "Too Tall" Jones and a young lineman named Harvey Martin anchoring the line alongside the talented but little-noticed Larry Cole and the hulking Jethro Pugh, an outstanding player now free from the long shadow of Bob Lilly. Behind them were linebackers Lee Roy Jordan, D. D. Lewis, Dave Edwards, and Randy White. In the backfield were Mel Renfro, Cliff Harris, Charlie Waters, and Mark Washington, plus the rookies. Thomas Henderson played on all the special teams. He not only ran back kickoffs, but he was also on the field when the Cowboys kicked off and punted. Wherever he was, Henderson terrorized the other team. Throughout the training camp, he had seemingly refused to learn Landry's system, but his natural talent was immense.

In the season opener against the Los Angeles Rams, the Cowboys defense held the opposition to a lone touchdown in an 18–7 victory. The Rams, led by quarterback James Harris, could neither run nor pass. This new crew of defenders was, in short, awesome. Said Too Tall Jones, "I thought if we could win this one, that's it. We can win 11 or 12, if not all of them."

Lee Roy Jordan: "We had a great draft in 1975 and so we had a lot of young guys, people like Randy White, who we knew were going to be players. When we finally put Randy at defensive tackle, after about a day of watching him there, you knew that's where he was going to be.

"Thomas Henderson was brash. He was loud. Thomas was a very talented athlete. I always liked Thomas, admired him and respected him. But he had some other things that didn't fit too well. He didn't have much of a work ethic. His deal was he always had a slight injury. He didn't need to practice. He was one of those guys who had played on teams where he was so good if he was ready to play on game day, the coach was glad to let him play. But our program has always been one that if you didn't practice all week, or even part of the week, you didn't play on game day. Thomas certainly was talented enough to take anyone's place, but he didn't study, didn't learn what to do very well. He just thought it would be automatic that he would take D.D.'s job or my job or anybody else's job. I was always having to tell him what he would have to do to fit into the program as far as working and studying and learning his responsibilities as far as the secondary, as far as the defensive line.

"Those rookies renewed our enthusiasm after being out of the playoffs. We came back with a real committed attitude. We had a great off-season training program, and like myself, I was committed to 'Hey, I can compete for a few more years, and I want to do the best I can,' and the attitude we had with the young guys, Burton Lawless, those guys, 11 or 12 of them, and Randy Hughes on defense, Rolly Woolsey was a defensive back, so we had a number of good players come out of that draft."

Roger Staubach: "In '75 we started with a team that wasn't supposed to do a whole lot. We played the Rams the opening game of the year, and we made some big plays. Fortunately, I was healthy again at the start of the year, and Drew Pearson was in stride, and our defense fought and scratched, and so all of a sudden we were a team. It was the best year we ever had as a team the whole time I was with the Cowboys.

"We had these young guys, we had old guys, and we'd win games any way we could. In that Rams game, for example, I ran for over 100 yards. But it was a real team effort. The defense played well. We scrambled, and that became the way we played all year long. We fought and scratched and clawed together the whole year. Everybody pitched in, and as the year went on you could see the depth of these guys. 'Cause no one was sure what Randy White was going to do, they moved him around, and then all of a sudden he was at defensive tackle, and it became, 'Geez, this guy is something.' Thomas Henderson, Bob Breunig, Randy Hughes, Scott Laidlaw—as the season went on, these rookies got better and better."

The 1975 Cowboys won their first four games. Against the St. Louis Cardinals, Thomas Henderson had suffered a serious hip pointer just before halftime, and he could barely walk when special-teams coach Mike Ditka told him the Cowboys were going to open the second half with him running a double reverse on the kickoff.

"I don't know if I can," said Henderson.

"Can you go?" asked coach Jerry Tubbs.

Said Henderson gritting his teeth, "Yeah, I think I can run that sucker."

The Cards kicked deep to rookie Rolly Woolsey. Henderson faked as though he were blocking, then turned and doubled back. Woolsey had fumbled, confusing things further, and finally picked it up as Henderson ran toward him. At the 3-yard line, Woolsey made the transfer and ran to his right. Henderson went left and turned upfield. Ditka had set the blockers perfectly, and the Cards defenders fell one after the other. Randy White made the final hit, and Henderson completed his 97-yard run for a touchdown. After he crossed the end-zone line, he ran under the goal post and thrilled the Texas Stadium throng by dunking the ball over it.

Against the Giants, starting running back Charles Young badly sprained a toe, forcing Landry to play veteran Preston Pearson, who had been picked up during training camp from the world champion Pittsburgh Steelers on waivers. Pearson had walked the picket line wearing the "No Freedom, No Football" slogan, angering Steelers coach Chuck Noll so badly that Pearson was the final cut. Preston Pearson would turn out to be the needed piece of Landry's plan to turn this mystery team into surprise champions.

Roger Staubach: "Getting Preston Pearson on waivers from the Steelers was a big deal, a great move. That helped us a tremendous amount. Preston really brought a great ability out of the backfield to catch the football. And we really weren't a backfield-type passing team. Our passing game was oriented more downfield because back then you couldn't hit the receivers downfield, so people were going back deeper, and linebackers were going back in support, so you were dumping the ball off a lot. And Preston brought with him the ability to come out of the backfield and catch passes. Also, we went to the shotgun formation where we could use him. And Preston was the sort of receiver who could adjust well to the defense. He'd turn in when he was supposed to, so he really took a lot of pressure off Drew Pearson."

After a close loss to the Green Bay Packers, the Cowboys played the Philadelphia Eagles in Veterans Stadium. The Eagles hated the Cowboys and punished them physically on every play. It was an important test that the Cowboys passed, 20–17.

Drew Pearson: "Everybody had it in for us. And the reason they did was because of our arrogance. Not so much the Cowboys players on the field—we respected our opponent to the utmost, but it was what Tex Schramm was projecting for the Cowboys as a team. They saw coach Landry nicely dressed, wearing a tie, a hat on the sideline, and their coaches are in a coaching shirt, a little ugly green jacket. It was what we projected. We projected class. When we traveled, we wore ties. You don't think people recognized that? Sure they did. And if they recognized it, they were going to write about it, and they were going to tell about it. 'This team is class. They project the image of their coach. They wear ties on the road. And they do it this way, do it that way,' and a lot of people got tired of hearing that crap. They just got tired of hearing it. And our opponents used that to help psych themselves up, help motivate themselves to want to beat us. And that's why every time we played anybody, I don't care who it was, the worst team or the best team, they played us like it was their Super Bowl.

"We had to be ready for each and every opponent, and thank God, we were. Because we as players knew what we were. They saw Landry's system, coming out with the movement, the Flex defense, Drew Pearson running across the backfield back and forth. 'What is all this crap?' They felt all that stuff was unnecessary, and they thought we were trying to finesse our opponents and beat them that way, and so everyone labeled us as a 'finesse' team. And everybody we played always tried to intimidate us physically, and they found out that didn't work, because even though we did those type of things, football is not a finesse game. Basketball might be a finesse game, but football is not. We were still physical. But we were smart enough to take advantage of our physical qualities and try to make it easy for us."

The Eagles were leading 17–10 when Dallas took over on their own 33 with 3:50 remaining. Roger Staubach hit fullback Robert Newhouse coming out of the backfield for 18 yards, and gained 15 more when Eagles defensive back Bill Bradley slugged him late. The Cowboys were down to the Eagles' 31. This was the year Staubach and Drew Pearson were getting to know each other, and with time running out, the two were making up plays as they went along.

"What do you have?" asked Roger.

Pearson ran a curl but then altered the route when he saw Bradley and Cliff Brooks in his path. He cut inside and headed for the goal line, where Staubach hit him between the two furious Eagles defenders. The score was tied.

Dallas got the ball back on its own 40 with 35 seconds left. In that short time, somehow Staubach ran seven plays. The biggest was a second-and-10 from the Eagles' 45. With seconds left, Staubach lined up in the shotgun. Landry called a pass to a running back. Staubach changed it. He told Pearson to run a deep sideline route. Staubach let fly, and with Brooks and Randy Logan bumping him, Pearson leaped back for the ball, caught it, and stepped out of bounds. The brilliant reception allowed Toni Fritsch to kick the winning field goal. Said Landry, "I don't know how he got it, and I don't know how he got out of bounds."

After losses to the Washington Redskins and the Kansas City Chiefs, the Cowboys rebounded with wins against the New England Patriots and the Eagles.

The Cowboys were 7–3. In the locker room before the next game against the Giants, Lee Roy Jordan made a short, memorable speech to the rest of the team, reminding them that a lot of vets in the league had never gone to a Super Bowl. Erroneously, he cited Preston Pearson as an example. Pearson, in fact, had been there the year before with the Steelers and had been there once before with the Baltimore Colts. No matter. Lee Roy was making a point, and everyone was listening.

Lee Roy Jordan: "We'd hold team meetings at times during the year—just the team, not the coaches, and this was an opportunity where I felt I needed to impress on these guys that, 'Hey, a lot of guys were here 10, 12 years before we got an opportunity to go to the Super Bowl, and here are a lot of young guys who might get to go there the first time out of the chute.' And so I tried to impress on them how important it was to play hard every play, and the great thing about it, I was always challenging them. 'Hey, who's going to make the play this time?'

"And what I was trying to do was challenge them again this particular time. 'Many teams and many great players have never been to the Super Bowl. Here we are with a chance to be in the playoffs, an opportunity that we *can* do it this year.'"

Drew Pearson: "Lee Roy was that type of leader. We all respected him. He'd kick your ass if you didn't respect him. And if you didn't like him, he didn't care. And that's why he got respect. He wasn't trying to win friends or be favorites with certain players. He treated everyone the same, and hey, if you were sloughing off, he didn't care if you were the Pope. He'd let you know it. And not just verbally, sometimes physically. If he'd have to jack you in the corridor, throw you up against a locker, he would. And that's the way football was played back then. We were all for one and one for all, and we all had to be together."

The Cowboys won the game 14–3. Staubach hit tight end Jean Fugett with a 54-yard touchdown pass right down the middle of the field. It was third-and-ten, and Staubach called a hook-and-go, a surprise play that angered the Giants into calling it a "Mickey Mouse" play. After the game Giants defensive back Jim Steinke fumed, "That's something you might make up in the street." Little did Steinke realize that he had identified Roger Staubach's greatest asset: his ability to improvise heroically at crucial times.

All the scoring came in the first period, and time after time the Cowboys defense stifled Giants quarterback Craig Morton in his attempts to score against Lee Roy Jordan and his team of tormentors. Morton was sacked four times, and he threw three interceptions on this futile afternoon of work.

Lee Roy Jordan: "Morton never beat the Cowboys, not ever. We always felt we had the pass rush that could get to Craig, and if we didn't have it out of our front four, we would certainly put it into a blitz package. We were not a high-percentage blitz team, but we always looked for an opportunity to blitz a guy and make sure we got to him. And if that meant an all-out blitz, that's what we would do.

"And we sacked him four times. That was a game where we felt we could do that and certainly create some turnovers by speeding up his delivery of the football, if he got rid of it. And so we had three interceptions as well."

After a loss to the Cardinals, the Cowboys won their last two games, against the Washington Redskins and New York Jets. With the 31–10 win over the

Redskins, the Cowboys assured themselves of a playoff spot. Said Landry, "A 9–4 record is beyond my imagination."

In the next and final game, Landry's gang of old vets and young kids made it 10–4 with a 31–21 win against the New York Jets behind the quirky Clint Longley, who played to allow Roger Staubach's various injuries to heal before the playoffs. The Jets went out in front 14–0, but Longley brought the Cowboys back. With the score tied 14–14, Harvey Martin put a hit on Joe Namath that finished Namath and ended any chances of the Jets winning.

Chapter 54

Hail Mary

The Cowboys entered the 1975 playoffs as the Eastern Conference wild-card team behind the St. Louis Cards, who had won the division with an 11–3 record. The opening-round opponent was the Minnesota Vikings, the Central Division champions. Led by coach Bud Grant, the Vikings had streaked to a 12–2 record and were clear favorites to beat Dallas. Vikings quarterback Fran Tarkenton was rated the number one quarterback in the NFL, and fullback Chuck Foreman was one of the top backs in the league.

Drew Pearson: "When we got into the playoffs as a wild-card, we knew we had a chance then, because at that time, even though we had 12 rookies, by that time most of those rookies were pretty educated as to what was going on in the NFL.

"That first wild-card game we played the Vikings, in Minnesota, and they were a pretty good football team. I mean, *nobody* was expecting us to win. We went up there, of course confident we could win, but we also knew that this obstacle in front of us was pretty stout."

The Cowboys led in the third quarter by a field goal, but Tarkenton then led a 70-yard drive, capped by a 1-yard plunge by back Brent McClanahan.

The score was 14–10 Vikings with 1:51 left in the game and the Cowboys on their own 15. It appeared the Cowboys were going nowhere. With less than a minute left in the game, they had the ball fourth-and-16 on their own 25.

Roger Staubach: "We were doing just what we could do going into that last series. We were in a shotgun formation, and John Fitzgerald got hurt; he hurt his elbow, and Kyle Davis came in. We were fourth-and-16 from our own 25 because of bad snaps in the shotgun. And Drew had not caught a pass the whole game."

Drew Pearson: "Yeah, I was very frustrated, very disappointed. Even though this Vikings team was better than us, no question, we still had played them tough, even though we didn't play that well on offense—our defense played very well that day to hold them to 14 points. But our offense didn't play well at all, and that's where my frustration came, because when we were not playing well that's when I felt most frustrated, especially if I didn't get to contribute. I was thinking that I could make some plays. I was saying to Roger, saying to

Landry on the sideline, to the other coaches, 'Call my name. Call my number. I can make something happen.'"

Lee Roy Jordan: "It was amazing to look at that sideline. There were a lot of faces that showed they had about given up, but there were a lot of us who had been in games when we had come back before, and that was something about our team as a defense: we always felt we could get the ball back, and we knew if we got it back, Roger, given a chance, could do it. He had done it before. So what we were trying to keep up was the attitude that even though they had made some plays against us and moved the ball on us, we could still win. With seconds to go we were a long way from scoring a touchdown, but I knew we still had a chance."

Unlike the veteran Jordan, rookie Thomas Henderson was mentally packing his bags and heading for home.

Thomas Henderson: "During that last series I was sitting on the bench. We were so far away I was packing. I was packing out of my apartment. I was going to go back to Oklahoma City. I was sitting on the bench thinking, 'Give up. It's over. Can't wait to get out of this cold motherf***er. . . .' And so I stood up and walked over to the sideline."

Drew Pearson: "We had a long way to go, and I don't know why we should have had confidence, because we hadn't moved the ball very well all day. But when we started that last drive I got excited because Roger was asking me, 'What have you got? What can you get open on?'

"We didn't have time to get plays sent in from the sideline. We didn't have time to confer with people in the press box. We had to go *now*. It had to be feeling, gut-type things. So Roger asked me, 'What can you get open on?' Early in the drive we kept running these turn-ins. I had caught one turn-in, then a sideline pass, and then we got bogged down because John Fitzgerald's arm was hurting and he messed up the snap. John snapped the ball, and Roger fumbled it around, and after he recovered it for a loss, we had a fourth-and-16.

"Roger just asked me. He said, 'What can you get open on?' I said, 'I don't know, but we have to get enough for this first down.' So Roger said, 'Why don't you run a post-corner.' And he said, 'Make sure you run a good post to get Nate Wright to bite on that.' And the last thing he said coming out of the huddle was, 'Make sure you get enough for the first down.'

"I took it downfield running a post, and I could feel Nate on my shoulder, which was right where I wanted him. I gave him that little move like I was shifting to that next gear to go deep on a post, and that gave me what I needed to break outside, and Nate kind of swiveled on his turn, and by that time the ball was in the air. Roger threw this ball. This might have been the best pass of his career. I mean, he drilled this ball, and I ended up catching it going out of bounds for 22 yards, got hit as I was going out of bounds, but I still think I could have gotten my feet in if I didn't get hit. But because I was forced out, it was called a good catch. I was sliding across the ice there, and I later found out that a security guard from the Vikings came across and kicked me.

"But anyway, we got 22 yards on the play, got the first down."

Roger Staubach: "After we hit the fourth-and-16 Drew was tired. We were at the 50, and I said to him, 'Hey, what can you do?' He said, 'I'm too tired right now.' So I called a play and threw the ball to Preston Pearson, and he dropped it, which was good, really. We would have probably gotten off another play, but it would have been different. Anyway, he dropped it. There were 26 seconds left in the game."

Drew Pearson: "We had no timeouts. If Preston had caught it and they had tackled him and held him down, then we'd have eaten up significant time, valuable time off that clock. And we might not have gotten another play off, and even if we had, it would have been a desperation play."

Roger Staubach: "Drew came back to the huddle, and I said, 'Remember against the Redskins how you made that in-route? Why don't you try that move on Nate Wright and go deep?' And that's what he kinda did. We were trying to get him isolated on one guy [Wright] and let him jump for the ball. I wanted him to make that little in-route and hold that one safety [Paul Krause] there and break back out, and then release [go long] and stay right. I'd try to keep Paul Krause away from running over there. I told everyone to block, to give me some time."

Drew Pearson: "Our bread-and-butter play still was the deep turn, the 16 route, so we figured we could get Nate Wright to bite on that. Roger said, 'I'll pump Paul Krause to hold him in the middle,' so when I came out of my break, I'd be man-to-man with Nate Wright."

Roger Staubach: "What I did, I pumped Krause. Krause was the safety in the middle of the field. If he realized I was looking to throw the ball to Drew, he would have been running across the field, and he would have been there. In fact, if you see the film, he got to the play—late—and started to yell at the referee while Drew ran another five yards. But he got there late, so he wouldn't have affected the pass. But he could have made the tackle. That was a weird deal.

"When I threw it, I actually underthrew it a little bit, because I pumped and then I turned to throw. Drew had taken off down the sideline, and he actually came back and caught the thing underneath his arm."

Drew Pearson: "When I came out of my break, Nate Wright and I were even. He might have had a step ahead of me on the play, but when I looked back to try to find the ball, I saw it was underthrown, and I was able to do the swim move, to come over the top of Nate Wright, and when I was doing so, the ball was there, and it hit my hands, and I thought I had dropped it, but I was bent over, and the ball slithered through my hands and just stuck between my elbow and my hip, stuck right there, and I was as surprised as anybody that I had caught the football.

"Nate Wright fell on the play, and they said I pushed him. You know, there *was* contact. When I brought my arm around, there *was* contact. And that might have been what knocked him off balance. But there was never, ever any deliberate push or anything of that nature. How can you push somebody and make the catch at the same time? I'm not that good. But anyway, I was able to make the play and take it into the end zone for that touchdown."

Roger Staubach: "Drew says he didn't push Nate, that Nate kind of slipped. There is no angle to show he flagrantly pushed him. And to this day Nate Wright doesn't say Drew pushed or shoved him, though he *did* slip.

"After I threw the pass I got knocked down. It was an away game, and when I didn't hear any screaming, that was good. And then I saw some objects coming on the field. I thought they were flags, but they were oranges the fans threw on the field. The Super Bowl was in the Orange Bowl that year. I guess that's why they had the oranges there. But the place was just stone silent. It was the eeriest feeling I ever had in a stadium.

"So then all of a sudden I realized, 'God, he scored!'

"It got even eerier when a Vikings fan threw a whiskey bottle and hit the referee in the head.

"Here we were, this unknown bunch of new guys. The Vikings were a *really* good team. They thought that this was going to be their best team. And because the Vikings got beat, the Rams thought they had it made. We were just happy to get out of there. We couldn't believe it. It was like ecstasy."

Lee Roy Jordan: "It was an unbelievable reaction and feeling on the sideline when we saw Drew in the end zone and the official with his hands up. If he doesn't catch it, we go home. The season is over. And it would have been a great season at that, for this young team. We had been out of the playoffs the year before. We turned it around, came back, would have been a good season anyway. But not nearly as good as going on to the championship game in L.A."

Drew Pearson: "People ask me about the emotions of doing that. When it happens, you're just being a football player. You're just reacting. You don't realize what you've done until all the media surrounds your locker. You fly back to Dallas, and bam, there's hordes and hordes of people out at Dallas/Fort Worth Airport, and they can't wait to see you. As a matter of fact, my teammates, man, they made me get off the plane first to distract the crowds so they could go the opposite way: 'All they want to do is see you, Drew, so you go up there.' They made me get off the plane first. Everybody swarmed to me, and here I am, a couple years in the league, but I've never done anything like this. So it was nice. I was riding high. I was on cloud nine, very excited, couldn't sleep that night.

"I think the controversy surrounding the play, whether I pushed Nate Wright or not, because of that controversy, it keeps it alive. There never was a final chapter, because they don't think they should close the book on it because there is still discussion about it, so it's kept alive, and it's been exciting for me to be part of that now. It was exciting then, but even 20 years later, it's still exciting, and even though I made a lot of other significant catches throughout my career, that's the one people remember most, the one they want to talk about the most.

Even in business speeches, motivational speeches I give, I refer to that story. I refer to two stories actually: my rookie year when I caught that 83-yarder and how Roger had confidence to go to a rookie in that situation and then the Hail Mary, how the odds were against us and how if everybody sticks together, pulls together, you have a chance to overcome those odds, not guaranteeing you will, but at least you have a chance, and that's all you want.

"So those are the things. That play is what people associate Drew Pearson with more than anything. That play labeled me as a clutch receiver, labeled me as 'Mr. Clutch.'"

Chapter 55

Super Surprise

In the first preseason game of the 1975 campaign, the Los Angeles Rams had defeated the Cowboys in a rout, 35–7. Before the rematch for the National Football Conference title, Lee Roy Jordan told reporters, "I bet nobody thought we'd be back for the championship after that." Few experts had given the surprising Cowboys a chance. And now, with a trip to the Super Bowl in the balance, even fewer thought the Cowboys would succeed.

Drew Pearson: "We went out there to L.A. to play the Rams in the Coliseum. For championship games you have to go out there two days before, and we had to read in the press how we didn't even have a chance, and how the Rams were so prepared, and 'Get your Super Bowl tickets immediately following the game,' and all this kind of crap. We relished that role of being the underdog and not being taken seriously. Here's a team that comes in as a wild card, 12 rookies; we beat a great Vikings team, but look how we had to beat 'em. Everyone said, 'They're just lucky to be here.' And we could have easily said this was enough. Nobody expected us even to be in L.A. We could have easily rolled over and let them kick our ass. But man, we were on a mission. We wanted to win that football game, and all the negative talk kind of inspired us to go after them."

The hometown crowd in the Los Angeles Coliseum had little to cheer about. On defense, the Cowboys were spectacular. They didn't allow a single first down. They held star back Lawrence McCutcheon to 10 yards on 11 carries and sacked quarterback Ron Jaworski five times for minus-51 yards, as Too Tall Jones, Harvey Martin, Randy White, and Jethro Pugh led a pass rush that never let up all game long. Linebacker D. D. Lewis starred, making two interceptions, and Lee Roy Jordan, the play caller and motivator, orchestrated the Flex, which held the 12–2 Rams to but a single touchdown.

Lee Roy Jordan: "Drew's catch against the Vikings propelled us into a great frame of mind. Everyone was really high during practice for the game against the Rams. We had a level of confidence that was just unbelievable, and God, we went to that Rams game high. We believed our defense was really going to do a job on their offense—and we did. And we created some plays, too, some turnovers that helped us."

Though he was "only" a special-teams player, one of the defensive standouts was rookie Thomas Henderson, who punished the Rams with his mouth *and* his body. The play that really set the Rams off took place on the opening kickoff, when Henderson clobbered the Rams kicker, Tom Dempsey. Few would have noticed had it been any other kicker, but Dempsey was born with a withered arm and a deformed foot. Dempsey played with a prosthesis made of metal for his right foot, and with it he once kicked a 63-yard field goal, the longest in NFL history. Special-teams coach Mike Ditka wanted to make sure Dempsey wouldn't be a factor. He enlisted Henderson in his quest.

Dempsey dropped his head to look at the ball and kicked off. Henderson raced down the field and hit Dempsey in the chin with his helmet before he had time to look up. Said Henderson, "He went down like he was dead."

Lee Roy Jordan: "Thomas didn't have mercy on a lot of people. 'Hey, if you're a player, you're a player, man. No matter whether you have short toes or not.'"

Dempsey's later kickoffs were short. And in the third quarter when Dempsey lined up to kick a field goal, Henderson yelled for the Rams to hear, "I'm gonna take Dempsey *out*!" He blocked the kick.

On offense, Roger Staubach threw four touchdown passes, the only time he ever did that. Three went to Preston Pearson, who time after time beat Rams linebackers for big gains. Pearson finished the game with seven catches for 123 yards. The running game was good enough. Fullback Robert Newhouse, who ran for 930 yards during an outstanding season, rushed 16 times for 64 yards. Staubach himself ran the ball for 54 yards, running like an experienced halfback. Toni Fritsch had three field goals. In all, the Cowboys rolled up 37 points.

Roger Staubach: "It was the most perfect football game we ever had as Cowboys. Everything we executed worked. We had the shotgun, used the shovel pass, everything I threw seemed to have eyes. I threw three touchdown passes to Preston and one to Golden Richards. It was just one of those games where everything worked perfectly, and the Rams were shocked. They were a *very* good team. We were *big* underdogs. We beat them 37–7."

Drew Pearson: "They had called our offense 'rinky-dink,' but we blew them out. We beat the Rams 37–7. We kicked their ass, man. At halftime we felt like we were going to the Super Bowl, and that was a damn good feeling.

"We had a great game plan on offense. I wasn't included very much in it, which I expected, and we expected them to pay a lot of attention to me after that Hail Mary, and that's what opened up Preston, and made him the go-to guy in this game. They disparaged our shotgun, but it eventually was that shotgun that blew them away, 'cause they couldn't cover it. They couldn't cover it all day. And they certainly couldn't cover Preston. They stopped some things. We didn't run very well against them, but we really didn't have to. Roger was on, and Preston was on, and that's what we rode on into the Super Bowl, and we needed that Super Bowl that year because if we didn't get there that year, it might have been quite some time before we even got close again. So that was a big victory for us, to get us into that Super Bowl."

The Cowboys' opponent in Super Bowl X was the Pittsburgh Steelers, a powerful defensive team that was back for its second year in a row. Pittsburgh had defeated Minnesota in Super Bowl IX by a score of 16–6. That the Steelers could hold Fran Tarkenton to six points was a testament to the defense's quickness. "Mean" Joe Greene, Ernie Holmes, Dwight White, and L. C. Greenwood were a formidable front line, and middle linebacker Jack Lambert was a wild man in the mold of Dick Butkus.

Upon the urging of special-teams coach Mike Ditka, the Cowboys game plan began with a surprise. Though Thomas Henderson was a linebacker, he could run the 40 in 4.5. Against the Cardinals on a reverse he had run a kickoff back 97 yards for a touchdown, and before the game Ditka explained to the rookie that he was to do it again. For one of the few times in his life, Thomas Henderson had butterflies.

Thomas Henderson: "I think Landry didn't want me to. Landry was very, very concerned that a linebacker was handling the ball. I think Ditka had to live with the decision. Someone told me this: Landry didn't want me handling the ball. He liked the results, but he was always nervous about a linebacker handling the ball, which is a legitimate concern.

"Let me tell you about how I was feeling before that game. You're talking about a guy who was nine years from witnessing his mother shooting his stepfather with a gun, just six years from his best friend getting shot at close range and dying, just a year out of Langston University. I had played that season in the NFL and had run for a touchdown. But to be in the Super Bowl . . .

"And I'd already wrapped up. I got elbow pads on, and all this extra padding, hand pads, got pads everywhere, because I'm going to be kicking butt on these special teams. And Ditka came over to me after we warmed up and came back in and he said, 'If we win the toss, we're going with the reverse.' And of course, I had to take all that shit off. I had to put stickum on. It scared me to death. It was like, 'Geez, you're going to let me handle the f***ing ball the first f***ing play of the Super Bowl?' I mean, there were times in my life when I've been afraid. This was the first stage fright I ever had—because of the pressure. Again, I agreed with Landry at that moment. I'm a linebacker. Jesus Christ, give the f***ing ball to somebody else. But, on the other hand, 'Give me the f***ing ball. Let's go.' 'Cause I was a running back in high school, in my early days, I knew how to run.

"They kicked it off, and I had to fake my little deal, and Preston Pearson took it deep, and I had to go around. I was standing on the 30-yard line, and I had to go back to him at about the 10. He started my way, and I went his way. He gave it to me, and I took it the other way, and a wall set up. When I turned the corner, everything looked pretty good, except the Steelers weren't quite as fooled as the

Cardinals had been. At some point, I thought I could have cut back. I figured, 'If I cut back, I don't know. . . . '

"I'll tell you what I did: I ran the play the way it was designed, not freelance and make something happen. Ditka was like that. He didn't like you to go out there and start doing your own tap dance. 'No ad-libbing, goddamn it.'

"So I ran the play the way it was designed, which was better for me. And they were very pleased. The only Steeler who could have stopped me was the kicker, Roy Gerela, and I was going to see if Gerela could stop me. I was going to see if I could run over him. If I could run *over* him, I could score."

Henderson couldn't run over him, and the two tumbled out of bounds on the Steelers' 43-yard line. When Gerela was untangled from the collision, he had broken ribs that affected his kicking the rest of the game. Henderson's 48-yard run was the longest kickoff return in Super Bowl history, and it gave the Cowboys great field position for the first set of downs. A 29-yard touchdown pass from Staubach to Drew Pearson gave the Cowboys a lead they would be able to hold until the final period.

What Cowboys fans remember about that game was the brutality of the Steelers and the refusal of the referees to curb it. For the entire game the Steelers defenders were holding, punching, and elbowing Drew Pearson and Golden Richards, who finally had to leave the game battered and bruised.

Drew Pearson: "Their whole MO going into the game was to be physical, be intimidating. Again we had to live down that finesse image, not being a physical football team, and that was pretty much the Steelers' style anyway, so they were pretty much playing the way they normally play. They wanted to be extra physical and not take anything from us, and if it was any kind of talk or arguing, they weren't going to stand for that, they were going to put their hand in your face, and try to intimidate you, and little extra stuff after the play.

"Even though they were being physical, they weren't intimidating us. They broke Golden Richards' ribs. They spit on him throughout the game.

"I'm not saying they didn't intimidate *all* of us, because they did intimidate a couple of our players. I wouldn't call any names, but it was very evident that certain guys just didn't want to go out there."

Roger Staubach: "The Steelers were tough. That was probably the best team we ever played. Their defensive team, I think, was the best defense that's ever played in the NFL. And they intimidated us. They kicked Preston Pearson when he was down, and our team didn't react where they should have.

"I screamed at Jack Lambert, calling him every name in the book when I saw Lambert kick Preston. But we didn't retaliate against him. We let him get away with that, so they won the war of intimidation."

Lee Roy Jordan: "I still don't think they beat us because they intimidated us. I feel like we were very competitive with them. As a young football team we just made some mistakes in the secondary, where we had them in a tough position, and we made mistakes and they made big plays."

Despite the Steelers' rough play, the Cowboys led 10–7 going into the final period. Great players win important games, and after a safety on a blocked punt and two Roy Gerela field goals, the Steelers seemingly put the game away when receiver Lynn Swann made a sensational 64-yard touchdown reception on a pass from Terry Bradshaw. That Swann was even in the game was remarkable. Two weeks before he had suffered a concussion playing against the Oakland Raiders. He had bleeding in his brain, and after the bleeding finally stopped his timing was off in workouts and he was dropping passes. In the days before the game Swann was not sure whether his presence in the lineup was a good idea.

But in the final minutes against the Cowboys, Lynn Swann was the difference. His touchdown with 3:02 remaining gave the Steelers a 21–10 lead. Swann finished with 161 yards on the day, a Super Bowl record.

Thomas Henderson: "Lynn Swann was one of the great receivers off the ground. He loved to jump. Because he was a long jumper in college. And it just seemed like he loved to jump, and Bradshaw *loved* to throw it up for him to go get. And he made some great catches. He had great concentration. That catch he made against Mark Washington [in the second quarter, when he went high in the air to grab the ball away from the defensive back], that was something."

The Steelers held their 21–10 margin with only three minutes left in the game.

Drew Pearson: "We almost came back to win. We got behind, and then we started to open things up. That's what we should have been doing the whole game. 'Cause if you become conservative against that Steelers defense, you're playing right into their hands. But if you play like you're in a frenzy, then you got a chance to beat those guys, because maybe they'll make a mistake somewhere along the line. They were so seasoned and so well schooled in their defense, had such an understanding of the personnel around them on both offense and defense, they very seldom made mistakes, and even if they made one, someone was there to cover up. They had a *great* team. There is no question going into that game, we knew they were the better team, but we felt we were the team of destiny that year, and we felt because of that, it gave us a lot of confidence that we could beat them."

Roger Staubach: "We started on the 20. We had a tight end offense going into that game, which really hurt us, too, because in the second quarter Jean Fugett pulled up lame, and that was a big factor in that game as far as what we were trying to do. The Steelers had a double-coverage-type deal on Drew and Golden.

"We were trying to figure out a way to get Drew and Golden open. They were a big, physical team. They had big cornerbacks who hit our backs downfield, and if a receiver went inside, the rule was you could hit him as long as the ball wasn't in the air. You could hit him 20 yards downfield. Mel Blount and Glen Edwards were really killing our wide receivers, to the point where they hurt Drew and seriously hurt Golden Richards. His ribs were banged up, so Percy Howard had to come in. And I finished the drive with a 34-yard touchdown to the Bird. That's what we called Percy. It was the only pass Percy ever caught with the Cowboys.

"After we got the ball back again there were 12 seconds left in the game when I threw Percy a pass that would have won the game: he went down the right side, and he was jumping to catch the ball—he was a big basketball player—but he was interfered with in the end zone, but the refs just weren't going to call it. The Steelers didn't have a single penalty called against them in that game. The defensive back just pulled him down by his shoulders. And the ball was right there. He could have had another one, and it would have been one of the most *unbelievable* stories of football. Percy could have had two touchdown passes to win the Super Bowl, the only two passes he ever caught! We came very close, but it wasn't to be.

"And even at the end we had a shot to win it. We played a very good football game against a really, very great football team. That Super Bowl was a tough one, but we did have a shot."

Drew Pearson: "The last play of the game was another Hail Mary to me. Roger threw it up as far as he could, and I ran down the field as fast as I could. I wanted to go up between the three guys who were back there, who eventually converged on the football, and my first thought was to go up and try to outleap them and come away with the football, but if that didn't happen, then I was going to try to make a reaction off the football once it was hit up, try to find it and make the catch. But there wasn't any Hail Mary in that script.

"They were looking for me on that play. They were laying back already for that. Glen Edwards picked that one off."

The Cowboys lost 21–17 in what was billed as the most exciting Super Bowl game ever.

Drew Pearson: "Turnovers cost us that football game. It wasn't anything else. Turnovers and a couple of great catches by that other No. 88, Lynn Swann. He was well covered on a couple of plays, and he just made fantastic Super Bowl–type catches, the kind of catches you dream about making in a Super Bowl. So he made them, and that hurt us more than anything—that and the turnovers. But other than that, I thought we played them head-up."

Said Landry about this Cowboys team, "This was the best group I've had from the standpoint of character, morale, spirit, and teamwork. They're the type who give you your greatest reward from coaching, who really make it enjoyable."

Chapter 56

Roger's Ordeal

Quarterback Clint Longley thought of himself as an outlaw. Born in Wichita Falls, Texas, on July 28, 1952, Longley was the son of a career IRS executive. After his family moved to a small town in Colorado, he had a desultory high school career because the coach featured a running game, but Longley returned to Texas to attend Abilene Christian College, where he became a small-college All-American. His senior year he threw 28 touchdown passes and gained 3,167 yards leading his team to an undefeated season and an NAIA championship.

He became known as the "Mad Bomber" because he loved to throw long. He had talent, but some wondered about his common sense. One time Clint went out into the Abilene brush and with a forked stick captured a bucketful of rattlesnakes. He interrupted a meeting of his coaches when he walked in and dumped them out on the floor. Clint thought it uproariously funny as the coaches scrambled to tabletops to avoid the snakes.

After Clint joined the Cowboys he continued to see himself as a rebel. He told reporter Bob St. John, "I like the Western movies and things like that. I like guns, the six-shooters. My uncle was Bill Longley. He was an outlaw who ran around with John Wesley Hardin. Only he didn't live very long. They hanged him for stealing a horse. I wouldn't have liked that part."

Longley also pictured himself as an NFL star. During the few times coach Landry had let him play, he had been electrifying, throwing long touchdown passes in Cowboys victories. But Landry demanded his players be disciplined, that they do things his way and not freelance. Landry wanted team players, not outlaws, and by 1976 the difference between Longley's dreams and reality began to take a toll on his psyche.

At the start of the 1976 training camp, Longley announced, "I'm going for number one." But by the end of the 1976 training camp not only wasn't Longley number one, he wasn't sure he was even number two. The Cowboys had signed Danny White, formerly a star at Arizona State and a refugee from the World Football League, and White, like Staubach, was a highly disciplined athlete, the kind favored by Landry. White didn't have as strong of an arm as Longley did, but he showed he could move the offense. Longley might have been as talented as Danny White, but he became the odd man out, and his resentment grew.

Drew Pearson: "You could see the tension between Clint and Roger. Roger tried to get to know Clint and bring him around, but Clint was very much against that, and I think Roger had a problem with that, because I don't think he ever had a teammate who didn't like him. But Clint didn't like him. Clint didn't like Danny. Clint didn't like coach Landry. He didn't like those guys. That's just the way it was. They were just different from him, and they tried to make him change, and because of that, he didn't like them, and so Clint always was doing things the opposite of what should have been done.

"This one day we were working out in training camp after practice. I must have run 100 routes all through practice in the two and a half to three hours we were out there. Now we had to run more, so I was a little pissed off anyway, and Clint was pissed off because he had to be out there, and I ran a quick out, five yards and out, and Clint threw it over my head. He did it on purpose.

"I said something to him: 'I'm not going to run any more routes for you if you're not going to throw the ball right.' And Roger said something to him, and that ignited it. When I said something back at Clint, Clint said something derogatory toward me, like, 'Screw you'—for lack of a better word—'you skinny-leg mother huh huh,' and Roger heard it, and he said, 'What? You're the one who's wrong.' Clint wanted to fight right there, but Roger said, 'I'll fight you down the hill.' And they went down the hill. They walked over there, and we were standing there watching. And the next thing you know, I saw Clint's feet up in the air, and Roger slamming him to the ground. And the fight was over.

"It was so funny, man. Clint's feet were straight up in the air. I don't know what Roger did. He put one of them Vietnam holds on him, that kung fu fighting. Next thing you know, Clint was down and his feet were up in the air.

"Roger came back, but he wasn't going to brag about nothing like that. He was more embarrassed about that than anything. But the media saw it. They jumped all over that, and so the next day in the paper it said 'Roger Staubach Wins Round One.' And Clint Longley didn't think he had lost the fight, so he was furious. He was going to get back at Roger.

"The next day when Clint decided to get revenge on Roger, it was a beautiful day, another day in paradise in Thousand Oaks. Another day you regretted having to go to practice because it was so beautiful. We were preparing for the afternoon practice, and everything was going as normal. What was abnormal was finding Clint sitting in the locker room. The quarterbacks and kickers and punters are usually the first ones to hit the practice field, so it was unusual for Clint to be there. That was a very unusual day, a very eerie situation because Clint was there, sitting in the locker room, waiting. He had his pants on, no socks, a little half T-shirt, and he was sitting there kind of bent over, his foot on the brace of the chair flicking up and down nervously, and he was supposed to be out on the field. That was kind of strange to see him just sitting there and not really talking to anybody, just staring straight ahead. I came by and said, 'Clint, you need to go out there.' He didn't say anything, didn't respond.

"Roger wasn't there yet, because he had an engagement in town, but we did not notice that as anything unusual because since we didn't see him, we thought he was already out on the practice field. When Roger arrived, he was late getting to practice, so he was rushing and hurrying, and he had put on his pants real fast, and he started to put his shoulder pads on, and I didn't see him because I had gone to the back part of the locker room, but I heard the rumbling, the tremendous commotion. And then I ran in to see what was happening, and I saw Roger and Clint really going at it on the concrete floor of the locker room, and there was blood all around, and I found out later the blood was the result of Clint's initial attack on Roger. When Roger got his pads over his head, he couldn't use his arms, and that's when Clint decked him. Roger was caught off balance and went flying back onto the scale that was there for us to weigh in and weigh out before and after each practice, and he was falling backward, and he turned, and as he turned, his head hit the scale, and blood went gushing everywhere. These two guys were grappling in the middle of the locker room floor, and the space was limited.

"Everybody was trying to separate them and nobody could. They were grappling on the floor, and blood was just flying everywhere. It was a gusher coming out of Roger's head. Randy White went in there, and he was the one who separated them. He grabbed one and grabbed the other and pulled them apart. Roger was still very upset and was really trying to get back at Clint, and once Randy let Clint go, he grabbed his stuff out of his locker and was gone.

"Clint took off to the dorm, because apparently this was all premeditated, and he knew what the consequences were going to be, and he was packed up ready to go. I went outside to watch Clint, to make sure of what he was up to, make sure he didn't go get a gun, make sure he really was gone, because in training camp Clint had guns. From his dorm window he used to shoot at rabbits and anything else that came near the dorm all night long. He was crazy. You'd be sleeping and hear, 'Boom, boom, boom.' You'd think, 'That's just Clint.'

"As Clint was going out, Tom Landry was coming in. Clint walked past Landry and didn't say anything, and Landry could see Clint was all red, had blood on him, and I was the first person Landry came in contact with. He said, 'What happened?' I said, 'Clint jumped Roger, and Roger's in the training room.'

"The trainer came in and stopped the bleeding, and Roger said, 'I'm OK. I'm all right.' The guys were holding him back, and the trainer was holding a bandage to his head, and Roger said, 'I'm OK. I'm all right. Everything's fine.' So Randy let him go, the other guys let him go, and Roger, zoom, he took off. He started running toward the dorm to go get Clint. We had to damn near tackle Roger to stop him from going back over there.

"Landry of course couldn't believe what was going on, and of course that was the end of Clint Longley."

Roger Staubach: "In 1974, his rookie year, Clint didn't care that I was the starting quarterback ahead of him. He sat with me on all the team planes that year. He was like my buddy.

"And then in '76 Danny White came, and he [Longley] went to the third team, and then he quit talking to us. And I confronted him on that, and we got into a little skirmish in practice, and the next day he took the cowardly route out.

"If he really wanted to fight like a man, he could have come into my room and said, 'Hey, let's finish up what we started on the field,' which he didn't want to do. The thing the team understood was that he was a chickenshit guy.

"The thing about Clint, he really wasn't into learning the system. Danny White came in, and he knew the system better than Clint did. Danny was a good player, and Danny took his job as backup quarterback, and when Clint didn't play in the last exhibition game in '76, that's when Clint really went weird. And I've never seen him since."

After Longley's departure, Danny White stepped in for Staubach as needed, and the Cowboys didn't miss a beat in winning their first six games. The offense scored consistently, despite a subpar running game, and the Doomsday Defense was solid, behind the front wall of Ed Jones, Harvey Martin, Jethro Pugh, and Larry Cole.

After a loss to the Cards, the team flew to Chicago to play the Bears. Early in the second quarter Staubach ran four yards for a touchdown. As he reached the end zone, defensive back Virgil Livers' helmet collided with Staubach's right hand, which held the ball. Staubach played the rest of the second quarter, but the hand began to swell and hurt. X-rays at halftime revealed a fractured hand. Danny White came in and threw two touchdown passes in a 31–21 win. The team's record ran to 6–1.

Staubach returned against Washington and had his passing hand stepped on, which led to a sore arm. Staubach could not pass effectively the rest of the year. Before the injury he was passing at 70 percent. After it, it was under 50 percent. With both Robert Newhouse and Preston Pearson hobbled by injury, the offense had to struggle the rest of the season.

After beating the Buffalo Bills 17–10, the team record stood at 9–1, but there was considerable dissension on the team. Coach Landry had praise only for O. J. Simpson, the outstanding Bills running back. Blaine Nye complained about the performance of the offensive line. Ralph Neely complained about the running game.

Drew Pearson: "Our standards of performance were always, I think, too high. But that's OK, because we always worked to try to strive for that. Expectations were high. The year before we were in the Super Bowl, and of course, when we blew everybody away at the start of the season, and then Roger hurt his hand, that's when we started having trouble offensively, because all you have to do is look at the numbers. We scored only 17 points on Buffalo, and then we lost to Atlanta, scoring 10, had only 19 points in a win over St. Louis, scored 26 to beat Philly, oof, we really did have a rough hoe. We lost the final game to Washington to finish 11–3, but that was a tough year for us, no doubt."

Roger Staubach: "In '76 we started out winning on big plays. I was having the best year I ever had. The passing game was just going crazy. But we were relying on it. Robert Newhouse was banged up a little bit; Preston pulled a stomach muscle. And then I broke my finger against the Bears, and after I was hurt, the passing game faltered, and we limped into the playoffs and lost to the Rams."

The opening playoff game was against the Los Angeles Rams. The Cowboys led 10–7 going into the fourth quarter. A last-minute touchdown plunge by Lawrence McCutcheon beat them.

Drew Pearson: "We were at home. Everything was in our favor. We should have beat them. We were just having a bad time. We were not able to come out of a negative December and turn it into a positive through the playoffs. We struggled through the second half of the season, and when the playoffs hit, we didn't have that momentum going in. The Rams were a team we should have beat. It was just disappointing, because the Rams were looking for a measure of revenge, because we had beaten them in a championship game the year before. They came in fired up, but still, losing 14–12, to give only 14 points and lose . . . the defense was playing very well. The offense . . ."

Roger Staubach: "I was so frustrated by the first-round loss to the Rams, I went to Landry to suggest a trade. I felt personally responsible for the team getting beat—and all because of that little finger of mine. I was in a highly emotional state.

"Landry told me, 'That's crazy. The team had problems with its running game, and you were injured. You played well under the circumstances. We just didn't have much support in other areas.'"

Harvey Martin: "We simply had no running game, and being forced into passing on every down rendered Roger less effective.

"One player, I moaned to myself, just one running back, and we'd be the best damn team God ever gave breath to."

Chapter 57

TD

On February 18, 1977, the NFL entered a new age as the league and the players signed to a new basic agreement that increased the likelihood of free agency and much higher salaries. Under the five-year pact, the Rozelle Rule was officially dead. The only compensation for signing a free agent could be a draft pick or two.

A month later Tex Schramm and Gil Brandt again proved their ability to keep the Cowboys franchise well armed when they traded four draft choices to the Seattle Seahawks for the second pick of the draft, University of Pittsburgh running back Tony Dorsett, a three-time college All-American. Dorsett had led Pitt to a 12–0 record and, after becoming the first college runner ever to run for over 6,000 yards, was awarded the Heisman Trophy.

The first pick in the draft, selected by the Tampa Bay Buccaneers, one of the worst franchises in the history of the NFL, was Ricky Bell. The trade with Seattle had been contingent on Tampa Bay taking Bell, not Dorsett.

Shortly after the Bucs announced their choice of Bell, Schramm marched hard into the pressroom of the Cowboys offices on the 11th floor of Expressway Towers by the Central Expressway with a blue and white jersey tucked under his arm.

"Gentlemen," he announced to the 50 or so reporters in the room, "I don't have our draft choice here with me, but I do have his jersey." He drew it across the back of a chair. The shiny blue letters read D-O-R-S-E-T-T above the No. 33. A few reporters chuckled, figuring it was a joke Tex was playing, an indication of his wistfulness. Soon it was clear he was serious.

The Cowboys had traded their first pick and three second-round picks for Dorsett. One of the picks had been obtained when they exiled Pat Toomay, another when they discarded Clint Longley. The Seattle draft picks turned into guard Steve August, tackle Tom Lynch, linebacker Terry Beeson, and, after making other trades, center Geoff Reese and receiver Duke Fergerson.

Seattle general manager John Thompson said he was pleased with the deal. Sure he was. He wasn't going to have to give his top draft choice $1 million, as Dallas did. The year before Seattle could have had Chuck Muncie but instead let New Orleans pay the freight. It settled on Steve Niehaus, a defensive tackle, instead.

A grinning Tex Schramm immediately praised Seattle for stocking its fine team and then returned to the truth when he crowed that Dorsett was the best running back to come along since O. J. Simpson. He was, in fact, the most dangerous Cowboys offensive threat since Bob Hayes.

Said a furious Bud Grant, coach of the Minnesota Vikings, "Dallas and Seattle must be sleeping together. I don't understand it at all." Insightful Baltimore Colts general manager Ernie Accorsi said, "The Cowboys got themselves a Hall of Famer for four draft choices."

When Dorsett arrived at the Dallas camp, the other players saw his flair. He drove a midnight black Porsche and wore a full-length mink. He gravitated to the North Dallas night spots, looking for pretty girls, white or black, and he wasn't in town a week when he learned something about being black in Southern society. At the Number 3 Lift, a disco bar, the bouncer, unhappy that this well-dressed black man wearing sunglasses was seeking entry, began baiting him. He was stopped and carded. He produced plenty of identification, but no ID satisfied the bouncer. The bouncer told Dorsett he didn't like the fact that he was wearing sunglasses at night. After the bouncer finished getting his jollies at Dorsett's expense, he finally allowed Dorsett inside.

Once there, the bartender continued the race-baiting. It was ladies' night, and Dorsett wanted to dance with white women, and the bartender told him straight out that he didn't want him coming around on ladies' night.

The bartender then accused Dorsett of not paying for the drink that sat in front of him. He had, in fact, paid, but Dorsett realized that what the bartender was insinuating was that because he was black, he was stealing something, and it made him furious.

The bartender then asked him to leave the bar area, saying he was in the way of the waitresses. The guy was quoted as saying, "Well, we don't want you standing here anyway. Get away right now." Dorsett indignantly refused to budge. The bartender then picked up his drink and walked it to the other end of the bar.

"I couldn't understand why he was telling me this," said Dorsett. Finally, Dorsett told him, "If you want me to move, you'll have to come over and move me."

The bartender then came around the bar to get him. Dorsett slugged him. The bartender began calling him foul names, including racial epithets.

The cops came, and Dorsett was charged with assault, though the charges were later dropped.

It had not been this way in Pittsburgh. In that city, where he was more famous than the mayor, he was accepted anywhere, including the ethnic neighborhoods. He found it hard to adjust to the racism and to a mind set bent on keeping the two races apart.

Despite the incident, Dorsett talked about how happy he was to be living in Dallas. Dorsett told Mary Elson, a reporter for *The Dallas Times Herald*, "I've been recognized everywhere: supermarkets, gas stations, restaurants. The people down here in Dallas are so friendly it's unbelievable. They all come up and say they're so happy I'm here. But let me tell you, they're no more happier than I am to be here."

That was his public face. In private, Dorsett was unhappy not to be as free as he had been in the city of Pittsburgh.

Mel Renfro: "He came out of the East Coast, from Pittsburgh, where he had lived by a different set of rules. In Pittsburgh, *everybody* loved him. In Dallas and the South, although the blacks were treated OK, he couldn't do what he did back home, and so Tony had a bitterness. He resented that even though he was such a good athlete, even though he was popular in the sense that the people liked his football performances, he still couldn't live the way he was used to living."

What Dorsett found equally hard to take at first were Landry's military-like practices. At Pitt, football had been fun. Not in Dallas. Like most rookies, he was having difficulty learning the system. The veterans chided him for not being more serious.

Then in preseason he was injured and missed most of the exhibition games. He felt animosity and envy coming from some of the vets. Not only had he won the Heisman Trophy and Walter Camp Award, but his paycheck was much bigger than theirs, and some of them weren't happy about that. When the season began, coach Landry used Dorsett in a spot role. Preston Pearson continued as the starter, and for the first three games, he carried a total of 21 times. Dorsett was uncomfortable and unhappy with the limited duty.

Drew Pearson: "Tony was the first Cowboys player to get $1 million. That didn't bother me at all. Tony was a Heisman Trophy winner from a national champion Pittsburgh Panthers, and he was the number two pick in the draft. So that warranted a certain salary level, and back then draft choices were getting more money than the veteran players. It was something understood. What it did, it created a new salary scale for us to go by. There was no resentment there, because players better than anybody understand the finances of the NFL. They know when you have your opportunity to get your money, you got to get it, whether you're a rookie or a 10-year veteran, you might only get one opportunity, and you gotta get it while you can.

"And quickly, Tony showed us he was special. That year we were 12–2 in the regular season. We scored over 340 points. We were a machine, and Tony was the game-breaking piece that we needed in our offense. He could turn a game around at any point on the field at any time in the game with just one quick hit up the middle. Preston started in our opening win against the Vikings, and then in the second game of the season when we beat up on the Giants, Tony ran seven times and scored two touchdowns."

In the third game, a solid 23–7 defeat of Ricky Bell and Tampa Bay, Dorsett ran 10 times for 72 yards. After the game he showed himself to be a harsher critic of himself than even Tom Landry could have been. After the game he told reporters, "Mentally I just collapsed . . . totally. I stopped two drives with my mistakes. I lined up wrong once and we had to call timeout because of that. Another time I didn't block the right man. I had a misunderstanding of who I was supposed to block." He concluded, "I still have a long way to go."

Drew Pearson: "A lot of people thought he was aloof because of his personality and his demeanor, but once you got to know him, you found out that's just the way he was, and you accepted that.

"The next game was against the St. Louis Cardinals, who we beat 30–24, and against the Cards Tony ran only 14 times, but he ran for 141 yards, including a 77-yard touchdown run.

"We had everything going for us. Against the Redskins, Roger hit me with a 59-yard touchdown pass. He threw for over 250 yards and two touchdowns, and he had his old form back. Roger was having a great year. He was throwing the ball. We had had an excellent off-season of work. We had an excellent preseason, and it was carrying right over into the season. Roger was the key, the igniter, and he made us go. He was having a great year.

"We beat the Eagles, and then we shut out the Detroit Lions, 37–0, then beat the Giants big to go 8–0, the best in our history."

Roger Staubach: "Tony Dorsett made a *big* difference when he came in '77. Getting Dorsett was a real shot in the arm. This guy was a sensational player. He had speed, and he was tough, could run inside. He took a lot of the pressure off me. With him we had a very balanced game. That year Tony Hill also came, and when you have Tony and Drew and Tony, we were one heck of an offense.

"Tony Hill was a good guy, yet he was very outgoing, very precocious, and he could drive you crazy. I think I had better control of Tony than anybody. I was able to control him, and he really made a lot of great plays, made them for Danny White too, won *a lot* of big games. But Drew was a Hall of Fame receiver, and Tony got lost in his shadow. When we hit the field offensively, we were *really good*."

The question was whether the Cowboys could go undefeated. Landry said he didn't think they could. What was required was for Staubach to stay healthy. In the next game, against the Cardinals, the Cowboys were leading by a touchdown with nine minutes left when Staubach sprained the thumb on his passing hand. As a result, he was ineffective at the end and Cards quarterback Jim Hart threw two touchdowns, one to Mel Gray, the other to Jackie Smith, to break the streak.

After the one loss, the Dallas writers were wondering in print whether the Cowboys were going to choke. Tony Dorsett, patient no longer, then told Landry he wanted to start. Landry called the rookie into his office and told him how unhappy he was with the progress he was making. Dorsett, who was not afraid of the coach, told Landry he was bored and dissatisfied with the way he was being used. "We've been expecting you to be starting for us," Landry said. "But the way you've been going, I have my doubts about all that."

"Coach," said Dorsett, "I have my doubts that I would ever be starting this season. It is not my favorite thing to do—to come into a game, to come out of a game."

"Well," Landry said, "if you showed some intensity in practice, some more hard work, it might be different."

Dorsett told Landry, "Coach, with not starting and not feeling a part of things, I was getting ready to write it off and get ready for training camp next year and try to win me a job."

Landry told him, "That's not the correct attitude. We have big plans for you right now. But you've got to get more into things."

"Well, I guess what we have is more a problem of miscommunication than anything," said Dorsett. "I admit I could have applied myself a little more. But if you'd told me in training camp that later on I would be starting for the Cowboys, I would have busted my butt more."

"It's not too late," said the coach.

That week Dorsett worked especially hard in practice, and Landry started him against the Pittsburgh Steelers, replacing an angry Preston Pearson, who felt he was being made a scapegoat. Said Landry, "The move has nothing to do with Preston. We felt Tony had been running very hard, and we wanted to see how he looked starting."

Though the Cowboys didn't win the game, a second loss in a row, Dorsett looked just fine. He ran 17 times for 73 yards, including one 13-yard touchdown run, as he fought to learn the Cowboys' complicated Multiple Offense system.

Drew Pearson: "The loss to St. Louis was disappointing, but we were right in that football game right up to the end. Then we came back and lost to Pittsburgh up there. That was the most disappointing loss, 'cause we wanted to beat the Steelers, and wanted to beat them at a time when it really counted. The only time we ever beat them was in the preseason exhibition games. We went up to Pittsburgh to win that football game. Roger got knocked out in that game, and they whipped our butts again. We didn't think there was any real concern for our football team. We knew we could get it back together."

In the next game, against the Washington Redskins, Dorsett ran for 64 yards, most of them in the second half, and scored the winning touchdown in a close 14–7 slugfest.

Drew Pearson: "It was a very physical football game. The Redskins had some great players. I do remember Tony Dorsett staggering back to the huddle after one hit by Chris Hanburger or somebody—I don't know whether it was Hanburger or Neal Olkewicz or this other guy who got killed out on a highway fixing a flat, the middle linebacker, Harold McClinton. He was an unsung hero on that defense, but he was a sledgehammer. He could knock your head off. But Tony staggered back to the huddle after one lick on the sideline. I was straightening his shoulder pads out. I asked him, 'Tony, are you all right?' He said, 'Yeah, but these guys are *men*.' That's when he realized he was in the NFL and it was a little different, because these other defenses were very strong and very tough, but Washington got more up to play us and kicked Tony's ass.

"And then against the Philadelphia Eagles, Tony ran for 206 yards, breaking Calvin's record for one game by 53 yards. Tony was a great player, man. He could hit that daylight and the next thing you knew, he was gone in the defensive secondary.

"And with Tony breaking Calvin Hill's rookie record, we finished the regular season 12–2 and had to face the Bears in the opening game of the playoffs.

"We were confident. We had beaten a very good Denver Broncos team that last game of the season in a very physical game. I remember so clearly getting racked up by Billy Thompson coming across the middle on a play. It was a physical game, but we won, and we felt we had momentum going, and we knew Chicago would have a hard time beating us. For them to beat us, we would have to beat ourselves, and we certainly didn't do it. We were clicking. We beat them 37–7, and then we beat the Vikings 23–6, another tough team, and a playoff nemesis, a team that always gave us a lot of trouble in the playoffs, but again, we had Doomsday. We talk about our offense, but Doomsday was being mighty effective, too, and the Vikings had some very good offensive weapons still, but we shut them down pretty good. We were rolling right on into that Super Bowl."

Super Bowl XII pitted the Cowboys against the Denver Broncos, a team led by former Dallas quarterback Craig Morton. Craig had toiled three years for the New York Giants before going to Denver, and not once had Morton been able to defeat the Cowboys. The Morton factor, as much as anything else, gave the Cowboys players added confidence going into the game.

Mel Renfro: "In our first game against the Giants when Craig played quarterback, I picked him off. He never once beat the Cowboys, because we knew how to get to him. We knew what to do. We pressured him. Blitzed him. Went after him. Didn't give him time. If you give him time, he'll throw the ball pretty well. So you don't give him time. He wasn't able to scramble because of his knees. We knew he wasn't mobile, and that's what happened in Super Bowl XII. We knew he didn't have good mobility, and if we didn't give him time, we could pretty much shut him down. We had Harvey Martin and Randy White plus Ed Jones, so we had the line where we could do it."

Drew Pearson: "We blitzed in a lot of situations throughout that football game, and we just kept constant pressure on Craig Morton. Even though the final score was 27–10, for a long time it was close, a tough game, but when the Denver Broncos started having success moving the football, it was when Craig left the game and they brought in Norris Weese, and he started scrambling around back there trying to avoid the rush, and that's when Denver started moving the football."

The star of the game offensively was running back Robert Newhouse, who not only threw a 29-yard touchdown pass to Golden Richards but ran 14 times for

55 yards, filling in for Dorsett after the rookie star sprained his knee and didn't play the second half.

Drew Pearson: "Robert's role was mainly short yardage, goal line, the lead back to block for Tony. Newhouse was a role player throughout his career with the Cowboys. There is no question he had the ability to be a starter and to start for a long time, but for some reason Landry never gave him—I don't want to say he didn't give him opportunities to start—but Landry never really saw him as the starter. There always seemed to be somebody else, Walt Garrison, Scott Laidlaw, Timmy Newsome, who would seem to end up getting more playing time than Newhouse. But Newhouse was never one to complain. He was the consummate team player, and whatever role Landry wanted him to play, Newhouse was willing to play it and not just play it, but play it well."

Roger Staubach: "We had played Denver the last game of the season and really fought like crazy to beat them 14–6. Denver had a great defense—the Orange Crush. We knew their defense was tough, and this Super Bowl, *our* defense made it easy for us. If their offense had been on and playing well, it would have been a heck of a game, but once we saw our defense was in control, we became very conservative.

"We hit this play to Butch Johnson, which was kind of a made-up kind of deal, but other than that, we were conservative because the defense dominated.

"We'd been watching film, and I saw that Bernard Jackson, their weak safety, liked to gamble a lot. He wouldn't get back into coverage. He'd be looking for things over the middle. So the play was sent in, a strongside play to the fullback or to Billy Joe Dupree, our tight end. Butch, who brought in the play from coach Landry, was supposed to run an in-route.

"I told Butch, 'You run a real strong post.'

"He said, 'No, I'm supposed to run an in-route.'

"I said, 'Butch, you just run a good post route, and I will throw it to you if Jackson is not back in his coverage.'

"If I had called '83-Y post' in the huddle, everybody would have said, 'Roger's going against the coach.'

"Butch ran a great post route. Steve Foley was playing to the outside a little bit. He should have prevented anything to the corner or the outside. And Jackson was the guy who should have made the play. Well, Jackson was cheating, so I threw it over his head, and I actually thought I threw it too far, and Butch Johnson made a sensational catch. It was controversial, because Denver said he didn't have control as he crossed the goal line, but when you see the film, you could see he had possession. It was just a great catch. Butch had a flair for making those kinds of catches.

"That really put the game away. We led, 20–3.

"But our defense just totally dominated the game. They could have had Jim Thorpe at quarterback for Denver, and he would have been in trouble. So it wasn't Craig Morton's fault. Craig Morton didn't have a shot in that game. Craig had a great season for Denver that year. They beat the Raiders in the playoffs. Craig had a great year. In fact, Craig was MVP in the AFC."

Drew Pearson: "We were pretty happy, elated. I was kind of hurting, just drained, dehydrated, and cramping up quite a bit. Winning the Super Bowl was kind of anticlimactic that year. Because we felt we *should* have won it. Landry put it in perspective by saying it was the 'challenge of the chase' that gave us our real satisfactions, all the things we had to overcome to get to the Super Bowl and win it was what was really satisfying to us, not necessarily just winning that one game, but just winning all season long and finishing 12–2 in the regular season, 15–2 overall. We knew we had accomplished a lot. So we were happy and elated and having a good time, but it was also businesslike. It was something we expected to do."

Chapter 58

The Assassin

After the 1977 Super Bowl XII victory, Harvey Martin and Randy White were awarded the co-MVP trophies and given cars. Martin had four tackles, two of them quarterback sacks. White had five tackles and a sack. But it could certainly have been argued that the Most Valuable Player on the team had been a part-time defender who starred on the special teams and at linebacker on third downs. His name was Thomas "Hollywood" Henderson.

Thomas Henderson: "Let me tell you something. The '77 Cowboys defense was one of the greatest defenses of all time, if anybody would ever study the caliber of players, the speed, the experience, the quickness. You go down that lineup, with Thomas Henderson, Too Tall Jones, Jethro Pugh, or Bill Gregory, Randy White, Harvey Martin, D. D. Lewis, Breunig in the middle, Benny Barnes, Mel Renfro, then Charlie Waters and Cliff Harris. What an ensemble! Jethro was this steelworker. He came in with the beat-up lunch pail. Him and Larry Cole were the unsung heroes of the Dallas Cowboys.

"Me and Too Tall made the same NAIA All-America team in 1973. Maybe he *was* too tall. Too Tall was a great player, but people always expected more out of him. I found him to be a great football player.

"That year I intercepted a pass against Tarkenton in the Minnesota game, and against Tampa Bay I intercepted a pass and returned it 79 yards. Then I dunked the ball over the crossbars. Yeah. I'm different, man. See, Landry didn't like that. I antagonized Tom Landry. To get Landry's praise it took me whipping Russ Francis' ass in Texas Stadium in '78 after the papers had said 'Russ Francis is the best tight end in the world ever, and if you don't think so, watch him drag Hollywood around Texas Stadium.' And I flat whipped his ass for four quarters.

"To start the game I punched Francis in the mouth—f***ing knocked him out, just bam. I whipped him so bad it hurt my back. That's how bad it was, and Landry came into the meeting room that Monday and took a moment, the first time in my career, and he said, 'I want to say something here. Thomas Henderson had a great challenge.' He said, 'Men who step up to those challenges are men who I like. I want to say this. Thomas Henderson is a pro.'

"Tom Landry called me a pro, and I never heard him call anybody else a pro. I played there five years and never heard Landry call anybody a pro. All the years he coached football, there were some people he looked at and said, 'That's a pro.' I know he thought Roger Staubach was a pro. But I don't think he thought everybody was a pro. I would like someday to find out what he meant by that. I never have confirmed what he meant by 'Thomas Henderson is a pro,' but I knew it was the highest compliment, had to be because I never heard him call anybody else that since then.

"I've said it before. I was the best linebacker to ever play in the National Football League. And I didn't play long. But I was the best there was. Before there was an L.T., there was a T.H. I made 56 the glamorous number that it is today. Everybody thinks it started with L.T., Lawrence Taylor. Lawrence Taylor wore 56 because I wore it. So when I say that, historians will say, 'Yeah, the son of a bitch was good.' I never had anybody argue with me when I say I was the best all-around linebacker. What I mean by that, I could play the run. I played the strong side as a 210-pound linebacker. I played the run; I played the pass excellently. I could blitz.

"The year Landry fired me [1979] I had 12 quarterback sacks. And Landry loved me blitzing because he knew when he called a sara 33 or a blitz for me that I was going to get to the quarterback. I picked the lines that were effective to get things done.

"People can talk about Jack Ham and all the other linebackers, but I would put my game-to-game film against any linebacker in history. I played the run perfect. You couldn't block me. I could control with power. I could escape. I caused major problems. I understood *how* to f*** up a play.

"My philosophy was to do my job, and then I went to help. 'OK, Landry, you want me to do this little shit of yours, OK.' 'Take this step, OK, Landry, how you like that?' Because he was watching me on Monday. He had to watch the whole team on Sunday. He would sit and criticize on Monday. So I would go and take my little step for Landry. 'Here, Landry, one-two,' and then I would take off. That's how I became an All-Pro in Landry's system.

"I remember in Super Bowl XII playing one of my finest games. Mike Ditka, the consummate competitor, said to me, 'Thomas'—and he knew I loved doing shit like this—'on the first punt, if you get a shot at Rick Upchurch, take the penalty. Just take him out. Not hurt him, but get his attention. Make sure he's going to be looking for you the rest of the day.' 'Cause we were afraid of him. We felt that Rick Upchurch could beat us returning kickoffs and punts.

"I flew down the field with my mission orders, and I took a 15-yard penalty. I just creamed Upchurch. I came to the sideline, and Ditka had moved away, and I had to see Landry. I basically said, 'Well f***, Ditka told me to do that.' And Landry turned to look for Ditka and couldn't even find him!

"Another play in that game, I was on the kickoff return team, and I was over there on the sideline bullshitting with the Denver coach, Red Miller, saying stuff like, 'Hey, Red, we're gonna whip you'all's ass today. You ain't got a f***ing chance to win, buddy.' I said, 'Watch this,' and I don't even remember the player—I was supposed to block the third guy from the end. That's the way we set those plays up. And I did something I learned at Langston, which was to take not a forearm, but more of an elbow to the head. And this guy came running down the field doing 22.6 miles an hour, and I clocked him just right upside the head with an elbow, just flat-out knocked him out. And Red was hollering at the officials, 'Fifty-six, you can't do that.' I said, 'But I already did it. What do you mean I can't do it? It's already done.' The guy was lying out on the ground, and Red was telling me I couldn't do that. I said, 'What do you mean I can't do that? You should have told me that 10 minutes ago.'

"I played against Riley Odoms, who was the tight end who rated himself far better than he was. He was basically whipped and noneffective. He didn't do shit. But he talked the whole day as if he was doing something, and to this day, and the history of Super Bowl XII, it was like he wasn't even there.

"In '77 I felt, and do to this day, that was the finest football team ever to be assembled. We just couldn't be beat. We had too many ways to hold you, too many ways to beat you. We had a great chemistry. It was a great team."

Chapter 59

HOLLYWOOD

In 1978 the Cowboys started slowly, compiling a 6–4 record and all the while putting up with the antics and carryings-on of Thomas Henderson. When the fleet middle linebacker arrived as a rookie in 1975, he was called "Thomas." But after that season he discovered *the big time*—a new lifestyle introduced to him by the Hollywood entertainment crowd. He began a romance with one of the Pointer Sisters, and he also started his love affair with cocaine. One of his druggie partners was comedian Richard Pryor, another victim of the cocaine epidemic of the late seventies.

When he came to camp in 1978, gone was Thomas Henderson. In his place was a larger-than-life, in-your-face character named Hollywood Henderson. For two short years, supernova Hollywood Henderson became the mouth of the South, the outrageous, braggadocian public persona of the Dallas Cowboys.

Thomas Henderson: "America discovered cocaine for the first time in the midseventies. Back then cocaine was the drug you heard about. It was Donna Summer and Barry White and disco music and limousines and Holly*woooood.* And if you wanted to be hip, slick, *and* cool, you eventually moved toward it. The reason I ended up with a severe drug problem was that I *liked* cocaine; I *loved* it. I savored it; I worshiped it. I had a relationship with it. I had sex on it. I had sex with it. I had parking lot sex. I had sex in clubs.

"I've been sober since 1983, and I remember telling someone recently, 'You know, back in the seventies, it would be about 4:15 in the morning when I'd get laid, and have these ménage à trois and these orgies.' I said, 'Today I'm asleep at 11:00.' So if I was going to have sex these days, I'd be shit out of luck, because I can't be awake at 4:15 to do *anything.*

"How prevalent was it on the Cowboys? Let me break it down like this. Five whites and seven blacks I knew of, including myself, who were using marijuana, pills, cocaine, and other mind-altering substances.

"It was sometimes a secret and sometimes you made a love connection. I would get some for some friends, and they would get me marijuana, or they would provide me with pills. It was not a loud thing. It was a very covert operation.

"When I came to training camp in '78, I had a deviated septum from doing so much coke, but it didn't affect me on the field. I was vicious. I was 215 pounds of assassin, explosive, physical, terminator. I was rude. And physically and in strength and explosion and power, you couldn't match up with me. So it didn't matter that I was f***ed up on drugs. I was 25 years old. I was in the middle of the prime of this physical superiority.

"The only problem I had was that I had contracted hepatitis. It was real bad, because I didn't know I had it. I kept waking up trying to feel better, 'cause I've often thought that the body can heal itself. But that hepatitis had my weight down from 210 to 185 pounds.

"I went to work one day, and the trainer, who had served in the military, looked at me and said, 'Goddamn, Henderson.' My eyes were yellow. By the time they put me in the hospital what I had had killed Elvis Presley's mom. The degree, my blood levels, all the readers, it had killed her. And here I was smoking marijuana, drinking white lightning, and snorting and smoking cocaine.

"The one thing Landry knew was, if I didn't start, I really hated it. I liked being introduced. I liked the publicity of it. I was the best f***ing player he had, so why the f*** wouldn't I want to be a starter? Why is he going to put some f***ing slugs on the field? Out of your 50 guys, I'm the best f***ing guy here.

"And after a point it didn't matter I was sick. What mattered was that Landry took personally what Thomas Henderson did. And he shouldn't have.

"In the second game of the season against the Giants, I was really hurt. I took Larry Csonka on a near g.o., which means the tight end blocks down and the fullback blocks the linebacker. I stepped across to take on Csonka, and I had great position. I had taken on this type of block many times, but I didn't have my back foot on the ground by the time Csonka and I collided.

"My collision with Csonka went from the top of my head out my ankle, all the force going back down to the ankle. I was putting the foot down, so by the time the force got down there, I just snapped. I remember laying in the training room a few days after that and saying to my coach, Jerry Tubbs, 'I'll be back next week.' And I had every intention of coming back, but my ankle was about 25 inches around.

"I think I broke it, but they didn't tell me that. I ended up missing five weeks. I became depressed. I was putting my foot in ice and getting gloomy. I was coming off an All-Pro year, and I asked our equipment man, Buck Buchanan, 'Buck, I need some high-tops.' He got me a pair. I went across the street to the Tom Thumb grocery store and bought six or seven tins of black shoe polish, and I went to my locker, sat there with ice on my ankle, and I painted these white high-tops black. And I did a horrible job. I got black on the soles, and they were just ugly looking, just the worst paint job, like if you let me spray paint your car. It just looked horrible. And when I returned in a game against the Philadelphia Eagles, I wore the black high-tops.

"First thing, I wore them to practice. I was trying to limp a little bit out there, and they were ugly. To see Thomas Henderson, who always wore the white socks rolled down and the nice feet . . . So I wore them when we played the Eagles, and I had a good game. It was my first game back. My ankle was sore. I had had a little injection in there for the pain, and I did a good job. And all Landry could say was that he didn't like my shoes. You know? Of all the things a coach could be doing, thinking about, contemplating, planning, this man called me into his office and said, 'Thomas, I don't want you to wear the black shoes anymore.'

"I told him, 'Have you lost your f***ing mind? What does wearing black shoes have to do with me playing football?' I said, 'You're out of line.'

"And I continued to wear my black shoes, until they became obnoxious to me, and I finally just threw them away. I wore them a couple more weeks just because he asked me not to. What kind of deal is that? I'm sure he wouldn't want to take that to the people: 'I'm benching Henderson because he won't take off those black shoes.' I mean, he had a bad position, and I knew it. I mean, Landry was a guy who grew up in the forties when they all wore black shoes. He *came* from black shoes.

"We finished the regular season 12–4. We beat the Falcons in the first playoff game when Danny White came in after Roger was knocked out. Then we played the L.A. Rams. Before the game I said that the Rams didn't have enough class to go to the Super Bowl, and they proved it when they tried to hurt me during the game. One of the things I did pretty good was block field goals. I used to jump that gap and get through there and block the ball on the kick, and the Rams knew that I did that, and when I said they had no class and didn't have enough class to go to the Super Bowl, I think they just decided to hurt me.

"When a guy goes to block a field goal, he gets around that corner and in the gap and lays out with his hands extended trying to block the ball as the guy goes to kick it, and in that position you're vulnerable, because you're not expecting anything. The worst thing you can do is run into some tackle. So the Rams designed a play for the linebacker on the other side; instead of him blocking his responsibility, he turned and like a pulling guard came to hurt me. The Rams appointed a linebacker, No. 50, Kevin McLain, to hurt me on this play. And what happened, I jumped the gap and laid out, and I saw Kevin coming and I was surprised. 'Why the f*** is he coming?' But he missed me. And the Rams missed the field goal. But that was one of the most chickenshit designed plays I've ever seen or heard of in my life.

"I went after Rams coach Ray Malavasi after that, called him a 'fat f***ing drunk.' Oh yeah. I told him, 'I'm going to single-handedly beat your fat ass today.' And I did it. I ran back an interception 68 yards to add insult to injury.

"It was too wet in the Coliseum to dunk the ball over the goal post, so I did a George Gervin finger roll. We were going back to the Super Bowl.

"And when I made the cover of *Newsweek* magazine, the first thing I did was to look to see whether there was any cocaine showing in my nose. I knew it was there. I told reporters, 'I'm more famous than the shah of Iran.' And I was. When

I arrived in Miami before our game with the Steelers, I told the reporters, 'Bradshaw is so dumb, he couldn't spell *cat* if you spotted him the *c* and the *a*.'

"I was concerned before the game. Remember when Fred Williamson was the 'Hammer,' and the Green Bay Packers ran a sweep around him in Super Bowl I after he ran his mouth, left him out there standing at attention laying down? You're *always* concerned. Also, at the time I had a nose problem. It was always stopped up or bleeding, but no one knew I was shoveling cocaine into it. My problem was that I couldn't get flaky cocaine in my nose any more. I had to put it in a liquid, and so it became a part of my addiction, but more so, a part of maintenance, because once your nose gets as f***ed up as my nose was, you need cocaine just to keep your eyes from watering. Without the cocaine, it would hurt me physically. I needed it. Cocaine became a maintenance thing.

"But in Super Bowl XIII, like Elvis' voice, my legs never failed me. If I could get there, I was going to do the job. So that day I played the finest football game of my career. Anybody who wants to get the special-teams reel, the defense reel, the third-down reel, go get that film and look at the performance of Thomas Henderson. You won't see a better performance of a football player."

Chapter 60

A Crushing Defeat

The game against the Pittsburgh Steelers—Super Bowl XIII—was for the title Team of the Decade. The game has been called the best in Super Bowl history. The winner would become the first NFL team to win three Super Bowls.

Roger Staubach: "At the beginning of the year, we lost a couple games, lagged at the start of the season, and then we got our act together, and we won eight in a row going into that Super Bowl.

"The Steelers were tough, too, but we had them. At the end of the half it was 14–14, and Tony Dorsett ran out of bounds around their 25-yard line, and a guy hit him late, and the ref threw the flag, and as Tony was coming back onto the field, he shoved the ball in the guy's face. So instead of having a 15-yard penalty, there were offsetting penalties.

"We had a play-action pass called to Drew Pearson past Jack Lambert, the linebacker. Lambert was the one I was worrying about. I threw it past Lambert, and Mel Blount made a great play and intercepted. Blount should not have been where he was. But he saw the motion, came off his coverage and intercepted, and as he caught the ball, Billy Joe made a great tackle, and the refs gave him a 15-yard penalty for roughing, and on the last play of the half, Rocky Bleier scored, and the Steelers went ahead 21–14. It was a real crime.

"We dominated the whole third quarter, should have tied the game. We missed a play to tight end Jackie Smith that could have been a touchdown.

"The play was a brand-new goal-line play put in a couple days before the game. It was a play with three tight ends. One of the tackles was the third tight end.

"On the play I was to look for Billy Joe, the tight end on the other side, to go to the corner, and I was to come back looking for the fullback out of the flat. The fullback was there strictly as an outlet receiver. What Jackie was supposed to do was get into the back of the end zone.

"We were on the 11-yard line. It was a third-and-one, and Landry sent in this play. I realized he was sending in a goal-line play, but I noticed we didn't have the right receivers in the game, so I had to call timeout.

"There was no time left on the [play] clock, so I went off to the side, and I said, 'Coach, that's a goal-line play.' He said, 'Well, you're right.'

"We had been practicing that from the 1- or 2-yard line. Jackie was to go to the back of the end zone and stand there and wait for the ball. But in this case we were on the 11.

"Landry said, 'Run it anyway, because they'll be in a goal-line type defense.' And he was right. It was not a bad play. Landry said, 'Look for your keys and make sure we get the first down.' In other words, he wanted me to hit the fullback out in the flat for a first down.

"I called the play in the huddle. I said, 'We're going to run the goal-line play.' And sure enough Mel Blount went with Billy Joe to the left, so he was out of the play. The fullback went into the flat and took a defender with him. And Jack Lambert blitzed up the middle, and as he was coming in, Scott Laidlaw just cleaned him, actually knocked the wind out of him. Lambert had to leave the game after that.

"And no one was near Jackie Smith, who was running to the back of the end zone, where he was supposed to go. Now if he would have just stopped at the goal line, it would have been perfect. But that's not what he was told. He knew his job was to get to the back of the end zone, which was 21 yards instead of 11 or 12. So he was running into the end zone, and I saw him wide open. I was seeing the whole thing. I'm saying, 'Oh my God, there is no one near Jackie Smith.' No one is even close to him. They let him run free.

"I released the ball, and I took something off it, because Jackie was not totally turned. He was just starting to turn when I was throwing the ball. And I think it surprised him that the ball got to him that fast. I really do. And I threw it a little bit low, and he kind of slipped.

"And the thing was, he really hadn't run that play. If he would have stopped at the goal line, he would have been standing there waiting. And it would have been real easy to hit him, and he would have caught it.

"But see, he was running to the back of the end zone, and I was getting blitzed, so I'm throwing it, and he just ran too deep, 'cause the play was perfect. It was a great call, a great play if Pittsburgh blitzed, and they loved to blitz deep in their territory, so it worked like a charm.

"But Jackie was surprised, and the ball hit him in the chest, and he couldn't catch it. We had to settle for a field goal, so it was 21–17 Pittsburgh instead of a tie.

"Even so, we were still in charge. The Steelers didn't have a first down in the third quarter. We got the ball back, and we should have scored, but we had to punt, and they got the ball back with just a few minutes left in the third quarter, and Terry Bradshaw threw the ball up for grabs to Lynn Swann, and the officials made the worst call in the history of football. I mean, the back judge was right there, swinging his arms to indicate the pass was incomplete, when from the middle of the field Fred Swearingen, who was not the referee, was just the field judge, threw his flag. He said that Benny Barnes had interfered with Swann. He shouldn't have made that call. Back then, even if you threw a flag, it didn't matter. You didn't overrule the call of the referee.

"But on this play that's what they did even though Swearingen saw the play differently from every other person in the Orange Bowl. And because of that penalty, they went in and scored on a run by Franco Harris after the referee ran into Charlie Waters, who would have stopped him.

"And the bad thing about it, they kicked off, and Roy Gerela slipped and squibbed the ball to Randy White, who had a broken hand, and Randy tried to run the thing back, and he fumbled on our own 18. On the next play Bradshaw threw for another touchdown. So they made 14 points in a matter of two minutes, and they hadn't even had a first down.

"It's not an excuse, but let me tell you, that's a big swing in that game, 'cause I really believe we had them confused. We were moving the football, and of course, we continued to do that, but we didn't have enough time.

"With six minutes left we trailed 35–17. We moved the ball and scored twice. Billy Joe Dupree caught a touchdown pass, and then Butch Johnson caught one to make the score 35–31, and we had the ball again when we tried an onside kick, and the Steelers recovered the ball. Unfortunately, we should have done that in the third quarter. And that's why it was so unfair to blame Jackie. He got hammered on the deal, which was so unjust. There were so many plays in that game that made a difference. I threw an interception, Randy White fumbled, the flag on the bogus interference call, and who got the hammer? Jackie, which was so unfair. It was a tragedy for him.

"This was the most disappointing game I ever played in, because we had this great team. Breaks were going to determine that game. No one dominated the other. To me, the '78 team was the best team we *ever* had in Dallas."

Drew Pearson: "We lost 35–31, and when it was over I was more disappointed in losing that game than any other. It was a tough loss to take. We had done so much and overcame so many obstacles, and we wanted it so bad. We wanted the back-to-back Super Bowls so badly that we could taste it, we could feel it, we lived it. We were a committed team, the players, the coaches, the organization, and nothing less than winning the Super Bowl was acceptable. There was no joy unless we could have won it all, and we didn't, and so it was sad and disappointing. It took a lot out of myself and a lot of players. It was really tough to take, but we dealt with it as professionals and gave credit where credit was due."

Chapter 61

America's Team

At the end of the 1978 season Bob Ryan of NFL Films called Cowboys public relations director Doug Todd to suggest a possible title for the Cowboys' highlight film: *Champions Die Hard.*

"I don't like that," said Todd. "We're not dead or dying."

"Then how 'bout something that projects the Cowboys as a national team? We've got all this footage of people in stadiums all over the league waving Cowboys pennants. How 'bout calling it *America's Team*?

"I like that," said Todd. "That sounds good."

The title *America's Team* was hated by the Cowboys players, because it smacked of that same arrogance that for years the Cowboys had been accused of displaying. Tom Landry didn't care for it, because it gave opposing teams one more thing for which to hate the Cowboys. "It gives the appearance that we are saying that we are the best team in the country," said Landry.

Tex Schramm, the marketing whiz, loved it.

By the late seventies, no sports team in America was as popular as the Cowboys, not even the New York Yankees. The Cowboys had 225 radio stations in their network, including 16 in Spanish. The *Dallas Cowboys Weekly* had ninety-five thousand subscribers, more than even *Pro Football Weekly.* A full 30 percent of apparel sold by NFL Properties had the Cowboys name on it, much of it with Roger Staubach's No. 12 on the back. (The Pittsburgh Steelers were second, with 8 percent of the market.) The cheerleaders sold more than 1 million posters. The Cowboys' made-for-TV movies, *Dallas Cowboys Cheerleaders* I and II, drew bigger ratings than even *Roots* or *Jesus of Nazareth.* In every town where the Cowboys played, there were significant numbers of Cowboys fans. America was Cowboy crazy.

Art Spander of *The* (San Francisco) *Examiner* made this analysis of the phenomenon: "These are difficult, complex times in America. Inflation, court-ordered busing, oil crises, lack of leadership. People seek a simpler life, a hero. That would be the cowboy—small *c*—and the Old West.

"Levi's, boots, 10-gallon hats are now worn as often in the East and Pacific Coasts as they are in the Southwest.

"And what's in Texas? Not much, really. Flat land, tall steel buildings, oil wells, and yes, with a capital *C,* the Cowboys, the most stable entity in America. In their 20 seasons of operation, they have had one owner, Clint Murchison, one president, GM Tex Schramm, one head coach, Tom Landry, one personnel director, Gil Brandt.

"Our best cars are from Europe. Our best electronic equipment and cameras are from Japan. What happened to the Great American Dream of working harder, producing better? It's alive and living in Texas Stadium."

Drew Pearson: "Our popularity was at an all-time peak, and it wasn't just in Dallas. It was on a national basis. I was running the Cowboys basketball team at that time, and we would go all over and sell out not just gyms but arenas. We played the Pittsburgh Steelers up in Pittsburgh, and nine thousand people came. We played a group of All-Stars in San Antonio in the HemisFair Arena, and ten thousand people were there for that game. So we understood our popularity and what success and winning had brought to us, and we liked it. We wanted to keep it going."

But for America's Team to continue winning, it had to stay intact, and in 1979 it lost several of its key pieces, including Jethro Pugh, who retired, and its entire strongside trio of Ed "Too Tall" Jones, Charlie Waters, and Hollywood Henderson.

Before that happened, there were smaller tremors. On June 8, 1979, Gigi Clayton, Tony Dorsett's 18-year-old girlfriend, died mysteriously. She had been a child actress, an honors student, and they were going to be married. Out of the blue, she had become paralyzed. Doctors could not find the cause. A week later she died. Then on June 14 John Murchison, Clint's brother, died suddenly while addressing a dinner of Boy Scout volunteers.

A week after that Ed "Too Tall" Jones shocked everyone when he announced that he was quitting the Cowboys to become a professional boxer. Jones had played out his option in 1978 and had become a free agent, and he was asking for $250,000 from Tex Schramm. When Schramm wouldn't give it to him and no other NFL team contacted him, Jones retired to go into boxing. Because Jones was 6'9", the media scoffed, but when Jones was growing up in Tennessee, he had won the state Golden Gloves championship. Boxing was his true love. Jones was training with Murphy Griffith, the uncle of boxing champ Emile Griffith.

Losing the 6'9" defensive end was a huge loss for the Cowboys. Jones, whose Tennessee State teams lost just two games in the four years he was there, could run the 40 in 4.75 and high jump 6'10".

When Jones announced his resignation, Landry told reporters, "Too Tall had great ability but limited desire. If he had been motivated to be the best of all time, he could have become consistent and become the best." His teammates disagreed. Said Thomas Henderson at the time, "The Cowboys are saying he had a motivational problem, but he was motivated every game. He made the big tackles. He was hurt because he didn't get the recognition."

With first Jethro Pugh in retirement and then Jones, Landry was glumly realistic. "Their loss has weakened us considerably," he said.

July was quiet, but then in August it was reported that Tony Dorsett had suffered a broken toe after he dropped a heavy mirror on it. Two days later Danny White broke his thumb, Thomas Henderson was hospitalized with a hiatal hernia, and in an exhibition game against the Seattle Seahawks, defensive back Charlie Waters suffered a serious knee injury, underwent an operation for torn ligaments, and was lost for the season.

Despite all this and Henderson's increased friction with Landry, the Cowboys machine rolled on. In 1979 Landry let Staubach loose, and Staubach began having monster days, and Tony Dorsett continued his climb toward greatness.

Roger Staubach: "In '75, '77, and '79 I played football as well as I ever did as far as what I had to do. Seventy-nine was the first time Landry opened up the passing game. Today you see quarterbacks throw for 350 yards—in '79 we were that type of team. Drew and Tony Hill both went over 1,000 yards, and we were a big-play team. We would hit the key third downs.

"Third down was the measurement. We got them, and we would score. The question always is: how do you get the ball into the end zone? When we got down there, we could use Dorsett, could use Drew, could use Tony. That's where I felt my strength was. I could figure out how to score. That was my job. No matter how you cut it, the quarterback has got to get his team in the end zone. Guys can have great statistics and not get it in. The thing was, we had the people, and different people. We also had Billy Joe Dupree, a big tight end. He made a lot of key plays. So we really had a lot of good players."

The Cowboys were 7–1, but in a 14–3 loss to the Pittsburgh Steelers, who taunted them for being America's Team, L. C. Greenwood tackled Roger Staubach as he tried to scramble and sent him backward hard to the ground, knocking him out. No one knew it at the time, but Greenwood's hit would later change the course of Cowboys history.

Drew Pearson: "It was a very physical game. As a matter of fact, I got my bell rung twice in that football game. I was knocked out twice—once in the first quarter by Dennis Winston, who was playing middle linebacker in place of Jack Lambert, who was hurt, and the other time was in the fourth quarter, just before Roger got hurt on the same pass pattern, by the same guy, Dennis Winston.

"But I remember Roger scrambling around. We were trying to run a pass pattern. He was scrambling around, and I was actually coming back to him, coming back to the ball, and L.C. caught up to him, and it wasn't a vicious hit. L.C. led with his head, and he caught Roger in the midsection, pulled him down with his legs, but when Roger was going back, the force, the momentum, was so great that his head hit that hard turf in Three Rivers Stadium, and you could actually see his head bounce, like L.C. was dribbling his head on the turf. I knew it was a severe hit. Of course, Roger was out. He was totally out. He didn't know what hit him, what happened. And as a matter of fact, he didn't become coherent until we were on the airplane flying back to Dallas after that football game. We used to sit across from each other, and I could tell when he snapped to.

"He was conscious—you're conscious when you get your bell rung. These concussions, I've had almost one a year throughout my whole career. I had a concussion, got my bell rung in the first quarter against the Tampa Bay Buccaneers one game in Texas Stadium and played the whole half of the game unconscious, but conscious. Caught a couple passes and everything. When I finally came to, I couldn't believe we were in the locker room in halftime. What had happened to the first half? How did we score? So it was the same thing with Roger. He just came to on the plane, and he asked what happened, and I told him, 'L.C. gave you one of those great hits.' But it was tough. Not even Roger Staubach could sustain that one."

Despite the concussion, Staubach didn't miss a game, and the next week against the New York Giants he pulled the game out in the final minute on a 36-yard touchdown pass to Drew Pearson, followed by a Rafael Septien field goal, as the Cowboys won 16–14. Then came two losses, to the Philadelphia Eagles and the Washington Redskins. In the third period of the Redskins game, the cameras caught Thomas Henderson mugging and fooling around. Linebackers coach Jerry Tubbs caught Henderson's act and was angry and upset. He told Landry. The next day Landry kicked Henderson off the team, saying that Henderson would never play in Dallas again. In all the reporting, there was not a single mention of Henderson's cocaine addiction.

Drew Pearson: "I was surprised that Thomas had let it get to that point. But he had become a disruptive force within our football team. And then when I found out he was doing cocaine on the sideline during that game, then hey, I wanted to kick his butt. Here we are playing a big football game, and everything's on the line, and you're doing cocaine while we're out here risking our lives? You're playing high? It was a disappointment to me. We didn't deserve to win if we had one player on our team doing something like that; we didn't deserve to win, 'cause you can't condone that. You can't do those things and expect to win, and we shouldn't have won."

In 1979 Henderson's downward spiral continued. The year began when he went to the Bahamas to participate in the Superstars competition and he was almost busted by local authorities. His season—and with it his Cowboys career—ended on November 18. It was not until 1983 that he was able to put his life back on track.

Thomas Henderson: "They should have busted me in the Bahamas. It might have changed the course of history. I had an ounce of cocaine, some marijuana, and the customs inspector took my bag off my shoulder, opened it up, looked in my bag, opened up my drug compartment, looked at me, looked back at my bag, looked at me, and in a Bahamian accent, he said, 'Have a good time, Hollywood.'

"I was so f***ing arrogant and so f***ed up, I'm not sure I was even scared. I was just nuts. I was world-famous. I had just done that commercial for 7-Up, 'America's Turning 7-Up.' This was all basically done on the self-promotion of Thomas Henderson. The great PR guy Tex Schramm never f***ing promoted me, only the people he wanted to promote, so everything Thomas Henderson received in the perks department was his own doing. And it was one of those deals. But I *played* myself into that 7-Up commercial, too. You know, I wish I had kept drinking that shit instead of drinking booze.

"I arrived in training camp in a limo and announced I wanted my contract renegotiated. I was underpaid. I was going to make $90,000 or $100,000, and it had gotten to the point where my performance and my work didn't match my money. I was so nuts that I pulled up at the training facility at Thousand Oaks and had the limousine driver drive the car up on the field and sit there on the shoulder. And it pretty much disrupted practice, because as they were practicing, they kept wanting to know who was in the limo, and I was in the limo snorting coke, smoking marijuana, and drinking champagne. After I held them in suspense for 40 minutes, I got out of the car with cowboy boots, shorts, cowboy hat, sunglasses, and I walked out on the field, and Landry knew I was going to come right over and shake his hand, and he shook my hand like George Bush would shake Saddam Hussein's hand, with no firmness, no look in the eyes.

"And then in August, right before the Seattle exhibition game, I had a freaky thing called a hiatal hernia. You can look it up. The symptoms of it are very similar to a heart attack. It's where the flap on your esophagus doesn't function properly, and the flap stays down, which causes you to have gas on the chest, and it really mimics a heart attack.

"And even though I had that, Landry wanted me to travel. If Staubach would have had a hiatal hernia, Landry would not have asked him to get on an airplane to fly to Seattle for a preseason game. But because my name is Thomas Henderson, and because I don't like to practice and I don't like his meetings and I don't like him, even with a team of doctors standing over me with scalpels, his only decision is out of some prejudice against me, and so he said he wanted me to travel, and I told Landry, 'I ain't flying to no motherf***ing Seattle to stand up and watch no f***ing game.'

"Well, his punishment to me was, 'If you're not going to Seattle with us, go to Dallas to the hospital.' So they sent me to Dallas. Of course, Landry didn't want to leave me at Thousand Oaks. He figured I'd go up and get some pussy when he was gone.

"The hernia hung around for longer than normal. I don't know how many days or weeks it's supposed to last, but this thing got on me and stayed a couple of weeks. It is something you operate on if that flap doesn't open up. The scar is from the middle of your back all the way around. They crack your ass like a coconut and look in there and fix stuff.

"I flew to Dallas, and they put me in Baylor Hospital, and I felt a lot better when I got to Baylor. That's when I started feeling better, because they had me sleeping in almost a standing position. With a hiatal hernia, they put your feet down and your head up. They have you sleeping at an angle. They put a policeman by my door. And I climbed out the window.

"I recovered, and against Houston in a preseason game, I stopped Earl Campbell all by myself on the goal line. It was one of the greatest hits in football, but see because of Tex Schramm—if D. D. Lewis would have made that play, it would have been on NFL Films for the history of the game. If Bob Breunig would have made that tackle, same thing. But shit, I had to go *find* that f***ing play on the game films. Damn right. I found it by calling the Cowboys after Jerry Jones took over. So I now have it.

"Matter of fact, real fans of the Cowboys and of me, whenever I'm in Texas or around the country, will come up to me, and they'll go, 'Man, let me tell you something. I saw you hit Earl Campbell. The damnedest hit I ever saw in my life.' I still get those comments.

"The Cowboys had a 7–1 record, and we were going to play the Steelers when Landry came up to me and said, 'You know what our deal is.' Right then, I knew Landry'd lost his mind. He had started focusing so much on discipline with me that he lost all reason with Thomas Henderson. He started treating me differently. He started treating me a little like Duane Thomas, and I wasn't going to have that. I had been sick. I had just come off hepatitis. I had the hiatal hernia, so I did not have a good summer. I was legitimately sick, and I had the flu, man. I mean, I had the flu bad, and the doctor and the trainer told me to take off a couple of days. I'm talking about nose stopped up, snot rags, headaches, weak, chills, just sick, but Landry, of course, made up these rules that said to me in effect, 'If you don't practice every day, you don't start on Sunday.' 'Hey, you're the boss. Make up whatever f***ing rules you want.'

"But you have to have a waiver on illness. He came over to me, and he said, 'You know what our deal is, Thomas. Hegman is going to start. You missed practice.' Well, Bob Breunig was sitting there, and he could see me, a black man, turn red. He was going to start Mike Hegman, play him a series, and then put me in, 'cause he knew who his horse was. And I said, 'F*** that.'

"I got up and went over to Landry's breakfast table in front of Stallings, Stautner, Tubbs, the whole crew, and I tapped him on the shoulder. Landry looked around, and I said, 'Let me just tell you this. If I don't start, I ain't playing today. Now, you handle that.'

"I guess nobody in his life had ever done that to him. I went over to the stadium, and my uniform stayed in the locker. I didn't tape my ankles. I just sat in my locker, and at some point Landry came over to me and said, 'I talked to the trainer,' as if he didn't know, and he backed off, said I was starting. And one more time my teammates saw something they had never seen before. They saw somebody challenge Landry. And it was probably the only time in my life I was right and he was wrong.

"But my days as a Cowboy were coming to an end. I was even losing Mike Ditka, who had always championed me on his special teams. The one thing between Ditka and me, I always knew that Ditka was a great football player, and Ditka knew I was a great football player. So we had a common knowledge of each other, and although he was coaching, I always knew that if I ever played against Mike Ditka, I'd a had a full day's work. But Ditka finally came to me one day and said, 'You know, Thomas, Buffalo Bill was a Cowboy.' And it wasn't long after that that I was released. Ditka knew something was in the works. Landry had probably said to him, 'I don't know how much longer I'm going to put up with this f***ing Henderson.'

"So we played the Redskins in Washington, and I was still sick. I was ill that year. The tight end, he just owned me that day. And that doesn't mean he abused me. I just couldn't get around him. I had no strength. I just couldn't play. I was weak, but no excuses. I played. I remember one time I blitzed, and I hit John Riggins, and bam, I just slid down to the ground and he took off. So it just wasn't a good day. Wasn't the worst day, but it was not a good game for me.

"And after the game somebody came up to me and said something like, 'You shouldn't have been looking at the camera.' I said, 'Aw f*** you. What do you mean?' I just went ballistic on whoever said it to me, and then on the airplane going home, I basically got drunk and walked up to first class, and said, 'You all can kiss my ass,' 'cause Jerry Tubbs had come to me and said, 'Thomas, you shouldn't have been looking in the camera.' Well, f*** you. They put the camera in my face. What do you want me to do, stick my head in my ass? But the camera incident was the culmination of a lot of things, not *the* thing. The next day Landry called me in to say he was letting me go. And I told him, flat out, 'Landry, you're never going to win another Super Bowl,' 'cause I had been telling Gil Brandt and Tex Schramm that all along. I said, 'I am you'all's main ingredient on this f***ing team. I f***ing block punts; I cover your f***ing punts; I cover your kickoffs, shut down all these great-ass return men.'

"I believe this: I wasn't the only weapon, but I was a very efficient weapon for the Dallas Cowboys. I contributed to the key areas of success of the Dallas Cowboys. From the time I was a rookie, playing on every special team, I was an impact player. And when Landry didn't have me on the defense, Mike Hegman went back to being Dave Edwards, a boring-ass linebacker on the strong side. So Landry lost that component. He lost me on third down, lost me on punt coverage, lost me on kickoff returns; he lost one of the best players in the National Football League.

"He had Staubach, Dorsett, Charlie Waters, but I *was the difference.* I made a difference. I always made something happen. I caused a turnover. I made a touchdown. I blocked a punt. I tackled the best f***ing punt-return guy in the league. I did all those things that average players don't do.

"He should have showed me some respect. He could have got a lot of miles out of me with some respect. I always felt that Landry looked down on me, I know that Landry is not a racist, but he acted like one. If it was not that he acted like a racist, he acted holier than thou—it was just that he was better. That was his persona. That is all not true, but that's the way he did it. I never had a conversation about anything normal with Tom Landry until *long* after my career was over.

"You know what Landry should have done? Landry claims they knew about my cocaine addiction. See, I think Tex Schramm knew and Gil Brandt knew that I had drug problems. I'm not sure they told Landry. And that's the kind of way the Cowboys were run in those days. They insulated and protected Landry from that sort of thing. I don't know that Landry could have done anything else because I was the drug addict, the alcoholic, the crazy motherf***er. If anything, when it came time for him to get rid of me, if he knew that I had a drug problem, if he loved me, if he cared about me, 'OK, I've been a bad boy.' But if you know why, if you know 'You've been a bad boy because you've been on drugs,' then if he says he knew, if he *knew* that, why didn't he send me to treatment? Say, 'Thomas, either you're going to a clinic for the drugs you're on or I'm going to release you.'

"In response to Landry releasing me, I announced my retirement. Yeah, it was one of those drunk-defying moments, like growling at the bartender. 'Ah, ah ah ah ah. They can't fire me. I quit.'

"But the Cowboys [under Landry] never did get back to the Super Bowl without me. They missed Thomas Henderson."

Chapter 62

CASUALTIES

When Ed "Too Tall" Jones embarked on his boxing career in 1979, the player slated to replace him as the strongside defensive end was the Cowboys' number one draft pick of 1978, Larry Bethea. A defensive tackle out of Michigan State, the 6'5", 250-pound Bethea could run the 40 in 4.8 seconds and bench-press 390 pounds. In 1977 he was named the Big Ten's MVP, the first lineman to be so honored since Dick Butkus in 1963. His senior year he had 45 solo and 44 assisted tackles. He finished his college career with a school-record 43 sacks. When the Cowboys drafted Bethea first in 1978, Gil Brandt told reporters, "He's no gamble at all."

During his rookie season, Bethea showed great ability but little heart for the game. Thomas Henderson, who was always very good at reading people, called him "Papa Bear." After one play during practice, he wanted to rest. He would refuse to play with minor ailments, not caring that competing players were taking his place for the few extra plays, something unheard of when you're trying to beat out others for a job.

During training camp in 1979, Bethea didn't show the necessary aggressiveness to play left end, which required him to charge from a left-handed stance into the teeth of the other team's attack. How, Bethea wondered, could he be mean while having to think about so much?

Tom Landry moved him inside to left tackle. Larry Cole was shifted to end. Skip Bayless reported that Bethea was too nice and nicknamed him "No Mean Bethea," a takeoff on the nickname of "Mean" Joe Greene, the Steelers behemoth.

Bethea had turned down offers to go to Harvard and Yale so that he could play football at Michigan State. By his second training camp, he was openly regretting his choice. "I'd be in law school by now," he said. Bethea told Bayless that because he was so big, everyone expected him to play football. "Yeah, when I was back in high school I had more forethought than most. Everybody else was into stars and heroes, and I had bigger plans. My coaches and counselors all wanted me to go into premed and prelaw, but they just didn't mix with football. I was athlete of the year in Virginia, and everybody just *expected* me to . . ."

Bethea discovered that he couldn't devote himself to the game the way Landry's system demanded. He also could not adjust to the brutality of the pro game. He would watch Randy White maul opposing players in practice and ask him, "What turns you on?" White answered, "Wearing the uniform turns me on."

Bethea responded the way he figured coach Landry would want him to: "Come Saturday," he said, "I'll show all those nice folks out there I can be a crazy SOB. Yes, sir, ole No. 76 will show 'em." The words, however, were hollow. Like a lot of players, Bethea also had great difficulty grasping the Flex. He would ask teammates and reporters, "Man, am I just not good enough?"

By the end of Bethea's second training camp, Gil Brandt was singing a different tune. "I just wish there was a way to stick a needle in a guy's arm and find out whether he wants to play or not. That will be the next breakthrough in scouting."

When Ed Jones returned for the 1980 season, Bethea's opportunity to start for the Cowboys was over. He began snorting cocaine, an addiction that captured him for the rest of his too-short life.

Thomas Henderson: "In terms of pro football players, Larry Bethea was not a good football player. He was a mistake. Whenever you pick a guy number one he should end up as a starter. The Cowboys have had some of those guys throughout their history, like Bill Thomas, Aaron Kyle, Billy Cannon Jr., and so Larry was a decent football player, but Larry was *not* a number one draft choice. And I'm not sure what the criteria was for picking him. It was probably his ability to run. He could run a 4.8 40. But Larry was a good little soul, but here he was playing behind Too Tall Jones and Harvey Martin, and he didn't measure up.

"Larry and I never talked about our cocaine habits. I never had those conversations. But by the time I was talking to Larry, we couldn't even talk. We'd look at each other, and our lips wouldn't move. We were smoking that [much] cocaine. The only conversation we were having was how we could get some more dope."

Bethea continued as a backup through 1983, when his name was mentioned by Tex Schramm in connection with a federal cocaine investigation along with four other Cowboys players. No charges were ever filed. When the Cowboys offered him only a small raise and no bonus to re-sign in 1984, he signed a three-year contract for $550,000 with the Michigan Panthers of the United States Football League (USFL). When he left Dallas, he was bitter, complaining that Landry had never given him much of a chance to be a starter.

He went from the Michigan Panthers to the Oakland Invaders, then to the Houston Gamblers, and when the USFL folded, so did Bethea's football career. His life after football was a steady spiral downward.

In July 1985 he was arrested for setting three fires in Mount Rainier National Park in Washington state. He pleaded guilty and was ordered to pay a $1,000 fine and undergo psychiatric evaluation. A few months later he asked Gil Brandt for his severance pay but didn't give a return address because he was homeless, living on the streets of Seattle.

In mid-1986 Bethea returned to live with his mother in Newport News, Virginia. According to Johnny Yu, a convenience store owner who knew him in Newport News, no local businessman would give him a job.

In August 1986 Bethea was arrested for stealing his mother's life savings of $64,000 from the attic safe. When he was brought in, he had $61,375, mostly in $20 bills, in his pockets. That day he had gone to the home of his estranged wife and bloodied her lip and scratched her arm in a scuffle. Adding to the confusion, Bethea's wife claimed half ownership of his mother's money, saying she was entitled to it under a divorce petition. Bethea was sentenced to four years in jail, but the judge suspended the sentence and ordered him to pay back his mother.

Ed Jones ran into Bethea not long after the incident with his mother. He was hoping Bethea was getting help, but he could see that Bethea wasn't straight.

In March 1987 Bethea applied for a job at a local 7-Eleven store. He was a regular customer there. He didn't get the job. At the time he was living on biweekly checks of $332 for retirement benefits from the Houston Gamblers. According to Yu, Bethea spent most of the money on cigarettes, beer, and cocaine.

On April 23, 1987, Bethea went to Yu to cash his final paycheck. He was depressed because it was for half the usual amount. He told Yu he had to get out of town. He cashed the check and went out and bought cocaine.

Bethea stole a gun from a parked car and robbed two convenience stores that evening. The stores were near his mother's home, and he was recognized as the robber in both instances. One of the stores was the 7-Eleven where he had applied for a job.

A few hours later he was found in the backyard of a run-down boarding house where a childhood friend had been staying. The friend, Tony McNight, had not been seen for a week. McNight's brother, Jason, told Susie Woodhams of *The Dallas Times Herald* that he thought Bethea had gone there to be in a familiar atmosphere.

When police found Bethea by the side of the boarding house, a bullet from the gun used in the robberies had ripped through his right temple. He had killed himself. He was 30 years old.

Jason McNight, who had himself been arrested and convicted of drug use, blamed himself for Bethea's death. "If I'd been there," McNight said, "I could have taken the gun and sent him home."

No one in Dallas could believe what had happened to him. Bethea had been so intelligent, so sensitive, so together. His motto had been "A man is only as good as his word." But he had been unable to control his drug habit, and the cocaine made him an animal, a creature forced to do terrible things so he could buy drugs he apparently no longer could stand doing. Hating himself for his drug habit and his twilight zone existence, Larry Bethea put himself out of his misery.

Thomas Henderson: "My heart always goes out to those afflicted by the disease of alcoholism and drug addiction. He shot himself in the head after he robbed a store of people he knew. And I understand where Larry had been."

Thomas Henderson had been fired from the Cowboys in the middle of the 1979 season. Petulantly, Henderson announced he had retired, a big mistake, because then the Cowboys still owned his contract. Had he allowed them to put him on waivers, he could have cut a rich deal with whoever picked him up. He ran off to Las Vegas. When he returned to Dallas, his cocaine habit had reached $400 a day. No longer a Cowboy, his safety net was gone. After 12 federal agents raided his hotel room, he flew to California to play for the San Francisco 49ers. The cocaine, however, made it almost impossible for him to function. He fell asleep at meetings, even at practice. He told the team doctor about his addiction and asked for help, but none was forthcoming. Henderson wore out his welcome in San Francisco when he did coke with one of the 49ers secretaries, who was busted and asked to tell what she knew about Henderson. Meanwhile, Henderson's wife, Wyetta, called 49ers coach Bill Walsh and told him about Henderson's cocaine habit. That evening he was put on waivers. Said Henderson, "I had asked for help, but instead of trying to heal me, the 49ers were letting me go."

His next stop was the Houston Oilers under Bum Phillips. Henderson had just about broken his neck in San Francisco, and in his third week in Houston, a hamstring popped. His heretofore perfect body was cracking under the strain of the drug habit, which by now had climbed to a one-day record of $2,100. He began freebasing, the ultimate high. In nine weeks, Henderson spent $110,000.

He moved out of the home he shared with his wife. "Thomas" Henderson was no longer in his body. In his place was a madman. He was paranoid. One night he packed his paraphernalia, sure he was going to be busted, and walked 15 blocks from his room in the Marriott Hotel to the Astrodome, certain he would be safe there. He sat down in the middle of the parking lot. He was sure the cops were watching him. He pulled his coat over his head—and smoked his cocaine.

He started screaming at the rustling bushes at the edge of the parking lot: "I know you cops are there." He shouted that if they came after him, he would break his pipe on the pavement and throw the coke all over the parking lot.

He sat under his coat for 45 minutes, peeking out and screaming. Only after the pipe clogged was he able to stop and stand up. He flung the pipe across the parking lot. It smashed into shards. "I threw the coke away," he yelled. "I don't have any drugs on me. I'm going back home now."

He walked back to his hotel room. He was holding more rocks of coke in his hand.

Amazingly, some time after this incident, his hamstring healed, and he returned to football. He had missed seven games. Football didn't matter. There was only cocaine. He was put on waivers and then reinstated at the end of the season in the final game against the Vikings. Incredibly, Henderson made the interception that saved the game for the Oilers. In the playoffs, they lost to the Oakland Raiders. Henderson was having blackouts, and he couldn't remember much of the game. He was drooling.

He flew back to Dallas. In three weeks he went through $15,000 in cash and another $5,000 he had borrowed. A girlfriend asked him, "Where, in this sickness, lives this man?"

Henderson couldn't say a word. He was running, and he couldn't stop. He thought to himself, "I am going to die."

Not knowing where to turn, Henderson was watching Super Bowl XV on TV when he saw Charlie Jackson, the head of NFL security. He called Jackson in New Orleans and told him he was freebasing and needed help. "It's ruining my life. I'm spending all my money. I'm going crazy," he said.

Jackson gave him the name of a psychiatrist and said he would help get him into a drug rehab center. But when the psychiatrist asked Henderson about his children, he exploded and ran off.

Henderson was sent to Camelback Hospital in Scottsdale, Arizona, the first NFL player ever to admit to drug addiction. While in the clinic, his wife served him divorce papers. He got drunk that night. He was put in psychiatric lockup.

Even after 60 days of treatment, his cravings for cocaine were very strong. Any time he drank a beer or smoked marijuana, the craving returned. He flew back to Dallas, and he returned to freebasing.

Henderson wanted to play football again, and he called Don Shula, who said he could try out for the Miami Dolphins in May 1981. To pay for his coke, Henderson sold his dream house in North Dallas.

At camp he was heavy, but he could still run. He scrimmaged with the rookies, and Shula personally accompanied him to AA meetings. But one of the rookies was freebasing, and Henderson could not say no.

In the last preseason game he took off his neck protector. In the second quarter against the Kansas City Chiefs, running back Joe Delaney hit him so hard he felt he had been hit with a sledgehammer. He blacked out. The tingling wouldn't stop. He started to feel numb. On the next snap, he ran *away* from the play. This time his neck was broken. He lay in the clubhouse the rest of the second half until the game was over.

Instead of being sent to the hospital, he was sent home, where he couldn't sit, couldn't lie down. The next day he could not get out of bed. His arms and legs didn't work. He started screaming. There was no one to hear him. He screamed from 4:00 A.M. until almost 8:30 in the morning. "Please, help me!" Finally, a maid heard him. She went and got help.

The doctor came and said he had a pinched nerve. Henderson told him he was sure his neck was broken. A CAT scan proved him right. His football career was over.

Henderson moved back to Dallas and found a new coke connection. He was getting a check for $6,000 every week based on a $125,000-per-year salary with the Dolphins, but the money was going to buy cocaine. Nothing else mattered to him but the pipe.

By December 1981 Henderson was broke. His money was gone. His house had been sold. He had no possessions. He pawned his Super Bowl rings and smoked that money. All he had left were his Mercedes and his clothes.

For over a year Henderson lived with singer B. J. Thomas, who supported him that whole time.

He got a job in an executive recruitment firm. He started to get into the nuances of drinking lunch. He began having blackouts. From beer at breakfast, he became a full-blown alcoholic. Now he had a double addiction. Then he began having seizures.

B. J. Thomas had to finally ask him to leave. To rent an apartment he had to borrow money. As collateral, he put up his precious car. In February 1983 he stopped paying rent and lost the car.

On his 30th birthday, March 1, 1983, he was dead broke. He owed everyone in Texas money, so he fled to California in the car he was supposed to turn over to his ex-employer.

Speeding across Texas and Arizona, his only thought was: I really want to die.

Then on November 2, 1983, Henderson and two underage girls shared some coke and had sex. The cops were at his door. His arrest, of course, made national headlines. He freebased heavily, hoping to die. Said Henderson later, "I wanted to stick a gun in my mouth and blow my brains out, but the police had my gun."

Four days later he checked into another treatment center. He met people as sick as he was. When he was finally able to admit he was an alcoholic, his life began to change. He finally recognized that if he didn't change, he would die, that if he freebased, he would die.

He was sentenced to four years and eight months for statutory rape. He was seven months and three days sober when he went to prison.

He got out on October 15, 1986. He was sober, which he has remained to this day. Now living in Austin, Thomas (no longer Hollywood) Henderson has become one of the preeminent spokesmen on alcohol and cocaine addictions.

In a way, Thomas Henderson has become a symbol of the excesses of the seventies, a professional football player who threw away a certain niche in the Hall of Fame because of drugs. But really, the symbol should have been Larry Bethea, who had been unlucky enough to be holding a gun at the same time his drug habit had defeated him. When Henderson wanted to die, he was unarmed. As a result, Bethea is dead, Henderson alive.

"I'm the most famous ex–cocaine addict in the world," he states as a matter of record. And that is true, but what Thomas Henderson is most proud of is that he has been sober since 1983, and since that time he has been able to help hundreds of other addicts who were where he had once been. And that, in the end, should be Thomas Henderson's legacy.

Chapter 63

Roger in Mothballs

Two weeks after Thomas Henderson's dismissal in midseason of 1979, the Cowboys suffered another serious setback when Drew Pearson was injured. He had just caught his second touchdown catch of the day against the New York Giants when he attempted to spike the ball. In doing so, he took a misstep, twisted an ankle, and severely damaged his knee. He returned to catch yet another touchdown pass, but it was to be his last game of the season.

Drew Pearson: "I caught three touchdowns in the December 2 game against the Giants. That game I had three touchdowns, and I was all fired up because it was against Terry Jackson, who was a nemesis of mine. We just had an ongoing war. When he came in as a rookie, I had been in the league a few years. I had known his brother, Monte Jackson of the Raiders, real well, and Monte was the type of guy you could do anything to, and he would never say anything throughout the whole game. You could spit on him, kick him, cut him, hold him, and he wouldn't say a thing. Push him. Nothing. So I thought Terry was the same way. When we played the Giants in the first game we played against him, I went right at Terry Jackson. I was going to knock the shit out of this guy and have him scared the whole game. And I went after him, but the only thing, Terry wasn't intimidated. It made him mad as hell, and he came back fighting like hell. So from then on, we had a feud.

"We were friendly and respectful after the game, but during the game he was trying to kill me and I was trying to kill him back. It was whoever got to whom first, so I scored early in that football game on Terry, and then scored another one on him, and I got so excited on the second one, I jumped up and didn't know whether I wanted to throw the ball in the stands or spike the ball, and I decided to throw it in the stands, but by that time I was on my way down and landed wrong. My ankle turned, but my knee hyperextended, and I went down like someone had shot me from the stands. The knee was hurting. It swelled up immediately, but I was embarrassed and didn't want Landry to be too upset with me so I went back out there on our next series, and I caught a 44-yard touchdown pass, this time on Ray Rhodes, who was playing cornerback at the time for the Giants. I limped through this pass route, I mean, literally limped through it. But I had to go back out there to save face, and I ended up catching it for 44 yards, but then I had to come out of the game after that, and the next day my knee just blew up.

"That was my 100th straight game, and I couldn't play my next one, against Philly, and that was a big game, for the title. We beat them when Butch Johnson came in and caught the winning touchdown pass, and then we came back against the Redskins in Texas Stadium, where we were losing 17–0 and came back and won. John Riggins burst down the sideline for 66 yards to make the score 34–21, and it looked like the game was lost, and then we came back. Roger hit Tony Hill going away in the end zone over Lemar Parrish, and we won that game. I remember that game well because I started that game, but I couldn't finish, because of my leg. But we came back and won that game, 35–34, one of the best games in Texas Stadium, and it not only won us a division title, got us into the playoffs, but it knocked the Redskins out of the playoffs as well.

"Then in the opening round of the playoffs against the L.A. Rams, we lost 21–19, with two minutes left on a 50-yard bomb to Billy Waddy. We fell flat on our face. We didn't play worth a damn. I don't know. I think we went in with a big head, full of ourselves, and the Rams came in and surprised us. That was a disappointing loss. That loss hurt very bad, 'cause we felt we had a good team. We could have been in our third straight Super Bowl, should have been.

"We had one last chance to win at the end. I don't know what happened. We just didn't move the ball. You gotta give guys like Jack Youngblood and Fred Dryer and Larry Brooks credit because they kept pressure on Roger all day, and that was Roger's last NFL game, and to let you know what kind of day it was, his last completed pass went to Herb Scott, an offensive lineman. Roger was scrambling around and just threw it. It was illegal, and we got a penalty and gave up the ball on the play. But that was Roger's last pass—to Herb Scott."

In 1979 Staubach had suffered five concussions, the worst from the hard hit by the Steelers' L. C. Greenwood, and at the end of the year he announced his retirement. A long and glorious era had ended. Since he began playing in Dallas in 1969, Roger Staubach had become the heart and soul of America's Team. He was a military veteran, a football hero, a poster boy for decency and Christian brotherhood, yet as fierce a competitor as ever put on shoulder pads. Twenty-three times, the last being the great 35–34 victory against the Washington Redskins, Staubach led the Cowboys to come-from-behind wins; 14 of those wins came in the last two minutes. Most of these occurred on national television. As long as there was time, Staubach believed the Cowboys could win, and because of this competitive confidence, so did his teammates. Part of the surprise about his retirement was that no one thought he would step down after failing in the opening round of the playoffs to the Rams. Everyone thought he'd come back for at least one more year to try to take the team back to the Super Bowl.

Roger Staubach: "I did a lot of soul-searching before I decided to retire. I was 38. In the '79 season I had three concussions where I had to leave the game and couldn't return. And against the Rams in the playoffs, Jack Reynolds grabbed me and drove me into the ground. I was dazed, really wasn't totally with it at the end of the game.

"It really bothered me the way we ended the game. I was thinking to myself, 'Hey, I'm 38, I really want to make this decision on my own.'

"After a total exam, Dr. Fred Plumb in New York told me I definitely should retire. He saw a difference in reactions between my right and left sides. They were very minimal, but he said it could be the beginning of scar tissue syndrome.

"Dr. Paul Williams here in Dallas didn't feel that way. He said he didn't see any difference. But Dr. Williams said there had been enough concussions that retiring was probably not a bad idea. So it was part of the factor.

"If I had been 34, I would not have retired. But being 38, I told myself it was time. We had been in three Super Bowls in four years, and Danny White was definitely ready to play. So I wasn't abandoning a good team. It was a *very* good team, and I would have had fun with that team. I wish I would have had more years with Drew and Dorsett. We could have won a lot of Super Bowls.

"And Danny White did one hell of a job, really. They just lost some tough games. But it still was a very good team for three or four years.

"I wish I were still playing. But I never second-guessed that I retired. I did miss it a lot more than I would have thought. Maybe if I had known that, knew how much I'd miss it, known that Ed Jones would come back, that Charlie Waters would come back, maybe . . . 'cause see, '79 was a tough year. We played pretty well that year, but Jones wasn't there, Charlie tore up his knee in the exhibition season, Randy White hurt *both* his insteps, Benny Barnes had a bad knee, so we kind of limped through the year. And then everyone came back healthy in '80, and I would have enjoyed quarterbacking that '80 team, that '81 team.

"But Danny quarterbacked them very well. They scored. The big mistake Landry made was giving Gary Hogeboom a chance, not that Gary wasn't a fine athlete, but he wasn't Danny White. That hurt Tom, and when Danny came back he started playing well again. And then Tom tried [Steve] Pelluer, who was another fine athlete, but Pelluer couldn't handle the deal emotionally. He had to call three timeouts in the first quarter of one game. So there were games that were lost that could have been won.

"I think losing Mike Ditka and Dan Reeves as coaches hurt, too, because they were that link to the players, and Tom listened to both those guys, and then all of a sudden Tom surrounded himself with yes-people. And Ditka and Reeves weren't like that. He needed their influence, because the league was becoming decentralized. You couldn't do it all yourself. I don't know if he would have made the Herschel Walker trade, but if he had had Troy Aikman, he would have won again.

"We were a great team. We had a better seventies than the Steelers. The Steelers won four Super Bowls, but we had nine winning, great seasons. We won so many games, but you are graded on whether you win the Super Bowl. We were the only NFC team to win a Super Bowl in the seventies. But we were very competitive in all of them. In '75 the Steelers were *the* team. I think we over-achieved that game. We played a great game that day, and we still could have pulled it off. And we should have won both the Colts games and the second Steelers game. Those were the tough ones. I don't want to sound greedy. It's just that I hate to lose."

Chapter 64

Close, but No Cigar

At the time he announced his retirement in mid-March 1980, Roger Staubach was rated the number two passer of all time in the NFL behind Otto Graham. Third was Sonny Jurgensen, with Lenny Dawson fourth. The retirement of Staubach was a shock, but it was blunted some when Ed "Too Tall" Jones announced he would abandon his boxing career and return to the Cowboys. Jones had earned $300,000 boxing, but he learned that he didn't have the overhand right, which was necessary to get him to the top of the boxing game. Jones would star for Dallas from 1980 through the 1989 season, becoming one of the most durable players in franchise history.

The year before, Tex Schramm had liberated talented defensive lineman John Dutton from a deteriorating situation in Baltimore under owner Robert Irsay. And so in 1980 the starting defensive front four were Ed Jones, Harvey Martin, Randy White, and Dutton.

On offense the only change was Danny White for Roger Staubach. It took a while for White to understand that it was more important for him to fit into the team than the other way around.

Drew Pearson: "We had a pretty good year in 1980, finished 12–4. We overcame a lot. Our offense was high powered, scored a lot of points. Danny did a nice job. The thing is, all he had to do was fit in. We took the driver out and put a new driver in. All the other pieces to that puzzle were still in place. Initially, Danny tried to do too much, tried to establish his own identity. And he tried to carry the team, and that wasn't necessary. All he had to do was fit in.

"It took him about halfway through the season to understand that. But you see what we had back. That's why I'm saying Roger was very tough to lose. He could have played that next year. You see the success we had with Danny, and not to slight him any, but, you know, if Roger was there, we could have had that same success. We were in position to go to another Super Bowl."

After the Cowboys thumped the L.A. Rams in the opening round of the playoffs, White engineered a tremendous victory over the Atlanta Falcons with a winning touchdown pass to Drew Pearson with 49 seconds left, but in the NFC title game against the Philadelphia Eagles and their star receiver Wilbert Montgomery, the Cowboys were able to score only one lone touchdown and lost 20–7. White had a poor day, and Tony Hill was criticized for not playing hard.

In 1981 the Cowboys, led by Tony Dorsett's 1,646 yards rushing, again finished 12–4, the 16th winning season in a row for the Cowboys under coach Landry. In the playoffs they seemed invincible, shutting out Tampa Bay, 38–0. Then against the San Francisco 49ers, Dallas led 27–21 and was getting close to field-goal range, but Danny White misfired on a pass to Doug Donley, and the Cowboys had to punt with only minutes remaining.

Behind young quarterback Joe Montana, the 49ers drove the length of the field and scored when Dwight Clark made an acrobatic catch in the end zone to give the 49ers the 28–27 lead with less than a minute left.

The Cowboys had one more chance. White connected with Drew Pearson, who would have scored, but Eric Wright pulled him down by his uniform shirt. Then with seconds remaining, White dropped back to pass to Tony Hill, but he tripped, fell, fumbled, and the 49ers recovered. It was possibly the most disappointing loss in Cowboys history. It also prevented Danny White from getting the acclaim he deserved. Had the Cowboys won that game and gone on to the Super Bowl, White would have had a far more esteemed place in Cowboys history. The loss to the 49ers, though, was so devastating, it caused everyone to forget all the games played up to then and forced everyone to focus on the defeat.

Drew Pearson: "I was stunned. It was just so disappointing. We had done what we had to do to get that lead, and heck, if we were going to turn the game over to anybody, why not our Doomsday Defense, because they had played well all season long? We expected them to be able to stop the 49ers. We never expected the 49ers to be able to drive it like they did, 90-something yards, and to win the game. I thought somewhere along the line we'd stop them and make them punt and work to get the ball back or they'd kick a field goal and try to cut the lead that way. For them to come all the way down the field was devastating.

"We came back after that. Danny hit me on a play over the middle for big yardage, and I thought I was gone actually. I got caught from behind. I never saw the guy, Eric Wright. He just reached out and was able to grab my jersey. He was able to enforce it by grabbing the shoulder pads, and he yanked me down. But still, that was one play in that drive. We could have come back. I came back to the huddle, and I wanted Danny White to line me up on the other side and instead of my going inside this time, wanted him to send me out and bring it. That would have given us another 20 yards, but Danny called Tony's number, and Tony took a little longer than normal to get downfield trying to avoid coverages, and Danny waited on him instead of looking away and going to the other side, and waited and waited, and he finally got hit and fumbled, and that was the end of that game."

In 1982 everyone expected that it was the year the Cowboys would return to the Super Bowl, but a crippling player strike temporarily changed everyone's plans. The issue was severance pay, and the strike caused seven games to be canceled.

What hurt the Cowboys as much as anything was the anger directed at Danny White, who met with Tex Schramm and tried to end the strike behind the backs of the other players. White had taken a pro-management stance, and afterward the sentiment was that the team didn't want White as their quarterback anymore, but preferred instead backup Gary Hogeboom.

Drew Pearson: "Nobody wanted to strike. Taking eight games off your career, that's hard to get back. You can get the money back, but you can't get those eight games back, 'cause time waits on no one.

"I was player rep at that time going through all that, and here was Danny White going behind our backs, trying to solve the strike by meeting with Tex Schramm. We didn't take too kindly to that. It might have been different if he had discussed it with us, and we blessed it—we all wanted to end the strike. We were disappointed Danny took that approach. I think he meant well in what he was trying to do, but his approach got him in trouble, and that's when the feud between him and Gary Hogeboom started brewing. The players resented Danny for doing that, and they started getting on Hogeboom's bandwagon.

"Hogeboom didn't turn out to be the quarterback he was cracked up to be. Hogeboom had us all infatuated, including coach Landry. I think Gary Hogeboom would have turned out to be a pretty good quarterback, but there was one game after I retired, we were playing the New York Giants, and Hogeboom was having a pretty good year, but Lawrence Taylor steamrolled him on a blitz, and looking at Hogeboom's stats from then on, he was never the same player. He took a devastating hit, and he never recovered from that hit, and he became happy feet back there from then on, and then he became a journeyman. He went from potentially the next great quarterback for the Cowboys to a journeyman.

"In 1984 it was announced that Clint Murchison was putting the team up for sale. I realized there would probably be some changes because Clint, from all we saw, was the ideal owner. He let football people run football business. It was Tex's deal. Tex paraded himself as the owner, and rightfully so, because he was perceived that way, because Clint gave him that type of clout. It was perceived as Tex's team. When the sale happened, you wondered how things were going to shake out, and who was going to get caught up in the transition.

"Around that same time in the winter of '84, I was going through a divorce, and then I fell asleep at the wheel after driving home from a basketball game and rammed the back of a semi that was parked on the shoulder, and that was it for me. When I announced my retirement in August, I had a huge hole in my liver. There was no way I could play again.

"I had planned on playing another three or four more years. I was on the verge of signing a new contract. Actually it was the first time I played out a contract with the Dallas Cowboys, 'cause I kept renegotiating all the time, trying to make up the loss I had coming in as a free agent at such a low salary. So I was on the verge of signing a big lucrative contract in the $500,000-a-year range, so I was looking forward to continuing to play. But because of the accident everything was gone, so I had to scramble around to find out what I was going to do. When the Cowboys made it clear my current contract and their financial obligation to me ran out in August, I said, 'Oh Lord, I have to find something to do,' because I had gotten divorced in February, and in that divorce I gave up just about everything I had because I wanted it to be a smooth transition, not only for my ex-wife but for my kids. I felt I had a lot of earning power, and I was willing to give that up as long as I could go forward with everything else in place and that being mine.

"When it was announced a few weeks after the accident that I was going to retire, a few people in the TV business were interested, NBC and CBS, and they both offered me opportunities to join their broadcasting teams as a color analyst, and I ended up signing with CBS. I enjoyed that, did seven NFL games that first year. Rudy Martzke's *USA Today* voted me Rookie of the Year, and I enjoyed the work and was looking forward to another season after a year of learning. My agent, David Falk, approached CBS about renewing the contract, and CBS decided, 'Hey, we don't want the guy.' Yeah, well. 'We want to go in another direction.' So I was really really shocked, didn't know what I was going to do, and that's when I started talking about a comeback. 'If they are not going to let me talk about the game, then I will give them something to talk about.' So I was going to go back out there and play.

"After almost a year of being out, the liver regenerated itself and the hole closed up and went from the size of a softball to a silver dollar, so I asked my doctor if I could play again, and he said yes. So I was working to make a comeback and called Tex Schramm and asked his feelings, and he was elated, ecstatic, but the last thing he said, 'Of course, we want our doctors to check you.'

"So I told coach Landry how I was working out and how I had my weight up and felt good, and some of the guys saw me at the practice field and said I looked like Drew of old, maybe even a little quicker. But they sent my x-rays up to the University of Pittsburgh to Dr. Stargell, who's the leading liver specialist in the world, and he said I could play again, but he would not give me 100 percent clearance. He gave me 99, and coach Landry and I discussed that, and we came to the conclusion that if we were going to do this, it had to be 100 percent OK. We were both in accordance with that. I said, 'If I had in the back of my mind that something could happen,' and even Dr. Stargell said if something does happen, if you get hit, you'd have to get hit squarely on that spot, and even if it did start hemorrhaging, which was the biggest fear, that you could probably stop or control it before it became life threatening. But having that in the back of my mind, I knew I'd have trouble being the same type of player that I was, that fearless guy going over the middle, and so coach Landry and I concluded over the phone, he said it was probably in the Cowboys' and my best interest not to pursue it.

"And after we decided I wasn't going to play anymore, he offered me an opportunity to come out to training camp to work with the new wide receivers, to coach them in training camp, to help them develop and get them ready. So I did that for five weeks, and I kind of enjoyed it. It was good because they had two rookies, Leon Gonzales and Karl Powe, small-college receivers, had ability but were very green, very raw, who ended up making the team, and the big reason they made it was my guidance and coaching. The other two receivers were Mike Renfro and Tony Hill, so those two guys were set in their ways. My main concern was those two young guys. Since these two guys were on the team, coach Landry needed them to continue to learn and progress, so he asked me if I wanted to stay on as a part-time, full-time assistant. It was only part-time in pay, but full-time in hours. Doing that for a year, I found out that coaching wasn't for me, and so I got out and had some opportunities as a sportscaster down in San Antonio, doing the weekend sports, did that for six months. And there were a lot of things I tried, had my hand in, but the real deal was after I quit the Cowboys; I had already started this business, and I knew that was going to be my security. I found out that TV was like football, here today, gone tomorrow.

"While I was still playing I started a company that intended to make sports caps using the logos of the various professional sports teams. The problem was that we were not able to get licensing agreements from any of the pro leagues. We had our struggles, no question. We were no different than anybody else. These licensing agreements, arrangements, are commodities and very difficult to get. It wasn't anything personal. It was just a business decision these leagues were making. They wouldn't give us the opportunity to do business. This is true of any black entrepreneurs trying to break into the white establishment, which was why we didn't take it personally. It's tough for anybody, let alone if you're a minority, to try to get those opportunities. And even beyond that, it was tough just being an ex–football player. They don't take you seriously. 'You were a good wide receiver, but what the hell do you know about business?' And at that time I didn't know much about business, but I was eager and committed and willing to learn, and I tried to surround myself with business partners who had the expertise I didn't have so I could learn. It was a tough road, but I understand what the NFL and the other leagues were doing.

"Our first agreement was with the United States Olympic Committee. They saw a need to hire a minority vendor in connection with the '88 Olympic Games, and we were the vendor that they hired for headwear. And when we got that, we didn't know what we were doing, so we hooked up with another headwear company who had been bidding for the opportunity, but lost out, and we rode their financial strength, their sourcing capabilities, and their overall marketing expertise during that first year. They did a decent job with the Olympic head-wear, but we ended up losing money on the program. But in the meantime, it gave us a lot of credibility in the market, and all of a sudden, 'Who are these guys?' and, 'How did they get an Olympic license?' And so it gave us credibility. We had some nice products.

"And then in '87 Al Campanis made those negative statements about blacks and minorities, about why they aren't fit to be in coaching positions and front-office positions, that they don't have the 'necessities,' the mental capacity. And then Jesse Jackson jumped all over that, and he started the 'fairness in sports' committee [the Rainbow Coalition for Fairness in Athletics Commission], and I joined that committee.

"They had their first meeting in Chicago in connection with the Rainbow Coalition conference, and I went up there without an appointment but with an agenda, and my whole agenda was to try to get in front of Reverend Jackson to let him know there is another issue that needed to be put on the table and brought to light, that these sports leagues don't do business with any minorities either. And so that was like, 'Ooh, really?' And so they had this big national press conference, and everybody spoke on the discrimination against minorities in sports, coaching, management, but Reverend Jackson gave me the opportunity to speak on the discrepancies in minorities doing business with these entities. And from there Major League Baseball contacted us, and they were willing to give us an opportunity, a chance, and after I left that meeting in Chicago, I came back to Dallas and went right to a meeting I had scheduled with Tex Schramm.

"My whole point in the meeting with Tex was to make him aware of an opportunity they could take advantage of 'right now' to try to ease this negative situation, and that was to get us a license to do business with them, to publicize that, and get the name Drew Pearson out, and it would go a long way. I explained it would take a long time to hire coaches and the same thing in office positions, so he will continue to have this pressure, so I said, 'This is something you can do immediately and release some pressure.' He saw the value of doing that.

"It just so happened that weekend the NFL owners were getting together in San Diego, and Tex promised me he would talk to Pete Rozelle at that meeting. And that meeting happened, and on Monday we got a call in our office, 'When can you come to New York to meet with Robert Carey, the president of NFL Properties?' So we went up there to meet with them, and they gave us kind of a token-type category, the golf cap category, where you can use all the teams' logos, but it has to be on a golf-style hat, which means it has to have the braid in front and a leather strap in the back. So we said, 'Fine. We'll take that and develop that.' It was a way to get in, and eventually they found out they really didn't want to give us that, so they called us back into New York, and we had them pretty much over a barrel, because by giving us that category, they stepped on some toes of other licensees, and they were putting pressure on them. Robert Carey admitted he was reneging on what they had promised us. So we said, 'Fine.'

"We knew we were in a pretty good position, because they didn't want this to get out, and they were willing to work with us. We asked them, 'If you take this back, what can you give us?' So they gave us the low-end market on headwear, which at that time was no market. But we took it, and we developed it and made it work, and now we are one of their top licensees, in the million-dollar club, which means for the last three years we've been paying NFL Properties over $1 million in royalties off the hats we sell.

"One of the biggest thrills for me was at one of the NFL awards dinners one evening, the first year we made the million-dollar club. It was a big thrill for me to go up there to the stage to be called and accept this trophy, which is in our lobby for our recognition for reaching that million-dollar club. And standing up there in front of all those licensees who were out there, guys who gave us a hard time—and they know they gave us a hard time, negatively talking about us and trying to run us out of the business—knowing we had overcome that, knowing we did it right and that we had made a significant contribution to NFL Properties, more so than a lot of people sitting out there who tried to keep us from doing it, it was a tremendous feeling of satisfaction. It was as much fun as winning the Super Bowl. It gave me the same satisfaction."

Chapter 65

CLINT GOES UNDER

The beginning of the end for Clint Murchison, Tom Landry, Tex Schramm, and Gil Brandt came on June 14, 1979, when John Murchison, a partner so silent that few knew he owned half interest in the Dallas Cowboys, died shortly after speaking at a fund-raising dinner for a group of Boy Scout volunteers.

John Murchison was visiting the home of Governor William P. Clements. In the middle of an informal talk, John began coughing, and he excused himself. A highway patrolman drove John to the hospital, and on the way John's breathing became labored. The trooper driving the car loosened John's tie.

The driver sped up, and at the intersection of Avondale and Oak Lawn around 9:00, as the vehicle raced through a red light, another car ran into it broadside. John had a heart attack. He was transferred to a fire department ambulance and taken to the hospital, but he died an hour later. The medical examiner said the collision had nothing to do with his death.

John, though an equal partner, had little interest in or enthusiasm for football, and so John had received none of the prestige from the Cowboys, nor did he desire any. John's wife may have resented Clint's fame and attention as a result of his ownership of the Cowboys, but John never did. In the news about his death, it did not even mention that John Murchison co-owned the Cowboys with his brother.

John, in fact, in many ways was disgusted by his brother's behavior. Clint, though quiet and demure in appearance, was a swinger. He lived to party. During his marriage to his wife Jane, Clint enjoyed stepping out. He liked the chase, thrilled to the challenge of getting a young woman into bed. For personal thrills, Clint bought a penthouse apartment at the southeast corner of Park Avenue and fifty-seven Street in Manhattan, an aid to an obsessive quest for an unending string of young female conquests. To enhance his ability to lure beautiful young women into his circle in Dallas, in 1972 the Cowboys officially added sex to their image. Clint and Tex Schramm hired 18 beautiful young women; had them don short shorts, halter tops, push-up bras, and white go-go boots; and had them wildly shake their breasts and their comely rear ends to the suggestive beat of rock and roll in front of the Dallas fans during breaks in the action on the field. These magnificent, scantily clad women were named the Dallas Cowboy

Cheerleaders, but they led no cheers, except for the libidinous reaction from the male fans every time they went into their routine. The "cheerleaders" only served to enhance Dallas' image as a town that both hates and loves sin, sometimes at the same time. As the owner of the team, Clint Murchison made personal forays, romancing a cheerleader when the spirit moved him, until the cheerleaders got so famous by 1977 that he decided he was in too much danger of suffering from adverse publicity and backed off.

In 1972 his wife Jane divorced him. After the divorce Murchison admitted that his womanizing wasn't as much fun.

By the midseventies Clint found he was having some difficulty making love to his lady of the night, so he added cocaine to his vices when he discovered its power to aid him in lovemaking. Like some of his players who were chastised for their drug use, by the midseventies Clint Murchison also was acting erratically. He had tongues wagging when he started seeing Anne Farrell Brandt, the wife of his chief scout, Gil Brandt, and the tongue ran faster when Anne divorced Gil and in June 1975 Anne and Clint announced they would marry. Clint became Anne's fourth husband. And though Gil lost his wife, he didn't lose his job.

After the marriage Clint had little time for Anne, who devoted herself to charity work and to religion. By the middle of the next decade, Anne would sit by and watch as Clint turned a billion-dollar family fortune into dust.

At the height of their success in the midsixties Clint and John Murchison had owned 100 thriving companies with a value of more than $1.25 billion. But the Murchison brothers had an Achilles heel, which was that Clint Murchison had a self-destructive streak that he worked to hide from his more conservative and responsible brother. Where most people seek out wealth, Clint already had it. He wanted more out of life than mere wealth: he craved excitement like a gambler who can't stay away from the roulette wheel but who insists on putting a tall pile of chips down on the number with the longest odds.

Without telling John what he was doing, Clint began risking everything the brothers had worked for on increasingly risky investments, beginning with a string of real estate deals in California. He began building single-family apartment complexes and residential developments up and down the West Coast.

Then Clint got involved with an Australian named Richard Baker, a man with *big* plans who fascinated him. The first deal was the purchase of a 46-acre estate near Washington, D.C. Baker paid $4.5 million too much for the land. Clint didn't care.

Beginning in 1973 Clint let himself be taken in by another wheeler-dealer, Lou Farris Jr., who involved him in ten real estate projects, eight of which lost money because the deals involved little cash flow. Refusing to listen to his associates, Clint argued that real estate values would always climb and contended he was satisfied merely to own the properties.

He continued his plunging. One venture was supposed to turn cow manure into natural gas. Clint, who in his own quiet, intellectual way was as much a rogue as his dad, named the company Calorific Reclamation Anaerobic Process, or CRAP. Clint wasted $10 million before the process proved the accuracy of its acronym.

By the midseventies Clint appeared intent on sabotaging his empire. It seemed that the less likely the success of a project, the more he wanted to invest. The worst thing an adviser could tell him was, "Clint, that will *never* work." Once that was uttered, chances are he would invest. As an example, Clint spent millions financing a ski resort in Iran.

From 1975 through the end of his life, Clint made borrowing more and more money an obsession. Clint sometimes even gave his personal guarantee on a loan, a step considered folly even in sure-thing deals.

While his brother John became more and more conservative in his dealings, borrowing less and less, Clint, without the knowledge of his brother, was running up a gigantic debt. When John finally learned the extent of Clint's borrowing, he ordered his brother to consult him before running up more debts, but Clint ignored his warning.

By the end of the seventies inflation had jumped as high as 18 percent, and sales of real estate had come to a standstill. With little cash flow, the bank notes on Clint's loans kept coming due. Murchison was borrowing money to pay existing debts. At this point Clint was no longer addicted to women or coke. His new addiction was borrowing money.

Finally in 1978 John had enough, and the brothers agreed to dissolve the partnership no later than October 1981. Unfortunately for John and his family, untangling the complex maze of corporations to determine who owned what seemed almost impossible. They were still entwined when John died in June 1979.

With the passing of John Murchison, his son Dabney, who preferred to be called John Jr., began looking into his father's affairs and discovered that Clint had borrowed heavily against his $30 million trust. Afraid he would never see the estate left to him by his father, in 1980 John Jr. sent his uncle a memo demanding the trusts be dissolved and paid out. Clint, as was his habit, ignored the memo. But John's son didn't tolerate Clint's arrogance the way his father had. As coexecutor of the estate, John Jr. was on a mission to save Murchison Brothers from the reckless, self-destructive Clint. He continued writing memos, demanding accountability. Clint kept ignoring them. A frustrated John Jr., fearful that Clint would bankrupt everybody, then sued for a final dissolution of the partnership.

In self-defense a proud Clint Murchison lied to his brother's widow, Lupe, that their financial problems were being caused not by him but by John Jr., whom Clint disparagingly referred to as the "Punk." Clint was so persuasive that he managed to get Lupe and her three daughters to sue John Jr. to remove him as coexecutor of his father's estate. The trial was scheduled for April 1981.

A few weeks before the trial, Lupe and a date returned to her mansion after having dinner. Two gunmen were waiting for them. The gunmen blindfolded the date, threw him in the back of her Mercedes, and threw Lupe in the trunk. When the youngest daughter, Barbara Jeanne, arrived home with two friends, the intruders tied them up. Four hours later the gunmen left with a few pieces of jewelry. No one was hurt. The intruders were never caught.

Rumors abounded that Clint had planned the robbery, hoping Lupe would think John Jr. had set it up. It was a "prank" reminiscent of Clint's seeding of RFK Stadium with chicken feed prior to the release of hundreds of chickens or another of his anti–George Preston Marshall schemes whereby Clint hired helicopters to hover above RFK Stadium and release ten thousand silver and blue Ping-Pong balls, only to be foiled at the last moment by the Federal Aviation Administration.

At the trial, John Jr. was vilified. Lupe's attorneys portrayed him as a "vicious and ungrateful son." That night John Jr. caved in to the pressure. He resigned as coexecutor, and in exchange, his mother agreed to loan him $3 million at an 18 percent interest rate to be adjusted annually.

John Jr. had lost a battle, but he was determined to win the war, and he had the funds to wage it against Uncle Clint. In February 1981 John Jr. sued Clint and his four children claiming Clint had used funds from his trust and demanded $30 million and an injunction forcing Clint to segregate John Jr.'s assets from the family trusts.

At the same time the value of oil and real estate was dropping steadily as interest rates were climbing. Clint had a flood of debt and little cash to pay it off. Banks were calling Clint every day for money. He had to scramble each day to keep the doors of Murchison Brothers ajar.

The very wealthy tend to believe they are too smart for things to go terribly wrong, and as late as 1982 Clint still believed interest rates would fall and save him. But that was the year the Arab oil-supplying nations began fighting among themselves, and as the warring countries began glutting the market with oil, the world price of oil dropped sharply, causing Texas real estate values also to crash. By 1982 interest rates were at almost 20 percent, and Clint was paying $80 million just to service the interest on his notes. He could pay only a fraction of that amount.

Clint's fortune was built on a house of cards, and once John Jr.'s suit revealed the shakiness of his position, Clint was doomed to bankruptcy. Under the terms of John's lawsuit, Clint was forced to take the liens off some of his properties so that John's trust fund would be unencumbered.

Against his brother's orders, Clint had invested heavily in a computer company called OSI, and in October 1981 John Jr. forced Clint to release his assets from all debts connected with OSI. Clint still had another $24 million of encumbered trust funds to go. Making Clint's life harder was a temporary injunction obtained by John Jr. stopping Clint and his children from refinancing any debts on assets in the trusts. Around this time John Jr. also began threatening Clint with going to the press to reveal the extent of his uncle's indebtedness.

In December 1981 Clint might have survived the crisis had he acted reasonably and fairly toward John Jr. But he was the great Clint Murchison, and so when John Jr. offered to give up his interest in two companies in the trust with assets of $4 million and forget the damages if Clint would pay out the remainder of his trust, Clint laughed at him. But unable to bluff any longer, in April 1983 Clint finally removed the debts from the remainder of John Jr.'s assets and turned them over to him.

By this time the other five Murchison children were becoming nervous that Clint was on a course that would leave them penniless. Around this time Lupe finally figured out that of the two combatants, John Jr. had right on his side. The family met to force the liquidation of Murchison Brothers. Lupe took some assets, and the children took their trusts, leaving Clint with a mound of debts.

In early 1983, with Clint's ship about to sink, his law firm announced it would no longer represent him, despite the fact that it had been Clint Sr. who had made the firm what it was. Around this time the Dallas banks, which for years had been reticent to force Clint to pay up, started turning the screws. Many had figured that because Clint owned the Dallas Cowboys, he would be good for any debts, but as the rumors began to spread through the banking community about Clint's precarious financial position, the nervous bankers began to panic, and the cry for payment became a chorus. Those who screamed loudest got paid first, but Clint didn't have nearly enough money to pay everyone.

Adding to Clint's accumulation of crushing problems was the diagnosis in 1983 that he was suffering from an extremely rare degenerative nerve disease, similar to Lou Gehrig's disease and just as deadly. In the spring of 1983 Clint invited Tex Schramm to his home and asked him to find a buyer for the Cowboys.

Clint knew he would have to give up his most precious asset, but before he did so, he made sure that his two most loyal employees, Tex Schramm and Tom Landry, were well taken care of. Murchison gave Schramm a $2.5 million bonus and raised his salary to $400,000 per year. He gave Landry a $2 million bonus and raised his salary to $650,000 per year. Gil Brandt's salary was raised to $225,000.

In late 1983 Schramm found a buyer, Dallas businessman Harvey R. "Bum" Bright, who paid $63 million for the team and $20 million for the stadium. (To demonstrate Clint Murchison's bad timing, after the market turned around Bright sold the team and stadium in 1989 for close to $150 million.)

Large portions of the proceeds from the sale were used to pay off Clint Murchison's most boisterous creditors. After the sale was announced, the remaining creditors panicked big time and lawsuits against him came in an avalanche. By this time Clint was wheelchair ridden, as the disease continued to get worse.

Two months after selling the team, the suits totaled $75.7 million, most of the debt coming from bad real estate deals. Clint, weak and unable to go to the office, sought to hold off creditors by telling everyone that they would be paid in full when the oil business turned around. But by the summer of 1984 creditors demanded payment.

That year he began losing lawsuits. By the end of the year his judgments amounted to $100 million. Sixteen banks held liens on his home and property. Complicating matters was that Clint had often borrowed money or made investments without putting anything down on paper, and because of his disease he was losing his ability to communicate. By January 1985 the claims against him had reached $185 million.

When three creditors summoned the courage to force the almost-paralyzed man into bankruptcy, more creditors stepped forward, until the demands totaled $560 million. By the time his assets were distributed, his creditors ended up with between 10¢ and 30¢ on the dollar.

In the fall of 1986 Clint and Anne had to sell their mansion, and they moved across the street into an ordinary middle-class development home where Clint spent his last days in a tiny room, alone much of the time, relying on his wife and a nurse to aid him. In mid-March 1987 he contracted pneumonia and was hospitalized. On March 29 his ex-wife, Jane, came to see him, as did John Jr. The following day Clint became unconscious, and in the evening the 63-year-old founder of the Dallas Cowboys passed away.

At the service there were four eulogies, including one given by Tom Landry. Some of Clint's closest friends were appalled at the Christian Fundamentalist nature of the service. Others were embarrassed by it. They knew Clint was antireligion, and they blamed his wife, Anne, who was born again and deeply religious. But still others realized the hypocrisy of the moment, and they laughed it off as "Clint's last prank."

In a tribute, Tex Schramm said about Murchison, "He's what kept the whole thing here together. He was the glue. Our 25-year record is a tribute to him. I don't think he ever got the credit he deserved." Schramm said that what made the Cowboys was not that Murchison was absent but that he was so supportive: "It was his support of all those people that made it possible. You can stay out and not contribute, but his whole thing was he gave the support and backbone to the organization that allowed people to have the confidence to perform their jobs."

Clint Murchison was not the only one to lose everything, only one of the first. In 1988 alone, 113 Texas banks failed, more than half of the 200 banks that failed around the country. Among those to lose big were the Hunt brothers, William, Nelson, and Lamar. Nelson would later be involved in a scheme to corner the silver market. Another who lost big was former Texas governor John Connolly, who had invested heavily in Texas real estate and lost most of what he had, including his home.

Clint Murchison Jr. had lacked so many of his father's traits, especially shrewd judgment and common sense, as well as his father's uncanny ability to adapt to changing circumstances. But after Clint Sr. had thrust his son, a man who had wanted to become a teacher, into a position of economic importance he really hadn't ever wanted, perhaps the son's exercise in frittering away his huge fortune had been part of an unspoken plan to make sure he wouldn't do to his kids what his father had done to him. By not leaving his kids money, they would have to be resourceful and make it on their own in an occupation of their choosing. Perhaps that's what Clint had intended by his recklessness. If that had been the case, then in that he succeeded Texas-style.

In the end Clint Jr.'s children not only didn't get their trusts, neither did they receive any inheritance. Clint had made repeated promises to pay them, but he never did, even though he could have at any time, and after his death in 1987, they were left bitter and angry at their father's betrayal.

Clint had taken a company worth $1.25 billion and in less than a decade created a debt of more than $500 million. As pranks go, that's one that's very hard to top.

Chapter 66

Bum Bright

On November 13, 1983, word leaked to the press that Clint Murchison had put Tex Schramm in charge of selling the Dallas Cowboys. By then, Murchison's problems had grown so serious that he had no choice. The Cowboys had been Texas' darlings, the premier franchise in the National Football League. They had been in five Super Bowls, winning twice, and in the previous 18 years had been in the playoffs 17 times. This was a *very* desirable property.

Schramm knew he had to be very careful finding a buyer, lest he lose his job. Murchison was leaning toward selling the team to a syndicate headed by Vance Miller, a former business partner, and W. O. Bankston, a Dallas car dealer and oilman.

In the early eighties Miller had involved Murchison in a deal in which he didn't have to put a cent down. The deal netted Murchison $8 million. They were close friends.

For the playoff game against the Rams the previous December, Miller and Bankston had plunked down $550,000 for the remaining available tickets so the local TV blackout would be lifted. They gave the tickets away. Miller and Bankston were offering Murchison about $90 million, but Schramm kept putting them off. Tex wanted assurances that his job was safe, and he wasn't getting them, and so Schramm steered Murchison toward a deal with another old friend of Clint's, H. R. "Bum" Bright, an acquaintance since they were boys. (He got his nickname as an infant because his father thought he looked like a hobo when bundled up in blankets.)

As early as 1983 Schramm had been in contact with Bright, who as a boy had been a roughneck in the Oklahoma oil fields. After graduating from Texas A&M in 1942, at the age of 27, he became a petroleum engineer. He had 12 bucks in his bank account, and he and his partner ate peanut butter sandwiches for lunch. Four years later he was a millionaire. Folksy, persistent, and ruthless, he began trading oil leases, and after 15 years, he proved a wizard at it. One time he persuaded one woman to lock her recalcitrant husband out of their bedroom until he signed over an oil lease on his property. Another time he strapped a pen to a hospital patient to get him to sign over a contract. He acquired a trucking company by warning the aging owner that he'd drive him to his grave and then buy the firm from his relatives at a discount. "I play to win," said Bright. "I don't care if it's checkers or gin rummy or the oil and gas business. You play the game to win."

He branched out into real estate in the early fifties and then became involved in trucking, insurance, and providing mortgages, and he was successful in them all. His advertising slogan: "The future is Bright."

When the Arab oil embargo forced the price of oil from $3 to nearly $40 a barrel, Bright was amassing a fortune. Natural gas prices also rose from less than $1 per thousand cubic feet to nearly $5.50, and by 1984 Bright was selling $60 million worth of it every day. Construction boomed. Real estate prices soared, and by 1984 Bum Bright was one of the 50 richest men in the world, worth an estimated $600 million. The AP had named him one of the 10 most powerful Texans.

A devoted family man with four children, Bright and his family sat down for a formal dinner every Sunday night. Like most oilmen, Bright's politics were very conservative. Like most right-wingers, he distrusted the federal government. "I have no use for government meddling in private affairs," he said. He raised large sums of money for Barry Goldwater and George Bush.

Bright had never been a raging Cowboys fan. His energy and money had been directed toward the football program of Texas A&M, where he was chairman of the board of regents. But once Bright assured Schramm that if he bought the team, he would have no interest in running it, Schramm did all the arm-twisting he could to make sure Bright ended up as owner of the Cowboys, even if one of the arms Schramm had to twist belonged to Bright himself.

When in 1983 Schramm initially told Bright that Murchison wanted him to buy the Cowboys, Bright said he wasn't interested. Two days before the purchase Bright had had Sunday dinner with his family and hadn't even mentioned it. What changed Bright's mind was a phone call from Charles Pistor, chairman of the board of Republic Bank. Bright was also on the Republic board. Murchison owed the Republic Bank money. Pistor told Bright the bank would benefit greatly if Bright bought the Cowboys and as an inducement offered Bright a very favorable loan if he would buy the team from Murchison. Bright was making $8 million per month in his oil business. In 1983 the Cowboys had made a stated profit of $600,000. But Republic was making it painless to buy the team. Bright finally thought, "Aw, it'll be fun."

Bright, along with minority investors (including Schramm at 3 percent), agreed to buy the Cowboys and the 30-acre tract of land in Valley Ranch where the new team headquarters were being constructed for $60 million, and to buy the remaining 65 years on the Texas Stadium lease for about $20 million. The total price was $84.5 million. Bright's participation was only 17 percent, despite an NFL policy that it preferred one investor to own a majority of the stock. But Schramm believed that his best chance of remaining with the Cowboys for the rest of his life rested on the shoulders of Bum Bright, and Schramm got NFL commissioner Pete Rozelle, his former Rams employee, to help push through the sale regardless.

The sale transferring the Dallas Cowboys from Clint Murchison to Bum Bright took place on March 19, 1984. Though the sale price was $84.5 million, not a penny went to Murchison. It all went to his creditors and to lawyers.

Bum Bright: "[The sale] had to be at 7:00 A.M. because a Saudi bank needed a [Murchison] note paid by 2:00 P.M. There were 11 different lawyers [mostly representing members of the Murchison family, who wanted their rightful shares]. There was a lot of hostility and maneuvering. When everyone got paid, there was $365,000 left. But Henry Gilchrist [Murchison's lawyer] said, 'Conditional precent to closing: legal fees!'

"I said, 'Aw, Henry, send him a bill.' But Henry said, 'I've been sending the son of a bitch a bill for two years . . .'

"So in the end poor old Clint got not a penny."

As part of the deal, Bright officially named Tex Schramm "designated managing partner," giving him authority to run the team. Schramm stated publicly that he had been looking for another Clint Murchison, someone who would sit in the background and take a low-profile, hands-off approach. For the time being, the jobs of Schramm and coach Landry seemed safe.

Schramm had planned wisely, because only a few months later the $130 million Key West Resort development, a 200-acre resort planned by Tex Schramm and two partners and financed by Clint Murchison, went under. The plan called for 597 condominiums to be built around a championship golf course. With Murchison's financial and personal health failing, Schramm needed to keep his day job.

A month later Bum Bright, through a holding company he controlled called Texas Federal, bought the Texas Federal Financial Corporation and merged with Trinity Banc Savings Association. Bright predicted he would turn the thrift into a "financial juggernaut." He began buying up other savings and loans and investing heavily in commercial real estate. The savings-and-loan craze was on. Ronald Reagan's go-go hands-off government of the eighties was in full swing.

When the Cowboys opened their 1984 season, seven of their veterans were no longer on the team. Harvey Martin, Billy Joe Dupree, and Pat Donovan retired; Larry Bethea, Glenn Carano, and Bruce Huther signed with the United States Football League; and Butch Johnson was traded to the Houston Oilers. When Drew Pearson was injured in a car crash during training camp and had to retire, he became number eight.

Landry opted to see if backup QB Gary Hogeboom could do a better job than Danny White, and it turned out he couldn't. The team started strong, with Hogeboom throwing for 343 yards in a win against the L.A. Rams, but by the heart of the season he lost to a winless Buffalo Bills team, prompting Frank Luksa of *The Dallas Times Herald* to ask, "Who ruined the Cowboys?" It was about this time that reporters, including Luksa, began questioning whether Tom Landry was too old, whether his ideas were passé. When the Cowboys lost to the Miami Dolphins, 28–21, after Dan Marino threw three touchdown passes to

Mark Clayton in the last game of the season, the 9–7 Cowboys were eliminated from the playoffs for the first time in 10 years. "Three against America's Team," Clayton shouted in the locker room after the game.

In 1985 Landry did one of his best coaching jobs, leading a mediocre team back to the NFC East title. Bob Breunig retired, and the linebacking corps was mediocre at best. Without dominant linebackers, Tom Landry's Flex was looking very weak.

Some of the losses were brutal: 44–0 to the Chicago Bears, 50–24 to Cincinnati, 31–16 to San Francisco. But a patched-up defensive backfield, called "Thurman's Thieves" by Danny White, captured the public's imagination. The group of low draft picks and free agents—Dextor Clinkscale, Mike Downs, Everson Walls, Bill Bates, Ricky Easmon, and Dennis Thurman—intercepted 33 passes, all in key situations. Only the Chicago Bears, the Super Bowl winners, had more, with 34.

By the end of the season defensive coach Gene Stallings instructed his defensive backs to abandon the Flex. They began playing a 46, blitzing on almost every down.

Before their Monday night game in St. Louis, the Thieves went to Union Station and bought Indiana Jones fedoras, like Tom Landry's hat, only with more flash. But while Landry looked astute, the Thieves looked like gangsters.

An hour and a half before kickoff, Dallas TV station WFAA did a live remote from St. Louis. It was a quickie interview staged outside the locker room. The Thieves showed up wearing their new hats.

A couple of the white players, Randy White and John Dutton, resented what this group of black defensive backs (plus Bill Bates) was doing, seemingly making fun of Landry, cutting up, showing off. Jim Jeffcoat, who is black, didn't like it either.

In the third quarter of the game, Thurman told linebacker Jeff Rohrer and end Jim Jeffcoat, who had just blown a play, that they had to communicate better. A furious Randy White interceded. "What the f*** are you talking about?" he asked. Thurman told White he wasn't talking to him. White pushed him, forcing Thurman into a confrontation. Players had to break them up.

When Landry asked the Thieves to stop wearing the hats, they refused. When the Thieves appeared on a popular poster wearing the hats, the other faction was not pleased.

Nevertheless, without Dennis Thurman and his Thieves, the 1985 Cowboys would have been far less successful. In the first round of the playoffs, against the Los Angeles Rams, the Thieves did a number on quarterback Dieter Brock, but Eric Dickerson ran for 248 yards in a 20–0 Rams victory.

This was the year Tom Landry should have retired. But Landry hated to leave the team when it was on the way down. And when Schramm asked Landry to train younger coaches, Landry said he would, though he was constitutionally unable to do so. It had always been Tom Landry's way or no way, and it would be that way to the end.

Chapter 67

The Fall of the Cowboys

In an article dated January 31, 1973, in the *Fort Worth Press*, Tex Schramm bemoaned the fact that the rest of the NFL teams had caught up with the Cowboys' scouting technique. Before 1973 other teams would ignore or not be aware of great players from small colleges, who the Cowboys would take in late rounds. No longer. "They have caught up with us, I'm afraid," said Schramm. "Every guy drafted through the first two rounds was just about the way we had them rated. Our scouts have seen it coming. They say it's like a jungle out there. Every place they go to look at a player they run over half a dozen scouts from other teams."

The Cowboys had struck gold in 1975 with their Dirty Dozen, and the team made the NFC playoff almost every year after that. Meanwhile the NFL had exploded in size, adding Minnesota in 1961, Atlanta in 1966, New Orleans in 1967, and 10 American Football League teams in 1970; Tampa Bay and Seattle were added in 1976. All of which meant that when it came time for the Cowboys to take their first player, by 1977 they were getting the 28th pick of the draft, the equivalent of the last second-round pick 10 years earlier. The Cowboys had been able to get Tony Dorsett that year after Schramm hoodwinked the Seattle Seahawks by swapping four draft choices for him. But after that heist, the Cowboys' well virtually ran dry when the ground rules changed. In 1978 the other teams organized a league-wide scouting combine, bought computers, and added software that would lead to better player selection, and the draft was moved from late January to late April, giving everyone more time to scout the college kids.

Once the scouting reports of opposing teams matched theirs, the Cowboys found themselves cut off from being able to draft impact players, and so rather than choose the obvious players, guys rated as solid but not outstanding, Schramm, Brandt, and Landry decided to take chances on players with athletic ability who may have been missing something else. "Because we had great success and our only goal had been to reach the Super Bowl, our whole goal was trying to find players that would be stars on a Super Bowl team," said

Schramm. "But when you draft late, you have to take people who haven't demonstrated that kind of talent but have the potential. We felt you had to take a gamble, and if he hits . . ."

Usually their gambles failed. Beginning in 1976 with Aaron Kyle, a string of Cowboys first-rounders provided little production. Larry Bethea didn't have the requisite toughness or desire. Robert Shaw didn't make it, and neither did Howard Richards or Rod Hill, a little-known cornerback from Kentucky State who was traded a year later for a sixth-round draft pick, or Billy Cannon Jr., a player with a marquee name who was badly injured early on. Jim Jeffcoat, the first pick in 1983, became a fine defensive lineman, but all in all by 1986 the Cowboys were old, and they had few young studs to fill in for the creaky veterans.

It was in 1985 that observers began to crucify Gil Brandt, chiding him for an alarmingly poor draft record over the previous eight years. In 1985 only 14 picks from those eight drafts were still on the Cowboys roster. In the previous five drafts, only six players had made the team. Only one first-round pick, Jim Jeffcoat, had become a regular. Six years later critics would recall that in 1979 Joe Montana had been available, but the Cowboys took Doug Cosbie instead. Of course, at the time Roger Staubach was months from retirement, and in addition to Staubach, the Cowboys had Danny White and Glenn Carano, but years later Schramm would say that not picking Joe Montana was one of the worst mistakes the Cowboys ever made.

Then in 1983, with White and Gary Hogeboom on the roster, the Cowboys passed on Dan Marino and took Jim Jeffcoat instead. But four other QBs had been taken before Marino in that draft. Who knew?

Said Ernie Stautner in 1985, "Gil Brandt should have been let go 10 years ago. I'd suggest defensive linemen, but they wouldn't listen to me."

Mel Renfro, who was working on the Cowboys scouting staff, said the same thing.

Mel Renfro: "I saw it coming. In '77 I told Gil, 'If you guys don't start preparing to replace these old guys, we're going to be in trouble. You have to get some guys to shore up these positions.' They had draft picks who were not going to be able to carry the team. But they wouldn't listen to me.

"I showed them guys. I said, 'These guys will help you.' Gil would say, 'We don't want them.' Why? Because Gil didn't discover them. I scouted for the Cowboys almost a year, and I went out and saw guys who could play, and they would show up on other teams as stars. Just because I said, 'This is the guy you need,' Gil disregarded it. Gil was the one.

"They didn't know what they were doing. They were reading statistics. They could no more go out and watch a guy. . . . Even when I was playing they would bring guys to me and say, 'Mel, work him out and write a report on him.' And this was *after* they paid him money and brought him in. I said, 'Why are you asking me to do this? You already gave him all that money, and he's here.'

"And oh man, they brought people in there, and I'd say to myself, 'What's going on here? This guy can't play.' They would send these guys over to me and say, 'Mel, what do you think?' I'd say, 'You've got to be kidding. Give me a little bit of that money.' They had the nerve to ask my opinion after the fact."

One of the first indications that things were changing on the Cowboys came in April 1986 when Brandt lost half his job. In the past Brandt had been in sole charge of personnel. He had been the scouting genius. But in 1986 that genius was coming into question.

To bolster their front office, Schramm hired Bobby Ackles, a man whose job it was to know intimately every opposing player in the NFL so that when the Cowboys sat down to trade, they would be more knowledgeable. "He can bring a new dimension to us, and that's what I want him to do," said Schramm.

During training camp in 1986 Landry upset his vets when he released the two ringleaders of Thurman's Thieves, Dennis Thurman and Dextor Clinkscale. They had had their picture taken with machine guns. They were pretending to be "bad dudes," and when Landry sent Thurman and Clinkscale packing, there was outrage among the black players. Said Everson Walls, "This is a terrible blow for this team." The year before the Cowboys had made 33 interceptions. This year the number would drop to 17.

Landry would also begin a simmering feud with Bum Bright. The new owner had told Schramm he would be silent like Murchison, but only Murchison was so idiosyncratic that he would own a $90 million corporation and not be interested in having input into the way it was run. Every man who watches football on TV thinks he knows as much as the coach, and in this respect Bum Bright was no different. Despite the fact that the Cowboys had led the league in passing yardage in 1985, the next year Bright wanted it changed. He wanted it more imaginative, more open, more exciting, regardless of whether Landry wanted it that way or not.

Bright had first met Landry after Bear Bryant left Texas A&M for Alabama after the 1957 season. Bright was helping to conduct the search for Bryant's replacement, and Landry contacted him. According to Bright, he interviewed Landry for the job and was "singularly unimpressed."

Bright may have even been looking for a sometime-down-the-line replacement for Landry when he asked Texas A&M offensive coordinator R. C. Slocum to name someone to rejuvenate the Cowboys offense, and Slocum in good faith recommended a young coach by the name of Paul Hackett. Hackett was a guy who had a history of making good quarterbacks better. Hackett had developed Steve Bartkowski and Joe Roth at California and Vince Evans and Paul McDonald at the University of Southern California. He helped Brian Sipe become MVP with the Cleveland Browns in 1980. Hackett had worked under Bill Walsh in San Francisco, and Joe Montana raved about him.

When Hackett joined the Cowboys, sportswriter Skip Bayless warned him that he would not be able to work with Landry. Said Bayless, "You might feel you'd gone from the funny farm to solitary confinement. Landry runs everything."

When Landry met Hackett, he didn't know a whole lot about him. When they sat down to talk, it turned out that Hackett's offensive philosophy was diametrically opposed to Landry's. Hackett came from the Don "Air" Coryell–Bill Walsh school of offense. His philosophy was that you ran certain plays no matter what the other team was using. If the primary receiver is covered, you throw to the secondary guy. If he's covered, you go to number three. If no one is open, the receivers have to adjust and try to get open. To Tom Landry, this was heresy.

But Landry was also a good soldier, and he knew Hackett was there on orders from Bright and Schramm. Landry told reporters he believed that the offense could integrate Hackett's system, because he had Danny White, an intelligent, experienced quarterback. White thus would be able to employ both systems, using Hackett's systems while continuing to read Landry's keys. Under Hackett, White would become the leading passer in the NFL.

If there was any controversy in training camp in 1986, it came from star running back Tony Dorsett. Dorsett's agents had helped get him in terrible financial trouble with some unwise investments. Each month the IRS was taking his check. He also had borrowed $500,000 from the Cowboys and had three years left on a contract that specifically forbade him from renegotiating it. Dorsett pleaded for Schramm to help him.

Tex did. Schramm restructured the contract so he could pay the IRS, draw a decent salary, and have an annuity of $50,000 per year for five years. Schramm had saved him.

And then Schramm signed former USFL star Herschel Walker, giving him a $5 million bonus to play for the Cowboys. Landry knew that the Cowboys' future would be the 25-year-old Walker. Walker, moreover, was a coach's dream. He was a rare individual, a star with humility who was always eager to learn. In meetings he always sat in the front, pencil in hand. All-Pro Dorsett, at 33 and running out of time, was pleased with the acquisition of Walker, until he found out the Cowboys had given him $5 million as a signing bonus. Once he learned that, Dorsett bolted training camp. "I'm not playing second fiddle to anyone," he said. Dorsett threatened to become a "very disruptive force on the team."

Dorsett did return, and he started, and Landry used Herschel Walker to advantage in spot situations.

Everything started out swimmingly. Hackett was dismayed at how weak the offensive line was. "But we'll trick 'em," said Hackett. In the Monday night opener against the New York Giants, the Cowboys gained 378 yards and scored 31 points against the team that would finish with the best defensive statistics in the NFL. During the game Hackett suggested the plays, and usually Landry went with them.

By midseason the Cowboys were 6–2. Their two losses were to the Atlanta Falcons and Denver, the latter when Danny White was injured and couldn't play. White came back, but against the New York Giants, Carl Banks blitzed and no one blocked him. After White extended his arm to pass, Banks crashed his helmet or shoulder pad into it, fracturing White's wrist and ending his—and the Cowboys'—season. The injured wrist would plague White—and Tom Landry—the rest of his career.

White was replaced by Steve Pelluer. With three minutes to go, the Cowboys trailed, 17–14. Pelluer dumped a screen to Tony Dorsett, who ran 30 yards to the Giants' 6. But tackle Phil Pozderac, who had already been caught holding twice in the game, got nailed again, and the play was called back. Then Pelluer hit Timmy Newsome for another 30-yard gain inside the Giants' 10. This time Pozderac, who could not hear the snap count, was suckered offside by Giants end George Martin.

Hackett did not blame Pozderac. He blamed Landry and Schramm and Brandt. "We cannot win in this league with the tackles we have," he said. "It is staggering how poorly this team has drafted for the last eight years. You compare this team to the 49ers, man for man, two deep, and it's a joke."

The great irony was that when Hackett was with the 49ers, Bill Walsh had sent him to the University of Washington to scout Pelluer. Hackett reported back that he wasn't impressed. Now Pelluer was all he had.

The end came the following week against the Los Angeles Raiders. Dallas dominated but led only 13–3 at the half. A touchdown was called back on a hold by Glen Titensor, and the Raiders went on to win when Jim Plunkett lofted a 40-yard touchdown pass that Dokie Williams caught in the end zone above three Cowboys defenders.

During the game it was apparent that Herschel Walker's ankle hurt him badly and would limit his play. That season Walker ran for 737 yards and set a Cowboys record with 75 receptions. Moreover, Tony Dorsett's knees were limiting his ability. He had to miss three games, breaking his streak of 94 games started consecutively. He ran for 748 yards, the first season in a brilliant career that he failed to reach the 1,000 mark.

Pelluer was hit so much, he became confused when he was urged to stay in the pocket. By the end of the year he was punch-drunk. In one game alone, he was sacked 11 times. Said Hackett, "I'm not sure any quarterback has ever taken a worse beating for a longer period and kept getting up."

In the season finale held in Texas Stadium, head coach Mike Ditka of the 14–2 Chicago Bears took pity on the Cowboys during a 24–10 win. Quarterback Doug Flutie threw only eight passes in the second half, scoring but a field goal, as Ditka fought to hold the score down against his mentor. The Cowboys looked so inept that after the game the Bears players were sympathizing with Tom Landry. The Dallas fans, of course, were less sympathetic. There was a banner that read, "Remember the Alamo; Remember the Cowboys." Several fans wore paper bags over their heads.

Dallas finished the second half 1–7, 7–9 on the season. A string of 20 straight winning seasons had come to an end; the last time the Cowboys had not enjoyed a winning season was 1965, when they finished 7–7. (To show how remarkable that is, at the time the team that was second in consecutive winning seasons was the Miami Dolphins, which had six.)

The last three weeks of the season Landry took away all of Hackett's authority. He went back to calling the plays for Pelluer.

At the end of the 1986 season Landry said, "No, I won't be retiring, unless someone decides to fire me, and that could be a possibility. We will try to bring this thing back up where it belongs. That will be a tough job."

In the spring of 1987 Hackett was offered the head coaching job at the University of Southern California. Hackett told Schramm, who asked him to be patient just a little longer. Hackett turned down the USC job, a terrible mistake.

It was clear that Hackett was Bum Bright's choice to replace Landry, but Schramm was more loyal to Landry than he was to Bright. Landry, his job no longer as secure under Bright as it had been under Murchison, told Schramm he wanted a three-year contract at $1 million per year, a figure comparable to what was being paid to Bill Walsh, Joe Gibbs, Don Shula, and Chuck Noll.

Bright told Schramm to give Landry three contracts at $800,000, $900,000, and $1 million. But Bright also ordered him to be sure to give him three one-year contracts, not three guaranteed years. Bright would not find out for several weeks that Schramm had ignored his orders and given Landry the three years guaranteed.

Once Landry had his three years guaranteed, Hackett became persona non grata. And under new coach Larry Smith, USC went to three consecutive Rose Bowls.

Training camp began and ended disastrously in 1987. It started with accusations against Rafael Septien, the best place-kicker the Cowboys ever had. Septien was accused of having sex with the 10-year-old daughter of a friend. Landry needed Septien and wanted Schramm to give him another chance. Schramm refused. Landry then released star receiver Tony Hill, a starter since 1978 and one of the great receivers in Cowboys history, saying he was overweight and could no longer make the grade. The year before Hill had been on schedule to catch 1,000 yards worth of passes, but halfway through the season Landry stopped calling his number, as Mike Sherrard became the team's go-to pass catcher. Hill needed 11 catches to break Drew Pearson's record of 490 receptions by a Cowboys receiver. When in 1987 Landry cut him in training camp, Hill never got that chance. Sherrard would be penciled in to be the Cowboys' new game-breaker.

Then in a seven-on-seven passing scrimmage against the San Diego Chargers, Sherrard, the top draft choice in 1986 and the best receiver on the team, ran a simple pass pattern and was knocked off balance by Chargers defender Carl Brazley. One cleat hit the opposite shin, shattering it. Teammates said they could hear the *cur-rack* from 20 yards away. "From the way it sounded, it was like two helmets had collided," said receiver Mike Renfro. Sherrard's bone protruded through the skin, and he was lost for the season. Danny White was so heartsick, he left the field saying he couldn't continue. As Sherrard was carried to an ambulance, Paul Hackett cried. Wrote sportswriter Jim Dent, "Tony Hill doesn't look that overweight now."

Then came the players' demand for free agency, followed by the threat of a strike if they didn't get it. In his negotiations with the players association, Schramm, who was a member of the owners' negotiating team, told union president Gene Upshaw that "there will never be free agency even if the players remained on the team for 30 years."

Recalled Upshaw, "He said the players are like cattle and the owners are ranchers, and the owners can always get more cattle."

The cattle went on strike. It was the most bitter players' strike in NFL history. After three regular-season games were canceled, Tex Schramm and the other owners hired scabs to replace striking athletes. The first three games of the 1987 season were played with a team consisting of replacement players and stars whom Schramm strong-armed into participating.

The reason the Cowboys vets played is that Schramm had boxed them into a corner so they had no choice. Anticipating a strike, Schramm had inserted clauses in contracts of some of his top players that if the player missed a game or practice for any reason other than injury, he would lose a large annuity built into his pay. Schramm, smart and ruthless, forced Danny White, Randy White, Too Tall Jones, Tony Dorsett, Doug Cosbie, and Everson Walls to face the decision whether to cross the picket line or stick with their teammates and lose hundreds of thousands of dollars.

Randy White crossed the first day, telling reporters, "I just can't walk away from the money I'm earning now." Striking would cost White $45,000 per week. Many of White's teammates were furious, because in 1984 he had held out for more money, and they had supported him, going so far as to wear No. 54 on their jerseys. Tony Dorsett labeled him "Captain Scab." A few days later a sheepish Dorsett (nicknamed "Captain Stab" by the strikebreakers) joined White when Schramm pointed out that if he didn't play, he stood to lose $6.4 million in annuities. All but Cosbie and Walls crossed the line and played with the replacement players. Dorsett played while hating every minute of it.

The venom directed at Randy White was nothing compared to how the players reacted when Danny White crossed the line. Danny White also cited the clauses in his contract. At the time Danny was facing a federal investigation for mail fraud in connection with a used truck parts company he owned. He admitted to owing creditors $230,000 but said he was innocent of committing fraud.

But Danny had an ulterior motive for crossing the picket line, said several of his teammates, who charged that Schramm had given him a $300,000 salary advance to solve his financial problems in exchange for playing. The strikers were furious, with both White and Schramm. Only the Cowboys were forcing their veterans on the field with the strikebreakers. Other owners even called Schramm to ask him not to play them. Schramm refused, and the Cowboys became a marked team. Said veteran tackle John Dutton, who was waived in midseason, “Tex Schramm made a marked team out of us.” Added a disgusted Everson Walls, “People used to hate us out of respect. Now they hate us out of disrespect.”

Tom Landry, to his credit, didn’t play Danny White, Tony Dorsett, or Mike Renfro, who also crossed the picket line. He played the replacement players, and in their first game, played before twelve thousand fans in the Meadowlands against the replacement Jets, quarterback Kevin Sweeney led the replacement Cowboys to a 38–24 win.

Schramm had anticipated the Cowboys having to use replacement players, and he hired an excellent replacement team, led by Sweeney. Sweeney had set passing records at Fresno State and had been drafted by the Cowboys in the seventh round. But Paul Hackett was convinced Sweeney was too small at 5'11" and too slow to do much but throw deep. Schramm loved the kid, but Hackett had cut him. As the strike loomed, Schramm wooed Sweeney into coming back and playing for the ersatz Cowboys.

In a poll conducted by *The Dallas Times Herald*, 82 percent of the six thousand people polled said that they supported the owners in the strike. Clearly, Texans extended their antiunion stance to football. Those Texans, moreover, were more enthusiastic about their replacement players than they had been about their veterans.

By the second replacement game, Kevin Sweeney was the new Texas hero. The second replacement game took place before forty thousand fans in Texas Stadium. As the replacement Cowboys met the replacement Eagles, one sign read, “White’s a Weenie. We Want Sweeney.” The replacement Eagles were a bad team because coach Buddy Ryan refused to give legitimacy to these games. Tom Landry, however, played it like it was the real thing. On the first play Landry called a reverse that split end Kelvin Edwards took 62 yards for a touchdown. After the replacement Cowboys won the game 41–22, Ryan called Landry “a hypocrite and a phony.”

In the final strike game against the Washington Redskins, 60,612 Cowboys rooters came to Texas Stadium to watch “Kevin from Heaven,” as reporter Skip Bayless called him. There was a fierce debate over whether the Cowboys quarterback should be Danny White or Kevin Sweeney. Bum Bright wanted Sweeney in there because the fans loved him so.

But rather than start Sweeney, Landry went with Danny White. Some fans even asked for their money back. White did not play very well as Washington won, 13–7. Once the strike was settled, Landry returned Danny White to his starting role and put Sweeney in mothballs.

Landry also set in motion the end of Tony Dorsett’s Cowboys career. Against New England in mid-November, Landry started Herschel Walker at halfback. Dorsett sat on the bench all but six plays. By the three-quarter mark in the season, Dorsett had disappeared. “It was pure meanness,” said Dorsett, who told Schramm and Landry he wanted to be traded. "Tom Landry didn't run me out of town," said Dorsett. "Tex Schramm didn't run me out of town. Not playing me ran me out of town. They chose not to use me, and that was something I wouldn't stand for."

There was an aura of bitterness that lingered long after the strike had ended that almost resulted in Tom Landry's dismissal. In part because Landry had played Danny White instead of Kevin Sweeney and in part because Bum Bright resented what he called Tom Landry's "unapproachable arrogance," Bright had a burning desire to fire Landry. Bright told Schramm, "Tex, it's a goddamn business. Call Landry, and let's fire him."

"No, we can't do that just yet."

"OK, call him, and I'll fire the son of a bitch."

"No, let me handle it my way."

It was during that conversation that Schramm informed Bright that he had just signed Landry to a three-year guaranteed deal that would cost Bright $1.9 million if he fired Landry then and there. Bright was furious. Schramm apologized, telling Bright "he didn't remember" Bright telling him not to guarantee the three years.

There was a time when Bright might have forfeited the $1.9 million just to get rid of Landry, but Landry had luck on his side because by this time Bright's empire had shrunk by $200 million, and Bright wasn't willing to toss away more money.

As the owner, however, Bright could, and did, make things rough on Landry. Once the regular players returned, it became clear that the Cowboys were fielding a lackluster losing team. They lost to the Eagles badly when a vengeful Buddy Ryan ran up the score. They lost 44–38 to Minnesota, three weeks after a loss to Detroit, which had won but one game. After the game Schramm said on his regular Monday night radio program, "I'm not sure it's all on the players. There's an old saying, 'If the teacher doesn't teach, the students don't learn.'"

Then after the Cowboys lost to another bad team, the Atlanta Falcons, Bum Bright unleashed a withering attack on Tom Landry. He told one reporter, "I get horrified sometimes at our play calling. I've heard we're not using certain players because they haven't been brought along yet. Maybe the problem is we can't utilize the talent of certain guys because we don't have anybody to direct how to use them. It doesn't seem we have anybody in charge that knows what they're doing."

Schramm, who was also unhappy with the poor performance of the team, told another reporter that the Falcons game was "the absolute low point of my years with the Cowboys." Tex's remark hurt Landry far worse than Bright's. Said Landry, "It was easier to discount Bright's comments because he knew nothing about football."

Landry, who wasn't used to this sort of criticism—disparaging comments losing coaches had heard in cities all across America since the days of Red

Grange and Bronko Nagurski—defended himself: "We have a quarterback with a bad wrist, an offensive line that keeps getting banged up—and we lost our best receiver before the season even started. Oh, nobody is ever really fair when it comes to coaches, but that's just the nature of the business."

The season ended 7–8. In the final game Landry installed Steve Pelluer at quarterback. Using his tried-and-true Multiple Offense with Pelluer at the commands, Landry proved the worth of his system, as Dallas beat two playoff contenders, the Los Angeles Rams, 29–21, and the St. Louis Cardinals, 21–16. Herschel Walker ran for more than 100 yards in each game.

Everyone had hope going into 1988. But it was to be false hope. Tom Landry's hourglass had run out of sand.

Chapter 68

Bum Bright's Payback

The Dallas Cowboys had the 11th pick in the 1988 player draft, and with it they selected Michael Irvin, a wide receiver from the University of Miami. "This will speed our return to the living," said Tex Schramm.

When Irvin arrived at the Cowboys training camp the other players couldn't help but notice that he wore enough jewelry to be a Hollywood movie producer. He had on an earring, gilt-edged sunglasses, a designer watch, and flashy rings, and he was driving a brand-new BMW. Irvin had specifically told the dealer *not* to tint the windows because he wanted to be recognized inside.

In practice, he never allowed the defenders to forget he was there, taunting and talking trash to the defenders he beat: "It's a nightmare having to cover me, isn't it? How can lightning keep striking like this?" But at the same time, on the field he worked harder than anyone, and he made catches that didn't seem possible for a runner lacking the blazing speed possessed by others.

Taking Irvin would turn out to be the highlight of a dismal season that would feature a starting lineup without either of the Whites, Danny or Randy, both hobbled with injuries. Danny would appear in but two games before a knee injury put him out for good. Two defensive starters, linebackers Jeff Rohrer and Mike Hegman, would go down before the season even began. Top draft pick Ken Norton had to go on injured reserve. A free agent, Garry Cobb, turned out to be the team's best linebacker.

Tom Landry decided he would take total control of the offense, because if the ship (or plane) was going to go down, it was going to go down his way. For 20 years his teams had won using his tried-and-true Multiple Offense system. Paul Hackett wasn't going to tell him what to do. Neither would Tex Schramm or Bum Bright. He was going to go with what he knew best. Landry planned a simpler, more basic offense that he felt would be better suited to a young team and an inexperienced quarterback, Steve Pelluer. Herschel Walker would be the main weapon in the offense. Landry knew the team was green, but he was optimistic.

The season opener set the tone for the season. Trailing by three points late in the game, the Cowboys had a third-and-two at the Steelers' 4-yard line. Landry called a play that was supposed to result in a touchdown to tight end Doug

Cosbie. Pelluer was supposed to fake, roll out, and pass to Cosbie in the right corner of the end zone. If Cosbie was not open, he was to throw the ball out of bounds. But Pelluer got mixed up, and he ran the wrong play. He threw the ball in the direction of three Steelers, the ball was intercepted, and the Cowboys lost.

In another game, the Cowboys lost by two points to the Giants when the referees mistakenly gave the Giants a safety. In yet another game, against the New Orleans Saints, they lost when end Thornton Chandler dropped a pass in the end zone.

Against Philadelphia, the Cowboys had a 20–0 lead with only seconds remaining in the first half. They were on the Eagles' 23, close enough to kick a field goal, but Landry wanted to get the ball closer because he was wary of the reliability of kicker Roger Ruzek, who had missed all of training camp in a contract dispute. He had Herschel Walker to go to, but instead he called for a rollout by Pelluer.

On the play Pelluer was cornered, and instead of eating the ball, he threw it away. After Pelluer was penalized for intentional grounding, the Cowboys lost 12 yards and were out of field-goal range. They had to punt.

The Eagles won 24–23 when Randall Cunningham led his team on an 85-yard drive, throwing a two-yard touchdown pass with two seconds left in the game. Landry took a roasting for losing that one, as the Cowboys' record sank to 2–6.

After the game Landry was asked about the play. He said, "I hadn't been comfortable with the ball on the 30." Of course, the reporters knew that the ball had been on the 23, not the 30.

On TV that night one of the commentators accused Landry of a memory lapse. For the first time came the kiss-of-death accusation for any coach: he's too old. The next day in the Dallas papers, the mantra was picked up.

Landry tried to defend himself, saying he didn't care whether the ball was on the 23 or the 30, he still didn't want a field goal at that time. He had wanted a first down, regardless.

This was one time that Tom Landry needed an ally. He needed an assistant coach or Tex Schramm or the owner to back him. But Landry's loyal lieutenants had left for head coaching jobs with other NFL teams: Mike Ditka was in Chicago, Dan Reeves in Denver, Raymond Berry in New England, John Mackovic in Kansas City, and Gene Stallings in Phoenix.

For years Landry had panicked in high-pressure situations late in the game, but in the past he had had veteran quarterbacks—Don Meredith, then Roger Staubach, then Danny White—who usually pulled him out of the fire because they were exceptional and because his system had given them the tools to do so. This time he had a quarterback with little experience, Steve Pelluer. And his offensive coordinator, Paul Hackett, would not cover for him. Hackett felt he had been betrayed by Landry. Why should he show loyalty to a man who had showed him none? When the reporters ran to Hackett, Hackett told them the truth: Landry messed up and was blaming his quarterback for his mistake. "Tom just lost it," he told Skip Bayless. "Completely lost it. It was total chaos on the sideline. Steve Pelluer played his heart out, and now he'll be the goat again. I just don't know how much more of this I can bear to watch."

This was nothing new. Landry had always panicked at the end of close games. And he had always made his quarterback the scapegoat for his mistakes. But this time, for the first time, Landry was unprotected, on his own. The wolves were at the door, and it was turning out to be a screen door. The reporters keening for Landry's head roared louder.

Bum Bright had wanted Landry out, and in interviews he was not supporting his coach. Even Schramm was talking openly of replacing Landry with Jimmy Johnson, Michael Irvin's old coach at the University of Miami. Schramm even contacted Johnson when he heard the Philadelphia Eagles were after him. But Schramm was hesitant to broach the subject with Landry. In Dallas, Tom Landry was still God.

The losses mounted. The Cowboys led the Phoenix Cardinals 10–0 but lost 16–10. They led against Houston 17–10 in the third quarter and lost when Cornell Burbage fumbled a kickoff with 4:32 left.

Bright had not lost his affection for Kevin Sweeney, and in part to boost fan interest, Schramm persuaded Landry to start Sweeney against the New York Giants. Hackett, knowing how small, slow, and brittle Sweeney was, prayed he didn't get hurt. But against the Giants, Sweeney was terrific, throwing for three touchdown passes as Hackett called the plays for him. The Giants still won, however, 29–21.

Landry started Sweeney against the Minnesota Vikings. In that game Sweeney threw four interceptions and was sacked in the end zone for a safety in a 43–3 shellacking.

Pelluer went back to quarterback against the Cleveland Browns, and Landry went back to calling the plays. The team lost 24–21 when two field goals were nullified by penalties.

Late in the game, trailing by three, Pelluer had the Cowboys within scoring distance. With a third-and-four on the Cleveland 22, Landry called a play in a way it had not been practiced before. Herschel Walker, who had split out right, didn't understand the call. Neither did Kelvin Martin, also spread right. Before calling signals, Pelluer had to reroute them. Pelluer's pass to Martin fell incomplete, and the Cowboys lost. After this game Skip Bayless in *The Dallas Morning News* called Landry "Mount Senility."

The Cowboys lost 10 games in a row. During that stretch they had lost five of seven games in the final minute. Interceptions on the goal line by the opposition cost them three of the ballgames.

Unlike the reporters, who saw gloom and doom and were looking to hang those responsible at high noon, Landry saw an inexperienced team that couldn't make the big play to hold a lead. He saw immaturity. But he also saw character and potential. Throughout the year, the players worked hard. No one gave up.

No one stopped giving his all. "The team's reaction to adversity gave me real reason for hope for the future," said Landry.

In the next-to-last game the Cowboys defeated the Super Bowl champion Washington Redskins, 24–17. Pelluer was 21 of 36 for 333 yards and threw three spectacular touchdown passes to the Cowboys' newest hopeful, Michael Irvin.

There was great celebration after the victory. The win had eliminated the hated Redskins from the playoffs. The party was as raucous as after Super Bowl victories. In the clubhouse after the game, lineman Tom Rafferty, who was one of only four players remaining from the Cowboys' 1975 Super Bowl team, stood up before the team to award Tom Landry the dirt-caked game ball. "This is for the guy who stuck by us when we were 2–12," said Rafferty, tears streaming down his cheeks. "He's taken a lot of shit. And he's the guy who's going to get us back on top." Rafferty handed the ball to Landry, who also stood with tears in his eyes as his players chanted, "T.L., T.L., T.L., T.L."

Said Randy White about Landry after the game, "He deserves a game ball each week. If you're on the inside, you know this is one of the best coaching jobs he's ever done here. We've lost 12 games, but nobody's quit. That comes from the top. He's still out there coaching every position. If they leave Tom Landry alone, he'll turn this team around. This guy's one of the greatest coaches who ever coached anything. And he still is."

It was one of Landry's most memorable wins. And it would be his last.

In the season finale, Buddy Ryan and the Philadelphia Eagles clobbered the Cowboys 23–7. The team finished 3–13, worst in the league, worst since Landry's inaugural season in 1960, when they were 0–11–1. Said Schramm, "I honestly never thought the day would come when I would be having a press conference on the last game of the season for being the poorest team in the league. It's nothing we're proud of. But now I guess it's a reality." On the upside, the loss assured the Cowboys the first pick in the draft.

The day after the final game Tom Landry went on his regular radio program and said that 1988 was the most difficult season he had ever coached. "Next year we're going to be a much better team coming out of training camp because we now have a higher experience level. Then we can start thinking about going back to the playoffs." It was not what Bum Bright and Tex Schramm wanted to hear.

After the season Landry took steps to strengthen his position on the team. He demoted Paul Hackett to special projects, assuring that Hackett's influence had ended. When Hackett applied for several college head coach jobs and a couple in the pros, he was turned down every time. Desperate, he took a job as offensive coordinator for the University of Pittsburgh.

Jerry Rhome, an old Landry favorite, replaced Hackett. "I'm a soldier," said Rhome. "He's the general."

But for Schramm to OK the firing of Hackett, Landry had to do something for Tex in return. That "something" was the abandonment of his beloved 4-3 Flex, a defense that opposing teams had seemingly figured out. Tex wanted a change, and Landry agreed to replace it with a 3-4 defense in 1989.

It was announced that the Cowboys were sacking Ernie Stautner, who had worked under Landry for 23 seasons. Stautner was being put in charge of those same "special projects" that Paul Hackett was supposed to be running. Replacing Stautner to oversee the change would be George Hill, an expert in the 3-4 who had been unfairly fired in Indianapolis by Bob Irsay.

Stautner did not see Schramm's hand in his firing. Rather, he saw himself as Landry's scapegoat. When he left the Cowboys, like most everyone else before him, he did so feeling bitter and unappreciated.

Landry went off on a Caribbean cruise, and when he returned he told reporters at Valley Ranch that he "definitely" planned to coach in 1989. "I might even coach into the nineties," he said.

But for the first time since Landry began as coach of the Cowboys, there was a real question about that. Said Schramm enigmatically, "If [Landry returning] is in the best interests of the Cowboys, I'm for it. If it isn't, then there will be a change."

In the fall of 1988, Bright's financial empire, like Clint Murchison's before him, was crumbling. Bright had begun his banking empire by buying Trinity Savings and Loan for $15 million. In 1984, right after buying the Cowboys, he bought Texas Federal Savings and Loan for $71 million and merged it with Trinity Savings and Loan. A year later he added Dallas Federal Savings and Loan for $107 million, making him the seventh largest privately held mortgage broker. These were top-of-the-market prices, though of course Bright could not have known that at the time. The other thing Bright didn't know was that many of the loans made by Texas Federal Savings and Loan were shaky at best with collateral on real estate projects that would never be completed.

Bright could not have anticipated what would happen to him, because he could not foresee the economic quagmire that lay ahead. He had fallen into the same trap of all the other get-very-rich-quick investors who saw the value of their real estate investments double and were counting on these investments to continue their precipitous climb. Through the eighties, investors schemed to buy land, then overvalued its worth even more in order to borrow money to buy more land from friendly banks glad to pocket the commissions. It was like *The Emperor's New Clothes*. Everyone knew the land was worth 20¢ on the dollar. But as long as no one would admit it, the game could continue.

Then in 1988 the house of cards holding up the investors and their banks collapsed. The price of real estate dropped so steeply that the real estate holdings became albatrosses to the title holders. And when the owners couldn't sell the land at inflated prices, they couldn't pay back the money borrowed to buy the land. Banks all over America were forced to declare bankruptcy.

At the same time oil prices were falling fast, dropping to $26 per barrel, as a result of global overproduction. By February 1986 the price of a barrel of

West Texas Intermediate Crude fell below $10 and put the Texas economy in the toilet.

Bright Banc was one of those S&Ls in free fall. Billions had been loaned against wells that were being capped and against real estate projects that were being abandoned. The irony was that the federal government, hated so deeply by Bright and under the presidency of his own George Bush, moved in to shove him off the board of the First Republic Bank Corporation just before the once-mighty bank-holding company collapsed. Federal regulators then seized his tottering $4.7 billion savings and loan association and began serving as conservators.

Before the government could step in and clean up the disaster, the Bright Banc alone would cost taxpayers $1.4 billion. Several years later the government accused Bright and his son-in-law James "Boots" Reeder of fraud, negligence, making misrepresentations to federal bank regulators, and breaking their duties to the thrift and its depositors. The government sought damages of $160 million. Bright called it an "unprincipled witch hunt." He added, "This suit is nothing more than another suit in a recent string of cases against honest men and women to extort money from them."

Bright accused the government of causing his downfall, arguing that the Tax Reform Act of 1986 took away investors' depreciation advantages. "That was why the banks and most savings and loans started to fail," said Bright.

Bright had built 118 luxury suites in Texas Stadium, but more than 100 remained unsold because the fans were unwilling to shell out so much money for a facility they could use only 10 times per year.

When word of Bright's problems began bubbling, Bright's desire to sell the Cowboys was also made known. Several potential buyers surfaced. One group, a consortium of Japanese businessmen, told Bright to name his price. But Bright still had not forgiven the Japanese for Pearl Harbor and World War II, and he turned them down.

Another potential buyer, Don Carter, the owner of the Dallas Mavericks, wanted the Cowboys but not Texas Stadium. Carter was also a great admirer of Tom Landry. But Bright needed to sell the stadium as well as the team, and he also wanted to make sure Landry would get what he felt he deserved, and so Carter was dismissed as a potential buyer.

The third candidate was an Arkansas oil driller by the name of Jerry Jones. While fishing with his son in Cabo San Lucas, Mexico, he noticed an item in *The Wall Street Journal* that Bum Bright had retained Solomon Brothers to find a buyer for the Cowboys. From Mexico, Jones called Solomon Brothers, who put him in touch with Bright.

Jones had played football at the University of Arkansas. He had been a teammate and at times a roommate of Jimmy Johnson, the head coach of the University of Miami. Jones satisfied Bright that he had enough money, and in their first meeting Jones had said the magic words. He told Bright that if he bought the team, he would fire Tom Landry and Jimmy Johnson would be his new coach.

In fact, during talks with Bright, Jones would bring Johnson along with him. The negotiations dragged on through the winter of 1989. Bright was demanding almost $150 million, and Jones was looking at the negatives and arguing that Bright's asking price was too high. For one, the value of NFL franchises had stopped rising along with that of the condos and shopping centers. For another, because more and more players were becoming free agents, the payrolls were rising swiftly. And Jones could certainly argue that a 3–13 Cowboys team had far less value than one fighting for a playoff berth.

Jones dragged his feet, hoping to get Bright to lower his price as his financial problems mounted. In the battle of two tough hombres, Bright held firm. For four days straight the two men negotiated, getting no sleep. The final impediment to closing the deal was a disagreement over $300,000 in closing fees. Bright suggested a coin flip to settle the issue: "Winner take all." Jones agreed. Bright produced a quarter. Jones called tails. It came up heads. Jones paid full price. Bright had the coin mounted and a week later presented it to Jones.

When the deal to sell the Dallas Cowboys to Jerry Jones was completed in February 1989, Bright had not only managed to extricate himself from a difficult financial situation, he had also gotten his revenge, the firing of Tom Landry. And even better, Bright wouldn't even be blamed for it; Jerry Jones would take the heat for that.

When Jones was introduced as the new Cowboys owner, Bright told the crowd, "What we have here is a new generation, someone with the competence and intelligence to help make the Cowboys what they once were."

Few paid attention at the time, but Bright was setting into motion events that would cause great upheaval for the Cowboys and their fans, though in the end, his words would prove prophetic.

Chapter 69

End of an Era

Tom Landry and his staff were preparing for the upcoming draft. UCLA's Troy Aikman, the best quarterback to come along since John Elway, would bring the Cowboys back, Landry was certain. Schramm and Landry were excited.

Landry had settled the quarterback situation in his own mind. He felt good about Steve Pelluer, and he thought the team would be better served if Troy Aikman learned behind him. In 1989 Landry decided he would return to the basic passing game he had used for so many years. With Hackett gone and his own former quarterback Jerry Rhome to replace him, he would also return to calling the plays for the quarterback and not leave it to an assistant. Tom Landry would rebuild the Cowboys his way.

Then on Thursday, February 23, 1989, there was a report from KXTV Channel 5 on the 10:00 news that the sale of the Cowboys was imminent. Neither Tex Schramm nor Tom Landry knew anything about it. The next day Schramm called Bum Bright, who told him to meet with him the next day. Meanwhile Don Shula, the head coach of the Miami Dolphins, called Schramm to tell him that Jimmy Johnson had asked his son, David, if he wanted to join him in Dallas as an assistant coach.

At Tom Landry's home the phone rang incessantly as a string of reporters called wanting to know whether he was going to be fired.

Late on Friday Schramm and Landry met. Schramm told his coach of 29 years, "Tom, I think it's over." Landry shrugged and took a breath. There was nothing either of them could do about it. Landry and Schramm didn't know it for sure, but the reports in the newspaper that the buyer, Jerry Jones, had flown University of Miami coach Jimmy Johnson into Dallas in his private plane were accurate. The draft was coming up soon, and Jones wanted to talk to Johnson about his coaching staff.

With entire sports staffs of newspapers searching high and low in the high-rent Dallas hotels for Jimmy Johnson, on Friday, February 24, Jones and Johnson were holed up in two rooms at the Embassy Suites Hotel trying to stay out of sight. That night, they got hungry for Mexican food. Fearing that Jimmy Johnson would be recognized, Jones asked the bellman to recommend an "out-of-the-way little place." He sent them to Mia's, a local Tex-Mex place on Lemmon Avenue. The two out of towners figured it would be a quiet dinner, that no one would see them.

But they couldn't have known that Mia's was not only Tom Landry's favorite Tex-Mex restaurant but a shrine to him as well, with photos of Landry all over the walls. Jones, Johnson, and their wives entered and sat down in a small opening next to the cash register to wait for a table. Ivan Maisel, a college football reporter with *The Dallas Morning News,* looked up from his nachos to discover he had the scoop of the year. Maisel had spent the afternoon staking out the Mansion hotel, hoping to ask Jimmy Johnson if he was replacing Tom Landry. And here were Jimmy Johnson and Jerry Jones ordering a round of beers. Maisel walked behind Johnson and tapped him on the shoulder.

"Oh, shit. What are *you* doing here?"

"I live a block from here," said Maisel. "What are *you* doing here?"

Johnson answered vaguely, and Maisel snuck off to look for a telephone. He exited through the kitchen, jogged to a nearby Chinese restaurant, and called the paper to request a photographer pronto. When the cameraman arrived, he asked Jones, Johnson, and their wives to smile for the birdie.

Said Johnson, "No, no, no, we don't need this! Jerry, dammit, tell him we don't need this!"

Jones wasn't concerned: "Aw, go ahead and shoot. This is a done deal."

Their picture, prominently featuring beer cans on the table, appeared in the paper the next morning. The picture said it all: here they sat in Tom Landry's favorite restaurant grinning and seeming so jubilant. The Dallas faithful, who months earlier were calling for Landry's head, fumed at the way these "furriners" were now treating him.

According to Bum Bright, that Friday Schramm had told Landry to stay close to Valley Ranch so Bright and Jones could talk to him about his dismissal, but instead of waiting around, the next day, a Saturday, Tom Landry got out of Dodge, piloting his Cessna 210 to his weekend retreat in Lakeway, just west of Austin. His children, Kitty, Lisa, and Tom Jr., met him there. While Bright was trying to get in touch with him at his home, calling in the morning every 30 minutes for three hours, Landry was out of town on the golf course, whistling in the wind, making believe that Jerry Jones' guillotine was not made of tempered steel. For almost 30 years countless players had tried to run and hide from Tom Landry's tyranny. Now it was his turn, and he would be no more successful than his former players had been.

Though it was Schramm's job to fire Landry, Tex wouldn't—or couldn't—bring himself to do it, not for Bum Bright, and not for Jerry Jones. Schramm told Jones that the honorable thing for him to do was to dismiss Landry face-to-face, not do it over the telephone. He said to Jones, "Before you have any press conferences or make any announcements you need to talk to Tom, and I strongly suggest you do it in person." Jones naively agreed. Schramm was setting up

Jones to be the bad guy in the scenario. Schramm was Iago, Jones Othello, and the Cowboys were Desdemona. When the negative reviews flooded in, Jones didn't know what hit him.

That Saturday morning Schramm met with Jones, Bright, and Johnson to defend the team's policies to the new owner. After the meeting Schramm interrupted Landry's golf game to tell him things didn't look good. Schramm said they were flying to Austin to meet with him. Landry finished the round as though nothing had happened.

Jones and Schramm boarded the Learjet with the Cowboys blue star insignia for the short flight from Dallas to Austin. Jones and Landry shook hands. Landry told the new owners, "If you're just coming down here for a publicity stunt, you need not have bothered."

Jones told him, "Oh, Tex insisted I talk to you. He felt we should meet face-to-face. I'm here now, and so is Jimmy."

The meeting lasted 40 minutes. In the end, Landry was no longer head coach after 29 years with the Dallas Cowboys. Landry's 270 wins were third-most in NFL history, behind Don Shula, who had been so successful with Baltimore and Miami, and George Halas, who had owned and coached the Chicago Bears for 40 years.

After the meeting Landry went back to the golf course, where he had dinner with his family. Never one to worry about things he couldn't control, Landry carried on, stoic as ever.

At 8:00 P.M. that Saturday night Schramm scheduled a press conference to announce what everyone knew: Jerry Jones was the new owner, Jimmy Johnson was the new coach, and Tom Landry was out. At the press conference Jerry Jones was introduced. At what reporters perceived as a wake for Landry, Jones pounded the podium like Nikita Khrushchev once did at the UN and talked only of the (Landry-less) future. "This is like Christmas for me . . ."

Jones began extolling the virtues of his friend, Jimmy Johnson, whom Jones called "the best coach in America." Reporters rolled their eyes as Jones began praising the new king without first holding the requisite tribute for the old one. When his remarks appeared in the morning newspapers, every Dallas Cowboys fan who loved and cherished Tom Landry hated Jerry Jones.

Summing up his years with the Cowboys, Landry told reporters, "I don't know if any team in professional football will ever duplicate what happened. The success of that era is something of which all of us who were a part are very proud. It was a great accomplishment."

On Monday Landry spoke to his players. "This will be our last meeting together," he began. He told the players not to worry about him, that he was going on with his life. "We will all go on," he said. "You . . . you'll . . . forget me . . . in a couple of weeks."

Tears came to his eyes. The players lowered their heads, embarrassed for him. He continued, "The way you react to adversity is the key to success. Right now . . . the situation around here is in turmoil and how . . . we react will be important . . . important in how the season goes next . . . year. I . . . don't want anyone to concern themselves with what has happened to me but to . . . to look . . . forward to playing football in September. . . ."

Tears fell from his face. He asked the players to do all they could do to make the Cowboys an elite team again. "That's . . . important for . . . you know, to know that you didn't quit, that . . . we didn't quit."

He broke down and couldn't go on for a while. The room was quiet.

Finally, "The things . . . I'm going to miss the most . . . are the coaches and you . . . the players." As Tom Landry sobbed, many of the players cried, too. When Landry recovered, he said, "I'll be with you in spirit, always. I love you guys. God bless you and your families."

The players gave him a standing ovation.

After posing for pictures with the staff, Landry got into his car with his son Tom Jr. and drove away. Cowboys players and staff stood on the steps outside the main building or looked through their office windows and watched him drive away.

Not long after his firing, "Landry for Governor" bumper stickers started to circulate. One billboard read, "Tom Landry. Thanks for 29 Great Years." Then in April 1989 came his "Hats Off to Tom Landry Parade."

On April 22, 1989, more than fifty thousand people turned out for Tom Landry Day. Volunteers raised $90,000 to pay for the celebration. When Roger Staubach first asked Landry about it, his response was, "Why would anyone want to hold such a thing for me?"

People were lined up six and seven deep for a mile along the streets of downtown Dallas. The governor of Texas and mayor of Dallas were there, and Staubach read telegrams from George Bush and Billy Graham. Bob Hope called to congratulate him.

When he saw the huge turnout, Jones, a decent man who had been placed in the role of villain, was happy for Landry. "I would have been more concerned if there had been apathy," said Jones.

There were 86 floats in the parade. Roger Staubach rode on one, as did Herschel Walker, Tony Dorsett, Drew Pearson, Ralph Neely, and Walt Garrison. Then a 1954 Buick carried the Landry family. "I don't deserve this," said Landry, "but I am so thankful for it." Tom waved as the fans shouted, "We love you, Coach."

The parade was held partly in response to his firing by new owner Jerry Jones. Before Landry had been a hero. Now he was a martyr. The next year he was enshrined in the Pro Football Hall of Fame where thousands gave him a thundering standing ovation.

Fans fondly recall his 270–178–6 lifetime record with the Cowboys, the 18 playoff seasons, the five Super Bowl appearances. Cowboys fans see the calm Tom Landry standing on the sideline wearing his famous cloth hat, impassive, concentrating, and they smile at the memory. In retrospect, for many fans, Tom Landry *was* the Cowboys. His players for the most part have forgiven him his shortcomings, and the fans have forgotten the final years of futility and recall only the good times.

Tom Landry: "We started tough, no draft, no players. Don Meredith and Don Perkins were the only two players who were considered draftable. We had hoped to turn it around in three years, but when we didn't get any draft choices, it became obvious it would be hard to build that fast. I had developed the 4-3 defense back when I was with the Giants, and everybody started using it, so when I became the Dallas coach, I had to come up with an offense that could beat my defense. And so we put in multiple sets, shifting up and down, moving our players around at the last moment, so the defense couldn't determine what was going to happen before the snap of the ball. At the beginning we didn't have good enough players to make the system work, and at the same time the players had to believe in me, believe in my ability to do it. If they didn't adhere to what we were doing, they wouldn't be there. And we struggled those early years. And yet in 1962 our offense tied with New York and Green Bay. We scored more than 400 points that year, even with the players we had. We slipped in '63, but I never changed my theory, and we were very fortunate to have a great draft in '64, and that was the thing that enabled us to turn the corner. It wasn't until 1965 that we won as many as we lost. And from then on, we kicked off.

"I really was always very confident in what we were doing and in the players we had to play for us. We were very fortunate to have players like Don Meredith in his beginning. Don was a good quarterback in a tough era. When you had to play in the sixties with the Cowboys with what we had—the punishment—Don was probably the toughest player that I had. He played hurt. He was kind of a happy-go-lucky guy, but he was really intent on doing the job. We were always at odds a little bit, because he wasn't Roger Staubach, who was my type of quarterback. But Don was a good guy. He was just kind of like a chip on your shoulder. When you worked with him, he didn't particularly want to be like I was, very disciplined. He didn't want to be that way. He was a funny guy. I remember an exhibition against the New York Giants one season, he came out of the huddle and looked at the defense, and he couldn't read it, and he said a four-letter word, you know, and he turned around and walked back to the huddle. And he was frustrated by it. But he was that kind of guy.

"We had some great teams with Don. The 1966–67 teams were great teams. And then Roger took over at quarterback. I didn't think Roger would ever play. I remember he was still in the service when he came out to training camp, and we'd give him a playbook, and Pete Gent used to say to him, 'Don't worry about it, Roger. They all get killed in the end,' 'cause that playbook was so thick. And I never paid much attention to him. He would be out there throwing, and I'd be working getting ready for the year, and he'd be out passing and trying to work out. I never thought he would stay, and then when he came to us and played that great game against the 49ers, a fantastic football game, for him to come off the bench and win a football game like that against an excellent football team, was really an amazing eye-opener for us. And then I had to make a tough decision.

"Craig Morton was signed as quarterback. And I enjoyed working with Craig. He was really a fine person, and you had to make that decision. I had those two quarterbacks. We were very fortunate we were able to have that kind of caliber player at quarterback through those years and even into Danny White. If Danny hadn't been hurt against New York that time, we would have gone to another Super Bowl or two, just because of his ability, because he was an excellent quarterback. And so, that's kind of where it ended, as we went into the eighties, and we were fighting to try to stay up, because we were drafting so late for so long, and we were very fortunate. If we hadn't drafted Too Tall or Dorsett or Randy White—those were all first-round choices we traded for—without them, we'd have been nose-diving long before then.

"As far as personal satisfaction, looking back, you have to be extremely proud of your first Super Bowl win, mainly because it meant so much to a team that couldn't win the big one for four years. Before we went to our first Super Bowl, I'll never forget, we played St. Louis on a Monday night game, Howard Cosell was up there and Meredith, and we were behind by two games and this was a very important game, and we got beat 38–0. Well, we lost everybody, including my old buddies in the press box, Gifford and all the rest of them. But the next day when we went into our meeting there, boy, they were down. Their heads were down. They were just defeated, and finally they had a little talk, and when I came in, 'Fellas, let's go out and play touch football.' And so they went out and played touch football and got real relaxed, and we went on to win all the rest of our games, got beat in the Super Bowl on a field goal at the end. That was a great turnaround. But that only happens when you have character. If you have character, you can turn a club around. If your team doesn't have the character, then they'll fall. They won't come back. But that team had character.

"It was almost five years before we won the big one. And that was very satisfying. As we were getting ready for the game, I remember Dave Edwards came up to me. 'Hey, Coach, if we're not ready, we're never going to be ready.' They were so confident that they could beat the Dolphins at that time. There wasn't any doubt in their minds. I don't get that feeling as a coach. I can't say before the game, 'We're going to win regardless.' It's very hard for me to say that, because I've seen it turn around so many times. But those players for that game, they really knew they could win. And they went out and won.

"I think the most enjoyable and most satisfying season was the season we went to the Hail Mary pass in 1975. Because that year we had a lot of people retiring. We had 12 rookies, and nobody expected us to go anyplace, and we were almost defeated in Minnesota when the Hail Mary pass came.

"You know, on that field, the old field, it wasn't the Dome, and therefore you're on a baseball field, and both teams were on the same side, and we were down on our own 20-yard line, and that's where we took over the ball. We had to go all the way. And I really couldn't hardly see the play when Drew caught it, because we were blocked off by the Minnesota team, and so I didn't recognize it. And I tell you, I was almost in shock, when you think about it, that he did catch it, he did score. It was amazing because this was one of Minnesota's best football teams. Of all of Bud Grant's teams, this one was really a good one, because of their defense, and to pull this off really was a miracle.

"They said when Roger came off the field after that, he sat down by Doc Knight, and they sat there for a while, and Roger turned to Knight and said, 'Can you believe that?' He was in doubt. Everybody was. The thing that was so amazing about that drive was that Preston Pearson was in there on a third-down play, and we didn't go to him because we were out of timeouts. So we were down about the 30-yard line, and Roger, instead of downing the ball, threw it to Preston. If Preston catches it, the game is over with. Time runs out. And Preston dropped it. And he never dropped it. And then came a fourth-down play, which was to Drew on a sideline, and one of the funniest things that happened on that thing, the guard who was walking up and down the sideline to keep people off, he was right there where Drew caught the ball, and Drew hit the ice and fell and slid, and the guard came up and kicked him in the ribs! We didn't see that until we saw the film the next day. But that was an amazing drive, a greater miracle than the one against the 49ers out in San Francisco that time.

"Duane Thomas was one of the great football players. If Duane Thomas would have stayed with us and Calvin Hill, too, if they would have stayed with us, if we had had the strength of those two players, we would have competed very strongly against Pittsburgh in the seventies. But it was very difficult. In Duane Thomas' case, it was a shame. He came to us kind of surly. But he was OK that first year. We ended up going to the Super Bowl against Baltimore. And the next off-season, he went to California, went to Los Angeles. He got into the drug scene there, and it was really a shame.

"Really, in those days, football coaches had no idea about drugs. I had never seen drugs. I wouldn't have any idea about drugs. And so we didn't know how to handle it. We were negative in the way we faced it, because we just didn't understand it. But when he came into training camp the next year, he was a Dr. Jekyll and Mr. Hyde. That next year we went to the Super Bowl again and won it, you remember he wouldn't talk to anyone, and he was amazing, and the next year I had to get rid of him because he was just so disruptive. So that was the era we were in.

"Nothing would have corrected Duane. No. Regardless of what Tex had offered him. After he went to L.A., and after he came back again and went to that Super Bowl we won, there was no turning back with him. Yet, I spoke a couple years ago out at Albuquerque. He and his wife came over from Las Cruces; they came down and visited at the banquet for the Fellowship of Christian Athletes. He was very friendly. And he tried. I don't know where Duane is now. He was trying hard. But boy, when you're on drugs. . . . What a great team we'd a had had he stayed.

"Thomas Henderson was a good guy. He was so unusual. I remember we sent a scout out to see him down in Oklahoma where he went to school, and the scout came in and was on the sideline and Thomas Henderson was in street clothes. They were out there scrimmaging. And he was in street clothes. He said to our scout, 'Would you like to see me play?' And so he goes in and changes clothes, puts on his uniform, comes out and puts himself into the scrimmage, plays for a while in there, and then he came over and said, 'Have you seen enough?' And so he went in and put on his clothes again. That's the lack of discipline of that era. You know? There was *no* discipline. And that's what happened from the late sixties well into the seventies. There just wasn't any discipline at all.

"I was very fortunate. I spent two careers with two great teams, New York and Dallas, and it was something you really enjoyed, being in Dallas and being a part of what took place. I love Dallas.

"The way the people responded to me personally, the Tom Landry Day after I was released, was really special. That's something you don't realize will happen, with the parade and all the things that took place there. They were wonderful times for us, and most people thought I should be bitter. I wasn't bitter. I wasn't bitter at all.

"When I left football, I just left it completely. I have been to Texas Stadium twice, never been at the practice field, never invited. None of us were.

"The Ring of Honor was one time I was there, and I went for Randy and Dorsett. Those were the only times. And it's a shame. I kind of feel sorry the way things have worked out with them. It's a new era, the hot-dogging and all that, the big salaries, people like Deion. It's just not football as we knew it."

NOTES

Chapter 1

3 *just a fun thing*, Wolfe, *Murchisons*, p. 239.
4 *if the railroad could do it*, *Ibid.*, p. 20.
4 *a very unethical approach*, *Ibid.*, pp. 32–33.
5 *give them a dollar*, O'Connor, *Oil Barons*, p. 127.
6 *cash makes a man careless*, Wolfe, *Murchisons*, p. 118.
6 *owe more than you can pay*, *Ibid.*, p. 61.
6 *American Liberty pipeline was so hot*, Priestley, *Saga of Wealth*, p. 173.
8 *just the shyest little boy*, Wolfe, *Murchisons*, p. 65.
8 *have at it*, *Ibid.*, p. 160.
8 *I saw him yesterday*, *Ibid.*, p. 285.
10 *afford to go broke once*, *Ibid.*, p. 168.
10 *feared that Clint Jr. was unbalanced*, It was almost 30 years before Murchison Sr.'s instincts would be proven correct.

Chapter 2

12 *tell him to go to hell*, Wolfe, *Murchisons*, p. 29.
16 *football is no place for soft people*, Wismer, *Public Calls It Sport*, p. 30.
16 *he knew he was wrong*, *Ibid.*, p. 60.
17 *you couldn't make that sort of basic boo-boo*, "Bobby Baker Talks to Texas Journalist Larry King," *Playboy*, June 1973.
See also Don Kowet, *Rich Who Own Sports.*

Chapter 4

26 *wasn't a prettier smelling place on earth*, Landry, *Autobiography*, p. 1.
27 *wondered how much greater he might have been*, *Ibid.*, p. 74.
29 *acute hatred for receivers*, *Ibid.*, p. 100.
35 *only one man who could have done this*, St. John, *Man Inside*, p. 87.

Chapter 5

37 *such a big challenge intrigued me*, St. John, *Man Inside*, p. 93.

Chapter 7

See Leslie, *Dallas City Limit* and Payne, *Big D.*

Chapter 9

54 *Cross gave the boy a pan*, Stowers, *Journey to Triumph*, pp. 15–16.

Chapter 10

64 *I never even had aspirations*, Stowers, *Journey to Triumph*, p. 27.

69 *playing against Bob Gain*, *Ibid.*, p. 35.

Chapter 11

77 *Eddie had been playing well*, Stowers, *Journey to Triumph*, p. 31.

Chapter 12

80 *he was like some damn animal*, Garrison, *Once a Cowboy*, p. 91.

86 *I had definitely not had a good day*, Stowers, *Journey to Triumph*, p. 36.

87 *all along Tom knew what he wanted*, *The Dallas Morning News*, June 6, 1968.

Chapter 16

104 *gravy*, Landry, *Autobiography*, p. 146.

104 *look sharp, men*, *Ibid.*, p. 148.

107 *get off Caroline's tricycle*, Payne, *Big D*, p. 309.

108 *go out and raise money*, *Ibid.*, p. 314.

111 *start thinking about life after football*, Landry, *Autobiography*, p. 147.

Chapter 17

115 *by the end of my first season*, Stowers, *Journey to Triumph*, pp. 104–5.

Chapter 18

119 *we were in a team meeting*, Stowers, *Journey to Triumph*, pp. 87–88.

122 *the most courageous and gutsy season*, Landry, *Autobiography*, p. 149.

123 *wasn't really a matter of courage*, Bud Shrake, "A Cowboy Named Dandy Don," *Sports Illustrated*, September 16, 1968.

Chapter 22

147 *completed an embarrassing 38 percent*, Landry, *Autobiography*, p. 159.

148 *finally I called Meredith into my office*, *Ibid.*, p. 159.

Chapter 23

160 *don't bother reading it, kid*, St. John, *Man Inside*, p. 119.

Chapter 24

163 *the guy has shown me a lot*, Stowers, *Journey to Triumph*, p. 133.

165 *Dallas will be the world champion*, *The Dallas Morning News*, October 22, 1966.

168 *what if I'd missed it*, *The Dallas Morning News*, November 14, 1966.

168 *this team loves that guy*, *Ibid.*

Chapter 26

180 *I can't tell the difference*, St. John, *Man Inside*, p. 129.

Chapter 28

192 *like standing in a pot of ice, The New York Times*, January 14, 1996.

Chapter 33

225 *Morton was like Meredith*, Garrison, *Once a Cowboy*, pp. 192–93.
226 *when Ditka joined the Cowboys, Ibid.*, pp. 197–99.
227 *Bob Lilly brought in a hunting knife, Ibid.*, pp. 111–12.

Chapter 35

237 *Roger Staubach was the epitome*, Garrison, *Once a Cowboy*, pp. 186–92.
238 *seemed innocent enough to me, Ibid.*, p. 189.
238 *the team was split, Ibid.*, pp. 193–94.
242 *I listened to some of the game on the radio, Fort Worth Star-Telegram*, June 4, 1970.

Chapter 36

243 *my 20th year in professional football*, St. John, *Man Inside*, pp. 137–38.
246 *our playoff defeats hung over everything*, Rentzel, *All the Laughter*, p. 194.

Chapter 37

249 *I'll try to handle him*, St. John, *Man Inside*, p. 153.

Chapter 41

269 *I know [Manders] recovered it*, Stowers, *Journey to Triumph*, p. 167.
270 *I looked across the room, Ibid.*
271 *I'm not taking any shit about this game*, Toomay, *Crunch*, p. 61.

Chapter 42

273 *if we discriminated against them*, Wolfe, *Murchisons*, p. 307.
273 *so that God can see His team play, Ibid.*, p. 368.
276 *when I saw Bob Lilly and Jethro Pugh*, Thomas, *Fall of America's Team*, pp. 95–96.
277 *I don't think Tom ever understood, Ibid.*, p. 95.
278 *a rumor going around camp, Ibid.*, p. 80.
281 *once we were playing the Giants*, Ditka, *Autobiography*, p. 118.
281 *how did you and Duane get along*, Garrison, *Once a Cowboy*, pp. 69–70.
282 *I think Landry looked at Duane, Ibid.*, pp. 70–71.
See also the Duane Thomas interview with Will Grimsley in *The Dallas Times Herald*, March 15, 1972.

Chapter 43

284 *Landry's responsibility as the head coach*, St. John, *Man Inside*, pp. 167–68.
285 *a group of the Cowboys started riding motorcycles*, Garrison, *Once a Cowboy*, pp. 102–4.

Chapter 45

296 *you have paved the way*, Bayless, *God's Coach*, p. 109.

Chapter 46

299 *I don't understand it, The Dallas Morning News*, November 24, 1972.

Chapter 47

310 *what position does she play, The Dallas Times Herald*, October 10, 1973.

310 *I was coming out of a bar on Lemmon Avenue, Fort Worth Star-Telegram*, July 31, 1994.
See also Frank Taggart's 1973 *The Dallas Times Herald* interviews with John Niland (September 11) and Rabbi Max Zucker (October 2).

Chapter 49

324 *Tom was* shocked, Bayless, *God's Coach*, p. 126.

Chapter 50

332 *a bad place to be*, Frank Luksa, *The Dallas Times Herald*, August 21, 1974.

Chapter 51

On Bob Hayes' drug bust, *see* Carlton Stowers, "Tarnished Star," *Dallas Observer*, September 26, 1991. *See also Austin American-Statesman*, August 21, 1991.

Chapter 55

360 *the best group I've had from the standpoint of character*, St. John, *Man Inside*, p. 215.

Chapter 56

361 *I like the Western movies, The Dallas Morning News*, July 20, 1975.

365 *we simply had no running game*, Martin, *Texas Thunder*, p. 92.

Chapter 57

367 *I've been recognized everywhere, The Dallas Times Herald*, July 10, 1977.
See also Dorsett, *Running Tough.*

Chapter 61

385 *it's alive and living in Texas Stadium, The* (San Francisco) *Examiner*, September 9, 1979.

Chapter 65

See Wolfe, *Murchisons.*

Chapter 66

419 *poor old Clint got not a penny*, Bayless, *God's Coach*, p. 217.

Chapter 67

422 *singularly unimpressed*, Bayless, *God's Coach*, p. 51.

428 *they chose not to use me*, Dorsett, *Running Tough*, p. 173.

429 *that's just the nature of the business*, St. John, *Landry Legend*, p. 70.

Chapter 68

432 *I just don't know how much more of this I can bear*, Bayless, *God's Coach*, p. 270.

Chapter 69

439 *I don't know if any team in professional football will ever duplicate what happened*, St. John, *Landry Legend*, p. 24.

440 *God bless you and your families*, *Ibid.*, p. 35.

Bibliography

Anderson, Terry. *The Movement and the Sixties.* New York: Oxford University Press, 1995.

Bahas, Dr. Gabriel. *Keep Off the Grass.* Pleasantville, NY: Readers Digest Press, 1976.

Bayless, Skip. *God's Coach.* New York: Simon & Schuster, 1990.

Blair, Sam. *Dallas Cowboys: Pro or Con?* New York: Doubleday, 1970.

Ditka, Mike, with Don Pierson. *Ditka: An Autobiography.* Chicago: Bonus Books, 1986.

Dorsett, Tony, with Harvey Frommer. *Running Tough.* New York: Doubleday, 1989.

Garrison, Walt, and John Tullius. *Once a Cowboy.* New York: Random House, 1988.

Gent, Pete. *North Dallas Forty.* New York: William Morrow, 1973.

Harris, David. *The League: The Rise and Decline of the NFL.* New York: Bantam Books, 1986.

Henderson, Thomas "Hollywood," and Peter Knobler. *Out of Control: Confessions of an NFL Casualty.* New York: G. P. Putnam & Sons, 1987.

Kowet, Don. *The Rich Who Own Sports.* New York: Random House, 1977.

Landry, Tom, with Gregg Lewis. *Tom Landry: An Autobiography.* New York: Zondervan Publishing, 1990.

Leslie, Warren. *Dallas City Limit.* New York: Grossman Publishers, 1964.

Martin, Harvey. *Texas Thunder.* Rawson Associates, 1986.

O'Connor, Richard. *The Oil Barons: Men of Greed and Grandeur.* Boston: Little, Brown, 1971.

Payne, Darwin. *Big D: Triumphs and Troubles of an American Supercity in the 20th Century.* Dallas: Three Forks Press, 1994.

Powledge, Fred. *Black Power and White Resistance.* Cleveland and New York: World Publishing Co., 1967.

Priestley, James. *A Saga of Wealth.* New York: G. P. Putnam & Sons, 1978.

Rentzel, Lance. *When All the Laughter Died in Sorrow.* New York: Saturday Review Press, 1972.

St. John, Bob. *The Landry Legend.* Dallas: Word Books, 1989.

———. *Landry: The Man Inside.* Dallas: Word Books, 1979.

———. *Tex!: The Man Who Built the Cowboys.* New York: Prentice Hall, 1988.

Schaap, Dick. *Quarterbacks Have All the Fun.* Chicago: Playboy Press, 1974.

Staubach, Roger, with Frank Luksa. *Time Enough to Win.* Waco, TX: Word Incorporated, 1980.

Stowers, Carlton. *Journey to Triumph.* Dallas: Taylor Publishing, 1982.

Thomas, Duane, and Paul Zimmerman. *Duane Thomas and the Fall of America's Team.* New York: Warner Books, 1988.

Toomay, Pat. *The Crunch.* New York: W. W. Norton, 1975.

Wiley, Ralph. *Why Black People Tend to Shout.* New York: Birch Lane Press, 1991.

Wismer, Harry. *The Public Calls It Sport.* New York: Prentice Hall, 1965.

Wolfe, Jane. *The Murchisons: The Rise and Fall of a Texas Dynasty.* New York: St. Martin's, 1989.

INDEX